Global Minority Rights

The International Library of Essays on Rights
Series Editor: Tom Campbell

Titles in the Series:

Sexuality and Rights
Nicholas Bamforth

Disability Rights
Peter Blanck

Democratic Rights
Corey Brettschneider

The Right to a Fair Trial
Thom Brooks

Global Minority Rights
Joshua Castellino

Indigenous Rights
Anthony J. Connolly

Civil Rights and Security
David Dyzenhaus

Language and Cultural Rights
Leslie Green

Group Rights
Peter Jones

Human Rights and Corporations
David Kinley

Genocide and Human Rights
Mark Lattimer

Animal Rights
Clare Palmer

Gender and Rights
Deborah L. Rhode and Carol Sanger

Economic, Social and Cultural Rights
Manisuli Ssenyonjo

Health Rights
Michael J. Selgelid and Thomas Pogge

Citizenship Rights
Jo Shaw

Theories of Rights
C.L. Ten

Bills of Rights
Mark Tushnet

Environmental Rights
Steve Vanderheiden

Global Minority Rights

Edited by

Joshua Castellino

Middlesex University, UK

Routledge
Taylor & Francis Group
LONDON AND NEW YORK

First published 2011 by Ashgate Publishing

Published 2016 by Routledge
2 Park Square, Milton Park, Abingdon, Oxon OX14 4RN
711 Third Avenue, New York, NY 10017, USA

First issued in paperback 2017

Routledge is an imprint of the Taylor & Francis Group, an informa business

British Library Cataloguing in Publication Data
Global minority rights. – (The international library of essays on rights)
1. Minorities–Legal status, laws, etc. 2. Human rights.
3. Human rights–History.
I. Series II. Castellino, Joshua.
341.4'8–dc22

Library of Congress Control Number: 2011925717

ISBN 13: 978-1-138-11100-4 (pbk)
ISBN 13: 978-1-4094-2463-5 (hbk)

Contents

PART IV FUNDAMENTAL NORMS IN THE PROTECTION OF MINORITIES

PART V SPECIFIC RIGHTS OF MINORITIES

PART VI HUMAN RIGHTS LAW AND MINORITY RIGHTS LAW

Acknowledgements

The editor and publishers wish to thank the following for permission to use copyright material.

American Society of International Law for the essay: Thomas M. Franck (1992), 'The Emerging Right to Democratic Governance', *American Journal of International Law*, **86**, pp. 46–91.

Brill Academic Publishers for the essays: Fernand de Varennes (1999), 'Equality and Non-discrimination: Fundamental Principles of Minority Language Rights', *International Journal on Minority and Group Rights*, **6**, pp. 307–318. Copyright © 1999 Kluwer Law International; Obiora Chinedu Okafor (2005), '"Righting," Restructuring, and Rejuvenating the Postcolonial African State: The Case for the Establishment of an AU Special Commission on National Minorities', *African Yearbook of International Law*, **13**, pp. 43–64. Copyright © 2005 African Foundation for International Law.

Cambridge University Press for the essay: Andrew Ubaka Iwobi (2004), 'Tiptoeing Through a Constitutional Minefield: The Great Sharia Controversy in Nigeria', *Journal of African Law*, **48**, pp. 111–64. Copyright © 2004 School of Oriental and African Studies.

European Centre for Minority Issues for the essay: Will Kymlicka (2002), 'Multiculturalism and Minority Rights: West and East', *Journal of Ethnopolitics and Minorities Issues in Europe*, **4**, pp. 1–25.

John Wiley and Sons, Inc. for the essay: Howard McGary Jr (1977), 'Justice and Reparations', *Philosophical Forum*, **9**, pp. 250–63.

MIT Press for the essay: Mark Mazower (1997), 'Minorities and the League of Nations in Interwar Europe', *Daedalus*, **126**, pp. 47–63.

Oxford University Press for the essays: Patrick Thornberry (1991), 'Historical Background: International Law Moves from Protection of Particular Groups to Norms of a Universal Character', in Patrick Thornberry, *International Law and the Rights of Minorities*, Oxford: Clarendon Press, pp. 25–37; Will Kymlicka (2008), 'The Internationalization of Minority Rights', *International Journal of Constitutional Law*, **6**, pp. 1–32. Copyright © 2008 Will Kymlicka. Oxford University Press and New York University School of Law; Christopher McCrudden (1998), 'Merit Principles', *Oxford Journal of Legal Studies*, **18**, pp. 543–80; Kevin Boyle Kevin and Anneliese Baldaccini (2001), 'A Critical Evaluation of International Human Rights Approaches to Racism', in S. Fredman (ed.), *Discrimination and Human Rights: The Case of Racism*, Oxford: Oxford University Press, pp. 135–191.

Texas International Law Journal for the essay: Elisa T. Beller (2004), 'The Headscarf Affair: The Conseil d'État on the Role of Religion and Culture in French Society', *Texas International Law Journal*, **39**, pp. 581–623.

Thomson Reuters for the essay: Sandra Fredman (1997), 'Reversing Discrimination', *Law Quarterly Review*, **113**, pp. 575–600. Copyright © 1997 Sweet & Maxwell and Contributors.

The Johns Hopkins University Press for the essays: Philip Vuciri Ramaga (1992), 'The Bases of Minority Identity', *Human Rights Quarterly*, **14**, pp. 409–28. Copyright © 1992 The Johns Hopkins University Press; Berdal Aral (2004), 'The Idea of Human Rights as Perceived in the Ottoman Empire', *Human Rights Quarterly*, **26**, pp. 454–82. Copyright © 2004 The Johns Hopkins University Press.

United Nations for the essays: Marc Bossyut (1998), 'Comprehensive Examination of Thematic Issues Relating to the Elimination of Racial Discrimination: The Concept and Practice of Affirmative Action', Preliminary Report submitted to the *Economic and Social Council of the United Nations*, E/CN.4/Sub.2/1998/5, pp. 1–24; Gay McDougall (2009), 'Minorities, Poverty and the Millennium Development Goals: Assessing Global Issues', *Report of the Independent Expert on Minority Issues*, United Nations: Human Rights Council, pp. 1–23.

United Nations Research Institute for Social Development for the essay: Jomo K.S. (2004), 'The New Economic Policy and Interethnic Relations in Malaysia', *Identities, Conflict, and Cohesion Programme*, Paper No. VII, Geneva: United Nations Research Institute for Social Development, pp. i–vii, 1–22. Copyright © 2004 UNRISD.

University of Pennsylvania Press for the essay: Radhika Coomaraswamy (1994), 'To Bellow Like a Cow: Women, Ethnicity and the Discourse of Rights', in Rebecca Cook (ed.), *Human Rights of Women: National and International Perspectives*, Philadelphia: University of Pennsylvania Press, pp. 39–57.

Every effort has been made to trace all the copyright holders, but if any have been inadvertently overlooked the publishers will be pleased to make the necessary arrangement at the first opportunity.

Series Preface

Much of contemporary moral, political and legal discourse is conducted in terms of rights and increasingly in terms of human rights. Yet there is considerable disagreement about the nature of rights, their foundations and their practical implications and more concrete controversies as to the content, scope and force and particular rights. Consequently the discourse of rights calls for extensive analysis in its general meaning and significance, particularly in relation to the nature, location of content of the duties and responsibilities that correlate with rights. Equally important is the determination of the forms of argument that are appropriate to establish whether or not someone or some group has or has not a particular right, and what that might entail in practice.

This series brings together essays that exhibit careful analysis of the concept of rights and detailed knowledge of specific rights and the variety of systems of rights articulation, interpretation, protection and enforcement. Volumes deal with general philosophical and practical issues about different sorts of rights, taking account of international human rights, regional rights conventions and regimes, and domestic bills of rights, as well as the moral and political literature concerning the articulation and implementation of rights.

The volumes are intended to assist those engaged in scholarly research by making available the most important and enduring essays on particular topics. Essays are reproduced in full with the original pagination for ease of reference and citation.

The editors are selected for their eminence in the study of law, politics and philosophy. Each volume represents the editor's selection of the most seminal recent essays in English on an aspect of rights or on rights in a particular field. An introduction presents an overview of the issues in that particular area of rights together with comments on the background and significance of the selected essays.

TOM CAMPBELL
Series Editor
Professorial Fellow, The Centre for Applied Philosophy and Public Ethics (CAPPE), Charles Sturt University, Canberra

Introduction

Global Minority Rights Law: A Commentary

The idea of protecting the weak from the strong is a powerful concept in human history, and although much history can be defined in socio-legal terms as quests through which the powerful have erected structures to protect their own interests, there is a rich, detectable trend of those who have sought to agitate for the interests of the weak in what was otherwise a relentless push for total dominance.[1] The growth of minority rights law as a discipline owes its heritage to those who struggled to create standards to protect the numerically inferior and non-dominant communities from the excesses of the majority. Minority rights issues provided an important axis along which public international law itself evolved, with early treaties such as the Promise of St Louis of France (1250) being instrumental in highlighting that the condition of the Maronites was a legitimate concern of international society and not merely of the territorial entity within which they lived.[2]

The growth of the discourse can be tracked through a range of bilateral treaties as regional rivals, such as Greece and Turkey, Austria and Russia, and Austria and Turkey, came to terms with how to address divided loyalties arising from populations swearing allegiance to one entity but living as a minority within the territory of another.[3] Although these concerns paint a sophisticated perspective of minority rights within Europe, they were not germane to European colonization. Thus, the colonial activities of European states were not subject to evolving standards at home, which had little impact on the manner in which territory was illegally acquired and demarcated in Latin America, Africa and Asia (Korman, 1996). Internal conflicts between majority and minority, usually dominated by powerful minority groups, often led to intense compromise in the construction of state identity. The dominance of the minority rights discourse by European perspectives is striking, even though one of the most sophisticated early sources of minority rights protection actually existed in the Ottoman Empire's demarcation of religious autonomy (Hashemi, 2006).

By the time of the establishment of the League of Nations, minority rights in Europe had taken centre stage, as reflected in its prominence within the heart of the institution's mandate (Stone, 1932). Nonetheless, the palpable failure of this regime to deliver protection and the lack of resistance to the Nazi project, coupled with the ebb of failure over the years to tackle Europe's invidious discrimination against minorities, highlighted the paucity of commitment

---

1 For a historical source that focuses on this and reflects the heritage of the discourse, see Janowsky (1945). See also Macartney (1934).

2 General background information on St Louis and the treaty can be found on the website of *Encyclopaedia Britannica* at: http://www.britannica.com/EBchecked/topic/348849/Louis-IX (accessed 8 August 2008).

3 See the Convention of the Settlement of the Frontier between Greece and Turkey, 1881, available in Hurst (1972, p. 592); and also, for example, the Treaty of Carlowitz, 1699, available in Fouques-Duparc (1922, p. 79) and The Convention of Constantinople, 1879, available in Hurst (1972, p. 583).

to enshrine protection. The events of World War Two signalled its ultimate defeat, with the League being unable to prevent the genocide of Jews and other minorities – one of the most dramatic violations of minorities in human history.

Minority protection under the United Nations (UN) is subject to two seemingly conflicting trends: first, the UN Charter placed emphasis on the prevention of interstate conflict; and, second, human rights were enshrined as part of the hard-wiring of the new system. The former signalled that attention had moved away from how states behave towards their populations. The principle of state sovereignty, expressed as article 2(7) of the Charter, drew a protective veil over issues considered as occurring within the domestic jurisdiction of states.[4] Six decades of state practice during the UN era has revealed that states avoid scrutiny of their records with respect to minorities by seeking refuge under the principle expressed in this article. This provides protection for the state when faced with self-determination movements emanating from communities living as *de facto* minorities within their jurisdiction. The second trend emphasizes the inherent dignity and worth of all individuals, and began a process through which states were required to imbibe protection within domestic law to uphold this standard. With such all-encompassing protection, a *lex specialis* for minorities or other groups became redundant.

While these developments at the UN stalled the development of 'international' minority rights law, the salience of the discourse grew as post-colonial countries arrived at independence with inherited populations that were the result of vested colonial boundary-line demarcation, rather than group cohesion (Castellino, 2008). It became apparent that boundary demarcations in post-colonial entities would ultimately determine whether a particular group existed as a minority or a majority within the new state.[5] The extent to which the typical post-colonial state, consisting of competing nations and identities, could arrive at a model of protection brought minority questions to the forefront. Today, global minority rights law as a discourse draws sustenance from comparative constitutional law, rather than from discussions of standards and processes framed at the international level (Castellino and Domínguez Redondo, 2006; Castellino and Keane, 2009; Castellino and Cavanaugh, 2012 forthcoming).

The academic writing on global minority rights law reflects its Western origins and subsumes rich and complex discussions concerning nationalism (see, for example, Keating and McGarry, 2001), electoral reform (see, for example, Rule, Zimmerman and Johnpoll, 1994), multiculturalism (Kymlicka, 2001), accommodation (see, for example, Reynolds, 2002), the role of the individual (see, for example, Oestreich, 1999), and questions of individual versus collective protection (Van Dyke, 1974). Such discussions inevitably subsume questions concerning ownership of resources (see, for example, Bannon and Collier, 2003). The literature includes models for 'protection-oriented' rights, with great relevance derived from the recent growth of international criminal law and the codification of crimes against humanity, war crimes and genocide as punishable under the Rome Statute of the International Criminal Court. The case law from the International Criminal Tribunals for Rwanda and the former Yugoslavia signpost the extent to which the worst excesses during war tend to be perpetrated against minorities (Schabas, 2006). Saddam Hussein's use of lethal gas against the

4 For more on the drafting history and interpretation of article 2(7) see Simma (2002).

5 This issue is addressed in an article by Goldie, 'The Critical Date' (1963). See also Andrews (1978).

Kurdish community at Halabjah and the flight of Christians from Iraq highlight the continued vulnerability of minorities (Minority Rights, 2010).

Minority rights questions do not arise only in the context of war. The belief that multiculturalism could provide a panacea of freedom in which different communities could pursue their agendas has been thrown into focus as Europe has reacted sharply to the growth of political Islam in its midst (Rath *et al.*, 2001). Formerly libertarian-oriented states have turned integrationist as clashes between majority and minority have sparked emotive debates on the freedom of expression (Keane, 2008) and hate speech (Cortese, 2006), appropriate dress in public places (Langlaude, 2006) and the extent to which parallel faith-based systems can coexist alongside established legal regimes (Benda-Beckmann, 2002). These debates are underpinned by xenophobic hysteria concerning migration that has affected its tone. In the United States, the election of an African-American as president was hailed as an important step towards the equality of standing of African-Americans. Yet while this momentous occasion may raise aspirations among various communities, it does not necessarily reflect the systemic changes necessary to forge a state based on equal opportunity.

In the emerging economies of Brazil, Russia, India and China, minority issues manifest themselves prominently, as historically excluded groups seek a stake in fast-expanding economies. In some instances this has resulted in separatist forces (for example, Chechnya, Kashmir, Xinjiang) seeking greater interests,[6] but in every case it has raised questions about the extent to which domestic structures are hardening along lines of historical exclusion.

In Latin America, recent developments, led by political processes in Bolivia and Venezuela over indigenous ownership of resources, have brought issues concerning indigenous heritage to the forefront. However, Latin America's African-Caribbean minorities languish at the bottom of most nationwide socio-economic indicators, unable to access the fruits of the rights theoretically available to all citizens.[7] Access to resources continues to strike a strident tone in many African states, fuelled by the positive African Commission decision regarding Ogoni rights in the Niger Delta.[8] At the opposite end of the spectrum, attempts to forcefully dismantle Zimbabwe's unfair land tenure system through resort to violence by Robert Mugabe's militias have created new vulnerability for white Zimbabweans (see, for example, Spierenburg, 2004). In addition to problems associated with forging national identities, African states face additional challenges over the arbitrary nature of their boundaries.[9] This means that social engineering and legal modelling with a view to inclusion is imperative if African states are to take the next steps towards political consolidation and socio-economic development.

It is difficult to estimate the relative contributions made by various pieces of writing. Since the discourse developed in a European context, historical sources focus on this region. However, as its salience has grown in the context of the challenges faced by post-colonial states, several authors have tried to examine comparative models in a bid to understand the means available through which protection can be constructed. Much literature has been

---

6 For a general source on this issue, see Coppieters and Sakwa (2003).

7 For a historical source that examines the plight of African-origin Latin Americans, see Andrews (2004).

8 *The Social and Economics Rights Action Centre and the Centre for Economic and Social Rights* v. *Nigeria* (African Commission Communication No. 155/96). See also Ako and Okonmah (2009).

9 For one of the most comprehensive pieces of works on African boundaries, see Brownlie and Burns (1979).

devoted to understanding the nuances of multiculturalism and the Canadian model (see, for example, Kymlicka, 1996). A primary reason for this is the extent to which Canada sought to forge a genuinely multicultural state, enshrined with protection on the basis of a number of grounds, including language rights. In recent years, however, awareness has grown that the Canadian model is of limited utility as states face problems that are difficult to imagine in the relatively sanitized context of Canadian domestic policy (Choudhry, 2008).

To provide readers with a structured approach to understanding global minority rights law, this volume is divided into six Parts, namely:

- Historical Development of Minority Rights Law
- Conceptual Development of Minority Rights Law
- Contemporary Challenges of Minority Rights Law
- Fundamental Norms in the Protection of Minorities
- Specific Rights of Minorities
- Human Rights Law and Minority Rights Law.

Part I provides a historical and contemporary focus on the development of the discourse itself. Part II seeks to reflect on an age-old question haunting the discipline: 'Who is a minority?' The most widely used definition, with its attendant faults, is one proposed by Francesco Caportorti in 1977, which defined a minority as:

> … a group, numerically inferior to the rest of the population of the State, in a non-dominant position, whose members being nationals of the state possess ethnic, linguistic or religious characteristics different from the rest of the population, and who maintain if only implicitly a sense of solidarity directed towards the preservation of their culture and identity. (p. 96)

Part III tackles an area that remains controversial in the context of global minority rights law. If all human beings have rights, then the need to attribute specific rights to minorities is questionable. However, when rights are hindered by the extent to which individuals are defined externally with regard to personal identifiers such as 'race' or ethnicity, language or other distinguishing features, fundamental questions arise over the efficacy of legal regimes designed to protect the inherent dignity and worth of *every* individual. Part IV highlights the essence of global minority rights law – notably, the promise of non-discrimination, equality and equality of opportunity while Part V reflects on particular rights that have merited attention in legislative policy, with a view to demonstrating the role that exists for policy-makers in the design of effective models. Finally, Part VI returns to the issue of the mainstreaming of minority rights and addresses the challenges this holds.

It could be argued that the most fundamental minority right is a cultural one. Guaranteeing that those who may be different from the rest can effectively maintain their difference, is essentially a privileged articulation of a cultural right. Yet this cultural right is no more than a vehicle through which protection can be gained for particular communities in order to promote the essence of their identity, as determined by each given community. This raises the spectre of conflicting rights, notably in situations where the pursuit of minority rights may be in direct contradiction with human rights. Part VI raises an important challenge to the discourse itself: namely, the extent to which privileging 'minority rights' may encourage fragmentation and division, providing ammunition to identity-entrepreneurs who seek more aggrandized roles than currently on offer. These are challenges to be addressed for the discourse to continue to provide real answers to the entrenched question of how to create egalitarianism and effective equality against the backdrop of homogenization and modernity.

Historical Development of Minority Rights Law

Part I of this volume consists of three essays that reflect the historical development of the subject and is designed to provide readers with three 'snapshots' to locate the subject from its origins in pre-Westphalian treaties through a significant failure to protect in the interwar period, to its contemporary relevance. The first essay (Chapter 1) is taken from Patrick Thornberry's highly regarded 1991 book, *International Law and the Rights of Minorities*, which demonstrates the rich heritage of the discipline and how it evolved from the Promise of St Louis. Thornberry's book traces contemporary developments and normative frameworks, although only the first, historical chapter is reproduced here. Minority rights discourse throughout the ages has been dominated by questions of who ought to be covered under the taxonomy of 'minority' or 'national minority' or even 'minority nationality' (Castellino and Domínguez Redondo, 2005). These distinctions are more than a question of academic classification, since any modelling to be undertaken in favour of minority protection necessarily needs a target audience in mind.

Mark Mazower's essay (Chapter 2) casts light on the extent to which a global regime for minority rights law could be framed. As a historian reflecting on the creation of a system of protection for minorities during the interwar period, Mazower effectively demonstrates that the prominence given to the minority question by the League of Nations proved inadequate in generating forces opposed to the subsequent destruction of groups during World War Two. The essay serves as a reminder of the limited role that international institutions can play in the implementation of protection measures for communities. Two other notable contributions, not included in this volume, provide further insight into the challenges of minority protection during this period; Julius Stone (1932) highlights the mechanism of the League's minority treaty system, and Joseph Kunz (1954) makes the link between minority rights and genocide. These articles provide further analysis of the issues covered by Mazower.

The final essay in Part I, by sociologist Will Kymlicka, is offered to reveal the extent to which the discourse of minority rights is now a significant factor in identifying policy issues within different societies. While the literature may be dominated by discussions concerning European models of protection, contemporary challenges emerging in several states reveal its global salience. Li-Ann Thio's writing should also provide further discussion for those interested in the issues raised by Kymlicka's hypothesis concerning the internationalization of minority rights (see Thio, 2005).

Conceptual Development of Minority Rights Law

In Chapter 4 Philip Ramaga seeks to explore issues concerning the constitution of 'minority' identity by reflecting on a range of different criteria and writings that examine what ought to be considered when identifying 'who' is entitled to claim minority status. His essay cuts across the oft-cited debate within the literature on 'subjective' and 'objective criteria' and whether definitions are needed or whether minority status is constitutive rather than declaratory. The literature is dominated by attempts to understand the constituent elements of minority identity, but, despite these, deep conceptual problems remain (Rodley, 1995).

In raising the gendered dimension of this issue, the UN Committee for the Elimination of Racial Discrimination has passed a general comment on multiple discrimination, highlighting the situation of women from minority communities.[10] Radhika Commaraswamy's essay (Chapter 5) provides a conceptual basis to this dilemma and has been selected for this reason. In minority rights literature this issue could be classed as the 'Sandra Lovelace question', after the famous legal case of a native Canadian who was denied the right to return to her reservation in the aftermath of her marriage to a non-Canadian.[11] This has also been reflected upon in a different context with similar issues in the famous Indian Supreme Court case of Shah Bano, in which the court, mindful that the protection of Shah Bano's rights as a member of India's Muslim minority was less than the protection afforded her as any other woman in Indian society, controversially extended the latter protection to her. Thus, 'human rights' trumped 'minority rights', although both derived from the same constitution (Castellino and Domínguez Redondo, 2006, pp. 82–86). One of the most central challenges for minority rights law within societies is the extent to which such rights, awarded on a collective basis, may violate individual rights' standards that are higher outside the minority regime. This fear of oppressing vulnerable groups within the minority needs to be uppermost in the minds of policy-makers who attempt to accommodate minorities within society.

Although the essays in Part I established the European heritage of the discourse of minority rights, Berdal Aral (Chapter 6) reflects that the first system of minority rights protection may be significantly older than admitted. His explanation of the Ottoman system serves to highlight the Eurocentric dimension of this subject. Early attempts to provide autonomy to tightly knit communities in the Middle East under the Ottoman Empire resulted in *laissez faire* practices by the Sultan, with religious personages given the scope to organize activities within the community in accordance with their own custom. While this system existed against a backdrop of discrimination in general activities, the segregated nature of the communities meant that its impact was contained to those who sought to enter 'mainstream' Ottoman society rather than live within their respective constituencies. The development of the so-called 'millet system' in the Middle East, commencing from a degree of autonomy for groups such as the Maronites and the Druze in Mount Lebanon is not merely a historical footnote: it has materially impacted on the question of minority rights in the Middle East to this day (Castellino and Cavanaugh, 2011 forthcoming).

Contemporary Challenges of Minority Rights Law

As indicated above, it could be argued that overcoming the challenge of the 'minority within the minority' is one of the most significant hurdles for the perpetration of standards governing the collective rights of minorities. This issue is therefore given prominence in the first essay of Part III by Elise Beller (Chapter 7). This essay about the role of religion and culture in French society also offers an opportunity to understand how the issue of minority rights could be actualized in a society that avowedly challenges the need for such a discourse. The position of

[10] UN CERD Gen. Comment XXV (56th session, 2000).

[11] *Lovelace* v. *Canada* (Comm. No. 24/1977).

France (and, to a lesser extent, Turkey) is that there is no need for *lex specialis* for minorities, since such rights are already catered for in its human rights provisions. Thus, France has a reservation to article 27 (the minority provision) of the International Covenant on Civil and Political Rights to emphasize its position. In recent years the issue of identity has come to the fore in this and other European societies, attributable to the growth of 'Islamaphobia' across Europe. Many legal questions have been raised at the European Court of Human Rights concerning issues such as the wearing of religious symbols, the right to don particular kinds of attire, and even the right to profess and proliferate certain beliefs (Howard, 2009). The Court's decisions and parallel discussions conducted through the media in many European states suggest that the question of the position of minorities in society is one that continues to have salience (Langlaude, 2006). That these discussions are often cloaked in an xenophobic meter reveals that despite a focus on minority rights in Europe, including the disasters of World War Two, sentiments against individuals from particular communities still invoke fiercely negative reactions.

Andrew Iwobi's essay (Chapter 8), framed in the context of Sharia law in Nigeria, raises a different kind of challenge: namely, the extent to which the construction of a regime promoting particular kinds of culturally-oriented rights may clash with better-established norms of human rights. This issue has been raised in the context of the above-mentioned Shah Bano case in India, but its importance needs to be emphasized since the growth of religion in the public space and the recent resonance of religious discourse has often meant that cultural rights, delineated on the grounds of religion, are being stressed and are causing strains on the human rights agenda. Many authors have sought to understand the implications of this phenomenon and have suggested solutions that may make the rearticulation of these systems compatible with human rights law (Baderin, 2008), but its relevance is particularly heightened when religious law, enacted or construed in favour of a faith-based minority, is allowed to coexist alongside mainstream legal systems. With the increased emergence of multiple identities, such articulations are likely to present minority rights discourse with its most significant challenge in the decades ahead.

The essay by Jomo K.S., written in the specific context of Malaysia's attempt to erect permanent privileges for the Malay presents the flipside of the construction of special regimes. The theory of affirmative action forms the underlying basis of minority rights, as explored in an essay by Marc Bossuyt in Part IV. For such measures to be justifiable they have to be driven by the objective of achieving socio-economic and political parity for groups that have faced historical discrimination. Thus, affirmative-action measures are simply an attempt to socially re-engineer or recalibrate society in a bid to arrive at greater equity and equality in the medium and long term. In the context of Malaysian policy, however, article 153 of Malaya's constitution controversially makes such rights permanent. As a result, Malays are given special privileges which are denied to its ethnic Chinese and Indian counterparts and which may be accessible only to its indigenous peoples (the *Orang Asli*) with some difficulty (see Castellino and Domínguez Redondo, 2006, pp. 147–92). Malaysian policy highlights the dangers that can exist in societies that erect special regimes ostensibly aimed at the 'development' of communities. While the Malaysian system cannot be compared to the odious apartheid system in South Africa since it has a genuine basis in attempting to correct historical inequality, its solidification into a permanent regime is a reminder of how 'special rights' can perpetrate, rather than correct, inequality if not carefully monitored.

Fundamental Norms in the Protection of Minorities

Three principles lie at the heart of the quest to create a special regime for minorities – namely, non-discrimination, equality and affirmative action. The principle of non-discrimination is well established in global legal systems and is a norm of *jus cogens* in public international law. It forms the fundamental basis of human rights law in articulating a vision to protect the inherent dignity and worth of each individual. In human rights documents the principle of non-discrimination forms a fundamental core to each existing right – a principle enhanced by the quest to achieve equality. This latter principle, which requires a significantly more active role for the state, is immensely difficult to achieve, especially in legal systems that are *laissez faire* in nature. In terms of human rights law, however, the principle of affirmative action is well established and forms the vehicle through which policies can be framed in a continuing quest to achieve equality. Writers such as Christopher McCrudden and Sandra Fredman have made significant contributions to the literature through their sustained work on questions of equality and non-discrimination, and the extent to which these principles can be embedded and realized within the domestic system as basic guarantees to ensure that the rule of law is truly ensconced within the legal system. Chapters 10 and 11 by McCrudden and Fredman respectively reflect both the sophistication of this equality agenda and the extent to which it shapes domestic policy. Outside the contested realm of self-determination and differentiated regimes for property rights, the twin issues of non-discrimination and equality of opportunity are fundamental to the domestic pursuit of rights for minorities and other vulnerable groups. Minority rights literature, often focused on debates at the international level, sometimes misses this crucial step in the discourse. Yet, without the theoretical foundation provided by the discussion on equality of opportunity in particular, any emerging discourse that aims to tackle minority rights questions would inevitably fall short.

Marc Bossyut's working paper on affirmative-action measures (Chapter 12) is the logical step derived from ensuring that the principles of non-discrimination and equality of opportunities inform domestic legal systems. As highlighted above, the most visible distinguishing tool of minority rights law is the acceptance of a positive obligation upon states to take action to remedy the historical and continuing discrimination against individuals based on their membership of a group. Such measures necessarily include designing affirmative action (or positive discrimination) measures, although understanding the manner in which such mechanisms could work is a complex and particularist project, depending on the variables existing in society. It is clear that a poorly designed affirmative-action package discriminates against the majority, attracts negative attention to the minority and harms any process of reconciliation between the majority and minority. Yet, a failure to design such a package simply perpetuates the cycle of discrimination into the future, relying on the passive statement of *de jure* equality while failing to take steps to address its *de facto* manifestations of inequality that exclude populations on the basis of on their identity. Bossyut's ECOSOC working paper provides a lens on to this debate, which is necessary for all who accept that active social engineering may be necessary to translate *de jure* promises into *de facto* realities.

Specific Rights of Minorities

Having established the historical evolution of the discourse, its conceptual frameworks and challenges, and their underpinning theories, in Part V this volume turns to specific rights of minorities that have evolved over time. In many situations, states and minorities often appear to be locked in conflict on the matter of how such rights ought to be constituted. By far the most controversial of these discussions focuses on the right to 'self-determination'. Framed as a right of 'peoples' without an accompanying definition of the constituents of such peoplehood, many groups which have considered themselves as nations that are living submerged within states have sought to assert their claim for self-determination. Indigenous peoples, distinct from minorities, have had some success with this argument in cases before the UN Human Rights Committee and in the express inclusion of self-determination in the Declaration on the Rights of Indigenous Peoples. However, customary law reiterates that minorities do not have the right to self-determination (see generally Ghanea and Xanthaki, 2005). The difficulty with this assertion is that groups which ought to be classed as minorities assert claims to peoplehood instead. As a result, the self-determination question locks minority rights into a zero-sum game in which the state is unwilling to engage in discussions that could potentially fragment it and minorities are frozen out of discussions of greater rights entitlements by virtue of their potentially separatist claim. Instead, attention has switched to notions of 'internal' self-determination or 'democratic entitlement'. Thomas Franck's essay (Chapter 13), written at the end of the Cold War, appeared to offer hope that a right to democratic governance was emerging in state practice. Franck analyses the origins of this right, deriving it from the American Declaration of Rights, but, while articulating the concept of what constitutes 'democratic entitlement', his essay raises questions about the extent to which democracy, as a numbers game, may hold out hope for minorities. The fact remains that democracy as a system of values offers minorities far greater hope than a strict adherence to numbers whereby minorities may be easily outvoted.

One claim from minorities, which is often made in public life but which has merited inadequate attention, is for reparative justice. At the international level, the issue of past violations is often obscured from view by the operation of the intertemporal rule of law, which argues that activities can only be gauged against the temporal context existing at the time of their commission or omission. Consequently, discussions concerning reparations for colonization and slavery have often forestalled in important fora such as the Durban World Conference on Racism, 2001. Yet, models for reparative justice exist, notably in successful claims made by relatives of Holocaust victims and others. In the first decade of the twenty-first century the discussion on transitional justice gained prominence as societies sought to understand and reconcile their histories with the present, using a range of tools such as truth and reconciliation commissions or special criminal tribunals. However, these issues have not been reflected upon from the perspective of minorities who are the most usual victims of past excesses. In Chapter 14 Howard McGary offers a lens through which to understand not only these issues, but also the importance that is placed on such processes among minority communities that have been victims of gross violations of human rights in the past.

It could be argued that the concept of multiculturalism is the consequence of living in societies in which multiple identities have become the norm rather than the exception. The writings of Will Kymlicka have been studied by those seeking to create interethnic harmony within societies in which different ethno-linguistic identities exist in close proximity. In Chapter 15 Kymlicka argues that it is clearly desirable for individuals to have choices in determining their own identity, with society arranged in a manner designed to accommodate the consequences of such choices. Multiculturalism would thus appear to be an ideal solution to clashes between communities in multi-ethnic societies. However, it clearly functions better in societies where there is already a degree of tolerance towards the Other, as well as a willingness to engage across ethnic boundaries. When the boundaries prove insurmountable, the concept flounders, and it remains difficult to imagine it working in contexts where identities are contested. Even in Europe where states display vestiges of multiculturalism, its salience is becoming frayed in the context of Muslim identity. Nevertheless, despite its deficiencies, multiculturalism has obvious benefits over every other system, since it imagines a state that genuinely tries to engage with several strands of culture rather than imposing a dominant narrative on recalcitrant and distinct communities.

The essay by Fernand de Varennes (Chapter 16) has been selected to reflect the immense impact that the denial of linguistic rights has had on the formation of minority identity. In many instances it is the imposition of a particular language and the denial of the right to speak any other language that has instigated cohesion among individuals who may otherwise not have had a sense of community. Linguistic activism has formed an important part of the advocacy agenda of minority communities as they seek application of the principle of equality and non-discrimination in regard to their use, development and promotion of their own language. The issue of linguistic rights is also important since it is the right that is most often governed by choices over numbers. Thus, language policy is often determined with regard to the practicability of being able to offer differentiated rights to linguistically distinct communities.

Human Rights Law and Minority Rights Law

Part VI of this volume returns to the question of whether adequate minority-specific tools have been developed to advance the situation of global minorities. The UN emphasis on human rights partly obscures the need to develop *lex specialis* for minorities; however, the fundamental difficulties of access to justice indicate that a significantly more active perspective is necessary to tackle ingrained inequality within societies. Kevin Boyle and Anneliese Baldaccini (Chapter 17) attempt to provide an assessment of this in the context of racism which is particularly apt to the plight of minorities, who are often victims of racism. There are clear indications that the system, as currently configured, offers inadequate remedies for minorities whether in the context of racial or other discrimination. The challenges of globalization and its impact on minorities is a further area of concern. The two essays by J. Oloka-Onyango and O. Okafor included as Chapter 18 and 19 respectively, reflect on the contemporary challenges for law in a range of post-colonial settings. Oloka-Onyango analyses these challenges in the specific context of what he labels 'marginalized rights' and the impact upon these rights by processes attendant to globalization. Okafor on the other hand, focuses more on remedies, and calls for the establishment of a special mechanism that is focussed on minorities and is regionally based. Such a mechanism does exist in Europe in the personage of the High Commissioner for National Minorities under the auspices of the Organization for Security and Cooperation in Europe, which has accumulated a significant list of both achievements and failures over the years of its operation. However, what is clear from the functioning of that body is that while it may be able to set standards and identify best practice, it could not provide an effective remedy mechanism for violations of minority rights.

The final essay in this collection (Chapter 20) comes from Gay MacDougall, formerly United Nations Independent Expert on Minority Issues. McDougall's contribution raises the fundamental question of the extent to which solutions being proposed to issues of underdevelopment and poverty tackle the plight of minorities. Economist Paul Collier (2007) articulates a stark vision for what he labels 'the world's bottom billion': inhabitants of sub-Saharan Africa and other least developed countries (LDCs), who, according to his analysis, live in fourteenth-century feudalistic conditions, unable to imagine the twenty-first century conditions either enjoyed or aspired to by the other 6 billion of the world's population. This analysis, based on decades of socio-economic research, has contributed to the articulation of the Millennium Promise and the Millennium Development Goals (MDGs), whose chief advocate, Jeffery Sachs, has argued that it is through investment that the poverty trap in LDCs can be sprung (Sachs, 2005). However, framed as macro-economic indicators, the MDGs may still be achieved without material improvement in the socio-economic status of minorities. Also, studies of the incidence of poverty may indicate that the 'bottom billion' live within a range of states, and its inhabitants are usually differentiated from the rest of the population of that state on the basis of ethnic, linguistic or racial identity. Thus, MacDougall's essay is a timely reminder of the coincidence of poverty indicators with minority status, and how any attempt to tackle the former without due attention to the latter is unlikely to deliver us the kind of socio-economic justice that writers such as Amartya Sen (2009) believe are possible.

Conclusion

The objective of this volume is to focus attention on the general principles of law and social policy that underpin the debate concerning minority rights at the international and domestic level. One question that remains relevant is 'What are the rights of minorities?' Rather than attempting to generate a list, the general trend in the literature has been to accept minority rights as all the human rights that exist, with a particular focus on the need to make these accessible to vulnerable groups. In an early UN human rights convention, the International Convention for the Elimination of All Forms of Racial Discrimination, passed in 1965, the drafters made an effort to list the rights that should be enjoyed free from racial discrimination. This list, contained in article 5 of that Convention, is effectively a précis of existing rights, accompanied by a General Observation from the Committee for the Elimination of All Forms of Racial Discrimination that the list presented is non-exhaustive.[12] Consequently, it could be argued that there is no need in a collection of this kind to have a special article focused on 'what' minority rights are: they are simply all the existing human rights, to be administered on the basis of non-discrimination, with a particular emphasis on ensuring full access to those who have traditionally been excluded.

Having identified this caveat, much writing has concentrated on what could be considered the 'fundamental rights' of minorities. In addition to the right to existence, (addressed separately in the context of war crimes, crimes against humanity and genocide in a separate

[12] UN CERD General Comment XX (48th Session, 1996).

Ashgate volume edited by Nikos Passas (1996)), the most fiercely contested ground between majorities and others, and between the state and minorities, lies over questions of entitlements. An emphasis on political participatory rights is thus a necessary corollary of the right to self-determination. While self-determination could be considered the 'first' human right, owing to its pre-eminence in the two human rights covenants, this right is not a feasible starting-point for discussions over minority rights. Instead, a common manifestation of the right within domestic situations is a focus on the right to political participation. In this context, the work of Brendan O'Leary on consociational democracy ought to be considered by those seeking to understand what such participation entails in the context of divided entities (see McGarry and O'Leary, 2009).

The cultural right of minorities could be identified as another fundamental 'right', or as a combination between the notion of cultural rights and the right to existence as a group or entity. Article 15 of the International Covenant on Economic, Social and Cultural Rights remains the only significant provision on cultural rights within the UN treaty mechanisms. Yet, from a minority perspective, it is primarily a differentiated culture (classed in religious, linguistic or ethnic terms) that distinguishes a minority from a majority. As a result, minorities have historically been subjected to processes of cultural assimilation and integration within the dominant culture. Where such integration or assimilation occurs with the consent of the group it could be deemed positive since it engenders cohesive national identity. However, assimilatory processes, whether implicit or explicit, threaten the existence of minorities through the destruction of their identities.

One right which merits inadequate attention and could be fundamental to the growth of the minority rights discourse and processes in the future is the complicated question of reconciliation and restitution. The obligation posited upon states to undo past injustices that have subjugated minorities within states is one justification for affirmative-action measures. Yet, for states to pursue this objective with commitment there would need to be consensus within society on the injustice perpetrated and a desire to engage remedies to repair the damage and prevent its cascade *ad infinitum* into the future.

Assimilatory processes of 'nation-building' (Deutsche and Foltz, 1963), especially in post-colonial entities, have signalled adoption of identities usually based on the majority community. Post-colonial states established on the territories of colonial predecessors have often adopted legislative, administrative and judicial measures designed to create 'national cohesion' by specifying linguistic and religious affiliations. The difficulty with boundary demarcation has left many from different linguistic and religious traditions explicitly (where perceived as a threat) or implicitly excluded. As a result, communities identifiable through a shared history based on a common language or religion agitate for equal rights as citizens of the new state.

Overall, minority rights provides the ultimate lens through which to examine the compliance of states with human rights norms on the basis that if domestic legal systems cannot provide remedies to *all* within the state, they fail the fundamental premise of protecting the inherent dignity and worth of every individual. The remnants of empire and the constant movement of peoples throughout human history has created communities that are exponentially less homogenous. This heterogeneity has resulted in a rich admixture of cultures, but has heightened tensions between communities as some cultures have come under threat. Creating a system that allows for the continued development of every community to the extent it desires, while still allowing individuals to choose to opt out is likely to be one of the most significant challenges of law in the twenty-first century.

References

Ako, Rhus T. and Okonmah, Patrick (2009), 'Minority Rights Issues in Nigeria: A Theoretical Analysis of Historical and Contemporary Conflicts in the Oil-Rich Niger Delta Region' in *International Journal on Minority and Group Rights*, **16**(1), pp. 53–66.

Andrews, George Reid (2004), *Afro-Latin America, 1800–2000*, Oxford: Oxford University Press.

Andrews, J.A. (1978), 'The Concept of Statehood and the Acquisition of Territory in the Nineteenth Century' *Law Quarterly Review*, **94**, pp. 408–27.

Baderin, Mashood (ed.), *International Law and Islamic Law*, Farnham: Ashgate, 2008.

Bannon, Ian and Collier, Paul (2003), *Natural Resources and Violent Conflict: Options and Actions*, Washington, DC: World Bank.

Benda-Beckmann, Franz von (2002), 'Who's Afraid of Legal Pluralism?', in 47 *Journal of Legal Pluralism*, **47**, pp. 37–83.

Brownlie, Ian and Burns, Ian R. (1979), *African Boundaries*, London: C Hurst & Co./Royal Institute of International Affairs.

Capotorti, Francesco, Special Rapporteur (1977), *Study on the Rights of Persons Belonging to Ethnic, Religious and Linguistic Minorities*, UN Doc. E/CN.4/Sub.2/384/Rev.1.

Castellino, Joshua (2008), 'Territorial Integrity and the "Right" to Self-determination: An Examination of the Conceptual Tools', *Brooklyn Journal of International Law*, **33**(2), pp. 503–68.

Castellino, Joshua and Cavanaugh, Kathleen (2011 forthcoming), *Minority Rights in the Middle East: A Comparative Legal Analysis*, Oxford: Oxford University Press,.

Castellino, Joshua and Domínguez Redondo, Elvira (2005), 'Minority Rights in China: A Legal Overview', *European Journal of Minority Issues*, **5**, pp. 51–83.

Castellino, Joshua and Domínguez-Redondo, Elvira (2006), *Minority Rights in Asia: A Comparative Legal Analysis*, Oxford: Oxford University Press.

Castellino, Joshua and Keane, David P. (2009), *Minority Rights in the Pacific: A Comparative Legal Analysis*, Oxford: Oxford University Press.

Choudhry, Sujit (2008), 'Does the World Need More Canada? The Politics of the Canadian Model in Constitutional Politics and Political Theory', in *Constitutional Design for Divided Societies: Integration or Accommodation?*, Oxford: Oxford University Press, pp. 141–72.

Collier, Paul (2007), *The Bottom Billion*, Oxford: Oxford University Press.

Coppieters, Bruno and Sakwa, Richard (2003), *Contextualizing Secession: Normative Studies in Comparative Perspective*, Oxford: Oxford University Press.

Cortese, Anthony (2006), *Opposing Hate Speech*, Westport, CT: Praeger.

Deutsche, Karl and Foltz, William (1963), *Nation Building*, New York: Atherton.

Fouques-Duparc, Jacques (1922), *La Protection des Minorités de Race, de Langue et de Religion*, Paris: Librairie Dalloz.

Ghanea, Nazila and Xanthaki, Alexandra (eds) (2005), *Minorities, Peoples and Self-determination*, (Leiden and Boston, MA: Martinus Nijhoff.

Goldie, L.F.E. (1963), 'The Critical Date', *International & Comparative Law Quarterly*, **12**, pp. 1251–84.

Hashemi, Kamran (2006), 'The Right of Minorities to Identity and the Challenge of Non-discrimination: A Study on the Effects of Traditional Muslims' Dhimmah on Current State Practices', *International Journal on Minority and Group Rights*, **13**(1) pp. 1–26.

Howard, Erica (2009), 'School Bans on the Wearing of Religious Symbols: Examining the Implications of Recent Case Law from the UK', *Religion and Human Rights*, **4**, pp. 7–24.
Hurst, Michael (1972), *Key Treaties of the Great Powers*, Vol. 2, Newton Abbot: David & Charles.
Janowsky, Oscar I. (1945), *Nationalities and National Minorities*, New York: The Macmillan Company.
Keane, David P. (2008), 'Cartoon Violence and the Freedom of Expression', *Human Rights Quarterly*, **30**(4), pp. 845–75.
Keating, Michael and McGarry, John (eds) (2001), *Minority Nationalism and the Changing International Order*, Oxford: Oxford University Press.
Korman, Sharon (1996), *The Right of Conquest: The Acquisition of Territory by Force in International Law and Practice*, Oxford: Clarendon Press.
Kunz, Joseph (1954), 'The Present Status of the International Law for the Protection of Minorities', *American Journal of International Law*, **48**(2), pp. 282–87.
Kymlicka, Will (1996), *Multicultural Citizenship: A Liberal Theory of Minority Rights*, Oxford: Clarendon Press.
Kymlicka, Will (2001), *Politics in the Vernacular: Nationalism, Multiculturalism, and Citizenship*, Oxford: Oxford University Press.
Langlaude, Sylvie (2006), 'Indoctrination, Secularism, Religious Liberty and the ECHR', *International and Comparative Law Quarterly*, **55**(4), pp. 929–44.
Macartney, C. (1934), *National States and National Minorities*, London: Oxford University Press.
Minority Rights Group International (2010), *State of the World's Minorities*, London: MRG.
McGarry, J. and O'Leary, B. (2009), *Consociational Theory*, New York: Routledge.
Oestreich, J.E. (1999), 'Liberal Theory and Minority Group Rights', *Human Rights Quarterly*, 21(1), pp. 108–32.
Passas, Nikos (ed.) (2003), *International Crimes*, Aldershot: Ashgate.
Rath, Jan, Penninx, Rinus, Groenendijk, Kees and Meyer, Astrid (eds) (2001), *Western Europe and its Islam*, Leiden and Boston, MA: Brill.
Reynolds, Andrew (2002), *The Architecture of Democracy: Constitutional Design, Conflict Management, and Democracy*, Oxford: Oxford University Press.
Rodley, Nigel (1995), 'Conceptual Problems in the Protection of Minorities: International Legal Developments', *Human Rights Quarterly*, **17**(1), pp. 48–71.
Rule, Wilma, Zimmerman, Joseph F. and Johnpoll, Bernard K. (eds) (1994), *Electoral Systems in Comparative Perspective: Their Impact on Women and Minorities*, Westport, CT: Greenwood Press.
Sachs, Jeffery (2005), *The End of Poverty*, London: Penguin.
Schabas, William A. (2006), *The United Nations International Criminal Tribunals: The Former Yugoslavia, Rwanda and Sierra Leone*, Cambridge: Cambridge University Press.
Sen, Amartya (2009), *The Idea of Justice*, London: Penguin
Simma, Bruno (2002), *The United Nations Charter: A Commentary* (2nd edn), Oxford: Oxford University Press.
Spierenburg, Marja J. (2004), *Strangers, Spirits, and Land Reforms: Conflicts about Land in Dande, Northern Zimbabwe*, (Leiden and Boston, MA: Brill.
Stone, Julius (1932), 'Procedure under the Minority Treaties', *American Journal of International Law*, **26**(3), pp. 502–13.
Thio, Li-Ann (2005), *Managing Babel: The International Legal Protection of Minorities in the Twentieth Century*, Leiden: Brill.
Van Dyke, Vernon (1974), 'Human Rights and the Rights of Groups', *American Journal of Political Science*, **18**(4), pp. 725–41.

Part I
Historical Development of Minority Rights Law

[1]

Historical Background: International Law Moves from Protection of Particular Groups to Norms of a Universal Character

Patrick Thornberry

Throughout the history of international law[1] there are examples of protective treaties concluded for the benefit of specific groups; the treaty is the paradigmatic instrument recognizing the right of minorities to fair treatment. The treaties produce a wilderness of single instances rather than any comprehensive scheme. There is, however, a certain similarity in the occasions and circumstances resulting in a treaty, even though the occasions and circumstances did not produce this result in all cases. Occasions for instituting a protective treaty were similar to those relating to the protection of aliens; a bond between protecting Power and protected minority, whether of religion, nationality, or culture. The minority could, indeed, consist of former nationals of the protecting Power on ceded territory. Hence the association of minority rights with cession of territory. An early example is the Treaty of Oliva of 1660,[2] by which Poland and the Great Elector ceded Pomerania and Livonia to Sweden, guaranteeing the inhabitants of the ceded territories the enjoyment of their existing religious liberties. Article 2(3) of the treaty provides that the 'cities of Royal Prussia, which, as a consequence of this war, have become the property of . . . (Sweden), will maintain all the rights, liberties and privileges which they have enjoyed . . . in the ecclesiastical or the lay domain.' A later example is the multilateral Convention of 1881 for the Settlement of the Frontier between Greece and Turkey.[3] Article III provides that 'The lives, property, honour, religion, and customs of those of the inhabitants of the localities ceded to Greece who shall remain under the Hellenic administration will be scrupulously respected. They will enjoy exactly the same civil and political rights as Hellenic subjects of origin.' Article VIII complements this in providing:

> Freedom of religion and of public worship is secured to Mussulmans in the territories ceded to Greece. No interference shall take place with the autonomy or

[1] Works cited, *supra*, ch. 1, n. 1.
[2] Fouques-Duparc, *La Protection des Minorités de Race, de Langue et de Religion.* 75–6.
[3] Hurst, *Key Treaties of the Great Powers*, vol. 2 (Newton Abbot: David & Charles, 1972) 592.

hierarchical organisation of Mussulman religious bodies now existing, or which may hereafter be formed; nor with the management of the funds and real property belonging to them. No obstacle shall be placed in the way of the relations of these bodies with their spiritual heads in matters of religion.

The convention also provides for the retention of property[4] titles to religious and educational institutions, and the autonomy of local religious courts.[5]

The Convention of Constantinople, 1879, between Austria-Hungary and Turkey[6] respecting the occupation by the former of the Provinces of Bosnia and Herzegovina is another example of a wide-ranging guarantee of religious liberty on a cession of territory. The guarantee is not confined to Mussulmans; Article II provides: 'the freedom and outward exercise of all existing religions shall be assured to persons residing or sojourning in Bosnia and the Herzegovina. Especially, entire freedom is assured to Mussulmans in their relations with their spiritual chiefs.' The Austro-Hungarian authorities promised that they would protect the honour, customs, freedom of religion, personal security, and property of Mussulmans. Further, all aggression against them, their property or religion, would be severely punished.[7]

It may be seen that the protection of such 'new' minorities could be generous in spirit. The identification of beneficiaries was in terms of religious affiliation, but the guarantee extended beyond the religious aspects of the minorities' existence to customs, property, educational institutions, and law. No distinction is made between religious belief and outward exercise of religion; the latter issue has been troublesome in recent times when States purport to accept freedom of religious belief, but curtail its exercise in terms of public order, etc. The rights in the conventions described are not limited in this fashion; they are simply declared.

Aspects of the treaties are emblematic of earlier, less disciplined societies despite the privations undoubtedly suffered by minorities; Article IV of the last convention provides that 'The Ottoman currency shall continue to have free circulation in Bosnia and the Herzegovina.' The stringency and discipline of modern societies provide an added element of threat to minorities which may produce similar culture disintegrating effects to the cruder methods of earlier times. The centralizing, homogenizing, and organizing tendencies of modern States are as great and perhaps greater than in earlier epochs. The Convention of Constantinople provides that the minorities are under the sovereignty of Austria-Hungary; they are not apparently compelled, as minorities are in many modern States, to subscribe to a national (or international) ideology as a condition of their continued existence.

Of course, not all treaties were so generous on their face and the condition of minorities was perilous over continents and centuries. Relations

[4] Article IV.
[5] Article VIII.
[6] Hurst, *supra*, n. 3, p. 583.
[7] Article II.

between Christian and Islamic powers were frequently strained and gave rise to early instances of protection. An example which belongs to the protection of minorities rather than the protection of aliens is the promise by St Louis of France in 1250 to protect the Maronites as if they were French subjects.[8] The promise was contained in a letter to the Emir, Patriarch, and Bishop; it was renewed in 1649 by Louis XIV in a communication to the Maronite Patriarch of Antioch and the Maronite nation, and by Louis XV in 1737.[9] These were unilateral acts; the earliest treaty in this context appears to be the Austro-Ottoman Treaty of 1615, article 7 of which reads:

Ceux qui professent être le peuple de Jésus – Christ et qui obéissent au Pape, de quelque dénomination que le soit, écclesiastiques, moines, ou Jésuites, auront le droit de construire les églises dans les Etats du sérénissime Empire des Turcs où ils pourront d'après leur usage, conformément au statut de leur ordre et d'après l'antique rite, lire l'évangile, se réunir en assemblées et vaquer ou service divin; ils seront traités avec bienveillance par le sérénissime empereur des Turcs et par ceux qui dépendent de lui . . .[10]

Many treaties followed the one of 1615, as the status of France as a Christian protector was rivalled by Austria and Russia in relations with the Sublime Porte. The Treaty of Carlowitz, 1699, provided a method of implementing guarantees in article 7:

les religieux catholiques româins, partout où ils ont leurs églises, pourront, sans empêchement, exercer leurs fonctions et vivre en toute sécurité, conformément aux ordres émanés de la Sublime Porte, et il sera permis à l'ambassadeur de Pologne près de la Sublime Porte d'exposer devant le trône impérial toutes les demandes qu'il aura ordre de faire au sujet de la réligion.[11]

In the Treaties of Koutchouk-Kainardji, 1774,[12] and Adrianople, 1829,[13] Russia obtained the right to make representations on behalf of Orthodox Christians.

If these instances were a melancholy reflection of relations between Christian and Moslem powers, the Reformation gave rise to the pressing need of protecting one Christian sect from another when religious wars and spontaneous changes resulted in the partisans of one faith finding themselves within the territory of a prince belonging to a different confession. Therefore, several treaties dealt with the rights of Protestants in Catholic

[8] A brief analysis of pre-Westphalia instruments protecting minorities is provided by Wintgens, *Der völkerrechtliche Schutz der nationalem, sprachlichen und religiösen Minderheiten*. See also Heyking, 'The International Protection of Minorities—the Achilles Heel of the League of Nations', *Transactions of the Grotius Society*, XII (1937), 31; Rosting, 'Protection of Minorities by the League of Nations', *AJIL*, 17 (1923), 641.

[9] Fouques-Duparc, *La Protection des Minorités de Race, de Langue et de Religion*, 79.

[10] Ibid.

[11] Fouques-Duparc, 79

[12] *Parrys Treaty Series*, 45, 349.

[13] Hurst, *supra*, n. 5, vol. i, 188.

territory, and vice versa. The Treaty of Oliva may be cited as one example. Others include the Treaty of Vienna, 1607, signed by the King of Hungary and the Prince of Transylvania, granting to the Protestant minority in the latter region the free exercise of their religion.[14] The Peace of Westphalia, 1648,[15] between France, the Holy Roman Empire, and respective allies, while confirming the rule of *cuius regio, eius religio* set out in the Religious Peace of Augsburg, 1555,[16] provided safeguards for minorities, though the protection was applied incompletely. Thus, Protestant worship was excluded in the Dominions of the House of Austria as a whole. The Treaty of Nijmegen, 1678, between France and Holland, is another example of an inter-Christian treaty;[17] this guaranteed freedom of worship to the Roman Catholic minority living in the territories ceded by France to Holland. To similar effect is the Treaty of Ryswick, 1697,[18] concluded between the same parties. The emphasis in early treaties is on freedom of conscience and worship, though sometimes even these freedoms were subject to restrictions in favour of public order. Article 14 of the Treaty of Peace between France and Great Britain, 1713, by which France gave Hudson Bay and Acadia to Great Britain is one example:

> it has been expressly agreed that in all the territory and colonies which by virtue of this treaty must be ceded or returned by [the King of France], the subjects of the said King will have the liberty of leaving within a year with all their movable properties. Those who, nevertheless, would choose to stay and remain under the domination of Great Britain, must be able to enjoy the exercise of the Roman Catholic religion, *in so far as the laws of England permit it.*[19]

Similarly, the Treaty of Paris, 1763, provides in Article 4 that the King of Great Britain 'agrees to grant to the inhabitants of Canada the freedom of the Catholic religion: consequently [he] will give the most precise and most effectual order, that his new Roman Catholic subjects may profess the worship of religion according to the rites of the Romish church, *as far as the laws of Great Britain permit*'.[20] By contrast, other treaties, for example, those of Oliva and Nijmegen, provided more precise guarantees in that they simply reaffirmed the status quo. An extreme example is provided by the Treaty of Dresden, 1745,[21] between the King of Prussia and the Elector of Saxony: Article 8 stipulated that the Protestant religion would be main-

[14] Balogh, *La Protection Internationale des Minorités*, 23 (Paris: Les editions internationales, 1930).

[15] *Parrys Treaty Series*, 1, 119, 271.

[16] Wintgens, *Der völkerrechtliche Schutz der nationalem, sprachlichen und religiösen Minderheiten*, 62–3.

[17] Ibid. 72.

[18] Israel, *Major Peace Treaties of Modern History 1648–1967*, 152 (New York: Chelsea House, 1967).

[19] *Parrys Treaty Series*, 27, 475.

[20] *Parrys Treaty Series*, 42, 320..

[21] Toscano, *Le Minoranza di Razza, di Lingua e di Religione nel Diritto Internazionale*, 16.

tained in the territories of the two parties, in accordance with the Treaty of Westphalia, without it ever being possible to introduce the slightest innovation.

After the Congress of Vienna, treaty clauses for protection of minorities become more detailed and there is a shift from protection of religious minorities to protection of national minorities. At no time would it appear that any doctrinal 'purity' was maintained in treaty practice in conferring rights on individuals or collectivities: churches, religious courts, those who profess to be the people of Jesus Christ, inhabitants of ceded territories, were all mentioned in texts as objects of protection. One writer surmises that there is a difference between inter-Christian instruments and the Christian and Turkish treaties in that the former tended to confine protection to ceded territories and the latter were more wide-ranging, applying throughout the Ottoman Empire. One reason for this may be that minority clauses were in contradiction to the spirit of the law in European states, whereas in Turkey the traditional *Millet*[22] system granted religious freedom to minorities throughout the Empire.[23] From the end of the fifteenth century to the 1920s each religious community (*Millet*) in the Empire enjoyed wide-ranging autonomy in civil and religious matters: *Millets* controlled education, records of birth and death, marriage, and wills. *Millets* could tax members, subject to paying a tribute to the Sultan. The origins of the system in the fall of Constantinople may have been inglorious for minorities in that it derived from the Moslems' contempt for Christians, whom they thought unworthy of the community of the faithful.[24] It was none the less a beneficial autochthonous system, not imposed by treaty.

The new era in Europe, building upon the French and American Revolutions, developed treaty protection in a more secular style: the French revolution of 1789 established in France the principle of freedom of religion and public worship; the First Amendment of the Constitution of the United States of America provided that Congress could 'make no law respecting an establishment of religion or prohibiting the free exercise thereof'. The emergence of nationality as a principle for nation building and identifying 'alien' minority elements within nation States did not mean that religious differences were of no account is the institution of treaty regimes. The religious distinction was always an element in the Turkish treaties, and national and religious differences between majority and minority coexisted:

[22] Capotorti, 'Study on the Rights of Persons belonging to Ethnic, Religious and Linguistic Minorities', UN Doc E/CN.4/Sub. 2/384, Add. 1–7, Intro., para. 6.

[23] Laponce, *The Protection of Minorities*, 84–5.

[24] Ibid. 84. Thus, the Sultan gave the Orthodox Patriarch, the Armenian Patriarch, and the Great Rabbi extensive jurisdiction over their respective religious communities (Millets). Members of the Millet did not have direct relations with the Turkish administration, but were required to act through the Community, which had legal personality. Compare the Kahal system, by which mediaeval kings of Poland allowed Jews to organize their own local government, the Kahal: see Laponce, *The Protection of Minorities*, 91.

the conflict in Northern Ireland is a striking contemporary example of such coexistence; it is at once a religious, an ethnic, and a political conflict. The Congress of Vienna, 1815,[25] provided for various categories of minority. Article 77 provided that the inhabitants of the Bishopric of Basle and those of Berne, united to the Cantons of Berne and Basle, should 'enjoy, in every respect, without any distinction of religion . . . the same political and civil rights which are enjoyed, or may be enjoyed by the inhabitants of the ancient parts of the said Cantons'.[26] Act XIV, annexed to the Treaty, on cessions made by the Kingdom of Sardinia to the Canton of Geneva, regulated the rights of populations in ceded territory, in case the Protestant tradition of the Canton might result in oppression of the Catholic minority. Article 3 provides:

> Sa Majesté [the King of Sardinia] ne pouvant se résoudre a consentir qu'une partie de son territoire soit réunie a un Etat, où la religion dominante est diffŕehte, sans procurer aux habitants du pays qu'elle cède, la certitude qu'ils jouiront du libre exercise de leur religion, qu'ils continueront à avoir les moyens de fournir aux frais de leur culte, et à jouir eux-mêmes de la plénitude des droits de citoyens.[27]

Protection of the Poles was on the basis of nationality. Article 1 of the Treaty, reflecting the dismemberment of the Polish State, makes provision for the Polish nation so that Polish nationality could be preserved: 'The Poles, who are . . . subjects of Russia, Austria and Prussia, shall obtain a Representation and National Institutions, regulated according to the degree of political consideration, that each of the Governments to which they belong shall judge expedient and proper to grant them.'[28] Annex X to the main treaty, concluded between Austria and the Netherlands, proclaiming the unification of Belgium and Holland, contained guarantees for the Belgian Catholic minority.

The tradition of protecting minorities by treaty continued throughout the nineteenth century. A tendency to devise multilateral instruments is evident throughout the century. The practice also demonstrates distinctions between States, since obligations were imposed on some States, indicating a second-class citizenship. The gravitational centre of the 'minorities question' moved eastwards: it was perceived as a predominantly Central and East European problem. An example of these tendencies is the Treaty of Berlin, 1878:[29] Bulgaria[30] and Eastern Roumelia[31] were recognized as autonomous principality and province, respectively, under the Sultan, provision being made, in both cases, for religious liberty. Article XXVI recognized the independence of Montenegro. Article XXVII relates that the 'High Contracting Parties agree on the following *conditions*' and there follows provision for non-discrimination on religious grounds and freedom of religious

[25] Hurst, *Key Treaties of the Great Powers*, vol. i, 76.
[26] Ibid.
[27] *Parrys Treaty Series*, 64, 318.
[28] Hurst, vol. i, 45.
[29] Ibid. vol. ii, 551.
[30] Article I.
[31] Article XIII.

worship. The independence of Serbia is also recognized by Article XXXIV 'subject to the *conditions* set forth'. Clauses on non-discrimination and freedom of worship similar to those for Montenegro are set out.[32] A more extensive array of conditions is provided for Romania, which is recognized as independent. Article XLIV provides: 'In Romania, the difference of religious creeds and confessions shall not be alleged against any person as a ground for exclusion or incapacity in matters relating to the enjoyment of civil and political rights, admission to public employments, functions and honours, or the exercise of the various professions and industries in any locality whatsoever.' The second paragraph provides that 'freedom and outward exercise of all forms of worship shall be assured to all persons belonging to the Romanian State, as well as to foreigners, and no hindrance shall be offered either to the hierarchical organisation of the different communions, or to their relations with their spiritual chiefs'. The final paragraph is headed 'Equal Treatment of Foreigners' and stipulates that subjects and citizens of all the Powers shall be treated in Romania, without distinction of creed, on a footing of perfect equality.

This comprehensive clause encompasses civil and political rights, freedom and outward exercise of worship, and equal treatment of foreigners. It reflected rights in 'all persons' and in religious communities. Article XLIII repeats the conditional recognition formula. The freedoms are absolute in that there is no public order requirement. The 'conditions' related to religious minorities; elsewhere in the treaty, national minorities are the object of protection. Article IV provides in relation to Bulgaria that 'In the districts where Bulgarians are intermixed with Turkish, Romanian, Greek or other populations, the rights and interests of these populations shall be taken into consideration as regards the elections and the drawing up of the Organic Law of the Principality.' The 'populations' may be added to the list of right holders described in the treaty. The document describes itself as a treaty 'for the Settlement of the Affairs of the East'. Thus the Sublime Porte promised to guarantee the security of the Armenians against attacks by Circassians and Kurds,[33] and it made a 'spontaneous declaration'[34] in favour of the principle of religious liberty, as a preamble to an extensive article on this subject.

It has been mentioned that the *locus* of the minorities question was essentially East European through the nineteenth century. The treaties provided models for regulation in other continents where European Powers were involved. The Treaty of Tientsin, 1858,[35] between Great Britain and China, made provision for religious toleration in China. Article VIII stated that

> The Christian religion, as professed by Protestants or Roman Catholics, inculcates

[32] Article XXXV.
[33] Article LXI.
[34] Article LXII.
[35] Hurst, vol. i, 343.

the practice of virtue, and teaches man to do as he would be done by. Persons teaching or professing it, therefore, shall alike be entitled to the protection of the Chinese authorities, nor shall any such, peaceably pursuing their calling, and not offending against the law, be persecuted or interfered with.

It may be noted that this treaty protected only *Christian* sects.

The development of treaty protection of minorities exhibits organized, and unorganized features. It was more than a wilderness of single instances in that it tended to become localized (mainly Eastern Europe), and the occasions for guarantees displayed certain similarities. Analytically, there was a movement to broaden guarantees beyond freedom of worship to encompass the range of civil and political rights. The treaties reflect a movement to extend to Eastern Europe what had become accepted in the West. The terms were in the main not generous to minorities, and in some cases were extremely vague, such as the reference to Polish nationality in the Treaty of Vienna. The texts occasionally recognized existing privileges of groups, but did not create them: they reveal little attempt to compensate for the numerical inferiority of the minorities in the States. The tone of the instruments is one of tolerance rather than encouragement. Despite this, the existence of so many examples of treaty protection of groups makes it possible to describe a tradition of minority protection in international law. The tradition replenished itself whenever the factum of international power was presented with a suitable opportunity for regulation. The treaties were a symbol of international concern. They were forward-looking rather than retrogressive. The twentieth century has accepted the continuance of the tradition of protecting particular communities, while elaborating a much more ambitious 'universal' scheme.

The principal failing was implementation; this negative 'tradition' has maintained itself in the twentieth century in the difficulties with full international implementation of human rights, whatever the successes of regional and bilateral systems. Claude offers damning criticism of the early period: 'The system of minority protection based upon special treaties guaranteed by the great powers was condemned to failure by the inadequacy of its scope, the vagueness of its substantive provisions, the rudimentary nature of its machinery and organization, and the uncertainty, ineffectiveness and susceptibility to abuse of its sanctions.'[36] In terms of efficaciousness of procedures, the criticism is realistic. It is not necessary to outline the history of atrocities against minority groups to make the point. One merely needs to recall the well-known episodes[37]—the religious wars of Western Europe, the persecution of Romanian Jews and the *pogroms* against them in Russia, the Ottoman massacres (genocide) of the Armenians. All are matters of histori-

[36] Claude, *National Minorities: An International Problem* (Cambridge, Mass.: Harvard UP, 1955).

[37] Franck and Rodley, 'After Bangladesh: the Law of Humanitarian Intervention by Military Force', *AJIL*, 67 (1973), 271, 271.

cal record. Effective intervention on behalf of threatened groups was occasional and sporadic, outmatched by cases of non-intervention. Many scholars postulate none the less that there existed a customary law right of humanitarian intervention at least in the nineteenth century.[38] If this is so, it would substantially supplement the treaty tradition.

The right of intervention given by treaty was often rather limited. The Treaty of Koutchouk-Kainardji, 1774,[39] provided for ministers of the Imperial Court of Russia to make representations in favour of the Orthodox religion. Article IX(I) of the Treaty of Paris, 1856, takes note of the proclamation by the Sultan of a Firman 'recording his generous intentions towards the Christian populations of the Empire'[40] and Article IX(II) recites that

> The Contracting Powers recognise the high value of this communication. It is clearly understood that it cannot, in any case, give to the said Powers (Great Britain, Austria, France, Prussia, Russia and Sardinia) the right to interfere, either collectively or separately, in the relations of His Majesty the Sultan with his subjects, nor in the Internal Administration of his Empire.

The function of the conditional recognition clause,[41] on the other hand, may have been to grant a right of intervention.[42] Specific clauses in treaties could sometimes give grounds for intervention more forceful than a right to 'make representations'. The London Protocol of 1830 guaranteeing Greek independence contained a declaration by France, Great Britain, and Russia that each power 'would consider it its duty to interpose its influence with the Porte, so as to ensure to the inhabitants [of Crete and Samos] protection against "oppressive and arbitrary acts" '.[43] Apart from treaty-right, a number of interventions (defined by Oppenheim as 'the dictatorial interference by a State or group of States in the affairs of another State for the purposes of maintaining or altering the actual condition' of things therein[44]) point towards a right not limited by the terms of the treaty or limited to the parties to it. Examples are the intervention[45] by France, Great Britain, and Russia in Greece in 1827, consequent upon numerous massacres perpetrated by Turkey. In so far as States not parties to the Treaty of Koutchouk-Kainardji

[38] The development of the literature on intervention is surveyed by Fonteyne, 'The Customary International Law Doctrine of Humanitarian Intervention: its Current Validity under the UN Charter', *California Western International Law Journal*, 4 (1974), 203.

[39] *Supra*, n. 12.

[40] Hurst, vol. i, 320.

[41] *Supra*, text following n. 31.

[42] Lauterpacht, *Recognition in International Law*, 357 (London: Cambridge UP, 1948); Moore, *A Digest of International Law*, vol. i, paras. 27, 72–4 (Washington: Govt. Printing Office, 1906); Hackworth *Digest of International Law*, para. 34 (Washington: Govt. Printing Office, 1940–44).

[43] XVII *British and Foreign State Papers* (1827–30), 203.

[44] *International Law: A Treatise*, 305.

[45] Fonteyne, 203; Franck and Rodley, 271.

took part (that treaty only concerned Turkey and Russia), that action could not be based on the treaty. Further, the implementation provisions were weak. The Powers indicated that humanitarian and pragmatic motives[46] justified intervention. Another example is said to be the mandate given by the Powers for France to intervene on behalf of Christians in the Levant in 1860, again following massacres. However, this is a weak example in that the official grounds for justification were a Protocol of 1860[47] signed by France, Great Britain, Prussia, Russia, and Turkey; and the Treaty of Paris, 1856,[48] though the latter, for reasons described (the provision in Article IX(II)) is hardly sustainable as a treaty justification.

Other cases cited as instances of the doctrine display features which confirm rather than dispel doubts on its generality of application. Fonteyne cites the intervention in Bosnia, Herzegovina and Bulgaria from 1876 to 1878.[49] But this involved a formal declaration of war by Serbia and Montenegro against the Porte in 1876, and a subsequent declaration of war by Russia. Fonteyne writes that:

> the declarations of war by Serbia and Montenegro were officially justified by humanitarian solidarity with the oppressed populations in the neighbouring countries. On the other hand, the demands of the European Powers [six Powers indicated in a Protocol of 1877 their determination to watch over the fulfilment of the promises in the Treaty of Paris, 1856] as well as the war waged by Russia were formally based upon an invocation of Article IX of the Treaty of Paris.[50]

Doubtful interventions could always be legalized by a declaration of war given the general *laissez-faire* attitude to war in the nineteenth century so that this may not constitute a precedent. Further, despite its restrictive quality, Article IX of the Treaty of Paris is still invoked. Ganji provides a less restrictive interpretation of Article IX(II) of the treaty: 'The principle of non-intervention in the second paragraph of Article IX was embodied for the sole purpose of providing that, as long as the Sultan was acting in good faith in implementing the *Firman*, the European Powers were to abstain from intervening.'[51] Such an interpretation gives treaty-right a broader scope.

While it is not a case of intervention to protect minorities, the intervention of the United States in Cuba in 1898 is sometimes cited as a clear precedent to advance the general doctrine.[52] President McKinley's message

46 Fonteyne, 208.

47 Ibid. See also the Convention of 1861 Prolonging the Occupation of Syria, Hurst, vol. i, 408.

48 Fonteyne, 317.

49 Fonteyne, 211–12.

50 Ibid.

51 Ganji, *International Protection of Human Rights*, 30–1 (Geneva: Librairie E. Droz, 1962).

52 Behuniak, 'The Law of Unilateral Humanitarian Intervention by Military Force: A Legal Survey', *Military Law Review*, 17 (1978), 157.

to Congress stated that the United States was intervening 'in the cause of humanity and to put an end to barbarities, bloodshed, starvation, and horrible miseries'.[53] Even commentators generally sceptical about the doctrine admit this as a possible exception.[54] However, humanitarian concern was simply one ground for intervention; the most important ground appears to have been protection of American citizens and their property in Cuba, rather than protection of Cubans.[55] One commentator cites the 'powerful influence of endangered investments and trade'.[56] The point is not the hidden motives, but the public justifications for intervention. If humanitarian justifications are sufficient ground in themselves, it is supererogatory to cite a cluster of reinforcing reasons.

Further evidence of lack of confidence in a justifying principle is provided by the Powers' reticence in the face of persecutions of the Jews. Responses to persecutions were mainly verbal, sometimes harsh, but often couched in extremely courteous terms. Fairly typical is the instruction from the US Secretary of State to the United States Consul in Bucharest: 'You will not be backward in joining any . . . protest, or other measure which the foreign representatives there may deem advisable, with a view to avert or mitigate further harshness towards the Israelites.'[57] The Department of State, more cautiously, instructed its Minister in St Petersburg that 'it would . . . be inadmissible for the Government of the United States to approach the Government of Russia in criticism of its laws and regulations, except so far as such laws and regulations may injuriously affect *citizens of this country*'.[58] Clearly the United States Government was inclined to intervene when protection of US citizens was the issue and not for Russian citizens persecuted by their own Government.[59] In connection with massacres of Armenians by the Turks, the United States Ambassador in Constantinople wrote to the Department of State: 'It is difficult for me to restrain myself from doing something to stop this attempt to exterminate a race, but I realise that I am here as Ambassador and must abide by the principles of non-interference.'[60]

Jurists were not unanimous on the doctrine; more significantly, it is

[53] Franck and Rodley, 285.

[54] Ibid.

[55] President McKinley in his message to Congress, 28 March 1898, listed four grounds for the intervention: humanity; protection of United States citizens in Cuba; injury to American commerce; the constant menace to peace from the feebleness of Spanish rule in Cuba: Moore, *A Digest of International Law*, vol. vi, 219; Brownlie, *International Law and the Use of Force by States* (Oxford: OUP, 1963), 340.

[56] Fitzgibbon, *Cuba and the United States 1900–1935* (Menasha, Wis., 1935, reprint New York: Russell, 1964), 25.

[57] Moore, *A Digest of International Law*, vol. vi, 360.

[58] *Foreign Relations of the United States, Diplomatic Papers, 1880* (Washington, 1861–), 873.

[59] *Foreign Relations, 1882*, 451; Stowell, *Intervention in International Law* (Washington: Byrne, 1921), 76–8.

[60] Stowell, 295.

difficult to find a broad consensus which would include most of them. There are hints of a supporting doctrine in Grotius,[61] but Vattel wrote that 'if the Sovereign buries his subjects under taxes, if he treats them harshly, it is the Nation's business; no one else is called upon to admonish him, to force him to apply wider and more equitable principles'.[62] These sentiments were developed in an age when national sovereignty had not reached the sacred status which it acquired later. In the nineteenth century there are clearly two schools of thought. The non-intervention school includes Mamiani, Carnazza-Amari, Pradier-Foderé, Pereira, and Halleck.[63] Italian and Latin American scholars were generally non-interventionists. Pereira describes a typical position: 'Internal oppression, however odious and violent it may be, does not affect, either directly or indirectly, external relations and does not endanger the existence of other States. Accordingly, it cannot be used as a legal basis for use of force and violent means.'[64] The interventionist school included Creasy, de Martens, Wheaton, Woolsey, and Arntz.[65] Creasy declares a principle with direct application to minorities; 'we intervene on behalf of a grievously oppressed people, which has never amalgamated with its oppressors as one nation, and which its oppressors have systematically treated as an alien race, subject to the same Imperial authority, but in other respects distinct.'[66] De Martens, however, introduces what today is regarded as an unacceptable distinction and which was not delineated by all writers: 'vis-à-vis non-civilised nations . . . intervention by the civilised Powers is in principle legitimate, when the Christian population of those countries is exposed to persecutions or massacres . . . [this is] not applicable to the relations between civilised Powers.'[67]

In all this, it is difficult to discover an *opinio juris*. The strongest advocates of the doctrine came from 'strong' States such as the USA; the jurists of the 'weak' States developed principles from their often negative experience of intervention. This is still true today, the loudest advocates of humanitarian intervention are to be found in the USA.[68] It seems that there is a gulf here which cannot be bridged. Treaty-right remained the surest ground for

[61] *De Jure Belli ac Pacis*, 2, 'Grotius on the Rights of War and Peace', tr. W. Whewell, Cambridge: CUP, 1853, ch. xxv, 438.

[62] *Le Droit des Gens*, 2, cited by Fonteyne, *supra*, n. 38, 215.

[63] Fonteyne, 215 ff.

[64] Fonteyne, 217.

[65] Fonteyne, 216.

[66] Creasy, Sir E., *First Platform of International Law* (London: John van Voorst, 1876), 303–5.

[67] De Martens, *Traité de Droit International*, cited Fonteyne, 219.

[68] Lillich, 'Forcible Self-Help by States to Protect Human Rights', *Iowa Law Review*, 53 (1967), 325; Lillich (ed.), *Humanitarian Intervention and the United Nations*; Behuniak, 'The Law of Unilateral Humanitarian Intervention by Military Force: A Legal Survey'; Moore, *Law and Civil War in the Modern World* (Baltimore: Johns Hopkins, 1971)—compare the articles by Brownlie, 'Humanitarian Intervention', p. 217, and Lillich, 'Humanitarian Intervention—A Reply to Dr Brownlie and a Plea for Constructive Alternatives', p. 229; McDougal, Lasswell and Chen, *Human Rights and World Public Order* (New Haven: Yale UP, 1980).

intervention, and collective action was preferable to unilateral action. In the context of minority protection, whatever position is taken on the legal status of humanitarian intervention, it is clearly a defective approach to the resolution of minorities issues. Humanitarian intervention by individual States could hardly serve as a model for the future. It is something of a blind alley, dangerously destabilizing to international society and ultimately counter-productive for its intended beneficiaries. International law could hardly afford such a doctrine in the age of advanced technological wars.[69]

[69] Perhaps the best overall review of the twentieth century doctrine is Ronzitti, *Rescuing Nationals Abroad through Military Coercion and Intervention on Grounds of Humanity* (Dordrecht: M. Nijhoff, 1985). The doctrine of humanitarian intervention is hardly supported at all by post Charter State practice. It could not be otherwise in view of the prohibitions in the UN Charter (Article 2(4): 'All members shall refrain . . . from the threat or use of force against the territorial integrity or political independence of any State, or in any other manner inconsistent with the Purposes of the United Nations') and the development of the principle of non-intervention. Interventions in support of co-nationals do not escape the general censure. When the Sixth Committee of the General Assembly was debating the definition of aggression in 1954, Greece and The Netherlands argued in favour of a right of humanitarian intervention in cases where there were ethnic ties between the intervening State and the minority suffering persecution, Israel contradicted this view in clear terms: 'It seemed advisable to refrain from any action that might be construed as authorizing military intervention of a co-national minority. Humanitarian intervention had frequently been invoked to justify intervention, although the true motives had been very different. In the period between the two world wars, certain minorities had also been used for subversion against the States of which they were citizens. Since the second World War . . . the problem of minorities had been greatly reduced. Consequently, neither the realities of modern life, nor the accepted concept of legal and illegal use of force, nor the teachings of history, could justify the use of force in such a hypothesis'. Panama added that 'The representative of Greece had spoken of the hypothetical case of armed intervention by a State to halt the extermination by another State of part of the former's population on racial, religious or other grounds. Such intervention would certainly conflict with the principles of the Charter'. *GAOR* 9, Sixth Committee, 412th meeting, para. 35; *GAOR*, 9, Sixth Committee, 418th meeting, para. 13. Greece and The Netherlands appear to have taken a different view of the legitimacy of intervention in subsequent cases: Akehurst, 'Humanitarian Intervention', in Bull (ed.), *Intervention in World Politics* (Oxford: OUP, 1984). Some of the argument bases itself on the proposition that the international law on human rights has failed to make sufficient progress and that unilateral action by States in the service of human rights may be the only method of rectifying abuses. In view of the newness of the concept of universal rights in international law, (*infra*, Part III) and the painstaking efforts of the international community to make the rights a reality, this view cannot be accepted. A forthright condemnation of 'humanitarian intervention' was issued in *The Nicaragua Case* (Merits), *ICJ Reports 1986* at para. 268: 'In any event, while the United States might form its own appraisal of the situation as to respect for human rights in Nicaragua, the use of force could not be the appropriate method to monitor or ensure such respect'. See Rodley, 'Human Rights and Humanitarian intervention: The Case Law of the World Court', *ICLQ*, 38 (1989), 321.

[2]

Minorities and the League of Nations in Interwar Europe

Mark Mazower

THIS YEAR THE NORTHERN GREEK CITY of Thessaloniki is the Cultural Capital of Europe. A century ago, it was known as Selanik, one of the most fascinating cities in the Ottoman Empire. Roughly half its 150,000 inhabitants then were Jews, as many as lived in the whole of France. In addition to Turks and Greeks, there were also Armenians, Bulgarians, Vlachs, Circassians, Albanians, and the secretive Dönmeh—the crypto-Jews who had followed Sabbatai Zevi, their false Messiah, into Islam in the late seventeenth century. Foreign visitors were astonished to find bootblacks and porters on the docks who spoke six or seven languages.

How did polyglot Selanik turn, in the span of a few generations, into a modern metropolis of the Greek nation-state, with a population of more than one million Greeks, virtually no Turks, and fewer than two thousand Jews? Its "liberation" by the Greek army in 1912 is only the beginning of the story. In fact, the city's designation as the Cultural Capital is perhaps more fitting than the Eurocrats realized: the hellenization of Thessaloniki encapsulates the history of minorities in Europe in the first half of this century.

In 1943, while the young *Wehrmacht* lieutenant Kurt Waldheim was posted to the city, its large Jewish community was deported and exterminated within a few months at Auschwitz-Birkenau. But even before that point, Thessaloniki had turned into a predominantly Greek city. Nazi genocide was but the most extreme variant of the international experimentation in policy towards ethnic minorities that had begun with the disintegration of the

Mark Mazower is Reader in History at the University of Sussex.

Ottoman, Habsburg, and Romanov empires in the maelstrom of World War I.

Nothing contributed more to turning Selanik into Thessaloniki than the population exchanges that took place in the Balkans as the Ottoman Empire broke up. In 1919, under the Treaty of Neuilly, the Bulgarian inhabitants of the city and the surrounding region were "exchanged" with Greeks from Bulgaria. This was a striking innovation in terms of international policy, but the tens of thousands caught up in this supposedly voluntary transfer were small fry compared with the millions involved in the compulsory exchange of populations that took place between Greece and Turkey when fighting between them stopped a few years later. According to the 1923 Treaty of Lausanne, Muslim residents in Greece had to leave their homes and "return" to Turkey, while Orthodox Christians from Asia Minor were moved in the opposite direction. Hundreds of thousands of the latter settled in and around Thessaloniki, thus helping to "hellenize" Greek Macedonia.

Today, in the aftermath of the war in Bosnia with its ethnic cleansing and its massive enforced movements of population, the 1923 Greco-Turkish agreement has acquired new relevance. Its seeming tidiness appealed to some European policymakers then, and apparently still does today. But how successful was it? At the level of individual lives, it wrought—or acquiesced in—the destruction of centuries-old homes and communities; it transformed identities according to the logic of nationalism, turning Orthodox villagers from Anatolia, many of whom could not speak Greek, into Greeks, and Muslims from Crete, many of whom were the descendants of Islamized Christians, into Turks. It created a massive problem regarding the property these refugees left behind, which poisoned Greco-Turkish relations for several years. It also burdened governments in Athens and Ankara with the expense of resettling hundreds of thousands of refugees.

On the other hand, both the Greeks and the Turks saw the exchange as a means of bolstering their new nation-states and "homogenizing" the ethnic mix of their populations. More to the point, as far as international policymakers are concerned, relations between the two countries did improve over the next twenty years, before the Cyprus dispute poisoned them once more. Today, relations are perhaps as bad as they have ever been. Thus the jury remains out on whether such transfers of population actually ease international tensions in the long run.

In the interwar years, however, the international community proved strikingly reluctant to draw on the Greco-Turkish population exchange as a precedent. It was not emulated until Munich and the start of Hitler's own policy of repatriating the ethnic Germans from the South Tyrol, the Baltic states, and Bessarabia. Before that, in the heyday of Wilsonian liberalism, the minorities policy with which the League of Nations came to be associated, and which seems to me to remain an experiment of abiding interest, involved keeping minorities where they were and offering them the protection of international law, rather than uprooting and resettling them elsewhere.

The idea of protecting minorities by law emerged rather belatedly during World War I. The sudden collapse of the great empires of Central and Eastern Europe caught most policymakers by surprise. History seemed to have vindicated the dreamers of a "New Europe"—whether it was Wilson himself with his dangerously vague principle of national self-determination, crusaders for oppressed nationalities like Robert Seton-Watson and Arnold Toynbee, or national leaders such as Masaryk and Paderewski. But some liberals were also well aware that nationalism as a policy could open up a Pandora's box of conflicts and tensions. Years before, Lord Acton had warned that "by making the State and the nation commensurate with each other in theory, [nationality] reduces practically to a subject condition all other nationalities that may be within the boundary." "I do not myself believe," noted Robert Cecil, in the British Foreign Office in 1917, "that a European peace founded only on nationality and without any other provisions is likely to be desirable or even in all respects beneficial."[1]

Similar doubts were forcefully expressed by Jewish lobbying groups in both Washington and London. Ever since the Balkan Wars of 1912–1913, they had tried to alert the Great Powers to the dangers that "half-crazed nationalists" posed to ethnic minorities and international stability in southeastern Europe. During World War I, two national movements proved their point. The first was the Turkish attempt to wipe out the Armenians, which unfolded in all its horror in 1915 and led to the murder of between eight hundred thousand and 1.3 million people. This was perhaps the first example of the "war of extermination" that the British scholar Arnold Toynbee saw as the result of the extension of the principle of nationalism to the multi-confessional tapestry of the Ottoman Empire.[2]

On the heels of the Armenian genocide came the struggle for Poland in 1918–1920. At Versailles, proponents of an ethnically pure Poland clashed with those who advocated a multiethnic commonwealth under Polish leadership. The problem for the former was that Poles lived alongside Germans, Jews, Lithuanians, and Ukrainians in the claimed territory; the problem for the latter was that multiethnic harmony was a rather ambitious goal for anyone in postwar Eastern Europe. By the end of 1918, Polish troops were battling for supremacy with the Ukrainians. They also carried out a series of pogroms that forced Jews to form self-defense units. Balfour worried that an independent Poland, "so far from promoting the cause of European peace, would be a perpetual occasion of European strife." By mid-1919 Poland was only two-thirds Polish from an ethnic point of view. In the disputed city of L'viv someone pointed out the war damage to an American visitor: "You see those little holes? We call them here 'Wilson's Points.' They have been made with machine guns; the big gaps have been made with hand grenades. We are now engaged in self-determination, and God knows what and when the end will be."[3]

At the Paris Peace Conference, the struggle over the form of an independent Poland eventually brought into being an ambitious new international policy on minority rights. Behind the scenes, the influential New States Committee recognized the need for some such policy if ethnic civil war was not to spread through Eastern Europe and destabilize an area already under the shadow of Bolshevism. Despite bitter protests, the new Polish government was obliged to guarantee certain rights to its minorities as a condition of recognition: they included equality of treatment under the law and religious freedoms as well as rights to certain forms of collective organization in the educational and cultural spheres. The Polish Minorities Treaty was guaranteed by the League of Nations, which apparently meant that complaints could be brought to Geneva (though not directly by the minority concerned). In certain circumstances, the League's Council could take action.

The Polish Treaty took international law into uncharted waters. During the previous century, the Great Powers had often recognized new states dependent on a commitment to religious freedom and toleration; such had been the case, for example, in Belgium in 1830 and Romania in 1878. What was new in 1919 was the concern for "national" rather than exclusively religious rights, for collective rights rather than individual liberties, and the provision for international deliberation.

Poland provided the model for a whole series of minority rights treaties that the peacemakers in Paris drew up for Eastern Europe. Similar obligations were imposed on other newly-created states as well as on former belligerents like Hungary and older states like Romania and Greece, which acquired territory as a result of the war. The League of Nations came to stand for a system that, on the one hand, accepted the nation-state as the norm in international relations and, on the other, made a considered effort to tackle the minority issues that were thus created. It accepted (perhaps thereby sometimes encouraging the creation of) minorities as collective entities; their political weight and profile were increased through the annual meetings of the European Congress of Nationalities, which publicized their plight.

But the role of the League itself in this system was ambiguous. It was difficult to bring cases to the League's attention, and even more difficult to push them through the Geneva machine and have them taken up by the Council. Although the League had the power to refer cases to the Permanent Court of Justice in The Hague, it rarely acted on it. On the other hand, it jealously guarded this power and blocked proposals to allow minorities to appeal to the Court directly. The League Secretariat did not see itself as a "champion of minorities" but more modestly as an interlocutor helping governments carry out their own obligations. The League also had few sanctions against egregious offenders. Thus the notoriously repressive behavior of Yugoslav gendarmes in Macedonia went unchecked, as did the Polish government's bloody "pacification campaign" against the Ukrainians in 1930.

Polish or Serbian intolerance did not much bother the French, who were more concerned about the stability of their Eastern European allies than about minorities. Nor, increasingly, did it bother the British, who believed the minorities treaties were hindering the process of assimilation. "More harm would in the end be done by unnecessary interference than, even at the risk of a little local suffering, to allow these minorities to settle down under their present masters," wrote a Foreign Office official in London in 1922. "So long as these people imagine that their grievances can be aired before the League of Nations they will refuse to settle down and the present effervescence will continue indefinitely."[4]

Yet despite such indifference from the League's main sponsors, some groups pushed for more of an activist stance. Under the diplomacy of Gustav Stresemann, Weimar Germany entered the League and began to assume the role of the "defender of minorities" with an eye to the millions of ethnic Germans scattered across Eastern Europe. German and Jewish groups spearheaded the lobbying of the European Congress of Nationalities, while Stresemann identified himself closely with the cause of reforming the Geneva machinery by creating a permanent minority rights commission. His efforts had limited results, partly because they were suspected to form part of a more general effort to revise the Versailles settlement. Stresemann merely managed to convince German nationalists at home that the League would never adequately protect ethnic Germans abroad.[5]

At the same time, the minorities treaties were bitterly resented as a humiliation by the countries concerned. They were particularly irritated by the fact that there was no universal minority-rights regime; they wondered why they had been singled out when no such obligations had been imposed on Germany or on Italy when it persecuted the German-speaking minority in the South Tyrol.

It is true that of the approximately thirty-five million estimated minority inhabitants in interwar Europe, only some 8.6 million lived in Western Europe (roughly one in twenty of the total population) whereas about twenty-five million lived in Central and Eastern Europe (one in four). Thus the minorities question *was* numerically far more important in the East. Even so, the lack of a universal regime was an embarrassment for the Great Powers.[6]

Such an idea had in fact been considered in 1919 in Paris, only to be rejected. As James Headlam-Morley, one of the key figures behind the minorities guarantees, noted at the time, fundamental issues of state sovereignty were at stake:

> At first there was, so far as I recollect, a proposal that there should be inserted in the League of Nations some general clause giving the League of Nations the right to protect minorities in all countries which were members of the League. This I always most strongly opposed. . .for it would have involved the right to interfere in the internal constitution of every country in the world. As I pointed out, it would give the League of Nations the right to protect the Chinese in Liverpool, the Roman Catholics in France, the French in Canada, quite apart from the more serious problems, such as the Irish. This point of view was, I think, not seriously opposed by any except the unofficial bodies who wished the League of Nations to be a sort of super-state with a general right of guarding democracy and freedom throughout the world. . . . My own view was that any right given to the League of Nations must be quite definite and specific, and based on special treaties entered into because of definite exceptional cases, and that such a right could only be recognized in the case of a new or immature state of Eastern Europe or Western Asia. Even if the denial of such a right elsewhere might lead to injustice and oppression, that was better than to allow anything which would mean the negation of the sovereignty of every state in the world.[7]

Thus the Great Powers were happy to interfere in the internal affairs of "new" states but allowed no meddling in their own affairs. This supremely paternalistic stance assumed that "civilized" states such as those in Western Europe had evolved procedures to facilitate the assimilation of minorities that did not yet exist in "immature states." That view was, to some extent, true: it was easier for Welsh or Catalan children to make careers in the professions or the civil service than it was, say, for Ukrainians in Poland or Hungarians in Romania, where hatreds were more recent. Breton children might suffer at school, but they did not have their homes and villages burned down. The minorities treaties were a way of educating less civilized nations in international deportment.

But the underlying premise was that assimilation into the civilized life of the nation was possible and desirable. As a Brazilian delegate put it in Geneva in 1925, the goal of the treaties was not to perpetuate a state of affairs in which certain groups in society saw themselves as "constantly alien," but, rather, to establish the conditions for "a complete national unity."[8]

After 1933, however, the "assimilation thesis" (as it was dubbed by opponents) was spectacularly refuted with the rise of the Third Reich. Ethnic nationalism as practiced in Warsaw or Bucharest had limited scope for assimilation; racial nationalism of the kind that spread across Central and Eastern Europe in the 1930s allowed none. The rise of institutionalized anti-Semitism in Hitler's Germany therefore undermined the whole basis of the League's approach to minorities. A supposedly "civilized" state was rejecting the assimilationist idea in the most sweeping fashion possible. In October of 1933, Nazi Germany left the League. A year later, the Polish premier, Colonel Beck, drove another nail into the League's coffin when he denounced Poland's minority-rights obligations "pending the introduction of a general and uniform system for the protection of minorities." The number of minority petitions received at Geneva fell sharply from 204 in 1930 to fifteen in 1936. This drop can be taken as a barometer of the waning confidence felt by European minorities in the value of the League.[9]

Let us not, however, be too hasty in writing off the League's minority system altogether. In the first place, it did notch up a few successes that offered valuable lessons for the future and showed what was possible with astute and far-sighted government. If these today have been forgotten, it is perhaps only because they were too peaceful for the history books. The Aaland islands dispute between Sweden and Finland, for instance, was resolved quietly in 1921: the islands remained Finnish, but the Swedish islanders were granted a high degree of administrative autonomy. This compact formed the basis of a solution that removed a major source of tension between the two countries.

The Estonian government took the remarkable step of granting cultural autonomy to its "national minorities"; the Latvians did not go quite this far but did offer some concessions in education. These, to be sure, were exceptions. More usually, as in the Lithuanian and Polish cases, promises made were not kept. The number of Ukrainian schools in Poland, for instance, dropped from 3,662 to 144 in the interwar period. Too often, *numerus clausus* clauses kept minorities out of universities and the civil service.[10]

Those who condemn the League's minorities system might also ponder the alternatives. Nation-states were a reality, not merely a creation of wartime Great Power diplomacy. The conversion of the Ottoman Empire into a Turkish national state, for instance, could hardly be attributed to forces outside the country; Mustafa Kemal made the running there, not Lloyd George. And as the Turkish example demonstrates, there were several other ways of treating minorities. "First we kill the Armenians, then the Greeks, then the Kurds," a Turkish gendarme told a Danish Red Cross nurse in July 1915 as the war accelerated the Turkification of the Ottoman Empire. Even friendly German observers concluded that, beyond the professed concern for military security in border areas, the Turks aimed for "the planned extermination of the Armenian people." Later this would be termed "genocide" and, later still, "ethnic cleansing." Neither mass murder nor population transfer offered a way of solving Eastern Europe's ethnic problems that was acceptable to liberal opinion.[11]

If proof was needed of the horrors such alternatives held in store, it was provided by Hitler's use of both mass murder and population transfer in his own effort to construct an anti-liberal new order in Europe. The "final solution of the Jewish question" formed part of this thoroughgoing Nazi attempt to redraw the racial map of the continent. A policy based on international law and state sovereignty was replaced by one that repudiated the very foundations of both: Nazi legal theorists attacked Geneva's "juridification" of international relations and its pathetic belief in a "common rule of law" applicable to peoples of differing racial worth.[12]

The Third Reich proposed to replace international law with a doctrine that legitimized German intervention in the internal affairs of other states on behalf of ethnic Germans abroad. The state, after all, was merely the expression of the racial *Volk*. "Blood is stronger than a passport," wrote a prominent pan-Germanist in 1937.[13] The German minorities in Eastern Europe were "racial comrades" of Reich Germans. They could be protected through invasion—as in Austria and the Sudetenland—or through the "trustee rights" that Germany acquired in its Danubian client states in the second Vienna accord of August 1940. German commentators hailed this last step as a vast improvement on the old League system of minority protection. These "laws for the protection of the folk-group" gave the "mother country" the right to intervene directly with the host government on behalf of the minority. They turned the entire "folk-group" into a collective legal entity. Such legislation looked a lot more attractive at the height of German power than it did a mere four years later. By 1945 collective justice had been turned on its head, as millions of ethnic Germans were expelled westwards.

* * *

During the war itself, the League's record towards minorities came under scrutiny. Had its policy of protection by treaty been too ambitious or not ambitious enough? Had it failed because the machinery was unworkable or because the political will to operate it was absent? As plans emerged to replace the League with a successor organization, these questions could not be shirked. The racial basis of Nazi jurisprudence and Germany's abandonment of the accepted principles of international law had been regarded since the late 1930s as among the principal causes of the breakdown of order in Europe. Nazi aggression had undermined the very existence of an "international community." At the same time, Nazi treatment of the Jews persuaded many people that if the individual was to be protected against the state, the traditional doctrine of state sovereignty in domestic affairs would have to be reconsidered. A revival and reinvigoration of international law thus emerged as the natural adjunct to liberal concern for world peace and, in particular, for the safeguarding of human rights.[14]

"Effective international organization is not possible," wrote Quincy Wright in 1943, "unless it protects basic human rights against encroachments by national States." Wright observed that unlike Poland or Czechoslovakia, Germany had not been obliged to conclude a minorities treaty with the League of Nations, with the result that "there was no formal ground on which the League of Nations could protest against the beginning of the persecutions in Germany. It was a general principle that a State was free to persecute its own nationals in its own territory as it saw fit."[15]

But the protection of human rights required the existence of a body superior to the state to which the individual could have recourse. The Austrian jurist Hans Kelsen insisted that "a right consists only in the legal possibility to invoke a court. . . . [International law] can confer rights on individuals only under the condition that individuals have direct access to an international court." His colleague Hersch Lauterpacht warned that the international protection of human rights "touching as it does intimately upon the relations of the State and the individual. . .implies a more drastic interference with the sovereignty of the State than the renunciation of war." But in his aptly-named *Peace through Law,* Kelsen argued that only people who believed in a "theology of the State" refused to recognize the need for all states to be bound by international law. Sovereignty was simply a red herring. "We can derive from the concept of sovereignty," he went on, "nothing else than what we have purposely put into its definition."[16]

The limits of sovereignty, then, reflected political rather than jurisprudential or philosophical considerations. But who was going to make states acknowledge the supremacy of international law? Liberal thought in the interwar period had reposed its confidence in the pressure of world public opinion to safeguard human rights. It was obvious that a more effective instrument of enforcement would be required in the postwar period. What complicated matters was the Allies' commitment, as enshrined in the Atlantic Charter, to respect traditional ideas of state sovereignty. The postwar state, in other words, was being asked in some measure to acquiesce in its own weakening. Experienced lawyers like Kelsen and Lauterpacht saw no other realistic way to persuade individual states to make their international obligations a part of domestic law. The alternative was to push for some form of world state, but this they regarded as utopian.

At the heart of this debate was the question of whether the human rights to be enshrined in the new postwar order should be individual or collective. This was where the post-1945 order would deviate most sharply from Geneva's approach. The League of Nations had chosen the latter in its system of protection for ethnic minorities in Eastern Europe. The war had done little to diminish the gravity of the problem of ethnic strife. Indeed, Raphael Lemkin coined the term "genocide" in his 1944 study of *Axis Rule in Occupied Europe,* and called for the development of "adequate machinery for the international protection of national and ethnic groups against extermination attempts and oppression in time of peace."[17]

Yet despite the obvious importance of safeguarding minorities, strong arguments were advanced in favor of demolishing rather than improving the collective-rights approach pioneered by the League. President Beneš and the Czech government in exile denounced the League system on the grounds that experience had shown that it had actually jeopardized their national security. "Every protected minority will ultimately find its Henlein," warned one observer. In addition, the states of Eastern Europe resented the fact that they had been singled out for special obligations towards their minorities, whereas the Great Powers, including Italy and Germany, had not had to suffer such an indignity. "In the end," wrote Beneš in 1942, "things came to such an extraordinary pass that the totalitarian and dictator states—Germany, Hungary, and Italy—persecuted the minorities in their own territories and at the same time posed as the protectors of minorities in states which were really democratic." Rather than attempting to restore the League system, Beneš suggested that the postwar approach to minorities should be based upon "the defense of human democratic rights and not of national rights."[18]

In addition to this opposition from Eastern Europe, the major Allied powers—Britain, France, and the United States—also showed little enthusiasm for reviving a system that had succeeded in internationalizing the most serious source of tension in Europe without finding adequate means of resolution. As the postwar settlement in Europe would show, the main interest of the major powers was in limiting their obligations to minor states; this meant that they too were happy to bury the League's approach to collective rights. The result was that the UN's eventual commitment to individual human rights was as much an expression of passivity as of resolve by the Allies. It was a means of avoiding problems, not of solving them. This fact helps us understand why so few of the wartime hopes for a reinvigoration of international law were to be realized.

Behind the rhetoric, the UN's commitment to minority rights was as weak as its overall position in power politics. In terms of the protection of minorities, the UN Charter represented a definite step backwards from the League. The Universal Declaration of Human Rights of 1948 underlined the new status of the individual in international law and revealed a lasting mistrust of the Nazi doctrine of state supremacy, but it contained no provisions for enforcement. Minorities were scarcely mentioned, and their study was confined to an obscure Sub-Commission of the Human Rights Committee. A UN Secretariat study of 1950, which provided a sharp distinction between the League's outmoded approach and the new "general and universal protection of human rights," has been described by one commentator as "disastrous for the international protection of minorities."[19]

More far-reaching in its implications was the 1948 Genocide Convention—passed after a remarkable one-man crusade by Raphael Lemkin, who had been disappointed at the refusal of the International Military Tribunal at Nuremberg to judge acts committed by the Nazis before 1939. Lemkin and others had seen the war-crimes trials as an opportunity to secure world peace by increasing the powers under international law to take action against individuals as well as states. The Genocide Convention added an important new crime to those recognized under international law and imposed obligations upon ratifying states to act to prevent or punish its commission. But the convention's potential has been ignored by the international community, and there has been little evidence to back the UN's confident assertion that "the feeling will grow in world society that by protecting the national, racial, religious and ethnic groups everywhere in the world we will be protecting ourselves." Over four decades, a series of genocides went unpunished outside Europe; in 1992 that indifference extended to Europe itself.[20]

* * *

During the Cold War, Europe's minorities problems—already much reduced by the dramatic shifts of populations that took place in the 1940s—were simply put into a deep freeze. On each side of the Iron Curtain, potentially destabilizing disputes were managed bilaterally, under the gaze of the presiding superpower. Neither Austro-Italian differences over the South Tyrol nor Hungarian-Romanian disputes over Transylvania were allowed to jeopardize bloc cohesion. The German problem was no longer one of minorities—as it had been between the wars—but rather of a divided country. The brutal stability the Cold War brought to Europe disguised the fact that the international regime on minority rights had regressed rather than advanced after the interwar years. In the 1990s, as the international response to the outbreak of war in Yugoslavia showed, thinking on minority rights had to start from scratch again.

There is a striking contrast between the ambition and confidence of international policy in the 1920s and the uncertain, reactive style of the 1990s. Population transfer along the lines of the 1923 Greco-Turkish exchange may have appealed to some Western policymakers as they tried to manage the war in Bosnia, but none had the assurance to offer it explicitly as a solution. It remains instead one possible interpretation of that masterpiece of obfuscation, the Dayton peace accords.

As for a fully developed international regime of minority rights protection, the League's effort must seem from today's perspective the product of an almost unimaginably activist and idealistic political elite, confident of their right to reshape half a continent according to the tenets of Western liberalism. Their effort remains of interest as the most sustained attempt in Europe's history to solve the dilemmas of nationalism through international law. But today the map looks very different. The two great minorities of 1918, the Germans and the Jews, have in different ways been eliminated; minorities also generally form a smaller proportion of national populations in Central and Eastern Europe today than before the war. At the same time, liberal confidence in history as an engine of ethnic assimilation has disappeared, perhaps for good.

The international community has grown in size and shrunk in resolve; emulating Geneva therefore seems unlikely. There may be some talk of rewarding Eastern European countries for good behavior, but when the Council of Europe admits Tudjman's Croatia as a member, it is hard to take this very seriously. The breakup of Yugoslavia eventually impelled the Conference on Security and Cooperation in Europe (CSCE) to appoint a High Commissioner on National Minorities, and it accelerated the publication of the UN's own belated "Declaration on the Rights of Persons Belonging to National or Ethnic, Religious and Linguistic Minorities." So far, however, these initiatives remain tentative; the League's policies look forceful and coherent in comparison. Internationally as well as domestically, it seems as though history is more about forgetting the past than about learning from it.

Let me conclude, then, with a paradigm of forgetting. The island of Ada Kaleh was the site of a Turkish fortress on the Danube just above the Iron Gates. It contained a mosque, a library, and a small village. When the Ottoman grip on the Balkans slackened in the nineteenth century, Ada Kaleh was overlooked. It was apparently forgotten by the diplomats at the Congress of Berlin and remained a curious Turkish anomaly, stranded midstream between the newly-created kingdoms of Serbia and Romania. In 1919 its three hundred Muslim inhabitants were handed over to Romania. Tourists used to row across from the mainland to view these "human curiosities," drink their coffee, buy their figs and rose-water and Turkish delight, and peer inside the last remaining harem in Europe. At a time when Atatürk was creating a secular state in Turkey, these few islanders preserved the traditional Ottoman ways. Today one will search in vain on the map for Ada Kaleh. It lies beneath the waters of the Danube, sacrificed in the 1950s to the ambitious hydroelectric plans of Romania's communist rulers. Is not Ada Kaleh just as appropriate a symbol of our manner of dealing with minorities this century as any of Europe's Cultural Capitals?

ENDNOTES

[1]Acton, quoted by C. A. Macartney, *National States and National Minorities* (New York: Russell & Russell, 1968), 17; Robert Cecil in Victor H. Rothwell, *British War Aims and Peace Diplomacy, 1914–1918* (Oxford: Clarendon Press, 1971), 159.

[2]See especially Arnold Toynbee's deliberately titled *The Western Question in Greece and Turkey: A Study in the Contact of Civilizations* (London: Constable and Company, Ltd., 1922).

[3]See Mark Levene, *Wars, Jews and the New Europe: The Diplomacy of Lucien Wolf, 1914–1919* (Oxford: Oxford University Press, 1992); Israel Cohen, *Travels in Jewry* (London: E. Goldston, 1952), 87.

[4]Cited by P. B. Finney, "'An Evil For All Concerned': Great Britain and Minority Protection After 1919," *Journal of Contemporary History* 30 (1995): 536–537.

[5]C. Fink, "'Defender of Minorities': Germany in the League of Nations, 1926–1933," *Central European History* 5 (4) (1972): 330–357.

[6]Figures from Otto Junghann, *National Minorities in Europe* (New York: Covici, Friede, 1932), 116, 119.

[7]James Wycliffe Headlam-Morley, *A Memoir of the Paris Peace Conference, 1919* (London: Methuen, 1972), 112–113.

[8]S. Sierpowski, "Minorities in the System of the League of Nations," in Paul Smith, ed., *Ethnic Groups in International Relations* (New York: New York University Press, 1991), 27.

[9]Cited by Inis Claude, *National Minorities: An International Problem* (Cambridge, Mass.: Harvard University Press, 1955), 30; numbers of petitions in Macartney, *National States and National Minorities*, 504, and Jacob Robinson et al., *Were the Minorities Treaties a Failure?* (New York: Institute of Jewish Affairs of the American Jewish Congress and the World Jewish Congress, 1943), 252.

[10]A. J. Motyl, "Ukrainian Nationalist Political Violence in Inter-War Poland, 1921–1939," *East European Quarterly* 19 (1) (March 1985): 46.

[11]Manoug J. Somakian, *Empires in Conflict: Armenia and the Great Powers, 1895–1920* (London: Tauris Academic Studies, 1995), 137, 86; Arnold J. Toynbee, *The Western Question in Greece and Turkey*, 2d ed. (London: Constable, 1923), 16–17.

[12]J. Herz, "The National Socialist Doctrine of International Law and the Problems of International Organization," *Political Science Quarterly* 44 (4) (December 1939): 536–554.

[13]Cited in United States, Department of State, Division of European Affairs, *National Socialism: Basic Principles, Their Application by the Nazi Party's Foreign Organization and the Use of Germans Abroad for Nazi Aims* (Washington, D.C.: US Government Printing Office, 1943), 70.

[14]Raphael Lemkin, *Axis Rule in Occupied Europe* (Washington, D.C.: Carnegie Endowment for International Peace, 1944), xiv; W. Friedman, "The Disintegration of European Civilization and the Future of International Law," *Modern Law Review* (December 1938): 194–214; J. Herz, "The National Socialist Doctrine of International Law," *Political Science Quarterly* (December 1939): 536–554.

[15]World Citizens Association, *World's Destiny and the United States* (Chicago, Ill.: World Citizens Association, 1941), 102–105.

[16]Ibid., 113; Hersch Lauterpacht, *An International Bill of the Rights of Man* (New York: Columbia University Press, 1945), vi; Hans Kelsen, *Peace through Law* (Chapel Hill, N.C.: The University of North Carolina Press, 1944), esp. 41–42.

[17]Lemkin, *Axis Rule in Occupied Europe,* xiii.

[18]E. Beneš, "The Organization of Postwar Europe," *Foreign Affairs* 20 (1) (January 1942): 226–242; Claude, *National Minorities: An International Problem,* 55–59.

[19]I. Szabo, "Historical Foundations of Human Rights and Subsequent Developments," in Karel Vasak, ed., *The International Dimensions of Human Rights* (Paris: UNESCO, 1982), 11–42; Hersch Lauterpacht, *International Law and Human Rights* (New York: F. A. Praeger, 1950), 353; Hersch Lauterpacht, *Report: Human Rights, the Charter of the United Nations and the International Bill of the Rights of Man* (Brussels: n.p., 1948), 22; P. Thornberry, "The UN

Declaration: Background, Analysis and Observations," in Alan Phillips and Allan Rosas, eds., *The UN Minority Rights Declaration* (Turku, Abo: Abo Akademi University, Institute for Human Rights; London: Minority Rights Group, 1993), 15.

[20]Nehemiah Robinson, *The Genocide Convention: A Commentary* (New York: Institute of Jewish Affairs, World Jewish Congress, 1960), 52; see also Hans Kelsen, "Collective and Individual Responsibility in International Law with Particular Regard to the Punishment of War Criminals," *California Law Review* XXXI (December 1943): 530–571; Hersch Lauterpacht, "The Subjects of the Law of Nations," *Law Quarterly Review* LXIII (October 1947): 438–460; *Law Quarterly Review* LXIV (January 1948): 97–116.

[3]

The internationalization of minority rights

Will Kymlicka*

Debates concerning integration and accommodation are a familiar feature of the domestic political life of many countries. But these debates increasingly have an international dimension as well. International organizations can strongly influence the way state–minority relations are framed and resolved, endorsing some models of accommodation while discouraging others. This paper attempts to explore which models of state–minority relations and, hence, which types of minority rights, have been endorsed by international organizations, for which types of groups, and in which contexts. These are not simple questions to answer. Many international organizations have struggled with this issue for the past fifteen years without any clear resolution, and their current policies and practices are full of ambiguities and inconsistencies. The goal of this paper is to bring out some of these complexities, focusing particularly on how the rights of indigenous peoples have been elaborated at the United Nations, and the way in which the rights of national minorities have been discussed within European organizations. Very different assumptions and principles underlie the two cases, and each raises its own moral and political dilemmas.

Around the world, one of the most pressing issues of constitutional design concerns the status and treatment of ethnocultural minorities. Should a constitution recognize a distinctive legal status for indigenous peoples? Should it provide official language status or self-government rights to territorially concentrated minorities? Should it guarantee political representation for dispersed ethnic minorities? In a recent study, John McGarry, Brendan O'Leary, and Richard Simeon have suggested that countries have two broad choices in this regard—either "integration" or "accommodation." The former seeks to integrate all citizens on a nondiscriminatory basis into shared national institutions; the latter seeks to accommodate diversity through minority-specific institutions. The authors' study provides a helpful overview of the range of

* Canada Research Chair in Political Philosophy, Queen's University, Kingston, Ontario. Email: kymlicka@post.queensu.ca

arguments regarding these choices and the circumstances that affect how nations choose.[1]

In the past, the decision to opt for integration or accommodation (or to attempt some hybrid) was left largely to the discretion of individual countries. Today, however, the international community plays an increasingly important role in shaping policy in this area, endorsing some models of integration and accommodation while discouraging others.

Therefore, any comprehensive examination of the integration/accommodation debate must look closely at the attitudes of the international community. When does the international community favor integration, and when does it favor accommodation? McGarry, O'Leary, and Simeon state that integration "is the dominant strategy for regulating diversity," favored by Western states and by the officials of intergovernmental organizations such as the United Nations and the Bretton Woods institutions.[2] This is more or less correct as a generalization, but it obscures a much more interesting and complicated story. Various international organizations have struggled with this issue for the past fifteen years without any clear resolution and their current policies and practices remain full of ambiguities and inconsistencies. This essay aims to bring out some of these complexities and to highlight some of the challenges they raise for those involved in debates concerning integration and accommodation.

I will begin by examining the norms that have been formulated within the United Nations, which divide nondominant ethnocultural groups into two broad categories—"indigenous peoples" and "minorities." According to the UN, indigenous peoples have much stronger claims to self-government than minorities. I will argue that, while it is indeed important to distinguish different categories of ethnocultural groups, this particular categorization is inadequate to address the actual patterns of ethnic political mobilization and conflict around the world. I will then consider recent attempts by the Council of Europe to develop norms relating to the category of "national minorities," which potentially can take us beyond the UN's "indigenous vs. minority" dichotomy. However, I will argue, these attempts too have proven inadequate, in ways that raise deep questions about the capacity of international law to articulate and protect minority rights.

[1] *See* John McGarry, Brendan O'Leary & Richard Simeon, *Integration or Accommodation? The Enduring Debate in Conflict Regulation, in* CONSTITUTIONAL DESIGN FOR DIVIDED SOCIETIES: INTEGRATION OR ACCOMMODATION? (Sujit Choudhry ed., Oxford Univ. Press, forthcoming 2008).

[2] *Id.*

1. The basic international framework

What is the view of the international community toward integration and accommodation? This is, of course, a hopelessly vague question, since the "international community" is not a single monolithic actor with a single set of beliefs or attitudes. Even if we restrict our attention solely to such treaty-based intergovernmental organizations as the United Nations and its agencies or the World Bank and the Council of Europe, there is no one consensus position. Each has its own distinct mandate or function that gives it a unique interest in, and perspective on, issues of ethnic diversity. There are profound differences among, as well as within, these organizations in their approaches to the governance of that diversity.

Let us look first at the United Nations. The UN is a key actor in this debate, not only because it claims to represent and speak for all the peoples of the world but also because it has addressed the question of integration and accommodation explicitly and has developed formal statements of its position. Moreover, its official position is surprisingly simple; namely, that "indigenous peoples" have a right to accommodation, whereas "minorities" have a right to integration.

This basic distinction between indigenous peoples and minorities is reiterated throughout the UN's activities, be it in the field of environmental protection, economic development, or human rights. However, it is articulated most clearly in two key texts—the 1992 Declaration on the Rights of Persons Belonging to National or Ethnic, Religious and Linguistic Minorities[3] and the draft Declaration on the Rights of Indigenous Peoples, which remains a draft despite thirteen years of intensive debate.[4] The former adopts an integrationist approach for minorities, focusing on nondiscrimination and civil rights; the

[3] Adopted by the General Assembly in Resolution 47/135. *See* U.N. Doc. A/RES/47/135/Annex (Dec. 18, 1993).

[4] First introduced in the Working Group on Minorities in 1993, the draft declaration was approved by the Human Rights Council in 2006. *See* Human Rights Council Res. 1/2, Annex, U.N. Doc. A/HRC/RES/1/2/Annex (June 29, 2006). The Council approved it by a vote of 30 in favor to 2 against (Canada and Russian Federation), with 12 abstentions, and forwarded it to the General Assembly for consideration; as of this writing, action is still pending. However, despite its lack of legal force, its core ideas have been picked up by various organs and agencies within the UN system, and similar ideas have been articulated by the International Labour Organization and in the draft declaration on indigenous rights of the Organization of American States (OAS).

latter adopts an accommodationist approach for indigenous peoples, focusing on self-government and institutional pluralism.[5]

This basic approach has been reaffirmed by the two UN working groups that have developed and interpreted these key texts. In 2000, Asbjorn Eide and Erica-Irene Daes, the then chairpersons, respectively, of the UN's Working Group on Minorities and Working Group on Indigenous Populations explained their understanding of the differing rationales underlying the two documents.[6] Their statements point to three basic differences between minorities and indigenous peoples: (*a*) minorities seek institutional integration while indigenous peoples seek to preserve a degree of institutional separateness; (*b*) minorities seek to exercise individual rights while indigenous peoples seek to exercise collective rights; (*c*) minorities seek nondiscrimination while indigenous peoples seek self-government. These statements by important UN figures confirm the fundamentally integrationist approach of the minority rights declaration, and the fundamentally accommodationist approach of the indigenous rights declaration.

Daes gives a particularly clear statement of the distinction:

> Bearing the conceptual problem [of distinguishing indigenous peoples from minorities] in mind, I should like to suggest that the ideal type of an "indigenous people" is a group that is aboriginal (autochthonous) to the territory where it resides today and chooses to perpetuate a distinct cultural identity and distinct collective social and political organization within the territory. The ideal type of a "minority" is a group that has experienced exclusion or discrimination by the State or its citizens because of its ethnic, national, racial, religious or linguistic characteristics or ancestry.
>
> ... From a purposive perspective, then, the ideal type of [a] "minority" focuses on the group's experience of discrimination because the intent of

[5] I will use the accommodation/integration terminology adopted by McGarry et al., *supra* note 1, although it is potentially misleading. What they call integrationist models often involve some degree of accommodation of cultural diversity within common institutions. For example, a "duty to accommodate" is part of the immigrant multiculturalism policy in Canada, even though this clearly qualifies as an integrationist policy in their typology. Conversely, what they call accommodationist models can often be seen as a way of ensuring that self-governing groups are, nonetheless, connected to (and in that sense integrated into) a larger state. Provincial autonomy for Quebec accommodates an aspiration for autonomy, but it also integrates a potentially secessionist group into a larger federal political order. The terms "integration" and "accommodation" should be understood with these provisos in mind.

[6] U.N. Econ. & Soc. Council [ECOSOC], Comm'n on Human Rights, Sub-Comm. on Promotion & Prot. of Human Rights, Working Paper on the Relationship and Distinction between the Rights of Persons Belonging to Minorities and those of Indigenous Peoples, U.N. Doc. E/CN.4/Sub.2/2000/10 (July 19, 2000) (prepared by Asbjorn Eide & Erica-Irene Daes) [hereinafter Eide & Daes, Working Paper].

existing international standards has been to combat discrimination, against the group as a whole as well as its individual members, and to provide for them the opportunity to integrate themselves freely into national life to the degree they choose. Likewise, the ideal type of "indigenous peoples" focuses on aboriginality, territoriality, and the desire to remain collectively distinct, all elements which are tied logically to the exercise of the right to internal self-determination, self-government, or autonomy.[7]

The parallels between Daes's two "ideal types" and the ideal types of integration and accommodation developed by McGarry and his colleagues are both clear and direct.

It is worth noting here that although Eide and Daes are primarily concerned with explaining the different entitlements of the two kinds of groups, as envisaged under the relevant UN declarations, they are not simply talking about legal distinctions. They are also making claims about the *aspirations* of the two groups. If international norms accord different rights to minorities than to indigenous peoples, this is because the two groups are presumed to want different kinds of rights. According to Daes, "The facts remain that indigenous peoples and minorities organize themselves separately and tend to assert different objectives, even in those countries where they appear to differ very little in 'objective' characteristics."[8] Steven Wheatley makes a similar claim: "There is no objective distinction that can be made between groups recognized as minorities, national minorities, indigenous peoples and peoples. What distinguishes these groups is the nature of their political demands: simply put, minorities and national minorities demand cultural security; peoples demand recognition of their right to self-determination, or self-government."[9]

This, then, is the UN's basic theoretical framework for addressing these issues, although the organization's actual practices are more complicated than its formal declarations would suggest. The UN endorses integration and nondiscrimination for national, ethnic, religious, and linguistic minorities, even as it endorses accommodation and autonomy for indigenous peoples. We can see echoes of this approach in other major intergovernmental organizations, such as the World Bank or International Labour Organization, which have adopted similar formal policies espousing autonomy for indigenous peoples while endorsing nondiscrimination and integration for minorities.[10]

[7] *Id.* at paras. 48–49.

[8] *Id.* at para. 41.

[9] Steven Wheatley, Democracy, Minorities and International Law 124 (Cambridge Univ. Press 2005).

[10] *See* Will Kymlicka, Multicultural Odysseys: Navigating the New International Politics of Diversity (Oxford Univ. Press 2007) (chs. 6–7).

2. Limitations of the international framework

The UN approach has the virtue of simplicity; however, it is arguably inadequate to the real-world challenges of ethnic diversity. With regard to indigenous peoples, its approach is widely and rightly seen as beneficial, helping to empower historically subordinated groups and to disseminate best practices for the effective participation and self-government of indigenous peoples. The UN Working Group on Indigenous Populations has served as the nerve center for a vibrant transnational network of community activists, nongovernmental organizations (NGOs), academics, philanthropic foundations, and policy makers; with considerable success, this network has diffused the ideas and standards contained in the draft declaration on indigenous rights. It has been particularly effective in encouraging and legitimizing the mobilization of indigenous peoples in Latin America.[11]

The UN's approach to minorities, by contrast, has been less successful. Its Working Group on Minorities has not become the locus of a global network in defense of minority rights. And even though the UN's declaration on minority rights has a clearer normative status than the draft declaration on indigenous rights—since it has been adopted unanimously by the General Assembly—the former has not had nearly the same public impact and is rarely invoked by minorities around the world.

There are several difficulties confronting the UN approach to minorities; the central problem, however, is the underlying assumption that "ethnic, national, racial, religious or linguistic" minorities can all be lumped together, and that they all seek integration rather than accommodation. This is, at best, a drastic overgeneralization, and at worst a serious misinterpretation of the issues. As others discuss in depth,[12] there are many cases worldwide where minorities seek accommodation rather than integration. Some of the most well known and protracted struggles for autonomy around the world involve groups that are considered minorities rather than indigenous peoples by the UN—groups such as the Scots, Catalans, Chechens, Kosovar Albanians, Kurds, Kashmiris, and Tamils. Indeed, in the early 1990s, it was precisely the upsurge of ethnic conflicts involving autonomy-seeking substate nationalist minorities that led the UN to take an active interest in formulating standards regarding minorities.[13] And yet, remarkably, the text that resulted—the 1992 declaration on minority rights—far from providing guidance for dealing with such minority

[11] *See* Alison Brysk, From Tribal Village to Global Village: Indian Rights and International Relations in Latin America (Stanford Univ. Press 2000).

[12] *See* Constitutional Design for Divided Societies, *supra* note 1.

[13] *See* Kymlicka, *supra* note 10 at ch. 2, on the impetus given to the UN's standard-setting activities by these ethnonationalist conflicts.

claims for autonomy, actually renders them invisible by presupposing that minorities, by definition, are only interested in integration.

The problem is not simply that a model based on a stark dichotomy between autonomy-seeking indigenous peoples and integration-seeking minorities is inadequate to deal with a number of important real-world cases. The deeper problem is that this very way of dividing up the ethnocultural landscape may obscure the actual issues involved in the choice between accommodation and integration.

In order to understand the problem, we need to step back and examine the broader patterns of ethnic politics in contemporary democracies. Relations between the state and minorities in the Western democracies are highly differentiated by group. Certain generic civil and cultural rights are guaranteed to the members of all ethnocultural groups; however, there are also a number of "targeted" rights that apply only to particular categories of groups. The precise categories vary from country to country, but they typically fall into the same basic pattern. The most common distinction is between "old" minorities, which were settled on their territory prior to its becoming part of a larger, independent country, and "new" minorities, which were admitted to a country as immigrants after it achieved legal independence. The old minorities are often called "homeland" minorities, since they have been historically settled within a particular part of a country for a long period of time and, as a result of that historic settlement, have come to see that part of the country as their historic homeland. The minority's homeland is incorporated within a larger state or, perhaps, divided between two or more countries; nonetheless, the minority still has a strong sense of attachment to this homeland and often nurtures memories of an earlier time, prior to the origin of the modern state, when it had self-government over this territory.

There is a nearly universal tendency within the Western democracies to distinguish the rights of old homeland minorities from those of new immigrant minorities. As Perry Keller notes, this distinction is "found in the laws and policies of almost every European State."[14] The same is true in North America.[15]

Of course, these broad categories of old and new minorities are themselves quite heterogeneous. Within the category of new minorities, for example, many countries accord a different legal status to different subcategories, such

[14] Perry Keller, *Rethinking Ethnic and Cultural Rights in Europe*, 18 OXFORD J. LEG. STUD. 43 (1998). For a helpful overview of these distinctions as drawn in the Nordic countries, see Lauri Hannikainen, *The Status of Minorities, Indigenous Peoples and Immigrant and Refugee Groups in Four Nordic Countries*, 65 NORDIC J. INT'L. L. 1 (1996).

[15] For details of the Canadian case, see Will Kymlicka, *Ethnocultural Diversity in a Liberal State: Making Sense of the Canadian Model(s)*, *in* BELONGING? DIVERSITY, RECOGNITION AND SHARED CITIZENSHIP IN CANADA 39–86 (Keith Banting, Thomas Courchene & Leslie Seidle eds., Institute for Research on Public Policy 2007). For the American case, see the (dated) overview in Sharon O'Brien, *Cultural Rights in the United States: A Conflict of Values*, 5 LAW & INEQUALITY J. 267 (1987).

as asylum seekers, temporary guest workers, illegal immigrants, and permanent immigrants. These may be crucially important legal distinctions but, insofar as any of these new minorities are accorded minority rights, they fall on the integration side of the ledger. In many countries, some of these new minorities are not granted any minority rights and are subject to policies of either assimilation or exclusion. But even in those countries that grant minority rights to some new minorities, often under the aegis of "multiculturalism," these are based on ideas of integration, not accommodation, and do not entail territorial self-government, official language status, or legal pluralism.

Similarly, there are important distinctions to draw within the category of old minorities. The most important distinction is between indigenous peoples and other historically settled homeland minorities, often called national minorities. The former include the Indians and Inuit in Canada, the Aboriginal peoples of Australia, the Maori of New Zealand, the Sami of Scandinavia, the Inuit of Greenland, and Native American tribes in the United States; the latter include the Québécois in Canada, the Scots and Welsh in Britain, the Catalans and Basques in Spain, the Flemish in Belgium, the German-speaking minority in South Tyrol in Italy, the French- and Italian-speaking minorities in Switzerland, and Puerto Ricans in the United States.[16] Here, again, this is an important distinction for many legal purposes but, in relation to issues of minority rights, both types of old minorities fall on the accommodation side of the ledger. They both seek and, increasingly, are accorded various rights to self-government over their traditional territory, as well as the right to use their language and express their culture in its public spaces.

To understand the UN's approach, and its limitations, we need to examine this distinction between indigenous peoples and national minorities in more depth. To oversimplify, the term "indigenous peoples" arose primarily in the context of New World settler states and refers to the descendants of the original non-European inhabitants of lands colonized and settled by European powers. Most of the early work on indigenous issues at the UN, for example, focused on the so-called Indian populations in Latin America. "National minorities," by contrast, is a term invented in Europe to refer to the European groups that lost out in the tumultuous process of European state formation over the past five centuries, and whose homelands were incorporated (in whole or in part) into larger states dominated by a neighboring European people. National minorities were active players in the process by which the early modern welter of empires, kingdoms, and principalities in Europe was turned into the modern system of nation-states. However, they either ended up without a state of their

[16] The Flemish form a numerical majority in Belgium, but were historically subordinated to the French-speaking elite, and so are often considered a "minority" according to definitions that emphasize nondominant status rather than numbers per se, and as a case of "minority nationalism," in the sense of contesting the earlier French-dominated state nationalism.

own (as in the case of the Catalans) or found themselves on the wrong side of the border, cut off from their coethnics in a neighboring kin-state (as occurred with ethnic Germans in Denmark and Italy).

These are the core cases for the two categories. A preliminary and crude way of distinguishing them is to say that national minorities have been incorporated into a larger state dominated by a neighboring European people, whereas indigenous peoples have been colonized and settled by a distant colonial European power. But there are other ways of marking the distinction between the two types of groups that supervene on this basic historical difference. It is widely accepted, for example, that the subjugation and incorporation of indigenous peoples by European colonizers was a more brutal and disruptive process than the subjugation and incorporation of national minorities by neighboring societies, and that this has left indigenous peoples weaker and more vulnerable. It is also often assumed that there is a supposed "civilizational" difference between indigenous peoples and national minorities. Whereas national minorities typically share the same modern (urbanized, industrialized) economic and sociopolitical structures as their neighboring European peoples, indigenous peoples are often assumed to have retained premodern modes of economic production, engaged primarily in subsistence agriculture or a hunter-gatherer lifestyle. And, as a result of large-scale colonizing settlement, it is assumed further that indigenous peoples, unlike national minorities, have been relegated, typically, to isolated and remote areas.

Thus, both in their core cases and in everyday usage the two terms refer to quite different types of groups, each rooted in fundamentally different historical processes and differing in their contemporary characteristics, including degrees of vulnerability, modes of production, and habitats. Both, however, are old minorities, having a historic presence on their traditional territory that predates the formation of the current state. As such, they are both homeland minorities, living on or near a historic homeland that has been incorporated into a larger state dominated by another national group. In recognition of this fact, there has been a widespread tendency within Western democracies to adopt an accommodationist approach toward both types of groups. This typically involves some form of territorial autonomy, combined with official language rights (in the case of national minorities) and land claims and customary law (in the case of indigenous peoples). Both groups are distinguished from new minorities—those formed through immigration or refugee flows after the establishment of the state—whose cultural claims are typically addressed through a more integrationist approach, based on nondiscrimination, civil rights, and the reform of common institutions to make them more accessible to, and respectful of, the new minorities.

We now see how the UN approach to the accommodation/integration issue differs from the established practice of Western democracies. In two key contexts, UN norms and Western practices converge: both endorse a norm of accommodation for indigenous peoples, and both endorse a norm of integration for new minorities. They diverge, however, with regard to the central case of national minorities or, more generally, on the case of homeland minorities that do not qualify as indigenous peoples, whether it is the Scots in Britain, the Kurds in Turkey, or the Tibetans in China. In the practice of Western democracies, such national minorities are typically accorded accommodation, while, under the UN norms, they would be presumed to come under the integration approach. In the practice of Western democracies, national minorities belong with indigenous peoples on the accommodation side of the ledger; according to UN norms, they would belong, with the new minorities, on the integration side.

Why have UN norms diverged from Western practices in this way? I will return to this question below; however, part of the answer lies in the special vulnerability of indigenous peoples and, hence, in their more urgent need for accommodation. As noted earlier, the subjugation of indigenous peoples by European colonizers was typically a more brutal and disruptive process than the subjugation of national minorities by neighboring European societies, and this has left indigenous peoples more vulnerable and, hence, in greater need of international protection. As a result, there was a plausible moral argument for giving priority to indigenous peoples over national minorities in the development of rights to self-government in international law.

However, what began as a difference in the relative priority and urgency of the claims of indigenous peoples and national minorities has paved the way for an almost total rupture between the two at the level of international law. If we take the stance of international organizations as our reference point—rather than the practice of Western democracies—it would appear that rights of self-government are claimed legitimately only by indigenous peoples, rather than by homeland minorities more generally. Across a wide range of international documents and declarations, indigenous peoples have been distinguished from other homeland minorities, and claims to territory and self-government have been restricted to the former. Under the current UN framework, national minorities are lumped in the same category as new minorities, ignoring their distinctive needs and aspirations in relation to historic settlements and territorial concentration. As a result, the distinction between indigenous peoples and other homeland minorities has acquired a significance and a rigidity in the international community that is entirely missing in the theory and practice of Western liberal democracy.

The attempt to draw a sharp distinction between indigenous peoples and national minorities, and to put national minorities in the same legal category as new minorities, raises a number of difficult questions. It creates (*a*) moral inconsistencies, (*b*) conceptual confusion, and (*c*) unstable political dynamics.

The sharp distinction in rights between the two types of groups is morally inconsistent, because whatever arguments exist for recognizing the rights of indigenous peoples to self-government also apply to the claims for self-government by other vulnerable and historically disadvantaged homeland groups. Miriam Aukerman compared the claims of indigenous peoples with those of national minorities in postcommunist countries and noted the strong similarities in their underlying goals and justifications. As she puts it, "Indigenous peoples and Central-East European [national] minorities share the goal of preserving their distinctive cultures, and justify their claims to group-differentiated rights with similar appeals to self-determination, equality, cultural diversity, history and vulnerability."[17]

Indeed, this inconsistency becomes clear from the explanations and justifications offered for the proposed indigenous rights norms by the experts chairing the two UN working groups in 2000. As noted earlier, they accord targeted rights to indigenous peoples beyond those available to all other minorities because of three key differences: the former seek institutional integration, individual rights, and nondiscrimination, whereas the latter seek institutional separateness, collectively exercised rights, and self-government. These are all pertinent differences between indigenous peoples and new minorities, such as immigrants, but they do not distinguish indigenous peoples from national minorities. On all three points, national minorities typically fall on the same side of the equation as indigenous peoples.

In an earlier document prepared for the Working Group on Indigenous Populations, Daes offers a somewhat different account.[18] She states that the crucial feature of indigenous peoples, which distinguishes them from minorities in general, is their strong attachment to a traditional territory that they view as their historic homeland:

> [A]ttachment to a homeland is ... definitive of the identity and integrity of the [indigenous] group, socially and culturally. This may suggest a very narrow but precise definition of "indigenous," sufficient to be applied to any situation where the problem is one of distinguishing an indigenous people [from] the larger class of minorities.[19]

But this criterion—"attachment to a homeland"—obviously differentiates homeland minorities (including national minorities), in general, not

[17] Miriam Aukerman, *Definitions and Justifications: Minority and Indigenous Rights in a Central/East European Context*, 22 Hum. Rts. Q. 1011, 1045 (2000).

[18] U.N. Econ. & Soc. Council [ECOSOC], Comm'n on Human Rights, Sub-Comm. on Prevention of Discrimination & Prot. of Minorities, Working Group on Indigenous Populations, Working Paper on the Concept of "Indigenous People," U.N. Doc. E/CN.4/Sub.2/AC.4/1996/2 (July 6, 1996) (*prepared by* Erica-Irene Daes) [hereinafter Daes, Working Paper 1996].

[19] *Id.* at para. 39.

indigenous peoples, in particular. Elsewhere, Daes claims that it is "possible to identify at least two factors [in the case of indigenous peoples] which have never been associated with the concept of 'minorities': priority in time and attachment to a particular territory."[20] But here again, these factors apply to old homeland minorities, generally, not just to indigenous peoples.

In short, because virtually all of the moral principles and arguments invoked at the UN to defend indigenous rights also apply to national minorities, an attempt to draw a sharp distinction in legal status between national minorities and indigenous peoples is morally problematic. It is also conceptually unstable. The problem is not merely how to justify the sharp difference in their legal rights but how to identify the two types of groups in the first place. The very distinction between indigenous peoples and other homeland minorities is difficult to draw outside the original core cases of Europe and European settler states.

In the West, there is a relatively clear distinction to be drawn between European "national minorities" and New World "indigenous peoples." Both are homeland groups, although the former have been incorporated into a larger state dominated by a neighboring people, whereas the latter have been colonized by a remote colonial power. It is far less clear how we can draw this distinction in Africa, Asia, or the Middle East, or whether the categories even make sense there. Depending on how we define the terms, we could say that none of the homeland groups in these regions are "indigenous," or that all of them are.

In one familiar sense, no groups in Africa, Asia, or the Middle East fit the traditional profile of indigenous peoples. All the homeland minorities in these regions were incorporated into larger states dominated by neighboring groups rather than into settler states dominated by European settlers.[21] In that sense, they are all closer to the profile of European national minorities than to New World indigenous peoples. For this reason, several Asian and African countries insist that none of their minorities should be designated as indigenous peoples. In another sense, however, we could say that, in these regions, all homeland groups (including the dominant majority group) are indigenous. During the era of colonial rule, all homeland groups, majority and minority alike, were designated as "natives" or "indigenous" in relation to the colonial rulers. Thus, from that perspective, all homeland groups in postcolonial states (including the dominant group) are equally

[20] *Id.* at para. 60.

[21] *Cf.* Amal Jamal, *On the Morality of Arab Collective Rights in Israel*, Adalah Newsletter, Apr. 2005, at 12 (arguing that Israel should be included as a European settler state, and, hence, that the Palestinians fit the traditional definition of an indigenous people).

"indigenous." And, indeed, the governments of several Asian and African countries declare that *all* their historic groups, majority and minority, should be considered indigenous.[22]

These two approaches yield diametrically opposed results but the upshot in both cases is to undermine the possibility of distinguishing the category of indigenous peoples from that of national minorities. Whether we say that all homeland groups are indigenous or that none are, we end up in either instance without a basis for identifying a subset of minorities as indigenous peoples, distinct from national minorities or other homeland minorities.

For this reason, some commentators have argued that the legal category of "indigenous people" should apply only to European settler states in the New World and not to Africa and Asia.[23] If the UN adopted this approach, it would mean, in effect, that all minorities in Asia or Africa, both old and new, fall under the integration framework of the UN's minorities declaration, not the accommodation framework of the indigenous declaration.

The UN, however, has not taken this approach. Instead, it has made the assumption that some homeland minorities in Africa and Asia are as deserving of—and as much in need of—autonomy and accommodation as indigenous peoples in the Americas. In order to protect such groups, therefore, the UN has attempted to reconceptualize the category of indigenous peoples so that it covers at least some homeland minorities in postcolonial states. From this perspective, we should not focus on whether homeland minorities are dominated by settlers from a distant colonial power or by neighboring peoples. What matters, simply, is the fact of their domination by others and their vulnerability,

[22] *E.g.*, Zambia's report to the UN, which states, "Zambia does not have the classifications of indigenous populations and minority communities as defined by the United Nations Organization. Zambia has ethnic groups that are all indigenous" (UN Doc. CRC/C/11/Add.25, Nov. 19, 2002), para 470. Lennox describes this as "representative of the commonly held view" among African states. *See* Corinne Lennox, *The Changing International Protection Regimes for Minorities and Indigenous Peoples: Experiences from Latin America and Africa* (paper presented to Annual Conference of International Studies Association, San Diego, Mar. 2006) (on file with author and with I•CON). As Mamdani notes, however, there is often an important exception to this claim that all ethnic groups are considered indigenous; in many African countries, groups brought to the country during the period of colonial rule often are still considered immigrants or foreigners, such as the indentured laborers from India whom the British moved throughout the British Empire. *See* Mahmood Mamdani, Citizen and Subject (Princeton Univ. Press 1996) for a discussion of the ways these colonial-era migrant groups are (mis)treated by many postcolonial citizenship regimes in Africa. It remains true, however, that all precolonial groups are often called indigenous, including the dominant group.

[23] *See, e.g.*, André Béteille, *The Idea of Indigenous People*, 39 Current Anthropology 187 (1998).

and, thus, the need to find appropriate means to remedy these conditions.[24] If homeland groups are dominated and vulnerable, we should use the international norms of indigenous rights to protect them, even if their oppressors are their historic neighbors and not colonizing settlers from afar. Hence, the UN approach has encouraged groups in Africa and Asia to identify themselves as indigenous peoples in order to gain greater international visibility and protection.

The difficult question this raises, however, is how to identify which homeland groups in Africa or Asia should be designated as indigenous peoples for the purposes of international law and practice, and on what basis? Once we start down the road of extending the category of indigenous peoples beyond the core case of New World settler states, there is no obvious stopping point. Indeed, there are significant disagreements within various international agencies about how widely to apply the category to homeland minorities in postcolonial states. Some would limit it to those peoples who were especially isolated geographically, such as the hill tribes or forest peoples in southeast Asia or pastoralists in Africa.[25] Others would limit it to groups that fall outside the market economy—that is, to groups living as hunter-gatherers or subsistence cultivators but not involved in trade or the labor market. (This seems to be one of the World Bank's criteria, invoked to deny indigenous status to the Berbers in Algeria.)[26]

These narrow definitions of indigenous people are clearly inconsistent with the way the term is used in the New World. In Latin America, for example, the term applies not only to isolated forest peoples in the Amazon, such as the Yanomami, but also to peasants in the highlands who have been in intensive contact and trade with the larger settler society for five hundred years, such as the Maya, Aymaras, or Quechuas. Similarly many indigenous peoples in North America, such as the Mohawks, have been involved in either settled agriculture and/or the labor market for generations. To limit the category to groups that are geographically isolated or not involved in trade or the labor market

[24] According to Daes, attempts to distinguish long-distance colonizing settlement from incorporation into states dominated by neighboring societies rest on an "unjustified distinction." Daes, Working Paper 1996, *supra* note 18, at para. 63. Similarly, the Working Group on Indigenous Populations/Communities in Africa, established by the African Commission on Human and People's Rights (created by the Organization of African Unity [OAU]), has stated that "[d]omination and colonisation has [*sic*] not exclusively been practised by white settlers and colonialists. In Africa, dominant groups have also after independence suppressed marginalized groups, and it is this sort of present-day internal suppression within African states that the contemporary African indigenous movement seeks to address. . . ." (African Commission 2005: 92).

[25] World Bank, Operations Evaluation Dep't, Rep. No. 25332, Implementation of Operational Directive 4.20 on Indigenous Peoples: An Independent Desk Review, para 1.4. (2003).

[26] *Id.*, Box 3.1.

would be to exclude some of the largest and most politically influential indigenous groups in the New World.

Accordingly, other commentators would extend the category of indigenous peoples in postcolonial states much more widely in order to encompass all historically subordinated homeland minorities that suffer from some combination of political exclusion, poverty, or cultural vulnerability. (This seems to be the recent approach of the International Labour Organization [ILO], at least in southeast Asia).[27] On this view, the label "indigenous peoples" would become virtually synonymous with "homeland minority"; it would cease to be a subcategory of homeland minority. The difference between the narrower and broader conceptions of indigenous peoples is potentially enormous—estimates of the number of people who would qualify as "indigenous peoples" in Indonesia range from 2 percent to 60 percent of the population, depending on whether a narrower or broader definition is used.[28] There is an enormous literature on this question of how to apply the category of "indigenous peoples" in Africa and Asia, and on the relative merits of broader and narrow definitions.[29] This is a matter of ongoing debate within various intergovernmental organizations, each of which has adopted different definitions, to the consternation of commentators who wish that a single definition would be adopted across the international community.[30]

From my perspective, however, the fact that different definitions are being used by different intergovernmental organizations is not the only, or even the primary, problem. The more serious problem is that all of these proposed approaches, whether narrow or broad, invoke criteria that are clearly a matter of degree. Homeland minorities in postcolonial states form a continuum in terms of their cultural vulnerability, geographical isolation, level of integration into the market, and political exclusion. We can, if we like, set a threshold somewhere along this continuum in order to determine which of these groups are called "indigenous peoples" and which are "national minorities"; however, any such threshold is likely to appear arbitrary and incapable of bearing the weight that international law currently places upon it. International law treats the distinction between indigenous peoples and national minorities as a categorical one, with enormous implications for the legal rights each type of group

[27] *See, e.g.*, Manuela Tomei, Indigenous and Tribal Peoples: An Ethnic Audit of Selected Poverty Reduction Strategy Papers (ILO 2005).

[28] Pieter Evers, *Preliminary Policy and Legal Questions about Recognizing Traditional Land in Indonesia*, 3 Ekonesia 1–24 (1995).

[29] *See* Benedict Kingsbury, "*Indigenous Peoples*" *in International Law: A Constructivist Approach to the Controversy*, 92 Am. J. Int'l L. 414 (1998).

[30] For an overview of these variations, and the calls for greater consistency, see World Bank, Legal Note on Indigenous Peoples (Apr. 8, 2005); and World Bank; Implementation of Operational Directive, *supra* note 25.

may claim. In the postcolonial world, however, any attempt to distinguish indigenous peoples from national minorities on the basis of their relative levels of vulnerability or exclusion can only track differences of degree, not the difference in kind implied by international law.[31]

The attempt to preserve such a sharp distinction is not only morally dubious and conceptually unstable, it is also, I suspect, politically unsustainable. The problem here is not simply that the category of indigenous peoples has gray areas and vague boundaries, with the potential for being over- or under-inclusive. That is true of all targeted categories, and there are well-established techniques of democratic deliberation and legal interpretation for dealing with such boundary disputes. The problem, rather, is that too much depends on which side of the line the various groups fall, and, as a result, there is intense political pressure to change where the line is drawn. This pressure is pushing the UN in unsustainable directions.

As should be clear by now, the current UN framework provides no incentive for any homeland minority to identify itself as a national minority, since this category provides no rights that are not available to any other ethnocultural group, including new minorities. Instead, all homeland minorities have an overwhelming incentive to define, or redefine, themselves as indigenous peoples. If they present themselves to the international community as a national minority, they get nothing other than generic minority rights premised on the integration model; if they come, instead, as an indigenous people, they have the promise of rights to land, control over natural resources, political self-government, language rights, and legal pluralism.

The increasing tendency for homeland groups in Africa, Asia, and the Middle East to adopt the label of indigenous peoples is thus not surprising. An interesting case is the Arab-speaking minority in the Ahwaz region of Iran, whose homeland has been subjected repeatedly to state policies of Persianization, including the suppression of Arab language rights, the renaming of towns and villages to erase evidence of their Arab history, and settlement policies that attempt to swamp the Ahwaz with Persian settlers. In the past, Ahwaz leaders have complained to the UN Working Group on Minorities that their rights as a national minority were not respected.[32] But since the UN does not recognize

[31] See this frank admission of the chairman of the UN Working Group on Minorities: "The usefulness of a clearcut distinction between minorities and indigenous peoples is debatable. The Sub-Commission, including the two authors of this paper, have played a major role in separating the two tracks. The time may have come for the Sub-Commission to review the issue again… . The distinction is probably much less useful for standard setting concerning group accommodation in Asia and Africa." Eide, in Eide & Daes, Working Paper, *supra* note 6, at para. 25.

[32] For the Ahwaz Education and Human Rights Foundation's presentation to the Working Group on Minorities, see http://www.ohchr.org/english/issues/minorities/group/11session.htm. For the presentation to the Permanent Forum on Indigenous Issues, see http://www.ahwazstudies.org/main/index.php?option=com_content&task=view&id=2048&Itemid=47&lang=EN.

national minorities as having distinctive rights, the Ahwaz have run into a dead end. Thus, they have relabeled themselves as an indigenous people and begun participating in the work of the Working Group on Indigenous Populations. Similarly, various homeland minorities in Africa, which once sent representatives to the Working Group on Minorities, have now started rebranding themselves as indigenous peoples and participating in that working group, primarily in order to gain protection for their land rights.[33]

This is just the tip of the iceberg. Any number of minorities are now debating whether to adopt the label of indigenous peoples, including the Crimean Tatars, the Roma, or Afro-Latin Americans. Even the Kurds—the textbook example of a stateless national minority—are debating whether to redefine themselves as an indigenous people, so as to gain international protection. So, too, with the Palestinians in Israel, the Abkhaz in Georgia or Chechens in Russia, and the Tibetans in China.[34]

In all of these cases, minorities are responding to the fact that generic minority rights are "regarded as fatally weak"[35] and as "completely inadequate ... to their needs,"[36] since generic rights are premised on integration and do not protect any claims based on historic settlement or territorial attachments. Given international norms as currently conceived, recognition as an indigenous people is the only avenue for pursuing protection for these interests. Perhaps, in time, the Scots and Basques will also claim this status. After all, what homeland minority would not want the same rights—as currently formulated—that are accorded indigenous peoples?

While the tendency for national minorities to adopt the label of indigenous peoples is not surprising, it is also not sustainable. The net effect of such shifts in self-identification would be the total collapse of the international system of indigenous rights. Many states supported the UN draft declaration on indigenous

[33] For list of African organizations attending meetings of the Working Group on Minorities, see http://www.ohchr.org/english/issues/minorities/main.htm; for the (overlapping) list of African organizations attending the Working Group on Indigenous Populations, see U.N. Doc. A/HRC/Sub.1/58/22*. For a discussion of how groups move from one to the other, see Lennox, *supra* note 22.

[34] For examples and discussion, see Ursula Dorowszewska, *Rethinking the State, Minorities and National Security, in* Can Liberal Pluralism Be Exported? 126–134 (Will Kymlicka & Magda Opalski eds., Oxford Univ. Press 2001) (on the Crimean Tatars); Edo Banach, *The Roma and the Native Americans: Encapsulated Communities within Larger Constitutional Regime*, 14 Florida J. Int'l L. 353 (2002); and Ilona Klimova-Alexander, *Transnational Romani and Indigenous Non-Territorial Self-Determination Claims*, 6 Ethnopolitics 395 (2007) (on the Roma); Jamal, *supra* note 21; and Hassan Jabareen, *Collective Rights and Recognition in the Constitutional Process*, 12 Adalah Newsletter (Apr. 2005) (on the Palestinians); Lennox, *supra* note 22, (on Afro-Latinos); and Aukerman, *supra* note 17 (on various Eastern European cases).

[35] Russel Lawrence Barsh, *Indigenous Peoples in the 1990s: From Object to Subject of International Law?*, 7 Harv. Hum. Rts. J. 33, 81 (1994).

[36] Aukerman, *supra* note 17, at 1030.

rights only because it was seen as exceptional, relevant to a very specific and relatively small and peripheral set of groups, and not as a precedent that could be invoked by other, larger homeland groups, such as national minorities. As we will see below, various intergovernmental organizations have repeatedly and explicitly rejected attempts to codify rights of self-government for powerful substate national groups, in part, because of geopolitical security implications. They are not going to allow such groups to gain rights of self-government through the back door simply by redefining themselves as indigenous peoples. Yet there is very little within the current UN indigenous rights machinery that prevents such a shift from taking place.

If more and more homeland groups adopt the indigenous label, the likely result is that the international community will retreat from its current commitment to robust accommodation rights for indigenous peoples. Indeed, the first signs of such a retreat are already visible. There are a number of ways this retreat could take place. The most obvious is that member states may bring negotiations on the UN and Organization of American States (OAS) draft declarations to a halt.[37] Or they may gut these declarations of their substantive content—for example, by excising rights to land or self-government, and by moving toward a more integrationist approach. Or they may attempt to limit sharply the scope of application of these declarations—perhaps by limiting them to "remote" groups that do not participate in the wage economy, such as forest dwellers. Whatever the technique, the result of such a retreat would be to undermine the major progress that has occurred to date on behalf of indigenous people.

This suggests that the long-term future of the targeted track for the indigenous at the UN and other intergovernmental organizations is not yet clear. This track is often cited as the clearest success in the development of international minority rights, but this judgment may be premature. Indeed, it has been a success, but it is in danger of becoming a victim of its own success. Achievements in the New World, particularly in empowering indigenous peoples in Latin America, are encouraging intergovernmental organizations to redefine and extend the category in ways that are morally inconsistent, conceptually unstable, and politically unsustainable.

3. Rethinking the approach

The UN is not unaware of these difficulties with its current approach to minority rights. Many key actors within the UN realize that the simple distinction

[37] The Draft Declaration finally came up for adoption by the General Assembly in November 2006, and was widely expected to pass, but instead it was deferred, largely due to concerns by African countries about the definition of indigenous peoples. For the African Group's objections, see its Draft Aide Memoire (Nov 9, 2006), *available at* http://www.iwgia.org/graphics/Synkron-Library/Documents/InternationalProcesses/DraftDeclaration/AfricanGroupAideMemoireOnDeclaration.pdf.

between autonomy-seeking indigenous peoples and integration-seeking minorities does not capture the reality of ethnic relations around the world, and that many different types of homeland minorities—not just indigenous peoples—seek autonomy. Indeed, the UN has direct hands-on experience with these claims for autonomy, since such claims are at the root of some of the most difficult and violent ethnic conflicts around the world, which it is often called upon to help resolve. In many cases, the UN has intervened actively to support the autonomy aspirations of national minorities, as in Cyprus (for the Turkish minority), Sudan (for the Southern peoples), Iraq (for the Kurds), Indonesia (for Aceh and Papua), Sri Lanka (for the Tamils), and Burma (for the Karens and others). Indeed, in Cyprus, the UN essentially drafted a new constitution (the "Annan Plan") proposing federalization and consociational power sharing as a means to overcome the long-standing conflict between the Greek majority and Turkish national minority.

Analogous situations have arisen in postcommunist Europe, although in this context it has been European organizations (such as the European Union, the Organization for Security and Cooperation in Europe [OSCE], and NATO) that usually have taken the lead role in conflict resolution. In several cases of conflict between states and homeland minorities in postcommunist Europe, intergovernmental organizations have pushed for the adoption of some form of federal or quasi-federal territorial autonomy—for example in Serbia (for Albanians), Bosnia (for Serbs), Macedonia (for Albanians), Ukraine (for Russians in Crimea), Moldova (for Slavs in Trans-Dniestria), Georgia (for Abkhaz), and Azerbaijan (for Armenians).

Thus, in a wide range of cases, the UN and other intergovernmental organizations have endorsed an accommodationist rather than integrationist approach toward national minorities. Moreover, they have justified this preference for a more accommodationist approach by citing "best practices" from the Western democracies. The Annan Plan for Cyprus, for example, explicitly drew on strategies used in Switzerland and Belgium to accommodate their substate national groups. Similarly, the EU's proposals for the former Yugoslavia were based on the model of autonomy for the German national minority in Italy. These Western examples are presented as successful models of how a liberal-democratic state should deal with its national minorities; they were not understood as regrettable deviations from an ideal of integration. In these and other ways, the UN has been actively involved in diffusing the theory and practice of autonomy regimes for national minorities to policy makers, journalists, community leaders, and academics around the world.[38]

In short, the UN exhibits a degree of inconsistency regarding the appropriate treatment of national minorities. In terms of norms, the UN presupposes

[38] *See* Kymlicka, *supra* note 10 , for more on the role of international organizations in diffusing discourses and models of minority rights.

that national minorities seek only integration (and are entitled only to integration) and belong in the same legal category as new minorities. In the actual practice of case-specific conflict resolution, however, the UN has set aside this presupposition, acknowledged the necessity of considering accommodationist alternatives to integration, and helped to diffuse models and best practices of accommodation.

In my view, this willingness to consider accommodationist alternatives is essential if the UN is to play a constructive role in resolving conflicts between states and national minorities. There was (and is) no plausible alternative to autonomy in such countries as Sudan, Iraq, Indonesia, and Sri Lanka. However, the fact that the UN's recommendations for accommodation in specific cases deviate from the norms and expectations of its own minorities declaration does create some obvious problems. For one thing, its recommendations appear ad hoc: Why is the UN supporting autonomy for national minorities in Indonesia and not, say, in Pakistan? Why is the UN supporting autonomy for the Kurds in Iraq but not for the Kurds in Iran? Why are intergovernmental organizations supporting autonomy for Albanians in Macedonia but not for Hungarians in Slovakia? At best, these recommendations seem arbitrary, and, at worst, they appear to be rewarding belligerence. An obvious explanation for why the UN is supporting autonomy for some national minorities and not others is simply that the former took up arms and engaged in violent struggles. In virtually all of the cases where the UN has endorsed autonomy for national minorities, it is after the minorities resorted to violence. By contrast, where national minorities have peacefully and democratically mobilized for autonomy, they typically receive no support from the international community and, instead, are told that international norms on the rights of minorities do not recognize a right to autonomy.[39]

The perverse effect is to increase the incentive for autonomy-seeking national minorities to take up arms, as this is the only way they can obtain any international support. At the same time, this state of affairs may delegitimize the very idea of autonomy, since it easily could be perceived as a payoff to bellicose minorities, rather than as a principled approach to the management of ethnocultural diversity.

Obviously, it would be preferable if the UN or other intergovernmental organizations could find a more principled basis on which to evaluate national minority claims to autonomy. To pretend that national minorities do not seek

[39] The ethnic Hungarians in Slovakia and Romania have repeatedly complained that their peaceful mobilization for autonomy has received no support from international organizations and indeed has often been discouraged. *See* Margit Bessenyey-Williams, *European Integration and Minority Rights: The Case of Hungary and its Neighbours*, *in* Norms and Nannies: The Impact of International Organizationson the Central and East European States, 227–258 (Ron Linden ed., Rowman & Littlefield 2002).

autonomy, as the UN declaration does, is to bury one's head in the sand. To support autonomy only in cases of violent conflict, as the UN practice of case-specific intervention does, may unintentionally encourage aggression. Developing a more consistent and principled approach to national minorities would not only enable more effective international intervention but also would help to stabilize the current framework for indigenous rights since, as we have seen, the absence of any recognition of national minority rights puts unsustainable pressure on the policy track regarding indigenous peoples.

Unfortunately, the prospects for the development of new international norms regarding the rights of national minorities are not good. There has only been one attempt at the UN to develop such norms, and that was stillborn. In 1994, Liechtenstein circulated in the General Assembly's Social, Cultural and Humanitarian Affairs Committee a draft Convention on Self-Determination through Self-Administration, which recognized a right of internal autonomy for all "peoples," where peoples were explicitly defined to include not only indigenous peoples but also homeland national minorities.[40] However, this draft was never debated seriously and quickly disappeared from view.

A more sustained effort to develop new norms for national minorities has occurred at the regional level within Europe. I will describe these European initiatives in some depth, because I believe they shed light on the prospects for reform at the global level. Recent European efforts to codify new minority rights norms have run into difficulties that would also surface, perhaps even in stronger form, at a global level.

When the Berlin Wall fell and communism collapsed in 1989–1990, a number of violent ethnic conflicts involving national minorities emerged in the postcommunist countries, undermining the transition to liberal democracy. As a result, several European organizations attempted to formulate norms and standards for the treatment of national minorities that could guide these countries in dealing with such issues. This initiated a period of intense debate within Europe about the appropriate treatment of national minorities, and about whether autonomy, as a right or norm, should figure in that treatment.

This debate was particularly intense between 1990 and 1993. After the collapse of communism, the very first statement by a European organization on minority rights—the 1990 Copenhagen declaration of the Conference on Security and Co-operation in Europe (CSCE)[41]—explicitly endorsed territorial autonomy as a best practice. Article 35 of the declaration states:

[40] *See* U.N. Doc. A/C.3/48/L.17 (Nov. 1993). *See also* THE SELF-DETERMINATION OF PEOPLES: COMMUNITY, NATION, AND STATE IN AN INTERDEPENDENT WORLD (Wolfgang Danspeckgruber ed., Lynne Reinner 2002), where the draft convention is reprinted together with legal commentaries.

[41] The precursor to the OSCE.

> The participating States note the efforts undertaken to protect and create conditions for the promotion of the ethnic, cultural, linguistic and religious identity of certain national minorities by establishing, as one of the possible means to achieve these aims, appropriate local or autonomous administrations corresponding to the specific historical and territorial circumstances of such minorities and in accordance with the policies of the State concerned.[42]

An even stronger endorsement of territorial autonomy came in 1993, in Recommendation 1201 of the Council of Europe Parliamentary Assembly. It provides that

> [i]n the regions where they are a majority the persons belonging to a national minority shall have the right to have at their disposal appropriate local or autonomous authorities or to have a special status, matching this specific historical and territorial situation and in accordance with the domestic legislation of the state.[43]

Unlike the 1990 CSCE declaration, this recommendation recognizes territorial autonomy as a right, not merely as a best practice. It was widely hoped and assumed that this text's provisions would play a central role in the Council of Europe's Framework Convention for the Protection of National Minorities, which was being drafted at the same time.

In short, there was much talk of an emerging right to autonomy in Europe in the early 1990s. A concrete expression of this idea was the decision of the European Commission in 1991 to require Yugoslav republics seeking independence to establish a "special status" for regions where national minorities form a local majority, modeled, in part, on the example of South Tyrol.[44]

However, as it turns out, the Parliamentary Assembly's Recommendation 1201 reflects the high-water mark of support for territorial autonomy within European organizations. Since then, there has been a marked movement away from it. The framework convention, adopted just two years after Recommendation 1201, decisively rejected the Parliamentary Assembly's advice and avoided any reference to territorial autonomy. Not only is territorial autonomy not recognized as a "right," it is not even mentioned as a recommended practice. Nor does territorial autonomy appear in any subsequent

[42] Conference on Sec. & Coop. in Eur. [CSCE], *Document of the Copenhagen Meeting of the Conference on the Human Dimension of the CSCE*, at para. 36, June 29, 1990, 29 I.L.M. 1306–1309 (1990).

[43] Eur. Parl. Ass., Recommendation 1201 on an Additional Protocol on the Rights of National Minorities to the European Convention on Human Rights, 44th Sess., Rec. 1201, art. 11 (Feb. 1993).

[44] Richard Caplan, Europe and the Recognition of New States in Yugoslavia 30–33 (Cambridge Univ. Press 2005).

declaration or recommendation by European organizations, such as the series of Hague, Oslo, and Lund recommendations adopted by the OSCE from 1996 to 1999,[45] or the draft constitution of the European Union.[46] Moreover, the Venice Commission[47] has ruled that national minorities do not have rights of self-determination, even in the form of internal self-determination.[48] For all intents and purposes, ideas of autonomy have disappeared from the debate about "European standards" on minority rights.

There are a number of reasons for this. For example, there was strong opposition to the idea of entrenching a right to territorial autonomy for national minorities in the West and to the notion that there might be international monitoring of how Western states treated their minorities. France, Greece, and Turkey have traditionally opposed the very idea of self-government rights for national minorities, and, indeed, they deny the very existence of national minorities. Even those Western countries that accord autonomy to their substate national groups do not necessarily want their own laws and policies regarding national minorities subject to international monitoring. The treatment of national minorities in various Western countries remains a politically sensitive topic, and many countries do not want their existing majority–minority settlements, often the result of long and painful negotiation processes, reopened by international monitoring agencies. In short, while they were willing, at first, to insist that postcommunist states be monitored for their

[45] Org. for Sec. & Coop. in Eur. [OSCE], *The Hague Recommendations Regarding the Education Rights of National Minorities* (Jan. 1996), *available* at http://www.osce.org/documents/hcnm/1996/10/2700_en.pdf; OSCE, *The Oslo Recommendations Regarding the Linguistic Rights of National Minorities* (Feb. 1998), *available at* http://osce.org/documents/hcnm/1998/02/2699_en.pdf; OSCE, *The Lund Recommendations on the Effective Participation of National Minorities in Public Life* (Sept. 1999), *available at* http://www.osce.org/documents/hcnm/1999/09/2698_en.pdf.

[46] The European Free Alliance, a coalition of minority nationalist parties from various regions of Western Europe (e.g., Catalonia, Scotland, Flanders, South Tyrol), proposed that the EU constitutional treaty contain a clause that recognized "the right of self-government of all those territorial entities in the Union whose citizens have a strong and shared sense of national, linguistic or regional identity." The proposal was never seriously debated. Eur. Conv., Secretariat, *Democracy at Many Levels*, para. 3, CONV 298/02 (Sept. 24, 2002) (*prepared by* Neil MacCormick). See Neil MacCormick, *The European Constitutional Convention and the Stateless Nations*, 18 Int'l Aff. 331 (2004), for the failed efforts to strengthen the recognition of "stateless nations" in the European constitution.

[47] The European Commission for Democracy through Law, the Council of Europe's advisory body on constitutional matters.

[48] Eur. Comm'n for Democracy Through Law (Venice Comm'n), Opinion of the European Commission for Democracy Through Law on the Interpretation of Article 11 of the Draft Protocol to the European Convention on Human Rights Annexed to Recommendation 1201 of the Parliamentary Assembly, §3 (Feb. 21, 1996), *available at* http://www.venice.coe.int/docs/1996/CDL-MIN(1996)004-e.asp.

treatment of minorities, Western democracies had no wish to have their own treatment of national minorities examined.

This resistance from within the West might have been sufficient to scuttle any attempt to formulate a right to self-government for national minorities. But the more immediate difficulty was the growing recognition by European organizations that it was unrealistic to apply or expect to impose such a norm of self-government in the postcommunist region. Any idea of minority self-government was bitterly opposed by postcommunist countries as a threat to their very existence.

Why was there such resistance to autonomy for national minorities in post-communist countries? To answer this question, we need to step back and consider why Western democracies, over time, have become more comfortable with the idea of autonomy for their own national minorities. I would argue that there have been two key preconditions in the West that have lowered the risk to states and the dominant national groups in accepting national minority claims: (*a*) the existence of reliable human rights protections, and (*b*) the "desecuritization" of ethnic relations, such that the treatment of minorities is seen as an issue of domestic politics rather than regional geopolitics. Neither was present in postcommunist Europe in the early 1990s.

For majorities in the West, the consolidation of robust legal mechanisms for protecting human rights and the development of a human rights culture, generally, have provided guarantees that the accommodation of minority claims to self-government would not result in islands of tyranny in which the basic security or rights of citizens would be in jeopardy. These guarantees dramatically lowered the stakes involved in debates about minority rights. In postcommunist Europe in the early 1990s, however, these guarantees were absent. Dominant groups lacked the confidence that they would be treated fairly within self-governing minority regions. Indeed, in those cases where minorities seized territory and established their own autonomous governments, the results were often various forms of discrimination and harassment—even ethnic cleansing—against anyone who did not belong to the minority. Ethnic Georgians were pushed out of the Abkhazia region of Georgia when it declared autonomy and/or sovereignty; ethnic Croats were expelled from the Serbian-dominated regions of Croatia when they declared autonomy; ethnic Serbs were forced from Albanian-dominated Kosovo when it achieved autonomy—and so on. Neither side could rely on effective legal institutions and an impartial police to ensure that human rights were respected.

These fears for individual security were compounded by geopolitical fears regarding the security of the state. A crucial precondition for the adoption of self-government for national minorities in the West has been the desecuritization of state–minority relations. With respect to both national minorities and indigenous peoples in the West, there is no longer any anxiety that they will collaborate with enemies of the state, and this allows claims for self-government to be treated as part of normal democratic politics. In postcommunist Europe, however, the perception of homeland minorities as potential fifth columns likely to collaborate with neighboring enemies remains pervasive, and so ethnic relations remain highly securitized.

In order to understand this perception, we need to recall the history of the region. The current configuration of states in Central and Eastern Europe is the result of the breakdown of three empires after World War I—the Russian Romanov empire, the Austro-Hungarian Habsburg empire, and the Turkish Ottoman empire—and the more recent collapse of the Soviet empire in 1989. Each of these empires encompassed the homelands of several national groups, many of which became independent states emerging from the ashes of the former empires (for example, Poles, Romanians, Czechs and Slovaks, Bulgarians, Serbs, Latvians, and so forth).

This process of state formation in the aftermath of imperial breakdown created several distinctive security problems relating to homeland minorities. First, the boundaries of these newly independent states typically (and inevitably) left some members of the national group on the wrong side of a new international border. When the border between Germany and Poland was drawn, there were many ethnic Germans on the Polish side of the border. Similarly, there were large numbers of ethnic Hungarians on the Romanian side of the border with Hungary; ethnic Russians on the Latvian side of the border with Russia; ethnic Turks on the Bulgarian side of the border with Turkey; and ethnic Albanians on the Macedonian side of the border. Often, these kin-state minorities are thought to have a higher loyalty to their kin-state than to the states in which they live. As a result, there is anxiety that such minorities are irredentist—that is, that they wish to redraw international boundaries so as to unite (or reunite) the territory where they live with their adjacent kin-state. Indeed, it is often assumed that they would collaborate willingly with their kin-state if it militarily invaded the country in order to claim this territory, as, indeed, some have done at various times in the twentieth century. No state is likely to accord self-governing powers voluntarily to a minority under these circumstances.

Where homeland minorities take the form of irredentist kin-state minorities, there is a much greater likelihood that ethnic relations will be perceived as a threat.[49] But this is not inevitable. There are factors that can either alleviate or exacerbate the problem. If, for example, the neighboring states are close allies, integrated into larger regional economic and security organizations, such that the kin-state has no interest in destabilizing its neighbor, this will alleviate the problem. This, of course, is precisely what has defused the problem of kin-state minorities in Western Europe. In the past, Belgium, Denmark, and Italy resisted according strong rights to their ethnic German minorities

[49] By contrast, many of the paradigmatic examples of national minorities in the West do not have a kin-state (e.g., Catalans and Basques; Scots and Welsh; Québécois; Puerto Ricans).

because they were perceived as kin-state minorities with a primary loyalty to Germany. But once Germany became a close ally rather than a potential enemy, as a result of the EU and NATO, the transborder affiliations of ethnic German minorities became unimportant (and came to be viewed, for that matter, as a potential asset in ongoing processes of regional integration).[50] In the postcommunist countries in the 1990s, however, there was no equivalent of the EU and NATO to turn potential enemies into allies. In the absence of regional security arrangements, postcommunist countries were in an almost Hobbesian state of nature, distrustful of all their neighbors. And in this context, the presumed disloyalty of kin-state minorities was quickly perceived as a security threat.

Another key factor in these considerations is the balance of power between a state, its minorities, and the neighboring kin-state. The perceived threat to state security obviously is reduced if the state feels itself to be a strong state confronting weak enemies, whether these are internal irredentist minorities or their kin-states across the border. Unfortunately, in the postcommunist world, the balance of power has tended to exacerbate rather than alleviate the problem. In many cases, the national groups that acquired independence after imperial collapse view themselves as historically weak, confronted with minorities and kin-states that have been historically dominant. The result is the phenomenon known as "minoritized majorities"—majorities that continue to think and act as if they are weak and victimized minorities and, therefore, continue to live in existential fear for their survival.

This phenomenon is pervasive in the postcommunist world, as well as in much of the developing world, but is virtually unknown in the West (at least in a geopolitical sense), and so needs some explaining. If one simply looks at the numbers and ignores the historical background, it may appear that kin-state minorities in most postcommunist countries are fairly small and weak. Ethnic Hungarians in Slovakia, for example, represent about 15 percent of the population and, hence, are relatively powerless in relation to the overwhelming ethnic Slovak majority in the country. Historically, however, the Hungarians were members of the privileged and dominant group within the larger Habsburg empire and were active collaborators in Habsburg policies to create Hungarian hegemony in the region. The ethnic Slovaks, by contrast, were subordinated, subject to coercive Magyarization campaigns. Since independence, this hierarchy has, of course, been reversed; Slovaks are now the dominant group, and Hungarians are the threatened minority subject to Slovak nation-building policies. But the

[50] The same applies to other potential kin-state minorities in the West that are linked by ethnicity to a neighboring state. The French in Switzerland or Belgium are not seen as a fifth column for France; neither are the Flemish for the Netherlands nor the Swedes in Finland. This is a testament to the success of the EU and NATO in desecuritizing national minority politics in Western Europe.

memory remains. Slovaks view ethnic Hungarians not merely as a potentially irredentist group loyal to their kin-state but as a historically powerful and privileged group that had collaborated with a hegemonic imperial power to oppress the Slovak language and culture. In the absence of effective regional security arrangements, the fear persists that this could happen again—that is to say, that the Hungarian minority could collaborate with the Hungarian kin-state to subordinate Slovaks once again and crush their national independence.

We see the same phenomenon in Poland regarding the German minority or in Romania and Serbia vis-à-vis the Hungarian minority. The same state of affairs may be found in the Baltics, Ukraine, and Moldova regarding the Russian minority; in Croatia and Bosnia with reference to the Serbs; and in Bulgaria regarding the Turkish minority, to name but a few. In all these cases, minorities are seen (rightly or wrongly) as allies or collaborators with external powers that have historically oppressed the majority group, and the majority group, in turn, reacts as a "minoritized" majority.

In short, several factors were at work exacerbating the securitization of ethnic relations in postcommunist Europe. The phenomenon of homeland minorities seeking self-government can raise difficulties at the best of times, since it challenges the state's claim to represent a single people and to derive its legitimacy from an undivided popular sovereignty. However, this challenge becomes that much greater in a state where (*a*) the homeland minorities are potentially irredentist minorities with loyalty to a neighboring kin-state; (*b*) the national groups forming the majority in the state were historically subordinated by the neighboring kin-state in its former capacity as an imperial power; and (*c*) there are no regional security arrangements to guarantee nonaggression. Where these factors are present, as they were and are in much of postcommunist Europe, the likely result is a pervasive securitization of ethnic relations.

This securitization is reflected in three assumptions that dominate public debate on minorities in the region. The first is that minorities are disloyal, not just in the sense that they lack loyalty to the state (that is equally true of secessionists in Quebec or Scotland) but in the stronger sense that they have collaborated with former oppressors and will continue to collaborate with current enemies or potential enemies. The second assumption follows from the first: that a strong and stable state requires weak and disempowered minorities. Put another way, ethnic relations are seen as a zero-sum game; anything that benefits the minority is seen as a threat to the majority. Therefore—the third assumption—the treatment of minorities is above all a question of national security.

Thus, the two main factors that enabled dominant groups in the West to accept accommodation policies—namely, human rights guarantees and desecuritization—were absent, or only weakly present, in postcommunist Europe in the early 1990s. Given this fact, it is hardly surprising that attempts to promote autonomy were strongly resisted in postcommunist Europe.[51] The homeland minorities seeking self-government were often perceived as geopolitical threats to the security of the state, as well as threats to the individual human rights of people living in the potentially self-governing territory. Under these circumstances, it would have been surprising indeed if there had been much genuine interest in Western models of accommodating national minorities. Instead, most postcommunist states clung firmly to an integrationist agenda, maintaining the goal of turning themselves into centralized, unitary, and monolingual nation-states, premised on a singular and undifferentiated conception of popular sovereignty.

The distinctive history of imperialism and minority collaboration in the region also creates another important obstacle to the adoption or tolerance of autonomy—namely, perceptions of historic injustice. In many postcommunist countries, there is a strong sense that historical wrongs have not yet been acknowledged or remedied. Some say that this focus on historical rights and wrongs is unique to Eastern Europe, and that Western democracies have managed to get beyond this backward-looking obsession with history and to focus, instead, on forward-looking coexistence.[52] It is certainly true that feelings about historic injustice run deep in many postcommunist countries. But the same is true in many Western countries, as well. Appeals to historical injustice are increasingly common in the West. Consider the recent explosion of writing on the issue of reparations to African-Americans for the historic wrongs of slavery and segregation. Claims for the rectification of historic injustice are also a vital part of contemporary mobilization by indigenous peoples in New Zealand, Australia and Canada, and even of some immigrant groups—such as, for example, Japanese-Americans seeking compensation for their detention in World War II.

As we have just seen, however, there is an important difference in the nature of the historic hierarchies in the West and in postcommunist Europe. In the West, it is almost always a *minority* that is seeking apology and compensation from the state that has historically mistreated it. Hence the argument from historic injustice operates to strengthen minority rights claims, and to buttress the argument for greater equality between majority and minority. It is invoked to pressure the majority to say, in effect, that never again will we try to expel, subordinate, or oppress you.

[51] These are not the only reasons for opposition to territorial autonomy in postcommunist Europe. For a discussion of a range of other such issues, see KYMLICKA, *supra* note 10, at ch. 6.

[52] This is a familiar trope of the extensive literature that distinguishes a "forward-looking" civic nationalism in the West from a "backward looking" ethnic nationalism in the East. *See, e.g.*, MICHAEL IGNATIEFF, BLOOD AND BELONGING (Farrar Straus & Giroux 1993), and the discussion in WILL KYMLICKA, POLITICS IN THE VERNACULAR (Oxford Univ. Press 2001) (ch. 12).

In postcommunist countries, however, it is typically the *majority* that feels it has been the victim of oppression, often at the hands of minorities acting in collaboration with foreign enemies. Hence the majority wants the minority to express guilt, and to offer an apology, as a way of saying that never again will the minority be disloyal to the state. We see this in the Czech Republic regarding the German minority; in Slovakia with reference to the Hungarian minority; and in the Baltics, vis-à-vis the Russian minority. In short, the sort of historic injustice that is central to postcommunist debates, unlike that in the West, is the historical oppression of the majority group by its minorities in collaboration with a kin-state or foreign power. This truly distinguishes Eastern Europe from the Western experience, although there are, to be sure, comparable examples from Africa and Asia.[53]

In this context, arguments about historic injustice work *against* minority rights claims. In the West, homeland minorities typically would have been stronger had it not been for historic injustices perpetrated by the larger state—for example, there would have been more people speaking the minority's language and practicing its culture, over a wider area. Minority rights can be seen, in part, as a way of acknowledging and remedying that harm. In postcommunist countries, however, historic injustice is often understood as having expanded the scope and prestige of the minority's language and culture at the expense of the majority. Indeed, taken to their logical conclusion, arguments of historic injustice may suggest that minorities have no right at all to exist on the territory of the state, if their very presence is related to such an historic injustice. Were it not for unjust Russian and Soviet imperialism, there would be few Russians in the Baltics. But for unjust Ottoman imperialism, there would not be all that many Turks in Bulgaria. If the goal is to remedy the wrongs created by these historic injustices, why not try to undo the Russification of the Baltics, either by expelling the Russians or by insisting that they assimilate to Estonian and Latvian culture? Why not try to reverse the Turkification of Bulgaria under the Ottomans, whether by expelling the Turks or by insisting they assimilate to Bulgarian culture?[54]

[53] For example, members of the Sinhalese majority in Sri Lanka often expresses this sense of historic injustice. It is widely believed that the minority Tamils collaborated with, and were unfairly privileged by, the British colonizers, and remain willing to collaborate with neighbouring India against the Sri Lankan state in order to defend those privileges. *See* SANKARAN KRISHNA, POSTCOLONIAL INSECURITIES: INDIA, SRI LANKA AND THE QUESTION OF NATIONHOOD (Univ. Minn. Press 1999).

[54] This is precisely what Bulgaria, for example, tried to do in the 1980s, by forcing all the Turks to adopt ethnic Bulgarian names. The communist Bulgarian government argued that the coerced assimilation of the Turks was simply reversing the unjust pressure that the Ottomans had put on Slavs to convert to Islam and to assimilate to Turkish culture.

These profound differences between East and West in human rights protection, geopolitical security, and in the nature of historic injustices create, therefore, obvious grounds for opposition within postcommunist countries to the adoption of autonomy for national minorities.[55] Given these obstacles, it is not surprising that efforts to codify a right to autonomy for national minorities have failed. While the international community has shown some willingness to consider this idea in the case of indigenous peoples, internal self-determination has proven too controversial in the case of European national minorities. As then OSCE High Commissioner on National Minorities Max van der Stoel observed in 1995, claims to territorial autonomy meet "maximal resistance" in the states of the postcommunist region, and so it was more "pragmatic" to focus on modest forms of minority rights.[56] As a result, European organizations have not only backed away from formulating territorial autonomy, as a legal norm, they have also, in many cases, stopped recommending it as a best practice. The OSCE high commissioner, in particular, has said that territorial autonomy should be viewed not as a best practice but as a last resort and has discouraged various minorities from putting forth autonomy demands on the grounds that such demands are destabilizing under existing conditions of geopolitical insecurity.[57] Far from imposing provisions for minority self-government on postcommunist Europe, some European organizations are now actively discouraging it.

Predictably, then, when the European standards for national minority rights were finally codified, all references to self-government or autonomy were dropped, and a much weaker set of norms were proposed. Indeed, the Council of Europe's framework convention and the OSCE's recommendations are essentially updated versions of the UN's minorities declaration, founded on a clear integrationist approach.

However—as with the UN—this integrationist legal framework coexists alongside a political practice of case-specific interventions more supportive of autonomy. We have already seen how European organizations have intervened in several cases to support the autonomy aspirations of national minorities, in Serbia, Bosnia, Macedonia, Ukraine, Moldova, Georgia, and Azerbaijan. Unfortunately, as was also the case with the UN, these case-specific

[55] In all of these cases, it is important to distinguish objective facts about security threats and historic wrongs from the way these facts are perceived and discussed. Political actors make choices about whether or when to highlight (or exaggerate) these factors in public debate. The perception of kin-state minorities as a security threat and as collaborators in historic injustices against the majority is something that is deliberately inculcated and reproduced by certain political elites for reasons of self-interest.

[56] Max Van der Stoel, Peace and Stability through Human and Minority Rights: Speeches by the OSCE High Commissioner on National Minorities 111 (Nomos Verlagsgesellschaft 1999).

[57] *Id.*

interventions appear arbitrary, at best, and, at worst, as rewarding belligerence. In short, the European experiment in national minority rights reproduces many of the limitations of the UN approach.

4. Conclusion

If the analysis in this paper is correct, the international community's approach to minority rights is at an impasse. Intergovernmental organizations are operating with a legal framework that draws a sharp dichotomy between an accommodationist approach to indigenous peoples and an integrationist approach to minorities. This legal framework is wholly inadequate to deal with the actual patterns of ethnic relations around the world and, in particular, is unable to deal with the aspirations to autonomy by homeland national minorities. Yet these aspirations lie at the root of many of the most pressing ethnic conflicts in the world today. In order to manage these real-world conflicts, intergovernmental organizations supplement their legal norms with case-specific interventions that are more accommodationist. However, these case-specific interventions in support of autonomy are often arbitrary and ad hoc.

This combination of unrealistic legal norms and arbitrary case-specific interventions has a number of perverse results, including encouraging and rewarding the resort to violence. Yet it is difficult to see what would be a feasible alternative. Ideally, we might hope to develop a more adequate legal framework, one that moves beyond the simplistic indigenous–minorities distinction, in order to address the distinctive needs and claims of various groups, such as homeland national minorities, which do not fit into the current dichotomy. Such a new framework would recognize that, just as indigenous peoples have legitimate claims relating to history and territory that are not addressed by generic integrationist minority rights provisions, so, too, do other homeland minorities. Indeed, we might imagine this as the first step toward a new multitargeted system of international minority rights, with separate legal provisions not only for indigenous peoples and national minorities but also for other distinctive types of minorities, such as the Roma in Eastern Europe or Afro-Latin Americans. These groups also have needs and interests that are not sufficiently protected by the current framework based on the indigenous–minority dichotomy. Various proposals for such a multitargeted system of minority rights have been made.[58]

Unfortunately, the prospects for reform of the framework of international norms are poor. There is no support at the UN for revisiting the issue of the

[58] For example, several NGOs have proposed a "Charter of Romani Rights," to develop targeted rights for the Roma in Europe; and the Parliamentary Assembly of the Council of Europe called for a specific legal instrument regarding the rights of immigrant citizens (Recommendation 1492). For these and other proposals for new targeted rights, see Kymlicka, *supra* note 10, at ch. 6 and 8.

rights of minorities.[59] Furthermore, the one serious attempt that has been made at a regional level to address the distinctive issues raised by national minorities—namely, the European norms developed by the OSCE and Council of Europe—has retreated to a more cautious defense of generic integrationist minority rights. Some commentators have expressed the hope that other regional intergovernmental organizations—such as the African Union, ASEAN, or the League of Arab States—might take up the task of formulating their own regional standards of minority rights. It is unlikely this will happen, but, if it did, it is almost certain that they, too, would shy away from endorsing any right to autonomy for national minorities. They might be willing to endorse a norm of autonomy for small and isolated indigenous peoples but not for powerful substate national minorities.

Nor is this simply a matter of a lack of good faith or political will. The reality is that the conditions that have enabled a consensus to emerge within various Western democracies in support of autonomy for national minorities simply do not exist in many parts of the world. Indeed, all of the obstacles that have prevented European organizations from codifying a right to autonomy for national minorities apply just as powerfully in other regions of the world. The problems we have seen in postcommunist Europe—such as the securitization of state–minority relations; the fear of human rights violations; and the nature of historic hierarchies—are pervasive in Africa, Asia and the Middle East, as well. If anything, the willingness to consider autonomy for national minorities is even weaker in these postcolonial states than in the postcommunist countries of Eastern Europe.

Under these circumstances, the prospects for gaining an international consensus on a new and more accommodationist framework for addressing the claims of national minorities is virtually nil. For the foreseeable future, we are left with the status quo. As McGarry, O'Leary, and Simeon correctly explain, the status quo is predominantly integrationist. However, as I hope I have shown, the commitment of the international community to an integrationist approach is neither uniform nor stable; there are multiple, if unpredictable, avenues open by which accommodationist approaches may find international support. As international organizations become increasingly influential in shaping domestic choices concerning the rights of minorities, there are deep and unresolved questions about how this influence should be exercised.

[59] For example, longstanding calls to turn the 1992 UN Declaration on minority rights into a binding convention have essentially disappeared from the debate. Even Minority Rights Group, the main international advocacy group in the field, has stopped pushing this idea. *See* MRG, *Possible New United Nations Mechanisms for the Protection and Promotion of the Rights of Minorities*, Working Paper submitted to UN Working Group on Minorities, 9th Session, E/CN.4/sub.2/AC.5/2002/WP3. Other proposals to strengthen the codification and monitoring of international norms have also fallen by the wayside. *See* KYMLICKA, *supra* note 10, at ch. 6.

Part II
Conceptual Development of Minority Rights Law

[4]

The Bases of Minority Identity

Philip Vuciri Ramaga

I. INTRODUCTION

Although concerted interstate efforts to protect minorities began with the 1648 Peace of Westphalia, the dilemma of defining minority identity has existed throughout history.[1] Before the twentieth century, protective interstate arrangements focused on religious groupings.[2] The minority questions brought about by the repartitioning of post–World War I (WWI) Europe were resolved in special and general treaties.[3] This treaty approach under the League of Nations system was ad hoc, region-specific, racially oriented, and unconcerned with a general concept of minorities.[4] Nevertheless, the minority concept did include the elements of religion, language, and nationality or ethnicity. Whether or not these characteristics actually existed was not contended because the instruments recognized specific and undisputed groups.

The post–WWI protection system ended with the dissolution of the League. Before the introduction of the International Covenant on Civil and Political Rights (ICCPR), the United Nations Sub-Commission on the Prevention of Discrimination and Protection of Minorities (SCPDPM) had recommended a definition of minority identity to include only the possession

---

1. *See* Leo Gross, *The Peace of Westphalia, 1648–1948*, 42 Am. J. Int'l L. 20, 20 (1948); 1 Fred L. Israel, *Major Peace Treaties of Modern History, 1648–1967* 7–49 (1967).
2. These included the protection of religious groups under the Treaty of Vienna, 1815; of Christian minorities in the Turkish Ottoman Empire; of muslims in Greece under the Protocol of 3 February 1830 of the Conference of London and the 1881 International Convention of Constantinople; and the general protection of religious freedom in the new Balkan States under the Treaty of Berlin, 13 July, 1878.
3. These treaties did not deal basically with minorities but contained clauses for their protection. *See* Tore Modeen, *The International Protection of National Minorities in Europe* 50 (1969).
4. *See* Tennent Bagley, *General Principles and Problems in the International Protection of Minorities* 9 (1950).

of or wish to preserve ethnic, religious, or linguistic characteristics distinct from the rest of the national population.[5] This definition was criticized in the Commission on Human Rights (CHR) on the grounds, inter alia, that it might eliminate certain national groups deserving special protection.[6] Instead, a formulation of general principles to be used in the absence of criteria for establishing the need of special protection was proposed.[7]

In 1966 a universal minority regime was introduced through the ICCPR. Article 27 of this instrument provides:

> In those States in which ethnic, religious or linguistic minorities exist, persons belonging to such minorities shall not be denied the rights, in community with other members of the group, to enjoy their own culture, to profess and practice their religion, or to use their own language.[8]

Unlike the earlier treaty provisions, this article omitted the "race" and "nationality" identities which the League system had recognized.[9]

To date, the most substantial work on Article 27 is the 1979 report of the SCPDPM Special Rapporteur, Francesco Capotorti. Capotorti provisionally interpreted minority identity as "cultural, physical or historical characteristics, a religion or a language."[10] This interpretation would seemingly cover all the current and former criteria in identifying minorities, as it includes physical as well as historical elements. In its conclusion, however, the report included neither "physical" nor "historical."[11] This omission is relevant in discussing the exclusion of certain elements from current identification criteria.

Throughout history, minorities have been identified by a multitude of terminological criteria: religion, language, culture, ethnicity, nationality, and race. Owing to the different disciplines in which these terms have been used, they may not be self-explanatory for legal purposes. Synchronizing legal and non-legal usage requires clarity of purpose, and to be in accordance with principles of treaty interpretation, the legal usage must precisely reflect the situation the law addresses and enhance the achievement of its objec-

---

5. *See* U.N. Doc. E/CN.4/Sub.2/119 (1950), para. 32; U.N. Doc. E/CN.4/Sub.2/140/Annex I/ Draft res. II (1951); U.N. Doc. E/CN.4/Sub.2/149 (1952), para. 26.
6. Francesco Capotorti, *Study on the Rights of Persons Belonging to Ethnic, Religious and Linguistic Minorities*, U.N. Doc. E/CN.4/Sub.2/384/Rev.1 (1979), para. 224.
7. *Id.*
8. International Covenant on Civil and Political Rights, art. 27, *adopted* 16 Dec. 1966, *entered into force* 23 Mar. 1976, G.A. Res. 2200 (XXI), 21 U.N. GAOR Supp. (No. 16), at 52, U.N. Doc. A/6316 (1966).
9. *See, e.g.*, Minorities Treaty between the Principal Allied and Associated Powers and Poland (Versailles) June 28, 1919, in 13 Am. J. Int'l L. (Supp.) 432 (1919).
10. Capotorti, *supra* note 6, at para. 28.
11. *Id* at para. 568.

tives.[12] Thus, due to the historical vagaries of terminology, Article 27 faces a problem of interpretation.

This article discusses the meaning of group identities under Article 27 and assesses its implications for minority protection. The article uses the principles and practices of the League of Nations system and the preparatory work, the substance and conclusions, and the subsequent practices of states under the ICCPR to illuminate and explain the development of minority identity concepts. Because minority protection is viewed as an allowance for diversity, and not necessarily as an attainment thereof, it acts as a textual guard against actual and likely victimization. Consequently, this article considers minority identity within this context.

II. RELIGION

Religion has long been a prominent minority identity and is ordinarily used to refer to a broad description of faith. In common parlance, "religion" tends to be limited to the easily identified faiths such as Christianity, Judaism, Islam, Hinduism, and Buddhism. Yet the Reformation and Counter Reformation—causes of division among Christians—exemplify the usage of "religion" to refer to denominational (Catholic/Protestant) groups. Nevertheless, any practice in the semblance of religion poses the problem of ascertaining the boundary between religion and other practices.

Belief is the fundamental element in religion.[13] It may seem that provisions for religious freedom protect only "believers" and not "non-believers."[14] However, the common formulation "religion and belief" implicitly includes non-believers as well,[15] an indication that the protection given to religious groups would, on the basis of nondiscrimination, be equally given to non-believers. The absence of controversy over this is a result of the manner in which other practices or beliefs have existed in comparison with the established and institutionalized religions. For example, atheism is a form of belief in reaction to theism; but its philosophy has not encouraged the

12. These and the principle of grammatical interpretation are now embodied in the *Vienna Convention on the Law of Treaties* art. 31–32 (2d ed. 1984).
13. According to David M. Walker, *The Oxford Companion to Law* 793 (1980), "religion involves belief in, and conciliation of powers deemed superior to man which are believed to regulate and control the course of nature. It involves elements of belief, a body of dogma, acts of conciliation and worship."
14. "Nonbelievers" is used here in the ordinary sense to refer to nonfollowers of any of the acknowledged religions.
15. *See* Roger Clarke, *The United Nations and Religious Freedom*, 11 N.Y. J. Int'l L. & Pol. 197, 201 (1978); Richard Lillich, *Civil Rights*, *in* 1 *Human Rights in International Law* 115, 159 (T. Meron ed., 1984).

development of doctrine coherent with a universally accepted institutional structure, a development that would bring it nearer to the very religions that it challenges.

Tomuschat defined religious minorities as those "united by common creed" and noted the ease with which the term has been used.[16] Yet this definition does not touch the issue of equality between believers and non-believers. The question of the boundary between religion and other practices may appear theoretical, as the concept of minority protection developed when "religion" referred to universally recognized faiths. Nevertheless, in many parts of the world there exist belief systems, sometimes termed traditionalist or animist, the invocation of which in a claim under Article 27 would necessitate verification of the claimed religious status using internationally acceptable criteria. The Amerindian and Aboriginal practices are illustrative here, although they have usually been accounted for in cultural terms.[17] Uncertainty about the inherent characteristics of a way of life frequently leads to the general description of atypical religions as "culture."

It is significant that the terms religion, ethnicity, culture, and language were not defined during the drafting of Article 27. According to the SCPDPM, cultural characteristics were covered by the concepts "ethnic," "religious," and "linguistic,"[18] a view which does not deal with the complexity of religion as such. Past studies on religious rights have been inadequate in answering the above questions, apart from discussing the juridical status of religions and the enjoyment of the pertinent rights under domestic law. Juridical status does not go beyond the domestic recognition of minorities, however, and a state is likely to use its own defining criteria, which could be unfair to minorities, especially when the majority religion is recognized as the state religion. Even when there is no policy of recognition as a precondition to religious status, inequality of treatment is not necessarily excluded.[19]

In accepting the terms of Article 27, states had the major faiths in mind. Nonetheless, the practices of states and the treaty organs show that denominations also amount to religions, depending on the inter-group relationships in given states. For instance, in predominantly Christian Australia religious minorities are recognized to include various Protestant congregations,[20] just

16. Christian Tomuschat, *Protection of Minorities under Article 27 of the International Covenant on Civil and Political Rights, in* 81 *Vlkerrecht als Rechtsordnung Internationale Gerichtsbarkeit Menschenrechte* 949, 959 (1983).
17. *See* Andrew Gray, *The Amerindians of South America,* Minority Rights Group Report No. 15; James Wilson, *Canada's Indians,* Minority Rights Group Report No. 21; James Wilson, *The Original Americans: U.S. Indians,* Minority Rights Group Report No. 31; Keith D. Suter & Kaye Stearman, *Aboriginal Australians,* Minority Rights Group Report No. 35.
18. U.N. Doc. E/CN.4/Sub.2/SR.48 (1950).
19. Arcot Krishnaswami, *Study of Discrimination in the Matter of Religious Rights and Practices* at 47–48, U.N. Publications, U.N. Sales No. 60.XIV.2 (1960).
20. *See* Capotorti, *supra* note 6, at Annex III.

as in Spain, Catholicism is the state religion and Protestants are considered a minority.[21] Similar situations have arisen among Moslems.[22] As differences develop between members of the same denomination, there is every likelihood of narrowing the context further. The Human Rights Committee (HRC) and states have acknowledged these as minority situations.[23] This recognition points to the intended purpose of the law, which goes beyond the meaning that might have ordinarily been attached to religion.

III. ETHNICITY

Sociologically, an ethnic group has been defined as a "distinct category of the population in a larger society whose culture is usually different from its own," whose members are, or feel themselves or are thought to be, bound together by common ties of race, nationality, or culture.[24] Studies of such groups have usually revolved around group relations to the extent that it has even been argued that one must focus on the group dynamic rather than on racial or cultural differences.[25] Thus, ethnicity has been distinguished from racial grouping in that " 'race' stands for the attributions of one group, ethnic group stands for the creative response of a people who feel somehow marginal to the mainstream of society."[26] Furthermore, "race" and "ethnicity" may overlap in that a group labelled a race is often pushed out of the main spheres of society and made to endure deprivations, thus leading to the formation of an ethnic group. Consequently, "distinct languages, religious beliefs, political institutions [then] become part of the ethnic baggage."[27] The sociologist Cashmore concluded that an ethnic group is one

> possessing some degree of coherence and solidarity composed of people who are, at least latently, aware of having common origins and interests. So [it] is not a mere aggregate of people or a sector of a population, but a self-conscious

---

21. *Id.*
22. *E.g.*, the case of the Baluchis in Iran. *See* Minority Rights Group Report No. 48; Robert J. Wirsing, *The Baluchis and the Pathans*.
23. For example, the acknowledgement by a number of countries of denominational minorities in the country monographs preparatory to the Capotorti study. *See* Capotorti, *supra* note 6, Annex III, at 110–114. In the consideration of state reports under the ICCPR, this is acknowledged, at least tacitly, where the impact of denominational State religions or majority sects is questioned. *See, e.g.*, Report of the Human Rights Committee, U.N. GAOR 35th Sess., Supp. 40, at 82, U.N. Doc. A/35/40 (1980)(report of Costa Rica); U.N. GAOR 40th Sess., Supp. 40, at 93, U.N. Doc. A/40/40 (1985)(report of Spain).
24. H. Morris, *Ethnic Groups*, 5 Int'l Encyclopedia of the Soc. Sci. 167 (1968).
25. *Id.*
26. Ellis Cashmore, *Dictionary of Race and Ethnic Relations*, 86 (1984).
27. *Id.* at 86–87.

collection of people united, or closely related by shared experiences. Those experiences are usually, but not always, ones of deprivation.[28]

These definitions depict situations similar to those of minorities. The more generalized notions of "common origin and interests" and "shared experiences" differ significantly from the restrictive approach of Article 27, which is limited to linguistic, religious, and ethnic factors, where "ethnic" is not identical with the sociological interpretation above. Yet, while some sociologists consider race as an attribute of ethnicity, "race" was deliberately omitted from Article 27.

Moreover, while some sociologists do not treat culture as an attribute of ethnicity, it was implicitly so treated in the article. That "culture" in Article 27 was considered an attribute of ethnicity is deducible from the grammatical construction of the article and subsequent interpretations. The key phrases are: "ethnic, religious or linguistic minorities . . . to enjoy their own culture, to profess and practice their own religion, or to use their own language." Despite the acknowledged overlap between culture and religion on the one hand, and culture and language on the other, this has been the accepted understanding of the minority identity provision both in the SCPDPM's work[29] and in scholarly writings.[30] It is therefore appropriate to consider the usage of "culture" in order to understand ethnicity in this context.

A. Culture

Culture has generally been referred to as learned patterns of behavior.[31] According to Taylor, culture, "in its wide ethnographic sense, is that complex whole which includes knowledge, belief, art, morals, law, custom, and any other capabilities and habits acquired by man as a member of society."[32] That culture is distinct from race is acknowledged in the social sciences and by bodies involved with cultural development. Race refers to human sub-species, or physical characteristics such as Negroid or Caucasoid,[33] distinct from learned behavior. "Whereas race is a question of heredity, culture is

28. *Id.* at 85.
29. *E.g.*, Capotorti, as special rapporteur for the SCPDPM, follows the same. *See especially*, Capotorti, *supra* note 6, at Chap. IV.
30. John Claydon, *The Transnational Protection of Ethnic Minorities: A Framework for Inquiry*, 13 Can. Y.B. of Int'l L. 25 (1975).
31. Milton Singer, *The Concept of Culture* 3 Int'l Encyclopedia of the Soc. Sci. 527, 527–541 *passim* (1968).
32. *Id.* at 527.
33. Cashmore, *supra* note 26, at 217.

essentially one of tradition in the broadest sense."[34] The exclusion of "race" from Article 27 and the inclusion of "ethnic" and "culture" is thus not a contradiction in terms. While culture may be so embracing as to include religion and language, it suffices here to highlight certain issues in assessing the distinctness of a cultural group. The obvious reason for such assessment is that the element of culture is important for distinguishing a discrete group from the rest of the population.

Culture does not have a self-distinctive criterion for determining the cultural unit. According to Kroeber and Kluckhohn, "[the] lines of demarcation of any analysis are in large [part] a matter of abstraction and convenience for the problem at hand."[35] This culture-pattern approach is challenged by the social structure approach advocated by Radcliffe-Brown, who asserts that all social phenomena need be studied "not in abstraction or isolation, but in their direct and indirect relations to social structure, i.e. with reference to the way in which they depend upon, or affect the social relations between persons and groups."[36]

These approaches reflect the problem that there is no "natural" unit of society, especially in today's growing mixture of cultural groups. Overemphasizing social structure tends to negate the argument for minorities not living as one group but scattered within a country. Therefore, the culture-pattern approach would seem more appropriate given the absence of universal criteria for determining the existence of a "social unit," which could be a nation-state, religious group, linguistic group, or even the population of a geographical region in a country. Nevertheless, the approaches are complementary, and only in this way can culture be understood.

It must be concluded that however valid "race" may be in defining a social unit or group, it is still not one of the identities under Article 27. As acknowledged by Tomuschat, it is true that defining ethnic minorities in the absence of obvious racial and linguistic differences is more complex than when these characteristics exist.[37] Nonetheless, this does not make "race" a necessary factor; nor is ethnic origin in itself sufficient, for one's past, however rich in culture, may have nothing to do with one's life in the case of voluntary assimilation into a new society.

The above analysis does not, however, explain the factors that led to the racial categorization in the League times and the absence of race from Article 27. The usage of "race" in the two systems therefore requires examination.

---

34. Michel Leiris, *Race and Culture* 20 (UNESCO, 1951).
35. Alfred Kroeber and Clyde Kluckhohn, *Culture: A Critical Review of Concepts and Definitions* (1952), cited in Singer, *supra* note 31, at 217.
36. Singer, *supra* note 31, at 530.
37. Tomuschat, *supra* note 16, at 955.

B. The Racial Criterion in Perspective

Although "race" is omitted from the ICCPR, its categorical use in the League minority treaties,[38] its significance in group discrimination, and its common, though extra-legal, use in establishing ethnicity tends to merge it with the overlapping group identities. Distinction must first be made between the non-discrimination provisions of the minority treaties which protected all inhabitants of a country,[39] and those dealing specifically with group protection. Article 12 of the Polish Minority Treaty, an example of the latter, refers, inter alia, to racial minorities, as acknowledged in an advisory opinion of the Permanent Court of International Justice.[40] In the nineteenth and early twentieth centuries, "race" was commonly used as a synonym for "nation" or "ethnic group"; hence the phrases "French race" and "German race." Not surprisingly, this period covered the establishment of the League minority system, leading to the conclusion that "race" in the minority treaties likely referred to characteristics other than the physical or genetic. This was true, at least, of the European countries then inhabited by the same race, except for the Jewish populations, that were seen as another race, and descendants of black slaves, who could hardly stake any claims under the then prevailing circumstances.

The vagueness of "race" in the minority treaties was addressed in the drafting of the Genocide Convention, Article II of which borrowed the treaty's wording, "national, ethnical, racial or religious" in describing the groups protected, but the terms "national" and "racial" were particularly unclear.[41] In reality, "racial," "linguistic," and "religious" were interpreted to correspond with "nationality," which did not necessarily mean citizenship.[42] Today, "race" has changed meaning. Contemporarily, the term refers to a group socially defined in a given society as belonging together "because of physical markers such as skin pigmentation [and] hair texture," based on external visibility and not genetic relationship.[43] It is groups so identified by these criteria, the so-called "social races," which are today the target of substantial anti-discrimination laws, for these laws usually result from rac-

38. *E.g.*, Minorities Treaty between the Principal Allied and Associated Powers and Poland (Versailles) June 28, 1919, *supra* note 9, at art. 12.
39. *Id.*
40. *Acquisition of Polish Nationality*, 2 Ann. Dig. of Pub. Int'l L. Cas. 292, 293–294.
41. Warwick A. McKean, *Equality and Discrimination under International Law* (1983).
42. This is evident in the exclusion of political groups (discussed in U.N. GAOR, 3d Sess., Pt. I, 6th Comm., 69th, 74th, 75th, and 128th meetings (1948)), whose aspirations could be termed national (in a political sense) while "nationality" was included, which must refer to ethnicity or race. On the synonymous use of "race" and "nationality," *see infra* note 49.
43. Cashmore, *supra* note 26, at 217.

ism.[44] Otherwise, with intermarriage in multi-racial societies, the actual meaning of "race" has lessened.

The exclusion of "race" from Article 27 must also be seen in the light of the post-1945 human rights developments. Several instruments, and especially the 1965 Convention on the Elimination of Racial Discrimination, treated race under non-discrimination. This does not, however, explain why racism is distinguished from other forms of prejudice, i.e., cultural discrimination, although both have been causes of group victimization. It has been submitted that there is nothing inherently wrong in the disappearance of a race so long as it is by voluntary intermingling. The same would seem to be the case with culture. However, culture may possess an additional element as a means of survival, as in the case of the indigenous populations whose livelihood depends on their environment, which environment constitutes the basis of their cultures.[45] The sustenance of mere racial identity is not so dependent, as evidenced by the survival of the same race in different environments. The inclusion of a racial criterion in the Genocide Convention merely reflected the fears of physical destruction. Because the existence of race depends not on external factors but on genetics, its enjoyment, for want of a better word, need not be guaranteed by special protection as against other races. Only when a racial group also possess non-genetic characteristics, like religion and culture, may it be protected as a group.

An example is the history of Jews as a minority group. The fact of Jewish persecution by the Nazi regime, which saw them as a race, does not dismiss the common consideration of them as a religious or cultural group, for they have had these non-genetic traits as well.[46] This was acknowledged in the conception of minorities. In Czechoslovakia, one of the states with Jewish minorities, it was held in 1925 that:

> [r]ace and nationality were not necessarily identical[, but that i]n regard to the Jewish race it was well known that, although it had been partly assimilated by other nationalities, it conserved partly not only its racial individuality, but also the national one.[47]

This opinion reflected not only the significance of external factors in determining the need for protecting racial groups as minorities; it considered the

44. *Id.* at 218.
45. E.g. the lifestyle of the Sami depending on the arctic environment which enables the traditional economy of reindeer herding. *See generally* Mervyn Jones, *The Sami of Lapland,* Minority Rights Group Report No. 55 (1982). *See also* Gray, *supra* note 17, on the encroachment of modern economic activities on the traditional economies of the Amerindians.
46. Benjamin Akzin, *Who is a Jew? A Hard Case,* 5 Israeli L. Rev. 259 (1970).
47. *Czechoslovak Language of Minorities Case,* 3 Ann. Dig. of Pub. Int'l L. Cas. 314 (1925–1926).

conservation of a language by a racial group as an essential distinctive mark of nationality.[48]

The synonymous use of race and nationality in the early twentieth century was more clearly shown in the *Extradition* (*Albanian National*) case, in which Albania demanded the extradition of a person of Albanian nationality but of Hellenic race.[49] In rejecting this request, which was based on a treaty allowing only the extradition of nationals of the requesting state, the Court of Appeal in Greece held that "national" included persons of Hellenic race, though of a different nationality.

Janowsky's detailed study of the minority treaties reveals the effort of Jewish groups in focusing attention on racial and nationality criteria for minority status.[50] While those persons from Eastern Europe who had experienced heightened persecution pressed for "national" rights, by which they meant national autonomy, those from the West pressed for racial protection. The treaty provisions for racial minorities satisfied the lesser demand. The treaties did not provide for the "national" rights, which must not be confused with "nationality" appearing in the non-discrimination provisions applicable to all inhabitants of a country. Recognition was given only to racial, religious, and linguistic minorities.[51] To the Jewish delegations, the acceptance of the racial criterion was partial satisfaction of the greater demand for autonomy, for even as a racial group the communities, at least in those times, carried with them cultural and religious identities.

In contemporary societies with racism, a despised race may need protection even as a group, but this cannot be considered a protection of race rather than protection from racial prejudice. In other words, it is not a protection of race qua race, but of a particular race being despised with the consequence of victimization. Protecting race would play into the hands of racist regimes like apartheid South Africa, whose racial separation policy has constituted an effective medium of discrimination.

Given these difficulties with race, it is not surprising that in the drafting of Article 27 "ethnic" was used instead of "race," although "racial minorities" was used by the United Nations until 1950.[52] The basic reason given for the substitution was the non-scientific basis of racial categorization and the more inclusive meaning of "ethnic" as a reference to cultural, historical, and biological characteristics, as opposed to "racial," which refers only to

48. *Id.*
49. *Extradition of Nationals*, 5 Ann. Dig. of Pub. Int'l L. Cas. 281 (1929–1930).
50. See especially the response to the Jewish demand for recognition as "national" entities. Oscar I. Janowsky, *The Jews and Minority Rights* (1933).
51. *See supra* note 40, at 294.
52. *See* Capotorti, *supra* note 6, at para. 196.

inherited characteristics.[53] With due respect for these views insofar as they distinguish between "racial" and "ethnic," there has been a confusion of the fundamental issue.

Incoherence in the arguments for omitting "race" indeed led to the conclusion in the Capotorti report that "the substitution of the term 'ethnic minorities' for the term 'racial minorities' . . . would seem to reflect a wish to use the broadest expression and to imply that racial. . . minorities should therefore be regarded as included in the category of ethnic minorities."[54] To omit "race" for being unscientific, and yet to subsume it under "ethnic," which, as defined, covered biological characteristics, seems contradictory, unless "biological" is interpreted to exclude inherited characteristics. The recollection in the SCPDPM of "ethnic" in the Genocide Convention as covering cultural, physical, and historical characteristics is inappropriate in the context of minorities because the Genocide Convention concerns physical destruction, so that the manner of group identification is not material in determining the right in question—physical existence.[55] In the case of minority protection, however, the identity determines the nature of the right. Indeed, as far back as 1950 the UN Secretary General had observed that " 'community' as a reference to minorities did not imply 'biological unity'."[56] He further noted that the League system protected racial, religious, and linguistic groups because these were considered more or less objective and stable.[57]

If the all-inclusive interpretation of "ethnic" was the intention of the drafters of Article 27, at least the grammatical construction of the article and subsequent application proves the contrary. The article by necessary implication treats culture, professing and practicing of religion, and the use of language as corollary to ethnic, religious, and linguistic identity. The corollary of racial identity, which is not mentioned, would perhaps be the maintenance of a race as such. In states' reports under Article 40 of the ICCPR, racial groups are mentioned only as categories with distinct culture, language, or religion, but not as physically distinct groups.[58]

---

53. *Id.* at para. 197.
54. *Id.* at para. 201.
55. U.N. Doc. E/CN.4/Sub.2/SR.48 (1950); U.N. Doc. E/CN.4/Sub.2/119, at para. 31(1950).
56. *See Definition and Classification of Minorities*, U.N. Doc. E/CN.4/Sub.7/85, at para 18 (1950).
57. *Id.* at para. 43.
58. Even where State reports mention a minority, which is otherwise a racial group, it is seen in cultural terms. *See* Chile's report on the Mapuche indigenous people where, despite acknowledging the Mapuche as a racial group, the representative explained the government's aims as integrating the group and respecting their customs and traditions. Racism and racial discrimination were mentioned but reference to Chile's report to the Committee

C. Nationality

Though excluded from Article 27 and the group protection clauses of the minority treaties, "nationality" has, despite disagreements, been used since the League times to refer to the so-called "national minorities."[59] "Nationality" originated in Europe as a reference to groups identified with particular territories in which they had had long residence, but which had lost their sovereignty to some numerically superior people of different nationality.[60] Political and other aspects of their lives were usually subject to special laws, as in the case of the Czechs in the Austro-Hungarian Empire.

Immediately after WWI "nationality" referred mainly to populations whose allegiance had to change with the repartition of Europe in an era of strong nationalism. An affected group had strong feelings of belonging to its respective stock in a definite territory. The logical satisfaction of such feelings would have been to grant autonomy or even independence. That this was not granted in the minority treaties points to the fact that "nationality" as a connotation of independent political existence was not accepted. This confirms the usage of "nationality" as a synonym for race and, more importantly, for linguistic groups.[61]

The United Nations has not had the same experience with the concept of nationality as did the League. On the one hand, decolonization has been supported by the United Nations, but on the other, nation-states have perceived the idea of protecting "national minorities" as an affront to their jealously guarded sovereignty. Consequently, there has been little resolution of the disagreements on the usage of "nationality." As the term had traditionally been used to refer, inter alia, to groups speaking the same language,[62] or to the same ethnic group, it was considered appropriate because the less expansive and more homogeneous societies before the nation-state could justifiably be considered political entities. The imposition of the modern

---

on the Elimination of Racial Discrimination was implicit recognition that the subject did not fall precisely under the provision on minorities. Report of the Human Rights Committee, Vol. I, U.N. GAOR, 45th Sess., Supp. 40, at 48, U.N. Doc. A/45/40 (1990). Uruguay's report mentioned blacks but did not regard them as a minority because they shared the same language and traditions with other Uruguayans. Report of the Human Rights Committee, U.N. GAOR, 44th Sess., Supp. 40, at 71, U.N. Doc. A/44/40 (1989).

59. *See* the terminology, especially in Eastern European countries: sessional *HRC Reports*; Capotorti, *supra* note 6, at Annex III.

60. Arnold M. Rose, *Minorities*, 10 Int'l Encyclopedia of the Soc. Sci. 365 (1968).

61. *See supra* note 47, at 314.

62. This is reflected by the definition of "nation" as including racial or ethnic groups, *see* 10 *The Oxford English Dictionary* 235 (2d ed. 1989); of "ethnic" as pertaining to, *inter alia*, "linguistic characteristics, especially designating a group within a larger system," *see* 5 *The Oxford English Dictionary* 424 (2d ed. 1989); and of "language" as "[t]he whole body of words and of methods of combination of words used by a nation, people or race," *see* 8 *The Oxford English Dictionary* 634 (2d ed. 1989).

state system, however, aroused conflict between the new states and the constituent communities wishing to maintain their identity as against the dictates of the nation-state—a clash of "nationalisms." As a result, nationality, in ethnic terms, has been receding into history.[63] Despite its use in the traditional sense, "nationality" in modern times more correctly describes the product of the nation-state, as confirmed by the history of Article 27.

During the drafting of the ICCPR the Soviet Union's proposed inclusion of "national minorities" in Article 27 was rejected by the CHR on the reasoning that "national minorities" implied a higher threshold which would exclude minorities that might never become national minorities.[64] The Soviets countered that limiting protection to "ethnic or linguistic groups" amounted to denying protection to national minorities.[65] Whatever the motivations for these arguments, the outcome did not resolve the differences in interpreting the identifying term "national." Taking both arguments as genuine, there seemed no valid reason to treat the two drafts as mutually exclusive. The real issue was, however, no different from that posed in the drafting of the minority treaties.

The fears about "national minorities" had mainly to do with the assumption that the term necessarily implied a degree of political consciousness attributable to the demand for political autonomy, very similar, if not identical, to the pursuit of self-determination.[66] This fear explains the compromise Article 27 attempts to achieve. As stated by the Yugoslavian delegate:

> The . . . article did not affect the integrity of the State and should not be allowed to obstruct the process of assimilation of minority groups. But that assimilation must be free and unconstrained. There was a danger that, in order to encourage assimilation, a government might adopt measures detrimental to the interests of minority groups.[67]

While providing protection against detrimental government policy, the article was also designed to safeguard government interests. Of these interests, the danger of territorial dismemberment was one of the gravest. This view was expressed even when the body was considering a less controversial proposal that "the State shall ensure to national minorities the right to use their native

63. On the impact of the modern notion of "nation," see Alain Fenet, *The Question of Minorities in the Order of Law*, in *Minority Peoples in the Age of Nation-States* 12, 20–21. On the temporal precedence of ethnicity, see P.J. Simon, *Propositions pour un lexique des mote cles dans le domaine des etudes relationelles*, 4 Pluriel-debat 65, at 71 (1975), cited in Fenet, *supra*.
64. The proposal in U.N. Doc. E/CN.4/L.222 (1953), reproduced in the Report of the Human Rights Commission, U.N. ESCOR, 16th Sess., Supp. 8, Annex III, at 55, was criticized in U.N. Doc. A/CN.4/SR.369, at 13 (1953).
65. *See* Tomuschat, *supra* note 16, at 959–60.
66. *Id.* at 960.
67. U.N. GAOR, 3d Comm., at para. 14, U.N. Doc. A/C.3/SR.1104 (1961).

tongue and to have their national schools, libraries, museums and other cultural and educational institutions."[68] It was feared that this proposal would have retarded the process of assimilating immigrants and prevented the formation of a homogeneous society.[69] In addition, it would have encouraged separatist or irredentist movements and a multiplication of barriers and frontiers.[70] Also rejected was a proposal that "every person shall have the right to show freely his membership of an ethnic or linguistic group, to use without hindrance the name of his group, to learn the language of his group and to use it in public and in private life."[71] The reason given for this rejection was that it would be disruptive if "every person" were to claim the benefit of the rights of minorities. This circumstance resulted in the clause "in community with other members of the group."[72]

Essentially, the concern underlying these views was expressly the "national unity or security" of the state.[73] With the desire of nation-states to encourage common national identity, even the nature of obligation imposed on the signatories was formulated to conform with this integrative or assimilationist policy. The original formulation that "the State shall ensure to national minorities the right" was rejected,[74] for the reason that such a positive obligation would artificially awaken or stimulate minority consciousness.[75] Consequently, the final formulation in Article 27 implies a negative obligation to permit the free exercise of minority rights.[76]

The obvious implications of the above views have not deterred states and scholars from using the term "national minority." Despite its political connotations, "nationality" has been used to refer to distinct ethnic groups forming part of a political nation. In the drafting of the article, it was necessary to clarify whether the Soviet proposal was distinct from ethnicity in common parlance and referred to political identity. In any case, the history of minority protection contains sufficient proof that political loyalty is, and has been, a prerequisite for protection. For instance, a recent study commissioned by the SCPDPM states that a minority is a "group of citizens" of a state in which

---

68. U.N. Doc. E/CN.4/L.21 (1951).
69. U.N. Doc. E/CN.4/SR.257 at 3 (1952).
70. U.N. GAOR, 3d Comm., 6th Sess., at paras. 10–14, U.N. Doc. A/C.3/SR.361 (1951); U.N. Doc. A/C.3/SR.362, at paras. 71–72 (1951). *See also* U.N. Doc. E/CN.4/SR.368, at 10 (1953); U.N. Doc. E/CN.4/SR.370, at 6, 9 (1953); U.N. Doc. E/CN.4/SR.371, at 5 (1953).
71. U.N. Doc. E/CN.4/SR.368, at 5–7 (1953); U.N. Doc. E/CN.4/SR.369, at 8 (1953).
72. U.N. Doc. E/CN.4/SR.369, at 6 (1953).
73. *See id.* at 4, 5, 7, 11; U.N. Doc. E/CN.4/SR.368, at 10, 16 (1953); U.N. Doc. E/CN.4/SR.370, at 4 (1953).
74. U.N. Doc. E/CN.4/SR.369 at 4, 9 (1953).
75. *Id.* at 5, 11; U.N. Doc. E/CN.4/SR.368, at 9, 16 (1953); U.N. Doc. E/CN.4/SR.370, at 5 (1953).
76. U.N. Doc. E/CN.4/SR.368, at 12 (1953); U.N. Doc. E/CN.4/SR.369, at 12 (1953).

they are located.[77] Furthermore, contemporary usage of "nationality" as a synonym for ethnicity is notable especially in the Eastern European countries, where the recognition of a group as such does not amount to a go-ahead for secession. In this respect, Capotorti's conclusion that "ethnic" in Article 27 was intended to cover "national minorities" is easy to understand.[78] Yet, after strong objection to the inclusion of "national minorities" for its supposed implications, the exclusion of "national" could hardly have reflected the implication that national minorities fell under the category of ethnic minorities.

D. Nationality and Self-Determination

Exclusive of "nationality," the intention of the drafters of the ICCPR must be reconciled with the contemporary interpretations of self-determination. Terminologically, this may not concern their intention during the drafting, as self-determination then referred almost exclusively to decolonization. Today, the principle of sovereignty and the rejection of secession is generally accepted in the United Nations and regional organizations. But the rights expressed in later interpretations of self-determination that do not controvert the proven intention may be deemed to have been granted. This conforms with the principle of effective treaty interpretation.

In more recent years, self-determination has been interpreted with emphasis on the non-political aspects of economic, social, and cultural development. The cultural aspect has been emphasized in the UNESCO Declaration on the Principles of Cultural Cooperation.[79] At a regional level, the African Charter on Human and Peoples' Rights (African Charter) specifies peoples' right to assistance of state parties in their struggle against cultural foreign domination.[80] Although this acknowledgment of cultural self-determination tends to exclude intra-national domination, presumably due to fears of secession, it necessarily introduces a yardstick that cannot be ignored in proving the possibly non-political basis of self-determination.

In recognizing cultural self-determination, the argument that "national minorities" unwarily introduces a political element is weakened. The Amerindian situation in the United States and Canada is illustrative insofar

---

77. The study by J. Deschenes, *A Definition of Minorities* (1985), was adopted by the Subcommission together with a proposed definition: *See* U.N. Doc. E/CN.4/Sub.2/1985/31/& Corr.1, at 30 (1985); Res. 1985/6, U.N. Doc. E/CN.4/1986/5, at 85 (1985).
78. Capotorti, *supra* note 6, at para. 201.
79. UNESCO, General Conference Records, 14th Sess., Resolutions, at 86–89 (1966).
80. African Charter on Human and Peoples' Rights, *adopted* June 27, 1981, O.A.U. Doc. CAB/LEG/67/3 Rev. 5, at art. 20 (3).

as the Amerindians maintain their desire for separate settlement; the self-governing system in the areas reserved to them should be considered as cultural self-determination.[81] Indeed, their separateness has so little to do with political independence on the international plane as not to arouse fears of secession. If anything, they are intent on maintaining their identity, an effort enhanced by detachment from the modern cross-national influences of politics.

Despite the agreement that minority protection was designed to exclude groups striving for independent political existence, the problem remains of reconciling Article 27 of the ICCPR on the one hand, and common Article 1 of the ICCPR and the International Covenant on Economic, Social and Cultural Rights (ICESCR) on the other. The latter provides for the right to self-determination, itself a group right. It has been suggested that the omission of "national minorities" resulted from the forecast of a danger in blurring the boundary between a people, in the sense of Article 1, and minorities.[82] This view reflects the original idea of self-determination as implying not mere residual political authority, but total independence. "People," the bearer of the right, was therefore interpreted to mean a group entitled to political independence. With the changes in the concept of self-determination, this interpretation has had to change.

Following Cristescu's definition of "people,"[83] which included the elements of group identity and relationship with a territory ("even if it has been wrongfully expelled from it and artificially replaced by other populations"), and drawing from the various interpretations of self-determination, Kiss has correctly concluded that

> [t]he right certainly includes "external" as well as "internal" self-determination and confirms the principle that peoples are to approve all territorial changes which directly concern them, [and] that self-determination also means that internal autonomy should be granted to peoples which can be identified inside existing States if they so wish.[84]

The organization of the Amerindians is therefore an example of internal self-determination, even if taken politically and not culturally. They have both the characteristics of Cristescu's definition. Following this argument, it must be concluded that the terms "peoples" and "national minorities" are not mutually exclusive. The idea of "internal" self-determination has applied not only to indigenous groups. Nationalities, in the sense of groups associated

---

81. *See generally*, James Wilson, *supra* note 17.
82. Tomuschat, *supra* note 16, at 960.
83. Aureliu Cristescu, *The Right to Self-Determination*, U.N. Doc. E/CN.4/Sub.2/404/Rev.1, at 41 (1981).
84. Alexandre Kiss, *The Peoples' Right to Self-Determination*, 7 Hum. Rts. L.J. 165, 175 (1986).

with some past or present territory, continue to exist. Examples of groups associated with territory include the unassimilated groups of the United States, such as the Irish and Scandinavians in Wisconsin and Minnesota, and ethnic groups in the former Soviet Union, such as the Ukrainians.

In any territory of whatever political structure, individuals of common origin tend to congregate. This tendency is given political flavor where, especially in federal systems, boundaries of political units are demarcated along ethnic, racial, or linguistic lines. The history and current boundaries of the French-speaking Canadian region of Quebec reflects this tendency,[85] in much the same way as that of the former Ukrainian Soviet Republic.[86] These examples reinforce the notion of "internal" self-determination, and not solely in a cultural sense.

IV. LANGUAGE

As a minority identity, and similar to religion in this aspect, language has been considered self-explanatory, a tacit view reflecting the circumstances under which minority protection developed. The initial focus being Europe, the linguistic categories there were clear-cut, such as German and Polish. Prior to the early protection system, the range of Germanic languages in Europe had crystallized into identified languages which had in turn become instruments of nationalism. They were thus associated with definite political entities. Therefore, in the redrawing of boundaries after WWI, the political significance of linguistic groups was not surprising. The same could not and cannot be said of all parts of the world. In certain countries and regions with wide linguistic categories, determining whether a given form of speech is a language, dialect, or other linguistic variety arouses difficulty, especially in reconciling purely linguistic and legal criteria.

"Language" has been considered non-technical by linguists who prefer the substitute "variety," given the variability of speech form with social, political, and cultural circumstances.[87] Similar speech patterns occur within social groups and geographical barriers. Dialect, as distinguished from language, refers to a subordinate variety of language such as the Yorkshire

85. The original European settlers in the region were French, and although it was ceded to the British (English speakers) way back as 1763, it remains predominantly French with boundaries more or less conforming with the settlement pattern.
86. Recognized in the USSR as a nationality, the Ukrainians have always been distinct from the Russians, with, *inter alia*, the Ukrainian Catholic Church distinct from the Russian Orthodox Church.
87. S. Romaine, *Language Varieties*, *in* 2 International Encyclopedia of Communications 399, 399 (1989).

dialect of English. With time, however, a dialect may become a language, just as the old Germanic dialects became autonomous in such forms as the current English, German, and Dutch languages. Although no such change has occurred with respect to the languages of the groups recognized in the minority treaties, the universality of current minority protection would require a verification of the variety of speech of a group claiming linguistic minority status.

Empirical studies have shown that what are sometimes termed languages, and named differently, are actually mere dialects. For instance, Serbian in southern Yugoslavia and Croatian in the north have been proven to be as intelligible to each other as the localized English varieties of Texas and Boston.[88] In fact, in Hungary, these Yugoslavian varieties have been collectively termed Serbo-Croatian.[89] Similarly, in India, Hindi and Urdu are so intelligible as to be considered variants of the same language. Additionally, distinctions have sometimes been made between such variants on the ground of script. Written Croatian uses the Latin alphabet while Serbian uses the Cyrillic; Hindu is written in Devanagari script while Urdu is in the Persian-Arabic. Such distinctions, whether in name or orthography, reflect differing social relations. The difference between Croatian and Serbian results from the Catholicism of the former, endowing it with the Latin script, and the Orthodox tradition of the Serbians, resulting in their adoption of the script associated with the Orthodox Church. Similarly, the use of the Persian-Arabic script in written Urdu shows the impact of the early Muslim Arab invaders, whose religion, written in the same script, prevails among Urdu speakers. The evolution of Hindi with Hinduism is even more direct.[90]

Conversely, a language called by one name may actually comprise several. For instance, it is acknowledged that the common name "Chinese" represents related languages such as Cantonese, Hakka, and Mandarin, which are as different from each other as the romance languages of French, Spanish, and Portuguese; the sole reason for such reference is common script.[91] The fact of common script does not warrant the designation of any two languages as one, while common speech patterns do. The legal issue then is whether language should be determined with reference to speech or script or both.

Because minority protection concerns actual or perceived risks to a

88. Merritt Ruhlen, *A Guide to the Languages of the World* 2 (1975).
89. *See* Capotorti, *supra* note 6, at para. 489.
90. On the ancient language of the Hindus as a medium for religious knowledge, see *The Oxford Reference Dictionary* 389, 733 (1986). Paul R. Brass, *Language, Religion and Politics in North India* 129–30, 135, 194, 215 (1974) (discussing influence of ancient language on Hindi).
91. Ruhlen, *supra* note 88, at 1–2.

distinct group, the precondition to protecting linguistic minorities must be distinguished from general recognition of languages, which may belong to minorities or majorities. The need for protection necessarily implies that "language" must refer not to any distinct form of speech, but to those forms whose distinctness arouses, or is likely to arouse, group conflict or domination. To suggest otherwise would be as ridiculous as to imagine the special protection of Afrikaans in apartheid South Africa. "Language" cannot, therefore, be interpreted in a solely linguistic sense to exclude such aspects as script, which may serve as symbols of group identity and form a heritage rooted in culture or religion. The use of Arabic script by Urdu-speaking Muslims of India and Pakistan is especially illustrative, as script makes a significant difference as a medium of communication in a world of literacy. The imposition of one form of script on a society that has used a different type for ages could be a form of domination encompassing language both as merely a means of communication and as the medium of a particular tradition or religion.

The potential for such group relations is greatest where language serves as a status symbol. An example is Spanish and indigenous Indian languages in Latin America, the former representing the higher status. The same applies even to dialect variants, as was noted in Jamaica, where the British spoke English while the lower social class spoke Jamaican Creole, although Creole has an English root.[92] The question then is whether such variants have sufficient autonomy to constitute languages. An affirmative answer will be linguistically arbitrary. Yet the very criteria used in distinguishing between, say, German and Dutch have been as political and cultural as those distinguishing Jamaican Creole and English.[93] Such is the result of language standardization, as determined by literacy, nationalism, and cultural identity, and as enhanced by the dictionary, grammar, and teaching. This conceptualization renders the standard language, like English, autonomous, while all related ones become dependent on it as their reference.[94]

When language has social, cultural, and political attributes apart from the mere communication value, it can ease any scheme of domination. For example, to require a group that has for centuries used one script to use another in all official matters could mean the exclusion of its members from public service, even if the official language is intelligible to its members. Similarly, the exclusive promotion of one language could mean the growth of a generation of the speakers of the other language who are denied linguistic access to their religion or culture when they are transmitted through a par-

92. *See* S. Romaine, *supra* note 87, at 399, 400.
93. *See id.*
94. *See id.*

ticular script. Arguably, in this sense each of the language variants should be considered autonomous to constitute "language" in minority protection. Only then can there be effective redress of the situation.

By the same logic, however, external influence on language may play down significant linguistic differences. The widely spoken Arabic has dialects such as Moroccan and Palestinian, which are linguistically no closer to one another than French is to Spanish. Similarly, the relationship of classical Arabic to Arabic speakers is the equivalent of what Latin was for Old French, Old Italian, and Old Spanish in the Middle Ages.[95] The determinant factors are the common ethnic and religious (Islamic) bonds among the Arabs which overshadow the linguistic variations. This would seem to result in conflict between the ethnic and religious factors on the one hand, and the linguistic one on the other. Nevertheless, as linguistic distinctiveness is relevant only in the context of relations between dominant and non-dominant groups, where the different brands of Arabic are spoken in the same country their significance under Article 27 should be weighed against the said ethnic and religious bonds.

V. CONCLUSION

A rule or legal definition may be illustrative or exclusive. The history of the drafting of Article 27 illustrates that the identities specified in it were meant to be exhaustive, so that "race" is excluded. While the article specifies ethnicity, religion, and language, these terms need to be interpreted separately from their common meanings in sociology and linguistics. The difference between the League and UN criteria underlines the requirement of interpretation in the light of the particular circumstances of the situations addressed. Because social relations are dynamic, it should always be recalled that the reasons for designating one characteristic as cultural, religious, or linguistic in one age need be subjected to review when assessing their validity for minority protection in a different age. While a traditional understanding of these characteristics is basic in labeling any identifying attribute, the differences between variants of the characteristics should be a qualifying condition in all cases.

95. Ruhlen, *supra* note 88, at 2.

[5]

To Bellow like a Cow: Women, Ethnicity, and the Discourse of Rights

Radhika Coomaraswamy

> "Why have you appeared before this gathering?
> Why do you bellow like a cow in labor?
> Your time must be near.
> Shameless women with no sense of decorum
> Bellow in gatherings of respectable men."
> —Addressed to Bhola Moiraon Poetess Jogeswari and her female troupe, nineteenth century

Introduction

In *The Politics of Rights,* Stuart Scheingold writes:

> The appeals made by the myth of rights for the support of Americans are rooted in traditional values and closely associated with venerable institutions. The symbolic voice of the myth of rights can, moreover, be easily understood and readily adapted to political discourse. But just how compelling is it? How pervasive and widespread and uniform a grip do legal values have on the minds of Americans?[1]

Implicit in this argument is that, for human rights to be effective, they have to go beyond the normative, textual essence and become a part of the legal culture of a given society. They must strike a responsive chord in the general public consciousness with regard to political and civil issues. This resonance is therefore the clue to whether the "myth of rights" works in a given society to ensure the political and civil rights of all persons.

This chapter argues that in the area of women's rights as human rights there is the least amount of resonance, especially in the countries of South Asia, and that this lack of resonance has prevented the effective implementation of rights.

The barriers to the implementation of human rights are two-fold. First, the lack of proper implementation machinery to make rights real in the lives of women is an obstacle, as is women's lack of awareness of the rights machinery that would empower them. The second and more formidable barrier is the refusal to accept the values in and of themselves: an ideological resistance to human rights for women.

In saying this I do not want to get caught in what is called the "Orientalist trap."[2] It is easy to divide the world into bipolar categories: the west is progressive on women's rights and the east is barbaric and backward. The reverse of this argument from the eastern point of view is to accept the distinction, but to say that the east is superior, more communal, and less self-centered with no place for this "adversarial" concept of rights. I would argue that in South Asia both traditions exist. There are examples of personal laws and women's rights that informed issues such as no-fault divorce and the best interest of the child centuries before the west considered them. The Kandyan laws of the Kandyan Sinhalese are one example.[3]

The Privileged Female Personality

To analyze the barriers posed by culture, custom, and personal laws with regard to women's rights as human rights, it is important to analyze the underlying assumption about the female personality that accompanies any discourse of women's rights especially in documents such as the Convention on the Elimination of All Forms of Discrimination Against Women (the Women's Convention).[4] The personality that is privileged in such documents is the free, independent woman as an individual endowed with rights and rational agency. It is, in fact, the culmination of the enlightenment project, the "rights of man" now being enjoyed by women. This is perhaps exemplified in the most controversial, and therefore the most important, provision of the Women's Convention, Article 16.

Article 16 requires that the states parties on a basis of equality of men and women ensure that women have the same right to choose a spouse freely and to enter into marriage with their free and full consent.[5] It also requires the state to ensure the same personal rights for husband and wife, including the right to choose a family name, a profession, and an occupation.[6]

Though the Women's Convention's emphasis is on the principle of nondiscrimination, and not on the principle of empowerment,[7] there is the assumption that it privileges the free, independent, and empowered woman. The only female differences accepted by the Women's Convention relate to a woman's condition of maternity in the section on labor law[8] and with regard to special rights related to the redressing of historical grievances.[9] The highlighting of these differences is only to ensure that the state take necessary measures to ensure that a woman is given the opportunity to develop her individual identity, rooted in an enlightenment view of the human personality, a personality without fetters or community context.

I am in agreement with the enlightenment view of the human personality. But it would be wrong to assume that the values contained in the Universal Declaration of Human Rights are truly universal. Such an assumption would make more than half the world the subject of ridicule. However, to work toward this enlightenment ideal, it is important to expose the ideologies of power that sustain counter-ideologies which view women as inferior. It is also important to learn how Asian societies may in fact further the rights of women even beyond those contained in international conventions—those rights which are attached to a woman in the context of her class, her caste, and her ethnic group.

The Duality in Modern Law

For the greater part of the non-western world, the approach to women is couched in ambiguity. The Sri Lankan Constitution inspired by liberal, socialist norms is one such example. It states after a general nondiscrimination clause that includes sex:

> Nothing in this Article shall prevent special provision being made by law, subordinate legislation or executive action for the advancement of women, children and disabled persons.[10]

On the one hand, the drafters argue that this formulation is to allow room for affirmative action on behalf of women, but the juxtaposition of women, children, and the mentally retarded is an extremely interesting feature. It is especially so if we compare it to Article 4 of the Women's Convention:

> Adoption by States Parties of temporary special measures aimed at accelerating de facto equality between men and women shall not be considered discriminatory.[11]

The first formulation as expressed in the Sri Lankan Constitution does not accept responsibility for historical wrong while the second implicitly does. The reason for this lies also in the fact that Sri Lanka is a Buddhist society; many of its leading scholars feel that there was no traditional discrimination against women and that discrimination is a colonial legacy. This line of thinking is dominant—discrimination originated with colonialism.[12]

Second, the Sri Lankan Constitution, in juxtaposing women with children and the disabled accentuates the duality present in all laws with regard to women. On the one hand, there is nondiscrimination and an assertion of women's equality with men. On the other hand, there is the belief that woman is vulnerable and needs protection. In this paternalistic project, women, along with children and the mentally disabled, are denied agency—the right to protect themselves.

The special protection provision on behalf of women is also defended on the ground that the reality of working conditions in a developing country often puts a worker's health at risk. That proposition is indisputable. But the argument of nondiscrimination requires that men also be protected from the terrible working conditions that may impair health. Equality in this worldview is only present to help women, it is not reciprocal. This line of thinking is similar to the cases on social security that came before the U.S. courts in the early 1970s, where men as widowers, husbands, and dependents claimed social security benefits to which they felt entitled.[13]

The Anthropological Reality: Ideological Barriers

The Sri Lankan Constitution is a modern document drawn from liberal and socialist inspiration. In some ways the issues it raises are easily identifiable and are within the framework of discourse that characterizes legal thinking with regard to women's rights as fundamental rights. The barriers, though real, are thought out and solutions of various inclinations have been put forward. It is a modern problem in the realm of world history and rights discourse. While the so-called modern Constitution reflects this duality between freedom and vulnerability, the situation becomes still more complicated if one deals with what is often called the "anthropological reality."

The "extra-legal" factors that are barriers to the consideration of women's rights as human rights in South Asia are rooted in ideological aspects, especially as they relate to the tension between the law and civil society, as well as within the legal system itself. Let us begin with the former.

Law and Civil Society

Ashis Nandy, an influential Indian scholar, analyzes the roots of the modern Indian crisis in the disjunction between the traditions of Indian civil society and the colonial inheritance of a modern nation-state run on Weberian lines, with bureaucracy and the market being the central organizational features. The law is the central instrument in this colonial process that aims at erasing tradition and plurality, and restructuring civil society along modern lines. The law and the state are the special targets of hatred and the rights discourse is seen as a manifestation of this impersonal, homogenizing, activist state. Judicial activism is anathema to scholars such as Nandy.

Nandy is one of the most influential scholars in South Asia. His challenge to rights discourse is the best articulated response to modern statehood which, through the use of law, attempts to ensure equality. It is important to examine his argument to recognize the type of ideological barriers that we face in South Asia when we talk about women's rights as human rights. The speeches and pamphlets of religious and ethnic dignitaries are self-evident in their rejection of the west, including rights, in what may be considered the Orientalist encounter. But Nandy is a more sophisticated, and perhaps a more enticing, articulator of the rejection of the concept of an activist state intervening to impose a model of equality based on the values of the Universal Declaration of Human Rights.

In "The Making and Unmaking of Political Culture,"[14] he argues that India has a measure of cultural autonomy from western values and institutions and that this autonomy persists despite the best efforts of the government. He argues that in the worldview of traditional Indian culture politics was considered the Machiavellian art of the possible. It occupied only a very limited sphere, that of providing security to the population. Civil society was the arena for struggle and conflict in traditional India, and it was ruled by precepts of *dharma* and ethics. Tolerance, he claims, was an aspect of everyday life. In the hierarchy of power, power over self was valued above state power, which was the least respected and the most brutal. Nandy's argument is supported by Deepak Lal's two-volume work, *The Hindu Equilibrium.*[15]

In this view of the dichotomy between civil society and the state, the root of all evil is located at the colonial encounter where the Weberian concept of state was transferred to Indian soil. The competition among political parties, the struggle for state resources, and the supremacy of state power are what Nandy points to as the main reasons for what Atul Kohli calls "the crisis of governability."[16]

The implications of this scheme of analysis for human rights are not very clear. Nandy is not opposed to the substance of human rights, which he feels is at the root of popular culture, and the humanistic face of civil society. However, he is totally opposed to the mechanism employed for its enforcement—the law and the paternalistic state. He argues instead for strengthening human rights values in civil society.

Nandy's point of view has been criticized as a romanticized view of the Indian past and of Indian popular culture. The rigors of the caste system or sex-based oppression cannot all be laid at the doorstep of colonial India. Many practices in Indian civil society shock the conscience and cannot be willed away as an aberration. And yet there is a voice there that should also be heard.

If one looks at the Women's Convention and other international documents of human rights, every article begins with the word "states parties" and proceeds to unfold the obligation imposed upon the state. As states are the foundation of the international order, this is inescapable. However, if the state is entrusted with the responsibility of ensuring women's rights, if it is always viewed as active and paternalistic in a benign manner, then this does pose serious questions. The nation-state in the third world does not carry this "Scandinavian aura." In addition, there is a major problem of implementation in what Kohli calls the redistribution of poverty.[17] Nandy is correct in one sense, that unless these human rights values take root in civil society and unless civil institutions and non-governmental organizations (NGOs) take up the cause, then women's rights as human rights will have no resonance in the social institutions concerned.

There are situations, of course, where state action or inaction with regard to a particular community galvanizes an awareness of human rights as part of the struggle of elements within society. The Chipko movement in India is one such example. Women protected their livelihood by wrapping themselves around trees when the bulldozers, which were part of a larger development project, came into their areas.[18] In Sri Lanka ethnic and civil violence has galvanized groups into action from all strata of society and has in itself instilled values of the right to life and freedom from arbitrary arrest. Lived experience is the best fermenting ground for human rights awareness and action, including the rights of women. In that sense Nandy is correct. The future of human rights in the South Asian region does not lie with states parties but with the movements in civil society.

Where Nandy is wrong is that the law is not only an empty shell but also a catalyst for mobilization. Even if the future lies in civil society, there have to be standards by which one can hold individuals and states accountable. In addition, in some rare instances, the courts are also galvanized into action. In such a context this artificial separation into civil society where the popular will resides, and the state where the legal and bureaucratic will resides, may create more problems in the realization of women's rights. It is only a combination of the two, coming together at a particular historical moment that results in change, creativity, and social action. The first is only limited to mobilization and awareness, the second to articulation and implementation. Of course, after enactment, forces in civil society have to act as watchdogs to ensure that the rights guaranteed are protected. So Nandy's point is well taken: civil society is necessary for creating the conditions for law to be relevant. It is also useful in ensuring that law is enforced. But, at the same time, it has to be recognized that without law, any human rights activist will only be tilting at windmills.

While discussing issues of civil society, it may be important to reiterate here that the essentialist view that western civil society and law empowers women while the eastern only subordinates them is not strictly correct. There are instances where traditional laws have been more progressive than modern legislation and the colonial encounter actually robbed women of pre-existing rights. A case in point is the Kandyan law of the Sinhalese, where standards such as no-fault divorce and best interests of the child and even polyandry were recognized in the Kandyan areas of Sri Lanka, and still have some legitimacy under the modern system of law, although, of course, the practice of polyandry faded with the importation of western values.

In addition, the colonial encounter forced reinterpretation of law according to legal norms prevalent in the west. The Thesawalamai of the Sri Lankan Tamils had notions of community property akin to that of the Roman Dutch law, but Dutch drafters interpreted the notion of community property according to their law before the nineteenth-century reforms with regard to married women's property. They imposed on Tamil women the denial of the right of alienation of property without their husband's consent, with no reciprocal duty. Today, married Dutch women can freely buy and sell property acquired in their name, but married Tamil women, subject to this archaic law and its medieval interpretation, cannot do so and do not enjoy the rights given by the Married Women's Property Ordinance of the nineteenth century. And since Sri Lankan Tamil women are a minority, they have no access to change the law, which, for all purposes, may govern them until the end of time, regardless of the change in circumstances or the practices of the community.

Law and Other Ideologies of Empowerment

Since in the final analysis rights are about empowerment, what many South Asians argue is that the traditional roots of empowerment in South Asian societies are denied in rights discourse. The legal strategies that accompany rights discourse aim at an adversarial contest in the courts between the victim and the state. However, it is argued that women's empowerment in these traditional societies has manifested itself not through rights ideology but through family ideology. There have been in South Asia recently a spate of writings about "Mother, Mother-Community, and Mother-Politics."[19]

South Asia has the greatest concentration of women heads of state. India, Pakistan, Sri Lanka, and Bangladesh have all experienced women heads of state. There is ideological acceptance of women in the public realm, but this is because these women have appropriated the discourse of motherhood. Anthropologists have also noted a major rise in mother-goddess worship.[20] Of course, the glorification of woman as mother means the denigration of unmarried women, widows, childless women, and divorced women. And yet this ideology is so powerful that the present Tamil Nadu Chief Minister Jayalalitha has appropriated motherhood as a symbol even though she is neither married nor a mother. She is called the "Avenging Mother" from the context of being a protector of the poor and underprivileged.

Women activists argue that legal strategies do not allow women to touch base with their traditional sources of empowerment. In Sri Lanka the ideology of motherhood has been appropriated for political action, symbolizing the widows and mothers who have lost their husbands and children in the recent violence. The Mothers for Peace or the Mothers of the Disappeared, precisely because of their appropriation of the mother ideology, have found a great deal of political maneuverability which even politicians, caught within the same ideological construct, are hard pressed to overcome.[21]

There has been a lot of criticism about this type of strategy which uses indigenous symbols because of the other side of the same process. If one accepts mother ideology, how do we privilege the voices of the unmarried and widows? The strategy appears to divide the female community with no real, concrete, political goal save that of agitation. But what is significant is that rights discourse, because of its construction and its style of implementation, is not plugging into many of the dynamic social movements taking place in South Asia. Perhaps one should accept that one is the realm of politics, the other the realm of law. Either way, it is important to recognize that there is an important division within the sphere of social action.

Whose Equality?

Before we move on to a discussion of the law as a strategy for the attainment of women's rights through human rights, it seems important to consider for a moment the discourse of equality. Often at the same conference the word equality is used in diametrically opposite constructions. Even international documents vary. Under the Women's Convention equality is nondiscrimination—a constant measure of men against women. In other contexts equality is access to empowerment as individuals, not as a measurement of the final end that men versus women actually reaches. In some cultures, equality retains notions of separate spheres, the public and the private and separate but equal doctrines prevail, justified by the uniqueness of the maternal function.

In socialist societies equality carries with it the responsibility of the state to socialize maternity and maternal functions so as to allow a woman to work and fulfill her public life. To many others equality is an ideological disposition, rooted in attitudes and psychological make-up which can only be removed through strategies drawn from psychology and post-structuralism. For many others, equality of women is completely dependent on their class, caste, or ethnic group—if these attain equality, then women in these groups will also achieve equality. For feminists, of course, equality is the other side of patriarchy. Since every aspect of life seems to be infected by the gender bias and classification, equality will only be achieved if it is linked to social transformation of a very radical sort.

Given these diverse conceptions of equality, the law in many of these societies as well as at the international level has taken the easy way out. It is only in areas where discrimination can be factually ascertained through empirical data and actual case studies that law is relevant to the question of female equality. It is therefore not unusual that nondiscrimination remains the model legislation in all parts of the world when it comes to the equality of women. Women's rights couched in this limited human rights discourse are also confined to concepts of equality that are linked to the structure of the law and its relationship with the state in any particular society. In addition, in our part of the world, there is very little autonomy that law enjoys vis-à-vis the state and politics. Human rights are then confined to this post-colonial sector of the law, legislation, the state, the bureaucracy, and political party mobilization. This is the clue to its success as well as its failure.

Opportunities and Innovations

This is not to say that interesting innovations cannot take women's rights beyond nondiscrimination in certain constitutional contexts. Since the Indian Constitution recognizes the right to life and dignity, in a series of cases the Indian courts dealt with situations that were clearly not issues of measuring men against women but rooted in life and dignity. The living conditions of the women of Agra Remand was one such case.[22] There have been others dealing for instance with women under trial, women prisoners, and women construction workers.[23] In these contexts the principles contained in the Indian Constitution permitted a move away from simple nondiscrimination—or the redistribution of poverty as it is sometimes called in third world societies—to a more empowering stance focusing on the clauses relating to human dignity. Unfortunately many countries do not have these provisions or judges willing to interpret them in a holistic light.

Barriers: Family and Personal Law

This chapter is not about opportunities but about barriers. The issues of women, ethnicity, and rights discourse eventually come to a head in the area of family law or personal law. Labor law and other forms of economic and labor legislation have a certain similar standard, modeled on ILO recommendations and directing themselves to the urban labor force. In this context the vast majority of women (87 percent of the Sri Lankan women workers)[24] work in the agricultural sector and are unprotected by the law. The barriers relating to their rights are in the urban labor bias of labor legislation. The criminal law is, of course, the security safety net of any society, and though there are many issues to raise with regard to women and violence, issues that are not directly addressed in the Women's Convention, the provisions are generally similar and have a certain uniform structure.

It is in family law, however, that completely different and plural standards and constructions exist of how we must conduct our personal and social life. It is, in fact, the litmus test in any society with regard to legal norms and the status of women. It is also the area where the law, ethnicity, and ideology with regard to the rights of women merge to become a powerful ideological force. Before we come to any conclusions about the barriers that exist about women in this area, let us look at four case studies: (1) sati in India; (2) the Hudood Ordinance in Pakistan; (3) the recent attempts at divorce reforms in Sri Lanka; and (4) the well-known *Shah Bano* case in India.

Roop Kanwar: The Sati Case

On September 4, 1987, in Deorala, Rajasthan, Roop Kanwar was burned alive on her husband's funeral pyre. She was an eighteen-year-old university student, and her husband was an unemployed university graduate when he died. Her shrine became a place of pilgrimage. Many believed she was a goddess and that offerings to her shrine would cure them of cancer, the illness that took the life of her husband. There are conflicting versions of her state of mind before her death. Some have argued that she was willing to die, others that she was coerced, still others that she was unsure but in the end succumbed to family pressure.[25]

The newspapers carrying the story a week later kindled a huge controversy. Urban-centered women's groups as well as groups of women from throughout India were horrified and organized a march in Rajasthan. The Rajasthanis retaliated by filling the streets with thousands of their own ethnic group: the right to commit sati, they claimed, was part of their ethnic culture. After months of delay the police finally arrested Roop Kanwar's father-in-law and five other members of the family for abetment to suicide. Three months later the Indian Parliament passed a tough law banning sati, even though an old law already existed, as a sign of central government intolerance of these ethnic practices declared by Rajiv Gandhi to be "utterly reprehensible and barbaric."

Though the feminist movement had scored a legal victory, the case exemplified the terrible gulf between human rights and women's rights activists, on the one hand, and those who see the status of women as an integral part of their ethnic identity, on the other. A leading Hindi journal pointed an accusing finger at secular, western-educated intellectuals, arguing that only godless people who did not believe in reincarnation would denigrate Roop's brave act.[26]

The debate over sati and Roop raged for weeks in the newspapers. There were those who argued that if it was voluntary it was all right. Suicide is a time-honored Rajasthani practice and should be accepted. It was cultural discrimination to prevent those who really wished to commit sati from doing so. There were others, such as Nandy, who argued that, although sati was a terrible affair, it was no business of the state. The onus must lie with the people and communities of Rajasthan; they must be the ones to outlaw the practice, not the central government. There were women's groups that felt that sati was so offensive that if a woman died of burns in a public place the burden of proof, as in Indian penal provisions on custodial rape, should shift to the family to prove that sati did not take place. Human rights activists, many at the forefront of the struggle against arbitrary arrest and detention, called for the imposition of the death penalty on those who aid and abet sati. The international struggle against the death penalty was forgotten in the heat of the moment.

Roop Kanwar's case sent the human rights community of India into deep crisis. First, Rajput defiance and Hindi-language newspapers pointed to how human rights consciousness was not an Indian norm; it was increasingly attributed to the "urban Western intelligentsia." This marginalization is purposeful, but, given the fact that many of the leading activists are Delhi based, it carries a measure of credibility and supports the counter belief that these human rights people are out to denigrate national culture. Spectators in Rajasthan during those days saw the people as joyous, celebrating a great event and a courageous act: they did not see anything wrong. This realization alone was terrifying to most feminists working in the twentieth century. Ironically, although the state came down strongly on the side of the women activists there was a sense that the battle was lost. Everywhere there were echoes of Nandy's initial analysis. What is the point of all these laws if the people do not believe that putting an eighteen-year-old woman on a funeral pyre and denying her life is not a violation of the most basic fundamental right—the right to life? What is the point of all the Constitutional protection if "ethnic identity" is an acceptable justification for reducing the status of women according to diverse cultural practice? As one activist said in conversation, "something died in the Indian women's movement with Roop Kanwar; the innocence of believing that what shocks your conscience will also shock the world."[27]

The Case of Safia Bibi: The Hudood Ordinance

The second case in point is the celebrated Pakistani case of Safia Bibi. Safia was a blind girl who alleged that she was raped. She was still a minor so her father filed a complaint of rape two days before she delivered the child supposedly born of this union. Her parents claimed that Safia had told them of the rape, but that fear and humiliation had kept them silent. The alleged rapist retorted that the blind girl was of loose virtue.

Under the newly promulgated Hudood Ordinance, under the Offences of Zina Ordinance,[28] Safia and victims of rape faced a major dilemma. If Safia alleged rape and failed to prove it (rape conviction requires four male witnesses), then she could be sent to jail for "adultery" if she was married and "fornication" if she was single. This is precisely what happened. The Sessions Court found Safia in violation of the Zina Ordinance and sentenced her, despite her blindness, to three years rigorous imprisonment. There was a national and an international outcry. The Federal Shariat Court set aside the judgment on technical grounds. However the alleged rapist did not spend a day in jail because of insufficient evidence.[29]

Safia Bibi's case was another crisis for the women's movement in South Asia. It was, without a doubt, the mobilization of women's groups in Pakistan along with their international network, that exerted sufficient pressure on the judges to revise the judgment.

Safia Bibi raises a very different set of issues from those raised by Roop Kanwar. In the Kanwar case, practices in civil society that were against women suddenly re-emerged in the context of new power and class struggles.[30] In the case of Safia Bibi, civil society had become accustomed to certain colonial norms with regard to criminal and civil procedures. The state, in its infinite wisdom and under martial law, introduced laws that had not been applied in Pakistan for centuries, based on its own interpretation of the Qur'an. This act of state took place after Pakistan had joined the United Nations and was thereby bound by the Universal Declaration of Human Rights. The spirit of the Hudood Ordinance, in the section on Zina and even with regard to criminal procedure in certain types of moral offenses, was clearly contrary to the Universal Declaration. In this case, the state flouted international norms so as to articulate religious fundamentalist ideals when there was no pressure from below for their promulgation. This manipulative use of religion and religious codes to defy international norms is a new manifestation of the post-colonial nation-state—a trend that may increase in the near future. The only option against this type of activity is not the legal system, which has become perverted by political will, but political mobilization from within and international support from without. The Safia Bibi case is an indication that such international efforts may succeed in some instances.[31]

No-Fault Divorce Laws: Sri Lanka

In 1991 a Committee set up to look into reform with regard to the divorce laws of Sri Lanka came up with the following recommendations:

(a) The establishment of family courts.
(b) A non-adversarial approach to marriage break-up by adopting the theory of marital breakdown.
(c) A move away from fault-based divorce to consensual divorce after two years judicial separation and/or five years separation as evidence of marital breakdown.
(d) Introducing standards with regard to the best interest of the child as the grounds for custody rather than the concept of a natural guardian—in Sri Lanka under Roman Dutch inheritance the natural guardian is the father.[32]

The Committee's recommendations were far-reaching in terms of Sri Lankan law which was still fault-based and adversarial with concepts of natural guardian, but the recommendations were well within the trend of divorce reforms sweeping most of the legal world except the Islamic countries. The reaction to the reforms was vociferously negative even from an organization such as the Sri Lanka Women Lawyers' Association. They argued vehemently for maintaining the old system with a few minor changes, their argument being that the present divorce reforms as suggested by the Committee threatened the family unit and therefore went against the interests of women.

The case law of the country had already set a precedent when a Supreme Court judgment stated that even a guilty man could move for divorce after seven years separation, thus allowing room for the introduction of no-fault divorce.[33] But this was unacceptable to the women lawyers who challenged the efficacy of the judgment.

The consensus was so openly against the proposed reforms that they were not adopted. The main furor against the reforms was that no-fault divorce went against the interest of the family and especially the wife. Women were in the forefront in challenging the Committee, which comprised leading women academics and professionals.

This crisis among women and their perceptions concerning family and divorce raises some extremely interesting questions. The Women's Convention, to which Sri Lanka is a state party, clearly privileges an independent free woman, but in the case of Sri Lanka the ideology of the family remains supreme. It is the belief that the protection of a woman lies in the protection of the family. Ironically, however, the data show an increasing number of female-headed households and the female as the primary earner, whether on the plantations, in the free trade zones, or as a migrant worker. This gap between myth and reality is the ideological construction, the barrier toward formulating laws that will protect women and children at the margins, margins that are increasingly becoming mainstream.[34]

While the Indian and Pakistani cases show us the dilemma generated by the tension between civil society and the law, in this case the whole struggle has been within the framework of the law—the preference for standards that were set in the late nineteenth century over modern day formulations. These divorce laws, of course, do not affect the personal laws of the minorities but only the general population. Rights discourse with its notion of the empowered individual comes up against communitarian notions of the family: an ideological force far stronger than rights discourse and perhaps the most formidable obstacle women's rights activists face. In fact, it is only recently that Sri Lankan scholars could even talk about domestic violence without being considered family wreckers. So even in a context where colonial legal norms prevail and have been indigenized, where rights discourse would be the natural outgrowth of these systems, the ideological barrier of the sanctity of the family unit will not allow reform in these areas even if, in the long run, it would empower women and give them an equal stake as individuals.

The Shah Bano Case: India

The final case study is the celebrated Indian case of Shah Bano. In 1975 Shah Bano's husband made her leave his home after over forty years of marriage. Initially he paid her a small maintenance, but then that stopped. In 1978 Shah Bano filed a prevention of destitution provision under Section 125 of the Criminal Procedure Code for maintenance of Rs. 500 a month (her husband was a lawyer with a five-figure income). While her application was pending, her husband pronounced *Talak* on her and divorced her, returning the *mehr,* the money she brought as a dowry (Rs. 3,000). He then refused to pay maintenance. The magistrate, under the Criminal Code, ordered him to pay Rs. 25, the High Court raised the payment to Rs. 179.20. The husband appealed to the Supreme Court. His argument was simple. He was a Muslim and his marriage was governed by Muslim personal law. Under that law there is no duty of maintenance, only the duty of returning the *mehr.* The personal law, he declared, was superior to the Criminal Procedure Code in this respect.

Ten years from the year the case began, the Supreme Court dismissed the husband's appeal saying that the provision against destitution did not conflict with Muslim rules of maintenance. If the wife cannot maintain herself within the three-month period of *Iddat* (initial separation before divorce), then she can have recourse to the criminal procedure.[35]

The most controversial case of the decade, it points to the enormous problems and dilemmas that South Asian nations face when they promote women's rights as human rights. In this case it would be Article 16 of the Women's Convention that would be relevant, the Article to which India made reservations when it signed in 1980. Therefore, at the time, India was not internationally bound. In 1993, it ratified the Convention without reservations and is now bound by the entire Convention.

The forces taking sides with regard to this confrontation were:

(a) *For Shah Bano:* Women's groups, Hindu fundamentalists who wished to rid India of Muslim law, and a very few moderate Muslims.

(b) *Against Shah Bano:* The Muslim community and, in the end, the Indian state, when Rajiv Gandhi moved to appease the minority community by passing legislation to override the Supreme Court

> judgment. Today destitute Muslim women do not have the right to go to court under the penal law.

The problem of Shah Bano was compounded by the fact that she was a minority woman in a country with a hostile majority where communal prejudices run deep and are volatile and explosive. Her community considered her a traitor. She also lived in a country that, like most others in South Asia, accepted a formal framework of law which stated in effect: "All men are equal, but women are bound by the position relegated to them by the different systems of personal law, laws which govern the most important area of their lives, the family." In 1984 Rajiv Gandhi made it clear that personal law was superior to any provision in the Criminal Code—it is privileged over all other legal provisions that may have some bearing on the provisions of personal law.

In Shah Bano's case the state stepped in to protect the rights of the minority community at the expense of women; a state that, in other contexts, might not think it wrong to fan the flames of communalism when it comes to other issues, especially in Kashmir. So, as Hensman puts it, the triple oppression of Shah Bano is clearly demonstrated: She suffers as a woman, she suffers as a Muslim, and in this particular context, she suffers as a Muslim woman who wants to assert a different voice in her community.[36] She was indeed the subaltern voice that suddenly found itself in a court of law.

Initially Shah Bano received a great deal of support, not least of which came from the Supreme Court of the land. However, some of the Court's interpretation of the Qur'an angered many Muslims who accused it of being wrong and insensitive.[37] The support she received from Hindu fundamentalists was also terrifying. The leader of one of the Hindu movements said in anger that one country must have one law. Of course he meant a law acceptable to the majority—Hindus.[38]

Women's groups supported Shah Bano vociferously, but their discourse of rights and equality was muffled by the voices of communalism on both sides. Trapped in the middle, especially when riots ensued, their voice was naturally weakened. When a delegation went to see Rajiv Gandhi, then Prime Minister, he sympathized but added: "How many women can you get on the streets to defend the Supreme Court judgment and stop the rioting?" So it was, in the end, a question of numbers and of violence, fear and terror, the very factors that are least conducive to a rights regime.

In the end Shah Bano had no rights. She became a metaphor in the political discourse of communalism which has shaped the violent history of post-colonial South Asia.

Conclusion

Shah Bano's case, and the others mentioned earlier, are indicative of the many problems that translate into barriers for implementing women's rights as human rights in the South Asian region:

(a) Rights discourse is a weak discourse, secondary to other legal discourses, especially when it comes to women and family relations.
(b) The values of rights discourse as it relates to women are not part of the popular consciousness, and, in fact, in some contexts, the reverse may persist in the practices of civil society.
(c) The post-colonial South Asian state has played a very arbitrary and ad hoc role depending on its composition and priorities, siding with different parties, different discourses, depending on the political exigencies and the numbers game. While the state may intervene to stop sati, it will refrain from giving a Muslim woman maintenance. While it encourages modern commerce, usury and banking, it will invoke laws that impose extreme penalties with regard to issues of rape, adultery and fornication. It has mastered the art of cultivated hypocrisy with regard to women.
(d) Even if the conditions exist with regard to rights discourse, the Sri Lankan case shows clearly that even among women certain ideologies are far more powerful than that of individual rights. The sanctity of the family moves women more than the freedom and, perhaps, the responsibility that empowerment is supposed to bring.

In the late nineteenth century a renowned North Indian poet charged a poetess with "bellowing like a cow," denying decorum, and invading male public space. Ironically, with regard to the law at least, the public space, often governed by recent thinking in the law, grants equal access to women in most South Asian societies. In Sri Lanka, the most progressive of the South Asian societies, women comprise 50 percent of the medical faculty; 50 percent of the law faculty and more than 50 percent of the arts faculty at the university. Women are joining the urban labor force at an ever-increasing rate. Laws are also being drafted to assist women in the rural areas, women who for centuries have worked in the fields without protection.

It is, however, the private sphere, a distinction that came to us with a colonial inheritance of personal laws, that is the most impervious to change with regard to women's rights. Here women are divided not only by community but among themselves about whether a rights discourse is relevant or necessary. Unless we begin to examine the law's approach to the family and to private space in greater detail, and understand the dynamics more fully with regard to ideological constructions that resist legal change, we will not be able to bring rights home to the family. The task is daunting but necessary. Without equity in the family, it is argued, there will not be equity in society. Without mutual respect in the family, we can be sure that there will be no respect for the rights of others in society. As has often been repeated, the family should not be defined in a formalistic, nuclear construction as a husband, wife, and children. The family is the place where individuals learn to care, to trust, and to nurture each other. The law should protect and privilege that kind of family and no other.

Notes

1. See Stuart A. Scheingold, *The Politics of Rights* (New Haven, CT: Yale University Press, 1974), 62.
2. Ronald B. Inden, *Imagining India* (Oxford: Basil Blackwell, 1990).
3. Savitri Goonesekere, *Sri Lanka Law on Parent and Child* (Colombo: Gunasena, 1987). See sections on Kandyan Law.
4. Convention on the Elimination of All Forms of Discrimination Against Women, G.A. Res. 34/180, U.N. GAOR, 34th Sess., Supp. No. 46 at 193, U.N. Doc. A/34/46 (1979), adopted 3 September 1981. Hereinafter cited as the Women's Convention.
5. Women's Convention, art. 16(1)(b).
6. Women's Convention, art. 16(1)(g).
7. Women's Convention, art. 1.
8. Women's Convention, arts. 11, 12.
9. Women's Convention, art. 4.
10. Constitution of the Democratic Socialist Republic of Sri Lanka, art. 12(4), 1978.
11. Women's Convention, art. 4.
12. See generally Sri Lanka Foundation Institute, *Human Rights and Religions in Sri Lanka* (Colombo: SLFI, 1988), on Buddhism. See Joanna Liddle and Rama Joshi, *Daughters of Independence* (London: Zed Books, 1986), for the colonial encounter and women.
13. See Kenneth Davidson, Ruth B. Ginsburg, and Herma H. Kay, eds., *Sex-Based Discrimination* (St. Paul, MN: West Publishing, 1974), 35, "Men as Victims."
14. Ashis Nandy, "The Making and Unmaking of Political Cultures in India," in *At the Edge of Psychology*, ed. Ashis Nandy (New Delhi: Oxford University Press, 1980), 47.
15. See Deepak Lal, *The Hindu Equilibrium* (Oxford: Clarendon Press, 1988).
16. Atul Kohli, *Democracy and Discontent* (Cambridge: Cambridge University Press, 1991).
17. Kohli, *Democracy and Discontent,* note 16 at 303.
18. Elisabeth Bumiller, *May You Be the Mother of a Hundred Sons* (New York: Fawcett Columbine, 1990), 133.

19. C.S. Lakshmi, *Mother, Mother-Community, and Mother Politics in Tamil Nadu* (New Delhi: EPW, 1990).

20. Lakshmi, *Mother, Mother-Community,* note 19 at 73.

21. Sunila Abeyesekera, "The Subversion of Motherhood," presentation to ICES, Colombo, August 1992.

22. *Dr. Upendra Baxi v. State of Bihar,* W.P. 5943 of 1980.

23. See generally Upendra Baxi, "Taking Suffering Seriously," in *The Judiciary in Plural Societies,* ed. N. Tiruchelvam and Radhika Coomaraswamy (London: Frances Pinter, 1987).

24. Department of Labour, *Employment Survey* (Sri Lanka, 1981).

25. See Bumiller, *May You Be the Mother,* note 18 at 62 for first-hand account.

26. Bumiller, *May You Be the Mother,* note 18 at 72.

27. Kamla Bhasin in conversation, August 1990.

28. The Hudood Laws, promulgated 1979; enforced 1980. See also Asma Jahangir and Hina Jilani, *The Hudood Ordinances: A Divine Sanction?* (Lahore: Rhotas, 1990), pp. 23, 85–130.

29. Jahangir and Jilani, *The Hudood Ordinances,* note 28 at 88–89.

30. Ashis Nandy, "Sati: A Nineteenth Century Tale of Woman, Violence and Protest," *At the Edge of Psychology,* ed. Nandy, note 14 at 1.

31. See Jahangir and Jilani, *The Hudood Ordinances,* note 28 at 88.

32. *Report of the Divorce Reforms Committee,* Ministry of Justice, Colombo, 1992.

33. *Muthuranee v. Thuraisingham* 1 N.L.R. (1984), p. 381, Colombo, Sri Lanka.

34. See generally Carla Risseauw, *The Fish Don't Talk About the Water* (Leiden: Brill, 1988), for the type of power women have in the informal sector.

35. Rohini Hensman, "Oppression Within Oppression: The Dilemma of Muslim Women in India," *Thatched Patio* (1990): 22.

36. Hensman, "Oppression," note 35 at 22.

37. Hensman, "Oppression," note 35 at 24.

38. Hensman, "Oppression," note 35 at 26.

[6]

The Idea of Human Rights as Perceived in the Ottoman Empire

*Berdal Aral**

ABSTRACT

Although human rights doctrine has primarily been a product of Western history, non-Western conceptions and interpretations of issues which we may today link with "human rights" can undoubtedly enrich the debates on this topic. The Ottoman system prioritized the benefits of collectivities rather than those of individuals, and emphasized justice rather than freedom. This paper argues that both the Ottoman sultan as well as the courts took great care to observe the *Shariah* law, understood of course from a Sunni perspective, which accorded extensive rights to the individual, Muslim and non-Muslim alike. These rights included the right to life, property, fair trial, and social protection, as well as specific rights for women. Contrary to some claims, the state in the Ottoman case did not seek to take control of the "public sphere" unless politics set in. It is only after the *Tanzimat* reforms of the nineteenth century, influenced primarily by European laws and institutions, that the state came to predominate the public sphere, thus narrowing the scope for civic action.

---

* *Berdal Aral* graduated from the Department of International Relations of the Faculty of Political Sciences in Ankara, Turkey, in 1985. He received a M.A. from University of Kent, England, 1990, and received his Ph.D. from University of Glasgow 1994. His thesis was "Turkey and International Society from a Critical Legal Perspective." Currently, he works as a lecturer at the Department of International Relations, Fatih University, Istanbul. He has written articles covering such issues such as Turkey's approach to international law, Turkey and the European Union, human rights, and new international law.

The author would like to express his sincere gratitude to Muhammad Abdulkerim, Karen Wolfe, and Muhammad Bakari who assisted him at different stages by reviewing part of the manuscripts.

I. INTRODUCTION

Analyzing the evolution of human rights in Turkey, experts in this field still focus exclusively on the nationalist/republican era, from the 1920s to today, generally disregarding the Ottoman experience that preceded the modern era. The single most significant reason for this obvious lack of interest is the difficulty of relating the "modern" conception of human rights to the ideas, perceptions, values, and institutions characterizing the Ottoman rule, which lasted over six hundred years from 1299 to 1922. The other reason may be the fact that Turkish academics and other experts in human rights tend to take an unfavorable view of the Ottoman legacy. In those rare instances when the Ottomans are being studied from the perspective of human rights, it is usually limited to the final period of the empire, commonly known as the *Tanzimat devri* (the period of re-ordering that began in 1839), during which time the Ottomans came increasingly under the influence of Western civilizational standards.

This outright lack of interest in the classical period of the Ottoman Empire shows an unwavering distaste for the Ottoman *Weltanschauung, i.e.,* its perspective of life and conception of the world. This gives the impression of a number of accepted clichés about the Ottomans concerning human rights. Before the *Tanzimat,* the Ottomans were thought to represent the antithesis of what had been achieved to protect and promote the rights of the individual in absolutist states in the West. To be more specific, the Ottomans were hardly credited with respect to the following rights and liberties: the right to life; immunity from arbitrary actions by the state; independence of the judiciary; prohibition of torture; freedom of expression; the right to privacy; freedom to travel; and so on. In short, the Ottoman Empire continues to be depicted as a tyrannical state and as a typical example of "Oriental Despotism" in the Marxist sense.

Such explicit and/or implicit prejudice is based purely on the ignorance of, and disrespect for, evidence that the subjects of the Ottoman Empire seem to have been treated generally more humanely and justly than those of the empire's contemporaries, an inevitable conclusion in the light of research. It was the Ottoman Empire that granted refuge and sanctuary to the Jews of Spain when, in 1492, they were expelled en masse from the country. If we accept that the existence of respected human rights is implied by a people's confidence in a Ruler's justice; in their confidence that violation of the law will be punished; in an autonomous sphere of existence for individuals as well as communities; in the existence of a list of rights and freedoms sanctioned by written laws that bind not only the individuals but also the state; then we should accept that, on the whole, the Ottomans had a fairly good record of human rights protection.

Concerning the position of human rights under Ottoman rule in the pre-*Tanzimat* era, the focus of analysis primarily centers on the Ottomans' treatment of their non-Muslim subjects. This focus reflects the apologetic attitude of Turkish scholars who take a sympathetic view towards the Ottomans. This attitude is by and large the result of Western accusations of Ottoman abuse and maltreatment of their non-Muslim subjects. The scholars who have a positive view of the Ottoman Empire, thus, strive to show that, contrary to accusations of maltreatment, these subjects were treated humanely, as their distinct culture and identity was respected by their Ottoman rulers. Furthermore, another, yet no less significant reason, exists; in parallel to the undeniable split among Turkish scholars regarding the role which Islam should play in Turkey, two conflicting views predominate with regard to the legacy of the Ottoman Empire. The first current of thought, which may be described as "pro-Ottoman-nationalist," considers the Ottoman epoch as a kind of "age of felicity" (*Asr-ý Saadet*; the term denotes the time of the Holy Prophet and his four successors, *i.e.*, Caliphs, when, as Muslims believe, God's rule on earth reigned supreme). From this perspective, since harmony and mutual understanding characterized the interaction between state and society under Ottoman rule, one can only appreciate rather than criticize the Ottomans. The "secularist perspective," on the other hand, is based on the assumption that Ottoman rule represented the "dark age" of humanity when decisions were arbitrary and oppression prevailed. Therefore, there is no need to examine the Ottoman Empire from the perspective of human rights since human rights did not exist in that era. There can be no doubt that both of these views are too narrow to allow a true understanding of the issue in question, since, as ideologically biased, they are sure to be based on emotions rather than facts. The truth is found somewhere in between, as reliable scholarship has demonstrated.[1]

This article begins with a description of the modern conception of human rights, while at the same time exposing different categories of human rights. It then proceeds with an exposition of the Islamic conception of key political terms in the classical era, which may be linked to human rights as we understand it today. They are the *raison d'être* of the state, justice, rights, and freedom. The Shia school of Islam is also examined in this section. The article then examines the Ottoman conception of state, politics, and society,

1. As examples of this balanced and scholarly literature, we can mention the following: HALİL İNALCIK, OSMANLI'DA DEVLET, HUKUK, ADÂLET (STATE, LAW AND JUSTICE IN THE OTTOMANS) (2000), HALİL İNALCIK, THE OTTOMAN EMPIRE, THE CLASSICAL AGE 1300–1600 (1997); İSMAİL HAKKI UZUNÇARŞILI, OSMANLI TARİHİ (THE OTTOMAN HISTORY) (1965); STANFORD J. SHAW, HISTORY OF THE OTTOMAN EMPIRE AND MODERN TURKEY, Vols. I & II (with Ezel Kural Shaw in Vol. II) (1991 & 1988).

focusing on the main strands of thought as expounded by Ottoman thinkers on politics and society. Next, the human rights performance of the Ottoman Empire is exposed. The following section outlines the Ottoman *millet* system as the body of administrative principles giving a degree of autonomy to religious communities, and the extent to which this system guaranteed the rights and liberties of non-Muslim minorities. Under a subheading within this section, the paper draws on "interventions" by powerful European states in the Ottoman Empire beginning from the end of the eighteenth century upon claims of maltreatment, in particular, of non-Muslim subjects of the empire. The final part of this study elaborates on the compatibility between an Islamic perception of human rights and modern human rights doctrine in the light of the lessons which we may draw from this "Ottoman model."

II. MODERN CONCEPTION OF HUMAN RIGHTS

The concept of human rights here covers essentially two distinct types of rights and liberties: classical rights and economic, social and cultural rights. Classical rights require that the state should avoid interference. The classical rights, which are at various times called "civil and political rights" or "negative statute rights," essentially concern individuals and/or groups of individuals. They include the following rights and liberties: the right to life; prohibition of torture; equality before the law; principle of non-discrimination; independence of the judiciary; the right to a fair trial; right of ownership; freedom of expression; freedom of conscience and religion; freedom of travel; freedom of association; and the right to privacy. The second category of human rights consists of economic, social and cultural rights. They are also called "positive rights," as they require active intervention on the part of the state to ensure a decent life for the poor and destitute. This second group of rights includes: the right to work; to social security; to education; to a decent living; and minority rights.[2]

Dominant human rights doctrine in the West is based on the theory of natural law that was developed in the seventeenth century. The social and political forces behind the evolution of this doctrine developed as a result of the antagonistic social dynamics in Europe. They included religious and sectarian intolerance on the one hand, and popular revolts against oppressive and arbitrary rule on the other. Such dynamics of confrontation between the ruler and the ruled, which sometimes verged on civil war,

2. MUSTAFA ERDODDAN, ANAYASAL DEMOKRASİ (CONSTITUTIONAL DEMOCRACY) 125–52 (1996).

never developed in the lands of Islam.[3] For this and similar reasons, human rights never became an acute problem for the Islamic states of the past.[4]

III. ISLAM AND HUMAN RIGHTS

According to the Quran, the human being is the most exalted of all creatures, and is therefore especially valuable irrespective of his or her religion. Endowed with reason and the desire for freedom, the human being is the viceregent of God on earth which is a human's natural right from the moment of birth. Being human is the common thread that binds all humankind together *before* their separation by different faiths. This understanding underlines the universality of Islam, for this "first and last of all religions" embraces the whole of humanity without discrimination.[5] The importance of this aspect of Islam is emphasized in numerous verses of the Quran and in sayings of the Holy Prophet. According to the Holy Book, "killing an innocent human being, is like killing all humankind."[6] The Holy Prophet, in addressing his adversaries whom the Islamic army had crushed, assured them that their lives, property, and blood were inviolable.[7] Additionally, in accordance with some Quranic injunctions, interference with one's private and family life as well as one's home, is forbidden.[8]

Certainly, *Shariah* law, and specifically the Quran, has no regard for, and even dismisses, some of the cherished fundamentals of the human rights doctrine. Just as the human being is superior to all other creatures, some people are superior to others by virtue of their religion, sex, mental capacity, or skills. Accordingly, Islamic law does contain the principle of equality before the law, but a distinction is drawn between Muslim and non-

3. It must not be denied, however, that a cultural duality existed between the "center" and "periphery" of the empire, whereby the Ottoman subjects often felt themselves to be left out of the economic, political, and cultural processes. Adem Çaylak, Osmanlý'da Yöneten ve Yönetien: Bir Şerif Mardin Çözümlemesi (The Ruler and the Ruled during the Ottoman Centuries: An Analysis of Şerif Mardin), 104–22 (1998). However one must not fail to identify a number of compensating factors: The all-embracing character of Islam; the public access to religious orders and communities, which provided for meaningful social intercourse among the individuals; the abundance of charitable foundations; the proper functioning of the justice system even in the provinces. *Id.* at 123.
4. Ahmet Arslan, *Ýnsan haklarý ve Ýslâm* (*Islam and Human Rights*) 5 Liberal Düşünce 37, 42 (1997).
5. *Id.* at 53.
6. Sûra Mâide, verse 32.
7. Ahmet Akgündüz, Ýslâm'da Ýnsan Haklarý Beyânnâmesi (Declaration of Human Rights according to Islam) 20 (2d ed., 1993).
8. "O ye who believe! Enter not houses other than your own without first announcing your presence." Sûra Nûr, verse 27. "It is not righteousness that ye go to houses by the backs thereof." Sûra Bakara, verse 189.

Muslim, between man and woman. According to the Quran, Islam was enjoined upon the entire human race as the last and perfect religion to correct the distortion suffered by previous religions, all of which had been corrupted through human intervention. Therefore, Islam anticipates the conversion of the "People of the Book" as well as of the idol worshipers to this uncorrupted religion. However, if they insist on adhering to their own religion, non-Muslims, in accordance with Islamic rules, will still be protected by the Islamic state on the understanding that, in return, they will accept a status inferior to that of Muslims. It is within this context that the distinction between Muslim and non-Muslim, discussed in this paper, must be understood.

In accordance with Islamic law, the "People of the Book" (Christians, Jews, Sabeans) enjoy the right to live freely in accordance with their religion, excepting the right to propagate their faith. They have the right to change their religion only if their chosen religion is Islam. Muslims, meanwhile, are precluded from changing their religion. Muslims who disregard this injunction are called apostates (*mürted*), and, according to some commentators, it is lawful to kill them. Although a Muslim man may marry a woman belonging to the "People of the Book," a Muslim woman is not permitted to marry a non-Muslim man. In addition, when acting as witness in a court of law, non-Muslims do not enjoy equality of status with Muslims. Finally, in an Islamic state, non-Muslims are legally barred from occupying a position which would authorize them to rule over, to represent or to prosecute Muslims. In short, with regard to political and public rights in an Islamic state, non-Muslim subjects are not given the right to enjoy equality of status with Muslims.[9]

In Islam, certain distinctions of status are also made between men and women as explicitly laid down in the Quran. According to Sûra Bakara (The Cow), verse 282, a man as witness in court equals two female witnesses. Under verse 11 of Sûra Nisâ (Women), men are entitled twice as much inheritance as women. Verse 3 of the same Sûra permits men to marry as many as four women, and verse 34 declares that, as the head of family men are entitled to beat their wives as the last resort, if their wives disobey them.

As far as a penal code is concerned, we find in the Quran certain types of punishment which may, from the perspective of the modern human rights doctrine, appear degrading and cruel. To give an example, Sûra Bakara, verse 179, states that "there is life for you in retaliation" which reflects the principle, "an eye for an eye." Accordingly, excluding exceptional circumstances, a murderer would have to face the death penalty. The same

9. Sami A. Aldeeb Abu-Sahlieh, *Muslims and Human Rights: Challenges and Perspectives, in* Human Rights and Cultural Diversity 239–68, 244–45 (Wolfgang Schmale ed., 1993).

principle applies to those convicted of theft, as stated in verse 38 of Sûra Mâida: "As for the thief, both male and female, cut off their hands. It is the reward for their own deeds, an exemplary punishment from Allah."[10] Finally, in the case of adultery, if those involved are married, some commentators claim that they will face death by stoning (*ragm*); if they are single, each will be beaten a hundred times with a stick.[11]

The Islamic notion of freedom also needs some analysis here. No doubt Islam emphasizes justice and social harmony, while freedom, as we understand it today, does not appear to be its primary concern. Muslim political experience appears to reflect this attitude. In the classical Islamic tradition, freedom was viewed as the opposite of slavery. For classical Islamic thinkers, the term was also related to the ontology of the individual. According to Râgýp el-Ýsfahânî (d. 1108), an individual who overcame the worldly desires of the self could be said to be free. For Kuşeyrî (d. 1074), true freedom lay in the full devotion to Allah. Ghazâlî (d. 1111) considered that captivity to passions was the single greatest obstacle to human freedom. Fârâbî (d. 950) appears to be the first Islamic thinker to have considered freedom (*hürriyet*) outside of its classical meanings by drawing on its sociological and political dimensions. In his terminology, the term *hürriyet* has a number of meanings, one of which is the *freedom* of individuals to fulfill their desires. He describes a government founded on such societal values as peoples' government (*cemâî devlet*). However, for Fârâbî, the state whose members enjoy the liberty of acting as they please has too many defects. Such "free" societies would inevitably lack common morality and values. Individuals accordingly bring to power those who promise maximum levels of satisfaction for their hedonistic expectations.

While advocating the idea of state based on virtue and high moral standards, Fârâbî did not deny that, given the heterogeneity of varying approaches to morality and ideas in such self-centered societies, people of virtue, such as philosophers and poets, could flourish too. Many of Fârâbî's writings elaborate on the problem of "freedom versus state authority." Sadly, however, the Islamic thinkers after him showed scant interest in this problem. Until the end of the eighteenth century, in the Islamic parlance, the term *hürriyet* corresponded with generosity and "freedom from sensual

10. If the thief had acted out of desperation on account of poverty or urgent need, he/she would be acquitted. Considering the strictness of criteria required for the precise determination of a crime, it should not come as a surprise to observe that, during the Ottoman Empire, amputation was applied only in a few exceptional cases.

11. The punishment of stoning is not mentioned in the Quran. We are informed that, during the duration of the Ottoman Empire, only two cases of stoning occurred. This is mostly explained by the strictness of conditions set by the Quran and by Muslim canonical jurisprudence (*fýkh*). Arslan, *supra* note 4, at 52.

desires." The true freedom, as it were, lay in the complete devotion to Allah. Following the French Revolution of 1789, however, Ottoman thinkers began to consider freedom from a political, legal and social perspective as a fundamental human right.[12]

In light of what has been stated above, it must be admitted that Islamic law differs from the human rights doctrine in many significant aspects. The human rights doctrine relies on secular sources which claim "humanism" as their base, whereas the Islamic law is based on revelation and *not* on human reasoning and its *raison d'être* is the establishment of God's order on earth. The Islamic law is no doubt consistent with this objective. Unlike the modern human rights doctrine, this is a *community-oriented* system of law. Civil and political rights, or "classical rights," consist of rights and liberties gained by the individual through a struggle *against* the state. No such polarity between state and individual exists in Islam. According to Islam, individual, society, and state complement each other like organs of the body.[13] The rights granted the human race by the grace of God are set down in the Quran along with the *responsibilities* of every individual toward the Creator and toward other people. Any claim that ignores these differences between Islam and the human rights doctrine is bound to be false.[14]

This obvious difference between Islam and modern human rights doctrine does not imply that societies living under Islamic rule are subject to arbitrary rule or even to oppression. The following example should make this clear. Historians acquainted with the practices of Islamic states generally accept that Christian and Jewish subjects of Islamic states had a far better chance of living in a secure and pleasing environment than Muslims who lived under the rule of a Christian state. Non-Muslim minorities of differing ethnicity representing a multiplicity of cultures and languages maintained their distinct identities thanks to the tolerance and pluralism practiced by Islamic states, including the Ottoman Empire.

The school to which the Ottoman Empire officially attached itself was the Sunni branch of Islam.[15] The other widely recognized branch of Islam is Shiism. Shia Islam has been the officially-sanctioned school of Islam in Iran

---

12. Hürriyet (Freedom), ÝSLÂM ANSİKLOPEDİSİ (THE ENCYCLOPEDIA OF ISLAM) 502–04 (1998).
13. Bassam Tibi, *Islamic Law/Shari'a, Human Rights, Universal Morality and International Relations*, 16 HUM. RTS. Q. 277, 289 (1994).
14. ANN ELIZABETH MAYER, ISLAM AND HUMAN RIGHTS: TRADITION AND POLITICS 44–45 (2d ed. 1995). In her outstanding book charting the human rights dimension of Islam, Mayer convincingly argues that these natural differences have to be acknowledged as the basis of a genuine dialogue between the Islamic perception of human rights and those who stand for the modern human rights doctrine. Mayer points out that these differences are generally deliberately overlooked by experts engaged with Islamic human rights issues.
15. On the Sunni character of the Ottoman Empire, *see* HALİL İNALCIK, THE OTTOMAN EMPIRE, THE CLASSICAL AGE 1300–1600 (1997), *supra* note 1.

since the sixteenth century.[16] Before dwelling on Sunni Islam as practiced by the Ottoman polity, it may be useful to put the Ottoman conceptions in context by examining the distinctions and similarities between the two schools of Islam.

Today, as in the past, the two schools of thought have an elaborate body of ideas on politics, state, and law. Since the Sunni school is examined in the rest of this paper by virtue of the Ottomans' official adherence to it, this section provides a brief account of the Shiite school of Islam and compares some aspects of it with the Sunni school.

The first political school of religious law (*madhab*) in Islam is Shiism.[17] This school gained prominence as state religion and thus found a fertile ground, first and foremost, in Iran under the leadership of Shah Ismail in the early sixteenth century. The belief in the infallibility of the Twelve Imams was part of this doctrine. No doubt, both the Iranian and Ottoman states, as Islamic polities, accepted the *Shariah* law as the supreme law of the land.[18] However, the Shiites, unlike Sunnis, refused the idea that the Iranian state could adopt laws that remained outside the *Shariah* law (*örf-î sultanî*).[19]

Historically, Sunni states were ruled mostly by dynasties or armies. This was anathema to the Shiite school's insistence on the rule by those versed in Islam.[20] For Shia, unlike Sunnis, the imamate (the leadership of the *umma*) was not only a political/legal matter, but also a matter of faith. In the Sunni tradition the judiciary and the executive were separated, while the Iranian clerics (*ulema*) could perform both functions. The *Sheikhulislam*, as the highest religious authority in the Ottoman Empire, did not perform executive or legislative tasks. He only determined whether a particular statute or regulation was compatible with the *Shariah* law, allowing greater freedom of action for Sunni rulers in comparison to the Shiite rulers.[21]

As Shiite clerics were considered to represent the "hidden imam," the last of the Twelve Imams, the descendants of the Holy Prophet through the lineage of his daughter, Fatimah, who were considered innocent by the Shia

16. Shiism emerged as a sect of Islam soon after the Prophet of Islam passed away. Many of those who advocated the caliphate of Ali, the cousin and the son-in-law of the holy Prophet, as the successor of the Prophet of Islam, viewed the installment of Abu Bakr as the new caliph as usurpation of power. The death of Ali's son, Hüseyin, and his companions caused by the forces of Yezid, the sultan of the Islamic *umma*, in Kerbela, was seen as the martyrdom and Shiism turned into a mass movement of those who yearned for the rightful rule of the descendants of the Prophet (*Ehl-i Beyt*).
17. Muhammed Ebu Zehra, Ýslâmda Siyasî ve Ýtikadî Mezhepler Tarihi (A History of Political and Theological Schools in Islam) 49 (Ethem Ruhi Fýðlalý & Osman Eskicioðlu trans., 1970).
18. Taha Akyol, Osmanlý'da ve Ýran'da Mezhep ve Devlet (The *Madhab* and the State in the Ottoman Empire and Iran) 86 (2d ed. 1999).
19. *Id.* at 146.
20. Taha Akyol, Hâricîlik ve Þîa (Kharidjism and the Shia) 181 (1988).
21. *Id.* at 198–201.

school, lay beneath the authority and prestige of the Iranian clerics. The preservation of the traditional *madrasa* system[22] (institutions of learning), which always remained outside the control of the state in Iran, was a key factor behind the enduring prestige of clerics in Iran.[23] This autonomy extended into other aspects of religion that distinguished Iran from the Ottoman Empire, including Egypt.[24] *Mujtahids* (high ranking clerics) in Iran acquired revenues from religious endowments (*waqfs*). In the words of Zubaida:

> Every *mujtahid* had a network of followers who deferred to him in matters of belief and the regulation of daily life, in fact it was (and still remains) the duty of every believer to enter into a relationship of this kind (*taqlid*, imitation) to a *mujtahid*.[25]

By the end of the seventeenth century, the clerics (*ulema*) had already become a formidable political force in Iran.[26] In the Ottoman Empire, by contrast, religious scholars held little power relative to the sultan.[27]

According to the Shia doctrine, Muslims have a duty to establish an Islamic state headed by an *imam*, a political leader with impeccable moral integrity and leadership skills who should strive to lead his people along the right path. In other words, both prophets and imams are seen as acting to safeguard against ignorance and moral degeneration,[28] suggesting that imams are simultaneously worldly and spiritual authorities.[29]

In spite of the differences mentioned above, significant similarities between the Sunni and Shiite branches of Islam exist in regard to the functions of rulers.[30] As in the case of the sultan, the imam in Shiism is

---

22. Madrasas were the main institutions of higher learning in the Islamic world up until the twentieth century. These charitable foundations were often built in close proximity to mosques. The scholars, often of high quality, held lectures on Islamic and other sciences such as the study of Quran, hadiths (the sayings of the Holy Prophet), fikh (Islamic law), medicine, astronomy, mathematics and geometry. Students of these schools were generally boarded in accommodations available within the madrasas. The founders of madrasas, who were often prominent scholars, enjoyed a considerable degree of autonomy over administrative, educational and financial matters.
23. Hamid Algar, 22 Ýslâm Ansiklopedisi (The Encyclopedia of Islam) 410–11 (2000).
24. Sami Zubaida, Islam, the People and the State 56 (1993).
25. *Id.*
26. Ýslâm Ansiklopedisi, *supra* note 23, at 401.
27. Akyol, *supra* note 18, at 119.
28. Musa K. Yýlmaz, *Şia'da Din ve Devlet Ýlişkisi ve Velayet-i Fakih* (The Relationship Between Religion and State in Shiism and the Guardianship of the Jurist), *in* Din-Devlet Ýlişkileri Sempozyumu (A Symposium on the Relationship between Religion and State) 35, 40–41 (1996).
29. *Id.* at 44.
30. The historical distinction between the Shiite and Sunni branches of Islam still prevails today. With the marked exception of some heterodox sects or schools, Muslims are attached to one of the two schools mentioned here. The largest accumulation of Shiites,

expected to enjoin good and forbid evil, guide the Muslim community towards purity and decency, and protect his subjects' life, property, family rights, and good names. The head of state, the imam, ought to rule in the name of the entire Muslim community and not for partial interests. The imam should also take care not to interfere too much in matters that lie outside the political sphere, *i.e.*, communal affairs.[31]

This paper first exposes the defining characteristics of state and politics in the Ottoman Empire, then examines the Ottoman approach to certain rights and freedoms we may today associate with human rights. Since the extent to which a state permits its citizens to share in the decisionmaking process can be seen as an important manifestation of political rights, both issues are of course intimately connected.

IV. STATE AND POLITICS IN THE OTTOMAN EMPIRE

The Ottoman state structure was shaped like a pyramid, the peak of which represented the person of the sultan. The sultan symbolized the unity of people and state. To use the modern constitutional terminology, the sultan was the head of the legislative as well as of the executive authority, and he was also the commander-in-chief of the army. Although this concentration of power gives the impression of absolute rule, the sultan could exercise this authority only within more or less well-defined areas. To begin with, his legislative power was limited to areas not regulated by the *Shariah*. Furthermore, the statutes adopted by the sultan became law only after their ratification by a *Sheikhulislam*—then the highest authority dealing, through *fatwa*,[32] with matters concerning the canon law. Although the final authority rested with the sultan, the process of adoption of laws involved the Imperial Council *(Divan-ý Hümayûn)* and the Grand Vizier (*Sadrazam*).

The granting of religious autonomy within the *millet* system,[33] based on some degree of autonomy for religious communities, similarly limited the power of the sultan. The relative autonomy of Islamic orders and foundations and of tradesmen's guilds also limited the legislative authority enjoyed by the sultan.[34] The authority wielded by the ruling cadres of the empire

constituting about ten percent of all Muslims in the world, are to be found in Iran and Iraq. Meanwhile, the great majority of people in Turkey today are Sunni Muslims, a fact which underlines the continuity of religious tradition in Turkey.

31. *Id.*
32. A fatwa is a positive statement confirming that a particular piece of legislation is not contrary to Islam.
33. This topic will be delved into in part VI.
34. Shaw, *supra* note 1, Vol. I, at 165.

should not be overlooked either. It is indeed impossible to imagine that the affairs of a world power could be handled without an able class of administrators. Somewhat ironically, as a direct consequence of *Tanzimat* reforms of the nineteenth century, the Ottoman Empire developed into an authoritarian and centralized state.[35]

The Ottomans believed in a state based on their religion, *i.e.*, Islam. They formulated this through the concept *din-ü-devlet*,[36] *i.e.*, a state governed by religion as well as religion in the service of the state. In a way, Islam may be said to imply such identification, because the spread of a religion, believed to be the sole true faith and the primary *raison d'être* for the Ottoman Empire, naturally necessitated the creation of a strong state. However, the balance between state and religion was slightly in favor of the former,[37] and notably none of the Islamic states of the past, including the Ottoman Empire, achieved even a short period of complete identification of the state with religion. According to Şerif Mardin, this was related to the establishment of strong states. The idea of the interest of the state as separate from and above religion began to take hold, and the interests of the Muslim community were subordinated to "the interest of the state."[38]

From the beginning, the Ottomans inherited a particular understanding of law-making from the previous Turkic states of Central Asia and from the Mongolians, whereby a sultan was permitted to adopt rules independent of the *Shariah* law, consequently called *kanun* (statute) or *örf* (sovereign right of the monarch). Such rules, which were the prerogative of the sultan, regulated worldly matters. They had the dual consequence of giving a privileged status to the sultan within the hierarchy of the state and of giving priority to the interests of the state. The patrimonial character of the relationship between the sultan and public officers was closely linked to the status of the former as the apex of the state mechanism.[39] The absence of total correspondence of the sovereign's law with Islamic law is evidenced by the fact that during the Ottoman centuries, sovereignty always rested with the Ottoman dynasty. No doubt this arrangement was contrary to Islam which enjoins believers to delegate matters of the community to those who possess the right qualifications. In politics, this often means that the ruler should be elected by the people.

Islam does not permit the attribution of divinity to human beings. However, according to Article 5 of the first Ottoman Constitution, adopted

35. *Id.*
36. Carter V. Findley, *The Advent of Ideology in the Islamic Middle East*, 55 Studia Islamica 143, 155 (1982).
37. Şerif Mardin, Türk Modernleşmesi (Turkish Modernization) 111 (1991).
38. Şerif Mardin, Türkiye'de Toplum ve SiaYset (Society and Politics in Turkey) 22 (1990).
39. Çaylak, *supra* note 3, at 106–07.

in 1876, "His majesty the sultan is not accountable. His person is sacred."[40] The right of the sultan to eliminate his brothers, introduced by Muhammed the Conqueror in the fifteen century for the sake of the survival of the state, is a clear violation of the incontrovertible canon law (Islamic *nass*), for in Islam the victimization of parts for the sake of the whole is considered a deviation.[41] Nevertheless, this apparently incomplete harmony between state and religion did not deter Ottoman statesmen from relying heavily on Islamic discourse.

The idea of a world order (*nizâm-ý âlem*) that emphasized social balance also reaffirmed the privileged position of the state. For such a "world order" to survive both individuals and communities had to "know their place." There was a widespread belief that it was proper for the sultan, as the guarantor of the world order, to legislate statutes and regulations in addition to the *Shariah* law. The observance of justice by the state with regard to its subjects, however, was of cardinal importance. This fact should prevent us from unjustified accusations. In the words of Adem Çaylak, "[t]he absolute sovereignty of the sultan and the values which he espoused, were designed to preserve the social order which was based on justice and security."[42]

Indeed, the secret behind the long endurance of the Ottoman Empire must be seen in the efficiency of its justice system. The sultans frequently issued edicts promising greater justice (*adâletnâmeler*) that reminded the governing elite to avoid any maltreatment of the subjects and to act in accordance with justice. Given that the Ottoman sultans perceived their subjects as a whole as "the trust of God," this should not come as a surprise. Arbitrary treatment of the people and tax collection in excess by the governors of the provinces were regarded as "tyrannical" by the sultans and, consequently, they often ordered the punishment of those guilty of such violations.[43] Equally, the Ottoman administrators were of the opinion that,

---

40. The 1876 CONST. Kanunî Esasî, promulgated on 23 Dec. 1876 (ŞEREF GÖZÜBÜYÜK & SUNA KILI, TÜRK ANAYASA METINLERI 31–44 (1985)). According to Akşin, the domineering role of the state should, first and foremost, be related to the Iranian influence. Sina Akşin, *Prof. Dr. Ahmet Mumcu'nun "Osmanlý Ýmparatorluðunda Egemenlik Kavramý" Konulu Tebliði Üzerinde Yorum* (An evaluation on Ahmet Mumcu's presentation entitled The Concept of Sovereignty in the Ottoman Empire, Milli Egemenlik Sempozyumu), *in* A SYMPOSIUM ON NATIONAL SOVEREIGNTY, ANKARA, 24–25 NISAN 1985 (Ankara, T.B.M.M. Basimevi).
41. AKGÜNDÜZ, *supra* note 7, at 18.
42. ÇAYLAK, *supra* note 3, at 107–08.
43. İsmet Miroğlu, *Osmanlý Devlet Felsefesinde Ýnsani Deðerler ve Hukuka Saygý (Humanistic Values in the Ottoman Perspective of State and Respect for Law)*, *in* TÜRKLERDE ÝNSANI DEÐERLER VE ÝNSAN HAKLARÝ: OSMANLÝ ÝMPARATORLUÐU DÖNEMI (HUMANISTIC VALUES AND HUMAN RIGHTS AS CONCEIVED BY THE TURKS: THE PERIOD OF THE OTTOMAN EMPIRE) 73, 74–77 (1992).

since both Muslims and non-Muslims were the children of God, it was their duty to protect all subjects, particularly the interests of the tax-paying peasants.[44]

The relationship between the Ottoman state and Muslim and non-Muslim subjects was conducted on the basis of the principle of decentralization. Except for matters of defense, internal security, and to a certain extent, of justice, most social, economic and cultural activities were performed by individuals, social groups, and communities. Of primary importance among these were issues of health and education. For example, when considering that local cultures and traditions in those lands which came under Ottoman rule remained largely intact, it becomes obvious that the Ottoman influence over the lives, say, of the Middle-Eastern-Muslim peoples was minimal.[45]

Contrary to expectations, the introduction of European rules and institutions during the *Tanzimat* period and the gradual adoption of Western human rights doctrine by the state resulted in a sharp increase of complaints raised by subjects against the state. This observation holds true not only for Muslims, but for non-Muslim subjects as well. A sizeable percentage of non-Muslim subjects, foremost among them the Greek-Orthodox community, opposed *Tanzimat* reforms for a number of reasons. First, these reforms abolished the control of the religious leaders over the members of their *millet*, the adherents of their religion, since, alongside the church assembly, new and secular "peoples' assemblies" were being set up as a result of the *Tanzimat* reforms. Second, non-Muslim subjects of the empire were now obliged to perform military service from which they had previously been exempted. Finally, the Greek-Orthodox subjects that ranked second only to the Muslims in the hierarchy of the different *millets* were furious about having to accept an equality of status with other non-Muslim communities. It might indeed be asserted that, far from improving the integration and communication between Muslim and non-Muslim subjects, the *Tanzimat* reforms hastened the process of disintegration among the non-Muslim *millets*.[46] Eventually, the evolving human rights doctrine highlighted the

---

44. Vojtech Kopcan, *Osmanlý Ýmparatorluðu'nun Orta Avrupa Eyaletlerinde Ýnsani Deðerler ve Yasalara Saygý* (*Humanitarian Values and Respect for Law in the Central European Principalities of the Ottoman Empire*), *in* HUMANISTIC VALUES AND HUMAN RIGHTS AS CONCEIVED BY THE TURKS, *supra* note 43, at 367, 378.
45. MUHAMMED ABDURRAHMAN, OSMANLÝ YÖNETIM FELSEFESI (THE OTTOMAN PERSPECTIVE OF POLITICAL GOVERNANCE) 61, *in* HUMANISTIC VALUES AND HUMAN RIGHTS AS CONCEIVED BY THE TURKS, *supra* note 43, at 62.
46. CEVDET KÜÇÜK, OSMANLÝ ÝMPARATORLUÐU'NDA MILLET SISTEMI VE TANZIMAT (THE OTTOMAN MILLET SYSTEM AND THE TANZIMAT) 13, 20–21; Mustafa Reşid Paşa ve Dönemi Semineri (A Seminar on Mustafa Reşid Paşa and His Time), Ankara, 13–14 Mar. 1985 (Ankara, Türk Tarih Kurumu Basýmevi, 1987).

ethnic identities of distinct *millets*, which in turn precipitated the collapse of the Ottoman Empire.[47]

The *Tanzimat* period may be seen as the background of a new era which ended with the destruction of the Ottoman society. Deprived of its traditional foundations, the empire began to lose its cohesion, its inner strength, the basic rationale of its laws, and consequently, its powerful sense of identity.[48] The failure of the "new" policies resulting from the *Tanzimat* process in a way demonstrated the validity of the traditionally faith-centered perspective of human rights held by the Ottomans. The modern centralized state, established as a result of pressures and influences exerted by the great European powers, began to present itself as the locus of human rights protection while partially replacing *Shariah* law with Western law. This new process naturally extended the Ottoman state's capacity to intervene in the spheres of freedom enjoyed by the subjects. Such unforeseen consequences became evident when arbitrary practices and unnecessary interference became common in the second part of the nineteenth century.

The Ottoman perception of politics would be insufficiently understood without drawing on the individual perspectives of the Ottoman thinkers. Many of the Ottoman scholars who composed written works that covered issues such as state, society, and justice were part of the governing elite. Their influence should therefore not be underrated.

Only limited number of books were written by Muslim scholars on politics during the Ottoman Empire. This is mainly because views which we may today associate with politics were scattered among a number of other disciplines ranging from Muslim canonical jurisprudence to history, from Quranic studies to (Islamic) philosophy.[49] The treatises authored by Ottoman thinkers possessed some common features which are worth mentioning. First, criticisms which they raised were often linked to problems of implementation, not to the underlying ideas and principles of governance. Second, they addressed themselves mainly to the rulers and not to the Ottoman subjects. Finally, these treatises did not question the legitimacy of the state, but sought to fix the defects of the Ottoman system.[50]

In comparison to the originality and depth of studies undertaken by Muslim scholars during the classical epoch of the Islamic history between the seventh and thirteenth centuries, the quality of works written by Ottoman thinkers appears rather dim.[51] The Ottoman political thought drew

47. The distinguishing traits of the millet system will be analyzed in part VI.
48. Küçük, *supra* note 46, at 21–22.
49. Ahmet Ugur, Osmanlý Siyâsetnâmeleri (Ottoman Political Treatises) 41 (2001).
50. Coşkun Yýlmaz, *Osmanlýlarda Siyaset Düşüncesi* (*Politics as Conceived by the Ottomans*), 4–5 Akademi k Araştýrmalar Dergisi 43, 66.
51. Ahmet Yaşar Ocak, *Düşünce Hayatý XIV–XVII Yüzyýllar* (*Intellectual Life during the XIV–XVII Centuries*), *in* Ekmeleddin Ýhsanodlu, Vol. I Osmanlý Medeniyeti Tarihi (The History of Ottoman Civilization) 159 (1999).

its principles primarily from Islam and from the wealth of experience enjoyed by preceding Islamic empires.[52] This was largely the result of the two basic goals that Ottoman statesmen were supporting: engaging in holy *jihad* against non-believers and rooting out religious ideas and movements which contradicted Sunni orthodoxy.[53]

The intellectual environment prevailing during the Ottoman Empire prioritized the principal dogmas of the Sunni thought and thus centered on the practical needs of this school of thought. The writings of Ottoman thinkers dealing with issues which we may today associate with politics and human rights were mostly written as reports or treatises (*siyasetname*) containing solutions to various problems of the state.[54] Such reports were then presented to the sultans. As such works were mostly intended to resolve practical problems, their theoretical contributions to Islamic political theory remained negligible.[55]

Those whose works deviated from the Sunni school of Islam were generally punished, which naturally discouraged potential transgressors of the Sunni doctrine. The following views expressed by prominent Ottoman thinkers are described by a well-known Turkish scholar as simplified and pragmatic expositions of the works of the classical era. The political views and ideas they expressed, from Tursun Beð to Defterdar Sarý Mehmed Paşa, were colored by a strong tinge of statism, while failing to make meaningful contributions to the product of the Iranian and Arab thinkers of the classical Islamic era.[56] These authors of political treatises, mostly functionaries of the state, rendered significant services to the state by giving counsels to the Sultans and to other ruling cadres of the state about politics, justice, and morality before the introduction of the Western-inspired and, at times, "imposed" legal reforms in the nineteenth century. Such written works later, *inter alia* focused on the methods and instruments by which to reverse the tide of the Ottoman decline.

The Ottoman thinkers tended to agree with the Ottoman statesmen who considered their own state as the perfect embodiment of human experience gained through the great civilization of the past. From the end of the

52. This is not, however, to deny the role played by Persian, Greek and Turkic traditions in shaping the Ottoman institutions.
53. Ocak, *supra* note 51, at 162.
54. Such works include Koçi Beğ, Koçi Beğ Risalesi (Treatise of Koçi Beğ) (1997); Kâtip Çelebi, Dustûru'l-amel li'slâhil-halel of Kâtip Çelebi (The Guiding Principle for the Reform of Defects) (1982); Defterdar Sari Mehmed Paşa, Nesâyihul-vüzerâ ve'l-umerâ (Counsels for Viziers and Rulers) (1990); Hasan Kâfî el-Akhisârî ve Devlet Düzenine ait Eseri: Usûlü'l-hikem fî nizâmi'l-âlem (Hasan Kâfî el-Akhisârî and His Treatise on State: The Fundamentals of Wisdom in the Pax-Universalis) 10–11; Tarih Enstitüsü Dergisi (The Journal of the Institute of History) 239–78 (Istanbul 1981); Andreas Tietze, Mustafâ Âlî's Counsel for Sultans of 1581 (Nushatü's-selâtîn) Vols. I & II (1979–1982).
55. Yýlmaz, *supra* note 50, at 66.
56. Ocak, *supra* note 51, at 164.

seventeenth century up until the end of the nineteenth century when the decline of the empire was all-too-evident, the Ottoman thinkers proposed a return to the time-honored laws (*kânun-ý kadîm*) that had prevailed during the reign of Süleyman the Magnificent in the sixteenth century as a fixed standard. The enduring idea of "return" to a perfect age rather than "progress" towards a bright future meant that the Ottomans had a propensity to equate "change" with "degeneration."[57] This largely explains why politics and society, in the Ottoman perception, were premised on the preservation of the status quo.[58]

To begin with, Tursun Beð (d. 1490), who lived during the sultanate of Mehmed the Conqueror in the fifteenth century, advocated absolute power for the ruler. In his view, the ruler ought to secure the observance of certain values, such as social order, justice, and security.[59] Muslim thinkers and statesmen of the Ottoman epoch consistently emphasized the significance of "the circle of justice," which they viewed as the most essential condition for the vigor and integrity of the state.[60] According to Koçi Beð (d. 1648), a state standing on wrong religious ideas could survive while the one that stood on injustice could not.[61] This view was shared by many other thinkers.

In the view of Kýnalýzâde (d. 1572), the ruler of an Islamic state was both an imam and caliph. An imam had the authority to lead the faithful by virtue of his devotion to the Creator and of his integrity and knowledge of religion, while the caliph was the worldly ruler of his subjects. To Kýnalýzâde, the politics of such a state had to be based on virtue. The ruler should act according to the principles of justice grounded in the *Shariah* law. Only then could he become the viceregent and shadow of Allah on earth. He was also expected to keep in close contact with his people.[62] In Kýnalýzâde's view, the ruler should exercise full authority so that while the existing social and political order was maintained, he did not allow his subjects to transgress the acceptable limits of behavior. The head of the state should act in virtuous ways and in accordance with the law. In Kýnalýzâde's formulation, "the head of state maintains the existing order of society, good

57. Yýlmaz, *supra* note 50, at 51–52.
58. Ocak, *supra* note 51, at 165.
59. Mehmet Öz, *Klasik Dönem Osmanlý Siyasi Düşüncesi: Tarihi Temeller ve Ana Ýlkeler* (*Ottoman Political Thought in the Classical Era: Historical Fundamentals and Essential Principles*), 12 Ýslami Araştýrmalar Dergisi, 27, 29 (1999).
60. Ocak, *supra* note 51, at 172.
61. Öz, *supra* note 59, at 30. Such views as "the circle of justice," came to prominence in the official parlance more markedly in the 16th and 17th centuries, although this theme never lost its topicality during the course of the Ottoman Empire.
62. Kinalýzâde Ali Efendi, Devlet ve Aile Ahlâký (State and Family Morals) 187–90 (Ahmet Kahraman ed.)

governance keeps the head of state in power, and wisdom maintains the political order."[63]

According to Gelibolulu Mustafa Âlî (d. 1600), inaction in the face of injustice (*zulüm*) was a form of tyranny. He asked, "[h]ow can a mature mind accept the commands of rulers which undoubtedly constitute sin?"[64] Âlî entreated the rulers to observe justice, protect the well-being of subjects, avoid excessive spending, and treat their subjects with compassion.[65]

V. HUMAN RIGHTS IN THE OTTOMAN EMPIRE

It was almost impossible for the sultan to by-pass the *Shariah* law, as it was based on the incontrovertible verses of the Quran (*muhkem âyet*) and on the sayings and actions of the Holy Prophet (*hadith*) of Islam, or to act in violation of this law, since the Ottoman Empire regarded itself as the vanguard of Islam. The abandonment of this identity and the accompanying missionary zeal would no doubt spell the end of divine dispensation so that this new state of affairs would result in a series of crises of legitimacy and identity.

The role of the sultan as the benevolent provider of sustenance for his people was also intrinsic to this "Islamic sensitivity." The idea of a tacit contract between the sultan and his people was based on the common belief that the state and the sultan existed in order to establish an Islamic order. This general understanding can be traced to the Quranic injunction which holds that the rulers "should enjoin what is right and forbid what is wrong."[66] This concept of a tacit contract is so deeply entrenched within the Islamic political theory that many proponents of Islamic law regarded it as the "right of resistance" by the people, in case the ruler should disregard *Shariah* law.[67] This explains why, immediately after the outbreak of a revolt or rebellion against a supposedly deviant sultan, the rebels made sure to incriminate the sultan for breaching this tacit covenant, and, accordingly, in case they achieved their goal, promised a "return" to the previous, rightly guided state of the Islamic community.[68]

There's no doubt that the Ottomans, in accordance with the prevailing perspectives of the time, tried hard to observe the Islamic injunctions on a

---

63. *Id.* at 229.
64. Yýlmaz, *supra* note 50, at 62.
65. *Id.*
66. Sûra Âl-i Ýrân, verse 104.
67. Çaylak, *supra* note 3, at 217.
68. Mardin Turkish Modernization, *supra* note 37, at 114.

variety of issues which, today, are accepted as part of the baggage of human rights. They deserve attention.

A. Political Rights

In the realm of political rights, it must be borne in mind that the idea of freedom as understood by the Ottomans derived directly from Islam. Instead of an individual demanding certain rights from the whole, the collectivist perspective of freedom emphasizing the general good of society predominated in the lands governed by the Ottomans.[69] Maintenance of social balance, harmony, and justice were the key socio-political objectives here. It was perceived that the freedom and the rights of the individual would make sense if only these conditions prevailed. It should be emphasized, however, that contrary to the Islamic precepts and code of behavior, individuals and social groups were discouraged by the Ottoman polity from any meaningful involvement in the decisionmaking process. In other words, as far as the Ottoman rule is concerned, it is difficult to speak of an active political participation on the part of the people in general.[70]

Likewise, as regards the appointment of statesmen and public officers, the public opinion was ignored. Even members of the ruling elite were not immune from the arbitrary dispensation of the sultan. Contrary to Islamic precepts, members of the military and civil bureaucracy, known as the *kapýkulu,* were, as the term suggests, literally regarded as the servants of the sultan. In other words, the sultan had absolute authority over them.[71] This authority was exercised in two ways. On the one hand, members of the ruling elite could face the death penalty by a mere order of the sultan without regard to the proper judicial process. On the other hand, they could lose their property through arbitrary confiscation (*müsadere*) by the state in case of exile or death. The rationale behind this deliberate policy was to frustrate the emergence of political rivals.[72]

B. Judiciary

Under Ottoman rule, the judicial functions were performed by independent courts headed by the judge (*kadý*) who ruled on the basis of the Islamic

69. *Id.* at 121.
70. Findley, *supra* note 36, at 156.
71. Ahmet Mumcu, *Osmanlý Ýmparatorluðunda Egemenlik Kavramý ve Gelişmesi (The Concept of Sovereignty and its Evolution during the Ottoman Empire)*, 33–49, *supra* note 40, at 43.
72. Çaylak, *supra* note 3, at 112.

canon law. These judges performed not only judicial functions but also administrative tasks. They applied Islamic law as well as the *örfî* law, the sovereign prerogative, as a separate source of law that remained outside of the *Shariah* law. Even the most ardent critics of the Ottoman Empire admit that the Ottoman courts did not make any distinction between the rulers (excepting the sultan) and the ruled. The cases were reviewed within a reasonable period of time, and the rulings were considered by the people to be generally fair. The accused, in line with Islamic injunctions, were considered innocent until proven guilty by a court of law. In accordance with the *hadith*, the saying of the Holy Prophet, "No doubt, Allah will in the hereafter punish those who torment people in this world,"[73] torture was prohibited. Likewise, no one could be arrested without a warrant issued by a court of law.[74] The "weaker" sections of society—generally women, children, and orphans—were afforded special protection by the courts. The residents of a district where a court existed could have full confidence in the *Shariah* law and in the judge who would apply that law, and could be assured that the court's decision would not be disobeyed by public officers.[75]

C. Freedom of Religion

As far as the question of "freedom of religion and conscience" is concerned, it is discernible that Muslims as well as non-Muslims took full advantage of this freedom. Within the Ottoman political system religion was an important medium of communication between the "center" and the "periphery," *i.e.*, between state and society.[76] The Islamic orders (*tarikatlar*) performed the vital function of confirming the identity and satisfying the spiritual needs of the Muslim subjects. These orders were the "paths" of those who wished greater affinity with God. Under the guidance of the *sheikh* (head of the order), members learned to behave with humility, devotion, and brotherly solidarity. These orders remained outside the control of the state. An ordinary individual's views regarding state, society, and life were first and foremost shaped by religious orders. However, religious groups that represented heterodoxy, or that deviated from Sunni Islam did not find similar favor with the state. On the contrary, such groups excited suspicion and

73. This is not however to deny the likelihood of sporadic incidents involving torture. But they were by no means officially sanctioned.
74. Akgündüz, *supra* note 7, at 22–23.
75. Shaw, *supra* note 1, Vol. I, at 135. Again, this is not to deny that such cases did occasionally take place. In some cases, public officers may have abused their position.
76. Çaylak, *supra* note 3, at 124.

mistrust. Occasionally, their members were exiled or punished in some other way.[77]

D. Social and Economic Rights

In the realm of social and economic rights, we can see that the state was involved in the economic life of the country, particularly in order to prevent abuses and disadvantages to the poor. The sensitivity of the sultan concerning the welfare of his subjects was founded on the Islamic concept that "the subjects of a ruler are a trust of God."[78] These religious foundations served similar important public functions in caring for the basic material and spiritual needs of society. The foundations possessed juristic personality and channeled the energy of society into areas considered useful. Under Ottoman rule, endowments such as mosques, Islamic schools (*madrasas*), public baths, fountains, and refectories were generally put up and financed by foundations. Such endowments also constituted an important part of urban life.[79]

E. Rights of Women

According to Islam, as creatures of God, men and women are equal. Since women are "the trusts of Allah," men are prohibited from mistreating their wives. Under the Ottoman legal system which, unlike that enjoined by the modern human rights doctrine, primarily relied on Islam, men are regarded as the head of family. In Islam, women are guaranteed full competence in their dealings and actions, and possess significant rights within the institution of marriage: the right to alimony; immunity from the duty to contribute to the family budget; the absolute right to dispose of their property; the freedom to take up any employment (the conditions of which are not inimical to *Shariah* law or to morality); and, under certain conditions, the right to divorce. In addition, Islam encourages the education of women.[80] This legal framework was adopted by the Ottoman Empire, as the laws and courts of record testify.

77. *Id.*
78. *Id.*
79. SHAW, *supra* note 1, Vol. I, at 161.
80. *Id.* at 28–35.

VI. THE MILLET SYSTEM

As far as minority rights are concerned it is generally agreed that the Ottomans managed to establish a sophisticated and comprehensive system of protection. The continuous military expansion of the empire gave rise to an increasing population of religious minorities. Unlike today, the Ottomans did not regard ethnicity or language as a basis for granting minority status, which is important if one is to make sense of Ottoman policies regarding minorities.

As mentioned earlier, the legal arrangements dealing with the treatment of Muslim subjects under Ottoman rule had their origin in the *Shariah* law. Accordingly, "minorities" were grouped together on the basis of their religion or the religious sects to which they belonged. Such minorities were formed by Orthodox Christians, Catholic Christians, as well as by Jews. These minority communities were called *millets,* in reference to their religion as well as to their sect. By this definition, Muslims as a whole constituted a separate *millet* irrespective of their ethnicity or language.[81]

The legal basis of the state's relations with non-Muslims under Ottoman rule was in the latter's status as *dhimmis. Dhimmis* were the "People of the Book," namely Christians and Jews, who lived under the protection of a sovereign Muslim state. Their lives and property were protected by the state and they enjoyed religious freedom. In turn, the *dhimmis* had to pay a special tax. The Ottoman policies were not intended to assimilate minorities into the Muslim majority, but to ensure that they maintained their distinguishing features. In accordance with this overall perspective, minorities had the right to communicate in their own language, to regulate their civic matters according to their own (mostly religious) law, to enjoy freedom of religion and conscience, the right to set up foundations, and to arrange for their own education.

In matters of public law, non-Muslims were treated in accordance with the *Shariah* law, which contained special rules for them. Socially, culturally, and politically, Muslims and non-Muslims were subject to different codes and concepts.[82] *Shariah* law was applicable to non-Muslims only if a particular dispute involved Muslims or if the non-Muslim subjects themselves asked for its application.

---

81. Gülnihal Bozkurt, *Türk Hukuk Tarihinde Azýnlýklar (Minorities in Turkish Legal History)*, 43 A.Ü. Hukuk Fakültesi Dergisi 49, 50 (1993). The religiously conceived *millet* system is not peculiar to the Ottomans. Romans, medieval European empires and pre-Ottoman Middle Eastern Islamic states had a similar policy. The originality of the Ottoman Empire lay in the systematization of this policy. *See* Shaw, *supra* note 1, Vol. I, at 151.
82. Bozkurt, *supra* note 81.

This sharp distinction drawn between adherents of different religions may be seen as oppressive when looked at from the perspective of modern human rights doctrine. Equally, a number of impositions designed to facilitate the recognition of non-Muslims by those outside of their own community may be perceived as insulting: the house of a non-Muslim could not be higher than that of a Muslim; non-Muslims were banned from living in certain neighborhoods; they were not allowed to dress like Muslims; they could not carry arms without special permission; they could not serve in the army; a non-Muslim man could not marry a Muslim woman; non-Muslims could not take up employment in the public sector; they could not witness against a Muslim in a court of law; and it was forbidden to toll the church bell loud enough to be heard from outside.[83] All these examples indicate that difference of status between Muslims and non-Muslims was institutionalized under Ottoman rule in favor of Muslims. For that reason, the intermingling of different *millets* with Muslims was almost impossible.

Individuals gained status and a recognizable identity within the Ottoman society only through their own *millets*. Non-Muslim Ottoman subjects came in contact with the rulers through the medium of their community leaders. The status of a leader had to be confirmed by the sultan. The person gaining recognition as the leader of a particular millet was then given the title of *pasha* (the highest title of civil and military officials), whereby he could apply the rules of his religion within his community. The extent of authority exercised by these community leaders under Ottoman rule far exceeded that which they had enjoyed under their Christian governments. Charged with religious *and* social functions, community leaders played a pivotal role in ensuring that taxes were paid and all other duties were fulfilled by the members of their community.[84] The leader of a particular *millet* collected taxes, resolved private law disputes through the community court, and set up schools.[85] Unlike modern states, where the government concerned itself with all aspects of the individual's life, the Ottoman political and administrative model concerned itself with the individual only indirectly, and instead focused its attention on the community bodies. For the Ottomans, human rights was not an independent issue, but was a natural requirement for social peace and justice. We may then easily assert that the Ottomans favored a collectivist approach to human rights.

The fact that under Ottoman rule human rights were not perceived with the individual in mind should not lead us to the conclusion that minorities were generally oppressed by the state. Such an allegation could easily be

83. *Id.* at 51.
84. Shaw, *supra* note 1, at 151–52.
85. Bozkurt, *supra* note 81, at 52.

refuted by evidence that, right from the beginning, a significant proportion of the Balkan Christians freely chose to live under the sovereignty of the Ottomans. Until the arrival of "the wind of nationalism" in the early nineteenth century, the Balkan subjects of the empire were generally content with Ottoman rule. This is the most reasonable explanation for the speedy expansion and consolidation of the Ottoman rule in the Balkans from the fourteenth century onwards.[86] To give an example, in Hungary, which the Ottomans called Budin, the Ottoman Empire did not interfere with religious freedom, but instead protected the Christian subjects against local fiefs.[87] Therefore, the claim that non-Muslims began to enjoy human rights and liberties only after the *Tanzimat* reforms of the nineteenth century is patently false.[88] Except for the limitations imposed by the *Shariah* law and the deliberate policy of keeping the religious communities apart, Christians, Jews, and Muslims were treated equally under Ottoman rule. Among the rights they enjoyed were: civil rights; freedom of travel; freedom of religion and conscience; the right to education; and the right to privacy. It can be asserted with confidence that the Ottomans generally implemented the rights and liberties which the Quran grants the People of the Book (*ehl-il kitab*).[89] The registers of the court of records of Islamic canonical law amply prove that the Ottoman courts generally observed and respected the rights of non-Muslim subjects.

A. From the Millet System to the Ottoman Citizenry

Following the proclamation of the Imperial Rescript of Gülhane (or the Imperial Edict of Reorganization) in 1839, the Ottomans abandoned the faith-centered *millet* system, adopting instead Ottoman citizenry as the basis for the relationship between state and subjects. With the issuance of the Imperial Edict of Reorganization the sultan had accepted certain limitations to his authority. Under this edict the sultan undertook to guarantee the life, property, and good name of his people, including minorities. According to the edict, anyone who deviated from the *Shariah* law would be punished irrespective of status. The sultan also conceded the transfer of his exclusive prerogative to punish, in respect of certain issues

86. Miroğlu, *supra* note 43, at 75.
87. Kopcan, *supra* note 44, at 375.
88. Like the 1839 Imperial Rescript of Gülhane-Tanzimat Fermaný—which is also called the Imperial Edict of Reorganization, and the Imperial Reform Edict—Islahat Fermaný of 1856.
89. Akgündüz, *supra* note 7, at 40–48.

and individuals, to independent courts.[90] Interestingly however, rather than disowning or even disavowing *Shariah* law, it was stated in the edict that the root cause of the problems faced by the Ottoman Empire was digression from the same.

The definitive date by which the Ottomans began to break with *Shariah* law was the proclamation of the Imperial Reform Edict of 1856.[91] This edict promised to completely remove the legal and de facto inequality between Muslim and non-Muslim subjects. This signaled the end of the restrictions based mostly on the *Shariah* law, which differentiated between adherents of different religions. Among the restrictions and special arrangements replaced by new rules were: the capitation tax (*cizye*) that was collected from non-Muslims was abolished, the ban on employment in the public service as well as the ban on military service was lifted, and the prohibition of acting as witnesses against Muslims in a court of law was canceled. Under the terms of the Reform Edict, members of minority *millets* were accorded the right to be represented in local and regional parliaments as well as in important state institutions such as the Council of State (*Şûra-yý Devlet*), which served useful functions in legislative matters.[92]

A number of privileges which the non-Muslims had previously enjoyed continued throughout the *Tanzimat* period. If we are to use the modern terminology of human rights, we could say that the different non-Muslim *millets* were fully accorded their special minority rights. The Ottomans continued to recognize separate arrangements for minorities in matters of civil, family, and inheritance law until well into the second half of the nineteenth century.[93] By this absence of a "unitary" legal system, which is one of the defining features of nation-states, we can recognize that the Ottomans still had no nation-state despite their co-option into Western legal standards.

Contrary to expectation, the process that began with the Imperial Reform Edict of 1856 precipitated the disintegration of the empire instead of fostering its integrity. The Balkan nations sought to exploit their newly gained rights to achieve independence.[94] There is no doubt that the majority of the *ulemâ* and of ordinary Muslims opposed the *Tanzimat* reforms they considered to be in contradiction with *Shariah* law. Also the Muslims were

---

90. Mumcu, *supra* note 71, at 46.
91. This edict was reaffirmed by the Paris Peace Treaty, which was signed by the Great Powers of Europe, indicating that the real dynamism of Tanzimat reforms was the result of international pressure.
92. Bülent Tanör, Osmanli-Türk Anayasal Gelişmeleri 95–113 (4th ed., 1999).
93. Gülnihal Bozkurt, Gayrimüslim Osmanli Vatandaşlarinin Hukukî Durumu, 1839–1914 (The Legal Status of the Non-Muslim Subjects of the Ottoman Empire, 1839–1914) 208–09 (1989).
94. Küçük, *supra* note 46, at 19.

extremely disappointed with the loss of their previously superior legal status.[95] Beginning with the nineteenth century, the adoption of a new concept of law and justice from the European infidels, who had until then been regarded as the enemy, was deeply disturbing for the Muslim subjects of the empire. They lamented the loss of the ideal order shaped by Islam.[96] Not surprisingly, even long after the onset of *Tanzimat* reforms, on the whole, both the commoners and the ruling elite continued to trace the source of the sovereign power exercised by the sultan to *Shariah* law.

B. Humanitarian Intervention in the Ottoman Empire

Right from the beginning, the Ottomans were perceived in the European parlance as alien intruders who had been in the business of oppressing Christians that fell prey to the Ottoman yoke. Their different perception was very much reflected in their appreciation of the minority problem. What the Ottomans regarded as "rebellion and lawlessness," the European Powers considered the "honorable struggle of oppressed peoples" for independence. The magic slogan of "protecting Christian minorities" was thus frequently used to justify military excursions into the Ottoman territories.[97]

Indeed, by the late eighteenth century when the Ottoman Empire had already become too vulnerable to foreign penetration on account of its weaknesses, the European powers began to call for reforms that would improve the lot of non-Muslim subjects within the empire. In fact, highlighting the negative aspects of the empire suited the imperial interests of the European powers that were in search of expanding their influence in the Ottoman realms. Not surprisingly, the support that these states gave to nationalist movements in the Balkans from the end of the eighteenth century was considered by the Ottoman Empire as an intervention in its affairs.[98]

As historians generally agree, many revolts were either provoked and/or aided by European powers in this period. While Russia considered itself the protector of Christian Orthodox subjects, Britain and France claimed this role for Protestants and Catholics respectively. Indeed, Russia played a pivotal role in the Greek revolt of the early nineteenth century against the Ottoman rule. Russia was no doubt an autocratic state, and its actions in the Balkans were hardly inspired by its love of freedom or revolutionary

95. Most Muslims could not comprehend how they could possibly be treated equally with non-Muslims. This, to them, was an affront to the Shariah.
96. Calling this justified reaction "reactionarism" would be utterly simplistic.
97. Scott Davidson, Human Rights 8 (1993).
98. İlber Ortaylý, Ýmparatorludun En Uzun Yüzyýlý (The Longest Century of the Empire) 73 (1999).

politics. Instead Russia was seeking ways to extend its influence in the Balkans at the expense of its arch rival—the Ottoman Empire.[99]

In 1860, an inter-communal strife broke out in Lebanon and Syria that resulted in the death of thousands of Christians and the destruction of many churches and monasteries. France, Britain and a number of other European states either sent warships to the Beirut harbor or landed troops in the area.[100] Thus, the powerful European states claimed the right of humanitarian intervention to prevent the persecution of Christian minorities in the Middle East (and the Balkans) at the hands of the Ottoman Empire.

It is often forgotten that intolerance of minority political activities was a common attitude of all the empires in the nineteenth century, and such actions often evoked harsh responses by target states. The bias against the Ottoman Empire surfaced again when a crisis broke out in Crete in 1897. In this year about ten thousand men from Crete and mainland Greece revolted against the Ottoman Empire, occupied the island of Crete, and declared the union of Crete with Greece. In the words of Stanford Shaw, a well-known scholar of Ottoman history, the invading forces

> cut a swath of devastation, slaughtering thousands of Muslims. The powers tried to intervene to secure a settlement but the massacres continued, forcing the governor to flee on a Russian warship while the Ottoman soldiers responded by slaughtering Greeks as well as defending the Muslims. It was this act alone that seemed to catch the eye of the European press. The powers proposed a settlement with full autonomy for Crete and with all the Ottoman soldiers withdrawn.[101]

The Ottoman response was no doubt ruthless, but so was the cruelty of Greek nationalists. The incident in Crete was, as in many other cases involving Christian minorities, abused by Great European Powers determined to weaken the Ottoman Empire in the Balkans and the Middle East.

The differences of opinion between the Ottomans and European Powers survived right up to the disintegration of the Ottoman Empire at the end of the First World War. In the view of Abdulhamit (the ruler of the Ottoman Empire from 1876 to 1908) and the Party of Union and Progress (*Ýttihat ve Terakki*), which effectively held the reins of power between 1908–1918, any manifestations of political nationalism from subject nations such as Armenians and Arabs were an unforgivable treason since such actions threatened the integrity of the empire. Although the Party of Union and Progress advocated Ottoman citizenry as the basis of the relationship

---

99. Niyazi Berkes, Türkiye'de Çaddaşlaşma (Modernization in Turkey) 147 (1978).
100. Shaw, *supra* note 1, Vol. II, at 142–43.
101. *Id.* at 207.

between the state and its subjects, Armenian and Arab nationalists were convinced that this party represented the interests of Turkish nationalism.[102] This mistrust between the state and certain nationalities precipitated the eventual disintegration of the Ottoman Empire in the aftermath of the First World War.

VII. CONCLUSION

The issues which have been discussed here so far lead to the conclusion that in matters covered by the *Shariah* law, the Ottoman Empire generally respected the human rights of its subjects. In areas not covered by firm injunctions of the *Shariah* law, arbitrary rule sometimes prevailed. This discrepancy between law and legal practice was partly the result of the conspicuous absence of civic establishments involved in politics. In the Ottoman case, the state, out of fear of potential rivalries, never allowed the emergence of intermediary groups that could act as channels of communication between the individual and the state. In other words, seen as alternative centers of power, political formations such as the capitalist class and local fiefs were considered threats to the power of the state; accordingly, they were never allowed to become a significant force. Social groups centered purely around religious and cultural values and activities within various Islamic communities and religious orders (*tarikats*), foundations, village councils, and tradesmen's guilds did not excite animosity on the part of the state.[103]

For the Ottoman ruling elite, the ideal system of governance had to be sought on the basis of *Shariah* law. Even after Western-inspired reforms had been proceeding at full speed, the Ottoman statesmen seemed reluctant to do away with their basically Islamic political system.[104] Interestingly, even the opponents to the sultan's absolute rule (*istibdat*), who gained growing support among educated circles in the second half of the nineteenth century, took great pains to present their ideas in the context of Islamic discourse. For instance, in their search for a constitutional order that would confer more extensive rights to the individual, the Young Ottomans (*Genç Osmanlýlar*) were always keen to emphasize that their demands for reform were based on Islamic injunctions.[105] One of the most respected members of the opposition, Namýk Kemal, found the basis for representative government

102. Berkes, *supra* note 99, at 401.
103. Mardïn, *supra* note 38, at 30–40.
104. Findley, *supra* note 36, at 158–59.
105. *Id.* at 150.

in the Quranic principle of *şûra* which requires that matters concerning the community should be decided by mutual consultation (*meşveret*). Likewise, the opposition's demand for an accountable government was justified by referring to the experience of the early years of Islam when the Islamic community had given an oath of allegiance (*biat*) to the new caliph, on condition that he should not deviate from *Shariah* law.[106] This, in a way, proves the lack of full compatibility between the Ottoman legal order and the *Shariah* law.

This discussion aims to demonstrate that the issue of human rights does not have to focus on the individual *per se*. Alternative, legitimate ways to protect the human rights of individuals in society exist. The Ottoman experience resulted in: maintaining a reasonable equilibrium between different social groups; encouraging pluralism based on the maintenance of religious communitarianism; and striving for justice for all the subject peoples irrespective of religion instead of consecrating legal equality as the guiding principle. As Muslims, the Ottomans perceived human rights as natural rights of divine origin; and as a consequence, they were sacrosanct and therefore inviolable. The sultans and the ruling elite took great pains to ensure that the rights and liberties expressly conferred by the *Shariah* law were implemented in full. These features of the Ottoman legal system should be thoroughly considered when evaluating the degree to which human rights were implemented and respected during the Ottoman Empire.

It is difficult to disagree with the concluding statement of Gökçen Alpkaya's article on the exercise of human rights under Ottoman rule: "[c]onsidering the relativity of the concept of human rights, which consists of a universal list of imperatives, we should perhaps first question the concept itself."[107] Therefore, what is ultimately enlightening is to reach an understanding of the Ottomans' perception of human rights without attempting to judge it from the perspective of modern human rights doctrine. Only then will it be possible to appreciate that, with regard to the aforementioned doctrine, valuable lessons could be learned from the Ottoman experience without denying its shortcomings.

---

106. Berkes, *supra* note 99, at 283–92.
107. Gökçen Alpkaya, *Osmanlý Hukuk Reformu ve Kişi Özgürlükleri: 1839–1908 (The Ottoman Legal Reform and Personal Liberties: 1839–1908)*, 12 Ýnsan Haklarý Yýllýðý 167, 182 (1990).

Part III
Contemporary Challenges of Minority Rights Law

[7]

The Headscarf Affair: The Conseil d'État on the Role of Religion and Culture in French Society

ELISA T. BELLER†

SUMMARY

I. INTRODUCTION

On February 10, 2004, the French National Assembly voted 494 to 36 to pass legislation that would ban the wearing of an Islamic headscarf, or any other conspicuous religious symbol, within French public schools.[1] The bill passed the French Senate by a similar margin, 276 to 20, on March 3, 2004.[2] The text of the law is extremely terse, stipulating only: "In public schools, the wearing of symbols or clothing by which students conspicuously [*ostensiblement*] manifest a religious appearance is forbidden. Internal regulations state that the initiation of disciplinary proceedings must be preceded by a dialogue with the student."[3]

---

† Associate, Rosen Consulting Group, Berkeley, California. B.A., Williams College (2001); M.Phil., Cambridge University (2002).

The author would like to thank Dr. Robert Tombs, her Master's dissertation advisor, for his guidance in formulating and realizing this article. She would also like to thank Prof. Shanti Singham and Carissa Hessick for their advice and encouragement. The author dedicates this article to her father, the late Eric I.B. Beller.

1. Elaine B. Sciolino, *French Assembly Votes to Ban Religious Symbols in Schools*, N.Y. TIMES, Feb. 11, 2004, at A3.

2. *Le Sénat Français Adopte le Projet de Loi sur les Signes Religieux à l'École*, LE MONDE (Paris), Mar. 3, 2004, *available at* http://www.lemonde.fr/web/recherche_articleweb/1,13-0,36-355392,0.html (last visited Apr. 13, 2004).

3. Projet de Loi Encadrant, en Application du Principe de Laïcité, le Port de Signes ou de Tenues Manifestant une Appartenance Religieuse dans les Écoles, Collèges et Lycées Publics, No. 253, Assemblée Nationale, Douzième Législature (2004) ("Dans les écoles, les collèges et les lycées publics, le port de signes ou tenues par lesquels les élèves manifestant ostensiblement une appartenance religieuse est interdit. Le règlement intérieur rappelle que la mise en œuvre d'une procédure disciplinaire est précédée d'un dialogue avec l'élève."), *available at* http://www.assemblee-nat.fr/12/pdf/ta/ta0253.pdf (last visited Apr. 13, 2004). The remainder of the text consists of technical notes, a statement that the law will take effect at the start of the new school year, and a compromise provision that the law will be re-examined after being in effect for one year. Nathalie Schuck, *France Changes Ban on Religious Symbols*, ASSOCIATED PRESS, Feb. 7, 2004, *available at* www.boston.com/news/world/europe/articles/2004/02/07/france_changes_ban_on_religious_symbols/ (last visited Feb. 28, 2004).

The headscarf legislation of 2004 emerged as a direct response to the recommendations of a commission appointed in 2003 by French President Jacques Chirac. Chirac charged the Stasi Commission, composed of prominent politicians, scholars, and others, with examining the issue of *laïcité*, or secularism.[4] On December 11, 2003, the commission issued its recommendations, among them a ban on wearing the headscarf in public schools. One week later, with strong public opinion behind him,[5] Chirac came out in favor of legislation to put such a ban into effect.[6] The Commission's report provides a sweeping historical and philosophical overview of the principle of *laïcité*. While denying that *laïcité* mandates "a militant atheism"[7] or that *laïcité* is incompatible with Islam,[8] the report states that just as the state must abandon all authority within matters of personal conscience and spirituality, so must religion "renounce [its] political dimension. *Laïcité* is incompatible with any conception of religion that hopes to rule over . . . the social system or the political order."[9] This separation is mutually beneficial to both religion and the state,[10] as well as providing an equal footing to all individual citizens.[11] While addressing numerous other applications of the principle of *laïcité*, the Commission spends a particularly significant portion of its report discussing the reasoning behind its recommendation to ban the headscarf in public schools.[12]

The international attention that the report's release and then the law's passage have attracted serves as the latest demonstration of the power of the headscarf to crystallize the controversies over Islam, immigration, and national identity that have emerged in France and, in various other guises, other Western democracies.[13] This particular variation of the struggle to define French identity did not, however, burst forth suddenly, nor was it precipitated solely by wariness of fundamentalist Islam in the wake of the terrorist attacks of September 11, 2001. Understanding the origins of the headscarf issue in France is essential to the task of decoding the significance of the actions of the French executive and legislature in late 2003 and early 2004. Examining those origins—the subject of this article—is essential not only to a factual understanding of the context of the Stasi report and resultant law, but even more to a grasp of the light that these events shed on the functioning and structure of the entire French governmental and legal apparatus.

The issue of the headscarf first erupted onto the French political scene in October 1989, when the principal of a majority-Muslim middle school in the Parisian suburb of Creil suspended three Muslim girls for wearing their headscarves in the public school

4. Philippe Bernard, *M. Stasi Prône l'Interdiction des Signes Religieux et Politiques à l'École*, LE MONDE (Paris), Dec. 11, 2003, *available at* http://www.lemonde.fr/txt/article/0,1-0@2-3224,36-345565,0.html (last visited Apr. 13, 2004). The sole dissenting view within the twenty-member commission on the issue of the headscarf was that of historian and sociologist Jean Baubérot. *Id.*

5. *See* Keith B. Richburg, *French President Urges Ban on Head Scarves in Schools: Chirac Confronts Spread of Islam*, WASH. POST, Dec. 18, 2003, at A1, A44 (describing a survey conducted in December 2003 by *Le Parisien* that showed sixty-nine percent of the French public in favor of such a ban).

6. *Id.* at A1. Other banned symbols would include the Jewish *kippah* (skullcap) or a large cross, while discreet symbols such as small crosses, Jewish stars of David, or Muslim hands of Fatima would be permitted. COMM'N DE REFLEXION SUR L'APPLICATION DU PRINCIPE DE LAÏCITÉ DANS LA REPUBLIQUE, RAPPORT AU PRESIDENT DE LA REPUBLIQUE, § 4.2.2.1, at 58–59 (Dec. 11, 2003) [hereinafter STASI COMMISSION REPORT], *available at* http://www.laic.info/Members/webmestre/Folder.2003-09-11.4517/rapport-stasi.pdf (last visited Jan. 17, 2004).

7. STASI COMMISSION REPORT, *supra* note 6, § 1.1, at 12.

8. *Id.* § 1.2.3, at 14.

9. *Id.* § 1.2.1, at 11.

10. *Id.*

11. *Id.* § 1.2.4, at 16.

12. *See id.* § 4.2.2.1, at 54.

13. *See* STASI COMMISSION REPORT, *supra* note 6, § 2.3, at 32 (discussing approaches taken by other European countries addressing the separation of church and state).

classroom. France found itself deeply divided by the principal's action, but, as in 2003 and 2004, the fault lines this rift revealed were not those between a clearly defined Right and Left, or feminist and anti-feminist camps, or even pro- and anti-immigration factions. Indeed, each of these opposing groups were as likely to disagree as to agree amongst themselves about whether the girls should be allowed to wear their scarves. Some avatars of the traditional political left, for example, supported the girls' self-expression in the face of government coercion, while others insisted that allowing Muslims too much sway would dilute and perhaps ultimately undermine France's secular and liberal political heritage.[14]

An appeal by a government minister to the *Conseil d'État* (Council of State), France's highest administrative tribunal, provisionally resolved the controversy. Serving as the body responsible for holding the state to account—and therefore performing some functions of the U.S. Supreme Court but not others—the *Conseil d'État* seems a curious institution to the American eye. It polices the vast French bureaucracy, yet it is of the bureaucracy in the most profound way. Its members, culled from the top of the class at the school that prepares the nation's elite civil servants, generally have no specific legal training.

To better understand the *Conseil d'État*'s role in French governance and the significance of the structure of which it is a part, this article will explore the *Conseil d'État*'s ruling in the case of the excluded girls, the circumstances surrounding that ruling, and the *Conseil*'s subsequent holdings on the question of wearing a headscarf in a public school. This article will draw out the fundamental attributes of the *Conseil d'État*, assessing the tribunal's place in French governance and its effectiveness and suitability for dealing with the increasingly pressing claims of pluralism and religious expression in the French public sphere. Finally, this article will briefly assess the implications of the recent involvement of the executive and legislative bodies in the headscarf debate and suggest a new way of reading the shifting role of the *Conseil d'État*'s 1989 ruling and of the *Conseil d'État* itself in this controversy.

First, however, it is imperative to gain a grasp of the facts of the case and the social climate into which the Headscarf Affair was born. The controversy's start was marked by an article that appeared on October 4, 1989, in the daily newspaper *La Libération*, reporting the basic facts of the case.[15] Within a week of the *Libération* article, all of the national press was publishing on the event, and the weekly news magazines had made it their top story. In the early weeks while the press was having its say, few politicians or national groups spoke up about the Affair. On October 10, the principal, the girls, and their families reached a compromise, seemingly acceptable to all parties. The girls, they agreed, could wear their scarves everywhere in the school except the actual classroom. Ten days later, however, the girls refused to remove their scarves in the classroom and were again expelled. The first person associated with the government to comment on the case was Danielle Mitterrand, wife of socialist President François Mitterrand. On October 23, Mrs. Mitterrand came out in favor of letting the girls wear the veils, chastising the country for still being unwilling to accept religions other than Christianity even 200 years after the Revolution.[16] She did not make clear on whose behalf she spoke, however, and politicians of all stripes considered her to have irresponsibly muddied the waters.[17]

Finally, the Wednesday after Danielle Mitterrand's remarks, Education Minister Lionel Jospin became the first member of the government to announce an opinion on the

14. ADRIAN FAVELL, PHILOSOPHIES OF INTEGRATION: IMMIGRATION AND THE IDEA OF CITIZENSHIP IN FRANCE AND BRITAIN 154 (1998).

15. FRANÇOISE GASPARD & FARHAD KHOSROKHAVAR, LE FOULARD ET LA RÉPUBLIQUE 12–15 (1995).

16. *Id.* at 21.

17. *Id.*

girls' right to wear their headscarves in the classroom. During his weekly televised question and answer period with the National Assembly, Jospin told parliamentarians, "[t]he school cannot exclude, since it was made for welcoming."[18] This statement precipitated great controversy in the Assembly, with some members of Jospin's own party vigorously opposing him and members of the opposition applauding.[19] In late November, with pressure from politicians and journalists mounting, Jospin exercised his prerogative to refer the matter to the *Conseil d'État*, France's highest administrative tribunal.

The *Conseil* ruled, on November 27, 1989, that wearing religious symbols to school is permissible as long as those symbols are not so "ostentatious" [*ostentatoire*] as to "constitute an act of intimidation, provocation, proselytising, or propaganda; threaten the dignity and freedom of students or other members of the educational community[;]" or disrupt the school's normal functioning.[20] While this judgment seemed to decide the case in the girls' favor, the fact that it explicitly left interpretation and implementation of these conditions to individual school principals was widely criticized as inviting the rule of individual prejudice and caprice.[21] In fact, only a few years later, a different school principal took up the court's invitation to test its ruling's criteria. Between 1989 and 2003, several further controversies erupted over the removal from the classroom of girls wearing headscarves. In subsequent cases brought before it by parents of aggrieved students, the *Conseil* generally upheld the students' general right to wear their religious garb. In fact, between 1992 and 1999, the *Conseil d'État* ruled in favor of the headscarf-wearing students in forty-one of the forty-nine cases that it heard on the issue.[22] Nevertheless, ample room to prohibit the scarves in individual cases remained.[23]

As will be discussed below, Jospin issued a circular—a directive to members of the French educational establishment—clarifying some of the provisions set out in the *Conseil*'s ruling and empowering school principals to determine when the headscarf was appropriate.[24] Five years later, François Bayrou, then the education minister, issued an additional circular that confirmed principals' authority in evaluating instances of headscarf-wearing. In addition, the Bayrou Circular elaborated on the *Conseil d'État*'s discussion of ostentatious (*ostentatoire*) religious garb, emphasizing that some symbols are "so ostentatious that their meaning is precisely to separate certain students from the rules of the communal life of the school. Such symbols are, in and of themselves, elements of proselytism."[25] The circular goes on to distinguish between permissible, discreet symbols and forbidden, ostentatious symbols.[26] The circular employs the same term as the *Conseil*

18. *Id.* at 22.

19. *Id.*

20. PIERRE BIRNBAUM, THE IDEA OF FRANCE 231 (M.B. DeBevoise trans., Hill and Wang 2001) (1998); *see also* Conseil d'État, Assemblée générale (Section de l'intérieur), 27 Novembre 1989, *available at* http://www.conseil-etat.fr/ce/rappor/index_ra_cg03_01.shtml (last visited Apr. 13, 2004). For a reprinting of the opinion, see Jean Rivero, *Laïcité Scolaire et Signes d'Appartenance Religieuse*, 6 REVUE FRANÇAISE DE DROIT ADMINISTRATIF 1, 6 (1990).

21. BIRNBAUM, *supra* note 20, at 230–32.

22. OPEN SOC'Y INST., *The Situation of Muslims in France*, *in* MONITORING THE EU ACCESSION PROCESS: MINORITY PROTECTION 69, 93 (2002), *available at* http://www.eumap.org/reports/2002/content/09/250/2002_m_france.pdf (last visited Apr. 1, 2004).

23. See *infra* text accompanying notes 244–252 (discussing decisions rendered by the *Conseil* in November 1992 and March 1995 regarding the permissibility of headscarves in the classroom).

24. Lionel Jospin, Circulaire du 12 Décembre du Ministre d'État, Ministre de l'Éducation Nationale, de la Jeunesse et des Sports, J.O., Dec. 15, 1989, at 15577, *reprinted in* Claude Durand-Prinborgne, *La "Circulaire Jospin" du 12 Décembre 1989*, 6 REVUE FRANÇAISE DE DROIT ADMINISTRATIF 10 (1990); *see infra* text accompanying note 204.

25. François Bayrou, Circulaire no. 1649 du 20 Septembre 1994, *available at* http://www.assemblee-nat.fr/12/dossiers/documents-laicite/document-3.pdf (last visited March 6, 2004).

26. *Id.*

d'État's 1989 ruling—*ostentatoire*—to describe unacceptable religious symbols. Nevertheless, the circular's effect was generally to narrow the circumstances under which a headscarf would be considered permissible.[27] The circular did not have the authority to define which symbols schools should consider *ostentatoire*. Indeed, even after the circular's release, the *Conseil d'État* ruled that wearing a headscarf is not automatically *ostentatoire* and that expulsion is permissible only if the student's action constitutes a threat to public order over and above the mere wearing of the headscarf.[28]

The *affaire des voiles*, or affair of the scarves, as it has become known,[29] crystallized many of the conflicts in French society surrounding immigration and national and religious identity. As such, political scientists and historians—not to mention journalists and politicians—quickly seized upon the *affaire* as a prime case study in the evolving debate over these issues in contemporary France. Scholar Miriam Feldblum observes that the *affaire des voiles* raised four issues: the role of secularism in the public school system; women's rights; "the spectre of a fundamentalist, aggressive Islam proselytising France"; and the integration of North Africans and other non-European immigrants.[30] This is a heady, complicated *mélange* of issues, each complex enough in its own right. As Maxim Silverman wrote less than three years after the *affaire*, "[t]his debate would have been incomprehensible to outsiders who had not followed events in the years prior to this incident . . . . It would also have been incomprehensible to those who had no knowledge of the secular tradition in France or the development of the modern French republic."[31] This article, after examining the historical context to which Silverman refers, without attempting to replicate the full historical review that he and others like Pierre Birnbaum have provided, will argue that there is yet a third body of knowledge that the informed observer must possess in order to make sense of the *affaire des voiles*. Until the release of the Stasi Report, the primary agent of the *affaire*'s legal resolution had been the French judicial system. The precise legal nature of that resolution, as well as the ways in which it remained incomplete until the recent action on the part of the executive and legislative branches, is a crucial element to our assessment of what the unfolding of the *affaire des voiles* can teach us about France past, present, and future.

The experience of Muslims in France has figured prominently in a growing literature on a new model for citizenship in France, Europe, and the wider world—a model more fluid than its predecessor and more open to the influence of immigrants and of others who were previously considered outsiders. To understand the significance of this alleged shift, it is important to grasp tenets of the traditional French model for citizenship and civic participation. Part II of this article will delineate and examine the history of the republican

27. OPEN SOC'Y INST., *supra* note 22, at 93.

28. Dominique Le Tourneau, *La Laïcité à l'Épreuve de l'Islam: le Cas du Port du "Foulard Islamique" dans l'École Publique en France*, 28 REVUE GÉNÉRALE DU DROIT 275, 293–95 (1997). The Vice President of the *Conseil d'État*, R. Denoix de Saint Marc, identified the point of disagreement between Bayrou and the *Conseil* as concerning to what extent the headscarf has an intrinsic "symbolic charge." In words that resonate with the debate over the headscarf that occurred in 2003 and 2004, Denoix de Saint Marc added that if a veil had a symbolic charge, then we would have to attribute that same charge to a kippa or a cross. *Id.* at 294 n.80 (quoting Interview with Renaud Denoix de Saint Marc, Vice President of the Conseil d'État, with LA CROIX (Nov. 7, 1996)).

29. I will employ the term *affaire des voiles* or, simply, "the *affaire*" to describe these events. In direct quotations, however, I will preserve an author's original choice of phrase. The term *affaire des voiles* is interchangeable with *affaire du foulard* and *affaire des foulards*—"affair of the headscarf" and "affair of the headscarves," respectively. *See* FAVELL, *supra* note 14, at x.

30. MIRIAM FELDBLUM, RECONSTRUCTING CITIZENSHIP: THE POLITICS OF NATIONALITY REFORM AND IMMIGRATION IN CONTEMPORARY FRANCE 136 (1999).

31. MAXIM SILVERMAN, DECONSTRUCTING THE NATION: IMMIGRATION, RACISM AND CITIZENSHIP IN MODERN FRANCE 1 (1992).

ideal of citizenship, as well as the debate over this ideal's accuracy in describing French political and social history. The Part will conclude with an analysis of scholarly works concerning the current status of immigrants—particularly, Muslims of North African descent[32]—within the French state. In several such works, the author uses the *affaire des voiles* as evidence for the author's view that one trend or another defined French politics during the final two decades of the twentieth century.

This literature on multicultural citizenship has failed to examine closely the role of the French legal system in the affair's unfolding and, especially, in its partial resolution in late November 1989 when the *Conseil d'État*'s decision reinstated the three girls from Creil into their school. The *Conseil*'s pivotal role in determining the fate of those three girls and in framing the future of the debate raises dual questions about how France's legal system has affected and in turn been influenced by the country's debate over immigration, secularism, and national identity. As Pierre Birnbaum has written, the *Conseil*'s decision of November 27, 1989 was an "essential document, which was to leave its mark on the whole of contemporary French jurisprudence."[33] To assess the *Conseil*'s role fully, however, will require more than an analysis of the reverberations of its decision within the French legal system. We must also look at the very structure of that system in order to understand how this decision fit into the broader socio-political debate that was raging as the *Conseil*'s members reached their conclusions. Specifically, we must look at how the case came to rest on the *Conseil* members' desks—in other words, what channels were in place within the legal system to deal with this highly politicized dispute. Part III will explore the history of the *Conseil d'État* and its function within the French state. This Part will examine the *Conseil*'s organizational structure and recruitment methods—a case study of the highly formalized bureaucracy that is characteristic of the French Republican state.

Finally, Part IV will analyze the text of the *Conseil*'s 1989 judgment as well as those of subsequent rulings in 1992 and 1995, especially highlighting the evidence and support that these decisions claim from the constitution of the Fifth Republic and other pertinent laws and legal texts. Combining these pieces of legal, political, and historical evidence, the article will draw conclusions about how well-equipped the French government and legal system are to adapt to the new challenges to national identity that immigration raises.

II. THE REPUBLICAN CITIZEN IN FRANCE

The debate over how accurately the French model of citizenship actually describes French history from the Revolution until the late twentieth century is perhaps the most contentious historiographical dispute about immigration into France. Some, like Rogers Brubaker, contend that throughout this historical period France retained a relatively constant idea of itself as a nation whose residents, in order to be worthy of the title "citizen," must actively take on its culture, including the all-important French language, and participate in its political life.[34] While the idea of the citizen evolved, it always maintained its ideological and political function as a way of defining participation in French culture and civic life.[35] The cultural aspect of citizenship was always dominant, though not exhaustive in explaining the development of the French idea of citizenship.[36] The flip side of this definition of citizenship is that, in theory, anyone willing to embrace French culture is eligible and welcome to become a citizen. Taking account of this historically-continuous

32. I will sometimes employ the term *Maghrebi*, which is a person of North African origin.
33. BIRNBAUM, *supra* note 20, at 230.
34. ROGERS BRUBAKER, CITIZENSHIP AND NATIONHOOD IN FRANCE AND GERMANY 35–49 (1992).
35. *Id.* at 35, 39, 85.
36. *Id.* at 86.

conception, Brubaker contends, is the best way to explain the conflicts over the assimilation and rights of *Maghrebi* immigrants that raged during the 1980s.[37] In this view, the influx of immigrants from non-white, non-Christian countries and those immigrants' expression in the 1980s of their desire to retain their own culture and religion inevitably ran up against the brick wall of the French idea of citizenship.[38]

An increasingly strong chorus of scholars, however, rejects the notion that a single, relatively unchanging ideal of republican citizenship was active with equal strength throughout two hundred years of French history.[39] To be sure, the fact that the type of government that ruled France changed so many times during that period highlights the ebb and flow of competing visions of the French state during the nineteenth and twentieth centuries. Nonetheless, one could argue that the idea of a strong state, directly involved in and responsible for the formation of its citizens' personal identity, remained an important component of Republic, Monarchy, and Empire alike. These opponents of the traditional view that citizenship was a fairly unchanging ideal contend that even the less ambitious version of the continuity hypothesis masks important innovations and shifts in France's conception of itself as a nation.[40] If that conception cannot be taken for granted in the French political scene, then some alternative explanation must be sought to account for the clashes over culture epitomized by the *affaire des voiles*.

Most important for this article's consideration of the structure of contemporary French government is the extent to which France's Republics—especially the current Fifth Republic, which has operated under the same constitution since 1958—have governed according to a consistently "republican" idea of the nation. Gérard Noiriel's *The French Melting Pot* is a much-cited debunking of the notion that France was a culturally homogeneous country with low immigration rates until the second half of the twentieth century.[41] In fact, Noiriel demonstrates the relative neglect that immigration has suffered as an object of historical inquiry and argues that immigrants from European countries such as Portugal, Italy, and Poland, have long formed a notable portion of France's population.[42] In a similar vein, Eugen Weber's *Peasants into Frenchmen* refutes the belief that the populations living within modern France's geographical borders have or have always had a uniform cultural identity. Rather, Weber shows that the central government expended a good deal of energy during the late nineteenth century inculcating French language[43] and culture into residents of some outlying regions.[44]

Adrian Favell criticizes Noiriel for ignoring the genuine novelty of the issues that non-white immigrants from former colonies brought to France, as compared with the difficulties surrounding absorption of white, Christian Europeans.[45] Nonetheless, Favell's own project builds upon Noiriel's contention that immigration is no new phenomenon in French cultural and political life. Favell argues that French policy toward immigrants was

---

37. *Id.* at 138–48.

38. *Id.* at 145–51. *Contra* FAVELL, *supra* note 14, at 173–74 (noting that French responses to immigration have not been constant over time and therefore are not the result solely of an unchanging view of French citizenship).

39. *See, e.g.*, SILVERMAN, *supra* note 31, at 9 (noting that French culture has been "historically variable").

40. GÉRARD NOIRIEL, THE FRENCH MELTING POT: IMMIGRATION, CITIZENSHIP, AND NATIONAL IDENTITY 278 (Géoffroy de Laforcade trans., Univ. of Minn. Press 1996) (1988).

41. Charles Tilly, *Foreward*, *in* NOIRIEL, *supra* note 40, at vii–viii.

42. *Id.* at 150–52.

43. EUGEN WEBER, PEASANTS INTO FRENCHMEN: THE MODERNIZATION OF RURAL FRANCE 1870–1914, at 72–79 (1976).

44. *Id.* at 332–36.

45. FAVELL, *supra* note 14, at 64–65.

not always a matter of national controversy, as it came to be during the 1980s.[46] Even during the wave of North African immigrants during the 1960s, Favell contends, France pursued a policy relatively unconcerned with the degree to which the new arrivals adopted French culture and political ideology.[47] Maxim Silverman and others have further chipped away at the idea that French culture is a static, established entity that new immigrants, who arrive with their own pre-formed identities, must choose to take or leave.[48]

Whatever their differences over the historical trajectory of the ideal of citizenship, scholars generally agree that ever since the 1980s, the ideal of a citizenry that is culturally assimilated and accepts the primacy of public life over private has loomed large over the controversy surrounding the status of North Africans in French society.[49] The prominent role of this conception of the nation in the wake of increasing calls among Muslim North Africans to be treated as a community with particular common interests may be due more to political opportunism than to any other factor,[50] or they may constitute a genuine revival of the centuries-old debate.[51] That debate, if temporarily dormant, has never died.

To assess these competing claims requires a brief look at exactly what ideals the republican legacy is alleged to encompass, beginning with the Revolution of 1789. Though ideas of a strong, homogeneous state had their origins in France well before 1789,[52] the Revolution was seminal in transforming those notions of the strong state by making the people, rather than the absolute monarch, sovereign. Within a few years the Revolution spawned or gave way to—depending on one's perspective[53]—a regime intolerant of those with insufficient allegiance to its increasingly extreme ideals.[54] While advocates of reinstating the Terror are nonexistent in contemporary France (though royalists are not), there do exist proponents of the view that the state should promote cultural uniformity and strict secularism within the public arena.[55] The Revolution remains important to many of

46. *Id.* at 173–74.

47. *Id.* at 48–50.

48. SILVERMAN, *supra* note 31, at 13–17. Historians of colonization by France and other countries have similarly pointed out that the colonized people were not simply passive receivers of the colonial power; rather, the make-up of their pre-existing society and governance affected the unfolding of colonialism. *See, e.g.*, NEIL MACMASTER, COLONIAL MIGRANTS AND RACISM: ALGERIANS IN FRANCE, 1900–62, at 36 (1997).

49. *See* BIRNBAUM, *supra* note 20, at 244 (suggesting that "most French of North African origin accept secularism, the predominance of the common law over ethnic or religious traditions, and integration into the public sphere without assuming that this implies an abandonment of multiple loyalties").

50. *See, e.g.*, *id.* at 249 (stressing that French political parties, influenced by citizenry who passionately support a universalist public sphere, reject the idea of representing multiple ethnic and religious interests); *id.* at 250 (describing the limited success with which the fledgling attempts to organize politically along ethnic lines have met); FAVELL, *supra* note 14, at 152–55 (stipulating that political events led to the triumph of the new Republican consensus).

51. *See, e.g.*, BIRNBAUM, *supra* note 20, at 251 (suggesting that a republican community cannot require citizens to renounce their personal values); FAVELL, *supra* note 14, at 174 (noting that although the *affaire* initially appeared resolved, the tensions it released recur "like a bad dream"); *id.* at 170–71 (discussing the extent to which a debate that originally hinged on making people from all regions of France feel French had shifted to address the acculturation of immigrants).

52. This view of the nation was exemplified by Louis XIV's famous statement, "*L'état, c'est moi*;" *see also* ALEXIS DE TOCQUEVILLE, THE OLD REGIME AND THE FRENCH REVOLUTION 50 (John Bonner trans., 1856) (arguing that the French Revolution continued the trend of centralization already present in the *ancien régime*).

53. For the position that the Terror the reign of revolutionary violence during the rule of the Committee on Public Safety in 1793 and 1794 followed logically from the 1789 Revolution, see FRANÇOIS FURET, INTERPRETING THE FRENCH REVOLUTION (Elborg Forster trans., 1981) (1978). For the opposing argument that the Terror was the product of later, contingent events, see Isser Woloch, *On the Latent Illiberalism of the French Revolution*, 95 AM. HIST. REV. 1452 (1990).

54. BIRNBAUM, *supra* note 20, at 62–63.

55. *See id.* at 223–24 (quoting various church officials as suggesting that the church should promote secularism as a means to encourage a democratic society); *id.* at 204–05 (describing the politics of Jean-Marie Le Pen's far right National Front party).

France's contemporary political battles because partisans so often appeal to it. Though the first republican constitution, that of 1791, has been supplanted, the Declaration of the Rights of Man and of the Citizen of 1789 is still cited formally in legal analyses[56] (as will be explored in Part IV) and informally in political debate.[57]

The short-lived Second Republic (1848–1852), famously lampooned by Karl Marx,[58] brought few lasting changes to France's conception of itself as a nation.[59] The lengthy Third Republic,[60] however, spawned numerous new tenets that became essential elements of the republican ideal. These included mandatory primary education, instituted in 1882,[61] and the separation of church and state in 1905.[62] Education became the single most important point of contact between state and citizen; it was the prime way that French culture and active citizenship were to be conveyed.[63] The *instituteur*, or schoolteacher, was lionized as being on the frontlines of the republican crusade.[64] Clearly this orientation, which retained its power in the Fourth and Fifth Republics, sheds light on the high stakes of the *affaire des voiles*. So, too, does the fierce secularism, or *laïcité*, that became the official line when the separation of church and state was mandated. This secularism demanded that religion remain a wholly private matter, that it not intrude into public debate or public view in any way. Throughout the nineteenth century, the battles between clericalist and anti-clericalist forces—those favoring established religion and those opposing it—were especially fierce because of their origins in the church's status of privilege during the *ancien régime*, in which the religious establishment was inextricably linked to the monarchy and state power.[65] Combatants on both sides of the battle over religion in French political life have continued to be inspired by the church's historical link to the old political order and anti-clericalism's link to Revolutionary thinking. *Laïcité* became a central article of faith for any good Republican.[66] Freedom from the public influence of religion was considered critical to the state that the Republicans were creating—one based on meritocratic hierarchy and rationally ordered bureaucracy.[67] As education of new citizens and bureaucrats was integral to the establishment of that system and to the continuity of a

56. *See, e.g.*, Cons. const., 16 Juillet 1971, *Les grandes décisions du Conseil Constitutionnel*, Sirey, 267, 278–84 (showing the expansion of the *Conseil*'s jurisprudence to include the rights of the Declaration and its reliance on the Declaration as a source of general principles of law); Elissa A. Okoniewski, *Yahoo!, Inc. v. Licra: The French Challenge to Free Expression on the Internet*, 18 AM. U. INT'L L. REV. 295, 303 (2002) (comparing article 11 of the Declaration to the First Amendment rights given to U.S. citizens); Louis Henkin, *A Bill of Rights-and-a-Half*, 32 TEX. INT'L L.J. 483, 483 (1997) (quoting from the Declaration for the proposition that "any society in which the guarantee of rights is not assured, and the separation of powers is not established, has no constitution").

57. *See* Nan T. Ball, Note, *The Reemergence of Enlightenment Ideas in the 1994 French Bioethics Debates*, 50 DUKE L.J. 545, 558 (2000) (exploring the invocation of the Declaration in bioethics controversies and laws).

58. *See infra* note 149 and accompanying text.

59. ROGER PRICE, THE FRENCH SECOND REPUBLIC: A SOCIAL HISTORY 307–21 (1972) (discussing the fractured nature of French society during the Second Republic and the lack of ideological cohesion in response to the 1852 Bonapartist coup).

60. The Third Republic stretched from France's defeat in the Franco-Prussian War of 1871 until the early days of the Second World War in 1940.

61. WEBER, *supra* note 43, at 309.

62. BIRNBAUM, *supra* note 20, at 118.

63. WEBER, *supra* note 43, at 303.

64. *Id.* at 317.

65. *See* Jean Baubérot, *Secularism and French Religious Liberty: A Sociological and Historical View*, 2003 BYU L. REV. 451, 459–60 (stating that the nineteenth-century French anti-clericalist sentiment was directed against the religious political dominion over the country).

66. *Id.* at 460.

67. *Id.*

republican ideology, the schools were a venue in which secularism was particularly emphasized.[68]

Finally, France's relationship with and ultimate loss of its North African colonies during the early- to mid-twentieth century played a role in the high emotions that flared during the *affaire des voiles*. Some French citizens, particularly on the far right, regarded the loss of Algeria and Morocco as a betrayal of France's mission to bring its culture to the rest of the world. Moreover, France's experience as a colonial power left behind at least one policy with lasting consequences for the absorption of immigrants into France proper. Algeria was declared an extension of French soil, so its residents became French citizens.[69] Thus, many of the new arrivals to the "mainland" were in fact not technically foreigners at all.[70] Since Napoleon's time, as will be discussed below, the status of second-generation immigrants—children born on French soil to non-French parents—has been a central issue in debates about citizenship and nationality.[71] By the 1980s, the children of the North Africans who arrived during the wave of immigration following the end of French colonial control of Algeria and Morocco were entering adolescence and young adulthood. Nicknamed "*beurs*," these young residents of France were considered the most difficult to manage from the standpoint of national policy.[72] The primacy of inculcating "Frenchness" through education came to the fore. The students involved in the headscarf cases of 1989 and subsequent years were either second-generation immigrants or had arrived in France at a very young age.[73]

Having identified the periods in France's history most pertinent to an understanding of the *affaire des voiles*, let us now look more closely at those events, especially the language used to construct the idea of the homogeneous French nation. In a seminal work of the French Revolution, *Qu'est-ce que le Tiers État?*, Emmanuel-Joseph Sieyès asked in 1789: "What is a nation? A body of associates living under *common* laws and represented by the same *legislative assembly*."[74] Membership in the nation was contingent on one's acceptance of a particular legal authority. Conversely, this acceptance alone was necessary in order to constitute a nation; ethnic similarity was not a requirement.

The Declaration of the Rights of Man and of the Citizen, proclaimed by the self-constituted National Assembly on August 26, 1789, emphasized that the individual rights to self-preservation and self-expression are primary and any governmental authority must proceed from the "general will" of those individuals and must infringe on their individual freedoms only insofar as such infringement is necessary in order to safeguard the freedoms of others or to ensure public security.[75] The first sentence of the Declaration stated that "ignorance, disregard, or contempt for the rights of man are the sole causes of public

68. *Id.* at 461.

69. Richard Alba & Roxane Silberman, *Decolonization Immigrations and the Social Origins of the Second Generation: The Case of North Africans in France*, 36 INT'L MIGRATION R. 1169, 1174 (2002).

70. Kimberly Hamilton et al., *The Challenge of French Diversity*, MIGRATION INFO. SOURCE, May 2002, *at* http://www.migrationinformation.org/Feature/display.cfm?ID=21 (last visited Jan. 4, 2004).

71. BRUBAKER, *supra* note 34, at 85.

72. Alba & Silberman, *supra* note 69, at 1170–71.

73. Jennifer Joan Lee, *Expulsions over Veil Intensify French Debate on Secularity*, INT'L HERALD TRIB., Oct. 21, 2003, at 19.

74. EMMANUEL-JOSEPH SIÈYES, WHAT IS THE THIRD ESTATE? 58 (S.E. Finer ed., M. Blondel trans., Frederick A. Praeger 1964) (1789); *see also* BRUBAKER, *supra* note 34, at 6–7 (noting that this conception of the nation pre-dated the Revolution by at least one hundred years).

75. DECLARATION OF THE RIGHTS OF MAN AND OF THE CITIZEN art. 6 (Fr. 1789), *available at* http://www.conseil-constitutionnel.fr/textes/d1789.htm (last visited Jan. 4, 2004). For a translation of the Declaration, see DECLARATION OF THE RIGHTS OF MAN AND OF THE CITIZEN (Fr. 1789), *translated in* THE OLD REGIME AND THE FRENCH REVOLUTION (Keith Michael Baker ed., 1987), *reprinted in* THE FRENCH IDEA OF FREEDOM: THE OLD REGIME AND THE DECLARATION OF RIGHTS OF 1789, at 1–3 (Dale Van Kley ed., 1994) [hereinafter THE FRENCH IDEA OF FREEDOM].

misfortunes and the corruption of governments."[76] According to Sieyès, a declaration of rights must be universal and timeless, not responding to any particular set of historically contingent grievances, as he considered the American Declaration of Independence to have done.[77] The Declaration of the Rights of Man and of the Citizen devoted a good deal of attention to equality under the law, stating for example that the law must set down reasonable punishments and that no one should be treated by the state in a way not explicitly prescribed by law.[78] Of the Declaration's seventeen articles, two deal with private opinion and religious conviction:

> Article 10. No one must be disturbed because of his opinions, even in religious matters, provided their expression does not trouble the public order established by law. Article 11. The free expression of thought and opinions is one of the most precious rights of man: thus every citizen may freely speak, write, and print, subject to accountability for abuse of this freedom in the cases determined by law.[79]

The parallel between the "public order" exception in Article 10 and the exceptions set forth by the *Conseil d'État* in its 1989 *affaire des voiles* decision is striking. While the Declaration considered "the rights of man" to form the basis of a legitimate state, the leeway it allowed for intervention by the state based on the public good was so broad that it has often been considered more utopian and communitarian than liberal.[80] The idea that "the law is the expression of the general will"[81] is very suggestive in French political thought and history. Jean-Jacques Rousseau, in 1762's *The Social Contract*, posited the general will as the state's source of legitimacy, but he distinguished between the cumulative will of each individual within society and the general will—what is best overall for the society, not the sum total of what is best for each member of the society.[82] Democratic voting, wrote Rousseau, was usually, but not always, the most effective way to ascertain the society's general will.[83] Thus, the Declaration's appeal to the "general will" entails the subordination of the individual and of groups subdividing the populace to the larger "nation," which the Declaration's third article proclaims sovereign.[84]

Among those who would replace the *ancien régime* with a new form of government, debate raged as to whether both the right to hold particular private religious beliefs and the

76. DECLARATION OF THE RIGHTS OF MAN AND OF THE CITIZEN pmbl. (Fr. 1789).

77. Keith Michael Baker, *The Idea of a Declaration of Rights*, *in* THE FRENCH IDEA OF FREEDOM, *supra* note 75, at 158–59. Another suggestive criticism of the American Declaration launched by shapers of the French Declaration was that the separation of powers turned the state into a clash of arbitrary wills. *Id.* at 164–65. According to Baker, Condorcet and others reasoned that "tyranny would be destroyed . . . [not by separation of powers, but instead] by setting forth the first principles of social organization in a rational exposition of the rights of man." *Id.* at 165.

78. DECLARATION OF THE RIGHTS OF MAN AND OF THE CITIZEN art. 8 (Fr. 1789).

79. *Id.* arts. 10–11.

80. *See* Dale Van Kley, *From the Lessons of French History to Truths for All Times and All People: The Historical Origins of an Anti-Historical Declaration*, *in* THE FRENCH IDEA OF FREEDOM, *supra* note 75, at 72–73.

81. DECLARATION OF THE RIGHTS OF MAN AND OF THE CITIZEN art. 6 (Fr. 1789). For the Stasi Commission's statement that public order was its prime consideration in recommending a headscarf ban, see *infra* note 214.

82. JEAN-JACQUES ROUSSEAU, THE SOCIAL CONTRACT AND OTHER LATER POLITICAL WRITINGS 121–22 (Victor Gourevitch ed., Cambridge Univ. Press 1997) (1762); *see also id.* at 60 (noting that the general will does not find expression when the populace has divided into factions based on certain common interests).

83. *Id.* at 122–25.

84. DECLARATION OF THE RIGHTS OF MAN AND OF THE CITIZEN art. 3 (Fr. 1789).

right to express them in the public sphere should be protected.[85] It was not the individual person qua person, but the citizen—the enfranchised permanent resident and cultural participant—who was the unit of political life. Public participation in national life was paramount. On the other hand, the Revolution's attitude toward residents of geographical France who had been born elsewhere was more open than were certain later conceptions of who was and was not a citizen. Revolutionary France, Brubaker points out, defined itself in opposition to *étrangers*—literally, "foreigners"—but these could be either foreigners in the traditional sense or internal opponents of the new order.[86] Revolutionary leader Jean-Lambert Tallien famously said, "[t]he only foreigners in France are bad citizens."[87] While this quotation cannot be taken to mean that anyone who wanted to be a French citizen would be automatically accepted as such by state authorities, the nascent state's leaders saw the primary threat to their vision for France as coming from those ideologically opposed to their project, regardless of nationality.

A decade and a half after the Declaration of the Rights of Man and of the Citizen, Napoleon's comprehensive Civil Code underscored the prominence of law promulgated by the centralized state. One early and particularly strong disagreement regarding immigration policy arose during the drafting of the Code. On the basis of the military advantages the state might thereby gain, Napoleon argued that any child born on French soil should be accorded French citizenship; this doctrine is known as *jus soli*. Opponents responded that the simple fact of having been born in France would not necessarily give the child the feeling of being French necessary for real citizenship. In the end, the Code stipulated that children born to foreigners on French soil could choose French citizenship when they attained majority.[88]

Napoleon's influence also endured in the nation's educational system; he was instrumental in embedding in France a strong tradition of state schools channelling students into different areas of government service. Although a series of Revolutionary laws from 1791 through 1793 had abolished all universities, academies, and corporations, most of these older institutions survived under new names and with new purposes.[89] In the wake of this abrupt break arose the *École Polytechnique* (1794), which was meant to respond to the government's growing need for engineers and would soon become the flagship of a fleet of professional training schools known as the *grandes écoles*.[90] Individual schools for artillery officers, military engineers, civil engineers, and mining engineers soon sprang up to provide additional training to *École Polytechnique* graduates.[91] This system of channelling France's future civil servants through a set of specialized educational institutions also shaped the development of the justice system—and the *Conseil d'État* in particular—as Part III will discuss.

The *École Normale Supérieure*, founded in 1795, played a supporting educational role through the end of the Second Empire. Intended to train teachers and academics, it did

85. Raymond Birn, *Religious Toleration and Freedom of Expression*, *in* THE FRENCH IDEA OF FREEDOM, *supra* note 75, at 269–70; *see also* Shanti Singham, *Betwixt Cattle and Men: Jews, Blacks, and Women, and the Declaration of the Rights of Man*, *in* THE FRENCH IDEA OF FREEDOM, *supra* note 75, at 117–28 (discussing the actual treatment of a religious minority—in this case Jews—during the early Revolutionary period).

86. BRUBAKER, *supra* note 34, at 46–48.

87. *Id.* at 47.

88. *Id.* at 86–90. In practice, few of those eligible to claim French citizenship actually did so, thereby escaping military service. *Id.* at 91. During the 1990s, France's policy on this issue again came under debate. The Pasqua Laws of 1993 required French-born children of French soldiers to declare their intention to become French citizens, while a 1998 law made such children automatic French citizens on their eighteenth birthdays. Hamilton et al., *supra* note 70.

89. GEORGE WEISZ, THE EMERGENCE OF MODERN UNIVERSITIES IN FRANCE, 1863–1914, at 18–20 (1983).

90. *Id.* at 19.

91. *Id.*

not claim the prestige and power that the technical institutes enjoyed, failing to attract the nobility or upper-middle classes to its ranks.[92] But with the advent of the Third Republic, graduates of the *École Normale Supérieure* entered government service in great numbers. This development was historically significant not only for the evolution of education in France, but also because *normaliens*, as they were called, were so instrumental in shaping the ideology of the Third Republic.[93] They "created," as one historian put it, "the [new regime's] necessary ideological synthesis. They had a recognizable and legitimate identity, a strategic monopoly of power in the field of education, and sufficient breadth of outlook to be creative in new circumstances."[94]

This emphasis on education as the best way to shape future government officials and future citizens alike received a significant boost in 1882 with the passage of a law making primary school mandatory. Education was exalted as the main way that the government would discharge its duty to instill republican fervor in its youngest residents. Jules Ferry, one of the founders of the Third Republic along with Léon Gambetta, was the principal architect of the theory and implementation of the mandatory education law; this policy was at the heart of the Third Republican project.[95] In a letter he wrote in 1883 to France's *instituteurs*, Ferry referred to the recent founding of "*une éducation nationale*."[96] As Gaspard and Khosrokhavar, who quote the letter, point out, this phrase means far more than nationwide education. Rather, it indicated to Ferry an education that would help to *form* the nation by imparting the nation's values to its schoolchildren.[97]

The separation of church and state was another landmark of the Third Republic. Its specific historical timing had much to do with the Dreyfus Affair, as discussed below. In that Affair just before the turn of the century, a Jewish army captain was falsely convicted of spying for Germany. The falsification of evidence and other wrongdoing on the part of the military tribunal that tried him and others involved in the case eventually came to light, and Dreyfus' supporters rode the wave into political power, replacing a center-right government with a center-left government.[98] During the controversy, the church had sided heavily with its old conservative ally, the military, in arguing that Dreyfus' case should not be reviewed. Extricating the church from all involvement in governance (there were even some restrictions on individual Catholics' opportunity to become civil servants) was a way of asserting that the old sources of authority, including the church and the military, had no place in the Republic of meritocracy and individual freedom of belief.[99] Even after its prominent defeat in the political arena, however, Catholicism continued to be an important cultural force in French society.[100]

92. ROBERT J. SMITH, THE ÉCOLE NORMALE SUPÉRIEURE AND THE THIRD REPUBLIC 1–3 (1982).

93. *Id.*

94. *Id.* at 2.

95. GASPARD & KHOSROKHAVAR, *supra* note 15, at 178–79.

96. *Id.* at 178.

97. *Id.* at 177–79. The Stasi Commission contended that the school's mission, which is "essential to the Republic," is best achieved if the school is something of a sanctuary of learning that excludes the raging controversies of society at large. STASI COMMISSION REPORT, *supra* note 6, § 1.2.2., at 12–13; *id.* § 4.2.2.1, at 54.

98. ERIC CAHM, THE DREYFUS AFFAIR IN FRENCH SOCIETY AND POLITICS, at xii–xvi (1996).

99. *Id.*

100. In response to the 2004 headscarf controversy, Guy Coq asserted that the proposed headscarf ban could best be justified with reference to the Catholic Church's historical hostility to Republican ideals and the Republic's resultant distrust of religion in the public sphere. Guy Coq, *Scarves and Symbols*, N.Y. TIMES, Jan. 30, 2004, at A25. In its eagerness to establish that France's position is not one of bigotry, Coq's argument simplistically glosses over the fact that Catholicism was the established religion of France for centuries—a position very different from that which Islam currently holds. Catholicism was therefore a known enemy, in contrast with Islam's unfamiliar and allegedly alien character.

Finally, while the chronology of France's adventures in Algeria and Morocco need not occupy much space here, colonial history continued to be an important cause of strife in the 1980s and 1990s. As historian Neil MacMaster writes, "For many the Algerian presence on French soil was the ultimate insult: the former colonial subjects, perceived as inherently inferior, had not only been the victors but were now colonising the land of the 'civilised' masters."[101] MacMaster states that scholars have attributed France's particularly strong animosity toward North Africans, manifested during the 1980s, to some combination of dislike of cultural difference and bitterness stemming from Algeria's successful War of Independence of 1954–62.[102] MacMaster argues, however, that neither racism against North Africans nor *Maghrebi* immigration to France began with the Algerian War of Independence. On the contrary, Algerians were targets of racism significantly before the War of Independence, and between the World Wars they formed the largest group of colonial workers living in Europe.[103] According to MacMaster, between the World Wars, and then during and after the War of Independence, emigration from Algeria to France continued, mostly because of economic concerns such as a French labor shortage.[104]

If Noiriel and MacMaster are correct that immigration has been a part of French history for far longer than previously assumed—and the numbers are on their side[105]—then the question arises of why North African immigrants aroused such ire from defenders of the alleged Republican ideal during the 1980s. The theory that the animosity stemmed from the mere presence of practitioners of a non-French culture who wished nonetheless to live in France is no longer viable. Although by the 1980s many *Maghrebis* were requesting more public acknowledgement of their distinctive culture than had previous immigrants, most North Africans did not wish to maintain a strict separation between themselves and French culture.[106] As discussed in more detail below, Yasemin Soysal describes attempts by Muslim immigrants to base their claims to *le droit à la difference*[107] on the French ideals of individual liberty.[108] They attempt to show—to themselves, to fellow Muslims, and to others—that Islam and France, far from contradictory, are complementary if not mutually reinforcing. This attempt at synthesis is most prominent among second-generation immigrants who see their own identities as a mixture between the culture of their parents and the culture of their surroundings.[109]

101. MACMASTER, *supra* note 48, at 2. For example, Jean-Marie Le Pen, a leader of the Far Right, claimed that headscarves in the public schools represented "the colonization of France." BIRNBAUM, *supra* note 20, at 227 (quoting *M. Le Pen Dénonce la "Colonisation de la France,"* LE MONDE (Paris), Oct. 28, 1989, *available at* http://www.lemonde.fr (last visited Jan. 23, 2004)).

102. MACMASTER, *supra* note 37, at 1–3.

103. *Id.* The number of Algerians living in France increased tenfold between 1914 and 1930 to 130,000. *Id.* at 3. As MacMaster points out, a large number of these Algerians lived in population centers, like Paris and Lyon, where many members of the native French population would have come into contact with them on a regular basis. *Id.*

104. *Id.* at 20–21.

105. France had the highest rate of foreign population growth of any country in the world in 1930, and it has continued to be one of the countries with the highest proportion of foreign-born residents in the world. NOIRIEL, *supra* note 41, at 5–6.

106. BIRNBAUM, *supra* note 20, at 250–52.

107. This phrase, meaning "the right to difference," was used during this decade as shorthand for the right to embrace a culture other than the dominant one and to receive a certain amount of public acknowledgement and accommodation of that fact. *See generally* Ulla Holm, *The Implication of the Concept of the French State-Nation and 'Patrie' for French Discourses on (Algerian) Immigration* (2003), *at* http://www.ciaonet.org/wps/hou03/hou03.pdf (last visited Feb. 13, 2004).

108. Yasemin Soysal, *Changing Boundaries of Participation in European Public Spheres: Reflections on Citizenship and Civil Society*, *in* EUROPEAN CITIZENSHIP BETWEEN NATIONAL LEGACIES AND POSTNATIONAL PROJECTS 165–66 (Klaus Eder & Bernhard Giesen eds., 2001).

109. *Id.*

This explicit attempt to embrace a personal identity that is both Muslim and French raises the question of to what extent the French ideal of secular republicanism might be resistant to Islam in particular, rather than simply to organized religion in general. Some political commentators and leaders have answered that Muslims present undeniably tougher resistance to assimilation than did previous immigrants. Gaston Defferre, a former socialist interior minister, said in a 1984 interview:

> When Poles, Italians, Spanish, and Portuguese live in France and decide to naturalize, it matters little whether they are Catholics, Protestants, Jews, or atheists . . . But the rules of Islam are not simply religious rules. They are rules of living that concern . . . marriage, divorce, the care of children, the behavior of men, the behavior of women . . . These rules are contrary to all the rules of French law on the custody of children in case of divorce, and they are contrary to [French rules on] the rights of women with respect to their husbands. What is more, in France we don't have the same habits of living.[110]

This, writes Brubaker, is merely a more subtle version of the nationalist claim that Islam and the West are irreconcilably at odds.[111] While only the far right essentialized such differences, he writes, all parties in France had some members during the 1980s who espoused a variant of this view that Islam and France are masters no one could simultaneously serve.[112]

As the dispute over Islam brewed, another citizenship issue dating back to the Napoleonic Code came to the fore. Political pressure to make acquiring French citizenship a conscious personal choice was mounting. The Gaullist *Rassemblement pour la République* (RPR) party, of which Jacques Chirac was a member, called attaining French citizenship "a solemn pact based on mutual recognition and the will to live together."[113] Thus, only a person who could prove substantial participation in French civic life—speaking the French language, civil or military service, lack of criminal record, and so forth—should be allowed to acquire French citizenship.

This recurrence of a centuries-old dispute lends some fuel to the assertion that the debate over national identity and citizenship in the 1980s represented more than anything a continuity with French history since the Revolution. Brubaker has made much of the role of the traditional idea of republican citizenship in that debate. According to Brubaker:

> Revolutionary and Republican definitions of nationhood and citizenship—unitarist, universalist, and secular—reinforced what was already in the ancien régime an essentially political understanding of nationhood. Yet while French nationhood is constituted by political unity, it is centrally expressed in the

110. BRUBAKER, *supra* note 34, at 149 (quoting interview with Gaston Defferre, former Socialist Interior Minister, *in* LES TEMPS MODERNES, 452–453–454 (Mar.–Apr.–May 1984), at 1573–74).

111. *Id.* at 149.

112. *Id.* In the late 1990s, the question was even raised of whether wearing a headscarf should prevent a woman from being granted citizenship. While a lower court held that the woman could be excluded from citizenship because she wore a headscarf, the higher administrative courts twice ruled that the headscarf was not grounds for refusal of naturalization. OPEN SOC'Y INST., *supra* note 22, at 125–26.

113. BRUBAKER, *supra* note 34, at 150 (quoting Club 89, *Une Stratégie du Gouvernement, reprinted in* Catherine Bonnefoy, *Maitriser l'Immigration: Reconnaitre les Realites Qui Preoccupent les Francais—Engager une Politique Coherente et Responsible*, 1088 HOMMES ET MIGRATIONS 51, 60–61 (1986)).

> striving for cultural unity. Political inclusion has entailed cultural assimilation, for regional cultural minorities and immigrants alike.[114]

Since the Revolution, in other words, acceptance of and participation in French *culture* has been the criterion for citizenship in the French *state*. Brubaker contrasts this political vision with an ethnocultural German one that he dubs a "nation in search of a state" in which citizenship presupposes membership—by bloodline—in "an organic cultural, linguistic, or racial community."[115] Such comparisons between the two nations' conceptions date to the early nineteenth century, when first German and then French intellectuals formulated the basic differences, each proclaiming their own nation's conception superior.[116] Brubaker defends the view that France and Germany have represented characteristic and distinct conceptions of what constitutes a nation while admitting that much previous scholarship has caricatured the difference between nineteenth-century French and German conceptions in an attempt to account for Nazism.[117] In the face of that explanation's reductionism, Brubaker

> aim[s] . . . to recover the analytical and explanatory potency of this distinction [between French and German understandings of nationhood], by rescuing it from the status of the routine and complacent formula, ripe for criticism, that it had become. For the distinctive and deeply rooted French and German understandings of nationhood have remained surprisingly robust. Nowhere is this more striking than in the policies and politics of citizenship vis-à-vis immigrants.[118]

The distinction between French and German ideas of national identity are not absolute, but they are pronounced and sustained enough to warrant closer scrutiny. Brubaker is correct to utilize a comparison between different conceptions of nationhood in order to throw into relief the main assumptions that each conception is making. Nonetheless, he overreaches in attempting to fit French and German practices into their categories of nation based on culture and nation based on ethnicity, respectively. He fails to acknowledge, for example, the fact that allegiance to a homogeneous French culture was far from automatic among its geographical residents. Instead, the French state was compelled to strive actively to promote the centralized government and culture that it touted as its gift to lovers of liberty all over the world.[119]

Perhaps then the ideal of a culturally unified citizenry was never instantiated, but striving toward that ideal was certainly a prime feature of republican France. This conception of the strong state dominated the language of politics.[120] Critics from across the political spectrum, rather than arguing for a less homogeneous political culture, instead presented rival views of what the dominant ideology should be.[121] The battle between clericalist and anti-clericalist forces exemplifies this polarization. In the second half of the twentieth century, however, calls for softening the strength of the state and reducing the

114. *Id.* at 1.

115. *Id.*

116. *Id.* at 1–2.

117. *Id.* at 1–17.

118. *Id.* at 3.

119. WEBER, *supra* note 43, at 67–114.

120. BRUBAKER, *supra* note 34, at 13–15.

121. *Id.* at 159–61; *see* BIRNBAUM, *supra* note 20, at 207–79 (discussing in detail the rival political ideologies). Birnbaum points out that "French political parties reject . . . a system of dual representation as unimaginable in a nation-state whose citizenry remains passionately committed to the existence of a universalist public sphere." BIRNBAUM, *supra* note 20, at 249.

separation between public and private life emerged.[122] Henri Lefebvre's collection of essays explicates the new conception of citizenship: "[m]an is a complex being with multiple connections, which are his memberships."[123] These include geographical categories like city, country, and world; and communities like family, occupation, religion, age, social class, and political affiliation.[124] To take one affiliation to the extreme and forget all others is distorting and has historically led to such abuses as nationalism, and "to limit citizenship to one of these memberships—that of politics—is equally aberrant. Getting beyond this reductionism, this closing off [of identity]—this is what we have called 'new citizenship.'"[125]

Yasemin Soysal's work on Muslims within Europe demonstrates the shift in cultural definitions of citizenship and public participation to which Lefevbre's book refers theoretically. Soysal argues that not all Muslim residents of Europe have used their religious heritage to preach fundamentalism or separatism, ideologies that dominate press images of the group. Instead, some European Muslims are carving out a new place for themselves in their societies and in so doing altering the meaning of citizenship.[126] Such Muslims have used elements of their own particular heritage to engage in a "universalistic discourse on rights."[127] This is not equivalent, Soysal emphasizes, to sharing the values of their adopted country; instead, it means that a common conversation, using common terms, takes place among individuals and groups that have differing cultural backgrounds. Soysal relates that in 1994, participants in a pro-headscarf demonstration in Grenoble held placards with such slogans as "Yes to Laicism, and to my Scarf!" and "France is my Liberty, So is my scarf!"[128] To these and other Muslims, Islam and France were far from incompatible. While they asserted their right to engage in a practice that, historically, was highly unusual in France, they did so under the auspices of the universal language of French citizenship. In short, they were saying, it is a *French* thing to do for me to wear my scarf, and it would be a French thing to do for you to support me. To the demonstrators, French republicanism's emphasis on individual liberty, in fact, permitted or even demanded that they be allowed to wear their religious symbols to school.[129] Here is just one example of how participants on all sides of the *affaire* marshalled French history and symbolism to their side. This is not to say that all supporters of the girls' right to wear their scarves accepted one version or another of the Revolutionary political legacy; rather, it compels us to note that substantial disagreement over the republican legacy was a hallmark of the *affaire*.

Commentators such as Adrian Favell and Maxim Silverman have used the *affaire des voiles* to illustrate how participants on all sides of French politics have adopted immigration as a political issue. Silverman states, "the 'problem of immigration' was not a natural result of the changing pattern of migration flows and their effect on French society; it was the result of the way this evolution was perceived and interpreted at the end of the 1960s by a number of influential officials."[130] France experienced a good deal of immigration during

122. *See generally* HENRI LEFEBVRE & LE GROUPE DE NAVARRENX, DU CONTRAT DE CITOYENNETÉ (Henri Lefebvre ed., 1990) (containing essays by Lefebvre and other scholars compiled from 1985 to 1990 and serving as both a reflection on and a product of the political climate that gave birth to *l'affaire des voiles*).

123. Armand Ajzenberg, *Foreward* to DU CONTRAT DE CITOYENNETÉ, *supra* note 122, at 12.

124. *Id.*

125. *Id.*

126. Soysal, *supra* note 108, at 166–67.

127. *Id.* at 169.

128. *Id.* at 166.

129. The *Conseil d'État*'s 1989 decision largely agreed with the demonstrators' conception of French republicanism. *See infra* text accompanying notes 206–214.

130. SILVERMAN, *supra* note 31, at 78.

the 1960s, particularly from Muslim North African colonies and former colonies.[131] That wave of immigration was handled within a framework of *insertion*, a policy which instead of treating immigration as a vast, symbolic issue, consisted of a series of pragmatic steps, such as dealing with immigrants' need for social services on a local level.[132] To Favell, the battles that raged during the 1980s over immigrants' place within French culture were not the inevitable historical result of the republican ideal.[133] Rather, they were the result of a specific chain of events during which various political factions seized on immigration for their own political benefit.[134]

To comprehend the judicial system's role in revising the French model of national identity, we need not retrace this chain of events or assess its causal link to the *affaire des voiles*. We must, however, note Favell's observation that once the specter of French identity was thrown into the mix, it dominated all subsequent debate over the issue.[135] Perhaps this fascination arose because, as Miriam Feldblum points out, the language of group rights and ethnic politics, already so prevalent in the United States and Britain, was all but absent from the French political vocabulary of the time.[136] Even before the advent of increasingly vocal *Maghrebi* activism in the 1980s, Feldblum argues, the state was making quiet, case-by-case compromises of the principle of *laïcité* with Christian and Jewish groups.[137] Starting in the 1980s, according to Feldblum, the growth of immigrant and Muslim advocacy groups began to force the political establishment to take notice of ethnic politics.[138] In turn, those groups moved toward a more conciliatory stance themselves—demanding not a separate cultural and political space, but instead a place within existing French institutions.[139] During the 1988 presidential election, for example, the group France-Plus organized voter registration drives aimed at enticing citizens of North African origin to exercise their right to participate in the French political system.[140]

The *affaire des voiles* and similar controversies involving North African Muslim immigrants to France signal to Feldblum the halting, but necessary, emergence of a political space in France in which group rights are a legitimate topic of public debate. Feldblum's contention that the *Maghrebis*' cultural identity must be taken into account if the North Africans are to be treated fairly recalls philosopher Charles Taylor's point that the rights of individuals are, under some circumstances, not sufficiently protected under the framework of atomistic, individual rights. Instead, the *group* has a right to cultural expression that is part of what each individual deserves but is by its nature a collective right, not an individual one.[141]

---

131. Bill Ong Hing, *Immigration Policies: Messages of Exclusion to African Americans*, 37 HOW. L.J. 237, 252 (1994).

132. FAVELL, *supra* note 14, at 46–47.

133. *Id.* at 46.

134. *See, e.g.*, *id.* at 50 (suggesting that the shift in views of immigration was just one element in the rise of regionalism and decline of purely national identity in France during that period).

135. *Id.* at 174–83.

136. FELDBLUM, *supra* note 30, at 132. This rejection of group rights rests on an understanding of individual rights that requires a complete lack of intermediaries between the individual and the state. *Id.* "The concept of minority group is absent in French legal and legislative texts .... [It is therefore impossible] for policy makers, legislators, and jurists to think about the notion of a minority." *Id.* at 132 (citing Danielle Lochak, *Les Minorités et le Droit Public Français: Du Refus des Différences à la Gestion des Différences*, *in* LES MINORITÉS ET LEURS DROITS DEPUIS 1789, at 111 (Alain Fenet & Gérard Soulier eds., 1989)).

137. *Id.* at 133.

138. *Id.* at 46.

139. *Id.* at 134–35.

140. FELDBLUM, *supra* note 30, at 135.

141. Charles Taylor, *The Politics of Recognition*, *in* MULTICULTURALISM: EXAMINING THE POLITICS OF RECOGNITION 25–73 (Amy Gutmann ed., 1994).

The *Conseil d'État* has stated repeatedly that group or collective rights are incompatible with the French Constitution, which instead bestows rights solely upon individuals.[142] On the other hand, the French government made a gesture toward recognizing Muslims as a group when it established the French Council of the Muslim Faith (CFCM or *Conseil Français du Culte Musulman*) in April 2003.[143] The CFCM serves as a counterpart to the long-established Catholic, Protestant, and Jewish organizations that function as official conduits between the state and their respective communities, so in one sense the new group's creation is unremarkable.[144] In the current political climate, however, the creation of the CFCM is both an acknowledgement of Islam's prominence in France and an invitation for Muslims to speak to the government with one voice. Of course, any assumption that France's Muslims wish to speak with only one voice is quite mistaken.

A person of no less stature than Jean-Marie Cardinal Lustiger, archbishop of Paris, wrote an article in *Le Monde* at the height of the *affaire des voiles* in which he criticized many commentators on the *affaire* for not caring to learn what the headscarf actually meant to its wearers and to other Muslims.[145] Cardinal Lustiger was perhaps a bit condescending in saying that wearing the headscarf may be just a student's adolescent phase, hardly warranting the stiff opposition that it had in fact engendered. Nevertheless, his prescription that attention be paid to the actual religious and social significance of the scarf before any conclusions are drawn is a step towards cultural pluralism.[146]

Calls for treating different immigrant groups differently based on their cultures of origin fly in the face of the Revolutionary ideal articulated in the Declaration of the Rights of Man and of the Citizen. According to that ideal, each individual has full freedom of conscience but in the political sphere must stand alone as one citizen with one vote, owing allegiance only to the state and not to a subset of the populace with whom he believes he has interests in common.[147] France's political commentators are virtually united in wishing to avoid what they consider to be the Anglo-American model of interest group politics, in which many racial and other factions jockey for advantages for their respective groups while abandoning the common culture of the entire nation.

Instead of finding a sustainable mode of "cohabitation"[148] between Muslims and other residents of France,

> mainstream French political intervention, represented by the reports and the legislation that has been passed—together with the increasing public and media hostility towards Islam in France—has simply blown the problem up into one of exaggerated and dangerously unstable proportions.

---

142. OPEN SOC'Y INST., *supra* note 22, at 111, 112.

143. Nicolas Sarkozy, Speech at the Twentieth Annual Meeting of the Union of France's Islamic Organizations (Apr. 19, 2003), *at* http://www.info-france-usa.org/news/statmnts/2003/islam041903.asp (last visited Apr. 13, 2004).

144. OPEN SOC'Y INST., *supra* note 22, at 114.

145. GASPARD & KHOSROKHAVAR, *supra* note 15, at 15–16. In fact, Catholic, Protestant, and Jewish authorities all supported the girls' right to wear the headscarf. BIRNBAUM, *supra* note 20, at 225–26.

146. *Id.* It is possible, as discussed below with regard to the *Conseil d'État*'s decision, that such an investigation may compel one to take a case-by-case approach to individual instances of headscarf-wearing, which may invite uncertainty and create an environment of scrutiny that works against the cause of cross-cultural understanding and acceptance. *See* discussion *infra* Part IV.

147. DECLARATION OF THE RIGHTS OF MAN AND OF THE CITIZEN art. 3 (Fr. 1789).

148. Cohabitation is a French political term that indicates power-sharing within the government. For example, from 1997 to 2002, cohabitation existed in the French government while gaullist Jacques Chirac served as president and socialist Lionel Jospin as prime minister.

> This particular pathology of the French republican philosophy has continued to be an open sore. It is an inflexible blindspot that has, in the end, always put the deontological sacredness of the republican ideals ahead of a rational and pragmatic compromise . . . . Although the *affaire* initially seemed to have been resolved, the tensions it released keep coming back to centre-stage: returning like a bad dream, on each occasion the inflexible official line grating against the sore, adding more fuel to the militants' fire, further aggravating the general tendencies, and embedding majority public opinion deeper in anti-Islamic concerns.
>
> The repetition of the *affaire* a second or third time, of course, has an air of farce rather than tragedy.[149]

In the case of the *affaire des voiles*, ironically, the central government's reluctance to assert its power actually increased the state's purview over individual behavior. In this case, asserting central governmental power would mean denying local authorities broad discretion to act in individual instances. In some ways, Favell's characterization of compromise as the crucial element that the partial resolution of the *affaire des voiles* lacked is exactly wrong. The *Conseil d'État* rendered a decision that forged a compromise with unpredictable consequences. Had it sided strongly either with secular homogeneity or with multicultural and multi-religious heterogeneity, the *Conseil* might have prevented precisely the same issue from erupting again so soon after the original upheaval.[150]

As noted above, the French government historically pursued a distinctly legal strategy in its promotion of a common culture. Laws were devised at the center by the legislative branch of government and radiated outward from Paris.[151] Though France has been deemed a nation more governed by statute than by jurisprudence,[152] the headscarf controversy of 1989 was not the first time that a major, celebrated judicial case had exerted a strong influence on the nation's political and social trajectory, illuminating tensions that previous events had failed to throw into relief. Less than one hundred years before the *affaire des voiles*, a military tribunal's framing of a Jewish officer accused of spying for Germany provoked such a divisive national argument that it was the defining political issue for two full years.[153] Commentators on the *affaire des voiles* frequently remarked on the relevance of the Dreyfus Affair to that more recent controversy, calling attention to the questions of truth and justice and of the role of the outsider in French political life that both

149. FAVELL, *supra* note 14, at 174. This pronouncement, originally published in 1998, has all the more resonance in light of the legislative developments of 2004. This discussion of tragedy and farce is an allusion to Karl Marx's critique of the French Revolution of 1848. *See* Karl Marx, *The Eighteenth Brumaire of Louis Bonaparte*, *in* LATER POLITICAL WRITINGS 31 (Cambridge Univ. Press 1996) (1852).

150. The passage of a law definitively outlawing the headscarf in public schools would presumably eliminate this uncertainty. However, commentators have already pointed out that the distinction between ostentatious and discreet religious symbols will itself prove ambiguous. Jamin Raskin, *Chirac Urges Ban on Head Scarves in Schools*, WASH. POST, Dec. 18, 2003, *at* http://discuss.washingtonpost.com/wp-srv/zforum/03/sp_world_raskin121803.htm (last visited Jan. 26, 2004).

151. R.C. VAN CAENEGEM, JUDGES, LEGISLATORS AND PROFESSORS: CHAPTERS IN EUROPEAN LEGAL HISTORY 152 (1987).

152. *See generally id.* at 89–94 (discussing the historical aversion of French statutory law to jurisprudence). The 2004 headscarf legislation can be seen as a return to this traditional emphasis on statutory solutions.

153. *See* CAHM, *supra* note 98, at 86–109 (discussing the national reaction to the Dreyfus verdict). Those two years were 1898 and 1899, though the original verdict against Captain Alfred Dreyfus was handed down in late 1894. *Id.* at 195–98. While no allegations of government corruption featured in the *affaire des voiles*, as they had in the *affaire Dreyfus*, one of the central issues in both controversies was a basic disagreement over the appropriate role of government authority.

affaires raised.[154] In a somewhat dimmer view of the strong connection between the Dreyfus Affair and Headscarf Affair, Birnbaum has written, "[j]ust as the Dreyfus Affair had done a century earlier, the *affaire des foulards* unexpectedly dramatized the question of French identity while blurring exactly what was at issue."[155]

The two *affaires* were linked in at least two concrete historical ways, as well. One of the first three national advocacy groups to speak out on the *affaire des voiles* was the *Ligue des Droits de l'Homme* (League of the Rights of Man), a group whose founding during the Dreyfus Affair was intended precisely as a means to link that particular miscarriage of justice to the cause of individual rights under all circumstances.[156] In addition, Léon Blum, prime minister of France during the 1930s, first entered political action in order to agitate for Dreyfus' exoneration.[157] Blum was a member of the *Conseil d'Etat* from 1895 to 1919.[158] By the time he resigned the *Conseil* to assume a seat in parliament, Blum "had written into French administrative jurisprudence a series of important and enduring judgments and recommendations, many of them expanding and confirming the role of the *Conseil d'Etat* as a rampart against arbitrary state action."[159]

The role of the central government was notably different in the two *affaires*. During the Dreyfus Affair, the leaders of the Third Republic—by then well enough into their tenure at the top to have become averse to any destabilizing controversies—were extremely reluctant to take up Dreyfus' cause, siding instead with the military establishment. As Birnbaum has witheringly put it:

> It was not until the Republic found itself endangered by the mobilization of nationalist and populist leagues at the very end of the nineteenth century that its leaders finally pulled themselves together, took up the fight, heard the universalist message of the intellectuals, and—almost against their will—approved review proceedings in the trial of Captain Dreyfus . . . . Apart from a few dignitaries . . . , the apparatus of the republican state as a whole scarcely budged.[160]

In contrast, it was a minister of the government, Jospin, who brought the issue behind the *affaire des voiles* before the *Conseil d'État*, forcing a short-term conclusion.[161] And, of course, the role of the judiciary in the Dreyfus Affair contrasts with its role in the *affaire des voiles*. Corrupt court proceedings precipitated the former controversy, while a fairly

154. *See* GASPARD & KHOSROKHAVAR, *supra* note 15, at 11, 24; *see also* Pierre-André Taguieff, *La Lutte Contre Le Racisme, Par-delà Illusions et Désillusions, Introduction* to 1 FACE AU RACISME 43 (Pierre-André Taguieff ed., 1991). Taguieff contends that the contemporary imperative for intellectuals to fight against racism is the legacy of Émile Zola, Charles Péguy, and Bernard Lazare—all of whom were prominent intellectuals who took up Dreyfus' cause, though Taguieff does not even feel the need to identify them as such. *See id.*

155. BIRNBAUM, *supra* note 20, at 224.

156. GASPARD & KHOSROKHAVAR, *supra* note 15, at 14. The other two political groups to weigh in on the *affaire* during its earliest days were the *Mouvement contre le Racisme et pour l'Amitié entre les Peuples* (MRAP) (a group close to the Communist Party) and *SOS-Racisme*, a youth movement with ties to socialism born in 1984 in response to the rise of the extreme right. *Id.*

157. Encyclopedia.com, *Blum, Léon*, *at* http://www.encyclopedia.com/html/b/blum-l1eo.asp (last visited Jan. 28, 2004).

158. Le Conseil d'État, *Les Grandes Figures: Léon Blum (1872–1950)*, *at* http://www.conseil-etat.fr/ce/histoi/index_hp_gf09.shtml (last visited Jan. 28, 2004).

159. TONY JUDT, THE BURDEN OF RESPONSIBILITY: BLUM, CAMUS, ARON, AND THE FRENCH TWENTIETH CENTURY 31 (1998) (emphasis added).

160. BIRNBAUM, *supra* note 20, at 126.

161. GASPARD & KHOSROKHAVAR, *supra* note 15, at 21–22.

deliberated but ambiguous decision from the country's highest administrative court provided temporary resolution to the latter.

If a comparably controversial judicial matter had not occurred for nearly a century prior to the *affaire des voiles*, then was the role of the judiciary in its resolution simply incidental? Are these two affairs linked in the literature only because both are aberrations in French history rather than exemplars of any broader pattern? Both controversies were more intense because of the drama of a court case that must be decided in a short period of time, in contrast to the deliberation and revision that legislation requires. But beyond the importance of the judiciary in giving both controversies some of their emotional intensity lies the more important fact that both revealed something about the structure of the state that responded to them. In the case of the Dreyfus Affair, the use of the unaccountable military tribunal came under fire; eventually, leaders of the pro-Dreyfus camp gained control of the government and enacted the separation of church and state during the first decade of the twentieth century.[162] To assess the state's resilience in dealing with the challenge that the *affaire des voiles* represented requires us to examine the particular history and governmental role of the *Conseil d'État*, the quasi-court that adjudicated the three Muslim girls' claim. It is to this exploration that the following Part turns.

III. THE *CONSEIL D'ÉTAT* AND THE FRENCH LEGAL SYSTEM

The issue of whether the Muslim girls could wear their scarves in the classroom came before the *Conseil d'État* because Lionel Jospin, the education minister, asked the court to render a judgment. The *Conseil d'État* is one of three high courts in France, the other two being the *Cour de Cassation*, the final venue for appeals of cases involving two private parties, and the *Conseil Constitutionnel*, the tribunal that decides the constitutionality of laws under consideration by the parliament. Together, these three courts serve the roles that in the United States are performed by the Supreme Court, as well as some additional functions. The division of duties between the *Conseil Constitutionnel* and the *Conseil d'État* is of particular import for understanding the French judicial system in comparative context. The *Conseil d'État* stands at the top of a hierarchy of administrative courts that will hear cases brought by private citizens. In contrast, the *Conseil Constitutionnel* considers only questions put to it by a government official. While a bill is under debate or before a law has gone into effect, various members of the executive and legislative branches of government may refer the law to the *Conseil Constitutionnel* to rule on its compatibility with the constitution.[163] After a law has gone into effect, the *Conseil Constitutionnel* cannot pronounce on its constitutionality.[164] As explored below, the *Conseil d'État* has a history of more than two centuries, while the *Conseil Constitutionnel* dates only to the establishment of the Fifth Republic in 1958. Today, however, the latter body enjoys at least coequal status with the former in determining matters of policy.[165] In its advisory function, the *Conseil d'État* is sometimes influenced by its expectation of how

162. CAHM, *supra* note 98, at xiii.

163. Alec Stone Sweet, *Constitutional Dialogues: Protecting Human Rights in France, Germany, Italy and Spain*, *in* CONSTITUTIONAL DIALOGUES IN COMPARATIVE PERSPECTIVE 11 (Sally J. Kenney et al. eds., 1999). The government officials with the authority to refer a law to the *Conseil Constitutionnel* include the president of the Republic, the president of the Assembly, the president of the Senate, and, since 1974, any sixty assembly deputies or any sixty senators. *Id.* at 12. For a comparison of these specific provisions for constitutional review with the policies of other European countries, see *id.* at 11–14.

164. L. NEVILLE BROWN & JOHN S. BELL, FRENCH ADMINISTRATIVE LAW 21 (5th ed. 1998). In 1989, President François Mitterand proposed that individual litigants be able to challenge a law before the *Conseil Constitutionnel* if the law allegedly violates the individual's fundamental rights. ANDREW WEST ET AL., THE FRENCH LEGAL SYSTEM 161 (1998). The Senate rejected this proposal the following year. *Id.*

165. BROWN & BELL, *supra* note 164, at 22–23, 73.

the *Conseil Constitutionnel* would view a particular provision. Thus, the latter tribunal exerts indirect influence on the legislative drafting process.[166]

Sometimes the *Conseil d'État*'s ruling on a complaint against the state amounts to a pronouncement on national principles, as in the case of the *affaire des voiles*. Thus, though its function is clearly distinguished from that of the *Conseil Constitutionnel*, the *Conseil d'État* occupies a high enough position in the structure of the French government that questions involving the founding principles of the Republic could hardly help but come across its desk on occasion. As the 2004 headscarf legislation demonstrates, administrative *Conseil d'État* decisions can be overruled by an ordinary statute.[167] In contrast, a constitutional ruling by the *Conseil Constitutionnel* may be overcome only by amending the constitution. The very idea that constitutional law trumps parliamentary law is relatively new in France; the *Conseil Constitutionnel* has been much more active since 1974, when members of parliament gained the right to refer matters to the *Conseil*.[168] As Part IV will discuss in greater detail, references to the Constitution of the Fifth Republic and to 1789's Declaration of the Rights of Man and of the Citizen figure prominently in the text of the decisions concerning the wearing of the headscarf in public schools. The *Conseil d'État* invokes such constitutional texts side by side with recent statute, citing both types of evidence as bases for interpreting the responsibilities of the administrative body in question. While the topics the *Conseil* considers are sometimes of a dry and technical nature, the *affaire des voiles* is a prime example of a broadly accessible and hotly contested issue decided by this arm of the French legal apparatus.

The *Conseil d'État* is charged with two related, but largely distinct, duties. Along with its role as the final authority on complaints against the state, the *Conseil* has a separate, explicitly consultative function that it has retained since its founding by Napoleon, an event that will be discussed below. In most instances, for example, bills proposed before the legislature and decrees promulgated by the executive branch must be submitted to the *Conseil* so that it can recommend changes. Under some circumstances, the *Conseil*'s suggestions are considered binding on the government,[169] while in other situations they are not.[170] Most important for our discussion is the provision that the government may call on the *Conseil d'État* to advise it on a matter of public administration. It was this provision that Jospin exercised in November 1989.

In its judicial function, the *Conseil d'État*'s word is always considered definitive, not merely one opinion that the government must take into consideration. Though it is itself a branch of the administration, the *Conseil* is more than simply a learned advisor when it is asked to resolve a dispute over the actions of a state authority. Nevertheless, as is true of all of France's judicial system, the *Conseil d'État*'s caselaw is not considered a source of law, since any such judicial authority would usurp the legislature's exclusive right to make law,[171] though caselaw is of "persuasive value."[172] An account of the *Conseil*'s establishment and its evolving governmental role over the two centuries of its existence will help us to understand the niche it currently occupies. Napoleon created the *Conseil d'État* in 1799 to ensure that the strongly centralized state that he was creating would be

166. JOHN BELL, FRENCH CONSTITUTIONAL LAW 53 (1995).

167. *See* BROWN & BELL, *supra* note 164, at 64 (explaining that "parliament must retain complete freedom to adopt whatever text it pleases").

168. BELL, *supra* note 166, at 29–30.

169. BROWN & BELL, *supra* note 164, at 65.

170. *Id.* at 64. The *Conseil* has various additional advisory duties, as well. *See id.* at 64–67.

171. WEST ET AL., *supra* note 164, at 54.

172. WEST ET AL., *supra* note 164, at 57; *see also* CHRISTIAN DADOMO & SUSAN FARRAN, THE FRENCH LEGAL SYSTEM 41 (1996).

judged by a separate judiciary rather than be subject to the courts that judged other matters.[173] Just as remarkable as the *Conseil*'s continuity through several changes in regime is its retention of a reputation for impartiality. In Napoleon's time as now, the *Conseil* was considered unbiased and above politics and therefore respected. It may seem odd that a tribunal that considers only cases involving the state continues to be considered the legitimate judge of state actions even under a Republic, which assumes that sovereignty lies with the people. In fact, the *Conseil* continues to enjoy respect precisely because Napoleon's view that the state should not be judged by the same body as adjudicates private matters continues to prevail. Within the Republican context, this view takes the form of the argument that the elected government represents all the people and therefore should be treated with deference, especially by the unelected judicial branch of government. The elected representatives of the people should not be overruled lightly. Though the *Conseil d'État*'s members are hardly elected, they are some of the most elite members of the vast French bureaucracy.[174] As discussed below, they are more trusted as judges of governmental actions because of their participation in the grand tradition of the civil service. In fact, the *Conseil d'État*'s decisions are all officially rendered "in the name of the French people." Paradoxically, the *Conseil* is considered a democratically-responsible body precisely because of its elite composition.[175]

As legal scholars Neville Brown and John Bell point out, France's system of administrative law (*droit administratif*), of which the *Conseil d'État* is the apex, is not rigidly codified, despite its origins in the reign of Napoleon, the codifier extraordinaire. Indeed, Brown and Bell suggest this flexibility has allowed administrative law to be an integral component of government, a role it could not play were its operations more perfunctory and were questions of administrative law clearly subordinate to purely political or constitutional matters.[176] "The secret strength of the Conseil d'État . . . is to be found in the history of this unique French institution, in the methods adopted for the recruitment of its personnel and also in its career structure generally."[177] One must understand the *Conseil*'s history and structure, Brown and Bell argue, in order to understand its present-day role in the French government. To comprehend the *Conseil*'s role in the *affaire des voiles*, then, we must combine these historical and structural components of the court's identity with France's broader history of wrestling with the issues of national identity and citizenship discussed in Part II. There is no direct chronological correspondence between the role of the *Conseil d'État* and the particular idea of French national identity that held sway at a particular historical moment. Nonetheless, the present Part will argue that examining the *Conseil* illuminates the division between France's public and private spheres in a way directly relevant to the debate during the 1980s and 1990s over national identity exemplified by the *affaire des voiles*.

Under Napoleon, the *Conseil*'s members mainly drafted new laws and regulations and served as advisors to the executive branch on administrative matters. Although, in practice, the government almost always followed the *Conseil d'État*'s opinion during the latter's first several decades of existence, the *Conseil* received formal power to decide matters pending against the administration only in 1872.[178] This change in status at the advent of the Third Republic was symbolic of the rule of law that the republican form of government was

173. BROWN & BELL, *supra* note 164, at 46. Like the institutions of higher education mentioned in Part II of this article and indeed like the idea of a strongly centralized state, the *Conseil d'État* has roots in pre-revolutionary political arrangements. *Id.*

174. *Id.* at 82–83.

175. *See id.* at 78–88.

176. *Id.* at 2–3.

177. *Id.* at 7.

178. BROWN & BELL, *supra* note 164, at 47.

supposed to bring; the governmental bureaucracy was no longer even theoretically permitted to disregard the *Conseil d'État*'s pronouncement. Seventeen years later, the *Conseil d'État* declared that private citizens no longer had to go through a governmental administrator in order to bring a claim before the *Conseil*. Citizens were empowered to bring their own complaints against the administration before the court rather than first having to find an ally within the government.[179] In practice, though, the lower administrative courts were increasingly the default venue for hearing most such grievances, while the *Conseil* was reserved for final appeals.[180] The *Conseil* has undergone relatively little reform partially because those aiming to reform the French governmental system to make it more responsive to citizen concerns have typically focused their energies on amending the bureaucracy's decision-making process, not pinning their hopes on a subsequent correction of bureaucratic action by the *Conseil*.[181]

The *Conseil d'État* is one of four *grands corps d'État*—the most elite branches of the French civil service. The other three are the National Audit Office (*Cour des Comptes*), the Inspectorate of Finance (*Inspection Générale des Finances*), and the Foreign Service (*Quai d'Orsay*).[182] Brown and Bell describe the *Conseil d'État* as being "composed of the cream of the French civil service," possessing "something of the atmosphere of an exclusive club" as its three hundred members make their home in an opulent building in Paris' first arrondissement.[183] Most entering members of the *Conseil d'État* have just spent two years at the *École Nationale d'Administration* (ENA)—in English, the National School of Administration—having passed a rigorous examination in order to gain entrance there. ENA entrants have usually just finished their undergraduate degrees, though only a minority have law degrees; a separate examination provides current civil servants with the opportunity to compete for ENA slots. At the end of their tenure at the ENA, graduates are ranked according to their final examination marks and overall performance, and the *Conseil d'État*, *Cour des Comptes*, and *Inspection Générale des Finances* attract the highest scorers.[184] Roughly one quarter of the *Conseil*'s membership is composed of outstanding public servants from other areas of the administration who are specially recruited. Both those who begin at the *Conseil* and those who enter it with work experience almost always remain at the *Conseil* for the rest of their careers, though they will usually spend some amount of time on secondment to another administrative office. Promotions—except to the very top positions within the *Conseil*—are based on seniority, a provision intended to safeguard *Conseil* members' political independence.[185]

Although the lower administrative courts—the regional *Tribunaux Administratifs* and the *Cours Administratives d'Appel*—have attempted to emulate the *Conseil*'s system of recruitment, they must resort to casting a wider net to keep up with their increasingly heavy workload.[186] Those lower courts do not generally serve as feeder institutions for the *Conseil*'s personnel.[187] Thus, though their status was enhanced by reform measures in 1953, they are different in kind, not merely in degree, from the *Conseil d'État*.[188] The

179. *Id.* at 47–48.

180. *Id.* at 47–48.

181. *Id.* at 61. Historically, Brown and Bell suggest, the shift of the caseload to the lower administrative courts had much to do with the overload of cases in the early 1950s concerning members of the administration who had allegedly collaborated with the Nazis during the recent World War and occupation. *Id.* at 51–52.

182. BIRNBAUM, *supra* note 20, at 168.

183. BROWN & BELL, *supra* note 164, at 62–63.

184. *Id.* at 82–83.

185. *Id.* at 82–85.

186. *Id.* at 83.

187. *Id.* at 86.

188. *Id.*

Conseil is a self-contained institution that generally promotes from within, except for the minority of its members who enter it mid-career.[189] Judging from its composition, then, the *Conseil d'État*'s ties—political and intellectual—are more to the central French bureaucracy in general than to the administrative court system in particular.

The *Conseil*'s three hundred members are, at any given time, roughly equally divided among three groups: those who have been lent out to another government department or to a private company; those who perform the *Conseil*'s advisory functions; and those who work for its judicial section, the *Section du Contentieux*. The advisory branch is divided into sections devoted to particular government functions. The *Section du Contentieux* is divided into ten subsections, each of which includes members from several different levels in the *Conseil* hierarchy. Since 1980, each of these subsections has had the authority to make pronouncements on behalf of the entire *Conseil*, but most decisions are made by two or more subsections.[190] When members of the *Conseil* hear a judicial matter, a *commissaire du gouvernement* is appointed from within their ranks. He or she is charged with acquiring an independent and impartial understanding of the facts of the case and the applicable laws and regulations. The *commissaire du gouvernement* then presents before the subsection or sections, "following his conscience," as the *Conseil d'État*'s official website puts it, as to what he believes the *Conseil* should rule.[191] He then does not take part in the deliberation over the *Conseil*'s eventual ruling.[192] In accordance with their public nature, the *Conseil*'s decisions are announced in public, though this procedure has become a formality that occurs after a decision has been given to the parties involved and to anyone else who requests it.[193] What has remained constant about the *Conseil*'s procedure for announcing its decisions, the feature that presents the single most striking contrast to the American system, is that there is never a dissenting opinion disseminated. As Brown and Bell write, "such would be quite alien to the whole spirit of the French court as a collegiate body."[194] Further, none of the content of the deliberations that led to a decision can ever be released.[195] The *commissaire du gouvernement* is the only member of the *Conseil* who states his or her individual opinion publicly.

In its advisory function, one of the *Conseil*'s roles is to participate in drafting legislation and formulating administrative policy, while in its judicial function, it passes judgment on the fairness and efficacy of laws that concern the behavior of the state and the state's various arms. This could theoretically lead to a conflict of interest, or an appearance of a conflict, since the *Conseil* would be evaluating laws and regulations that it had a hand in constructing. In practice, the sections that adjudicate judicial matters remain segregated from the sections that perform the *Conseil*'s purely advisory role, so the problem of an administrative body judging its own handiwork is considered moot. Moreover, the *Section du Contentieux* has a strong historical record of holding the administrative sections of the *Conseil* to high standards.[196] Pursuing the question of whether or not this is a fully satisfactory answer, however, points directly at the issue at hand in this article—how well the state judicial apparatus is equipped to deal with challenges to the traditional French identity such as that presented by the *affaire des voiles*.

---

189. BROWN & BELL, *supra* note 164, at 82–85.

190. *Id.* at 75–76.

191. Le Conseil d'État, *Commissaire du Gouvernement*, *at* http://www.conseil-etat.fr/ce/outils/index_ou02_c.shtml (last visited Feb. 13, 2004).

192. *Id.*

193. BROWN & BELL, *supra* note 164, at 112–13.

194. *Id.* at 113.

195. *Id.* at 112–13.

196. *Id.* at 79–80.

On one hand, given the intricate nature of the French bureaucracy—and the primacy of bureaucracy within French governance as a whole—the *Conseil d'État*'s being a part of the civil service adds to its legitimacy in the eyes of those it judges, the administrators. As Brown and Bell put it:

> The Conseil d'Etat commands general respect of the administrator in action because he knows his judges are fully aware of the special problems besetting public administration. When called to account by the Conseil d'Etat . . . he has to acknowledge that his judges are not strangers to the administrative process; they are not amateurs throwing legalistic spanners into the administrative works, which is how British ministers have sometimes tended to regard their High Court judges. On the contrary, the French official is well aware that his judges are peculiarly expert in the field of administration.[197]

But this immersion in the administrative world by the members of the *Conseil d'État*'s judicial wing is both asset and potential liability. These *Conseil* members understand the challenges of administration and are therefore better equipped to judge what is acceptable interpretation and execution of the law and what is not. On the other hand, being situated squarely within the administration, the *Conseil* cannot gain the illuminating perspective that an outsider might bring to the task. The *Conseil*, therefore, may have difficulty weighing the challenges facing bureaucrats against the legal, political, and social effects of a given decision. Put another way, the *Conseil*'s place in the bureaucracy prevents it from functioning as part of a system based upon the separation of powers, as the Supreme Court does in the United States.

Another salient fact is that the *Conseil d'État*'s judicial branch has very little power of enforcement against an administrative section that it has deemed in the wrong. In practice, because its pronouncements are respected and obeyed, the *Conseil* rarely has any need for such power.[198] Again, this fact may tend either to bolster the *Conseil*'s efficacy within the French government or to diminish it. One may argue in favor of the current arrangement that if the *Conseil d'État*'s composition and its place within the French government mean that it does not need any enforcement powers, then that is evidence that its positioning is appropriate. Its impartiality is sufficiently respected that even those against whom it rules have agreed to be bound by its decisions. On the other hand, the *Conseil*'s lack of enforcement power renders it dependent on the rest of the bureaucracy's continuing perception of its impartiality. As it happens, the 1992 case concerning the headscarf involved an instance in which a school had acted blatantly against the *Conseil*'s 1989 decision.[199] In this case, the *Conseil* ruled against the school, which then obeyed its decision, but instances like this are troubling. If the *Conseil* is respected only because it is seen to conform to the same rules of the game as those it judges, then it would seem to be confined to a very narrow sort of purview over the administration. Evaluating whether existing protocol was followed and evaluating how well existing protocol answers to the legal, social, and political questions to which it must answer are two very different matters. To be an effective safeguard, it seems that an institution that judges the actions of the state

197. *Id.* at 81.
198. *Id.* at 113–14. Of course, this lack of enforcement power is a common condition among judicial bodies.
199. Conseil d'État, 2 Novembre 1992, *Recueil des Décisions du Conseil d'État*, Lebon, 389, 389.

must perform both the former and the latter function.[200] Does the *Conseil d'État*'s niche in the French government help or hinder it in reaching this goal?

To make this issue more concrete, let us turn to the *affaire des voiles* itself. In that instance, the presence of a court that hears only matters involving the state, not those between two private parties, provided a forum for resolution that was respected by the authorities whose actions might be curtailed by the court. The controversy was so divisive that a body that was perceived as political may well have had difficulty commanding the consent of the governmental officials involved. In this, the *Conseil d'État*'s presence was fortuitous.[201] On the other hand, the compromise ruling that emerged in November 1989 provided too much room for subsequent confusion and divergent implementation by different school principals. In examining the text of this and later, related decisions, Part IV will seek to uncover the factors that entered into the *Conseil*'s decision to frame this compromise as it did. It is possible that the *Conseil* specified exceptions that were too open-ended because it was too insulated from the raging political debates about Islam, integration, and secularism in the schools—failing to take account of the need for a strong principled statement that would prevent the matter from snowballing. The converse, too, is possible: that the *Conseil* was perhaps not insulated enough, understanding all too plainly the pressure facing the principals and therefore wishing to let them retain a good deal of autonomy even as it stated that wearing a veil in school did not contravene the principle of secularism. If the latter were the case, then the *Conseil*'s significant siding with the girls would remain to be explained. If the former, then the question would arise as to whether a more definitive statement by the *Conseil* would have fairly settled the matter. Ideally, a tribunal in the *Conseil*'s position would be just insulated enough from politics to deliver a ruling taking account of the current political climate without becoming beholden to it.

Of chief importance was the *Conseil*'s interpretation of *laïcité* as protecting religious expression in the classroom so long as no proselytism or provocation was intended. Many combatants on both sides of the melee over the headscarf's place in the classroom claimed that *laïcité* clashed with religious expression in the public sphere. The disagreement was over which value was more important. The *Conseil* chose not to take sides in that debate. Instead, its innovation was to state that there was no conflict, that in fact the principle of *laïcité* itself mandated that freedom of religious expression—and not just freedom of inward religious belief, as the commonly held view of *laïcité* would have it—be respected except when it clashed with another significant educational interest. This is the crux of the compromise that the *Conseil* carved out as it attempted to adapt the doctrine of secularism to the demands of adherents of a non-majority religion. As one commentator has noted, "[i]n reading the [*Conseil d'État*'s] opinion, one notices that the notion of *laïcité* evolves and must adapt itself to the evolution of society."[202] In light of the legislative and executive intervention into this issue in 2004, it may now be said that the *Conseil d'État* has lost this ideological battle, at least for the time being. Its proposed redefinition proved to be too radical a rethinking of the *laïcité* that is so fundamental to the French Republic.[203]

---

200. The legislature, which is the governmental body charged with rendering laws that address social and political questions, bears some responsibility for directing the actions of the government bureaucracy, but it rarely exercises its legislative authority in response to a particular interaction between the state and a private party.

201. As already noted, even under these circumstances, at least one school implemented rules in direct violation of the *Conseil*'s original decision. Conseil d'État, 2 Novembre 1992, Lebon at 390.

202. Nathalie Deffains, *Le Principe de Laïcité de l'Enseignement Public à l'Épreuve du Foulard Islamique*, 34 REVUE TRIMESTRIELLE DES DROITS DE L'HOMME 203, 213 (1998) ("A la lecture de l'avis, on s'aperçoit que la notion de laïcité est évolutive et doit s'adapter à l'évolution de la société.") (citing JEAN BAUBÉROT, VERS UN NOUVEAU PACTE LAÏQUE? 191 (1990)).

203. *See* STASI COMMISSION REPORT, *supra* note 6, at 7 (stating that *laïcité* forms part of the very foundation of the Republic).

The *Conseil*'s importance in the *affaire des voiles* and the larger controversy of which the *affaire* was emblematic stemmed from the tribunal's central role in shaping the terms of the debate in both the legal and the political arenas. For years following 1989, the *Conseil*'s was the single most important voice in deciding which precedents, laws, and principles were paramount in adjudicating this complex and delicate matter. The Jospin and Bayrou circulars made the *Conseil*'s decision more concrete and aided principals in interpreting the ruling. Even as the Bayrou circular added the term "discreet" to the discussion of headscarf standards, the circular was more a restating and refocusing of the *Conseil*'s 1989 decision than it was a radical shift in policy. As the highest legal institution with jurisdiction over the actions of the French state, the *Conseil d'État* wielded obvious power—and, at least as importantly, credibility—in shaping the government's position toward Muslim apparel in the public schools.

Two weeks after the *Conseil* handed down its opinion, Jospin released a circular—a binding directive to all those under the Ministry of Education's authority—that provided guidance to all members of the French educational system on how to implement the *Conseil*'s directive.[204] While the *Conseil d'État*'s ruling was binding only on Jospin himself, his circular became law for all educational administrators, bureaucrats, and teachers. In his circular, Jospin reassured the many members of the educational system who had been shaken by the *Conseil*'s interpretation of the principle of *laïcité*. He did this partially by making some of the *Conseil d'État*'s directives more concrete, but also by emphasizing the continuity between the *Conseil*'s opinion and previously dominant views of the role of private religion in the school system. In addition, as Part IV will address, Jospin's circular applied the logic of the *Conseil*'s decision to at least two issues that had not been directly implicated in the case of the girls from Creil.

We will now turn to the text of the decision of November 27, 1989; the circular of December 12, 1989; responses to those pronouncements from members of the French legal community; and the content and texts of subsequent decisions on the same issue. This examination will uncover how the *Conseil* justified its decision and how that justification served to enhance or detract from the decision's effectiveness. The exceptions laid out in the *Conseil*'s November 1989 opinion were no hollow provision intended to placate hard-line secularists and their allies. In fact, as it happened, in a number of later cases the *Conseil* ruled that the girls in question *had* engaged in specific behavior that justified their being banned from wearing their scarves. This was a compromise with teeth, one might say. No doubt, the *Conseil d'État* was called upon in 1989 to craft a delicate balance between competing claims. The question remains of whether the room it left for maneuvering was the necessary outcome of reconciling two legitimate but opposing principles, or whether subsequent cases could have been avoided with a firmer application of the legal precedent and of the *Conseil*'s own powers of purview over the administrators of the French state.

IV. THE *CONSEIL D'ÉTAT* RULES ON THE HEADSCARF CASE[205]

At the outset of its 1989 decision, the *Conseil d'État* lays out three questions: first, is wearing religious symbols in school compatible with the principle of *laïcité*; second, if so, under what conditions is regulation of such wearing permissible; and third, could the refusal to follow such regulations result in the expulsion of the offending student from the

204. Jospin, *supra* note 24, at 15577.

205. This Part relies on the author's translation of the *Conseil*'s decision.

school?[206] Following this declaration of the questions that the decision must address is a list of no fewer than twenty-three legal documents, statutes, decrees, and international conventions that the *Conseil* cites as having contributed to its pronouncement.[207] Heading this enumeration is the Declaration of the Rights of Man and of the Citizen, followed by the Preamble to the Constitution of 1946 (Fourth Republic), the Constitution of 1958 (Fifth Republic), and the European Human Rights Convention, enacted in 1950. The historical sweep of the French laws cited includes the 1882 law making primary school mandatory, the 1905 separation of church and state, and several provisions regarding education, the most recent being the immigration law of August 2, 1989.

The opinion proper declares early on that "*la liberté de conscience*"—freedom of conscience—is "one of the fundamental principles recognized by the laws of the Republic [and] is operative in the domain of education."[208] Furthermore, this case touches at the most basic foundations of the Republic because it implicates education—one of the state's primary responsibilities, enshrined in the preamble to the 1946 constitution and in numerous laws. The *Conseil* quotes the law of July 11, 1975, and its formulation of the importance of education within the French state: academic education allows a child "to acquire a culture [and] prepares him for a professional life and for the exercise of his responsibilities as a man and as a citizen."[209] The *Conseil* then quotes the recent education law of July 10, 1989, which invokes the guarantee that education will help pupils to "develop their personalities . . . to make themselves a part of social and professional life, to exercise their citizenship . . . ."[210] The opinion then goes on to quote the law of August 2, 1989, stating that schools must imbue their students with "respect for the individual, for his origins, and for his differences."[211] From these and other key provisions, the *Conseil d'État* distills the fundamental principles that the right to have access to an education is guaranteed to those living within French borders regardless of their religion; that the freedom of religion and of manifesting that religion outwardly are protected in public and in private unless they present a threat to public health, security, or order, or the liberties of others; that parents have the right to ensure that their children receive an education compatible with their religious beliefs; and that the state must promote understanding and tolerance among "all racial and religious groups."[212]

The *Conseil*'s formulation of the state's duty emphasizes the school's positive responsibility to recognize the religious and cultural differences among its students. While the laws and other legal documents that the *Conseil* cites state that freedom of religious belief is an unimpeachable value of the Republic, none go as far as the *Conseil* does in positing that the school has an obligation to facilitate the tolerance, if not acceptance, of students from very different cultural backgrounds than some of their classmates. Furthermore, the *Conseil* contends that the principle of *laïcité* not only permits but, in fact, requires the schools to respect the free expression of religion. This conception of the principle of *laïcité* goes beyond the total freedom of inward personal conscience that the

206. Conseil d'État, 27 Novembre 1989, pmbl.; Rivero, *supra* note 20, at 6–7.

207. Conseil d'État, 27 Novembre 1989, pmbl. The *Conseil*'s inclusion of international law in its consideration is noteworthy, demonstrating the seriousness with which it and the rest of the legal community took France's international obligations.

208. *Id.* § 1; Rivero, *supra* note 20, at 7.

209. Conseil d'État, 27 Novembre 1989, § 1; Rivero, *supra* note 20, at 7.

210. Conseil d'État, 27 Novembre 1989, § 1; Rivero, *supra* note 20, at 7.

211. Conseil d'État, 27 Novembre 1989, § 1; Rivero, *supra* note 20, at 7.

212. Conseil d'État, 27 Novembre 1989, § 1; Rivero, *supra* note 20, at 7. The provision concerning parents' rights to see that their religious beliefs are not overtly contradicted by their children's education is at odds with repeated assertions in education laws cited by the *Conseil* that the school has a central responsibility to impart French culture to its students. The idea that parents' religious beliefs and the school's views of French culture might never clash was highly unrealistic, as, indeed, recent developments have demonstrated.

principle had always represented to its supporters and its enemies alike. Perhaps the most succinct subsequent statement of this new interpretation of *laïcité* is David Kessler's: "[e]ducation is *laïque* not because it forbids the expression of different faiths but on the contrary because it tolerates all of them."[213] This debate over the meaning of *laïcité* is reminiscent, though with important differences, of the oft-perceived tension in American jurisprudence between the Establishment Clause and the Free Exercise Clause of the First Amendment. The *Conseil d'État* is very clear:

> It results from the constitutional and legislative texts and from France's international engagements cited above that the principle of *laïcité* in public education, which is one of the elements of the *laïcité* of the state and of the neutrality of all of the public services, requires that education be dispensed with respect, on one hand, for this neutrality by the programs and teachers and, on the other hand, for the students' liberty of conscience . . . .
>
> This freedom on the students' part includes the right to express and to manifest their religious beliefs inside educational establishments, [so long as such expression is done] with respect for pluralism and for the freedom of others, and without detracting from the [school's] educational activities [and] the content of [its] programs . . . .[214]

The freedom of belief is firmly enshrined in the cited texts; the freedom of expression inside a public school is the *Conseil*'s own extrapolation. The *Conseil*, however, admits of another exception to students' free exercise of religion. That freedom may be curtailed when it interferes with the mission with which the educational system is charged. Notably, this mission includes the acquisition of "a culture" (clearly a unifying French culture, though this is not specified), the preparation for the responsibilities of being a professional and a citizen, and the inculcation of respect for the individual and his origin and differences, and for the equality of the sexes.

This section of the *Conseil*'s opinion makes way for the most frequently quoted portion of the opinion, which states that wearing religious garb in a school "is not in itself incompatible with the principle of *laïcité*" but must not "constitute an act of pressure, provocation, proselytism, or propaganda" that impinges on the freedom of the other students or impedes the school's educational mission.[215] It is striking the way the *Conseil* so quickly follows its daring reinterpretation of the principle of *laïcité* with an expansive list of exceptions. The pronouncement that *laïcité* implies free exercise of religion earned the *Conseil d'État* much criticism, as the *Conseil*'s members must have known it would.[216]

213. David Kessler, *Neutralité de l'Enseignement Publique et Liberté d'Opinion des Élèves (à Propos du Port de Signes Distinctifs d'Appartenance Religieuse dans les Établissements Scolaires)*, *in* 9 REVUE FRANÇAISE DE DROIT ADMINISTRATIF 112, 114 (1993). Kessler was a member of the *Conseil d'État*, but not of the group that rendered the 1989 decision. He made this statement in his role as the *commissaire du gouvernement* for a later headscarf case that will be discussed below.

214. Conseil d'État, 27 Novembre 1989, § 1; Rivero, *supra* note 20, at 7–8. In contrast, the Stasi Commission states that, "after having heard all of the positions [on the headscarf], [we] conclude that today the question is no longer one of freedom of conscience but [rather] of public order." STASI COMMISSION REPORT, *supra* note 6, § 4.2.2.1, at 56.

215. Conseil d'État, 27 Novembre 1989, § 1; Rivero, *supra* note 20, at 8. The alliteration of the latter quotation is present in the original French text.

216. Gaspard and Khosrokhavar criticize those who opposed the *Conseil d'État*'s decision, accusing them of adhering blindly to an unexamined principle that they had not updated to fit contemporary circumstances. Some commentators, they write, behave "as if the word '*laïcité*,' brandished during a debate, is enough all by itself." GASPARD & KHOSROKHAVAR, *supra* note 15, at 177.

For example, in 1996, a member of the National Assembly called the headscarf "the sign of a ferocious fundamentalism possessing a totalitarian character, a menace to the Republican order and to the Muslim communities that wish to integrate themselves [into French society]. The *Conseil d'État* . . . places France in a system in which there is no longer a separation of Church and State."[217] We should not underestimate the power of the *Conseil d'État*'s statement of principle, nor the power of its application in this particular case in favor of the girls from Creil. Nevertheless, the text makes evident how easily an opponent of the *Conseil*'s interpretation of *laïcité* could contend that a given instance of headscarf-wearing should be prohibited. Not only is the question of what constitutes "provocation" extremely difficult to answer, but religious apparel could also be banned from a school if it impeded the school's perceived ability to impart French culture or the idea of gender equality to the wearer of the scarf herself. Under the 2004 headscarf legislation, the prohibition of "ostentatious" religious symbols provides a new space for challenges to the general rule.

In his article reviewing the 1989 decision, Jean Rivero contends that the limits placed on freedom are in fact the most essential part of freedom's character: "To affirm a freedom is necessarily to define its limits. All freedoms are exercised within a society. They cannot fail to take account of the requirements of living within a society [*la vie sociale*], of the freedom of others, and of the conflicts that can arise from their coexistence."[218] The exceptions, though necessary, cannot possibly have the same precision as the general prescription, writes Rivero. This statement, no doubt, applies to many cases in which exceptions to a general rule must be enumerated. It is particularly important, however, in a case such as the *affaire des voiles*, which rests on the state's authority to control individuals' behavior while they are participating in a public institution. The type of regard for society to which Rivero refers and which he attributes to the *Conseil d'État* falls firmly within France's Rousseauian and revolutionary inheritance and is at odds with the model of ethnic group rights proposed by Feldblum and others. According to Rivero, this is not a case merely of the conflict of one set of rights with another—the girls' right to wear their religious garb versus their classmates' right to be free of religious pressure or politically motivated distraction in their classroom.[219] If the situation presented only such a conflict, then "the requirements of *la vie sociale*" would be a redundant consideration. Instead, there is a separate entity with an interest in the proceedings of the *affaire des voiles*. Even beyond the state as represented by the school and its administrators, the school's teachers and students, and the girls and their families, there is another actor in this legal and social drama: French society, with its shared culture and values. This is a distinctive feature of French law—that the state's interest in instilling culture in its citizens is considered an ever-present party to any conflict over conduct in the public schools. This is no mere civic education in the Anglo-American vein. Rather, in France, the state, not the parent, is seen to have the ultimate responsibility to educate a child.[220] This state of affairs stands in contrast to the American model of education, in which local authorities exert much more control over the public education system than do national authorities.

The influence of the students' parents is another integral piece of the *affaire des voiles* puzzle. It is not only religious expression that the headscarf's opponents decry. A traditional culture that is not French, represented by parents who are first-generation

217. Le Tourneau, *supra* note 28, at 295 (quoting the interview of Ernest Chénière with LE FIGARO, Nov. 7, 1996).

218. Rivero, *supra* note 20, at 4.

219. *Id.* at 5.

220. This point is brought home by the fact that the Stasi Commission endorses full religious self-expression among university students, as they are no longer minors. STASI COMMISSION REPORT, *supra* note 6, § 4.2.2.2, at 58.

immigrants, can be one of the state's primary rivals in its central mission to impart French culture and prepare students for French citizenship. The *Conseil d'État*'s decision does not address this tension except to affirm the parents' right, mentioned above, to ensure that their children's education does not directly contradict the family's private religious beliefs. Rivero, on the other hand, slyly alludes to the sometimes-pernicious role of the students' parents in orchestrating a collective incidence of scarf-wearing. "A collective wearing of the headscarf, which reflects a decision which does not truly come from the students themselves, might constitute 'an act of pressure or of provocation.'"[221] This suspicion that parents may be using students to promote their own message or, by extension, to impress upon the student that she is separate and different from her classmates exacerbates the legal and social tensions of this case. (This is not to say, of course, that the suspicion is always misplaced.) The *Conseil d'État* does not permit itself to be distracted by such divisive points; instead it adheres to legal discipline and addresses only the administrative behavior that its role within the French government charges it to judge. The trade-off is that by addressing only the conditions within the classroom in its delineation of exceptions, the *Conseil* cannot make as full a statement as it otherwise might regarding the culture and preparation for the responsibilities of citizenship that the school is designed to impart to its students. The influence of parents was one of the central aspects of the public dialogue about the headscarf during 2003 and 2004.[222]

This is a general circumstance of the judiciary—it responds to particular cases, not to general societal trends. However, the *Conseil*'s conception of *laïcité* is not contained directly in the legal texts it cites, so it has already given credence to some other, more nebulous form of evidence.[223] Secondly, the exceptions that the *Conseil* sets forth invoke the mission of the school to impart French culture to its students.[224] A disruption to this function would be grounds for banning the headscarf. Thus, a potential tug of war between the student's family's native culture and that of France is already presupposed by the *Conseil*'s formulation of the reasons the headscarf may be banned.

Rivero picks up on this balancing act in which the *Conseil* is engaged between adhering strictly to the legal questions at hand and making a broader, socially relevant statement. He writes, "[i]f the *affaire des voiles* had concerned only the notion of *laïcité*, it is doubtful that it would have stirred up so much controversy, attracted to the *collège* in Creil so many press photographers, and mobilized the media [as it did]."[225] Rather, the *affaire* is fundamentally about more than the old battle of religion versus secularism, a distinction that some defenders of the headscarf ban, such as Guy Coq, ignore or miss.[226] The *affaire des voiles* stirred up deep political passions relating to the integration of North African immigrants and the native French population's fear that a fundamentalist Islam—one that the majority of Muslims arguably do not recognize as their own religion—will infiltrate France and French political life. Specifically, the *affaire* aroused the fear that the decision by second-generation immigrants to wear the headscarf represented a rejection of the process of integration.[227]

As it was, many—not least, some legislators and members of the civil service—disagreed with the *Conseil d'État*'s interpretation of *laïcité*. In such a polarized

221. *Id.* at 5 (quoting a portion of the *Conseil*'s formula for when students should not be allowed to wear a headscarf).

222. STASI COMMISSION REPORT, *supra* note 6, § 3.2.1.1, at 39.

223. Conseil d'État, 27 Novembre 1989, § 1; Rivero, *supra* note 20, at 8.

224. Conseil d'État, 27 Novembre 1989, § 1; Rivero, *supra* note 20, at 8.

225. Rivero, *supra* note 20, at 5–6.

226. Coq, *supra* note 100, at A25.

227. *Id.*

environment, a case-by-case approach to the problem is perhaps the most radical approach available, because such an approach put wholesale prohibition of the headscarf off limits.[228] But the *Conseil* was both enabled and hamstrung by the generality and universalism of the legal texts from which it drew its evidence and inspiration. Perhaps that legal backdrop prevented the *Conseil* from presenting an even more complete picture of the status of immigrants and Muslims within the school system. Rivero states that the status of Muslims was beyond the legal scope of the *Conseil d'État*'s decision, but the *Conseil* nevertheless succeeded in making clear that the principle of *laïcité* applies to Islam, all the while "leaving the door open to the chance for integration on which depends, in large measure, the homogeneity of tomorrow's society."[229]

Here, Rivero has hit on the crucial fact that the *Conseil d'État* must have viewed its decision as responding to the challenges of the present day, or it would not have taken the step of recasting *laïcité* as it did. It is disturbing that Rivero so blithely assumes that the welcoming of Muslims into the school system will lead to future homogeneity, and further that homogeneity remained one of the goods the *Conseil* was aiming to achieve in crafting its compromise ruling. The *Conseil*, on the contrary, shows every sign of granting freedom of religious expression as a principle, rather than as a sneaky means to the same ultimate end as previous versions of *laïcité* had sought. In any case, the reason the *Conseil* fails to present a complete picture of the political context of its decision is not that it is unconcerned with that issue. Rather, it attempts to demonstrate that, having taken account of the contemporary situation, it is impartially rendering a decision based solely on interpretation of the laws and other legal documents discussed above.

In the final portion of its decision, the *Conseil* addresses itself to the third issue it laid out at the beginning, that of the appropriate punishment for a student whose wearing of religious clothing is found to be unacceptable. Here the *Conseil* weighs the damage to the school and classroom that is effected by the presence of a "disruptive" student against the student's right to a public education. Since a parent may provide the student's mandatory education, there is no absolute right not to be expelled from a public school, states the *Conseil*.[230] Left unmentioned is the state's interest in maintaining control over the student's education by keeping him or her within a public school and out of a private, sectarian alternative. All of the acquisition of French culture and preparation for civic and professional participation in French life that the *Conseil* and its legal sources tout so highly are clearly impossible to carry out if the student withdraws from the state educational system altogether. Perhaps the *Conseil* would argue that by the time that a school is contemplating expulsion, the state's interest in influencing the student is obviously less significant than either the student's own right to education or the state's right to keep the schools safe and to promote other students' acquisition of culture and skills for citizenship. Nonetheless, the omission of this additional interest skews the choice in favor of the school's right to protect itself by removing the disruptive student. Were it not for the fact that some formidable punishment must exist for violating state regulations, the argument could even be made that the state could best promote cultural uniformity by continuing to educate the headscarf-wearing student. Further, some commentators have suggested that the furor over the headscarf has proven a distraction from the more important question of how to teach students to be good citizens.[231]

---

228. Kessler, *supra* note 213, at 114.

229. Rivero, *supra* note 20, at 6.

230. Conseil d'État, 27 Novembre 1989, § 3; Rivero, *supra* note 20, at 8–9.

231. Geneviève Koubi, *Des Propositions de Lois Relatives à la Laïcité dans les Établissements Publics Scolaires*, 73 REVUE DE LA RECHERCHE JURIDIQUE. DROIT PROSPECTIF 577, 584–85 (1998). Koubi adds that one of the central issues facing citizens is precisely the ability to navigate a pluralistic society, acknowledging diversity without sacrificing French unity. *Id.* at 585.

In fact, the *Conseil* rules that the school has the right to expel students who fail the test the *Conseil* has devised for the wearing of the headscarf. The head of a school, the *Conseil* writes, may refuse admission to an offending student "to the degree and for the duration necessary to re-establish" normalcy and order.[232] This would seem to grant rather broad power to the principal of the school, and it certainly prioritizes the normal functioning of teaching and school administration over whatever rights to public education the student may have and any state interest in continuing as the student's education provider. In a typical and indicative move, however, the *Conseil* closes the entire decision by emphasizing that the threat must be reasonably dire before it justifies refusing admission to a student. A refusal of admission, the *Conseil* writes, "will not be justified except by the risk of a menace to the order of the establishment or to the normal functioning of the service of education."[233] Thus, the *Conseil d'État* dances towards and away from mandating the specific ways in which local school administrators must handle the wearing of religious clothing in the public school.[234]

Recognizing the need for further practical instructions on how to put its general principles into practice, the *Conseil* states that the minister with jurisdiction over education may provide a guide to those beneath him on how schools must apply the new criteria laid out in the decision.[235] Minister Jospin took up the *Conseil*'s invitation in his circular fifteen days later. In his opening remarks, Jospin reiterates the centrality of *laïcité* to the Republic and to its educational system; explains that he had referred the case to the *Conseil d'État* because of the great difficulties in interpreting the relevant law; and declares his intention to help "all the members of the educational community" with their task of implementing the *Conseil*'s recent decision.[236] Though Jospin had been the first governmental official to express his personal support for the girls of the *affaire des voiles*, his circular is more pragmatic than was the *Conseil*'s decision, and in many respects that pragmatism tends to promote the wearing of the scarf somewhat less than does the *Conseil*'s reliance on broader constitutional themes.

The first directive that Jospin gives to the educational establishment is that as soon as a problem arises, school officials should immediately engage in dialogue with the student wearing the headscarf and with her parents. The officials should impress upon the student and parents that it would be in the interest of both the student and school if she ceased wearing the headscarf. "You must," Jospin writes, "dedicate all of your conviction to this dialogue," as many fights will be avoided simply through such communication.[237] The presumption, though, is that once a conflict has arisen over a student's headscarf, the school official must take the firm position that the student should stop wearing the scarf provided that the circumstances conform to the exceptions the *Conseil* laid out in its decision. Jospin is also bold enough to suggest a test for assessing whether an act of wearing a headscarf constitutes provocation or proselytism. He advises the school officials that the attitudes and

232. Conseil d'État, 27 Novembre 1989, § 3; Rivero, *supra* note 20, at 8.

233. Conseil d'État, 27 Novembre 1989, § 3; Rivero, *supra* note 20, at 9.

234. Some suggest that the ambiguity in the *Conseil d'État*'s ruling is due to the transitional phase in which France found itself at that time—caught between its own loss of homogeneity on one side and the American group rights model of society on the other. Under such circumstances, the *affaire des voiles* decision is "the reflection of a profound malaise." J.-P. Chapuisat, *L'Actualité et le Droit: Laïcité Scolaire, l'Avis du Conseil d'État sur le Port du Voile Islamique à l'École*, 1990 L'ACTUALITÉ JURIDIQUE DROIT ADMINISTRATIF 39, 45; *see also* Philippe Ségur, *Le Principe Constitutionnel de Laïcité*, 1996 ANNALES DE L'UNIVERSITÉ DES SCIENCES SOCIALES DE TOULOUSE 117, 134 (suggesting that *laïcité* is in a period of transition during which its outline is fairly clear, but "its center remains even today a prisoner of the fluctuating shadow of what has been left unsaid").

235. Conseil d'État, 27 Novembre 1989, § 2; Rivero, *supra* note 20, at 8.

236. Jospin, *supra* note 24, at 20.

237. *Id.*

intentions that the students and their parents demonstrate are crucial to the assessment of whether or not the wearing of the headscarf was intended as a benign, purely religious act.[238] This attention to intention rather than outcome (whether the wearer of the headscarf wanted to convey a proselytizing message versus whether anyone at the school actually felt preached to) seems plausible only in the context of the state's interest in preventing the non-French parents from impeding the acquisition of French culture by the headscarf-wearing student, rather than the state's interest in the education of her classmates. Jospin's decision to include the student's parents as full participants in whatever assessment and negotiations may occur underscores his focus on the political issues surrounding the legal matter. However, he does not explicitly address the issues concerning Islam and immigration that arose out of the *affaire des voiles*. Instead, he adheres to the *Conseil*'s precedent of referring to culture only in the context of the French culture with which the schools are entrusted.

Jospin's circular especially latches onto the implications contained in the *Conseil*'s ruling for political behavior within the school. Jospin writes that school officials must use the criteria enumerated in the circular to assess and deal with provocative political symbols that students might wear.[239] Presumably, Jospin would elaborate that the same logic should apply to religious and political expression, since both are fundamental liberties that should get presumptive protection in the absence of a threat to safety or to the school's mission, and yet both also impinge on the neutrality of the educational environment. The salient difference between these two types of expression, though, is that religious expression is governed by the principle of *laïcité*. According to the traditional view—and that still widely held among those, especially on the left, who opposed the girls' right to wear the headscarf—*laïcité* requires the state to project and promote a perfectly religiously neutral public space in which the businesses of politics and civil administration can proceed without hindrance from organized religion. According to this model, the school must be a sacredly secular place precisely because of the central role it plays in readying French youth to participate in political debate and discharge their civic duties.

If that is true, then one would expect freedom of political expression within the public school—especially expression by a student, not by someone in authority—to be subject to far fewer restrictions than religious expression. Jospin's formulation would seem either to diminish the protection accorded to political speech or to reduce the religious to the merely political. Under this view, religious expression in the school cannot help but be political expression, and the student expressing herself must know that, so religious expression should be treated as political expression would be. This formulation renders the headscarf in some ways less threatening and in other ways more threatening. If wearing the headscarf can be subsumed under the category of political expression—say, to promote Islamic influence in French policies—then it is a known quantity although it is still an opponent of traditional *laïcité* and the republican order. Thus, one need not make the effort to understand how wearing the headscarf could be part of a belief system that may in fact prove compatible with participation in French civic life but which must also be taken seriously on its own terms. If wearing the headscarf is automatically a political act, then that act is no longer foreign, no longer a challenge to the very way that the individual is assumed to interact with society in France. On the other hand, if religious expression automatically constitutes political expression, then there can be no "innocent" headscarf-wearing. Instead, all such incidents must be viewed as a potential challenge to the secular school. This view is in line with the fear (all the more prominent since the terrorist attacks

238. *Id.* at 21.

239. Jospin, *supra* note 24, at 20. Legal scholar Claude Durand-Prinborgne criticizes this move, noting that the criteria used for the permissibility of political symbols are more strict and that applying the religious criteria would run contrary to the principle of political expression. Durand-Prinborgne, *supra* note 203, at 13–14.

of September 11, 2001) that the girls' veils augured an attempted assertion of fundamentalist Islam in French politics. Both possible outcomes of Jospin's formulation oversimplify the meaning of the headscarf and represent an inability to reach beyond the traditional categories of French politics.

It seems strange that Jospin would state that religious expression deserves exactly as much protection as political expression does in a circular designed to convince the educational establishment to accept the *Conseil d'État*'s ruling. After all, the *Conseil*'s most stinging conclusion, from the perspective of that establishment, was that *laïcité* actually requires that the school actively protect students' free expression of their religion. To contend that religious and political expression should receive the same degree of deference would seem to expand religion's place in education even further and therefore to be a counterproductive step in the attempt to gain the educational community's acceptance. This tactic on Jospin's part seems best to fit the explanation that he was trying to make the religious expression represented by the headscarf seem less foreign by placing it into the same category as any other form of expression aimed at persuasion.

Toward the end of his circular, Jospin delves into another issue not implicated in the *Conseil*'s decision, that of teachers' personal expression. Because of their status as solemn representatives of the state, as models to their students both explicitly and implicitly, Jospin concludes that teachers "must avoid any distinctive philosophical, religious, or political mark that might diminish [their students'] freedom of conscience."[240] Here again, religious and political expression are placed into the same category, though their grouping together here is more intuitive, since Jospin is stating that *any* sort of personal view that the teacher might express would damage the neutrality that the educational environment must promote. Thus, "philosophical, religious, or political" may better be seen, in this context, more as a list of strong personal allegiances that a teacher would be tempted to express than as a significant grouping of types of ideologies. In other words, such expression is not forbidden to the teacher because of any particular similarity between political and religious expression, but rather because any introduction into the classroom of the teacher's personal views would tarnish the meticulously neutral environment that the school was meant to provide for its students.

It is beyond the scope of this article to assess the appropriateness of treating all political expression in the public school in the same way as the *Conseil d'État* had mandated that religious expression be treated. Suffice to say that, as we have seen above, equating these two types of expression is far from as obvious as Jospin's casual insertion of political expression might seem to indicate. Of note for the present discussion, however, is Jospin's engagement with the political dimensions of wearing a headscarf in the face of the *Conseil*'s sidestepping of the issue. Jospin, of course, never states that the *Conseil* has neglected this area. His circular, on the contrary, seems intended on first glance solely to reinforce the authority of the *Conseil d'État*'s ruling. And it certainly does that. Attention to the political dynamics of the ruling and its consequences is only natural on the part of a government minister. In this instance, the *Conseil d'État*'s membership in the French civil service was perhaps not enough to bridge the gap between a novel, if not daring, interpretation of a bedrock Republican principle and a skeptical, if not hostile, cadre of civil servants being called upon to put that new interpretation into daily practice. In order to take full account of the ruling's political consequences, Jospin clearly had to say something that the *Conseil*'s decision had not already expressed. The particular ways in which Jospin chose to insert politics into his circular, however, were not inevitable choices and did not necessarily clarify the matter and bring it closer to resolution. Nor were all of Jospin's

240. *Id.* at 22.

additions to the *Conseil*'s remarks of a political nature. One of Jospin's caveats, in fact, addresses a decidedly judicial matter; he stresses that any student accused of wrongdoing must be guaranteed the right to a defense.[241]

In an overall comparison of the circular's approach and that adopted by the *Conseil*, one would expect the former to be more concrete and practical, as it is. What is surprising is that the circular may well be the legal decision's equal with regard to breaking new theoretical ground concerning personal expression within the state-sponsored confines of the public school. Jospin's main objective is to rally his troops around the *Conseil*'s basic conclusions. He even ends the circular with a rousing, "[t]ogether we must give life to the ideal of *laïcité* and make that ideal understood."[242] Secondarily, though, he is attempting to mold the civil service's internal debate over religious expression. In this project, he sometimes obscures the issues that he had asked the *Conseil d'État* to consider, as when he adds provisions concerning personal expression by teachers.[243] In other instances, however, Jospin's politically aware approach illuminates portions of the larger debate that the *Conseil* chose to or was forced to ignore. His discussion of the role of parents as well as his excursion into the question of how to treat provocative political expression in the school demonstrate Jospin's desire to use this case to frame general principles as well as specific policies regarding the school's behavior vis-à-vis expressions of private matters within the public sphere.

The *Conseil d'État* issued its next decision concerning the wearing of a headscarf just under three years after the decision of November 1989.[244] In this second case, a *collège*—located, like the one around which the 1989 controversy swirled, in the suburbs of Paris—had adopted a rule that specifically prohibited the wearing of the headscarf. It subsequently revised this regulation, substituting a ban on all distinctive religious, philosophical, and political signs and items of dress. Meanwhile, parents of the students whose right to wear their scarves was under attack brought a case against the school. This complaint was heard first by the regional administrative tribunal of Paris, whose unfavorable decision the families appealed to the judicial branch of the *Conseil d'État*. The decision of November 2, 1992, consists in large part of a nearly direct quotation from the *Conseil*'s 1989 decision.[245] The 1992 decision breaks no new theoretical ground, nor is it intended to do so. Rather, it very briefly states that the regulation in place at the school in question is illegal due to "the generality of its terms."[246] The decision of the Paris tribunal is overturned, the *collège* regulation annulled, and the headscarf-wearing students returned to school.[247]

This decision follows closely the recommendation of David Kessler, the *commissaire du gouvernement* who handled the case. In his presentation he urges the *Conseil* to annul the decision of the tribunal of Paris and to reinstate the girls who wish to wear their headscarves. Kessler addresses himself to the deciding members of the *Conseil d'État*:

> [i]n confirming for the first time in the contentieux [the judicial section of the Conseil d'État, as opposed to its consultative branch] that the question of the Islamic headscarf is not an issue of principle but an issue concerning particular instances, and in reminding [the readers of the decision] that, because it is a

241. *Id.* at 21.
242. *Id.* at 22.
243. *Id.*
244. Conseil d'État, 2 Novembre 1992, Lebon at 389.
245. *Id.*
246. *Id.*
247. *Id.*

question of particular instances, no general prohibition [of the headscarf] can be tolerated, your decision will have great significance . . . .[248]

In other words, the confirmation by the *Section du Contentieux* of the centrality of freedom of religious expression would send the clear message that the question is closed as to whether, in principle, a headscarf is permissible in the school. The question of the headscarf's status remains open only on a case-by-case basis; particular instances of headscarf wearing may yet be forbidden, but headscarf-wearing as a general category of behavior may not.

It is very important, according to Kessler, that the judicial branch of the *Conseil d'État* demonstrate its willingness to enforce the requirement that schools give students the right to wear religious apparel unless specific exceptions apply. Kessler proclaims his agreement with the 1989 decision's claim that the freedom of religious expression in the public schools is included within the principle of *laïcité*. This is the correct interpretation, says Kessler, partially because of the protection of religious expression under numerous international conventions that France has signed in recent decades. But furthermore, Kessler argues, *contra* Durand-Prinborgne's position in his 1990 article, such a sort of religious liberty has been contained within France's own legal heritage from the start.[249]

A more complex application of the 1989 decision's criteria for when wearing a headscarf is acceptable was at work in a decision the *Conseil* issued in March 1995.[250] By 1994, some social commentators were complaining that the number of girls wearing the veil had grown from just a handful to seven hundred. This increased strength in numbers alone, journalist and essayist Christian Jelen wrote, was enough to constitute a threat to *laïcité* where perhaps one had not existed in 1989.[251] Many girls had taken their cue from the *Conseil*'s relatively favorable rulings in 1989 and 1992 and adopted the headscarf. Like its predecessor in 1992, the 1995 case had been brought by the parents of the expelled students, and the parents' claim had been rejected by a regional administrative tribunal. The school, this time in Lyon, had told two sisters that their headscarves prevented them from fully participating in physical education and that therefore the students must remove their scarves. The *Conseil* ruled that the school's regulation was not unduly restrictive and did not have the effect of outlawing headscarves altogether, as the students and their parents had claimed. Therefore, the students' refusal to remove their scarves constituted an interference with the normal functioning of their education, a disruptive violation of the school's order. The girls' expulsion was upheld.[252]

Thus the *Conseil* concluded its triad of cases concerning the wearing of headscarves in public schools. The first had been an opinion by the *Conseil*'s consultative wing, requested specifically by Minister of Education Lionel Jospin; the second, an affirmation by the *Conseil*'s judicial branch of the principles of the first opinion; and the third, an implementation of one exception to the rules laid out in the first opinion. The tribunal had stated the theoretical principles that must guide resolutions of such cases, implemented

248. Kessler, *supra* note 213, at 118.

249. *Id.*; *see* Durand-Prinborgne, *supra* note 204, at 19 (arguing that France's European and other international obligations have induced it to accept principles in tension with its own founding philosophy).

250. Conseil d'État, 10 Mars 1995, *Recueil des Décisions du Conseil d'État*, Lebon, 122–23.

251. GASPARD & KHOSROKHAVAR, *supra* note 15, at 29. In 2003, the Stasi Commission similarly stated that the present context was different from that of 1989 because "the demands of communitarianism" had grown so much stronger in the interim. STASI COMMISSION REPORT, *supra* note 6, § 2.2.3, at 27.

252. Conseil d'État, 10 Mars 1995, Lebon at 123. The decision also mentions that the father of the two girls in question had participated in a demonstration outside the school. The *Conseil* takes a dim view of this behavior, which it says aggravated the girls' original offense in refusing to remove their scarves. *Id.*

those principles, and implemented an exception to the principles. This collection of legal texts, especially the *Conseil d'État*'s treatment of the principle of *laïcité*, is a telling case study in the evolution of France's conception of itself as a nation. It is a prime example of the way in which standing legal and political principles may come to take on different meanings under different historical circumstances. If the meaning of French political ideals underwent such challenge and change during the late 1980s and early 1990s and then again in 2003 and 2004, then it seems futile to hope to find a single, constant French national identity dating back to the Revolution or further, even in the less rigid form that Brubaker seeks. Though the *Conseil*'s 1989 decision was based firmly on established legal texts and its 1992 and 1995 decisions were little more than applications of the doctrine set forth in 1989, the *Conseil* was engaged in redefining a revered principle, that of *laïcité*. The specific details of the *Conseil*'s shaping of the debate in 1989 are all the more important given the opposing political consensus that gave rise to the Stasi Commision's report and the 2004 law banning ostentatious religious symbols in the public school. Notwithstanding the modifications effected by the Bayrou Circular, France had operated under the *Conseil*'s redefinition of *laïcité* for fifteen years before the adoption of a statutory solution to the headscarf question. Whatever one thinks of the merits of the legislation, the return to a more traditional view of *laïcité* as excluding prominent religious expression from the classroom was not the result of knee-jerk prejudice or paranoia on the part of France's populace and politicians. This issue had been percolating through the French polity for all those years, and, in fact, ten pieces of legislation concerning *laïcité*—nine of them relating to the implementation of *laïcité* in the public schools—were proposed between 1989 and 2002.[253] Nor did the reassertion in 2004 of the strictly secular quality of the public school reflect only a distrust of organized religion, stemming from the Catholic Church's long association with an anti-republican political stance.

Instead, the events of late 2003 and early 2004 throw into relief the radical, even experimental, nature of the 1989 decision. Conversely, our analysis of that decision and the role of the *Conseil d'État* within the French state lends a depth of understanding that would otherwise be missing from the task of teasing out the meaning and implications of the 2004 legislation. Even as it proposed a redefinition of *laïcité*, the *Conseil d'État* rendered a decision ambiguous enough to increase rather than decrease the level of conflict over the presence of headscarves in France's public schools. Combined with the fear of fundamentalist Islam and the increase in the headscarf's popularity, the *Conseil*'s delegation of so much discretion to individual schools helped keep the issue simmering.

The *laïcité* law of 2004, intended to bring clarity to this issue, is itself subject to legal challenge. Specific instances of the implementation of the law's provisions may be challenged within the French administrative courts, but any attempt to invalidate the law itself would have to go through the *Conseil Constitutionnel* or the European Court of Human Rights (ECHR).[254] Fewer than sixty members of each house of parliament voted against the legislation, precluding a referral to the *Conseil Constitutionnel*. As a result, the ECHR will likely be called upon to interpret Article 9 of the Council of Europe's Convention for the Protection of Human Rights and Fundamental Freedoms:

> Everyone has the right to freedom of thought, conscience and religion; this right includes freedom to change his religion or belief and freedom, either alone or in community with others and in public or private, to manifest his religion or belief, in worship, teaching, practice and observance.

253. Koubi, *supra* note 231, at 578 n.7.

254. Foreign treaties take precedence in French law over statutes passed by the legislature. CONST. art. 55 (Fr.), *available at* http://www.conseil-constitutionnel.fr/textes/constit.htm (last visited Apr. 18, 2004); *see also* WEST ET AL., *supra* note 164, at 44.

> Freedom to manifest one's religion or beliefs shall be subject only to such limitations as are prescribed by law and are necessary in a democratic society in the interests of public safety, for the protection of public order, health or morals, or for the protection of the rights and freedoms of others.[255]

Past ECHR decisions indicate that France's new *laïcité* law may indeed be found to violate the Convention for the Protection of Human Rights and Fundamental Freedoms. The following is a brief introduction to the ECHR caselaw that may be relevant to the *laïcité* law. In *Kokkinakis v. Greece*, the court asserted: "While religious freedom is primarily a matter of individual conscience, it also implies, *inter alia*, freedom to 'manifest [one's] religion'. Bearing witness in words and deeds is bound up with the existence of religious convictions."[256] Here, the Court affirms the right to express one's religion in public, already mentioned explicitly in the Convention.

Further, according to the Court, any restriction of the right of expression must respond to a "pressing social need" and be "proportionate to the legitimate aim pursued."[257] These requirements introduce the possibility that the Court will fail to see a pressing need for the type of educational environment that the French state hopes to promote, or that the Court will judge the headscarf ban to be a disproportionate response to the threat to *laïcité*. The Court has deemed pluralism to be "indissociable from a democratic society,"[258] a statement which may clash with France's commitment to avoiding the language of multiculturalism and group rights.

Finally, should it suspect that the new headscarf law is intended to target Muslims specifically, the Court could also refer to its statement that, "[t]he right to freedom of religion as guaranteed under the Convention excludes any discretion on the part of the State to determine whether religious beliefs or the means used to express such beliefs are legitimate."[259]

On the other hand, the Court has on occasion proven willing to invoke the exceptions set forth in Article 9 of the Convention. In the case of a highly religious member of the Turkish Armed Forces, the Court ruled that Turkey was justified in forcing the officer to retire early because he had expressed his opposition to the secularism on which the Turkish state is based: "Article 9 does not protect every act motivated or inspired by a religion or belief. Moreover, in exercising his freedom to manifest his religion, an individual may need to take his specific situation into account."[260] However, this case concerns the behavior of a person *employed* by the government, so the exception that it invokes may not apply to students.

The *Conseil d'État* has also invoked Article 9 in a decision upholding the ruling that a woman cannot wear a headscarf in her photograph for official identification because in such an instance the interest in public order outweighs the interest in religious freedom.[261]

At the heart of France's struggle with its national identity is a debate over the relative strength of the public and private spheres within French life. The *Conseil d'État*'s 1989 administrative decision and the judicial rulings that followed remain significant

255. Convention for the Protection of Human Rights and Fundamental Freedoms, Nov. 4, 1950, art. 9, *available at* http://www.echr.coe.int/Convention/webConvenENG.pdf (last visited Apr. 16, 2004).

256. Kokkinakis v. Greece, 260 Eur. Ct. H.R. (ser. A) at 17 (1993).

257. Goodwin v. United Kingdom, App. No. 17488/90, (1996) 22 Eur. H.R. Rep. 123, 124 (1996).

258. Serif v. Greece, App. No. 38178/97, (2001) 31 Eur. H.R. Rep. 561, 562 (1999).

259. Manoussakis v. Greece, App. No. 18748/91, (1997) 23 Eur. H.R. Rep. 387, 408 (1996).

260. Kalaç v. Turkey, App. No. 20704/92, (1999) 27 Eur. H.R. Rep. 552, 552 (1997).

261. Conseil d'État, 27 juillet 2001, *Recueil des Décisions du Conseil d'État*, Lebon, 400, 401.

developments in that ongoing debate despite the 2004 headscarf legislation. The complete exclusion of private matters from the public arena, which a traditional French secularist would advocate, has the effect of homogenizing the public sphere, discriminating against those who wish to express a culture different from the state-promoted (or, less charitably, state-constructed) dominant French culture. The *Conseil d'État* is a symbol of the primacy of the public sphere in France. By its very existence, it demonstrates the special status that the state and the public sphere hold in French society. Its prestige and credibility are based on the prestige of the public sphere. As the conduit between public and private—the arena in which private citizens may launch complaints against the state—the *Conseil d'État* is in a particularly important position to help France reach a new equilibrium of private and public. The *Conseil*'s protection of a sphere of private expression through its reshaping of the principle of *laïcité* represented a significant step in asserting the permeability of the boundary between public and private. According to the *Conseil*, in order for the state to maintain neutrality—to maintain its public function—it must in fact allow private expression to flourish. Respect for private expression is not at odds with the school's mission but in fact part of it.[262]

The *Conseil d'État*'s most enduring contribution to the controversy over French nationhood is its reorientation of the debate. This contribution will endure even with the 2004 enactment of the law prohibiting the headscarf in public schools. The *Conseil*'s stature as a part of the state bureaucracy gave it the standing to shape the debate despite sometimes-fierce opposition within the government. Yet the litany of exceptions to the right to religious expression in the school tarnished the luster of the *Conseil*'s conceptual innovation. Bureaucratic channels to sidestep the implications of the new *laïcité* were constructed in the very document in which that new view of the French state was unveiled. The *Conseil* ultimately did not break free enough from its place in the bureaucracy to give real teeth to its new conception of *laïcité*. The compromise left open too much room for public officials to renege on the promise of respect for private expression. As France found itself increasingly alarmed at the rising prevalence of the headscarf, the push to counter the perceived threat to the educational sphere gained strength.

This analysis does not yield an easy prescription for how the French state in general, and the *Conseil d'État* in particular, could better balance France's tradition of valuing civic participation and public service against the individual freedoms that are another portion of what might be called the republican heritage. It does, however, point to the importance of knowledge of the French legal structure for an understanding of the political dynamics of France's struggle with its national identity. Because of its status as the only governmental body that can call the state to account for its enforcement of laws and interpretation of constitutional provisions, the *Conseil d'État* plays a role that cannot be ignored. The shortcomings of the *Conseil*'s decisions regarding the *affaire des voiles* are nothing less than reflections of the advantages and disadvantages in general of France's vast state bureaucracy—entered by merit but also rigidly specialized and hierarchical. Anyone may take the ENA entrance exam, but in attending and graduating from the ENA, the new civil servant accepts the strict specialization and regimentation that characterizes most civil service. The *Conseil d'État* stands at the intersection between this system and the foundational principles of the Republic. Its vision of *laïcité* suffered a very public setback during the events set off by the Stasi Commission's report. The extent to which this alternative vision of *laïcité* will resurface in French debate is as yet unclear. Nevertheless, the *Conseil d'État*'s role in the headscarf controversy was to reanimate public debate

262. Aspects of this attitude influenced the Stasi Commission on topics less well publicized than that of the headscarf. For example, the Commission's report advocated that Yom Kippur and Eid-El-Kebir be recognized school holidays. STASI COMMISSION REPORT, *supra* note 6, § 4.4, at 69. President Chirac did not endorse this particular recommendation, but its presence in the report is nonetheless noteworthy.

regarding the nature of the French state's foundational principles. In particular, the *Conseil* insisted upon the importance of individual expression even in the face of important government interests. Its situation within the French governmental structure positions the *Conseil* to continue to fulfill this function as France continues to grapple with newly urgent issues of national identity.

[8]

TIPTOEING THROUGH A CONSTITUTIONAL MINEFIELD: THE GREAT SHARIA CONTROVERSY IN NIGERIA

ANDREW UBAKA IWOBI*

INTRODUCTION

It has been stated by Mayer that "the role of constitutions in systems where Islamic law is applied remains a major point of contention".[1] The difficulties inherent in reconciling the operation of Islamic law with the constitutional arrangements of a modern nation state are vividly illustrated by recent developments in Nigeria. The current Constitution of the Federal Republic of Nigeria was promulgated in 1999.[2] This Constitution (hereafter referred to as the 1999 Constitution) laid the foundation for the reintroduction of civilian government after nearly fifteen years of military rule. Shortly after it came into force, various state governments in Northern Nigeria embarked on a process of reforms designed to restore the Sharia to the position of pre-eminence it had enjoyed within their territories in pre-colonial times.[3] An issue which has been debated loud and long is whether the Sharia reforms are in accord with the provisions of the 1999 Constitution. The aim of the present study is to contribute to this debate by seeking to determine what bearing the 1999 Constitution has on the Sharia reforms, with a particular view to establishing whether or not there are sufficient grounds for impugning the constitutional validity of these reforms.

A host of legal luminaries, influential academic commentators, politicians, religious dignitaries and other members of the Nigerian intelligentsia have pitched into the controversy. Ardent supporters and vocal opponents of the Sharia reforms alike have frequently invoked the authority of the Constitution to buttress their contradictory positions. The inevitable consequence of this is that opinion is deeply polarized on the constitutionality of the Sharia reforms. This state of affairs is hardly surprising given the legal and political landscape against which these reforms were both conceived and implemented. Before placing the Sharia reforms under the spotlight of the 1999 Constitution it is worth surveying this landscape. This survey will entail an examination of key episodes and notable developments in Nigeria's colonial and postcolonial constitutional history which

* LL.B. (Hons)(Jos); Ph.D. (Birmingham). Lecturer, University of Wales, Swansea.

[1] A.E. Mayer, "A critique of An-Na'im's assessment of Islamic criminal justice" in T. Lindholm and K. Vogt (eds.), *Islamic Law Reform and Human Rights: Challenges and Rejoinders*, Oslo, 1993, 37 at 49.

[2] Constitution of the Federal Republic of Nigeria (Promulgation) Decree, No. 24 of 1999.

[3] The affected states (which are variously described as "Sharia-compliant", "Sharia-implementing" or "Sharia-observant" states) are Bauchi, Borno, Gombe, Jigawa, Kaduna, Kano, Katsina, Kebbi, Niger, Sokoto, Yobe and Zamfara (which pioneered the reforms). Such reformatory zeal is by no means restricted to Nigeria's Northern states. On the contrary, "Islamic Law", as Oba points out, "is enjoying a wave of revival across the world [and] Muslims are now seeking to return to the pristine form of Islamic law". A.A. Oba, "Islamic law as customary law: the changing perspective in Nigeria", (2001) 51 *ICLQ* 817 at 821.

have created and exacerbated the religious fault lines running through the nation's body politic. As we shall see in this connection, the frictions and fissions engendered by the interplay of religion and politics within the constitutional setting have contributed significantly to the intense controversy generated by the ongoing debate on the constitutionality of the Sharia reforms.

The Interplay of Politics and Religion in Nigeria's Constitutional History

The colonial era

For several centuries before the advent of colonial rule, the Sharia had "in various ways and with various levels of intensity governed the lives of Muslims in Nigeria".[4] Northern Nigeria was declared a British protectorate in 1900 and soon thereafter became the testing ground for Lord Lugard's policy of indirect rule. A notable feature of this system of governance was that it sought to preserve traditional administrative structures and pre-existing institutions insofar as these did not undermine or militate against the hegemony of the colonial power. In accordance with this philosophy, the traditional ruling classes were co-opted into the lower strata of colonial government. Within the judicial sphere, these traditional authorities remained actively involved in the administration of justice and settlement of disputes. In those parts of the Northern Protectorate where Islam held sway, these judicial functions were discharged in accordance with the rules and precepts of the Sharia.[5] Although the colonial authorities gave assurances that they would not interfere with the Islamic way of life in Muslim communities, the verdict of modern-day Muslim scholars is that British rule severely compromised the Islamic character of these communities and substantially weakened the position hitherto enjoyed by the Sharia as the dominant legal order.[6]

The colonial authorities did undoubtedly initiate certain measures which circumscribed the manner in which the Sharia was administered by the Emirs' Courts and Alkali Courts and diluted certain aspects of the law which they perceived to be unduly rigorous. The most contentious and far-reaching of these colonial measures was the enactment of the Northern Nigerian Penal Code and Criminal Procedure Code on the eve of Nigeria's independence. These codes, which implemented the recommendations of

---

[4] A.S. Mohammed *et al.*, "Human Living Conditions and Reforms of Legal Systems: The Talakawa and the Issue of Shari'ah in Contemporary Nigeria". Paper presented at Conference on The Shari'ah and the Constitutional Process, Zaria, 1999. Available at http://www.ceddert.com/Article2.htm, last accessed 23 July, 2002.

[5] C.A. Quinn and F. Quinn, *Pride, Faith and Fear: Islam in Sub-Saharan Africa*, Oxford, 2003, 39–40. See also R. Peters, *The Reintroduction of Islamic Criminal Law in Northern Nigeria*, Lagos, 2001, 11–13. Available at http://europa.eu.int/comm/ europeaid/projects/eidhr/pdf/islamic-criminal-law-nigeria_en.pdf, last accessed 24 September, 2003.

[6] See T.M. Naninya, "History of the Sharia in some states of Northern Nigeria to circa 2000", (2000) 13 *Journal of Islamic Studies* 14 at 21; Oba, n. 3, above, 824–826; M. Tabiu, "Sharia, Federalism and Nigerian Constitution". Paper presented at International Conference on Sharia, London, 2001. Available at http://www.shariah2001.nmnonline.net/tabiu_paper.htm, last accessed 24 September, 2003; A.H. Yadudu, "Sharia Implementation in a Democratic Nigeria: Between Deference to Popular Will and Libertarian Challenges". Paper presented at Conference on the Study of Islam and Democracy, Arlington, Virginia, 2002. Available at http://www.amanaonline.com/Articles/art_184.htm last accessed 24 September, 2003.

an international panel of jurists, effectively abolished the substantive and procedural aspects of Sharia criminal law. In the case of the Penal Code this was slightly offset by the inclusion of certain Sharia offences and punishments which, according to Anderson, were preserved "as special concessions to Muslim sentiments".[7] From his vantage point as a member of the panel which had initially recommended the codes, Anderson acknowledged that they were enacted in the teeth of considerable opposition and was evidently gratified that the Northern Nigerian Government (which at this stage was headed by indigenous politicians) "not only saw the need for such a revolutionary change but also had the courage and determination to carry it into effect".[8] Present-day Muslim scholars take a less sanguine view of the matter, maintaining that the decision to dispense with the Sharia in the field of criminal law was orchestrated by the British colonial authorities and foisted on the Northern Regional Government during negotiations over Nigeria's Independence Constitution. Tabiu, for instance, signifies that the British colonial masters placed the political leaders of the North under great political pressure to accept the Penal and Criminal Procedure Codes by making the attainment of independence conditional on introducing the legal and judicial changes contemplated by these Codes. In the process, the colonial authorities impressed on these political leaders that these changes were necessary "if the self governing region was to fulfil its role in the federation of Nigeria and command respect among the nations of the world" and insisted that refusal to implement them "was bound to jeopardize the region's commercial and industrial interests financed by capital from abroad".[9] In Tabiu's assessment the current developments in the Sharia-compliant states of Northern Nigeria are proof positive that "Nigerian Muslims have never openly or silently accepted the triumph of colonial policy in undermining the Sharia and subordinating its judicial system".[10]

The post-Independence era

In the years since the end of colonial rule in 1960, Islam and Christianity, the two dominant religions in Nigeria, have in the words of Pobee, established themselves as "key players in national life".[11] During this period, relations between these two religions have not been characterized by harmony or tolerance. On the contrary, as Quinn and Quinn observe, the Muslim population of Nigeria, more than most other African Muslim communities, has been drawn into a competitive struggle with the nearly numerically equal Christian

[7] J.N.D. Anderson, "Criminal law reform in Nigeria: a major advance", (1961) 24 *MLR* 616, 618. See also Peters, n. 5, above, p. 13, and P. Ostien, "Islamic criminal law: what it means in Zamfara and Niger States", (2000) 4 *Journal of Public and Private Law* 1, at 2–3. Among other things, the P.C. criminalized the consumption of alcohol by Muslims (s. 403) as well as extra-marital sexual intercourse (ss. 387–388). The punishment stipulated for such offences is "*haddi* lashing as prescribed by Muslim law" (s. 68).

[8] Anderson, n. 7 above at 617.

[9] Tabiu, n. 6 above. The view that the colonial authorities coerced the Northern Regional Government into substituting the Codes for the pre-existing Islamic penal system is echoed by Yadudu, n. 6 above (see especially his footnote 6).

[10] Tabiu, n. 6 above.

[11] J.S. Pobee, "Religious human rights in Africa", (1996) 10 *Emory International Law Review*. Available at http://www.law.emory.edu/EILR/volumes/spring96/pobee.html, last accessed 24 September, 2003.

community.[12] The decade after the attainment of independence was a time of great political turmoil, which culminated in the demise of Nigeria's first democratic civilian government and a bloody and protracted civil war. For the most part, however, the upheavals which bedevilled the nation during this period were precipitated not by conflicts within the religious domain but by intense party-political rivalries and deep-rooted ethnic tensions.[13] Religion emerged as a highly contentious issue and forced its way to the top of the political agenda in the late 1970s during the constitutional debates that preceded Nigeria's return to civilian rule in 1979. The first salvo in what ultimately degenerated into an acrimonious war of words between Muslim and Christian adversaries was fired when the Constitution Drafting Committee (CDC) prescribed in article 17 of its initial draft that Nigeria was to be a secular state. In response to strenuous objections from Muslim members of the Committee this clause was deleted from the draft.[14] The CDC ventured further into the religious sphere when its sub-committee on the Judiciary recommended the creation of a Federal Sharia Court of Appeal as an intermediate court between the Sharia Courts of Appeal of the then six Northern states and the Nigerian Supreme Court. In the sub-committee's view, the establishment of this court would "give relevance to the moral, ethical and religious beliefs of all segments of [the Nigerian] society".[15] This recommendation was accepted by the CDC and duly incorporated into the draft Constitution which it prepared.

The creation of an additional court within a judicial hierarchy might at first sight appear to be an anodyne proposal. It was however evident from the outset that the proposed Federal Sharia Court of Appeal was not perceived as just another court. Because of the Islamic character of the court, the ensuing discussion of the merits of the so-called Sharia provisions was recast as a debate on the extent to which concessions should be given to Muslims in the judicial system prescribed by the Constitution.[16] This projection of religion into the mainstream of national life proved to be highly divisive. As Mottoh-Migan points out it created a situation in which members of each religious group increasingly came to perceive members of the other group as "them" while seeing their own religious group as "us".[17] The religious antagonisms fuelled by such perceptions made it almost inevitable that the proposed creation of a Federal Sharia Court of Appeal would turn out to be "easily the most controversial of all the Constitutional provisions put forward by the Constitution Drafting Committee".[18]

---

[12] Quinn and Quinn, n. 5 above at 48.

[13] See S. Bako, "Muslims, state and the struggle for democratic transition in Nigeria: from co-operation to conflict" in P.A. Beckett and C. Young (eds.), *Dilemmas of Nigerian Democracy*, Rochester, New York, 1997, at 283.

[14] M.H. Kukah, "Religion and the politics of national integration" in A. Mahadi *et al.* (eds.), *Nigeria: The State of the Nation and the Way Forward*, Kaduna, 1994, 445 at 450.

[15] D.D. Laitin, "The Sharia debate and the origins of Nigeria's Second Republic", (1982) 20 *Journal of Modern African Studies* 411. See also T. Mamman, *The Law and Politics of Constitution Making in Nigeria: Issues, Interests and Compromises*, Maiduguri, 1998, 209–210.

[16] A. Agbaje, "Travails of the secular state: religion, politics and the outlook on Nigeria's Third Republic", (1990) 28 *Journal of Commonwealth and Comparative Politics* 290.

[17] V.R. Mottoh-Migan, *Constitution Making in Post-Independence Nigeria: A Critique*, Ibadan, 1994, 31.

[18] T. Muhammadu and M. Haruna, "The Making of the 1979 Constitution" in P. Ekeh *et al.* (eds.), *Nigeria Since Independence. The First Twenty-Five Years: Vol. V Politics and Constitutions*, Ibadan, 1989, 49, at 54–55.

The controversy surrounding the creation of the Federal Sharia Court was at its most intense during the proceedings of the Constituent Assembly (CA). The CA, which was chaired by Justice Udo Udoma, had the task of reviewing and, where necessary, redrafting the contents of the CDC's draft Constitution. Realizing the explosive nature of the Sharia issue, Udoma created a special committee to revisit this matter and advise the Assembly on how to proceed. Contrary to the CDC's proposal, this committee recommended the operation of Sharia Courts of Appeal at the state level but proposed that appeals from these courts should lie to the Federal Court of Appeal rather than a separately constituted Federal Sharia Court of Appeal. According to Udoma's version of events, when this recommendation was first tabled it was accepted by all Assembly members. However once the Muslim members had found time to reflect further on the matter they became implacably opposed to the recommendation. The ensuing disagreement between Muslim and non-Muslim Assembly members rapidly escalated to such a degree that the Assembly's existence was almost brought to an abrupt end when the Muslim members boycotted its proceedings for nearly three weeks.[19] Laitin, who has undertaken a careful study of this fraught episode in Nigeria's constitutional history, indicates that as positions hardened "each side in this debate ... developed a whole arsenal of ideological and pragmatic contentions, mixed with both vague and explicit threats as to the consequences of their side losing".[20] It took the intervention of the Federal Military Government to break the impasse and prevent the derailment of the entire constitutional process, thereby ensuring that the Constitution was in place when civilian rule was restored in October 1979.[21]

A related matter which had preoccupied both the CDC and the CA was whether the Constitution ought to proclaim Nigeria to be a secular state. The 1979 Constitution avoided the use of the controversial "s" word and merely declared in somewhat Delphic terms that "[t]he Government of the Federation or of a State shall not adopt any religion as State Religion."[22] With regard to the specific issue that had produced the deadlock in the CA, no provision was made in the judicial hierarchy set out in section 6 of the Constitution for a Federal Sharia Court of Appeal. Instead the Constitution empowered states which wished to do so to establish their own Sharia Courts of Appeal. It further provided that appeals would lie, in matters of Islamic personal law, from these courts to the Federal Court of Appeal where they would be heard by judges learned in Islamic personal law.[23]

---

[19] U. Udoma, *History and the Law of the Constitution of Nigeria,* Lagos, 1994, 312–317.

[20] Laitin, n. 15 above, at 416.

[21] The Decree promulgating this Constitution was subsequently re-designated as the Constitution of the Federal Republic of Nigeria (Enactment) Act, Cap. 62, Laws of the Federation of Nigeria, 1990.

[22] S. 10 of the 1979 Constitution. As shall be seen below, the true import of the corresponding section of the 1999 Constitution is a matter of intense debate between the supporters and opponents of the Sharia reforms in the Northern states.

[23] See s. 240 (establishment of state Sharia Courts of Appeal) and ss. 217 and 223 (Appellate Jurisdiction of Federal Court of Appeal over Sharia Courts of Appeal). It shall be seen below that advocates and critics of the Sharia reforms disagree quite vehemently on whether corresponding provisions in the 1999 Constitution are to be read as restricting the jurisdiction of state Sharia Courts of Appeal to cases involving issues of Muslim personal law.

The promulgation of the 1979 Constitution only served to engender an uneasy and short-lived truce between those who felt aggrieved that the Sharia had been unduly marginalized within the Nigerian legal order and those who objected to the creation of Sharia Courts at the Federal level and were averse to extending the ambit of the Sharia. Religious passions were once again inflamed when news emerged in January 1986 that the Babangida-led military regime had surreptitiously taken Nigeria into membership of the Organisation of the Islamic Conference (OIC). According to Chukwulozie's account of the OIC imbroglio, this development generated bitter controversy between Nigerian Christians and Muslims. Muslims maintained that the OIC was nothing more than a cultural organization and suggested that significant economic benefits would flow from membership. Christians and other non-Muslims responded by insisting that membership of the OIC was incompatible with Nigeria's status as a secular state. Muslims countered by contending that the received common law encompassed rules and reflected moral perspectives which were essentially Christian in origin. Confronted by the prospect of civil unrest, the Federal Government sought to defuse the situation by setting up a committee consisting of leading Christians and Muslims as well as government representatives. The Committee failed to reach a consensus and its Christian members dissociated themselves from the report that it submitted to the government.[24]

While the controversy surrounding Nigeria's entry into the OIC rumbled on, the Babangida regime initiated a programme of transition which was ostensibly designed to reinstate civilian rule. The first step in the transition process occurred in January 1986 with the establishment of a Political Bureau, charged with the responsibility for formulating a blueprint for constitutional reform within the Federation. Non-Muslim members of the Bureau (who were in the majority) advocated the insulation of the Nigerian state from religious affairs and recommended in particular that the state should not belong to any religious organizations, operate religious schools or continue to finance religious pilgrimages. Their Muslim counterparts vigorously argued against the separation of state and religion, insisted that withdrawal from the OIC infringed the constitutional rights of Nigerian Muslims and renewed the demand for the establishment of a Federal Sharia Court of Appeal.[25]

Upon receipt of the Bureau's report the Government set up a Constitution Review Committee (CRC) to review the 1979 Constitution and draft a new Constitution. Section 11 of the CRC's draft Constitution echoed section 10 of the 1979 Constitution in prohibiting the adoption of a state religion by the Federal Government as well as state Governments. The CRC however appears to have been acutely sensitive to the hostility which the retention of the prohibitory section would provoke among the Muslim populace. The Committee sought to resolve this dilemma by emphasizing in its report that the word "secular" did not feature in the relevant section and suggesting that those who maintained that Nigeria was a secular state had misunderstood the import of the section. With regard to the controversy surrounding the establishment and jurisdiction of Sharia courts, the Committee did not accede to

[24] See T. Chukwulozie, ***Muslim-Christian Dialogue in Nigeria,*** Ibadan, 1986. See also T. Falola, "Christian radicalism and Nigerian politics" in P. Beckett and C. Young (eds.), ***Dilemmas in Nigerian Democracy,*** Rochester, New York, 1997, 265 at 272.

[25] See Agbaje, n. 16 above, 294.

Muslim demands for the creation of a Federal Sharia Court of Appeal. The Committee's draft Constitution did however provide for the extension of the jurisdiction of the existing Sharia courts beyond the realm of "Islamic personal law" (as designated in the 1979 Constitution) into other areas of civil law.[26]

The task of deliberating on the draft Constitution produced by the CRC was entrusted to a Constituent Assembly (CA) inaugurated in May 1988. The religious tensions simmering under the surface during the proceedings of the Political Bureau and the CRC became more acute and intractable when the CA began its work. As Ibrahim observes in this connection, it became evident from the outset that "Muslims and Christians were intent on reorganizing and remobilizing themselves into opposing camps in readiness for a resumption of the hostilities generated by the Sharia issue".[27] The intense acrimony, acute mutual suspicions and Machiavellian intrigues, which characterized the Assembly's deliberations on the Sharia issue, have been graphically described by its Chairman, Justice Aniagolu.[28] According to Aniagolu's account, the first skirmish in what escalated into open warfare occurred when Muslim members of the Assembly complained bitterly about the predominance of Christians on Committees 3 and 16, which were charged with the responsibility of reviewing the sections of the draft constitution dealing with judicial matters. The substance of their complaint was that the Christian members of these committees had been heard boasting that they would use their numerical advantage to outvote the Muslims and remove any reference to the Sharia Court of Appeal in the Constitution. This led to a stampede by assembly members to join these two committees and foreshadowed the turmoil that would eventually engulf the Assembly. Committee 3 was assigned the task of reviewing Clauses 1–13 of the draft Constitution. Clause 6 provided that the judicial powers of the Federation were to be vested in the courts enumerated therein, including Sharia Courts of Appeal. There were heated arguments as to whether Sharia Courts should be recognized and provided for within the Constitution. The Committee's non-Muslim members sought to strike out any reference to such courts in Clause 6 on the grounds that they were religious courts (like the Roman Catholic Canon courts). They argued that legislating for such courts in the Constitution would derogate from section 10 which prohibited the adoption by the state of any religion and insisted that entrenching such religious courts in the Constitution was not in keeping with the secular character of the government. The Muslim members of the Committee who favoured the preservation of Sharia Courts within the Constitution counter-argued that the Sharia was a way of life for Muslims and to oust any provision for the establishment and operation of Sharia Courts of Appeal from the Constitution would strike at the very root of the Muslim way of life. They maintained that the Constitution was meant for all Nigerians and had to articulate and provide for the needs of all segments of Nigerian society.

---

[26] Agbaje, n. 16 above, at 294–296.

[27] J. Ibrahim, "Religion and political turbulence in Nigeria", (1991) 29 *Journal of Modern African Studies* 115, at 130.

[28] A.N. Aniagolu, *The Making of the 1989 Constitution of Nigeria*, Ibadan, 1993. See also A.H. Yadudu, "Constitution-making and the politicisation of Shari'a in Nigeria", (1991) 18 *Journal of Islamic and Comparative Law* 19 especially at 28–33; Mottoh-Migan, n. 17 above (especially ch. 5); and J.S. Read, "Nigeria's new Constitution for 1992: the Third Republic", [1991] 35 *J.A.L.* 174, at 175–177.

Leaving the Sharia Court of Appeal out of the Constitutional equation amounted to expunging Muslims from the body politic of Nigeria and would signal the dismemberment of Nigeria. The more hardline members of the pro-Sharia faction sought to raise the stakes by contending that the Sharia courts ought to constitute a parallel hierarchy of courts existing alongside the British-type courts, right up to the level of the Supreme Court.[29] By mid-September 1998, the pro- and anti-Sharia factions in Committee 3 had become so inescapably deadlocked on the question of whether the Sharia Court of Appeal should be included in the list of courts enumerated in Clause 6 that the Committee Chairman (a Christian) put the matter to a vote. This was won by the anti-Sharia faction by a majority of 15 to 11. The pro-Sharia faction vociferously questioned the validity of the vote and refused to sign the Committee's report on the outcome of its deliberations. As a compromise, the report that was ultimately submitted to the Assembly Chairman simply set out the opposing standpoints of the two factions without signifying that the matter had been put to a vote.[30] Committee 16 was assigned, *inter alia*, the task of reviewing Clause 254 and other complementary clauses dealing with the composition and jurisdiction of state Sharia Courts of Appeal. Non-Muslim members of the committee sought to delete this clause from the Constitution and the Muslim members responded by calling on the Assembly Chairman to rule that the Assembly's Standing Orders, which empowered Committees to make amendments to clauses they were reviewing, did not authorize them to expunge such clauses. When it was ruled that the power of amendment extended to the expunction of clauses, this met with such relentless opposition that the Committee was ultimately unable to produce a report for consideration by the Committee of the whole house.[31]

Concerted efforts by Aniagolu and other prominent Assembly members to resolve the impasse between pro-Sharia and anti-Sharia factions proved to be of no avail. Matters came to a head when the whole Assembly began deliberating on the reports presented by its various committees. When the report of Committee 3 was tabled before the Assembly, Clause 6 did not appear on the order paper due to clerical problems. This excited the suspicion in the minds of Muslim members that a plan had been hatched to gloss over the Sharia issue and, once the fuss had abated, to present the Government with a "Sharia free" Constitution. Bitter recriminations ensued and the atmosphere within the Assembly Chamber became so combustible that proceedings had to be adjourned for a week in late November 1988. This state of affairs elicited a swift reaction from the Federal Government, which proceeded to exclude the Sharia issue from the CA's agenda and to impose its own solution. This solution attempted to strike a balance between the competing demands of the pro-Sharia and anti-Sharia factions by stipulating (a) that any state which required it could establish its own Sharia Court of Appeal, (b) that these courts were to exercise jurisdiction in civil proceedings involving questions of Islamic law and (c) that the jurisdiction of these courts was to extend only to cases in which all the parties were

29 Aniagolu, n. 28 above, at 50.
30 Ibid., at 55–64.
31 Ibid., at 54–55, 77.

Muslims.[32] These stipulations were in due course incorporated into the provisions of the 1989 Constitution which was supposed to have ushered in Nigeria's ill-fated Third Republic. Despite the monumental efforts which had gone into fashioning this Constitution, the annulment of the 1993 Presidential election and the subsequent seizure of power by the military regime of General Sani Abacha meant that these constitutional provisions never came into force.

In 1994, General Abacha convened a National Constitutional Conference with a view to producing a new Constitution to replace the stillborn Constitution of 1989. Participants at this conference spent a considerable amount of time debating religious issues and put forward several key decisions, notably:

(i) that the Nigerian state should remain secular and the Federal, State and Local Governments should continue to be prohibited from adopting any religion;
(ii) that no Government or State agency should promote or hinder the practice of any particular religion;
(iii) that the Government should not be a member of any international religious organization;
(iv) that the Government should not promote, patronize or fund religious pilgrimages.

According to Nwala, who was a participant at the Conference, the recommendations regarding the membership of international religious bodies and government funding of pilgrimages were vehemently opposed by conservative Muslims who contrived to ensure that these two measures were not contained in the 1995 draft Constitution produced by the Conference for submission to the Federal Government.[33]

The Federal Government took no steps to give effect to this draft Constitution while General Abacha remained alive. However, after his sudden death, General Abubakar, who succeeded him as Head of State, initiated a national debate on the 1995 draft Constitution under the guidance of a Constitution Debate Co-ordinating Committee (CDCC). The CDCC, which was inaugurated in November 1998, was mandated to pilot and co-ordinate constitutional debate and collate views and recommendations put forward by individuals and groups. It was required to submit its report by the end of December 1998. In his inauguration address to the CDCC, Abubakar identified a number of contentious issues connected with the 1995 draft Constitution in respect of which his Government would welcome fresh ideas. Significantly, none of these issues related to the place of religion in the Nigerian body politic either in general or with specific reference to the application of the Sharia and operation of Sharia courts within the legal system. The CDCC invited members of the public, various interest groups and provisionally registered political parties to submit memoranda and to participate in public hearings at various debate centres throughout the country. At the end of this exercise, the CDCC's report concluded that it was clear that Nigerians had opted for a

[32] Ibid., at 93–100, 140–145 See also Read, n. 28 above; and P. Koehn, "Comparative transition to civilian rule: Nigeria's first and second experiments", (1989) 27 *Journal of Modern African Studies* 401, 424.

[33] T.U. Nwala, *Nigeria: Path to Unity and Stability Abuja National Constitutional Conference 1994–1995 A Critical Review*, Nsukka, 1997, 95–96.

Constitution modelled on the 1979 Constitution with relevant amendments derived from the 1995 draft Constitution.[34]

Yadudu, who was a member of the CDCC, states that its report was considered by the Provisional Ruling Council (PRC) of the Federal Military Government amidst press speculation and insinuations that this body was being torn apart by the Sharia issue.[35] The outcome of the PRC's deliberations was that the provisions of the 1979 Constitution dealing with the non-adoption of a state religion and Sharia Courts of Appeal were reproduced with minor amendments in the 1999 version which came into force on 29 May, 1999. This did not however signal the end of the Sharia controversy. On the contrary, barely four months after the promulgation of the Constitution and the restoration of civilian rule in Nigeria, "the Sharia emerged on the scene, defying all the odds [and] throwing the whole nation into disarray".[36]

The Constitutional Implications of the Sharia Reforms

Overview of the Sharia reforms

The foregoing account vividly demonstrates the manner in which the deep-seated religious convictions, concerns and antagonisms of the Muslim and non-Muslim segments of the Nigerian populace have been played out in the constitutional arena in the past twenty-five years. In each of the Constitutions prepared during this period the standard approach to dealing with tensions engendered by religious differences has been to prohibit the adoption of any religion by the Federal and state Governments while at the same time providing for Sharia Courts of Appeal to operate on the same level of the judicial hierarchy as the High Courts. Bako alludes to the fact that Muslims, including intellectual leaders, see the Muslim side as having been disadvantaged at many points by these constitutional outcomes.[37] The paramount reason why these Constitutions were viewed askance in Muslim circles was that they were seen to inhibit the operation of the Sharia to a degree which many Muslims considered objectionable. From the Muslim perspective, little was done to rectify this unsatisfactory state of affairs either by the Muslim politicians of the Second Republic or by successive Muslim military rulers who assumed power in the years following the demise of the Second Republic.

With the restoration of civilian rule in 1999, the outlook has changed dramatically in most of the Northern states with predominantly Muslim

[34] See the speech delivered by the CDCC Chairman, Justice Tobi, at the formal presentation of the CDCC Report to General Abubakar. Available at http://www.nigerianscholars.africanqueen.com/debates/constitution/cdcc.htm, last accessed 24 September, 2003. See also N. Tobi, "The legitimacy of constitutional change in the context of the 1999 Constitution" in I.A. Ayua *et al.* (eds.), *Issues in the 1999 Constitution,* Lagos, 2000, 21, at 25–29 (hereafter referred to as Tobi (2000) n. 34.).

[35] A.H. Yadudu, "The amending process under Nigerian law and Constitutions" in Ayua *et al.* (eds.), above, n. 34, 302, at 317. See also K. Henneman, "Responding to Religious Conflict in Northern Nigeria". Available at http://www.maxwell.syr.edu/parc/Henneman%20Communal%20Conflict%20Paper.pdf, last accessed 24 September, 2003.

[36] I. Sulaiman, "Sharia Restoration in Nigeria: The Dynamics and the Process". Paper presented at International Conference on Sharia, London, 2001. Available at http://www.shariah2001.nmnonline.net/ibrahim_paper.htm, last accessed 24 September, 2003.

[37] S. Bako, n. 13 above, at 288. Although this remark was made with particular reference to the 1979 and 1989 Constitutions, it is equally applicable to the 1999 Constitution.

populations. Since then, twelve Northern state governments, starting with the Zamfara State Government, have sought to reverse the *status quo* by introducing far-reaching executive measures and legislative reforms designed to elevate the standing of the Sharia and enlarge the jurisdiction of the Sharia courts operating within their territories.[38] According to Yadudu, the paramount aim of these reforms was "restore the Sharia in its pristine purity, shorn of all the baggage it has acquired over a century of contact with the English common law ... ".[39] As Tabiu signifies, for those states which have embraced the Sharia reforms, this has necessitated a "transformation of their legal systems in conformity with the Sharia".[40] In this connection, the most significant measures taken by the Governments of these states have been directed at:

(a) extending the scope of the Sharia beyond the realm of civil law into the sphere of criminal law;
(b) reorganizing the courts responsible for administering the Sharia; and
(c) resuscitating and strengthening the social dimensions of the Sharia which had hitherto been abandoned or neglected, such as the reintroduction of community participation in crime prevention and detection; the resumption of state responsibility for the collection and distribution of *zakat* (obligatory alms) and the reinstatement of the ideals of the Sharia within the commercial sphere.[41]

As Ladan points out, there are certain differences in detail in the Sharia legislation enacted by various Sharia-compliant states. He however emphasizes that in spite of such differences the states have a great deal in common as far as the implementation of the Sharia is concerned. The common features identified by Ladan include the creation of quasi-governmental bodies to implement the Sharia in these states; the establishment of separate courts, separate penal codes and separate criminal procedure codes for Muslims in these states; the amendment of their Sharia Court of Appeal laws to enable these courts to hear appeals in criminal cases and the prohibition of certain practices and the punishment of Muslims and non-Muslims engaging in such practices within these states.[42]

Constitutional issues arising from the reforms

It is significant that the approach adopted by those intellectuals who have sought to champion the Sharia reforms is not to denounce the 1999 Constitution for unduly inhibiting the operation of the Sharia but rather to insist that the reforms are wholly consistent with the provisions of the Constitution. This

[38] See n. 3 above, for a list of these Sharia-implementing states.

[39] Yadudu, "Benefits of Shariah and Challenges of Reclaiming a Heritage". Paper presented at International Conference on Sharia, London, 2001. Available at http://www.shariah2001.nmnonline.net/yadudu_paper.htm, last accessed 24 September, 2003.

[40] Tabiu, n. 6 above.

[41] Tabiu, n. 6 above; Yadudu n. 39 above.

[42] M.T. Ladan, "Legal Pluralism and the Development of the Rule of Law in Nigeria: Issues and Challenges in the Development and Application of the Sharia". Paper presented at International Conference on Sharia, Penal and Family Laws in Nigeria and in the Muslim World: A Rights-Based Approach. Abuja, 2003. Available at http://nigerianewsnow.com/News/November03/231103_sharia.htm, last accessed 28 May, 2004.

places them at odds with critics of the Sharia reforms who are equally vehement in their insistence that the reforms derogate from the Constitution in several significant respects. Supporters and opponents of the reforms do agree on one point, namely that section 38(1) of the Constitution safeguards the rights of all Nigerian citizens, including Muslims, to manifest and pursue their religious beliefs in worship, practice and observance. Advocates of the reforms assert that this constitutional guarantee provides ample justification for the measures taken by the Northern state Governments which have sought to reclaim their Islamic heritage by embarking on these reforms. Their opponents contend that while it is imperative to safeguard the freedom of Muslims to worship and observe the tenets of their faith, this does not warrant the degree of governmental involvement within the religious sphere which has occurred in various Sharia-compliant states. The opposing camps now appear to have battled each other to a standstill and retreated to their respective bunkers, and it might seem tactless or even foolhardy to revisit such a sensitive issue at this juncture. It can however be surmised from the manner in which the debate is reignited whenever the Sharia courts sentence adulterers to death by stoning or order amputation for theft, that the issue will remain highly topical and contentious until the courts finally determine whether the Sharia reforms pass muster under the 1999 Constitution. While awaiting further developments within the judicial sphere it will nevertheless be instructive to explore a number of substantive issues pertaining to the constitutionality of the Sharia reforms. The issues which shall be addressed here relate to the following matters:

(a) *The legality and legitimacy of the Constitution*: Various critics of the 1999 Constitution have questioned the legality and disputed the legitimacy of this Constitution. Is it open to advocates of the Sharia reforms to contend on the basis of such criticisms that this Constitution does not afford a suitable frame of reference for determining the constitutionality of the Sharia reforms?
(b) *The battle for supremacy between the Constitution and the Sharia*: Is the doctrinal foundation of the Sharia amenable to the supremacy of the Constitution?
(c) *The effect of section 10 of the Constitution on the Sharia reforms*: Does the implementation of the Sharia reforms entail the adoption of a particular religion in contravention of section 10?
(d) *The jurisdiction of state Sharia courts*: Does the Constitution recognize the competence of such courts to adjudicate on criminal matters as prescribed in the Sharia Penal Codes currently in force in the Northern states or does it restrict their jurisdiction to matters of Islamic personal law?
(e) *The severity of the punishments sanctioned by the Sharia*: Can the infliction of traditional Sharia punishments such as amputation, stoning to death, crucifixion and retaliatory killing and wounding be reconciled with the proscription of cruel and inhuman treatment by the Constitution and by various international human rights conventions to which Nigeria is a signatory?
(f) *The discriminatory effect of the Sharia penal regime*: A significant consequence of the Sharia reforms is that the penal regime applicable to Muslims within the Sharia-compliant states is considerably stricter than that applicable to their non-Muslim counterparts in certain key respects.

Does this violate section 42(a) of the Constitution which provides, *inter alia,* that a Nigerian citizen who belongs to a particular religion shall not be subjected to disabilities or restrictions to which Nigerians of other religious persuasions are not made subject?

(g) *The constitutional implications of extra-legislative Sharia offences*: Some offences which are known to the Sharia have not been expressly defined as offences in the Sharia Penal Codes. What are the constitutional implications of imposing penal sanctions on persons who commit such offences? This issue will be explored with particular reference to the offence of apostasy.

(h) *The scope for the Federal Government's involvement in testing the constitutional validity of the Sharia reforms*: Since the Sharia reforms were devised and implemented by state governors and state legislative assemblies with no input whatsoever from the Federal Government, some commentators have argued that it is incumbent on the Federal Government to initiate judicial proceedings with a view to determining the constitutional validity of these reforms. The Federal Government has so far declined to intervene on the basis that it lacks the *locus standi* to do so. Is the stance adopted by the Federal Government justified or does it constitute an abdication of its responsibilities?

(a) The legality and legitimacy of the 1999 Constitution

Since the 1999 Constitution came into force its legality has been called into question by at least one influential commentator while doubts have been expressed in various quarters concerning its legitimacy. Advocates of the Sharia reforms might conceivably seize upon such doubts as a basis for contending that the 1999 Constitution does not provide a suitable reference point for judging these reforms.

As Ogowewo points out, "[a] Constitution is legitimate if it is the result of the popular will".[43] The desirability of involving the populace in constitution-making has also been stressed by the Presidential Committee on the Review of the 1999 Constitution (PCRC) which states that the process should ideally involve "wide ranging debate, extensive popular participation and expert consultation".[44] This theme is also taken up by Ekeh, who is one of Nigeria's foremost political scientists. He observes that a nation's Constitution is a most solemn document and that preparing it is a sacred and weighty undertaking not to be addressed lightly. He further declares that all worthy constitutions are made by citizens and their representatives and that a Constitution must be judged not only by its contents but also by the process through which it is formulated and ratified.[45] Commenting on the 1979 Constitution, the aborted 1989 Constitution and the 1995 draft Constitution, Ekeh states that all three constitutions "were decreed into existence by military fiat and ... their

[43] T.I. Ogowewo, "Coup proofing democracies: the need for a proactive approach" in J. Hatchard and T.I. Ogowewo, *Tackling the Unconstitutional Overthrow of Democracies: Emerging Trends in the Commonwealth*, London, 2003, 11.

[44] See the Report of the PCRC. Available at http://www.pcrconline.org/The_Report/1.shtml, last accessed 24 September, 2003.

[45] P. Ekeh, "Comments and Viewpoints on the Nigerian Constitution" (undated). Memorandum submitted by the Association of Nigeria Scholars for Dialogue to the Constitution Debate Co-ordinating Committee. Available at http://www.nigerianscholars.africanqueen.com/debates/constitution/ViewConst1.htm, last accessed on 24 September, 2003.

making was circumscribed by military commandments regarding areas that the constitution should not touch".[46] The 1999 Constitution falls into the same mould, having been sponsored by a military regime as part of a programme of transition to civilian rule, and it comes as no great surprise that the pivotal role played by the military in the preparation and promulgation of this Constitution has provoked a debate in legal and political circles about the legitimacy of this Constitution.

On the one hand, some commentators contend that the legitimacy of the 1999 Constitution has not been fatally compromised by the fact that it bears the legislative imprint of a military regime. This point of view has been eloquently canvassed by Achimu who maintains that:

> "There may be an unjustified overstatement of the position when critics of the Constitution state that the Constitution has been imposed by the military. That objection is obviously based on the realisation that the Federal Military Government placed the formal clothing of legality on the Constitution. It however fails to take into consideration the activities that preceded the formal signing of the Constitution into law as well as the source of the substantive parts of the Constitution. An examination of these issues will show that there has been some input which can be traced directly to the people.
>
> The erstwhile military government had set up a Constitution Debate Coordinating Committee. This committee had called for memoranda from Nigerians and conducted oral hearings in various centres in the nation. It would appear that the preponderance of the popular view was that the state should revert to the Constitution of 1979. This was presumably the basis of the recommendation that was made to the Provisional Ruling Council. It is clear that this recommendation was accepted because a close comparison of the two Constitutions discloses great similarities between the clauses contained in both.... [T]he truth of the matter is that the 1979 Constitution was adopted and accepted by the generality of Nigerians as meeting the constitutional needs of the State. It is submitted that the people having been just as involved in the formative stages of the 1999 Constitution would have no basis for questioning its legitimacy."[47]

Tobi, who chaired the CDCC, is equally convinced of the legitimacy of the 1999 Constitution and is adamant that the CDCC report which preceded this Constitution faithfully reflected the views of the Nigerian populace. He submits that the [Abubakar] regime "legitimately carried out the function of constitution-making" when it promulgated the 1999 Constitution and invokes the ideas and arguments of leading legal theorists such as Kelsen and Olivecrona to justify his position.[48]

The views expressed by Achimu and Tobi may be contrasted with the more critical stance taken by other commentators. Benjamin, for instance, declares that "[t]he main opposition to the 1999 Constitution centres around its being a product of official secrecy, an imposed constitution that was not subjected to popular debate or referenda. This is partly due to the manner in which General Abdulsalami Abubakar and the Provisional Ruling Council introduced the Constitution without consulting the opinion

[46] P. Ekeh, "Themes of the Wilberforce conference" in P. Ekeh (ed.), *Wilberforce Conference on Nigerian Federalism*, New York, 1997. Available at http://www.nigerianscholars.africanqueen.com/pubs/wilber2.htm, last accessed 24 September, 2003.

[47] J.V. Achimu, "The legitimacy of constitutional change: the enactment of the 1999 Constitution" in I.A. Ayua *et al.* (eds.), *Issues in the Nigerian Constitution*, Lagos, 2000, 1, at 10–11.

[48] Tobi (2000) n. 34 above, at 28, 33–37.

of the public. ... To this extent most Nigerians started to know what the Constitution looks like only with the departure of the military on 29th May 1999".[49] Similar reservations have been expressed by Igbuzor, who asserts that "[t]he people did not participate in the process of making the Constitution. This is why the preamble which begins with 'WE THE PEOPLE of the Federal Republic of Nigeria ... do hereby make, enact and give to ourselves the following Constitution' has been severely criticised as a false claim."[50] The Constitution has also been subjected to sustained criticism by the Presidential Committee on the Review of the 1999 Constitution. In its report, the Committee emphasizes that the CDCC was given less than two months to complete its task and comments adversely on the absence of wide-ranging debates and lack of extensive popular participation in the making of the Constitution. The report also acknowledges the widespread view that "the words 'WE THE PEOPLE OF NIGERIA' contained in the preamble tell a great lie since Nigerians never met to agree on the Articles of the Constitution" and suggests that "the Constitution of the Federal Republic of Nigeria (Promulgation) Decree No. 24 of 1999 being a military decree cannot confer legitimacy on the constitution along with the democratic structures which have resulted from it."[51] Ogowewo, who is perhaps the most trenchant critic of the 1999 Constitution, also opines that "in the conception and promulgation of the 1999 Constitution a great deceit was practised on the Nigerian people by the departing provisional ruling council (PRC) of the military government" and declares "that the Federal Republic of Nigeria is today being governed in accordance with a Constitution that is illegitimate is a fact that admits of very little doubt".[52] Indeed, Ogowewo does not only seek to impugn the legitimacy, and hence the moral authority of this Constitution but also goes further to question its legal validity. He argues at length that the Constitution is void for illegality since it breaches the supremacy clause of an earlier valid Constitution.[53] The earlier Constitution to which he refers is the 1979 Constitution which he maintains "was the product of a constituent assembly of elected citizens acting as representatives of the people"[54] and which he insists "expressed the will of the Nigerian people to govern themselves democratically in accordance with terms which *they* agreed upon".[55] He accordingly makes a case for the judicial annulment of the 1999 Constitution and the reinstatement of the 1979 Constitution.

In the light of the foregoing, advocates of the Sharia reforms might seek to contend that even if aspects of the reforms are inconsistent with the 1999 Constitution, the Constitution, being of doubtful legitimacy, is not

[49] S.A. Benjamin, "1999 Constitution: implications for political structure" in O. Ajakaiye and S.A. Benjamin (eds.), *Issues in the Review of the Nigerian Constitution,* Ibadan, 1999, 18 at 22.

[50] O. Igbuzor, "Constitution Making in Nigeria: Lessons for Making a People's Constitution". Paper presented at a Conference on Constitutional Development, Kibuye, Rwanda, 2001. Available at http://www.gamji.com/NEWS1557.htm, last accessed 24 September, 2003.

[51] See Report of the PCRC, n. 44 above.

[52] T.I. Ogowewo, "Why the judicial annulment of the Constitution of 1999 is imperative for the survival of Nigeria's democracy" in M. Andenas (ed.), *The Creation and Amendment of Constitutional Norms,* London, 2000, 265, at 266. This thesis is developed further at 274–278.

[53] Ibid., at 283, 297.

[54] Ibid., at 270, 296

[55] Ibid., at 272, 297.

imbued with sufficient moral authority and hence does not command sufficient loyalty or respect to deter the architects of the reforms from carrying them into effect. Furthermore, such advocates might be inclined to argue that if the 1999 Constitution is indeed tainted by illegality as posited by Ogowewo, the fact that the Sharia reforms might infringe certain constitutional provisions ought not to impair the legal validity of these reforms.

As the debate rages on regarding the legitimacy of the 1999 Constitution, and without seeking to discount the possibility that this Constitution might in due course be judicially annulled, it is significant that since civilian rule was restored in May 1999, the Nigerian courts have been confronted with several cases in which they have had to pronounce upon various aspects of the Constitution. On every such occasion, the courts have scrupulously interpreted and applied the relevant provisions of the Constitution and in so doing, have never called its legality into question nor have they given the least indication that its legitimacy is in any doubt within the judicial sphere.[56] It can be deduced from this that in the event of a judicial challenge to the constitutionality of the Sharia reforms, the courts are unlikely to uphold any defence of the reforms which proceeds on the premise that the Constitution is founded on an illegality or that the legitimacy of the Constitution is suspect.[57]

It is equally noteworthy that the Governors and members of the state Houses of Assembly who introduced the Sharia reforms were all elected to office under and derive their executive and legislative powers from the 1999 Constitution and allied military decrees promulgated as part of the Abubakar regime's programme of transition to civilian rule. This very fact creates a "Catch 22" dilemma for any supporters of the Sharia reforms who might be inclined to respond to claims that these reforms infringe the 1999 Constitution by seeking to challenge the legality of this Constitution. At the root of this dilemma is the fact that if the Constitution is void for illegality because of the circumstances in which it was promulgated, such supporters would be hard pressed to justify the legality of any laws or policies initiated or implemented by Nigeria's current civilian rulers including the Sharia reforms. As Tobi perceptively points out in this regard,

> "it was the same military regime of General Abubakar that promulgated all the Decrees which ushered in the civilian Government on the 29th of May, 1999.... Can Nigeria and Nigerians who took the benefit of the country returning to a democratic government and participating in elections under these decrees

---

[56] See, for example, *Attorney General of Ogun State & 4 ors* v. *Attorney General of the Federation* [2002] 18 N.W.L.R 232; (revenue allocation under ss. 162 and 163 of the Constitution); *Independent National Electoral Commission* v. *Musa* [2002] 17 N.W.L.R 412 (effect of ss. 221–229 of the Constitution on the formation, registration and operation of political parties); *Fawehinmi* v. *Inspector General of Police* (extent of the immunity from legal proceedings conferred by s. 308 of the Constitution) and *Medical and Dental Practitioners Disciplinary Tribunal* v. *Okonkwo* [2001] 7 N.W.L.R 207 (refusal of treatment *vis-à-vis* the right to privacy (s. 37 of the Constitution) and freedom of religion (s. 38 of the Constitution)).

[57] In any case, even if the courts do ultimately decide to dispense with the 1999 Constitution and recognize the continued operation of the 1979 Constitution, as proposed by Ogowewo, this does not significantly affect the analysis which follows, since the provisions of the 1999 Constitution which have a bearing on the Sharia reforms have replicated the corresponding provisions of the 1979 Constitutions with a few minor amendments not affecting their substance.

really condemn the same military government that made these events possible, for promulgating a Constitution which is the main plank of democracy? Is such a position not tantamount to eating one's cake and still trying to have it intact?"[58]

(b) The supremacy issue

Section 1(1) of the 1999 Constitution provides that "[t]his Constitution is supreme and its provisions shall have binding force on the persons and authorities throughout the Federal Republic of Nigeria". This is reinforced by section 1(3) which states that "If any other law is inconsistent with the provisions of this Constitution, this Constitution shall prevail and that other law shall, to the extent of the inconsistency, be void." The fundamental premise that the Constitution is supreme and that its provisions override all other laws is clearly at variance with the deeply held conviction among the Muslim faithful that the Sharia embodies the will of Allah and as such is eternally valid, immutable and not susceptible to review by any human agency. This perception of the Sharia as being divinely inspired goes a long way towards explaining the strong support which Mayer discerns among fundamentalist Muslims for the notion that not just laws but also constitutions must be drawn up or rewritten in accordance with Islamic criteria and that the Sharia is to be placed above the constitution.[59] This creates a veritable dilemma for any advocate of the Sharia reforms who insists that these reforms are entirely compatible with the Constitution. This dilemma is clearly discernible to Al-Zakzaky who signifies that Muslims who endorse the operation of the Sharia as one of the legal systems under the Constitution must contend with two conflicts. According to him, "One conflict will be with the Constitution which will claim superiority over the Shar'iah and will therefore place the Shar'iah under its control and regulation. The other conflict will be with the Shari'ah itself which as the law of Almighty God claims superiority over all laws and therefore cannot accept the Supremacy of the Nigerian Constitution".[60]

Several Nigerian Muslim legal scholars have articulated the belief that according to the fundamental tenets of Islam, the Constitution must defer to the supremacy of the Sharia. Sulaiman, for instance, declared with reference to the 1979 Constitution that "to believe that the sentences of [this] Constitution could drive Islam to the background is a mere adventure in aberration (sic)"; and also proclaimed that "the only way a Muslim can show his sincerity in his belief ... is to struggle wherever he is for the supremacy of the Shariah to the point of sacrificing his life".[61] By the same token, Adegbite asserts that "To the Muslims, the Constitution ... can only be supreme to the extent that it does not infringe any commitment emanating from Allah's

[58] Tobi, (2000) n. 34 above.

[59] Mayer, n. 1 above at 49.

[60] I.Y. Al-Zakzaky, "Application of the *Shari'ah* in the Contemporary World: Some Lessons from Muslim Countries". Part II of a Paper presented at Conference on Nature and Application of the Shari'ah, Kano, 1999. Available at http://www.muslimedia.com/archives/features00/shariah2.htm, last accessed 24 September, 2003.

[61] I.K.R. Sulaiman, "The Shari'ah and the 1979 Constitution" in S.K. Rashid (ed.), *Islamic Law in Nigeria (Applications and Teachings)*, Lagos, 1986, 52 at 53, 57.

injunctions. Therefore we must only talk of the limited supremacy of the Constitution".[62]

On the other hand, Ostien points to utterances by the Governors of several Sharia-implementing states which suggest that they have recognized and accepted the supremacy of the Constitution *vis-à-vis* Sharia law. Moreover, the preamble to the Zamfara Sharia Penal Code (upon which the corresponding codes of most other states are modelled) declares that the Code is subject to the provisions of the Constitution. As Ostien emphasizes, such a concession is no small thing for Muslims to make but is nevertheless absolutely necessary within the context of the Nigerian federation.[63] It remains to be seen which of these positions will ultimately prevail if the courts were ever to adjudicate that the Sharia as currently applied in these states infringes the Constitution in some material respect.

(c) The issue relating to the adoption of a state religion

Section 10 of the 1999 Constitution provides that "[t]he Government of the Federation or a state shall not adopt any religion as State religion". One of the most strenuous objections put forward by non-Muslims opposed to the Sharia reforms is that these reforms are unconstitutional because they infringe the prohibition of a state religion enshrined in section 10. Ardent supporters of the reforms have been at pains to negate any such impression. Yadudu, in particular, peremptorily dismisses suggestions that the Sharia reforms infringe the prohibition of state religion as "the loud and pious but self-serving declarations of the so-called legal luminaries who mask their Christian or atheistic biases and preferences".[64]

The debate regarding the true import of section 10 rages on unabated. A particularly contentious issue which is yet to be resolved is whether the section dictates that the Nigerian federation and its constituent states must maintain a secular outlook in the conduct of their affairs. Leading Muslim academics who support the Sharia reforms maintain that there is nothing in the Constitution to warrant the supposition that Nigeria is a secular state. Tabiu, for instance, asserts that a reading of section 10 "does not establish [the] claim that the Constitution describes Nigeria as a secular state" and emphasizes that "In fact the constitution does not use the word secularism or any of its derivatives at all".[65] The point is driven home by Yadudu, who poses the question: "Where does the Constitution declare Nigeria to be secular?"[66]

[62] L. Adegbite, "Political Agenda for Muslims". Paper delivered at Conference on Islam in Nigeria, Ilorin, 2000. Available at http://www.thisdayonline.comarchive/2001/04/15/20010415pol05.html, last accessed 16 August, 2002. See also Oba, n. 3 above, at 844, where he observes that Muslims are now challenging aspects of the Constitution that are not consistent with Islamic principles and ethics and demanding in particular that "the sovereignty and supremacy which resides in the constitution ... be expunged. Both they claim belong to Allah."

[63] P. Ostien, "Ten good things about the implementation of Shari'a in some Northern states of Nigeria", (2002) 90(2) *Svensk Missions Tidskrift (Swedish Missiological Themes)*. Available at http://twist.lib.uiowa.edu/gsncollo/section1/images/1.pdf, last accessed on 24 September, 2003.

[64] Yadudu, n. 6 above.

[65] Tabiu, n. 6 above.

[66] Yadudu, n. 39 above. It is however noteworthy that Yadudu's stance seems to be at variance with views he had earlier expressed in relation to the corresponding provision in s. 10 of the 1979 Constitution in A.H. Yadudu, "The separation of Church and State: Nigeria's Constitutional contrivance", (1992) 1(2) *Lawyers Bi-Annual Journal of Nigerian and Comparative Law* 14, at 22. Here Yadudu appears to have accepted that secularism became enshrined in the Nigerian Constitution

This view is contested by a host of non-Muslim commentators. The most notable of these commentators is Nwabueze who observes that "it is argued that Nigeria is not a secular state in as much as the Constitution does not make it one. All it does is to prohibit the adoption of any religion as the state religion .... This is not true. On the contrary, the constitutional prohibition of the establishment of a state religion does import the secularity of the state in the fullest sense of the term."[67] The view that the secular character of the Nigerian state is affirmed by the Constitution is echoed by Davies.[68] Referring to Smith's classic definition of a secular state,[69] Davies argues that Nigeria "is to all intents and purposes a secular state because s. 10(1) of the [1979] Constitution [which is identical in wording to s. 10 of the 1999 Constitution] specifically prohibits the state from adopting any religion as state religion. Secularity has thus been constitutionally guaranteed in recognition of the fundamental right of Nigerians to profess any religion". A third commentator, Ihenacho, asserts that a secular state is one whose government does not depend for its existence on religions and does not sponsor any religion and argues that Nigeria can aptly be described as a secular state in the light of section 10.[70]

The view that the Constitution has taken cognizance of Nigeria's secular status is by no means restricted to non-Muslim commentators. Thus, for instance, Mamman, like Davies, refers to Smith's definition of a secular state and similarly concludes that this conception of a secular state is "concretely reflected in section 10 of the 1979 Constitution".[71] Another commentator, Bunza, while noting that the term secular does not feature in the Constitution, maintains that "the status of the country remains secular" and refers in this connection to section 10 of the Constitution.[72] A third commentator, Sulaiman, while categorically dismissing secularism as a purely Western solution to a Western problem which has little relevance to the Muslim way of life, makes the significant concession that the secularization of the Nigerian state has been sanctioned by the Constitution.[73] Moreover, several years before the Sharia reforms were initiated, the Chief Judge of the North Eastern state of Adamawa, while delivering judgment in a dispute over the erection of a mosque in the office of the Deputy State Governor, is reported to have referred to the constitutionally guaranteed secularity of the state.[74]

with the adoption of s. 10, while maintaining that it was not clear from the wording of the section "which version of secularism the framers of the constitution dumped on the nation".

[67] B.O. Nwabueze, *Military Rule and Constitutionalism,* Ibadan, 1992, 282. See also B.O. Nwabueze, "The unconstitutionality of the state enforcement of Sharia law", *The* [Nigerian] *Guardian*, 3 July, 2000. Available at http://www.ogbaru.org/buezeon%20sharia.html, last accessed on 24 September, 2003 (hereafter referred to as Nwabueze (2000) n. 67).

[68] A.E. Davies, "Secularity and state practices in Nigeria" in A.E. Davies *et al.* (eds.), *Contemporary Issues in Nigerian Affairs*, Ibadan, 1995, 80, at 81.

[69] D.E. Smith, *India as a Secular State,* Princeton, NJ, 1963, 4. He defines a secular state as one "which guarantees individual and corporate freedom of religion, deals with the individual as citizen irrespective of his religion, is not constitutionally connected with any religion nor does it seek to promote or interfere with religion".

[70] D.A. Ihenacho, "Professor Auwalu H. Yadudu's Sharia apology: a response" (undated). Available at http://www.gamji.com/NEWS1310.htm, last accessed 24 September, 2003.

[71] Mamman, n. 15 above, 302–303.

[72] M.U. Bunza, "Islamism and secularism: a religious political struggle in modern Nigeria", [2002] 2 *Journal for the Study of Religions and Ideologies* 49 at 54.

[73] Sulaiman, n. 61 above, at 53.

[74] Reported in *The* [Nigerian] *Guardian*, 14 September, 1993.

It thus appears that the preponderance of opinion supports the view that Nigeria is a secular state. If this, indeed, is the true import of section 10, it seriously undermines the constitutional validity of the reforms initiated by the Governments of the Sharia-compliant states. The architects of these reforms have made it abundantly clear that their paramount objective is to reaffirm the Islamic faith and revitalize the Muslim way of life. The direct involvement of state Governments in the pursuit of this objective is clearly at variance with workings of the secular polity visualized by this interpretation of section 10.

On the other hand, even if Tabiu and Yadudu are correct in maintaining that it cannot be extrapolated from the wording of section 10 that Nigeria is a secular state, it still needs to be ascertained whether the Governments which have embraced the Sharia reforms have in effect adopted Islam as their state religion within the meaning of section 10. Advocates of the reforms have been at pains to negate any impression that this is the case. Yadudu, for one, lays considerable stress on the fact that the Governors of Zamfara and Niger States who pioneered the Sharia reforms have made pronouncements to the effect that Islamic law has not been adopted as the official state religion in their states.[75] He acknowledges that the Sharia legislation in these states derives its inspiration from Islamic religious norms but is adamant that such "legislative borrowings from a religious code" cannot be equated with the adoption of Islam as a state religion.[76] This is echoed by Tabiu who asserts that when a state acting within its sphere of legislative competence enacts legislation, such legislation is not rendered unconstitutional by the fact that it is sourced from a particular religion. Elaborating on this theme, Tabiu observes that

> "Opponents of Sharia seem to have been unduly carried away by the fact that the contents of the laws in question originated from the Sharia. But laws sourced from the Sharia as well as laws sourced from Christianity have always formed part of Nigerian legislation and no one ever said they violated the Constitution. For example the Penal Code contains provisions sourced from the Sharia and the Marriage Act was entirely sourced from Christianity. Both have been part of Nigerian law applied by Nigerian courts [for many years]."[77]

The Nigerian courts have not yet had occasion to consider whether the "non-adoption" clause in section 10 will be violated in instances where legislation enacted by the Federal Government or a state government embodies or articulates rules and doctrines inspired by or derived from a particular religion. In the absence of Nigerian authorities, useful guidance may be sought from pronouncements of the United States Supreme Court when dealing with disputes concerning the First Amendment to the United States Constitution which provides, *inter alia,* that "Congress shall make no laws respecting an establishment of religion". In this connection, it is pertinent to refer, for instance, to various state laws prohibiting or restricting the pursuit of commercial activities on Sundays. In *McGowan* v. *Maryland*[78] and other notable cases decided in 1961,[79] the Supreme Court held that these Sunday closing laws (or "Blue Laws" as they are commonly called) did not violate

[75] Yadudu, n. 6 above.
[76] Yadudu, n. 6 above. Yadudu, n. 39 above.
[77] Tabiu, n. 6 above.
[78] 366 U.S. 420 (1961).
[79] *Two Guys from Harrison Allentown* v. *McGinley* 366 U.S. 512 (1961); *Braunfeld* v. *Brown* 366 U.S. 599 (1961) and *Gallagher* v. *Crown Kosher Supermarket* 366 U.S. 617 (1961).

either the Establishment Clause or the Free Exercise Clause also contained in the First Amendment.[80] In coming to this conclusion the court accepted that these laws had their genesis in Christianity and were originally designed to effectuate concepts of Christian theology. However, the manner in which the laws had evolved through the centuries and the manner in which most of these laws were currently written and administered clearly suggested to the court that they were now invested with a secular rather than a religious character. In the court's view, the predominantly secular purpose of the laws was to provide a uniform day of rest for all citizens and the fact that this day was Sunday, which happened to be of particular significance for Christians, did not detract from their secular character. The court accordingly concluded that in their modern-day manifestation, these laws bore no relation to the establishment of a religion and accordingly did not infringe the Establishment Clause in the First Amendment.[81]

The focus of the Supreme Court on whether legislation in dispute before it had a religious or secular purpose was taken further in *Lemon* v. *Kurtzman*,[82] where Chief Justice Burger enunciated a three-pronged test (the so-called *Lemon* test). According to this test, when seeking to decide whether a particular enactment violated the Establishment Clause, the court would need to consider:

(i) whether it had a *bona fide* secular purpose or whether its purpose was to advance religion;
(ii) whether its principal or primary effect was to inhibit or advance religion; and
(iii) whether it pointed to an excessive government entanglement with religion.

The *Lemon* test has for many years provided the basis for determining whether Federal and State enactments are unconstitutional under the terms of the Establishment Clause, although its application to individual cases has proved somewhat problematic. In the past two decades the test has been criticized by various Supreme Court Justices who have sought to refine it [83] or to espouse alternative tests such as Justice Day O'Connor's Endorsement test;[84] Justice Kennedy's Coercion test;[85] and the Neutrality test.[86] Despite this sustained

[80] The operation of these Blue Laws is characterized by marked variations from one state to the next. The variable operation of these laws is exemplified by the fact that the sale and public consumption of alcohol on Sundays is prohibited or tightly regulated by legislation in states such as West Virginia, Colorado, Utah and Idaho whereas other states such as Massachusetts, New York, New Hampshire, Vermont, Delaware, Pennsylvania and Oregon have largely abandoned this tradition of keeping Sundays "dry".

[81] For an incisive analysis of the relationship between the Sunday Closing Laws and the Establishment Clause and the Supreme Court's jurisprudence in this area, see M.A. Stadtmauer, "Remember the sabbath? The New York Blue Laws and the future of the Establishment Clause", (1994) *12 Cardozo Arts and Entertainment Law Journal* 213.

[82] 403 U.S. 602 (1971).

[83] See e.g. *Agostini* v. *Felton* 96-553 (1971).

[84] See e.g. *Lynch* v. *Donnelly* 465 U.S. 668 (1984); *Santa Fe Independent School District* v. *Doe* 530 U.S. 290 (2000).

[85] See *County of Allegheny* v. *American Civil Liberties Union* 492 U.S. 573 (1989); *Lee* v. *Weisman* 112 S.Ct 2469 (1992).

[86] Originally propounded in *Everson* v. *Board of Education*. 330 U.S. 1 (1947) and recently embraced in such cases as *Zelman-Simmons* v. *Harris* [00-1751 S.Ct (2000)] and *Mitchell* v. *Helms* [98–1684] S.Ct (2000).

judicial onslaught against the *Lemon* test, the Supreme Court has not explicitly renounced it, nor has it officially been replaced by any of the other tests.[87] On the contrary, as Circuit Judge Carnes recently emphasized in *Glassroth* v. *Moore*[88] "[e]ven though some Justices and commentators have strongly criticized Lemon, both the Supreme Court and this circuit continue to use *Lemon's* three-pronged analysis".

While the Nigerian Supreme Court is not bound by the jurisprudence of the U.S. Supreme Court or its pronouncements on the First Amendment Establishment Clause, it seems reasonable to suppose that similar considerations will bear on the Nigerian Supreme Court and its subordinate courts when dealing with the non-adoption clause in section 10 of the 1999 Constitution. If this supposition is correct, it can first of all be extrapolated from cases such as *McGowan* that the mere fact that a particular Nigerian statute contains rules and principles emanating from Christianity or Islam does not invariably signify the adoption of that religion by the Government which enacted it. To this extent, Yadudu and Tabiu are both correct insofar as they suggest that instances of "legislative borrowing" or "sourcing" from a particular religious code (as exemplified by the Penal Code and the Marriage Act) do not necessarily entail a violation of the non-adoption clause. Referring first of all to the Penal Code, it is true that vestiges of the Sharia were preserved in a few of its provisions. However, it was never conceived by the Northern Regional Government which enacted this Code that it would serve as a vehicle for the furtherance of the Islamic religion. On the contrary, the main purpose of this Code was to introduce a predominantly secular penal regime applicable to the Muslim and non-Muslim inhabitants of the territory, and its primary effect was to supersede the Sharia-based system of criminal justice widely in force in pre-Independence Northern Nigeria. Turning to the Marriage Act, this statute does indeed define marriage in terms of the Christian conception of a union between one man and one woman to the exclusion of all others and accords recognition to marriages which are solemnized in accordance with Christian rites. This is however balanced by the fact that the Act also makes provision for civil marriages of a secular character, which may be contracted by Christians and non-Christians alike. Such civil marriages are accorded the same prominence by the legislation and enjoy the same legal status as Christian marriages, despite not being accepted as valid according to strict Christian dogma. Adopting the terminology of the *Lemon* test, the Penal Code is predominantly secular in terms of its purpose and its primary effect. As far as the Marriage Act is concerned it can be discerned from the manner in which its recognition of religious marriages is counterbalanced by corresponding provisions for civil marriages that its purpose and effect neither inhibit nor advance religion. Moreover, there is nothing in either statute pointing to an "excessive entanglement with religion" by the enacting governments. It thus seems that there is no basis for declaring either statute unconstitutional on the ground that its operation

[87] This state of affairs is typified by the Supreme Court's approach in the *Santa Fe Independent School District* case where the court made only cursory reference to the *Lemon* test while placing greater reliance on the Endorsement test without formally pronouncing that this test had superseded the *Lemon* test. See further E.C. Klingler "Constitutional law: endorsing a new test for Establishment Clause cases", [2001] *53 Fla. L.R.* 995–1004.

[88] 335 F 3d 1282 11th Circuit (2003).

within the Nigerian legal system is in any way indicative of the adoption of Islam or Christianity in violation of section 10.

In the case of the Marriage Act, it might arguably have been otherwise if, for instance, the government of a Christian-dominated state in Southern Nigeria, being consumed by religious fervour, proceeded to enact a statute ostensibly designed to regenerate Christian values within the state by treating as valid only those marriages celebrated according to Christian rites and prohibiting Christians within its territory from contracting civil marriages. If the *Lemon* test were to be invoked it could justifiably be claimed that such a statute was designed to advance the Christian religion within the state and that the government of the enacting state was becoming excessively entangled in religious affairs and was in effect adopting Christianity as its state religion in contravention of section 10.[89]

Applying the *Lemon* test to recent developments in the Sharia-observant states of Northern Nigeria it is quite evident from the events leading up to the enactment of the Sharia Penal Codes, the contents of these codes, and the manner in which they have been implemented and received that the paramount purpose and primary effect of the entire exercise has been to advance the Islamic religion. It is equally obvious that the state governments which have gone down this route have not just entangled themselves but have become almost inextricably enmeshed in the pursuit of an overtly religious agenda. The reforms introduced by these states go well beyond mere "legislative borrowings from a religious code" of the magnitude seen in such statutes as the Penal Code and the Marriage Act. On the contrary, the governments of these states, whether of their own volition or in response to public pressure, have embarked on programmes designed to restore the Islamic religion to its full vigour and propagate and promote the Islamic way of life in their territories, and have sought to utilize the legislative process in furtherance of these goals. In effect, the Sharia restoration programmes embarked upon by these states convey the distinct impression that they have indeed adopted Islam as their official religion contrary to section 10. This point of view has been most eloquently expressed by Agbakoba and Obeagu who insist that "[w]hat is required for a violation of section 10 to occur ... is the implementation of a measure or chain of measures that lead to the establishment of a state religion. It may be administrative, legislative or otherwise but once there is a pointer to the fact that a particular religion is [favoured] by government, the legal effect would be that a state religion is adopted".[90] The most significant element of the Sharia reform agenda has been the reinstatement of the penal aspects of the Sharia and there is considerable merit in the argument advanced by Peters that "Th[is] reintroduction of Islamic Criminal Law

89 There is also every likelihood that a statute framed in such terms would be adjudged unconstitutional (i) under the Coercion test on the ground that it coerced people to support or participate in a particular religion against their will; (ii) under the Endorsement test since the terms in which it was framed would convey a message to non-adherents that they were outsiders, and not full members of the community and (iii) under the Neutrality test since the enacting government could be perceived to be allying itself to the Christian faith in preference to any other religion.

90 O. Agbakoba and O. Obeagu, "Sharia Death Penalty: Legal Issues and Controversies" (Undated). Available at http://www.hurilaws.org/sharia_penalty_art.htm, last accessed 24 September, 2003.

necessitates an intensive involvement of the State and could be regarded as the adoption of Islam as state religion."[91]

This impression that the reinstatement of the Sharia in the Northern states is tantamount to the adoption of Islam as a state religion is reinforced when cognizance is taken of the declaration by N.H. Shah, the former Chief Justice of Pakistan, another nation which has embraced the Sharia. Shah states that "The Holy Qur'an lays down that Allah is the sovereign and lawgiver and his revealed law must be adopted as the law of the state".[92] In line with this reasoning, Al-Zakzaky maintains that "The total application of Sharia is only possible where the system of government is purely Islamic. Here the shari'ah as a legal system is seen as part of a complete Islamic system which encompasses all aspects of life".[93] This point is reiterated by Aluko who suggests that "Muslims cannot operate full Islamic law of Sharia (sic) except in an Islamic state".[94] It follows that if the rationale underlying the reforms instituted by the Northern states is to restore the Sharia in its pristine purity (as has been suggested by Yadudu) this can only be achieved within a Shariacratic framework.[95] Consequently, the greater the vigour with which the governments of these states pursue this objective, the more difficult it will be for them to counter the impression that Islam has been adopted as the basis of governance within their states. Conversely, if these governments are prepared to concede that their agenda is not to restore the Sharia to its pristine purity but to embrace a watered-down version of the Sharia, this would lend greater credence to their claims that they have not adopted Islam as the official religion of their states.

(d) The jurisdiction issue

The enactment of the Sharia Penal Codes has resulted in the uneasy coexistence of two distinct penal regimes in each of the Sharia-implementing states. This dichotomy has been rendered even more pronounced by the fact that in these states the pre-existing body of criminal law contained in the Northern Nigeria Penal Code and the Islamic system of Criminal Law embodied in the Sharia Codes are now administered by entirely separate courts. On the one hand, the offences contained in the Penal Code continue to be dealt with by the High Courts of these states (or by magistrates in the case of lesser offences). On the other hand, as part of the Sharia reform process, Zamfara and other states have enacted laws under which their Area Courts have been reconstituted into Sharia Courts.[96] By virtue of these Sharia Court Laws, the primary responsibility for trying offences created by the Sharia Penal Codes lies with these courts while appellate jurisdiction in

[91] Peters, n. 5 above, at 32.

[92] N.H. Shah, "Law and religion in Islam", (2000) 11 *Islam and Christian-Muslim Relations* 243.

[93] Al-Zakzaky, n. 60, above.

[94] S. Aluko, "The Social and Economic Implications of Sharia Law" Seminar Paper, Akure, 1999. Available at http://www.nigeriannews.com/Sam_Aluko.htm, last accessed 24 September, 2003.

[95] The term "Shariacracy" was devised by Mazrui to denote "governance according to the norms, principles and rules of Islamic law". A. Mazrui, "Sharia and Federal Models in the Era of Globalization: Nigeria in Comparative Perspective". Paper presented at International Conference on Sharia, London 2001. Available at http://www.shariah2001.nmnonline.net/mazrui_paper.htm, last accessed 24 September, 2003.

[96] See Peters n. 5 above at 16–17; Ladan n. 42 above.

respect of such offences rests, not with the state High Courts but with the state Sharia Courts of Appeal.[97] It is arguable that such laws are unconstitutional insofar as they appear to fetter the unlimited jurisdiction conferred on state High Courts in criminal matters by section 272(1) of the 1999 Constitution which provides that "the High Court of a state shall have jurisdiction to ... hear and determine any criminal proceedings involving or relating to any penalty, forfeiture, punishment or other liability in respect of any offence committed by any person".

In any event, it is a matter for debate whether state Sharia Courts of Appeal are in fact empowered by the Constitution to exercise criminal jurisdiction. Section 277(1) of the 1999 Constitution provides that a State Sharia Court of Appeal "shall, in addition to such other jurisdiction as may be conferred on it by the laws of the State, exercise such appellate and supervisory jurisdiction in civil proceedings involving questions of Islamic personal law which the court is competent to exercise in accordance with the provisions of subsection (2) of this section".

Section 277(2) elaborates on the scope of the jurisdiction conferred on Sharia Courts of Appeal by section 277(1). It provides that "For the purpose of subsection (1) of this section, the Sharia Court of Appeal shall be competent to decide:

(a) Any question of Islamic personal law regarding a marriage concluded in accordance with that law, including a question relating to the validity or dissolution of such a marriage or a question that depends on such a marriage and relating to family relationship or the guardianship of an infant;
(b) Where all the parties to the proceedings are Muslims, any question of Islamic personal law regarding a marriage, including the validity or dissolution of that marriage or regarding family relationship, a foundling or the guardianship of an infant;
(c) Any question of Islamic personal law regarding *wakf*, gift, will or succession where the endower, donor, testator or deceased person is a Muslim;
(d) Any question of Islamic personal law regarding an infant, prodigal or person of unsound mind who is a Muslim or the maintenance or the guardianship of a Muslim who is physically or mentally infirm; or
(e) Where all the parties to the proceedings, being Muslims, have requested the court which hears the case in the first instance to determine that case in accordance with Islamic personal law, any other question."

It was more or less universally accepted that a similar formulation in section 242 of the 1979 Constitution effectively limited the adjudicatory functions of Sharia Courts of Appeal to matters pertaining to Islamic personal law. Even the most vocal advocates of the Sharia conceded this point, while bitterly criticizing this state of affairs. Sulaiman, for instance, declared that the Constitution "reduced [the Sharia] to the narrow confine

[97] See, for example, the Zamfara State Shari'ah Courts (Administration of Justice and Certain Consequential Changes) Law No. 5 of 1999, the Zamfara State Area Courts (Repeal) Law No. 13 of 2000 and the Zamfara State Shari'ah Court of Appeal (Amendment) Law No. 6 of 2000. Note however that in two states (Niger and Kebbi) the Area Courts have been retained but their jurisdiction now extends to civil and criminal matters.

(sic) of Personal Status. This can be seen from the jurisdiction of the Sharia Court of Appeal.... Thus all other aspects of the Sharia have no relevance as far as those who drafted and those who ratified the Constitution were concerned."[98] Similarly, Kumo confirmed that Sharia Courts of Appeal were limited to matters of Muslim personal law but made it clear that he regarded this as "a serious and inexplicable diminution of what ought to be the jurisdiction of the Sharia Court of Appeal". He accordingly proposed the amendment of the Constitution so as to give the Sharia Courts of Appeal appellate jurisdiction in all cases where the proper law was Islamic law.[99]

Despite the foregoing, advocates of the Sharia reforms have sought to contend that the phrase "*in addition to such other jurisdiction as may be conferred on it by the laws of the state* ... " in section 277(1), empowers any State Government that so wishes to enlarge the jurisdiction of its Sharia Court of Appeal so as to enable it to adjudicate on the criminal offences prescribed in the Sharia Penal Codes.[100] Yadudu, for instance, asserts that "The provision of section 277 is not couched in an exhaustive term (sic) to preclude the jurisdiction of the Sharia courts. So long as Islamic penal system (sic) is enacted in a written law and punishments prescribed therein, that piece of legislation, it is submitted is constitutional."[101] According to this line of reasoning, Zamfara and other Northern states have not acted unconstitutionally by legislating for their Sharia Courts of Appeal to adjudicate on criminal matters arising under the new Sharia codes.

Taken in isolation, the reference to the conferment of additional jurisdiction on Sharia Courts of Appeal does indeed suggest that these courts may now be empowered by legislative fiat to try criminal cases. It is however submitted that section 277(1) should not be read in isolation but construed in conjunction with section 277(2) because of the cross-referencing between the two subsections. As Nwabueze correctly observes "the words 'in addition to such other jurisdiction as may be conferred on it by the law of the state' in subsection (1) above are controlled ... by the words in subsection (2) to the effect that 'for the purpose of this section, the Sharia Court of Appeal shall be competent to decide ...'. Any other view of the matter would do violence to the letter as well as the spirit of the provision."[102]

It can be discerned from a combined reading of both subsections that as the Constitution currently stands;

(i) the primary responsibility of a Sharia Court of Appeal is to exercise appellate and supervisory jurisdiction in civil proceedings which pertain to questions of Islamic personal law (which for want of a better word we designate the court's basic jurisdiction);

(ii) in addition to this basic jurisdiction, a Sharia Court of Appeal may also exercise such other jurisdiction as may be conferred on it by the laws of the state;

[98] Sulaiman, n. 61 above, at 54.

[99] S. Kumo, "The application of Islamic law in Northern Nigeria: problems and prospects", (1977) 7 *Journal of Islamic Law* 21, at 27, 29.

[100] See Peters, n. 5 above, at 33.

[101] Yadudu, n. 6 above. See also Yadudu, n. 39 above.

[102] Nwabueze (2000), n. 67 above.

(iii) both the court's basic jurisdiction and any additional jurisdiction conferred on it by the laws of the state must accord with the terms of subsection (2) which enumerates the areas of substantive law on which the court is competent to decide.

In effect, such a combined reading of section 277(1) and (2) suggests that while exercising its basic jurisdiction as well as any additional jurisdiction conferred on it, the Sharia Court of Appeal is only competent to hear disputes pertaining to those aspects of Islamic personal law specified in section 277(2). On this reading of section 277, the type of situation in which such additional jurisdiction might conceivably be conferred on a Sharia Court of Appeal by the laws of the state would be where the state legislature deems it necessary to invest the court with original jurisdiction in disputes relating to any of the matters set out in section 277(2).[103] If this interpretation of section 277 is correct, it would follow that the reference therein to such additional jurisdiction as may be conferred on the court does not justify the legislative measures taken by the Sharia-compliant states to invest their Sharia Courts of Appeal with criminal jurisdiction.

This view that section 277 as currently framed, does not extend the jurisdiction of Sharia Courts of Appeal from the sphere of Islamic personal law into the realms of criminal law is supported by cases such as *Alkali* v. *Alkali*[104] and *Maida* v. *Modu*.[105] In these cases, the Court of Appeal held that under the corresponding provision of the 1979 Constitution (i.e. section 242) the jurisdiction of the Yobe and Borno State Sharia Courts of Appeal did not extend to disputes relating to land. It can be deduced from this that if the legislative assemblies of these states enacted legislation purporting to confer on their Sharia Courts of Appeal the jurisdiction to entertain land disputes, the courts would deem such legislation unconstitutional. *A fortiori*, it seems that the enactment by the various Sharia-compliant states of legislation intended to enlarge the jurisdiction of their Sharia courts beyond the realm of Islamic personal law and into the criminal domain may be susceptible to judicial challenge on constitutional grounds.

The supposition that s. 277(1) permits state legislatures to invest their Sharia Courts of Appeal with criminal jurisdiction also fails to take cognizance of the fact that these courts do not function in a vacuum but operate within a judicial hierarchy clearly defined by the Constitution. The Supreme Court is the ultimate court and can only hear appeals emanating from the Court of Appeal. For its part, the Court of Appeal, which is the penultimate court in the hierarchy, exercises appellate jurisdiction over *all* the superior courts of record in a state, including Sharia Courts of Appeal. Section 244(1) of the Constitution, which provides for appeals from state Sharia Courts of Appeal to the Court of Appeal, specifically states that such appeals shall lie from decisions "in any civil proceedings before the Sharia Court of Appeal with respect to any question of Islamic personal law which the Sharia Court of Appeal is competent to decide". By contrast, section 241(1), which

[103] This might conceivably happen, for instance, in disputes over inheritance where the value of the estate exceeds a specified amount.

[104] [2002] 1 N.W.L.R. 453.

[105] [2000] 4 N.W.L.R. 99. See further, Oba n. 3 above, 833–834, and in particular the cases cited at 834 (n. 21).

deals with appeals from the Federal and State High Courts to the Court of Appeal, provides that such appeals shall lie as of right from "decisions in any criminal proceedings in which the Federal High Court or a [State] High Court has imposed a sentence of death". It follows from the foregoing that if it is correct that section 277(1) empowers individual states to extend the jurisdiction of their Sharia Courts into the criminal domain as has happened in Zamfara and other states, the Court of Appeal (and by extension the Supreme Court) would have no constitutional standing to entertain an appeal once the Sharia Court has given its verdict. The implication for this would be that if, for instance, a Sharia Court of Appeal has handed down or upheld a sentence of death for a *hudud* offence or in retribution for a killing, no provision exists for an appeal to the Court of Appeal; whereas if a person is found guilty of a capital offence by a State High Court which exercises co-ordinate jurisdiction with the Sharia Court of Appeal, the accused person will have recourse to the Court of Appeal as of right by virtue of section 241. It is extremely difficult to conceive that the framers of the Constitution would have contemplated the operation of Sharia Courts of Appeal as courts of last resort particularly in cases where the life of a citizen is at stake. Until this conundrum is resolved one way or another, the view that the dispensation of criminal justice by the state Sharia Courts of Appeal is constitutionally valid will remain open to question.

(e) The Sharia punishments vis-à-vis *the prohibition of cruel and inhuman treatment*

It has been observed by Al-Zakzaky that the one aspect of the Sharia "that attracts the attention of almost everyone, particularly non-Muslims, is the *hadd* (the prescribed punishments in the *Qur'an*), so much so that Shari'ah to them becomes almost synonymous with punishment".[106] The perceived severity of these punishments has been cited by the Council of Muslim Theologians as one of the main reasons why the Sharia "seems to arouse the most intense reactions of hostility, ridicule and misgivings among those who are not within the fold of Islam".[107] These punishments include flogging, amputation of the hand, cross amputation of hand and foot, banishment and death sentences which may be carried into effect by such traditional means as crucifixion, beheading and stoning to death (the *hudud* punishments). In addition, the Sharia allows for retaliatory punishments (*qisas*), which in their most extreme forms may entail killing and the infliction of severe physical injuries. Out of

[106] I.Y. Al-Zakzaky, "Application of the *Shari'ah* in the Contemporary World: Lessons from some Muslim Countries". Part I of Paper presented at a Conference on the Nature and Application of the Shari'ah, Kano, 1999. Available at http://www.muslimedia.com/archives/features99/shariah1.htm last accessed 24 September, 2003.

[107] Jamiatul Ulama–Council of Muslim Theologians, "The Shari'ah" (Undated). Available at http://www.jamiat.org.za/isinfo/sharia.html, last accessed 24 September, 2003. This perception that some Sharia punishments are unduly severe is by no means restricted to non-Muslims. Adegbite, for instance, has conceded that "by present standards some of the punishments prescribed by Islamic law are unduly harsh", L. Adegbite, "Human rights in Islamic law", (1977) 7 *Journal of Islamic and Comparative Law* 1, at 5. Mazrui, n. 95 above, also accepts that the Sharia punishments "are too severe and ought to be reconsidered". Amin, for his part, opines that "There is a widespread belief that the penalty of death for two consenting adults who committed heterosexual or homosexual offences in private is too harsh", S.H. Amin, *Islamic Law in the Contemporary World: Introduction, Glossary and Bibliography*, Glasgow, 1985, 27–28.

this range of penalties, the Penal Code which has been in force in Northern Nigeria since independence has only made provision for flogging (including *haddi* lashing for certain prescribed offences against the Sharia)[108] and the imposition of the death penalty for homicide (albeit by hanging).[109] The most controversial feature of the Sharia reforms undertaken by the Northern states is the assimilation of the classical punishments prescribed by the Sharia into their recently enacted Sharia Penal Codes.[110] Thus for instance, the Zamfara State Shari'ah Penal Code[111] has legislated in Chapter VII for such *hudud* punishments as stoning to death for the offences of adultery, rape, sodomy and incest when committed by married persons;[112] amputation for theft;[113] cross amputation for multiple thefts and robbery;[114] and crucifixion for robberies in which murder has been committed and property seized.[115] Moreover, since offences such as intentional homicide[116] and voluntarily causing grievous hurt[117] are categorized as "*Qisas* and *Qisas* related offences", it appears that those convicted of such offences may by way of retaliation be subjected to the same punitive treatment that they inflicted on their victims.[118]

In the view of commentators such as Mayer, the re-emergence of these *hudud* crimes and their extreme penalties in contemporary Islamic societies represents "a break with modern penological principles and human rights norms".[119] Speaking from the standpoint of a person outside the Islamic system she opines that "laws imposing penalties like amputations, cross amputations and crucifixions would seem to be an obvious violation of article 7 [of the International Convention on Civil and Political Rights (ICCPR)], which stipulates that no one shall be subjected to cruel, inhuman or degrading punishment."[120] In much the same vein, El-Affendi has declared that "[t]here are no doubt some areas where Islamic principles as understood by prevalent Islamic orthodoxy today, do clash with the current international norms on Human Rights such as the UN Convention against Torture and other Cruel, Inhuman and Degrading Punishments (UNCAT) ... The Islamic punishments for theft (amputation of the hand) and the right to retribution for

[108] S. 68, P.C.

[109] See Penal Code.

[110] See generally, Peters, n. 5 above, 18–28 and Ostien, n. 7 above.

[111] Law No.10 of 2000 (hereafter called the Zamfara State SPC). All specific references in this work to sections of the SPC shall be to the Zamfara State version.

[112] See ss. 127(b) (adultery); 129(b) (rape); 131(b) (sodomy) and 133(b) (incest).

[113] See s. 145.

[114] See s. 145 (multiple thefts) and s. 153(b) (robbery in which property has been seized but murder is not committed).

[115] See s. 153 (d).

[116] S. 200.

[117] S. 220(a).

[118] The case of Sani Rodi is particularly noteworthy. Rodi was the first person to be convicted of unlawful homicide punishable by death under the SPC having been found guilty of stabbing his master's wife and children to death. In passing sentence, the Katsina City Sharia Court directed that Rodi was to be killed with the same knife he had used on his victims. See G. Yonge, "Is this justice?", *The Guardian*, 10 January, 2002. The sentence was not carried out in the manner prescribed by the Sharia Court. Instead Rodi was put to death by hanging, a fact which was criticized by Sharia purists. See "Katsina Executes First Sharia Court Murder Convict", Available at http://www.thisdayonline.com/archive/2002/01/04/20020104news23.html., last accessed 24 September, 2003.

[119] Mayer, n. 1 above, at 39.

[120] Mayer, n. 1 above, at 47.

grievous bodily harm are deemed to contravene the UNCAT."[121] Commenting with specific reference to Nigeria, Ostien states that "[s]uch punishments are today thought by many throughout the world to violate the universal ban on cruel, inhuman or degrading punishment and treatment".[122] This view is echoed by Sunder, who notes that the Nigerian Government is a state party to several international human rights treaties, including the UNCAT and the ICCPR, and who highlights the incompatibility between the Sharia punishments and the terms of these treaties. She lays particular stress on the fact that the ICCPR prescribes that the death penalty should only be imposed for the "most serious crimes" and that the United Nations Commission on Human Rights has interpreted this to mean "intentional crimes with lethal or extremely grave consequences". She deduces from this that the punishment of stoning to death for a non-violent act such as adultery infringes international human rights norms.[123]

The point has been made by Mayer that "having formally accepted international human rights, governments of Muslim countries are bound by these norms and are also subject to being judged by them".[124] By the same token, El-Affendi signifies that "if a government accedes voluntarily to a treaty or convention then Islamic principles as well as agreed norms dictate that it should adhere to its obligations under these treaties. If it cannot, due to the conflict of these obligations with other norms it holds dear, then it should make this clear and withdraw from those international treaties and conventions."[125] Even though the Nigerian Government has shown no inclination to withdraw from treaties prohibiting cruel and inhuman punishments which it has duly ratified, the operation of these treaties within the Nigerian context has been vigorously contested by Muslim advocates of the Sharia reforms. The prevailing attitude in Muslim circles is vividly exemplified by a recent publication of the Supreme Council for Sharia in Nigeria (SCSN) which portrayed Nigeria's ratification of various United Nations instruments concerned with human rights as part of a "United Nations covert campaign against Islam". The SCSN was especially critical of the UNCAT on the ground that this Convention was "intended to make illegal most aspects of Shari'a *Hudud* (Islamic Punishments) as divinely ordained by Allah [thereby] violating the fundamental belief of all true Muslims in Nigeria in particular and the world in general".[126] Also pertinent are comments by Governor Sani of Zamfara State, who recently stated that he had received at least 8,000 letters from human rights and non-governmental organizations pointing out

---

[121] A. El-Affendi, "Islam and human rights: the lessons from Sudan", (2001) 91 *The Muslim World* 481, at 491.

[122] Ostien, n. 63 above.

[123] M. Sunder, "Beauty Marred: The 'Miss World' Riots, A Stoning Sentence and the Conflict between Religious and Secular Law in Nigeria" (Undated). Available at http://writ.news.findlaw.com/commentary/20021205_sunder.html., last accessed 23 September, 2003.

[124] A.E. Mayer, *Islam and Human Rights: Tradition and Politics,* Boulder, Colorado, 1999, 12.

[125] El-Affendi, n. 121 above, at 490.

[126] Supreme Council for Sharia in Nigeria, "Revisiting the plot to destabilise Nigeria using the United Nations (U.N.) covert campaign against Islam", *Daily Trust,* 22–28 February, 2002. Reproduced as Appendix One in J. Ibrahim, "Democracy and Minority Rights in Nigeria: Religion, Sharia and the 1999 Constitution". Draft of Paper presented at Conference on Globalisation, State Capacity and Self-Determination in Muslim Contexts, Santa Cruz, California, 2002. Available at http://www2.ucsc.edu/cgirs/conferences/carnegie/papers/ibrahim.pdf, last accessed 24 September, 2003.

that the world is now a global community which has gone beyond the age of amputation, flogging and so on. He dismissed such letters with the observation that their writers did not appear to appreciate that such punishments had been ordained by the Qur'an.[127]

Such views are not restricted to quintessentially Islamic organizations like the SCSN or the political architects of the Sharia reforms but have also been articulated by notable Muslim intellectuals such as Sanusi and Yadudu. Sanusi advocates the need for caution, enlightenment and sensitivity in interpreting and implementing the Sharia and favours the recognition of economic and other conditions as extenuating circumstances when applying the SPC. He however emphatically rejects criticisms by non-Muslims that penalties such as amputation are violations of established international human rights norms insisting that "these criticisms try to present a value-judgement as a statement of fact, even though it emanates from a different world view".[128] For his part, Yadudu appears to attach little weight to concerns about the incompatibility of the SPC with international covenants and conventions, pointing out that such concerns "have almost exclusively been voiced by non-Muslims to whom the Sharia does not apply".[129] Indeed even the celebrated jurist, An-Na'im, (whose credentials as a human rights activist are impeccable and who has not supported the imposition of such punishments in his native Sudan) responds to the assertion that such punishments patently violate the norms of international human rights with the retort that this proposition is not obvious at all from the standpoint of a person inside the Islamic system. He points out that the meaning of cruel, inhuman or degrading treatment or punishment in Islamic cultures may be significantly if not radically different from perceptions of the meaning of this clause in other parts of the world. He notes that UN agencies such as the UN Human Rights Commission, the European Commission for Human Rights and other bodies with a Western orientation have attempted to provide guidance on what constitutes cruel, inhuman and degrading punishment but queries the usefulness of such guidance when the focus is on non-Western perspectives on cruel, inhuman or degrading punishment.[130]

While it is undoubtedly true that the prohibition against cruel, inhuman and degrading punishment is a Western-inspired construct, it has nevertheless been assimilated into the African Charter on Human and Peoples' Rights

[127] *The* [Nigerian] *Vanguard*, 25 March, 2002.

[128] S.L. Sanusi, "Class, Gender and A Political Economy of 'Sharia'" (undated). Available at http://www.nigerdeltacongress.com/carticles/class%20gender%20and%20the%20political %20 economy%20of%20shar.htm, last accessed 24 September, 2003.

[129] Yadudu, n. 6 above.

[130] See A.A. An-Na'im, "Towards an Islamic reformation: responses and reflections" in T. Lindholm and K.Vogt (eds.), *Islamic Law Reform and Human Rights: Challenges and Rejoinders*, Oslo, 1993, 97 at 110; See also An-Na'im, "Towards a cross-cultural approach to defining international standards of human rights: the meaning of cruel, inhuman or degrading treatment or punishment" in A.A An-Na'im (ed.), *Human Rights in Cross-Cultural Perspectives: A Quest for Consensus,* Philadelphia, 1992, 19 at 28–37 especially 30 and 37. By the same token, some Nigerian commentators, such as Sobo and Amadi, who, like An-Naim, do not personally approve of the more severe Sharia punishments, are not convinced that Western Judeo-Christian mores provide an appropriate yardstick for judging their cruelty or inhumanity. See M. Sobo, "Constitutional Amendment in the Nature of a Substitute: God and Country" (undated). Available at http://www.gamji.com/muyiwa14.htm, last accessed 24 September, 2003; S. Amadi, "Repositioning the Sharia Debate", available at http://www.thisdayonline.com/archive/2002/09/19/20020919com02.html, last accessed 24 September, 2003.

(ACHPR), which is the principal international instrument through which the nations of Africa have sought to safeguard the fundamental human rights of their citizens.[131] Article 5 of the Charter affirms that every individual shall have the right to the respect of the dignity inherent in a human being and prohibits all forms of degradation of man including torture, inhuman or degrading punishment or treatment. In the case of Nigeria, this prohibition has effectively been "indigenized" by the enactment of the African Charter on Human and Peoples' Rights (Ratification and Enforcement) Act, 1983.[132] Section 1 of the Act states that the provisions of the ACHPR shall have the force of law in Nigeria and shall be applied by all authorities and bodies exercising legislative, executive or judicial powers in Nigeria. Ostien asserts the ACHPR sets limits within which the Sharia-compliant states must act.[133] Some support for this view can be found in the case of *Abacha* v. *Fawehinmi*,[134] in which the Nigerian Supreme Court was afforded the opportunity of pronouncing upon the legal status of the Charter within Nigerian domestic law. The Court decided by a majority of four to three that Chapter 10 was an existing law which had not been ousted by the promulgation of military decrees.[135] OGUNDARE, J.S.C., who delivered the lead judgment, made it clear that the ACHPR was not superior to the Constitution and that it was open to the National Assembly to effect its removal from Nigerian municipal law simply by repealing Chapter 10. At the same time, however, he declared that "[it] is a statute with international flavour. Being so therefore if there is a conflict between it and any other statute its provisions will prevail over those of the other statute for the reason that it is to be presumed that the legislation does not intend to breach an international obligation. To this extent I agree with their Lordships of the Court below that the Charter possesses 'a greater vigour and strength than any other domestic statute' ".[136] It appears from the foregoing that unless and until the National Assembly sees fit to remove the ACHPR from Nigerian municipal law by repealing Chapter 10, the various legislative assemblies in Nigeria are obliged to ensure that any Acts or Laws which they enact do not violate the articles of the Charter. It follows that the SPC may be open to judicial challenge if the punishments prescribed therein are adjudged to constitute inhuman or degrading punishment or treatment within the contemplation of article 5. Neither the ACHPR itself nor the recently formulated Robben Island Guidelines[137] provide any direct guidance on what constitutes "inhuman or degrading punishment or treatment". However Umozuruike, who has had the distinction of serving on the African Commission of Human and Peoples' Rights established under article 30 of the Charter, has declared that "the amputation of limbs as a criminal punishment would be entirely contrary to the African Charter and no argument that

[131] See generally U.O. Umozurike, *African Charter on Human and Peoples Rights*, The Hague, 1997; especially 30–31; V.O.O. Nmehielle, *The African Charter on Human Rights: Its Laws, Practice and Institutions*, The Hague, 2001, especially 90–92.

[132] Cap. 10, Laws of the Federation of Nigeria, 1990.

[133] Ostien, n. 63 above.

[134] [2000] 6 N.W.L.R. 228.

[135] Most notably, the State Security (Detention of Persons) Decree No. 2 of 1984.

[136] *Abacha* v. *Fawehinmi* at 289.

[137] The Guidelines and Measures for the Prohibition and Prevention of Torture, Cruel, Inhuman or Degrading Treatment or Punishment in Africa. These Guidelines were adopted by the African Commission on Human and Peoples' Rights in October 2002.

it is sanctioned by religious or traditional dogma will suffice."[138] If this view is correct, it follows *a fortiori* that the even more extreme Sharia punishments such as stoning to death and crucifixion will also run counter to the terms of the Charter.

Even if the ACHPR is ever expunged from Nigerian domestic law, the fact remains that the fundamental rights set out in Chapter IV of the 1999 Constitution include the entitlement of every individual to respect for the dignity of his person and the accompanying freedom from torture, inhuman or degrading treatment which are enshrined in section 34(1). Like the ACHPR, the Constitution does not elaborate on what constitutes torture, inhuman or degrading treatment. However, in *Uzoukwu* v. *Ezeonu*,[139] NASIR, P.C.A., commenting with reference to the corresponding provision in section 31(1)(a) of the 1979 Constitution, stated that inhuman treatment meant "any barbarous or cruel act or acting without feeling for the suffering of the other". In one line of cases decided under the Sharia Penal Codes, Sharia Courts in Zamfara State sentenced Buba Jangebei to amputation in 2000 for stealing a cow, and in 2001 imposed the same sentence on Lawali Isah for stealing three bicycles. In the same year, Sharia Courts in Sokoto State ordered the amputation of Umaru Aliyu for stealing a sheep as well as the cross-amputation of Sani Sheu and Garba Dandare for the theft of a policeman's beret, belt and bicycle, electronic equipment and a substantial amount of cash. It is arguable that these amputations and cross-amputations amount to inhuman treatment as conceived by NASIR, P.C.A., (or at the very least constitute degrading treatment) since all these men now carry an enduring and highly visible badge of dishonour which is manifestly disproportionate to the magnitude of their offences. If this is correct, it would seem to follow that NASIR, P.C.A.'s formulation on what constitutes inhuman treatment also encompasses an even more serious line of cases, in which persons convicted of sexual offences under the SPC have been sentenced to death by stoning by the Sharia courts of various states.[140]

The fundamental rights guaranteed by Chapter IV of the 1999 Constitution include not only the aforementioned right not to be subjected to inhuman or degrading treatment but also the right to life. This right is guaranteed by section 33(1) of the 1999 Constitution, which provides that "Every person has a right to life and no one shall be deprived intentionally of his life save in

[138] Umozurike, n. 131 above, at 31.

[139] [1991] 6 NWLR 708, 764.

[140] These include Safiya Husseini Tungar-Tudu, who was convicted of adultery by a Sharia Court in Sokoto State in October 2001; Amina Lawal, who was convicted of adultery by a Sharia Court in Katsina State in March 2002; Yunusa Chiyawa, who was convicted of adultery by a Sharia Court in Bauchi State in June 2002; Ahmadu Ibrahim and Fatima Usman, who were both convicted of adultery by a Sharia Court in Niger State in August 2002; Sarimu Mohammed Baranda, who was convicted of rape by a Sharia Court in Jigawa State in May 2002 and Jibrin Babaji who was sentenced to death by stoning for sodomy by a court in Bauchi State in September 2003. None of these sentences have so far been executed. Tungar-Tudu's conviction was overturned by the Sokoto State Sharia Court of Appeal. Baranda's sentence was overturned by the Jigawa State Sharia Court of Appeal which has ordered him to be detained in a mental institution until the State Governor decides to release him. Lawal's sentence has been overturned by the Katsina State Sharia Court of Appeal. More recently, the sentences imposed on Chiyawa and Babaji have been quashed by the Bauchi State Sharia Court of Appeal on the ground that their respective trials were unfair. Appeals by Ibrahim and Usman remain pending in the Niger State Sharia Court of Appeal.

execution of a court order in respect of a criminal offence of which he has been found guilty in Nigeria". Schabas, who is a leading advocate of the elimination of the death penalty in those countries where it still exists, argues that "[f]ull-fledged and complete respect of the right to life ... necessarily involves the abolition of the death penalty".[141] In the Nigerian context, a similar stance has been taken by influential human rights organizations such as the Human Rights Law Service which in the mid-1990s initiated a vigorous campaign for the abolition of hanging and execution by firing squad, the two modes of capital punishment in operation within the Nigerian judicial system at the time.[142] The abolitionists not only insisted that these penalties amounted to cruel and inhuman treatment but also contended that they violated the right to life enshrined in section 30(1) of the 1979 Constitution, which is identical in wording to section 33(1) of the 1999 Constitution. The issue as to whether such judicially sanctioned killings are consistent with the constitutionally guaranteed right to life has become all the more contentious since the SPC extended the ambit of the death sentence to encompass the punishments of stoning to death, crucifixion and retaliatory killings. This issue might arise, for instance, where a person intentionally stabs another to death. If this offence is committed in a Southern state, the traditional punishment would be death by hanging, whereas if it is committed by a Muslim in one of the Sharia-compliant states, the SPC stipulates that he may be sentenced to die in the same manner as his victim. The two modes of execution may differ materially but each would raise questions as to whether the legislation which prescribes the sentence violates section 33(1). By the same token, if an armed robber mounts a road block, steals a vehicle and kills its owner in the process, he faces the prospect of crucifixion if the robbery occurred in a Sharia-compliant state and he is a Muslim, whereas if it occurred in a Southern state the normal sentence would be execution by firing squad. Again, it would be equally pertinent to consider whether depriving the culprit of his life in such circumstances offends against section 33(1) irrespective of whether the prescribed punishment is execution by crucifixion or by firing squad. In the case of death by stoning for adultery, parallels are discernible between this mode of punishment and execution by firing squad since they both entail killing an offender by aiming projectiles at his body. It thus appears that any suggestion that execution by firing squad might not be permissible under section 33(1) applies with even greater force to death by stoning given the fact that where a firing squad is employed the offender is normally killed by a rapid volley of bullets whereas in the case of stoning, the missiles used are considerably slower, with the result that the pain endured by the offender is cumulative and the whole process is much more protracted.

The courts have not yet had the occasion to pronounce on whether any of the stoning sentences which have been handed down in the various

[141] W.A. Schabas, "The Abolition of Capital Punishment from an International Law Perspective". Paper delivered at the 17th International Conference of the International Society for the Reform of Criminal Law, The Hague, 2003.

[142] Hanging was prescribed for offences such as murder under the Criminal Codes of the Southern states and the equivalent offence of culpable homicide punishable by death under the Penal Codes of the Northern states; while execution by firing squad was specified by the Firearms (Special Provisions) Decree No. 47 1970 (later Decree No. 5 of 1984) for the offence of armed robbery.

Sharia-compliant states or any of the other forms of capital punishment that were resurrected by the SPC are permissible under the 1999 Constitution. Guidance may however be sought from the landmark case of *Onuoha Kalu* v. *The State*[143] where it fell to the Nigerian Supreme Court to determine whether section 319(1) of the Lagos State Criminal Code, which prescribed the death penalty for the offence of murder, contravened the 1979 Constitution. The appellant in this case had been convicted of murder by the Lagos State High Court and sentenced to death by hanging under the terms of section 367(1) of the Lagos State Criminal Code. He appealed unsuccessfully to the Court of Appeal and thereafter appealed to the Supreme Court. He was represented by Counsel from the Human Rights Law Service, as part of its campaign for the abolition of capital punishment in Nigeria. They argued on the appellant's behalf that the imposition of the death penalty for murder constituted a cruel, inhuman and degrading punishment and was inconsistent with the right to life as entrenched in section 30(1) of the 1979 Constitution.

If this line of reasoning had been upheld, this would undoubtedly have cast grave doubts on the constitutionality of the stoning sentences imposed by the Sharia Courts. However, the seven Justices of the Supreme Court who heard the appeal held unanimously that the death penalty did not infringe the right to life as enshrined in the Nigerian Constitution. IGUH, J.S.C, who delivered the lead judgment, stated that:

> "Under section 30(1) of the Constitution, ... the right to life, although fully guaranteed is nevertheless *subject to the execution of a death sentence of a court of law in respect of a criminal offence* of which one has been found guilty in Nigeria. The qualifying word, save, used in section 30(1) seems to me to be the unmistakable key to the construction of that provision. In my view, it is plain that the 1979 Constitution can by no stretch of imagination be said to have proscribed or outlawed the death penalty. On the contrary, section 30(1) of the Constitution permits it in the clearest possible terms, so long as it is inflicted pursuant to the sentence of a court of law in Nigeria in a criminal offence.... The plain meaning of this section of the Constitution cannot be derogated from in the absence of any ambiguity whatsoever. It simply guarantees and protects the right to life. But it also recognises deprivation of life so long as it is pursuant to the execution of the sentence of a court in a criminal offence of which the accused has been found guilty in Nigeria."[144]

Justice Iguh also disagreed with the submission by the appellant's counsel that insofar as the death penalty inflicted both physical and mental pain on the victim this, *per se*, amounted to torture, cruel and degrading treatment contrary to section 31(1)(a) of the 1979 Constitution. His Lordship observed that this Constitution conferred only a qualified right to life and drew attention to a host of cases decided by the courts of other countries such as Tanzania, Zimbabwe, India, the United States and Jamaica where the right to life has been similarly circumscribed by the terms of their respective Constitutions.[145] The conclusion he drew from his review of these cases was

---

[143] [1998] 13 NWLR 531. See also *Adeniji* v. *The State* [2000] 2 N.W.L.R 354.

[144] Ibid., at 587–588.

[145] Ibid., at 589–593. The cases referred to in this connection are *Mbushuu & Anor* v. *The Republic*, Criminal Appeal No. 142 of 1994. 30 January, 1995 (Tanzania); *Catholic Commission for Justice & Peace in Zimbabwe* v. *Att-Gen of Zimbabwe & Ors* (1993) (4) SA 239 (Zimbabwe); *Baca Singh* v. *State of Punjab* (1983) (2) SCR 583 (India); *Gregg* v. *Georgia*, 428 U.S. 153, 176–187 (1976), *District Attorney for Suffolk* v. *James Watson & Ors* (1980) 381 Mass 648, *Jureck* v. *Texas* 428 U.S.

that the death penalty, *per se*, was not intrinsically unconstitutional in the Nigerian context notwithstanding the inclusion within the Constitution of a provision which proscribed torture, inhuman or degrading treatment.

Counsel for the appellant also sought to persuade the Supreme Court that the mode of execution prescribed by the Lagos State Criminal Code, which entailed hanging a convicted murderer, was "barbarous and cruel and deprived the convict of all vestiges of human dignity". In seeking to substantiate this argument, counsel relied heavily on the South African case of *The State* v. *Makwanyane & Anor*[146] where the degree of suffering inflicted on the human body by the process of hanging was described in such graphic and gory detail that the South African Constitutional Court was left in no doubt that this method of execution was destructive of human dignity. In his judgment, Justice Iguh sought to differentiate between the death penalty as a form of punishment and the method of its execution. He maintained that the central question which fell to be determined in the present appeal was whether the death penalty as a form of punishment was constitutional and insisted that the alleged barbarity or otherwise of hanging as a method of execution was not directly in issue before the court. His Lordship did however concede that it may well be the case that hanging was destructive of human dignity, as opined by the South African Constitutional Court.[147] By the same token, UWAIS, C.J.N, while reiterating that "in this case we are not concerned with the manner of carrying out the sentence of death but by the sentence itself" nevertheless accepted that "[t]he manner of carrying out the sentence of death [i.e. hanging] could perhaps invoke the provision of s. 31(1)(a) of the [1979] Constitution".[148] Equally instructive is the judgment of KUTIGI, J.S.C, who while declaring that "death penalty *per se* ... cannot under any circumstance amount to torture or inhuman or degrading treatment which is what is prohibited under s. 31(1)(a)", went on to point out that "[w]hat may amount to torture, inhuman or degrading treatment will be the method of procedure or the manner or way in which a condemned prisoner is kept or executed."[149] On the other hand, OGUNDARE, J.S.C, reasoned that because the Nigerian Constitution only conferred a qualified right to life, the death sentence was constitutional notwithstanding the manner of its execution.[150] This was reinforced by OGWUEGBU, J.S.C, who stated categorically that "The death sentence *per se* cannot amount to torture, inhuman or degrading treatment. The manner of its execution by hanging cannot also constitute cruel or inhuman treatment".[151] The two remaining Justices, BELGORE and WALI, J.J.S.C., expressed no views on the matter. This raises the distinct possibility that if the Supreme Court had been adjudicating on whether hanging as a method of execution was cruel or degrading and consequently violated the Constitution, at least three (and perhaps more) of

(1976) and *Woodson* v. *North Carolina,* 428 U.S. 242 (1976) (United States); and *Noel Riley & Ors v Att-Gen for Jamaica* [1983] 1 A.C 719 and *Earl Pratt & Anor* v. *Att-Gen for Jamaica* [1994] 2 A.C 1 (Jamaica).

[146] (1995)(6) BCLR 665 (CC).

[147] *Onuoha Kalu.*, at 597.

[148] Ibid., at 604.

[149] Ibid., at 613.

[150] Ibid., at 622.

[151] Ibid., at 629.

the panel might have been inclined to hold that it did. Accordingly, even though the decision in *Onuoha Kalu* makes it highly unlikely that the Supreme Court will hold that introducing the death penalty for certain Sharia offences infringes either the constitutional right to life or the prohibition of cruel, inhuman or degrading treatment, it is quite conceivable that the court may in due course decide that stoning to death and crucifixion, as prescribed by the SPC, which are infinitely more agonizing and protracted than the two other forms of capital punishment not derived from the Sharia (i.e. hanging and death by firing squad), are inhuman or degrading methods of execution and hence unconstitutional.[152]

Even though the Supreme Court in *Onuoha Kalu* declined to hold that the imposition of the death penalty was unconstitutional, their Lordships held open the possibility that measures might eventually be taken by the legislature to secure the abolition of capital punishment in Nigeria. The point was succinctly made by IGUH, J.S.C, who acknowledged that "the arguments against capital punishment may be proper (sic) basis for legislative abolition of the death penalty";[153] and by OGUNDARE, J.S.C, who emphasized that "it is for the abolitionists of the death penalty to direct their attention to the legislature to effect the change they desire".[154] Nearly five years later, in response to the furore generated by the various cases in which persons accused of adultery have been sentenced to death by stoning, the Federal Government initiated a debate on the Death Penalty in the National Assembly. In order to facilitate this exercise, the Federal Ministry of Justice established a National Study Group on the Death Penalty in November 2003. This body, which has 12 members representing different facets of Nigerian society, has been mandated to take the debate to all parts of the country, to collate the views expressed at various consultation sessions held in the major cities of Nigeria and to produce a report by June 2004 setting out its findings and recommendations. It is envisaged that this report will provide the basis upon which the Assembly will decide whether or not to legislate for the abolition of capital punishment in Nigeria.[155] If at the end of this exercise, the Study Group unequivocally recommends the abolition of the death penalty, this would pave the way for the legislature to seek to alter the Constitution by elevating the right to life guaranteed by section 33(1) to an absolute and unconditional right. Such an outcome would not only negate the decision in *Onuoha Kalu* that death by hanging did not infringe the Constitution but would also lay to

[152] This view that the manner in which a death sentence is executed may amount to torture or inhuman treatment has also gained currency in the realm of international human rights law. Schabas, for instance, signifies that article 7 of the ICCPR which prohibits cruel, inhuman and degrading punishment is breached by "[m]ethods of execution that inflict superfluous or prolonged suffering on the condemned person—such as the gas chamber". See Schabas, n. 141 above.

[153] *Onuoha Kalu,* at 527.

[154] Ibid., at 624. See also to the same effect BELGORE, J.S.C, ibid., at 606 and OGWUEGBU, J.S.C., ibid., 631.

[155] See Amnesty International Report; "The Death Penalty and Women Under the Nigerian Penal Systems" Available at http://www.web.amnesty.org/library/print/ENGAFR44001 2004, last accessed 18 May, 2004; Amnesty International "The Death Penalty in West Africa" Available at http://web.amnesty.org/web/web.nsf/print/deathpenalty-westafrica-eng , last accessed 18 May, 2004 ; IRIN Office for the Coordination of Humanitarian Affairs: "Nigeria: Government Appoints Panel to Review Death Penalty". Available at http://www.irinnews.org/report.asp? REPORTID =37651&SelectRegion=West_Africa&SelectCountry=NIGERIA, last accessed 18 May, 2004; S. Olukoya: "Should the Death Penalty be put on Death Row?" Available at http://www.ipsnews.net/africa/interna.asp?idnews=21892, last accessed 18 May, 2004.

rest the ongoing controversy over whether the modes of capital punishment revived by the SPC are permissible under the Constitution. As a matter of practical politics, however, the process of securing such a constitutional amendment might well prove immensely difficult. Section 9 of the Constitution requires any proposed amendment to be supported by a two-thirds majority in both the Senate and the House of Representatives. Opposition from senators and members of the House of Representatives from the Sharia-compliant states with the support of their co-religionists from other states is likely to render this requirement unattainable. This is compounded by the fact that section 9 also requires any such amendment to be supported by resolution of the Houses of Assembly of not less than two-thirds of all the states. Fulfilling this requirement is likely to be problematic in view of the fact that the Sharia reforms have been embraced by 12 out of Nigeria's 36 states.

(f) The discriminatory effect of Sharia-based punishments

The proposition that all persons should be equal before the law has been characterized by Peters as "one of the most profound principles in human rights discourse".[156] This principle has become virtually sacrosanct within the domain of international human rights. Thus, for instance, article 26 of the ICCPR declares that "All persons are equal before the law and are entitled without any discrimination to the protection of the law." This is echoed by article 3 of the ACHPR, which states that "Every individual shall be equal under the law" and "Every individual shall be entitled to equal protection of the law". The principle of equality of treatment and protection against discrimination has also been embraced by successive Nigerian Constitutions including the 1999 Constitution which provides in section 42(1) that "A citizen of Nigeria of a particular ... religion ... shall not only by reason that he is such a person (a) be subjected either expressly by or in the practical application of any law in force in Nigeria or any executive or administrative action to disabilities or restrictions which citizens of Nigeria of other ... religions ... are not made subject...".

Commenting on section 39(1) of the 1979 Constitution, which is identical in wording to the aforementioned section 42(1), NASSER, P.C.A., signified in *Uzoukwu* v. *Ezeonu*[157] that the reference therein to "law in force in Nigeria" included Sharia law. It is significant in this connection that the offences created by the recently enacted Sharia Penal Codes as well as the punishments prescribed for such offences are targeted at the Muslim populace of the Sharia-compliant states. This is evident, for instance from the Introduction to the Zamfara SPC which provides, *inter alia,* that "Every person who *professes the Islamic faith* ... shall be liable to punishment under the SPC for any act or omission contrary to the provisions thereof of which he may be guilty within the state [emphasis added]."

The most notable consequence of this provision and similar provisions in the legislation of other Sharia-observant states is that Muslims in these states are likely to be penalized more harshly for their infractions than their non-Muslim counterparts. Thus, for instance, if a Muslim and his non-Muslim

[156] Peters, n. 5 above, at 37.
[157] Above, n. 139, at 766.

friend are caught in the act of stealing a bicycle in Kano, Kaura Namodo or Kontagora and there is sufficient evidence to prove their guilt, the Muslim culprit faces the daunting prospect of amputation while his non-Muslim co-offender will, at the very worst, be sentenced to a term of imprisonment (except in the highly unlikely event of his opting to be tried by a Sharia court).[158] By the same token, if two married persons commit adultery with each other and one of them happens to be a Muslim and the other a Christian, the former can be prosecuted and possibly sentenced to death by stoning, whereas the latter would undoubtedly have sinned against his or her religion but will not have to answer to a criminal charge.

The fact that the SPC dictates that Muslims are to be governed by a more draconian penal regime than non-Muslims has prompted suggestions that the Muslim inhabitants of the Sharia-observant states are being subjected to discriminatory disabilities and restrictions on account of their religion in contravention of the principle of equality enshrined in section 42 of the 1999 Constitution.[159] The most influential and widely publicized expression of this viewpoint is contained in a letter entitled "Prohibition of discriminatory punishments" written by Kanu Agabi in his capacity as the Attorney-General of the Federation (AGF).[160] In this letter, which was addressed to the governors of the Sharia-compliant states, the AGF began by drawing their attention to the deluge of letters he had received from all over the world protesting against the discriminatory punishments now imposed by some Sharia Courts for certain offences. The AGF conceded that the motive of these governors in conferring criminal jurisdiction on their Sharia Courts was "to ensure transparency and achieve a more orderly and disciplined society". He however cautioned that the Constitution must not be violated in seeking to achieve this laudable objective. He observed that the fact that the Sharia legislation enacted by these governors applies only to Muslims "makes it imperative that the rights of such persons to equality under [section 42(1) of] the Constitution should not be infringed". He then proceeded to argue that "[a] Moslem should not be subjected to a punishment more severe than would be imposed on other Nigerians for the same offence. Equality before the law means that Muslims should not be discriminated against. As an elected Governor, I am sure that you will not tolerate such disparity in the allocation of punishment." In the AGF's view, such disparate treatment was "not only against the Constitution but also against equity and good conscience".

Two possible objections might be raised in response to Agabi's pronouncement. In the first place, since non-Muslims are immune from the Sharia punishments, advocates of the Sharia reforms might argue that it is unduly presumptuous for the AGF or other non-Muslims to excoriate the SPC for discriminating against Muslims, when devout Muslims throughout the Sharia-compliant states regard it as a benefit rather than a detriment to be required to adhere to the more rigorous penal regime sanctioned by the Sharia. It is undoubtedly true that there are numerous fervent Muslims in

---

158 See Ostien, n. 63 above.
159 Peters, n. 5 above, 37–38.
160 G.K. Agabi, "Prohibition of discriminatory punishment", (2002) 1(2) *Jenda: A Journal of Culture and African Women Studies*. Available at http://www.jendajournal.com/jenda/vol1.2/agabi.html., last accessed 24 September, 2003.

the Sharia-compliant states who would consider it utterly abhorrent ever to engage in the types of acts which would attract the Sharia punishments. However, it is equally the case that there are some of their co-religionists who are either less devout or more susceptible to the sort of temptation which might impel them to indulge in such acts. It is submitted that the willingness of the former to be governed by the Sharia does not detract from the fact that the latter are subjected by the Sharia legislation to disabilities (such as amputation) and restrictions (such as the criminalization of extra-marital relations) to which non-Muslims in their state are not subject contrary to section 42(1) of the Constitution. The discrimination encountered by such errant Muslims is compounded by the fact that where they are convicted of any offence under the SPC which is punishable by death, there appears to be no scope under the Constitution for them to appeal beyond the Sharia Court of Appeal. By contrast, non-Muslims who are sentenced to death by a High Court are not subjected to such a disability but may appeal as of right to the Court of Appeal and thereafter to the Supreme Court.[161]

The second objection to Agabi's pronouncement is that there is nothing novel in the fact that certain offences and punishments have been specifically designated by the SPC to apply exclusively to Muslims. This point has been made by Peters[162] and by Governor Kure of Niger State,[163] who both signify that even before the advent of the Sharia reforms, adultery, consumption of alcohol and the like only constituted offences under the pre-existing Penal Codes of the Northern states when committed by Muslims. They suggest that the inclusion of such "Muslim-only" offences in the Penal Code generated little controversy and never prompted claims that the Code infringed the non-discrimination clause in earlier Nigerian Constitutions. It can however be counter-argued that if commentators did not see fit to question the constitutionality of the Sharia-based offences contained in the Penal Code, this is probably because the punishments prescribed for these offences were comparatively benign. The fact that the Muslim-only punishments set out in the SPC are considerably more severe has accentuated the discriminatory effect of today's Sharia-based penal regime and has quite understandably heightened concerns about the constitutionality of such discriminatory punishments. It is submitted that despite the censorious responses made by the architects of the Sharia reforms to the AGF's Sharia pronouncement,[164] he cannot be faulted for seeking to use his exalted office as a vehicle for articulating these concerns.

161 See pp. 137–138 above.

162 Peters n. 5 above, at 38.

163 Governor Kure's views are set out in a news report by K. Ehigiator, entitled "Sharia: Governor Sani Adamant, Rules out Dialogue". Available at http://www.vanguardngr.com/news/articles/2002/march/25032002/f2250302.htm, last accessed 24 September, 2003.

164 These responses are exemplified by the comments attributed by *The* [Nigerian] *Punch* newspaper of 25 March, 2002 to the Secretary-General of the National Council for the Implementation of Sharia in Nigeria, Nafiu Baba-Ahmad. According to this report, the Secretary-General dismissed Agabi's letter as the handiwork of anti-Islamic forces which have regrouped and want to launch an attack on Islam and Muslims in Nigeria and urged the Governors of the Sharia-compliant states "to throw Agabi's letter into the dustbin and wait for his next action". See also A.M. Ali, "2003 Elections: The Sharia in the Mix". Available at http://www.google.co.uk s.../20020330plu05.html+godwin+kanu+agabi&hl=en&ie+UTF-, last accessed on 29 July, 2003.

(g) The recognition of offences not specifically defined in the Sharia Penal Codes

Chapters IX to XI of the Zamfara SPC define and prescribe punishments for a wide range of offences. In addition it is provided in section 92 that "[a]ny act or omission which is not specifically mentioned in the [SPC] but is otherwise declared to be an offence under the *Qu'ran, Sunnah* or *Ijthihad* of the Maliki School of Islamic thought shall be an offence under the Code." An issue which arises is whether the recognition of such "general offences" (as they are called in section 92) violates section 36(12) of the 1999 Constitution. This subsection provides that "[s]ubject as otherwise provided by this Constitution, a person shall not be convicted of a criminal offence unless that offence is defined and the penalty prescribed in a written law". Peters makes the point that some Muslims would argue that the Sharia is written law because its rules and principles are enshrined in the sacred texts of Islamic jurisprudence.[165] On the strength of this, it might be contended that section 36(12) is not violated by section 92 SPC since the acts and omissions which are declared to be offences in section 92 are embodied in written law. It seems, however, that this argument is untenable as section 36(12) goes on to specify that "in this subsection, a written law refers to an Act of the National Assembly or a Law of a State, any subordinate legislation or instrument under the provisions of the law". It is therefore evident that the sacred texts of Islamic law mentioned in section 92 do not come within the fairly narrow compass of "written law" as contemplated by section 36(12) and that a person may be punished for offences prescribed in these texts only to the extent that these are also specifically defined in the SPC. It is submitted in the light of this that Peters is correct when he asserts that "a section [such as section 92 SPC] making punishable any act or omission that is an offence under the Sharia even if it is not mentioned in the Penal Code itself ... is ... patently repugnant to the principle of S. 36(12) of the Constitution as even some Muslim lawyers admit".[166]

Peters expresses the view that it is very possible that those who drafted the SPC had the offence of apostasy in mind when formulating section 92.[167] Ostien similarly cites apostasy as the most obvious example of a section 92 offence since it is not otherwise included in the SPC but is most certainly an offence under the Qu'ran.[168] Premodern Islamic jurists postulated that apostates were to be given an opportunity to repent and return to Islam but if they refused they were to be executed (if male) and imprisoned till they recanted (if female).[169] One Muslim scholar has suggested that the rule that renders apostasy punishable by death has become obsolete.[170] Another asserts that the practice of executing apostates "fall[s] short of the present day standard of

[165] Peters, n. 5 above, 37. See also Oba, n. 3 above, 832.

[166] Peters, ibid. The Muslim lawyer identified by Peters as having admitted that s. 92 of the Zamfara SPC and corresponding provisions in other Sharia Codes are in conflict with s. 36(12) of the Constitution is A-L. Adegbite, who is the Secretary-General of the highly influential Nigerian Supreme Council for Islamic Affairs. In this connection, Peters cites a paper by Adegbite entitled "Sharia in the Context of Nigeria", *The Sharia Issue: Working Papers for a Dialogue*, Lagos, 2000, 57–82.

[167] Peters, n. 5 above 38.

[168] Ostien, n. 7, above at 6.

[169] Mayer, n. 124, above at 49.

[170] R. Maydani, "*Uqubat*: Penal Law" in M. Khadduri and H.J. Liebesny (eds.), *Law in the Middle East, Vol.1: Origin and Development of Islamic Law*, Washington, D.C, 1955, 223, at 227.

human rights".[171] It is conceivable that the architects of the Sharia reforms may have been persuaded by such sentiments that the execution of apostates is unacceptable, hence its non-inclusion among the offences and penalties set out in the SPC. An alternative possibility is that the Northern state governments are reluctant to give their official seal of approval to the killing of people for their religious beliefs by making apostasy punishable by death in the SPC but are nonetheless tacitly supportive of the execution of apostates. This would not be an entirely novel development, for as Mayer points out, in some countries that have embraced Islamicization programmes, there are no express legislative provisions mandating the execution of apostates but such executions nevertheless occur as if the Sharia rules are binding in the absence of such legislative provisions.[172]

There are no reports of any Muslim having been sentenced to death or executed for the offence of apostasy in any of the Northern states since the advent of the Sharia reforms. On the contrary, in a recent case which received press coverage, two accused persons were arraigned before a Zamfara State Sharia Court charged with having renounced Islam and converted to Christianity. The presiding judge, Alhaji Jabaka, acknowledged that under strict Islamic law the punishment for converting from Islam to another religion was death. He however declined to sentence the accused persons to death as demanded by the local Sharia Implementation and Monitoring Group since the SPC had made no provision for converts from Islam to be punished in this manner.[173] Even if it is eventually established beyond peradventure that the SPC does not contemplate the execution of apostates, the argument may still be put that the very fact that apostasy is treated as a criminal offence by virtue of section 92 SPC is inconsistent with section 38 of the 1999 Constitution. It is especially relevant that the fundamental right to freedom of religion enshrined in this section is expressed to include the freedom to change one's religion. Insofar as the offence of apostasy is directed against the Muslim who renounces his or her faith, it clearly impinges on this freedom, irrespective of whether the legal sanction visited on the offender entails the loss of life or the lesser penalties contemplated by section 92.

(h) The involvement of the Federal Government in testing the constitutional validity of the Sharia reforms

A notable feature of the Sharia reforms is that they were introduced entirely at the instigation of state governments without the endorsement or support of

[171] S.H. Amin, *Islamic Law and its Implications for Modern World*, Glasgow, 1989, 57.

[172] Mayer, n. 124 above 154.

[173] See the *Daily Champion* newspaper, 27 April, 2002. At the same time, however, it has been reported that the Zamfara State Deputy Governor Mamuda Shinkafi recently issued a *fatwah* calling for a non-Muslim journalist to be "beheaded as a matter of religious duty" for writing an article which was deemed to be blasphemous to Muslims. See S. Kola-Balogun, "FATWA: Beyond Individual Human Rights". Available at http://www.thisdayonline.com/archive/2002/12/17/20021217law05.html, last accessed 24 September, 2003. See also "Nigeria: The Miss World Riots: Continued Impunity for the Killings in Kaduna", (2003) Human Rights Watch Report available at http://www.hrw.org/reports/2003/nigeria0703/nigeria0703.pdf last accessed 24 September, 2003; K. Somerville, "Controversy over Nigerian Fatwa", BBC News Report. Available at http://news.bbc.co.uk/1/hi/world/africa/2519595.stm, last accessed 24 September, 2003; Any such inclination on the part of a state government to orchestrate, sanction or otherwise acquiesce in the extra-judicial killing of an alleged blasphemer offends against s. 33(1) of the 1999 Constitution which prohibits the intentional deprivation of a person's life "save in execution of the sentence of a court in respect of a criminal offence of which he is found guilty".

the Federal Government. In principle, there is nothing inherently objectionable in this state of affairs since section 2(2) of the 1999 Constitution proclaims that "Nigeria shall be a Federation consisting of States". As Ostien points out, the whole point of adopting such a federal structure "is to permit wide local political variations within broad national limits".[174] Ardent supporters of the Sharia reforms argue with great vigour that the Nigerian Constitution invests the Federal government and the governments of individual states with executive and legislative powers within the respective spheres of competence assigned to them and that the states which have implemented these reforms are acting within their sphere of competence. The leading proponent of this viewpoint is Nigeria's immediate past Chief Justice, Muhammed Bello, who declares that

> "Section 4 of the constitution has divided the legislative powers of government between the federation and the states. In its second schedule, it specifies the exclusive legislative list on which only the federation may make laws and also the concurrent legislative list on which both the federation and the states may make laws. In addition it empowers the state to make laws on any other matters not included in the two lists. Sharia falls within the residue and consequently, a state has the Constitutional power to make laws relating to the Sharia".[175]

Careful scrutiny of the exclusive legislative list suggests that Bello's representation of the constitutional position is not entirely accurate. In this connection it is pertinent that the Second Schedule to the 1999 Constitution to which he alludes includes Evidence as an item within the exclusive legislative competence of the Federal Government.[176] It is therefore doubtful whether a state's constitutional power to make laws relating to the Sharia extends to the enactment of legislation providing for the operation of evidential rules derived from the Sharia. In effect, legislative provisions such as section 10 of the Sokoto State Sharia Courts Law, 1999 (which provides that the law of evidence to be applied in these courts shall be the Islamic law of evidence) and section 127 of the Kano State SPC and the Kebbi State SPC (which deal with proof of unlawful sexual intercourse in cases of adultery) may well be unconstitutional.[177]

Insofar as the Sharia-compliant states have purported to legislate on a matter which the Constitution specifically assigned to the federal domain, it might have been expected that the Federal Government, acting through the Attorney General of the Federation (AGF), would at the earliest opportunity initiate judicial proceedings with a view to challenging the constitutional validity of this aspect of the Sharia reforms. Contrary to such expectations, the two Senior Advocates of Nigeria who occupied the position of AGF during President Obasanjo's first term of office both displayed a marked disinclination to test the constitutional validity of the Sharia reforms within the judicial sphere. Kanu Agabi, who was the AGF during the critical period when the Sharia reform process was commenced by the Zamfara State Government in 1999, appears to have been unable to make up his mind at that juncture about

[174] Ostien, n. 63 above.

[175] M. Bello, as quoted in Tabiu, n. 6 above. See also Ostien, n. 63 above, who characterizes the measures taken by the Sharia-compliant states as "a good example of Nigeria's new found federalism at work".

[176] Part 1 of the Second Schedule to the 1999 Constitution (Item 23).

[177] See Peters, n. 5 above, at 33–34.

the constitutionality of these reforms. He is reported to have proclaimed that the reforms were unconstitutional,[178] but other reports disclose that he declared the reforms to be constitutional.[179] In the light of these contradictory pronouncements it is scarcely surprising that the Nigerian Senate felt constrained to request President Obasanjo to direct Agabi to approach the courts for a constitutional interpretation of the legal status of the Sharia reforms.[180] Agabi resolutely refused to go down this route, arguing that the Federal Government lacked the *locus standi* to initiate judicial proceedings against the Sharia-implementing states.[181]

In June 2000, Agabi was succeeded as AGF by Bola Ige. When questioned on the constitutionality of the Sharia reforms during a newspaper interview in 2001, Ige's response was that "To tell you the truth, none of the states which have passed what they call sharia law have violated any part of the constitution". Ige went further to state that "The second thing I would like to say in regard to Sharia is that no known Muslim in Nigeria has complained that the application of the Sharia has violated his rights, not one.... Now how then would the Attorney-General of Nigeria say he has a *locus standi* (sic.)".[182] Barely eight months later, however, in response to the imposition of a stoning sentence by a Sokoto State Sharia Court on a woman who had been convicted of adultery, Ige declared that the Federal Government would seek to ensure that the sentence was not carried out. Even though Ige did not go as far as to recant his earlier assertion that the Sharia reforms did not violate the Constitution, he nevertheless characterized the punishment in this case to be "harsh and crude" and is reported to have hinted that the Federal Ministry of Justice, over which he presided "could compel Sokoto state to comply with the Federal Constitution and provide judicial relief to Safiyatu [the alleged adulteress]".[183] The proactive approach favoured by Ige in this context is difficult to reconcile with his earlier insistence that the AGF lacked the *locus standi* to challenge the constitutionality of the Sharia within the judicial sphere and that this could only be done by those who complained that their constitutional rights had been infringed by the Sharia.

Following Ige's untimely death in December 2001, Agabi was reinstated as the AGF. It was shortly thereafter that he wrote to the Governors of the Sharia-implementing states to inform them that the discriminatory

[178] See "Tensions Rise over Islamic Law in Northern Nigeria". Available at http://www.domini.org/openbook/nigeria19991223.htm, last accessed on 24 September, 2003.

[179] See the news report "APP in Zamfara Urges FG to Call Agabi to Order over Sharia Matters". Available at http://www.thisdayonline.com/archive/2002/03/24/20020324news/16.html, last accessed 29 July, 2003. See also Ali, n. 164 above.

[180] The Senate's request is referred to in the 1999 Annual Report of the Human Rights Law Service. Available at http://www.hurilaws.org/1999_annual_report_and_accounts.htm, last accessed 24 September, 2003.

[181] See S. Hon, "Sharia: Attorney-General of the Federation has *Locus Standi* to Sue". Available at http://www.nigerdeltacongress.com/sarticles/sharia_attorney.htm, last accessed 24 September, 2003.

[182] C. Edomaruse and P. Omale, "The Attorney General's Sallah Gift ... Sharia is Constitutional Says Ige". Available at http://www.thisdayonline.com/archive/2001/03/04/20010304news01.html, last accessed 24 September, 2003.

[183] S. Babasola, "Sharia: F.G. won't allow Safiya to die—Ige", *The Vanguard*, 15 November, 2001. Available at http://www.vanguardngr.com/news/articles/2001/November/15112001/f4151101.htm, last accessed on 24 September, 2003. See also D. Isaacs, "Living on Nigeria's Death Row", BBC News, 5 December, 2001. Available at http://news.bbc.co.uk/1/hi/world/africa/1694027.stm, last accessed 24 September, 2003.

punishments provided for in their Sharia Penal Codes rendered the Sharia reforms unconstitutional.[184] Agabi's pronouncement was indignantly dismissed by these Governors who maintained that it was for the courts rather than for the AGF to determine the constitutionality of the Sharia reforms. This viewpoint was eloquently put by Governor Kure of Niger State who declared that "I need not remind the learned Senior Advocate of Nigeria [i.e. Agabi] that as the Chief Law Officer of the federation, the honourable course to take if you feel so strongly about the constitutionality of our actions is to lay the issue before the courts."[185] This view has been widely echoed in non-Muslim circles. Amadi, for instance, states that "The AG[F] has declared sharia unconstitutional. But this is an opinion. It does not lie in his mouth to say so with any juristic finality. The court[s], especially the Supreme Court must make that declaration.... A public policy response to the Sharia debacle should entail legal action by the AGF on behalf of the Federal Government to establish the constitutional extent and legitimacy of the Sharia".[186] Reference may also be made in this regard to an online petition sponsored by Women's Rights Nigeria urging Agabi "as the Chief Law Officer of Nigeria to seek judicial interpretation on the validity of the imposition of [the] Sharia Criminal Legal System into (sic.) Nigeria".[187]

In a wide-ranging press interview that he granted two months after his Sharia pronouncement, Agabi himself acknowledged that Nigerians expected the Federal Government to commence judicial proceedings against the Sharia-implementing states.[188] He however pointed out that the jurisdiction to entertain actions by the Federation against states was well defined. According to him, such jurisdiction resided in the Supreme Court and an action would lie only where the rights of the Federal Government had been infringed. He contended that in the absence of any such infringement, the court's jurisdiction did not extend to the ongoing controversy regarding the constitutionality of the Sharia reforms. He further argued that insofar as the imposition of discriminatory punishments under the SPC infringed the fundamental rights enshrined in the Constitution, the rights which were thereby violated were rights vested in private persons. He noted that a number of Nigerian NGOs had attempted, unsuccessfully, to challenge the constitutionality of the Sharia-based punishments through the judicial process.[189] He extrapolated from this that it was not open to the Federal Government to go to court to challenge the constitutionality of the Sharia punishments. Rather it was for those individuals who had been sentenced to be amputated or stoned to death under the SPC to seek to vindicate their constitutionally guaranteed rights within the judicial arena.

---

[184] See above, at 29.

[185] See n. 163 above. Governor Kure's view on the matter is also reported in the news item entitled "Let the Court decide on Sharia, Kure Tells Govt". Available at http://www.cometnews.com.ng/25032002/nn99608.htm, last accessed 24 September, 2003.

[186] Amadi, n. 130 above.

[187] This petition is available at http://www.petitiononline.com/wrw/petition.html, last accessed 24 September, 2003.

[188] "Why the Federal Government Will Not Test Sharia in Court, by Kanu Agabi". Interview with L. Okenwa, available at http://www.thisdayonline.com/archive/2002/06/25/20020625law.04.html, last accessed 2 January, 2003.

[189] See, for example, *Human Rights Law Service* v. *Attorney General of Zamfara State & Anor.* Unreported Case No ZM/GS/M36/2000 referred to in http://www.hurilaws.org/1999_annual_report_and_accounts.htm, last accessed 24 September, 2003.

Several observations may be made regarding the stance taken by the erstwhile AGF. In the first place the suspicion cannot be avoided that the AGF's evident desire to evade all responsibility for initiating judicial proceedings against the governments of the Sharia-implementing states may have been motivated by concerns over the political risks of alienating the governments of these states and inflaming religious passions among their citizenry. Kola-Balogun is highly critical of the AGF on this account, arguing that "As the Chief Law Officer of the Federation he has a duty to use the executive powers vested in him as a minister to execute and maintain the constitution.... Refusing to go to court on the Sharia because it is not politically expedient to do so even though the Constitution is being breached is an affront to the rule of law and the conscience of the Federal Republic of Nigeria."[190]

Secondly, in expressing his view on the Federal Government's standing to sue, the AGF failed to take due cognizance of the amplitude of powers conferred on the President and Federal Ministers by section 5 of the 1999 Constitution. This section states that the executive powers of the Federation shall be vested in the President acting directly or through Federal Ministers or public officers and further stipulates that these powers "shall extend to the execution and maintenance of this Constitution". According to Hon, "'the execution and maintenance of this Constitution' includes the right, power and duty of the executive branch of government ... to defend it against wanton breach".[191] More than any other Federal Minister or public officer, the AGF has a pivotal role to play in the process of executing and maintaining the Constitution. His designation by section 150 of the Constitution as the Chief Law Officer of the Federation casts him in the role of "the number one defender of this Constitution"[192] and makes it incumbent on him more than any other person to seek to test perceived breaches of the Constitution in court. In Hon's unflattering assessment a situation in which the AGF, after having declared the Sharia to be unconstitutional, simply sat back hoping that it would recede into oblivion "amounts to a breach of the Constitution and a despicable dereliction of duty".[193] In much the same vein, Ogowewo, who has written extensively on standing to sue under Nigerian law, declares that "Even under the present standing rule, a diligent Federal Attorney General should be able to invoke the courts to test the constitutionality of such a Sharia law, since he has a duty to do so pursuant to the combined effect of section 5(1)(b) and section 150(1) of the 1999 Constitution ...".[194]

A further criticism which may be directed against the AGF's reasoning is that it completely overlooks recent judicial pronouncements and academic commentary which suggest that the standing to sue is not necessarily limited to cases in which litigants can show that their private legal rights have been infringed. The AGF's insistence that neither the NGOs nor the AGF himself

[190] S. Kola-Balogun, "Sharia and the issue of Locus Standi". Available at http://www.thisdayonline/com/archive/2001/04/03200104031aw09.htm See also S. Kola-Balogun, n. 173 above.

[191] Hon, n. 181 above.

[192] Ibid.

[193] Ibid.

[194] T.I. Ogowewo, "Wrecking the law: how Article III of the Constitution of the United States led to the discovery of a law of standing to sue in Nigeria", [2000] XXVI(2) *Brooklyn Journal of International Law* 527, at 583 (n. 223).

had the standing to challenge the constitutionality of the Sharia reforms in court since their private legal rights had in no way been infringed by these reforms is completely at odds with this more flexible judicial and academic approach.

The case of *Adesanya* v. *President of the Federal Republic of Nigeria*[195] has for many years been the leading Nigerian authority on standing to sue. The appellant in this case was a Nigerian Senator during the Second Republic. He commenced proceedings claiming that the President's appointment of Justice Ovie-Whiskey as the Chairman of the Federal Electoral Commission was unconstitutional. During confirmation hearings in the Senate, the appellant had opposed this appointment but it had nevertheless been confirmed by a majority of Senate members. The appellant's standing to sue was challenged in the Court of Appeal which ruled that he had no standing. A full panel of the Supreme Court similarly affirmed the appellant's lack of standing. Although the lead judgment was delivered by FATAYI-WILLIAMS, C.J.N, the *locus standi* rule that gained judicial acceptance was articulated by BELLO, J.S.C, who adopted a test predicated on section 6(6)(b) of the 1979 Constitution (which has since been re-enacted at section 6(6)(b) of the 1999 Constitution). This subsection provides that "The judicial powers vested in accordance with the foregoing provisions of this section shall extend to all matters between persons or between government or authority and any person in Nigeria, and to all actions and proceedings relating thereto, for the determination of any question as to the civil rights and obligations of that person." Justice Bello pointed out that the judicial powers conferred on Nigerian courts by this constitutional provision "are limited in scope and content to only (sic) matters, actions and proceedings 'for the determination of any question as to the civil rights and obligations of that person [who seeks to invoke the court's jurisdiction]' It is only where the civil rights and obligations of [that] person ... are in issue for determination that the jurisdiction of the courts may be invoked". He then went on to signify that "standing will only be accorded to a plaintiff who shows that his civil rights and obligations have been or are in danger of being violated or adversely affected by the act complained of".[196] In a host of cases decided after *Adesanya,* the courts proceeded to treat Justice Bello's judgment as reflecting the position of the Supreme Court on the issue of standing to sue and to apply his "civil rights test" as a matter of course whenever a litigant's standing to sue fell to be determined.[197]

Ogowewo's analysis of *Adesanya* discloses how the application of the Bello-inspired test has resulted in a situation in which litigants are adjudged to possess the standing to sue only in the event of the infringement of their private legal rights (which in this context have been equated with the "civil rights" referred to in section 6(6)(b)).[198] In his later article where he comments further on this equation of civil rights with private legal rights, Ogowewo explains that the emergence of a standing rule predicated on

[195] [1981] 1 All NLR [Part 1] 1. *Adesanya* has been incisively reviewed in T.I. Ogowewo, "The problem with standing to sue in Nigeria", [1995] 39(1) *J.A.L* 1.

[196] *Adesanya* at 39.

[197] See Ogowewo, n. 195 above, at 8–9. See also O. Ilofulunwa, "Locus Standi in Nigeria: An Impediment to Justice". Available at http://www.hurilaws.org/locus_standi_art.htm, last accessed 24 September, 2003.

[198] Ogowewo, n. 195 above, at 4.

section 6(6)(b) left no room for a standing test which did not focus on an infringement or threatened infringement of a private legal right.[199] He maintains that the adoption of this rule by Nigerian judges effectively shut out many prospective litigants from the courthouse.[200] He points out that the fact that the rule was founded on a narrow concept of personal standing which focused on private legal rights meant that it afforded no scope for representative standing.[201] This suggests that the Nigerian standing rule as thus conceived would indeed preclude Nigerian NGOs from instituting proceedings to challenge the constitutional validity of the Sharia reforms, since they would be hard pressed to show that these reforms have infringed any of their private rights.

Ogowewo has however been relentless in his criticism of the standing rule formulated by Justice Bello. He states that "neither the text of section 6(6)(b) nor its pre-enacting history would suggest ... that it deals with standing to sue";[202] and decries the manner in which "[b]y some kind of alchemy the courts transmuted a constitutional provision that seemingly has no bearing on the standing principle into one that contains a rule of standing to be applied in all areas of the law."[203] He describes the rule in unflattering terms as "a gigantic conceptual mistake [which] has wreaked ... havoc across the entire face of Nigerian law".[204] He puts forward a compelling case for the abandonment of the civil rights test upon which the rule is founded. In so doing, he succeeds in demonstrating that, despite the weight accorded to Justice Bello's judgment in subsequent cases, *Adesanya* did not in fact decide that section 6(6)(b) laid down a standing requirement since the court was divided on the issue with no discernible majority. In particular, FATAYI-WILLIAMS, C.J.N, did not subscribe to the view that section 6(6)(b) laid down the restrictive standing requirement ascribed to it by Justice Bello. The only link which the Chief Justice could discern between the subsection and the question of standing to sue was that the effect of the subsection was to confer on litigants an unfettered right of access to the courts in constitutional disputes not connected with the fundamental rights provisions in Chapter IV. Elaborating on this theme, Ogowewo states that:

> "Even though it has been universally accepted that the Adesanya court decided that s.6(6)(b) laid down a standing requirement, a close reading of the case will reveal that this is not correct. The reasonings of the Chief Justice and Justice BELLO each commanded equal support on this point. While Justices NNAMANI and IDIGBE agreed with Justice BELLO,[205] Justices SOWEMIMO and OBASEKI agreed with the C.J.N. Justice UWAIS, who could have resolved this deadlock, quite surprisingly made the rather preposterous assertion that '... the interpretation to be given to section 6(6)(b) of the Constitution will depend on the facts or special circumstances of each case'."[206]

199 See Ogowewo, n. 194 above, at 548.
200 Ibid., at 540.
201 Ibid., at 529, n. 9.
202 Ibid., at 535.
203 Ibid., at p. 536.
204 Ibid., at 529.
205 It is noteworthy that even though NNAMANI and IDIGBE, J.J.S.C, signified in their judgments that they concurred with BELLO, J.S.C., certain pronouncements made by these two judges suggest that while they professed to endorse Justice Bello's civil rights test, they in fact favoured a less rigorous "sufficient interest" test. See Ogowewo, n. 195 above, at 4–5.
206 Ogowewo, n. 195 above, at 9–10. See also Ogowewo, n. 194 above at 556–559; Ilofulunwa, n. 197 above.

In the light of this, Ogowewo boldly asserts that "subsequent decisions including those of the Supreme Court which treat *Adesanya* as deciding that section 6(6)(b) lays down a requirement of standing exhibit a misapprehension of that decision".[207] In recent years, the courts have also displayed a similar inclination to question the authority of the standing rule formulated by Justice Bello. The first discordant note was struck by AYOOLA, J.C.A, in *First African Trust Bank* v. *Ezegbu*.[208] In his dissenting judgment, he opined that section 6(6)(b) dealt with the judicial powers of Nigerian courts and not with individual rights whereas *locus standi* was concerned with the rights of a party to sue. He therefore questioned the relevance of the subsection to the issue of standing to sue.[209] Justice Ayoola revisited the matter four years later in *NNPC* v. *Fawehinmi*.[210] He asserted in this case that

> "Section 6 of the Constitution which vests judicial powers of the Federation and the States in the courts and defines the nature and extent of such judicial powers does not deal directly with the right of access of the individual to the court. The main objective of section 6 is to leave no doubt as to the definition and delimitation of the boundaries of the separation of powers between the judiciary on the one hand and the other organs of government on the other ... Section 6(6)(b) ... is not intended as a catch-all, all purpose provision to be pressed into service for determin[ing] questions ranging from *locus standi* to the most uncontroversial questions of jurisdiction."[211]

Justice Ayoola's stance on the issue of standing to sue has been commended by Ogowewo as an "independent and bold piece of thinking".[212] Ogowewo goes on to suggest that even though the subject of *locus standi* has been hallowed through ritual incantations of the Constitution, Nigerian courts should now feel free to depart from those decisions, including those of the Supreme Court which treat Adesanya as deciding that section 6(6)(b) lays down a rule of standing.[213] Significantly, the Supreme Court itself has now taken the first step down the route suggested by Ogowewo in *Owodunni* v. *Registered Trustees of Celestial Church & Ors*,[214] where the authority of *Adesanya*- was reassessed. OGUNDARE, J.S.C, who delivered the leading judgment in this case, alluded to the general belief that in *Adesanya* the Supreme Court had adopted the position that the law of *locus standi* was now derived from section 6(6)(b). He declared that "I am not sure that this general belief represents the correct position of the seven Justices that sat on the case". He proceeded to quote excerpts from the judgments delivered in *Adesanya* and signified that "from the[se] extracts ... one can clearly see that there was not a majority of the court in favour of Bello J.S.C's interpretation of section 6 subsection 6(b) of the Constitution".[215] He added, tellingly, that "In my respectful view, I think Ayoola J.C.A (as he then was) correctly set out the scope of section 6 subsection 6 of the Constitution ... in *NNPC v Fawehinmi & Ors*".[216]

207 Ogowewo, n. 195 above, at 10.
208 [1994] 9 N.W.L.R, p. 149.
209 Ibid., at 236.
210 [1998] 7 N.W.L.R at 598.
211 Ibid., at 612.
212 Ogowewo, n. 194, above at 571.
213 Ibid., at 575.
214 [2000] 10 N.W.L.R at 315.
215 Ibid., at 341–345.
216 Ibid., at 345.

If it is indeed correct that the courts are now free to depart from the standing rule formulated by Justice Bello, it would follow that criteria other than whether a litigant can show that his private legal rights have been infringed will come into play in determining whether such a litigant has standing to sue. In the case of litigation within the realm of public law, Ogowewo suggests that discarding the section 6(6)(b) standing rule paves the way for the courts to adopt a liberal "sufficient interest" test when seeking to determine whether a litigant has standing to sue. With particular reference to proceedings instituted with a view to preventing the Constitution from being infringed or to seek a pronouncement that an infringement which has occurred is unconstitutional or to challenge the constitutional validity of any law, Ogowewo contends that Nigeria will do itself no credit if it continues to apply a standing test that focuses on private legal rights and maintains that a liberal sufficient interest test will be more apposite in this context. He points out that such a test accords with contemporary "communitarian" and "expository" principles of constitutional law adjudication. The communitarian principle proceeds on the premise that the public and not only victims of constitutional violations have a legitimate interest in ensuring that the state adheres to the Constitution. It enables persons with the genuine desire and capacity to challenge infringements of the Constitution even where the victim of the alleged violation of the Constitution refuses to sue. The essence of the expository principle is that the paramount function of the courts is not simply the resolution of disputes but the exposition of legal principles. According to this view, the standing rule adopted in the constitutional sphere should not focus on the characteristics of the plaintiff since judicial pronouncements within this sphere are liable to affect numerous persons and must therefore strive to clarify the proper interpretation of constitutional provisions not just for the case at hand but also for future interactions between the different tiers of government and between the government and its citizens. Ogowewo maintains that embracing such a communitarian and expository model of constitutional adjudication should accord Nigerian NGOs the standing to challenge the constitutionality of Sharia punishments even where the persons at the receiving end of such punishments are disinclined to initiate proceedings themselves.[217] The prospect that such proceedings can in fact be initiated by NGOs makes it difficult for any AGF to maintain with any degree of credibility that he has no standing to test the constitutional validity of the Sharia punishments.

The objection might conceivably be raised that insofar as the primary basis upon which such punishments have been impugned is that they infringe the

[217] Ogowewo, n. 194 above, at 581–584. Significantly, in *Owodunni*, Justice Ogundare, having concluded that it was not correct to say that the Supreme Court had decided in *Adesanya* that s. 6(6)(b) prescribed the *locus standi* of a person wishing to invoke the judicial powers of the court, went on to assert that "[t]he *Adesanya* case which is in the realm of public law seems to lay it down that to invoke the judicial powers of the court, a litigant must show sufficient interest or threat or injury he will suffer". It is however evident from *Fawehinmi* v. *Inspector General of Police*, n. 56 above, which also arose in the realm of public law, that this matter has not yet been conclusively settled. In this case, UWAIFO, J.S.C., after reiterating that "Section 6(6)(b) of the 1999 Constitution does not confer *locus standi* on any litigant" proceeded to declare that the litigant "must show that his civil rights and obligations have been infringed before section 6(6)(b) which vests judicial powers in the court and provides forum for litigation (sic) will enable the court to look into [his] grievance".

fundamental rights guaranteed by Chapter IV of the Constitution, the issue of standing to sue falls to be determined by reference to section 46(1) of the 1999 Constitution. This provides that "any person who alleges that any of the provisions of this Chapter has been, is being or is likely to be infringed in relation to him may apply to a High Court ... for redress." Referring to section 42(1) of the 1979 Constitution (which is identical to section 46(1)) FATAYI-WILLIAMS, C.J.N, signified *per obiter* in *Adesanya*[218] that this provision was "restrictive in nature" and appears to have inferred that only those persons whose fundamental rights had been, were being or were likely to be infringed had the standing to sue under the fundamental rights provisions of that Constitution. In response, it might be pointed out that both section 42(1) and its 1999 counterpart are framed in permissive rather than restrictive terms since they merely provide that the person whose fundamental rights have been infringed *may* apply for redress. As Ogowewo remarks in this connection "it is arguable that this provision only makes it abundantly clear that the person whose rights are infringed or threatened should be able to sue; and that it does not go as far as taking away a right to sue that is vested in a third party.[219] It appears from this that the fact that a person whose constitutional rights have allegedly been infringed by the infliction of discriminatory Sharia punishments is empowered to seek judicial redress under section 46(1) does not necessarily disqualify other parties such as the Federal Government and Nigerian human rights organizations from also challenging the constitutionality of such punishments once they can show that they have a legitimate and sufficient interest in safeguarding the fundamental rights of the Nigerian citizenry.

Furthermore, even if it is conceded that FATAYI-WILLIAMS, C.J.N, was correct in holding that it is only a person whose fundamental rights have been infringed who has the standing to sue under Chapter IV, there are other grounds upon which the Federal Government might possibly be able to challenge the constitutionality of the Sharia reforms without recourse to the fundamental rights provisions in Chapter IV. The Federal Government may wish to contend, for instance, that by providing for the operation of Sharia rules of evidence within their judicial systems, the governments of the Sharia-implementing states have strayed into an area which falls within the exclusive legislative competence of the Federal Government. Again the Federal Government may seek to challenge the conferment of jurisdiction on the Sharia Courts of the Sharia-implementing states to impose death sentences on the ground that under the Constitution, the only state courts which are competent to impose such sentences are those courts (i.e. the High Courts) from which appeals against the death sentence lie to appellate courts at the Federal level. It is submitted that ample scope exists under section 232(1) of the 1999 Constitution for the Federal Government, through the AGF, to institute proceedings against the governments of the Sharia-implementing states in respect of such hitherto unresolved constitutional issues. Section 232(1) provides that "The Supreme Court shall to the exclusion of any other court have original jurisdiction in any dispute between the Federation and a state or between states, if and insofar as that dispute involves any question

[218] *Adesanya*, at 23.
[219] Ogowewo, n. 194 above, at 584.

(whether of law or fact) on which the existence or extent of a legal right depends". A typical instance in which recourse has been had to the original jurisdiction of the Supreme Court is in the case of *Attorney-General of the Federation* v. *Attorney General of Abia State & 35 others*,[220] which involved a dispute between the Federal and state governments regarding the allocation of revenue from the Federation Account set up under section 162 of the 1999 Constitution. In this case the court had to determine the seaward boundaries of Nigeria's littoral states for the purpose of calculating the amount of revenue accruing to the Federation Account directly from any natural resources derived from these states. It is clear from the submissions of counsel and the judgment of the Supreme Court that the dispute before the court involved questions of law and fact on which the existence and extent of competing legal rights between the Federal and state governments depended. Equally, the issue of whether state governments are competent to legislate in a field which falls within the Federal Government's exclusive legislative list as well as the issue of whether a state court can displace the federal appellate courts as a final court of appeal in cases where death sentences are imposed are profound questions of law on which the existence and extent of competing legal rights between the Federal Government and the governments of the Sharia-implementing states depend. It thus seems that these are matters in respect of which the AGF is entitled to invoke the Supreme Courts original jurisdiction under section 232(1).

Finally, the manifest unwillingness of the Federal Government to initiate judicial proceedings with a view to challenging the constitutionality of the reforms introduced by the Sharia-implementing states may also have significant implications under international law. The position in this regard was clearly enunciated by the Secretary-General of the International Commission of Jurists in a letter to President Obasanjo.[221] In this letter she reminded the President that "the conduct of the Sharia courts is directly attributable to your Government" and drew his attention to article 4 of the draft articles on the Responsibility of States for Internationally Wrongful Acts, which was adopted by the International Law Commission at its fifty-third session in 2001. Article 4 provides that:

1) The conduct of a state organ shall be considered an act of that State under international law, whether the organ exercises legislative, executive, judicial or any other functions, whatever position it holds in the organization of the state and whatever its character as an organ of the central government or of a territorial unit of the state.

2) An organ includes any person or entity which has that status in accordance with the internal law of the state.

In the light of these provisions the Secretary-General concluded that "the conduct of the Sharia court—a judicial state organ—is imputed to your [i.e. the Federal] Government; as such your Government is legally obligated to take measures to prevent the violations of human rights at the hands of these courts". If this view is correct, it is submitted that the responsibility of

---

[220] [2002] 6 N.W.L.R 264.

[221] L. Doswald-Beck, "Sharia Court Ruling Violates Human Rights" (2002). Available at the Commission's website http://www.icj.org/news.php3?id_article=2645(+en, last accessed 24 September, 2003.

the Federal Government extends beyond pronouncing, through the AGF, that the discriminatory effect of the Sharia punishments renders the Sharia reforms unconstitutional. The least that might have been expected in the circumstances would be for the AGF to submit this matter to the courts for resolution instead of seeking to hide behind the fig leaf of lack of *locus standi*. It remains to be seen whether Akinlolu Olujimi who was recently appointed as the AGF, following President Obasanjo's re-election, will be bolder than his two predecessors in venturing into the judicial arena with a view to establishing the constitutionality or otherwise of the Sharia reforms.

CONCLUSION

What emerges quite clearly from the foregoing analysis is that certain facets and ramifications of the Sharia reforms are exceedingly difficult to reconcile with the provisions of the 1999 Constitution. I am inclined to agree with Ihenacho that despite their protestations to the contrary, advocates of the Sharia reform process "know that it is of its nature contradictory to the Constitution".[222] If this assessment is correct, those who have championed the reforms would do well to pay heed to the advice proffered by the erstwhile AGF in his aforementioned letter to the governors of the Sharia-implementing states in which he cautioned that "The stability, unity and integrity of the nation are threatened by such action [i.e. flouting the Constitution]. In order to implement policies or programmes inconsistent with the Constitution we must first secure its amendment. Until that is done, we have to abide by it. To proceed on the basis either that the Constitution does not exist or that it is irrelevant is to deny the existence of the nation itself. We cannot deny the rule of law and hope to have peace and stability."[223] In the same vein, Ihenacho suggests that the best way for the Sharia-implementing states to proceed is not by arbitrarily supplementing the Constitution with a body of laws that may be contradictory to its visions and objectives, but rather by endeavouring to amend the Constitution or repeal and replace it.[224]

One course of action, which might conceivably put the constitutional legitimacy of the Sharia reforms beyond dispute, would be to initiate a root-and-branch review of the constitutional arrangements currently in place within Nigeria.[225] Such a review has been advocated by Mahmoud, who envisages the reconstruction of the Nigerian state through the introduction of a new legal and constitutional order that will be capable of accommodating and diffusing the tensions and conflicts generated by the Sharia experiment.[226]

[222] Ihenacho, n. 70 above.

[223] Agabi, n. 160 above.

[224] Ihenacho, n. 70, above.

[225] The alternative course of action advocated by Ogowewo, (n. 52 above), which would entail the judicial annulment of the 1999 Constitution and the reinstatement of the 1979 Constitution will not achieve this end because the material provisions of the 1979 Constitution are substantially the same as the corresponding provisions of the 1999 Constitution.

[226] A.B. Mahmoud, "The Shari'a Project in Northern Nigeria and Governance in a Federal Nigeria". Draft of Paper presented at Conference on Globalisation, State Capacity and Self-Determination in Muslim Contexts, Santa Cruz, California, 2002. Available at http://www2.ucsc.edu/cgirs/conferences/carnegie/papers/mahmoud.pdf, last accessed 24 September, 2003. A review of the 1999 Constitution has in fact been undertaken by The Presidential Committee on the Review of the Constitution (PCRC) but this Committee did no more than tinker around the edges of the Constitution. With regard to the constitutionality of the Sharia reforms, the only

In view of the strains imposed on the Federation by the controversies surrounding the Sharia reforms, one vital issue which any thoroughgoing review would need to address is whether the current federal structure provided for by the 1999 Constitution remains a viable basis for governing the nation. Nwabueze, who is one of Nigeria's most eminent constitutional lawyers, considers it extremely difficult for "state enforcement of Sharia, in all the plenitude of its injunctions to co-exist with a truly federal form of political association". He accordingly argues for the restructuring of Nigeria into a loose confederation.[227] Mazrui, whose credentials as a scholar are equally impressive, takes a different view. He stresses that a federal system is capable of accommodating a degree of asymmetry within its constituent parts and argues that the introduction of such asymmetrical federalism in the Nigerian constitutional order will enable Nigeria to function effectively as a Federation while accommodating the Shariacratic aspirations of the Northern states.[228] Whether the outcome of such a review is that Nigeria continues to function as a federation or is transformed into a confederation, the fact remains that without a genuine commitment to preserving national unity and a greater willingness to compromise than has hitherto been shown there can be no guarantee that any meaningful progress can be made towards satisfying the genuine aspirations and desires of the advocates of the Sharia reforms while at the same time addressing the equally compelling concerns and fears of opponents of these reforms.

In conclusion, the challenge facing the Nigerian nation has been aptly summarized by Quinn and Quinn.[229] They declare that the nation is facing its "eleventh hour" and proclaim that what is required to diffuse the current explosive situation is a strong governmental effort at mediation coupled with a sustained effort at goodwill and co-operation by Muslim and Christian leaders. As they pessimistically observe, however, "No such positive forces appear on the horizon at this point but Nigerians have headed for the brink in the past and then pulled back. Without such a turning point the future is not hopeful."

---

recommendations put forward in the PCRC report were (i) that ss. 10 and 38 should be retained unamended and (ii) that the word "personal" used in connection with Islamic law should be deleted from section 277 and any other section of the Constitution in which it appears. See the relevant portion of PCRC Report. Available at http://www.pcrconline.org/The_Report/10.shtml, last accessed 24 September, 2003.

227 Nwabueze (2000) n. 67 above.

228 Mazrui, n. 95 above.

229 Quinn and Quinn, n. 5 above, at 63–64.

[9]

The New Economic Policy and Interethnic Relations in Malaysia

Jomo K.S.

Contents

Summary/Résumé/Resumen

iii

Summary

Malaysia's New Economic Policy (NEP) was first announced in 1970 as the principal policy response to the post-election race riots of May 1969, which also resulted in a significant regime change. This paper suggests that the events of May 1969 also involved a widespread popular rejection of the ruling Alliance coalition as well as a "palace coup" within the ruling United Malays National Organisation (UMNO) as the "Young Turks" supporting then-Deputy Prime Minister Tun Abdul Razak sidelined Prime Minister Tunku Abdul Rahman, who had led the UMNO from 1951 and the country to independence in August 1957. The Rahman regime was seen by the new Razak regime as having been too conciliatory toward the ubiquitous Chinese business community. The Razak NEP regime, through the NEP, was therefore committed to increased ethnic affirmative action, or positive discrimination policies, on behalf of the ethnic Malays in particular and *bumiputera* (indigenous Malaysians) in general.

The NEP had two prongs, namely "poverty eradication regardless of race" and "restructuring society to eliminate the identification of race with economic function". The NEP was supposed to create the conditions for national unity by reducing interethnic resentment due to socioeconomic disparities. In practice, the NEP policies were seen as pro-*bumiputera*, or more specifically, pro-Malay, the largest indigenous ethnic community. Poverty reduction efforts have been seen as primarily rural and Malay, with policies principally oriented to rural Malay peasants. As poverty reduction efforts had been uncontroversial and had declined in significance over time, the NEP came to be increasingly identified with efforts at "restructuring society" efforts to reduce interethnic disparities, especially between ethnic Malay and ethnic Chinese Malaysians.

The NEP has been associated with the *First Outline Perspective Plan* [OPP] *for 1971–1990*. The OPP sought to reduce poverty from 49 per cent in Peninsular Malaysia in 1970 to 16 per cent in 1990. The actual poverty rate in the peninsula in 1990 was 17 per cent, while the national rate was slightly higher. The NEP's main restructuring target was to raise the *bumiputera* share of corporate stock ownership from 1.5 per cent in 1969 to 30 per cent in 1990. The government's data suggest that *bumiputera* ownership rose to about 18 per cent in 1990 and slightly over 20 per cent in 2000. Although the government originally envisaged that much of the *bumiputera* corporate wealth would be held by trust agencies, private individual *bumiputera* ownership has risen from less than a third to over 90 per cent. Much of the measurement of NEP achievement has been subject to dispute. This has been exacerbated by the lack of transparency on socioeconomic data deemed sensitive.

The NEP has since ostensibly been replaced by the National Development Policy associated with the *Second Outline Perspective Plan for 1991–2000*, and then by the National Vision Policy linked to the *Third Outline Perspective Plan for 2001–2010*. Although the new policies have put far greater emphasis on achieving rapid growth, industrialization and structural change, there is the widespread perception that public policy is still dominated by the NEP's interethnic economic policies, especially wealth redistribution or "restructuring" targets.

These policies are believed to be especially important in terms of influencing public policies affecting corporate wealth ownership as well as other areas, notably education and employment opportunities. In other words, ethnic discrimination primarily involves the business community and the middle class, where interethnic tension is most acute. Interethnic business coalitions have become increasingly important over time, often with an ethnic Malay partner securing rents for gaining access to government-determined business opportunities, and the ethnic Chinese partner with access to capital and business acumen getting the job done. Such joint ventures have generated considerable resentment, especially among those denied access to such business opportunities.

With privatization opportunities from the mid-1980s largely decided on a discretionary basis by the government leadership, there has been growing resentment and criticism of rent-seeking iv

and cronyism. Such disbursement of privatization opportunities also strengthened the leadership's means for patronage, in turn encouraging competition for party and government political office and upward mobility. The selective nature of the bail-out processes and procedures following the 1997-1998 currency, financial and economic crises have strengthened, rather than undermined, these tendencies.

While there is little doubt that specific socioeconomic targets of the NEP have been largely achieved, later rather than sooner, it is not clear that such achievement has led to national unity, understood in terms of improved interethnic relations. Associating improved interethnic relations almost exclusively with reduced interethnic disparities among the respective business communities and middle classes has in fact generated greater ethnic resentment and suspicion on both sides. Ethnic affirmative action policies as implemented and enforced in Malaysia have associated the interests of entire ethnic groups with their respective elites, thus generalizing resentments associated with interethnic, intra-class competition. Thus, it is unlikely that the ethnic affirmative action policies will achieve the end of improved interethnic relations. An alternative approach needs to be found to create more lasting conditions for improved interethnic relations.

At the time of writing, Jomo K.S. was professor in the Applied Economics Department at the University of Malaya, Kuala Lumpur, Malaysia.

Résumé

En Malaisie, la Nouvelle politique économique (NPE), annoncée pour la première fois en 1970, était principalement une riposte politique aux émeutes raciales postélectorales de mai 1969, qui ont aussi entraîné un important changement de régime. L'auteur voit dans les événements de mai 1969 un vaste rejet populaire de l'Alliance au pouvoir, l'UMNO, ainsi qu'une "révolte de palais" au sein de celle-ci, lorsque les "jeunes Turcs", qui soutenaient Tun Abdul Razak, alors Vice-Premier Ministre, ont mis sur la touche le Premier Ministre Tunku Abdul Rahman, qui était à la tête de l'UMNO depuis 1951 et avait conduit son pays à l'indépendance en août 1957. Le nouveau régime considérait que le gouvernement Rahman avait été trop conciliant envers les milieux économiques chinois, omniprésents en Malaisie. Avec sa NPE, il était donc résolu à renforcer la lutte contre la discrimination ethnique pour redresser la situation en faveur des Malais de souche en particulier et des autochtones, dits *bumiputera*, en général.

La NPE avait un double objectif, soit "l'éradication de la pauvreté sans distinction de race" et "restructurer la société pour abolir l'identification de la race à une fonction économique". Elle était censée créer les conditions de l'unité nationale en atténuant la rancœur interethnique due aux disparités socio-économiques. En pratique, les mesures relevant de la NPE ont été perçues comme favorisant les *bumiputera*, ou plus spécifiquement les Malais, soit la plus grande communauté ethnique autochtone. L'action menée pour réduire la pauvreté est apparue comme dirigée essentiellement vers le monde rural et malais, les mesures prises visant essentiellement les paysans malais. Comme cette action n'avait pas été contestée et a perdu de son importance avec le temps, la NPE a été progressivement assimilée aux efforts de "restructuration de la société", destinés à réduire les disparités interethniques, en particulier entre les Malais de souche et les Malaisiens de souche chinoise.

La NPE a été associée au premier *Plan prospectif général* [Outline Perspective Plan—OPP] *pour la période 1971-1990.* Ce plan visait à ramener la pauvreté de 49 pour cent dans la péninsule malaise en 1970 à 16 pour cent en 1990. En 1990, le taux de pauvreté effectif dans la péninsule était de 17 pour cent, tandis que le taux national était légèrement supérieur. Le principal objectif de restructuration de la NPE était de porter la part des actions d'entreprises aux mains des *bumiputera* de 1,5 pour cent en 1969 à 30 pour cent en 1990. Les statistiques gouvernementales laissent à penser que la part que possèdent les *bumiputera* a atteint environ 18 pour cent en 1990 et dépassait légèrement les 20 pour cent en 2000. Bien qu'initialement le gouvernement ait prévu que les biens sociaux des *bumiputera* seraient détenus dans une large mesure par des sociétés de gestion, la propriété privée individuelle chez les *bumiputera* a progressé, passant de moins du tiers à plus de 90 pour cent. La quantification des résultats obtenus grâce à la NPE a donné lieu à de nombreuses querelles, qui ont été exacerbées par le manque de transparence des données socio-économiques jugées sensibles.

Depuis lors, la NPE a été ostensiblement remplacée par la Politique nationale de développement associée au *Deuxième plan prospectif général 1991–2000*, puis par la Politique de vision nationale, rattachée au *Troisième plan prospectif général 2001–2010*. Bien que les nouvelles politiques accordent beaucoup plus d'importance à une croissance rapide, à l'industrialisation et à l'aménagement des structures, la majorité de la population continue à penser que les orientations économiques interethniques de la NPE, en particulier les objectifs de redistribution des richesses ou de "restructuration sociale" continuent à dominer la politique publique.

Si ces orientations sont jugées importantes, c'est essentiellement parce qu'elles influeraient sur les politiques publiques touchant à la propriété des biens sociaux et à d'autres domaines, notamment l'éducation et l'emploi. Autrement dit, la discrimination ethnique est essentiellement le fait des milieux des affaires et de la classe moyenne, où la tension interethnique est la plus forte. Les associations économiques interethniques ont pris une importance croissante avec le temps; elles réunissent souvent un associé de souche malaise qui prend en charge le loyer pour bénéficier des possibilités économiques offertes par le gouvernement et un associé de souche chinoise qui a assez de capitaux et de sens des affaires pour faire marcher l'entreprise. Ces associations ont suscité une rancœur considérable, en particulier chez ceux qui se voyaient refuser ces chances de progrès économique.

L'équipe gouvernementale décidant dans une large mesure et de manière discrétionnaire des modalités de la privatisation depuis 1985 environ, le copinage et la recherche du profit sont de plus en plus montrés du doigt et suscitent un ressentiment grandissant. Ces rachats ont aussi renforcé les moyens dont disposent les dirigeants pour se faire une clientèle, ce qui a à son tour favorisé la course aux fonctions politiques au sein du gouvernement et dans les partis et la mobilité dans le sens de l'ascension sociale. Au lieu d'atténuer ces tendances, les méthodes sélectives appliquées dans le sauvetage des entreprises après la crise monétaire, financière et économique des années 1997–1998, les ont aggravées.

S'il n'est guère contestable que les objectifs socio-économiques de la NPE ont été largement atteints, plutôt tard que tôt d'ailleurs, il n'est pas certain que l'unité nationale en ait été renforcée, si l'on entend par là une amélioration des relations interethniques. En se bornant pratiquement, pour améliorer ces relations, à réduire les inégalités entre les milieux d'affaires et classes moyennes des diverses ethnies, on a en fait nourri la rancoeur et la méfiance des deux côtés. Les politiques ethniques d'action corrective telles qu'elles ont été appliquées en Malaisie ont assimilé les intérêts de communautés ethniques entières à ceux de leurs élites respectives, ce qui a généralisé le ressentiment qui va de pair avec la concurrence entre les ethnies ou à l'intérieur d'une même classe. Il est donc peu probable que les politiques ethniques d'action corrective atteignent leur but et améliorent les relations interethniques. Il faudra trouver un autre moyen pour créer des conditions qui permettent d'améliorer durablement ces relations.

Au moment où il rédigeait cette étude, Jomo K.S. était professeur au département d'économie appliquée de l'Université de Malaya, Kuala Lumpur, Malaisie.

Resumen

La Nueva Política Económica (NEP) de Malasia fue dada a conocer por primera vez en 1970 como la principal respuesta política a los disturbios raciales postelectorales que tuvieron lugar en mayo de 1969 y que también condujeron a un cambio de régimen importante. En este documento se indica que los eventos de mayo de 1969 también supusieron el rechazo popular general a la coalición de la Alianza, la agrupación política dominante, al igual que un "golpe de Estado" al interior vi

de la Organización Nacional para la Unidad Malasia (UMNO por sus siglas en inglés), el partido en el poder; ya que los "Jóvenes Turcos" que apoyaban al entonces Viceprimer Ministro Tun Abdul Razak rechazaron al Primer Ministro Tunku Abdul Rahman, dirigente de la UMNO desde 1951 y que había llevado al país a su independencia en agosto de 1957. El nuevo régimen de Razak estimó que el régimen de Rahman había sido excesivamente conciliador con los ubicuos círculos comerciales chinos. Por consiguiente, el nuevo régimen de la NEP de Razak se comprometió a fomentar la acción afirmativa étnica, o las políticas de discriminación positiva, en nombre de los malasios étnicos en particular y de los indígenas *bumiputera* en general.

La NEP tenía dos enfoques: "la erradicación de la pobreza con independencia de la raza" y la "reestructuración de la sociedad para eliminar la identificación de la raza con la función económica". En teoría, la NEP debía crear las condiciones para la unidad nacional, al reducir el resentimiento interétnico debido a disparidades socioeconómicas. En la práctica, las políticas de la NEP se percibieron como pro-*bumiputera*, o más específicamente como pro-malasios, haciendo referencia a la comunidad étnica indígena más grande. Los esfuerzos desplegados para reducir la pobreza fueron considerados esencialmente rurales y malasios, con políticas fundamentalmente orientadas a los campesinos malasios. Dado que estos esfuerzos no habían sido polémicos y habían perdido importancia con el tiempo, la NEP se identificó cada vez más con iniciativas encaminadas a la "reestructuración de la sociedad" para reducir las disparidades interétnicas, especialmente entre malasios étnicos y chino-malasios étnicos.

La NEP se ha asociado con el primer *Plan General de Perspectivas* [Outline Perspective Plan—OPP] *para 1971-1990.* El OPP pretendía reducir la pobreza en Malasia Peninsular del 49 por ciento en 1970 al 16 por ciento en 1990. En 1990, la tasa real de pobreza en la península se estimó en el 17 por ciento, mientras que la tasa nacional fue ligeramente superior. El principal objetivo de reestructuración de la NEP era aumentar el porcentaje de los accionistas *bumiputera* del 1.5 por ciento en 1969 al 30 por ciento en 1990. Según los datos del gobierno, éste ascendió al 18 por ciento en 1990 y a algo más del 20 por ciento en 2000. Aunque el gobierno preveía inicialmente que gran parte del capital en acciones de los *bumiputera* estaría en manos de compañías fiduciarias, el porcentaje de accionistas *bumiputera* individuales ha aumentado de menos de un tercio a más del 90 por ciento. La evaluación realizada de los logros obtenidos por la NEP ha sido motivo de gran polémica, exacerbada por la falta de transparencia sobre los datos económicos considerados confidenciales.

Desde entonces la NEP parece haber sido reemplazado por la Política de Desarrollo Nacional asociada con el *Segundo Plan General de Perspectivas para 1991-2000*, y luego con la Política de Visión Nacional vinculada con el *Tercer Plan General de Perspectivas para 2001-2010.* Aunque las nuevas políticas han puesto mucho más énfasis en lograr el crecimiento rápido, la industrialización y el cambio estructural; en general se percibe que la política pública sigue estando dominada por las políticas económicas interétnicas de la NEP, concretamente la redistribución de la riqueza o los objetivos "de reestructuración".

Estas políticas se consideran especialmente importantes en términos de políticas públicas influyentes que afectan la propiedad del patrimonio corporativo, así como otras áreas, en particular las oportunidades de educación y empleo. En otras palabras, la discriminación étnica abarca fundamentalmente los círculos comerciales y la clase media, donde la tensión interétnica es mayor. Las coaliciones de empresas interétnicas han adquirido una creciente importancia con el tiempo; en muchos casos cuentan con un socio malasio étnico que consigue el crédito para poder acceder a oportunidades comerciales determinadas por el gobierno, y con un socio chino étnico que tiene acceso al capital y suficiente perspicacia en los negocios para llevar la tarea a buen término. Tales empresas conjuntas han generado un resentimiento considerable, particularmente entre aquellos a quienes se les ha negado el acceso a tales oportunidades comerciales.

La captación de rentas y el favoritismo dieron lugar a críticas y resentimiento, debido al hecho de que las autoridades gubernamentales, desde mediados del decenio de 1980, decidían sobre las oportunidades de privatización de manera discrecional. Tal manejo de distribución de las oportunidades de privatización también aumentó los recursos de las autoridades para el patrocinio, lo que a su vez fomentaba la competencia para los cargos políticos y dentro del partido, al igual que la movilidad ascendente. La naturaleza selectiva del proceso y de los procedimientos que acompañan las licitaciones, sumados a la crisis monetaria, financiera y económica de 1997-1998 contribuyeron más bien a fortalecer que a debilitar esas tendencias.

Si bien no cabe duda de que la mayoría de los objetivos socioeconómicos específicos de la NEP se han alcanzado, más bien tarde que temprano, no está claro que este logro haya propiciado la unidad nacional, entendida en términos de unas mejores relaciones interétnicas. Asociar casi exclusivamente unas mejores relaciones interétnicas con la reducción de las disparidades interétnicas entre los respectivos círculos comerciales y las clases medias ha generado de hecho más resentimiento étnico en ambas partes. Las políticas de acción afirmativa étnica tal como se han llevado a cabo en Malasia, han asociado los intereses de grupos étnicos enteros con sus respectivas elites; por lo que se ha generalizado el resentimiento asociado con la competencia interétnica y dentro de las clases sociales. Así pues, es poco probable que las políticas de acción positiva étnica logren mejorar plenamente las relaciones interétnicas. Es preciso hallar una estrategia alternativa para crear condiciones más duraderas que mejoren las relaciones interétnicas.

En el momento de escribir este texto, Jomo K.S. era Profesor en el Departamento de Economía Aplicada en la Universidad de Malaya, Kuala Lumpur, Malasia.

Introduction[1]

Malaysia's New Economic Policy (NEP) was announced in 1970 as part of a package of measures introduced after the political crises of May 1969. It sought to "eradicate poverty" and to "restructure society to eliminate the identification of race with economic function" in order to create the conditions for national unity. Since then, poverty in Malaysia has decreased tremendously, as it has in neighbouring Thailand and Indonesia, which did not have comparable commitments to poverty reduction, but also experienced rapid economic growth and structural transformation. Not surprisingly, the NEP has been principally associated with "restructuring", that is, efforts to reduce interethnic economic disparities between the *bumiputera* (indigenous ethnic Malaysians) and the non-*bumiputera*, and especially between ethnic Malays and Chinese. Hence, "restructuring" has come to be associated with "positive discrimination" or "affirmative action" on behalf of the mainly Malay *bumiputeras*. Such state interventions have resulted in significantly greater *bumiputera* wealth ownership, business participation, educational opportunities and public sector employment and promotion, as well as representation among professionals and managers/administrators.

However, these measures have also resulted in greater resentment by those who feel deprived by such policies, resulting at various times in emigration, capital flight and ethnic mobilization. Resentment is arguably greatest among the middle classes, where ethnic rivalry is perceived to be greatest. Hence, while it is doubtful that the NEP has created the conditions for national unity, it has probably mitigated *bumiputera* resentment of non-*bumiputera* domination of business and the professions. Rapid economic growth over the last three decades, some economic and educational liberalization since the mid-1980s, as well as greater recognition of external challenges, have also served to mitigate interethnic resentment. Thus, it is useful to initiate a careful analysis of the Malaysian experience with a brief review of the background to the NEP.

Background

Malaya achieved independence in 1957 and formed Malaysia, including the Borneo states of Sabah and Sarawak in 1963. (Singapore joined in 1963, but seceded in 1965.) About half of the population of the peninsula at that time comprised ethnic Malays, with almost 40 per cent Chinese and 10 per cent Indians. In Sabah and Sarawak, there were almost no Indians, and over one-third of the population was Chinese. Of the indigenous *bumiputera* population, Muslims and non-Muslims were almost evenly balanced in Sabah, while less than a quarter of the population of Sarawak was Muslim.

During the 1960s, economic development not only maintained, but apparently even increased, income inequalities, including the income gaps within each major ethnic group in Peninsular Malaysia. Income distribution in Peninsular Malaysia apparently worsened between 1957 and 1970, with the rich becoming richer and the poor becoming poorer in all ethnic groups, especially among the Malays. While most Indians and many Chinese comprised the bulk of the working class, the vast majority of smallholder farmers in the peninsula were Malays. In Sabah and Sarawak, there were fewer wage earners and more working the land.

The ruling Alliance coalition in the 1960s was essentially a coalition of mainly ethnic-based parties led by the United Malays National Organization (UMNO). After the virtual elimination of the legal Left in the mid- and late 1960s,[2] essentially racialist or communal[3] political ideologies faced

[1] At the time of writing, Mahathir Mohamad was still Prime Minister of Malaysia.

[2] The incumbent government used the legal Left's opposition to the formation of Malaysia in September 1963 and the subsequent *Konfrontasi* (confrontation) by Indonesia to arrest and detain—indefinitely without trial—almost all leaders of opposition political parties and thousands of activists associated with the Socialist Front, including the Labour Party of Malaya, the Partai Rakyat Malaya (People's Party of Malaya) and the Parti Perhimpunan Kebangsaan (PPK, or National Convention Party), as well as the Sarawak United People's Party (SUPP).

[3] From the late 1940s, the British encouraged political mobilization along ethnic lines. The leaders of these parties came together in the early 1950s to form the multiethnic Alliance Coalition, which won the first-ever 1955 federal elections. This coalition has continued to

little competition. Consequently, the deteriorating socioeconomic and political situation in the 1960s came to be seen and interpreted primarily in ethnic terms. Many ethnic Malays believed ethnic Chinese economic hegemony to be responsible for Malay economic underdevelopment, although in the late 1960s, the commanding heights of the Malaysian economy were still primarily dominated by foreign (mainly British) investors. On the other hand, many non-Malays believed the UMNO-led Malay-dominated Alliance government to be responsible for official government discrimination against them. Most businessmen were ethnic Chinese and most government officials were Malays. Hence, Chinese capitalists, together with the Malay administrative-political elite, enjoyed most of the fruits of rapid economic growth in the 1960s.

In the third federal elections held after independence in May 1969, the ruling Alliance coalition retained a reduced parliamentary majority despite securing less than half the popular vote with the help of gerrymandered constituency delineations. In the May 1969 election, half of the Malays and the majority of non-Malays voted against the Alliance government. Although undoubtedly manipulated by certain politicians, the post-election race riots were easily triggered in the federal capital of Kuala Lumpur. As noted above, tensions had already been brewing before the elections due to ethnically perceived frustrations reflecting underlying class relations. After the elections, race riots broke out, apparently due to culturally offensive behaviour by jubilant opposition party supporters as well as armed mobilization by youthful supporters of an incumbent chief minister who had not secured a majority in his state legislative assembly.

After the 1969 election results and the subsequent riots, the prime minister, Tunku Abdul Rahman, was gradually eased out by his deputy, Abdul Razak. Razak, the deputy leader of the ruling party and coalition, is believed to have staged a "palace coup"—with the greater military-police role in response to the race riots—to take over political leadership with the support of party critics of Tunku, the incumbent party leader and prime minister. Thus, the replacement of the old UMNO leadership also reflected the ascendance of the so-called Young Turks within UMNO, who had challenged Tunku's leadership since the late 1960s. After the traumatic events of May 1969, UMNO dominance of the ruling coalition became more pronounced as it co-opted most opposition parties, which were also largely based on ethnicity, although they mobilized less explicitly along ethnic lines, unlike the parties in the ruling coalition. It is generally agreed that Malaysian economic policy making changed rather drastically in the aftermath of the race riots and the UMNO palace coup associated with 13 May 1969.

While government policy before the NEP was generally considered to be basically laissez-faire in approach, and responsive to, as well as supportive of, both foreign and domestic (predominantly Chinese) private sector interests, the 1970s were characterized by growing state intervention, primarily in favour of the emerging Malay elite. While such intervention generally did not threaten property rights per se, particular business interests—usually Chinese or foreign—felt threatened at various times. Seen against this background, the economic policies of Malaysia's fourth prime minister, Dr. Mahathir Mohamad, in the 1980s, suggest efforts to retreat from the excesses of 1970s-type state interventionism, for example through privatization, as in the creation of the concept of "Malaysia Incorporated",[4] deregulation and "flexibility in NEP implementation".

Adoption of the NEP was announced after the events of 13 May 1969 as one of several efforts to achieve national unity in view of the socioeconomic inequality inherited from the colonial period and consolidated in the post-independence years. The NEP was ostensibly declared to cre-

rule the country ever since. In the mid-1970s, it changed its name to the Barisan Nasional (National Front) as it expanded significantly to include some previous opposition parties after the traumatic post-election race riots of May 1969.

In popular discourse, ethnic groups are referred to as racial groups, and such parties are seen as racial parties. Insofar as they seek to mobilize all of those belonging to a particular ethnic group, they have been referred to as racialist. Racialism is thus the common term used to refer to ethno-populism in Malaysia, that is, cross-class mobilization of particular ethnic groups. Some early political scientists have introduced the term "communalism"—used in India to refer to religious populism—as a surrogate for racialism.

4 Although originally modified from the term "Japan Incorporated", referring to the close relationship between the Japanese state and business interests, the term has come to refer to efforts to ensure that the bureaucracy better serves private business interests after the former's ascendance during the 1970s, during the first decade of the NEP, when government intervention and the public sector grew significantly.

ate the socioeconomic conditions for achieving "national unity" through redistributive policies. The NEP had two objectives, namely to "eradicate poverty" regardless of race and to "restructure society" to eliminate the identification of race with economic function. An *Outline Perspective Plan* [OPP] *for 1971–1990* (Government of Malaysia 1971, 1973) identified medium- and long-term targets en route to 1990 for both NEP objectives.

The OPP included specific targets for poverty reduction and *bumiputera* wealth ownership in particular. It is often forgotten that these distributional goals assumed an average annual growth rate of 8 per cent over the OPP period. Initially, the NEP was widely accepted across ethnic lines, especially after the traumatic May 1969 events. Subsequent political developments enhanced UMNO and Malay political hegemony as several opposition parties joined the newly broadened Barisan Nasional (BN) ruling coalition.

The next section examines the extent to which the NEP's declared aims have been achieved. This survey is seriously constrained by the nature of publicly available official statistics, which improved briefly in the late 1980s, only to be reduced again in the 1990s and thereafter. Most older Malaysians seem to think that interethnic relations deteriorated in the 1970s and 1980s, and many were inclined to attribute this—at least partly—to the implementation of the NEP. On the other hand, there has undoubtedly been considerable success in achieving specific NEP objectives, as the following review demonstrates. According to available government statistics on NEP implementation, it appears that the OPP targets had, by and large, been achieved by 1990, except for a shortfall in Malay corporate wealth ownership. The final section examines implications of the legacy of the ethnic divide and its pre-eminence in the public imagination. This has had served as a huge constraint on political, as well as economic, options, and is likely to shape future political mobilization, as well as coalition building and economic policy packages.

NEP Targets, Expenditures and Achievements

Poverty reduction

The OPP stated that the official poverty level should be reduced from 49 per cent in Peninsular Malaysia in 1969 to 16 per cent by 1990. According to official government planning documents, the poverty rate had been reduced. Tables 1 and 2 summarize some official data on the incidence of poverty in Malaysia by sector for various years since 1970. They point to an overall poverty reduction from 49.3 per cent in 1970 (official estimate)—or 56.7 per cent, according to Anand (1983)—to 29.2 per cent in 1980 and 16.5 per cent in 1990 in Peninsular Malaysia alone. Poverty incidence in all of Malaysia, including Sabah and Sarawak, fell to 6.8 per cent in 1997, rose to 7.5 per cent in 1999 and fell again to 5.1 per cent in 2002.

Table 1: Incidence of poverty, 1970–2002 *(per cent)*

	1970 [a]	1980 [a]	1990 [a]	1997 [a]	1999	2002
Malaysia total	49.3	29.2	16.5	6.1	7.5	5.1
Rural	58.6	37.7	21.1	10.9	12.4	11.4
Urban	24.6	12.6	7.1	2.1	3.4	2.0
Hard-core poor	—	—	3.9	1.4	1.4	1.0

[a] For Peninsular Malaysia only. **Source:** Government of Malaysia 1973, 1981, 1991a, 1999, 2001a, 2003.

Table 2: Incidence of poverty by state, 1970–2002 *(per cent)*

	1970[a]	1976	1984	1987	1990	1995	1997	1999	2002
Malaysia total	49.3	37.7	20.7	19.3	17.1	8.7	6.8	7.5	5.1
Number of poor households *(thousands)*	791.8	879.3	649.4	649.1	619.4	370.2	294.4	360.1	267.9
Johor	45.7	29.0	12.2	11.1	10.1	4.2	1.6	2.5	1.8
Kedah	61.0	61.0	36.6	31.3	30.0	12.2	11.5	13.2	10.7
Kelantan	74.1	67.1	39.2	31.6	29.9	22.9	19.5	18.7	12.4
Kuala Lumpur	—	—	—	—	—	9.5	0.1	2.3	0.5
Melaka	34.1	32.4	15.8	11.7	12.4	3.2	3.6	5.7	2.7
Negri Sembilan	50.5	33.0	13.0	21.5	9.5	5.3	4.5	2.5	2.2
Pahang	56.1	28.9	15.7	12.3	10.3	6.8	4.1	2.7	3.8
Perak	52.2	43.0	20.3	19.9	19.3	4.9	4.5	9.5	7.9
Perlis	63.2	59.8	33.7	29.1	17.2	11.8	10.6	13.3	10.1
Pulau Pinang	52.7	32.4	13.4	12.9	8.9	9.1	1.6	2.7	1.4
Sabah	—	58.3	33.1	35.3	34.3	26.2	22.1	20.1	16.0
Sarawak	—	56.5	31.9	24.7	21.0	10.0	7.5	6.7	5.8
Selangor	42.7	22.9	8.6	8.9	7.8	2.2	1.3	2.0	1.1
Terengganu	65.1	60.3	28.9	36.1	31.2	23.7	17.3	14.9	10.7

[a] For Peninsular Malaysia only. **Source:** Government of Malaysia 1976, 1981, 1986, 1989, 1991a, 1999, 2001a, 2003.

Official statistics suggest very impressive reductions in poverty in the 1970s and early 1980s, especially in Peninsular Malaysia. Although there are many legitimate reservations about the quality and nature of this data, there are few observers who would doubt that poverty, as officially defined, has been significantly reduced, even though part of the decline in poverty may have been due to a lowering of the poverty line. In view of the generally rapid growth of the Malaysian economy in most of the 1970s and part of the 1980s, poverty—as defined by the government—could have been further reduced, if more just and effective redistributive policies had been implemented, government waste minimized, and government allocations ostensibly for poverty eradication used effectively for reducing poverty instead of enriching politicians and contractors securing rural development projects. More significantly, it appears that per capita income levels have generally risen with growth.

However, the significance, consistency and credibility of this data have been challenged on several grounds.[5] There is much doubt as to whether the definitions of income used in the various surveys concerned have been consistent, for example, with regard to the valuation of services provided by the government, how these have been calculated in determining house-

[5] For example, the poverty reduction between 1984 and 1987—reported in the *Mid-Term Review of the Fifth Malaysia Plan, 1986–1990* (Government of Malaysia 1989), and based on the presumably consistent first and second Household Income Surveys—raised more troubling questions. For instance, while the number of poor rubber smallholding households was reported to have risen from 68,500 in 1984 to 83,100 in 1987, poverty incidence among them was said to have fallen from 42.7 per cent to 40.0 per cent! This decline would require the total number of rubber smallholding households to have fallen by 23 per cent—from 207,800 to 160,400—over the same three-year period, a development unsupported by other evidence. And while the number of poor rubber smallholders is reported to have increased, poverty incidence among estate workers was inexplicably supposed to have dropped by 29 per cent—from 16,400 to 11,700—over the same period! Meanwhile, the number of poor rice farm households was reported to have dropped by 23 per cent—from 70,500 to 54,400—despite the reduction of government subsidies (for example, for fertilizer) and the officially fixed rice price from 1980 to 1990.

Similarly, the disclosure of the official poverty line in mid-1989 suggests that at least some of the poverty reduction, especially between 1976 and 1984, may have been due to the reduction of the per capita poverty line income from Malaysian ringgit (RM) 33.00 in 1970 to RM30.30 in 1987 in 1970 prices, or from RM74.15 in 1970 to RM68.09 in 1987 in 1987 prices. There is also no way of independently verifying the comparability of the data, for instance, in terms of methods of measurement, since they are not publicly available. Also, the different nature of the three kinds of surveys involved means that they are not strictly comparable from a statistical point of view.

hold incomes, and the actual measurement and estimation of poverty.[6] Other problems in using an income-based determination of economic welfare have also not been given adequate attention. While incomes undoubtedly influence economic welfare, it would be wrong to assume that welfare reflects expenditure, which is in turn largely determined by income. Another problem involves the estimation of income—and hence poverty—on a household basis rather than on a per capita basis. The *Mid-Term Review of the Fifth Malaysia Plan, 1986–1990* (Government of Malaysia 1989), suggests that if per capita income—instead of household income—is used, the official poverty rate in Peninsular Malaysia would go down fairly significantly. While this is quite plausible and even likely, the plan document did not elaborate on why this would happen.

It also seems likely that some methods of measurement may have changed. For example, the *Fifth Malaysia Plan, 1986–1990* (Government of Malaysia 1986:83) explicitly favoured a more comprehensive concept of income, which "takes into account the imputed values for own produce consumed at home and owner-occupied housing" as well as "the full value of public services enjoyed by households, either free or at subsidized rate (including) health, education, transport and utilities, and the various subsidies granted by the Government". There are, of course, merits in the income concept proposed, especially as a measure of living standards or economic welfare, but reducing poverty incidence by broadening the income concept, or by comparing essentially incomparable data, raises serious doubts about the actual extent of poverty reduction.

Nevertheless, for want of more acceptable alternative data sources, official figures will be used. The prevailing official poverty measures have used a household, rather than a per capita, poverty line income (PLI) yardstick.[7] According to the *Mid-Term Review of the Fifth Malaysia Plan, 1986–1990* (Government of Malaysia 1989:45), the PLI[8] has been defined as the minimum expenditure level to secure a certain standard of living, and "updated annually using the Consumer Price Index (CPI) to reflect changes in price levels". The PLI should be adjusted to reflect changes in the costs of specific items making up the PLI, as their relative weights differ from the breakdown of the CPI. Also, per capita consumption expenditure is probably a far better gauge of economic welfare than household income.

The current PLI approach to poverty measurement is based upon a notion of absolute poverty. There seems to be less official interest in, and concern about, relative poverty, that is, inequality and income distribution. There should be closer monitoring of distributional trends in economic welfare, expenditure, income and wealth to provide a more comprehensive and accurate picture of the welfare of the Malaysian population in relation to economic growth generally, and as a consequence of the implementation of the NEP—and successor policies—specifically. It is quite possible that such statistics would show relatively greater increases in incomes of poorer groups in all ethnic communities, as well as a significant reduction in differences among the average incomes of the major ethnic communities—trends which the Malaysian government could well be proud of. Available income data and the basket of goods and services constituting the PLI should also be made publicly available to facilitate meaningful public scrutiny of income and poverty reduction trends.

---

6 For instance, a household may well enjoy government-subsidized services valued above or below the value assumed in estimating the poverty line income (PLI). But if the full value of the services it enjoys pushes the household above the poverty line, whereas taking into consideration only the minimum quantum for the PLI would keep it below the poverty line, then clearly, the household is not receiving certain other basic needs despite being considered to be above the poverty line.

7 The *Mid-Term Review of the Fifth Malaysia Plan, 1986–1990* (Government of Malaysia 1989:47) noted that if a per capita measure is used instead of a household measure, the official poverty rate in 1987 would have been 12.4 per cent, instead of 17.3 per cent, in Peninsular Malaysia.

8 The different PLIs first published in the *Mid-Term Review of the Fifth Malaysia Plan, 1986–1990* (Government of Malaysia 1989) for Peninsular Malaysia, Sabah and Sarawak emphasize the considerable variation in living costs within a small country like Malaysia. For 1987, the PLIs were estimated at "about RM350 per month for a household of 5.14 persons in Peninsular Malaysia, RM429 per month for a household of 5.24 in Sarawak, and RM533 per month for a household of 5.36 in Sabah". Hence, the per capita PLI was 19.8 per cent higher in Sarawak and 45.5 per cent higher in Sabah than in Peninsular Malaysia. Yet, there have not been separate PLIs for urban and rural areas, implying that the true extent of urban poverty may well be underestimated compared to rural poverty, since the urban cost of living is significantly higher, especially in the Kelang Valley and Johor Baru areas. The PLI for 1999 was RM510 per month for Peninsular Malaysia for an average household size of 4.6, RM685 per month for Sabah for an average household size of 4.9, and RM584 per month for Sarawak for an average household size of 4.8 (Government of Malaysia 2001b).

Under the NEP, there was no official commitment to reducing income inequality except between ethnic groups, particularly between the *bumiputeras* and non-*bumiputeras*. Since poverty is officially conceived in absolute rather than in relative terms in relation to a poverty line income, income inequality can grow as the poverty rate declines if economic growth is sufficiently high. Income distribution trends do provide important indications of the welfare implications of economic growth and recession, especially as they affect interethnic, spatial[9] and other income inequalities.

Table 3: Mean monthly household income by ethnic group and stratum, Peninsular Malaysia, 1970–2002 *(Malaysian ringgit (RM))*

	1970	1973	1976	1979	1984	1987	1990	1995	1999	2002
Peninsular Malaysia total	423	502	566	669	792	760	1,167	2,020	2,472	3,011
Bumiputera (B)	276	335	380	475	616	614	940	1,604	1,984	2,376
Chinese (C)	632	739	866	906	1,086	1,012	1,631	2,890	3,456	4,279
Indian (I)	478	565	592	730	791	771	1,209	2,140	2,702	3,044
Other	1,304	1,798	1,395	1,816	1,775	2,043	955	1,284	1,371	2,165
Urban (U)	687	789	913	942	1,114	1,039	1,617	2,589	3,103	3,652
Rural (R)	321	374	431	531	596	604	951	1,326	1,718	1,729
Disparity ratio (C/B)	2.29	2.21	2.28	1.91	1.76	1.65	1.74	1.80	1.74	1.80
Disparity ratio (I/B)	1.73	1.69	1.56	1.54	1.28	1.26	1.29	1.33	1.36	1.28
Disparity ratio (U/R)	2.14	2.11	2.12	1.77	1.87	1.72	1.70	1.95	1.81	2.11

Note: The figures shown for 1970 to 1987 are in constant 1978 prices, and the figures shown for 1990 to 1999 are in constant 1990 prices. **Source:** Government of Malaysia 1981, 1989, 1996, 2001b, 2003.

Tables 3 and 4 show income distribution trends in Malaysia, especially Peninsular Malaysia, since independence, and particularly after the NEP was adopted. Between 1957 and 1970, income inequality apparently grew, with the rich getting richer and the poor getting poorer, although serious doubts (Anand 1983) have been raised about the comparability of the data involved. Some evidence since then points to growing income inequality during the 1970s, that is, from 1970, through 1973 and 1976, to 1979, but other data suggest otherwise. For example, in the 1970s, the average real income of the bottom 40 per cent increased, according to the *Fourth Malaysia Plan, 1981–1985* (Government of Malaysia 1981:37). These trends suggest that rising incomes and poverty reduction in the 1970s may have been accompanied by growing income inequality, but there is other evidence to suggest that income inequality declined during the 1970s and 1980s, and has not changed much since then. Average interethnic income disparities also declined during the NEP period, but appear to have risen in the 1990s.

9 Urban/rural and by state.

Table 4: Income share by income group, 1970–1999 *(per cent)*

	1970	1973	1976	1979	1984	1987	1990	1999
Malaysia total								
Top 20	55.9	53.7	61.9	54.7	53.2	51.2	50.0	50.5
Middle 40	32.5	34.0	27.8	34.4	34.0	35.0	35.5	35.5
Bottom 40	11.6	12.3	10.3	10.9	12.8	13.8	14.5	14.0
Urban [a]								
Top 20	55.0	—	—	—	52.1	50.8	[b]	48.9
Middle 40	32.8	—	—	—	34.5	35.0	[b]	36.7
Bottom 40	12.2	—	—	—	13.4	14.3	[b]	14.9
Rural [a]								
Top 20	51.0	—	—	—	49.5	48.3	[b]	48.0
Middle 40	35.9	—	—	—	36.4	36.7	[b]	36.7
Bottom 40	13.1	—	—	—	14.1	15.0	[b]	15.6
Gini Index	0.50	0.50	0.57	0.49	—	—	0.44	0.44
Theil Index	0.48	0.43	0.71	0.42	—	—	[b]	—

[a] The published figures for urban and rural Malaysia in 1987 and 1999 do not add up to 100 per cent due to rounding. [b] The 1990 figures have been omitted from this table because of the significant disparities involved. **Source:** Government of Malaysia 1973, 1976, 1979, 1981, 1986, 1991b, 2001b.

The first official Household Income Surveys in 1984 and 1987 suggest declining overall income inequalities in the 1980s. Inequalities between *bumiputeras* and non-*bumiputeras*, as well as those between town and country, appear to have declined fairly steadily from the 1970s in Peninsular Malaysia. The 1985–1986 recession apparently reduced all major income disparities with the relatively better off being more adversely affected than the relatively worse off. Evidence for Sabah and Sarawak, only available for 1984 and 1987, suggests greater inequality there, as well as similar disparity-reducing consequences of the mid-1980s recession.

The government probably has a successful story to tell with its data, and the credibility of the story would only be enhanced by better public access to it. It may also be useful to reconsider the composition of the PLI and to compare it with detailed consumer price trends in order to make more accurate inflation adjustments to the original PLI, and also to determine a more meaningful PLI with the benefit of hindsight and the experience of the last two decades of NEP implementation. Needless to say, significant regional and locational variations in living costs—for example, between urban and rural areas and perhaps even some of the major metropolitan centres (for instance, Kelang Valley and Johor Baru)—should be taken into consideration.

Despite the ostensible official concern about poverty, it is quite remarkable that after more than three decades of the NEP, there is still relatively little detailed information about the characteristics of the poor, which could help ascertain the reasons and causes of poverty, as well as appropriate, effective and efficient measures and efforts to overcome poverty. Such detailed analytical poverty profiles are especially urgent in view of the increasingly recognized phenomenon of "hard-core poverty", said to be relatively unaffected by existing poverty eradication policies.

The absence of a clearer understanding of the phenomenon of poverty has allowed policies to continue regardless of their efficacy with regard to its eradication. Of course, once certain policies are implemented, interest groups benefiting from such policies tend to ensure their continuation regardless of their effectiveness in terms of their ostensible aims. This has led to the suspicion that such policies are maintained to facilitate patronage by the ruling political coalition and for the benefit of certain rural interest groups and among contractors and other business interests, rather than for the purpose of poverty reduction, as claimed.

A great deal of what is officially classified as poverty eradication actually refers to expenditure for rural and agricultural development, much of which is certainly not for the benefit of the poor. Hence, it is crucial that expenditure for poverty eradication be provided in meaningful detail in order to ascertain the extent to which such expenditure actually benefits the poor. Such evaluation is crucial in order to minimize abuses in the name of poverty eradication. Careful comparative studies can also ascertain the degree to which poverty eradication expenditure actually contributes to relieving poverty.

The evidence so far seems to suggest that poverty reduction has been largely due to rising incomes. In rural areas, especially among the peasantry, it seems to be largely attributable to increasing productivity. However, rising productivity mainly benefits those who own their own economic resources, especially land. Inequality in resource allocation, both in terms of ownership as well as access, has therefore meant that such productivity gains have tended to benefit the well-to-do more than others. Hence, it is very likely that expenditure ostensibly for poverty eradication has actually brought greater benefits to the relatively affluent rather than the poor.

The demographic factor also needs greater consideration. The reduction of poverty among some of the "target groups" has been achieved by a reduction in the population involved, for instance, in rice cultivation, small-scale rubber growing, fishing and plantation labour. Hence, despite continued population growth, there have not been corresponding increases in the number and population shares involved in these activities. On the contrary, there may well have been significant declines, at least in some rural occupations.

With the ageing of the rural population as a consequence of urban migration largely by the young, it appears that the economically active proportion of the population involved in agriculture has declined, exacerbating the phenomenon of idle agricultural land, also due to the uneconomic size of the farm land involved.[10] With the average Malay fertility rate about double the Chinese rate at the end of the 1980s, and with the Indian rate slightly higher than the Chinese, it is also quite possible that per capita Malay income levels will continue to remain low, and poverty correspondingly high, simply due to larger household sizes.

The official focus on Malay peasant poverty has emphasized productivity-increasing efforts for self-employed rural producers at the expense of other measures to reduce poverty, consequently adversely affecting other impoverished groups. Even among the Malay peasant population, those with less access to economic resources, especially land, are ignored by the main thrust of poverty eradication efforts. Hence, peasant agricultural labourers have little to thank the NEP for. If their condition has improved, it has been due more to other extraneous reasons, such as full employment or productivity increases that have accounted for a rise in their wages, rather than as a consequence of NEP poverty eradication measures.

Similarly, other rural labourers—such as estate workers and mine workers, as well as public works and land development contract labourers—have been ignored by the NEP. The importance of immigrant and contract labour for some of these jobs has only served to worsen general working conditions and lower wage rates for these occupations, rendering them even more unattractive to Malaysians and depressing wage rates more generally in the labour market, especially for unskilled labour.

---

[10] Millions of acres of farmland have been abandoned, especially in parts of Peninsular Malaysia, for a variety of reasons. The most important reason is believed to be the uneconomic returns from continuing to farm the land, especially in the context of near full employment and the option of higher and/or more stable incomes as well as less onerous off-farm work. Old or absentee landowners can no longer find tenants or farm labourers to work their land for them at the incomes (crop share or wage) they are prepared to pay or at the rental rates they expect.

The current approach has also tended to ignore the poor, other than the primary target groups, namely the rice farmers, rubber smallholders, coconut smallholders and fishermen. Hence, the majority of the poor in Sabah and Sarawak are largely unaffected by poverty eradication measures, while some—for example, shifting cultivators as well as hunter-gatherers—feel their interests threatened by the logging, land development and other trends that go by the name of development. Those in the towns also feel ignored by poverty eradication measures that they perceive to be primarily, if not exclusively, rural in orientation.

However, while there are many groups of poor that have been bypassed by official poverty eradication measures, they may feel less neglected by official development efforts. Since "development", particularly the provision of infrastructure and social services, is intimately connected with government and party patronage, these poor communities—especially the *bumiputeras*, and particularly the Malays—do not necessarily feel themselves ignored by government development efforts generally, although they have not benefited from the government's poverty eradication measures.

"Restructuring society"

Despite the popular rhetorical commitment by politicians to poverty eradication, the 1970s and early 1980s saw growing emphasis on the NEP's other pronounced objective to "restructure society": to abolish the identification of ethnicity with economic function, especially to create, expand and consolidate the Malay capitalist and middle classes. As officially interpreted, "restructuring" is not meant to abolish or change socioeconomic relations between classes or economic interest groups; in practice, it mainly seeks to increase *bumiputera* capital ownership and ethnic proportions in the more attractive—mainly professional—occupations.

In practice, then, restructuring efforts have been largely aimed at increasing the share of *bumiputera* capital, as well as the number of *bumiputera* businessmen and professionals in the context of continued open capitalist development by using public sector and state intervention extensively. The NEP's restructuring strategy mainly involves the redistribution of corporate stock ownership, employment and education, with the latter two sometimes considered together. There is particular interest in ownership of the modern corporate sector, although only a small minority of the population is actually involved, reflecting the dominance of capitalist interests in defining supposedly ethnic or communal interests.

Wealth distribution

However, wealth restructuring—particularly the 30 per cent target for *bumiputera* share ownership by 1990, which has still not been reached—has remained the main obsession in most discussions about the NEP. Table 5 reflects the distribution of ownership of the corporate sector by ethnicity and residence between 1969 and 2002. The *bumiputera* share rose sharply during the 1970s until the mid-1980s from 1.5 per cent in 1969 and 2.4 per cent in 1970. While the original *Mid-Term Review of the Second Malaysia Plan, 1971–1975* target (Government of Malaysia 1973:84, table 4.8) of 9.0 per cent *bumiputera* ownership by 1975 was surpassed, only 12.5 per cent of the corporate sector was in *bumiputera* hands by 1980 (instead of the projected 16.0 per cent) and 19.1 per cent in 1985 (instead of the 23.0 per cent expected). Instead of the 30.0 per cent targeted for 1990, the *bumiputera* share hovered at around 19.4 per cent in 1988, 19.3 per cent in 1990, 20.6 per cent in 1995, 19.1 per cent in 1999 and 18.7 per cent in 2002.

Meanwhile, the ownership of share capital by foreign residents fell from 63.4 per cent in 1970 to 42.9 per cent in 1980, 33.6 per cent in 1983, 26.0 per cent in 1985, and 24.6 per cent in 1988, before rising to 25.4 per cent in 1990, 27.7 per cent in 1995, 32.7 per cent in 1999 and then dropping slightly to 28.9 per cent in 2002. Meanwhile, the Chinese share rose from 22.8 per cent in 1969 to 45.5 per cent in 1990[11] (when ethnically anonymous ownership of locally controlled companies

[11] This happened despite some official discouragement of Chinese investments and capital flight attributable to the Industrial Coordination Act (ICA), higher interest rates abroad, as well as emigration and investments overseas due to Chinese frustrations in Malaysia. The resilience of Chinese capital should not be underestimated, however. The decline in ethnic Chinese political influence after the 1960s has resulted in various responses and initiatives, varying with the specific interests concerned. From 1985, some of the more

was largely assigned to the Chinese), before declining sharply to 40.9 per cent in 1995, 37.9 per cent in 1999 and rising to 40.9 per cent in 2002. Meanwhile, the Indian share rose slightly from 0.9 per cent in 1969 to 1.2 per cent in 1985 and 1988, and 1.5 per cent in 1995, 1999 and 2002.

The government statistics that are most often cited tend to mislead by exaggerating the shortfall from the 30 per cent target (originally for 1990), with *bumiputera* ownership[12] hovering above 18 per cent since 1983. It is likely that *bumiputera* share ownership is much higher than suggested by such government statistics.[13] All the percentages cited earlier probably underestimate their respective proportions of share ownership. If we put aside the share capital held through nominee companies and locally controlled companies of unknown ethnic ownership identity, the total *bumiputera* share of ethnically and residentially identified equity in 1988 was 24.7 per cent, with the foreign resident and Chinese shares rising to 31.2 per cent and 41.4 per cent, respectively. It has been argued that the *bumiputera* and foreign shares would be even higher if shares held through nominee companies and locally controlled companies are taken into account, although there is no empirical basis for ascertaining the veracity of such claims.

politically inspired initiatives were exposed as business scams dependent upon political patronage or protection, exploited by politicians and businessmen for their own selfish ends. These exposures have further undermined the already seriously eroded position of the Malaysian Chinese Association (MCA), the second most important party in the ruling coalition. Despite its sizeable share of the economy, Chinese capital has limited control over the financial sector (for example, banking) and the "commanding heights" of the traditional capitalist sectors (international trade, primary production), which have mainly been taken over from foreign (especially British) capital by the state, ostensibly for the Malays.

12 In the mid-1980s, Mahathir announced to foreign investors and the Malaysian Chinese public (through the Chinese press) that NEP targets, particularly the 30 per cent objective, had been suspended in view of the economic recession in the mid-1980s.

13 Federal and state government share ownership other than *bumiputera* trust agencies have not appeared since 1969 in the official tables on ownership of share capital in limited companies.

Table 5: Ownership of share capital (at par value)[a] of limited companies, selected years *(millions of RM / per cent)*

Ownership group	1969	1970[b]	1975	1980[c]	1983	1985	1990	1995	1999	2002
Malaysian residents	**1,767.7 / 37.9**	**1,952.1 / 36.7**	**7,047.2 / 46.7**	**18,493.4 / 57.1**	**33,010.5 / 66.4**	**57,666.6 / 74.0**	**80,851.9 / 74.6**	**129,999.5 / 72.3**	**208,797.2 / 67.3**	**278,094.0 / 71.1**
Bumiputeras	**70.6 / 01.5**	**125.6 / 02.4**	**1,394.0 / 09.2**	**4,050.5 / 12.5**	**9,274.6 / 18.7**	**14,883.4 / 19.1**	**20,877.5 / 19.3**	**36,981.2 / 20.6**	**59,394.4 / 19.1**	**73,161.8 / 18.7**
• Individuals[d]	49.3 / 01.0	84.4 / 01.6	549.8 / 03.6	1,880.1 / 05.8	3,762.2 / 07.6	9,103.4 / 11.7	15,322.0 / 14.2	33,353.2 / 18.6	54,046.0 / 17.4	66,746.0 / 17.1
• Trust agencies[e]	21.3 / 00.5	41.2 / 00.8	844.2 / 05.6	2,170.4 / 06.7	5,512.4 / 11.1	5,780.0 / 07.4	5,555.5 / 05.1	3,628.0 / 02.0	5,348.4 / 01.7	6,415.8 / 01.6
Other Malaysian residents	**1,697.1 / 36.4**	**1,826.5 / 34.3**	**5,653.2 / 37.5**	**14,442.9 / 44.6**	**23,735.9 / 47.7**	**42,783.2 / 54.9**	**59,974.4 / 55.3**	**93,018.3 / 51.7**	**149,402.8 / 48.2**	**204,932.2 / 52.4**
• Chinese	1,064.8 / 22.8	1,450.5 / 27.2	— / —	— / —	— / —	26,033.3 / 33.4	49,296.5 / 45.5	73,552.7 / 40.9	117,372.4 / 37.9	159,806.9 / 40.9
• Indians	41.0 / 00.9	55.9 / 01.1	— / —	— / —	— / —	927.9 / 01.2	1,068.0 / 01.0	2,723.1 / 01.5	4,752.9 / 01.5	5,951.1 / 01.5
• Others	— / —	— / —	— / —	— / —	— / —	987.2 / 01.3	389.5 / 00.3	1,751.1 / 01.0	2,888.0 / 00.9	3,204.7 / 00.8
• Nominee companies	98.9 / 02.1	320.1 / 06.0	— / —	— / —	— / —	5,585.1 / 07.2	9,220.4 / 08.5	14,991.4 / 08.3	24,389.5 / 07.9	35,969.5 / 09.2
• Locally controlled companies[f]	471.0 / 10.1	— / —	— / —	— / —	— / —	9,249.7 / 11.8	— / —	— / —	— / —	— / —
• Federal and state governments	21.4 / 00.5	— / —	— / —	— / —	— / —	— / —	— / —	— / —	— / —	— / —
Foreign residents	**2,909.8 / 62.1**	**3,377.1 / 63.4**	**8,037.2 / 53.3**	**13,927.0 / 42.9**	**16,697.6 / 33.6**	**20,297.8 / 26.0**	**27,525.5 / 25.4**	**49,792.7 / 27.7**	**101,279.2 / 32.7**	**112,727.6 / 28.9**
Share in Malaysian companies	1,235.9 / 26.4	— / —	4,722.8 / 31.3	7,791.2 / 24.0	9,054.3 / 18.2	12,672.8 / 16.2	— / —	— / —	— / —	— / —
Foreign controlled companies	282.3 / 06.0	— / —	— / —	— / —	— / —	— / —	— / —	— / —	— / —	— / —
Net assets of local branches[g]	1,391.6 / 29.7	— / —	3,314.4 / 22.0	6,135.8 / 18.9	7,643.3 / 15.4	7,625.0 / 09.8	— / —	— / —	— / —	— / —
Total[h]	**4,677.5 / 100.0**	**5,329.2 / 100.1**	**15,084.4 / 100.0**	**32,420.4 / 100.0**	**49,708.1 / 100.0**	**77,964.4 / 100.0**	**108,377.4 / 100.0**	**179,792.2 / 100.0**	**310,076.4 / 100.0**	**390,821.6 / 100.0**

[a] The ownership of share capital (at par value) classification as adopted by the *Ownership Survey of Limited Companies* is based on the shareholder's residential address, and not on citizenship. Malaysian residents are persons, companies or institutions living in or located in Peninsular Malaysia, Sabah or Sarawak. This definition therefore includes foreign citizens residing in Malaysia. [b] Figures for 1970 do not add up to 100 per cent due to rounding. [c] The figures for 1980 are based on the *Ownership Survey of Limited Companies*, cited in Malaysian government plan documents. [d] This category represents ownership by individual *bumiputeras* including their funds channelled through institutions such as the Lembaga Urusan dan Tabung Haji (LUTH); Majlis Amanah Rakyat Unit Trust Scheme; various cooperatives; and the Amanah Saham Nasional (ASN) scheme. [e] This category represents ownership by trust agencies such as the Permodalan Nasional Berhad (PNB); PERNAS International Holdings Berhad (PERNAS); Majlis Amanah Rakyat; state economic development corporations (SEDCs); Bank Pembangunan Malaysia Berhad (BPMB); Urban Development Authority (UDA); Bank Bumiputera Malaysia Berhad (BBMB); Kompleks Kewangan Malaysia Berhad (KKMB); and Food Industries of Malaysia (FIMA). It also includes the amount of equity owned by the government through other agencies and companies that have been identified under the Transfer Scheme of Government Equity to Bumiputeras. [f] This reflects the total share capital of limited companies whose ownership could not be disaggregated further and assigned beyond the second level of ownership, to specific ethnic groups. [g] This category refers to the difference between the total assets and liabilities in Malaysia of companies incorporated abroad. This approach is used because the criteria for equity share capital cannot be applied to such companies. [h] Except for 1969, the totals exclude government holdings other than through trust agencies. **Source:** Government of Malaysia 1971:40, 1976:184, 1981:62, 1984:101, 1986:107, 1989, 1996:86, 2001a:64.

The share of "other Malaysian residents"—often wrongly equated with the non-*bumiputera* Malaysian share as this category includes foreigners resident in Malaysia—rose from 34.3 per cent in 1970 to 37.5 per cent in 1975, 44.6 per cent in 1980 and 49.7 per cent in 1982, slipping to 47.7 per cent in 1983, before rising to 54.9 per cent in 1985 and 56.0 per cent in 1988. After that, it fluctuated between 55.3 per cent in 1990, 51.7 per cent in 1995, 48.2 per cent in 1999 and 52.4 per cent in 2002. This category includes the ethnically unidentifiable residual share of "others", "nominee companies" and "locally controlled companies" that could not be assigned to specific ethnic groups, which had grown from 12.2 per cent in 1969 to 20.3 per cent in 1985 and 21.2 per cent in 1988.

Ownership of locally controlled companies was presumed to belong exclusively to non-*bumiputera* Malaysians from 1991, whereas such shares could also have been owned by *bumiputeras*, as well as foreign residents. Some analysts would argue that they are more likely to be owned by *bumiputera* individuals, especially politicians, who wish to obfuscate their business interests. But if we assume that these shares are divided according to the known ethnic proportions, the *bumiputera* share would rise to at least 22 per cent.

All such official figures only consider nominal share values, whereas estimates of the distribution of wealth held in shares should consider share prices, although there are many problems in estimating such market values. Since *bumiputera* and foreign share ownership tends to be concentrated in the larger, more successful firms, which have been able to restructure to meet government guidelines, it is likely that the actual market value of shares held by non-*bumiputera* residents is correspondingly less than nominal share ownership, whereas *bumiputera* and foreign wealth would be considerably higher. Hence, it is quite possible that the 30 per cent *bumiputera* wealth ownership target has been achieved. While the 1997–1998 financial crisis undoubtedly affected wealth, there is little evidence of ethnic implications, except for evidence that government interventions have tended to favour those best connected politically.

If market values are considered, instead of nominal or par values,[14] the proportion of publicly listed foreign and *bumiputera* shares would probably rise rather significantly, at the expense of the Chinese share. According to data from the Kuala Lumpur Stock Exchange (KLSE) *Annual Companies Handbook*, incorporating information up to September 1988, 29.4 per cent of equity by nominal value was owned by *bumiputeras*, with 41.9 per cent owned by "other Malaysians" and 28.7 per cent owned by foreigners. However, when market values based on closing prices at the KLSE on 1 March 1989 are considered, the *bumiputera* and foreign shares rose to 34.5 per cent and 32.2 per cent respectively, with the share of "other Malaysians" falling to 33.3 per cent (Fong 1989:table 5). Not surprisingly, this suggests that *bumiputera* shares are generally more highly valued in the market than those held by foreigners, and especially those belonging to other Malaysians.[15]

The official figures for distribution of share ownership do not take into account share ownership in private limited companies, which are generally smaller, but sometimes more lucrative. The distribution of share ownership does not accurately reflect wealth ownership in Malaysia, especially of non-corporate wealth held by private companies. It could also be reasonably argued that "net tangible assets" would provide a more accurate reflection of corporate wealth distribution than par values, or even market values. Also, share capital only represents a portion of economic wealth, albeit an important one.

Similarly, the assets of foreign branches and subsidiaries in Malaysia have been ignored by such calculations. Hence, it is likely that foreign wealth and wealth-generating capacity in Malaysia has been significantly underestimated by government statistics. A fuller picture of wealth dis-

[14] Nominal or par values refer to the price at which the share was first issued at the time of the initial public offer (IPO).

[15] The distribution of share ownership tracked by the government uses nominal or par values, whereas reference to subsequent market values would yield rather different wealth distribution shares. The government's wealth redistribution efforts have focused on the commanding heights of the economy, where large firms enjoy oligopolistic, if not monopolistic advantages, usually augmented by favourable government consideration in its allocation of lucrative business opportunities. Hence, it is not surprising that the *bumiputera* share has increased most when market values are considered, followed by the foreign share.

tribution and economic power has to consider other tangible assets, such as real property and agricultural land, together with other sources of economic power, including access to rent-seeking opportunities and corporate control, as distinct from ownership. Hence, the *bumiputera* percentage does not include shares owned by those who use nominee companies and other such devices that obscure the identity of the owner.

Not much is known about the trust agencies ostensibly set up to advance *bumiputera* share ownership and entrepreneurial and managerial capabilities. However, in the public eye, these trust agencies have been associated with the growth of the public sector under the NEP. During the heady early years of NEP implementation, public enterprises of various types proliferated. By the early 1980s, federal government officials were no longer quite sure how many such enterprises had been established, not only by the federal and state governments, but also by the various statutory bodies, regional development agencies and other such public sector bodies. The fiscal and foreign debt crises of the early 1980s led to the introduction of structural adjustment programmes.

In the mid-1980s, the government established a Central Information Collection Unit (CICU), run by Permodalan Nasional Berhad (PNB). Accounts from 1987 revealed that almost half of the 1,148 enterprises—mostly subsidiaries and companies associated with state enterprises—were still in the red, involving a net loss of RM1.9 billion. Some 562 companies had losses totalling RM7.5 billion, while another 446 had profits of RM5.6 billion, with the remainder inactive or in the process of closing down. Total public sector investments in the 1,148 companies came to RM15.3 billion, or about 71 per cent of the total paid-up capital of RM21.5 billion, with the state holding at least half the equity in 813 of these companies.[16]

The *Third Malaysia Plan, 1976–1980* projections (Government of Malaysia 1976:86, table 4.16) for the 30 per cent Malay share of the corporate sector in 1990 anticipated 7.4 per cent for "Malay individuals" and 22.6 per cent for "Malay interests". The *Fourth Malaysia Plan, 1981–1985* (Government of Malaysia 1981), however, reduced the share for *bumiputera* individuals to 5.2 per cent (or 17.3 per cent of total *bumiputera* ownership) and raised the share for "*bumiputera* trust agencies" to 24.8 per cent (or 82.7 per cent of total *bumiputera* ownership). However, since then, far greater emphasis has been given to *bumiputera* personal wealth acquisition. The share of *bumiputera* individuals rose significantly from 7.6 per cent in 1983 to 14.2 per cent in 1990, 18.6 per cent in 1995, 17.4 per cent in 1999 and 17.1 per cent in 2002. Meanwhile, the *bumiputera* trust agencies' share declined from 11.1 per cent in 1983 to 5.1 per cent in 1990, 1.7 per cent in 1999 and 1.6 per cent in 2002. Individuals accounted for 73.4 per cent of total *bumiputera* ownership in 1990, 91.0 per cent in 1999 and 91.2 per cent in 2002.

The share for *bumiputera* trust agencies correspondingly fell to 9.0 per cent of the total *bumiputera* share in 1999—a very dramatic reversal in a relatively short space of time, with important implications for the composition and nature of Malay capital as well as the character and role of state intervention and the public sector in Malaysia. Clearly, wealth accumulation by the state on behalf of the entire *bumiputera* community has been abandoned in favour of private accumulation by individual *bumiputeras*, although for private aggrandisement, much of this accumulation has been heavily reliant on government dispensation. Hence, capital accumulation has increasingly been determined by "know who" (political connections or influence), rather than "know how" (entrepreneurial ability or capabilities). While this might be more pronounced among *bumiputera* businessmen, it has also been true for others who have made their fortunes contingent upon opportunities involving government dispensation (Gomez and Jomo 1999).

In fact, the issue of wealth ownership—whether of shares or other wealth—only involves the interests of a small elite. The high concentration of share capital ownership within each ethnic community was almost definitely understated in the case of the Amanah Saham Nasional (ASN). The ASN scheme—superseded by Amanah Saham Bumiputera (ASB) from 1991—provides some indication of the degree of wealth concentration in Malaysia. The ASN and ASB schemes

[16] *South East Asia Digest*, 21 July 1989.

have had unusually high rates of participation owing to the government's efforts to maximize *bumiputera* participation.

Such concentration is even more pronounced in the rest of the economy in view of government efforts to promote widespread participation in the ASN and its successor ASB schemes and the previous RM50,000 (now RM200,000) ownership limit on share units per *bumiputera*. The level of concentration was also limited by the RM50,000 share ceiling for individual ownership. The ASN's and ASB's tax-free rates of return to investment have been consistently well above prevailing savings and fixed deposit interest rates. No other share-ownership scheme in the country, and probably in the world, has been able to attract such widespread nominal participation. Yet, although well over two million *bumiputeras* were involved by the late 1980s, the vast majority had invested RM500 or less, while about 1.3 per cent of all eligible *bumiputeras* owned 75 per cent of all ASN shares!

Ethnicity in employment and the professions

Government occupational statistics also suggest that employment restructuring has, generally speaking, been achieved. In fact, *bumiputera* employment in the public sector and agriculture greatly exceeds their overall demographic share. According to the World Bank, government remuneration is, on average, about 25 per cent higher than in the private sector. However, *bumiputeras* are still underrepresented in some of the most lucrative professions, such as medicine, accountancy and architecture, although much of this is temporary and will decline as the population ages. Nevertheless, as tables 6a and 6b show, for the vast majority of the population, employment restructuring goals had, by and large, been achieved by 2000.

Table 6a: Employment by occupation and ethnic group, 1970 *(per cent)*

Occupation	Bumiputera	Chinese	Indian	Other
Professional and technical	47.0	39.5	10.8	2.7
Administrative and managerial	24.1	62.9	7.8	5.2
Clerical and related	35.4	45.9	17.2	1.5
Sales and related [a]	26.7	61.7	11.1	0.4
Services	44.3	39.6	14.6	1.5
Agricultural	72.0	17.3	9.7	1.0
Production, transport and other	34.2	55.9	9.6	0.3
Ethnic share of total employment	51.8	36.6	10.6	1.0
Ethnic share of total labour force	52.7	35.8	10.7	0.8

Proportional equality index [b]

Occupation	Bumiputera	Chinese	Indian	Other
Professional and technical	0.89	1.10	1.01	3.38
Administrative and managerial	0.46	1.76	0.73	6.50
Clerical and related	0.67	1.28	1.61	1.88
Sales and related	0.51	1.72	1.04	0.50
Services	0.84	1.11	1.36	1.88
Agricultural	1.37	0.48	0.91	1.25
Production, transport and other	0.65	1.56	0.90	0.38
Index for ethnic share of total employment	0.98	1.02	0.99	1.25

[a] This line does not add up to 100 per cent due to rounding. [b] The proportional equality index is derived by dividing each ethnic group's occupation employment share by its total labour force share. **Source:** Government of Malaysia 1981.

Table 6b: Employment by occupation and ethnic group, 2000 *(per cent)*

Occupation	Bumiputera	Chinese	Indian	Other
Professional and technical	63.9	25.8	7.6	2.7
Teachers and nurses	73.2	18.4	6.9	1.5
Administrative and managerial	37.0	52.3	5.5	5.2
Clerical and related	56.8	32.9	8.6	1.7
Sales and related	37.3	49.8	6.8	6.1
Services	57.7	21.8	8.5	12.0
Agricultural	61.2	10.3	6.9	21.6
Production, transport and other	44.7	33.8	10.0	11.5
Ethnic share of total employment	51.5	29.7	8.3	10.5

Proportional equality index [a]

Occupation	Bumiputera	Chinese	Indian	Other
Professional and technical	0.97	1.02	1.03	2.26
Teachers and nurses	1.11	0.73	0.93	1.24
Administrative and managerial	0.56	2.07	0.75	4.30
Clerical and related	0.86	1.30	1.16	1.45
Sales and related	0.56	1.97	0.92	5.07
Services	0.87	0.86	1.15	10.00
Agricultural	0.93	0.41	0.94	17.97
Production, transport and other	0.68	1.34	1.35	9.59
Index for ethnic share of total employment	0.78	1.17	1.12	8.72

[a] The proportional equality index is derived by dividing each ethnic group's occupation employment share by its total labour force share (latter figure not shown; unavailable to author at time of publication). **Source:** Government of Malaysia 2001b.

As far as occupational restructuring is concerned, by 2000, *bumiputeras* were significantly underrepresented (that is, less than 45 per cent) only at the "administrative and managerial" levels (at 37.0 per cent) and in sales-related occupations (at 37.3 per cent). Nevertheless, the Malay proportions in these occupations have greatly increased since independence, and especially under the NEP, although the Chinese proportions—52.3 per cent and 49.8 per cent respectively—still exceed their population share.

Otherwise, occupational restructuring has largely been achieved, especially in low-income employment. The main sources of tension over employment restructuring involve access to business opportunities and the more lucrative occupations. This mainly affects and concerns the middle class. Tertiary education, as well as related employment and promotion opportunities, are the main concerns and primary sources of interethnic resentment and conflict, especially among the middle class, who correctly see these as determining their life chances. Both sides have been morally self-righteous about their interests and claims. On the one hand, many *bumiputeras* invoke indigenous or "native rights" and the need for "positive discrimination" and "affirmative action" to overcome historical disadvantage under colonialism. On the other hand, many non-*bumiputeras* protest "ethnic discrimination", "cultural oppression" and the official undermining of meritocracy.

Ethnic percentages in professional and technical occupations broadly reflect demographic proportions in the Peninsular Malaysian population, although *bumiputera* underrepresentation in the more lucrative and prestigious professions has been highlighted by the Malay middle class, politicians and the government. Nevertheless, as table 7 shows, the *bumiputera* proportion of the eight prized professions rose from 4.9 per cent in 1970 to 29.0 per cent in 1990 and 33.1 per cent in 1995, slightly declining to 32.0 per cent in 1997, before measurement changes reduced the number of professionals by 45.5 per cent in 1997, and the *bumiputera* share to 27.3 per cent in 1997, 28.9 per cent in 1999 and 37.2 per cent in 2002. (According to the official government statistics, the number of professionals they are tracking suddenly fell by almost half!) There may also be some underestimation of the *bumiputera* proportion as far as those in government service (such as the legal and judicial services) are concerned. Perhaps, more importantly, recent *bumiputera* advances into the professions mainly involve the younger age groups. Hence, the *bumiputera* proportion will continue to increase as the population ages, even if the current proportions remain unchanged. Malay professionals also seem to earn proportionately more, suggesting a likely ethnic premium in their professional charges[17] (Merican 1987).

Table 7: Registered professionals[a] by ethnic group, 1970–2002 *(number / per cent)*

	Bumiputera	Chinese	Indian	Other	Total
1970 [b]	225 / 04.9	2,793 / 61.0	1,066 / 23.3	492 / 10.8	4,576 / 100
1975 [c]	537 / 06.7	5,131 / 64.1	1,764 / 22.1	572 / 07.1	8,004 / 100
1979	1,237 / 11.0	7,154 / 63.5	2,375 / 21.1	496 / 04.4	11,262 / 100
1980	2,534 / 14.9	10,812 / 63.5	2,963 / 17.4	708 / 04.2	17,017 / 100
1983	4,496 / 18.9	14,933 / 62.9	3,638 / 15.3	699 / 02.9	23,766 / 100
1984	5,473 / 21.0	16,154 / 61.9	3,779 / 14.5	675 / 02.6	26,081 / 100
1985	6,318 / 22.2	17,407 / 61.2	3,946 / 13.9	773 / 02.7	28,444 / 100
1988	8,571 / 25.1	19,985 / 58.4	4,878 / 14.3	762 / 02.2	34,196 / 100
1990	11,753 / 29.0	22,641 / 55.9	5,363 / 13.2	750 / 01.9	40,507 / 100
1995	19,344 / 33.1	30,636 / 52.4	7,542 / 12.9	939 / 01.6	58,461 / 100
1997 [d]	22,866 / 32.0	37,278 / 52.1	9,389 / 13.1	1,950 / 02.7	71,843 / 100
1997 [d]	10,659 / 27.3	21,298 / 54.4	6,653 / 17.0	515 / 01.3	39,125 / 100
1999	15,321 / 28.9	28,565 / 53.9	8,183 / 15.5	884 / 01.7	52,953 / 100
2002	35,046 / 37.2	47,270 / 50.1	10,593 / 11.2	1,411 / 01.5	94,320 / 100

[a] Architects, accountants, engineers, dentists, doctors, veterinary surgeons, surveyors, lawyers. [b] Excludes surveyors and lawyers. [c] Excludes surveyors. [d] There was a significant change in the counting of professionals from 1997, including 1999 (Government of Malaysia 1999) and 2002 (Government of Malaysia 2003), with the total number of professionals and the *bumiputera* share dropping drastically. **Source:** Government of Malaysia 1976, 1979, 1981, 1984, 1986, 1989, 1991b, 1994, 1996, 1999, 2001b, 2003.

As far as tertiary education is concerned, the *bumiputera* population in government-accredited local universities and university colleges was 67 per cent in 1985 (Government of Malaysia 1986:490–491), up from 40 per cent in 1970 (Government of Malaysia 1973:193). The ratio was supposed to be 60 per cent as of the early 1980s, as part of a "compromise" resolution of the Merdeka University issue[18] from the late 1970s. The controversy over ethnic quotas for public university admissions has continued to the present. The vast majority of students in private tertiary institutions have been non-*bumiputera*. However, most of the thousands of *bumiputera* students abroad are believed to be government-funded, compared to only a small proportion of non-*bumiputeras*.

[17] One would not normally expect relatively younger professionals to earn more than their older counterparts, everything else being equal. However, it seems likely that the generally younger *bumiputera* professionals were earning more than their non-*bumiputera* colleagues because of a certain premium attached to their services, that is, they could charge more because it has been advantageous for their clients to utilize them for certain kinds of work, perhaps involving government procurement, contracts and so forth.

[18] The relatively well-organized Chinese-medium education movement had asked for the establishment of a Chinese-medium university from the late 1960s. This was rejected by the government in the early 1980s. Instead, the government suggested that the ethnic ratios for entrance to government universities would be set for *bumiputeras* and non-*bumiputeras*, ostensibly to the advantage of the latter because their ratio has been higher than their demographic share of the population. However, this "compromise" did not really address the issue of medium of instruction. Also, the *bumiputera* share is considered to have been higher than if university entrance was determined on an exclusively "meritocratic" basis, that is, on the basis of matriculation examination results. Also, the official records of university entrants since then suggest that the *bumiputera* ratios were generally exceeded, at least until the late 1990s.

Evidence on "restructuring society" also suggests considerable success in terms of changing ethnic proportions in various lucrative professional occupations and by sectoral employment as well as wealth ownership. Official concern appears to have shifted away from school enrolment ratios, where *bumiputeras* are now actually "overrepresented", owing to the generally larger size of *bumiputera* families, as well as the higher enrolment of non-*bumiputera* children in private tertiary institutions. Even interest in enrolment at the tertiary level has declined with the considerable *bumiputera* advances since the 1970s and the growing phenomenon of graduate unemployment since the mid-1980s. Instead, the focus is now primarily on the lucrative professions, where *bumiputeras* are still relatively underrepresented despite rapid progress, especially since the 1980s.

It is very likely that tertiary education, and especially access to these professions, will continue to preoccupy the middle class, who feel they stand to gain or lose most in this regard. For obvious reasons, focus on the lucrative professions is likely to remain. Such ethnic preoccupations previously constrained state approval of private initiatives in human resource development and domestic tertiary education development, despite the considerable foreign exchange savings that have since accrued.[19] However, the situation has changed significantly since the mid-1980s, as businesses have successfully invested in providing education services to secure tertiary educational credentials.[20] Continued regulation has provided lucrative opportunities for rentier marketing of such degrees. Such preoccupations, as well as the regime's obsession with controlling campus dissent, have stood in the way of urgently needed reforms to higher education in order to better prepare the Malaysian population for rapid cultural and technological changes.

Expenditure

After the NEP's inception, the state's commitment and priorities—as reflected by NEP expenditure allocations—increasingly shifted away from poverty eradication toward restructuring, until the *Fifth Malaysia Plan* (Government of Malaysia 1986). The ratio of allocations for restructuring, compared with poverty eradication, rose steadily from 22 per cent under the *Second Malaysia Plan* (Government of Malaysia 1971) to 37 per cent under the *Third Malaysia Plan* (Government of Malaysia 1976) and 47 per cent under the *Fourth Malaysia Plan* (Government of Malaysia 1981). According to the *Fifth Malaysia Plan*, the allocation ratio from the fourth plan was later revised upward to 57 per cent, while the ratio for actual expenditure was estimated at 59 per cent (Government of Malaysia 1986:231, table 7.3). However, this ratio was revised downward for 1986–1990 to 33 per cent under the fifth plan, and then further down to 26 per cent, and then 20 per cent with the *Mid-Term Review of the Fifth Malaysia Plan* (Government of Malaysia 1989). Only a small percentage of the *bumiputera* population benefits significantly from restructuring expenditures, compared with the far greater proportion of the Malay population (23.8 per cent in Peninsular Malaysia in 1987) still officially considered poor. Subsequent Malaysian five-year plan documents no longer provide the information necessary for analysis of subsequent trends.

There is considerable evidence that only a fraction of poverty eradication funds actually benefit the poor, considering the huge bureaucracy and other expenses involved. "Of the revised allocation for poverty eradication, about 40 per cent was directly channelled to the poor through programmes such as input subsidies and basic amenities, 31.8 per cent for indirect programmes such as purchase of equipment, credit facilities and training, while the rest was essentially for supporting programmes which included the construction of related office buildings and associated management costs" (Government of Malaysia 1989:60). The nature of poverty eradication expenditure also provides greater benefits to the non-poor; for example, the rice price support programme primarily benefits big farmers with large marketable surpluses of grain. Also, shifting the emphasis from poverty eradication to restructuring society probably tended to increase inequality

[19] It was very difficult to obtain official permission to set up private educational institutions because the government wanted to control access to educational opportunities, especially at the tertiary level. Many (mainly non-*bumiputera*) children were therefore sent abroad at considerable expense to their parents. This also involved foreign exchange outflows, which have been reduced as a consequence of some deregulation since the mid-1980s as the devaluation of the ringgit raised the costs of tertiary costs abroad.

[20] Private education is now big business in Malaysia, with many businesses investing in setting up private colleges that issue degrees from foreign universities through so-called "twinning programs".

within the Malay community, while the mid-1980s shift in the opposite direction may partly account for the reduction in Malay income inequality during 1984–1987.

To improve the effectiveness and efficiency of public expenditure, including poverty eradication efforts, strict "performance evaluation" has to be developed. Such comparative evaluation can help identify to what extent each poverty eradication measure is effective in reducing poverty or increasing incomes and economic welfare among target groups, among those who are poor as well as among others who are not poor. Such evaluations would be useful in identifying the most effective measures for eradicating poverty in the future, as they would have to take into account the efficacy of specific poverty reduction measures.

Conclusion

Malaysia's New Economic Policy was first announced in 1970 as the principal policy response to the post-election race riots of May 1969, which also resulted in a significant regime change. This paper suggests that the events of May 1969 also involved a widespread popular rejection of the ruling Alliance coalition as well as a "palace coup" within the ruling UMNO as the "Young Turks" supporting then Deputy Prime Minister Razak sidelined Prime Minister Rahman, who had led the UMNO from 1951 and the country to independence in August 1957. The Rahman regime was seen by the new Razak regime as having been too conciliatory with the ubiquitous Chinese business community. The new Razak NEP regime was, therefore, committed to increased ethnic affirmative action or positive discrimination policies on behalf of the ethnic Malays.

The NEP had two objectives, namely "poverty eradication regardless of race" and "restructuring society to eliminate the identification of race with economic function". The NEP was supposed to create the conditions for national unity by reducing interethnic resentments caused by socioeconomic disparities. In practice, the NEP policies were seen as pro-*bumiputera*, or more specifically, pro-Malay, the largest indigenous ethnic community. Poverty reduction efforts have been seen as primarily rural and Malay, with policies principally oriented to the rural Malay peasants. As poverty reduction efforts had been uncontroversial and had declined in significance over time, the NEP came to be increasingly identified with efforts to "restructure society" and reduce interethnic disparities, especially between ethnic Malay and ethnic Chinese Malaysians.

The NEP has been associated with the first *Outline Perspective Plan for 1971–1990* (Government of Malaysia 1971, 1973). The OPP sought to reduce poverty from 49 per cent in Peninsular Malaysia in 1970 to 16 per cent by 1990. The actual poverty rate in the peninsula in 1990 was 17 per cent, while the national rate was slightly higher. The NEP's main restructuring target was to raise the *bumiputera* share of corporate stock ownership from 1.5 per cent in 1969 to 30 per cent in 1990. The government's data suggest that *bumiputera* ownership rose to about 18 per cent in 1990 and slightly over 20 per cent in 2000. Although the government originally envisaged that much of the *bumiputera* corporate wealth would be held by trust agencies, private individual *bumiputera* ownership has risen from less than a third to over 90 per cent. Much of the measurement of NEP achievement has been subject to dispute. This has been exacerbated by the lack of transparency on socioeconomic data deemed sensitive.

The NEP has since ostensibly been replaced by the National Development Policy (NDP) associated with the *Second Outline Perspective Plan for 1991–2000*, and then by the National Vision Policy linked to the *Third Outline Perspective Plan for 2001–2010*. Although the new policies have put far greater emphasis on achieving rapid growth, industrialization and structural change, there is a widespread perception that public policy is still primarily influenced by the NEP's policies of restructuring society.

These policies are believed to be especially important in terms of how public policies affect corporate wealth ownership as well as other areas, notably education and employment opportunities. In other words, ethnic discrimination primarily involves the business community and the middle class, where interethnic tension is most acute. Interethnic business coalitions have become increasingly important over time, often with the ethnic Malay partner securing rents for gaining access to government-determined business opportunities, and the ethnic Chinese partner with business acumen getting the job done. Such "Ali Baba" arrangements[21] have generated considerable resentment, especially among those denied access to such business opportunities.

With privatization opportunities from the mid-1980s largely decided on a discretionary basis by the government leadership, there has been growing resentment and criticism of rent-seeking and cronyism. Such disbursement of privatization opportunities have also strengthened the leadership's means for doling out lucrative opportunities, and thus political patronage, in turn encouraging competition for party and government political office and upward mobility. The selective nature of the bail-out processes and procedures following the 1997–1998 currency, financial and economic crises have strengthened, rather than undermined, these tendencies.

While there is little doubt that specific socioeconomic targets of the NEP have been largely achieved, it is not clear that such achievement has led to national unity, understood in terms of improved interethnic relations. Associating improved interethnic relations almost exclusively with reduced interethnic disparities among the respective business communities and middle classes has in fact generated greater ethnic resentment and suspicion on both sides. Ethnic affirmative action policies, as implemented and enforced in Malaysia, have associated the interests of entire ethnic groups with their respective elites, thus generalizing resentments associated with interethnic, intra-class competition. Therefore, it is unlikely that the means of ethnic affirmative action will achieve the end of improved interethnic relations. An alternative approach needs to be found to create a better rapport among the various ethnic groups over the long term.

Quite predictably, it has been in the area of wealth ownership that there seems to have been the greatest false modesty all round. The main protagonists—the Malays and the Chinese—are both very insistent that the official figures exaggerate their respective shares of economic wealth. While there are grains of truth in such claims, the arguments are essentially self-serving. They are used to legitimize and support claims for greater shares, and for government intervention or withdrawal in this regard, as the case may be. But what is most telling, perhaps, is that increased wealth ownership for any particular ethnic group actually only involves a very small minority, who are nevertheless ever ready to proclaim that they embody the interests of the particular ethnic group with which they are identified.

The relations between wealth distribution and other interethnic economic disparities, such as income distribution, may be quite spurious. It is quite possible that there would be greater interest in raising incomes, rather than redistributing wealth. It is quite likely that there will be no further upward revision of the NEP's wealth restructuring targets above 30 per cent, despite continued Malay calls for wealth redistribution to reflect ethnic demographic proportions. As post-1990 (National Development Policy and *Second Outline Perspective Plan for 1991–2000*) and post-2000 (National Vision Policy and *Third Outline Perspective Plan for 2001–2010*) policies suggest, it is likely that the 30 per cent target, which has developed such great symbolic significance and is most closely identified with the NEP in the public imagination, will be indefinitely retained for achievement at some point in the future. Depending on how one chooses to measure corporate wealth distribution, it can be shown that the 30 per cent target has already been achieved or is close to being achieved.

However, adopting such measures to assuage *bumiputera* demands is likely to be politically risky. Furthermore, under the NEP, many who now control UMNO and the other BN parties at various levels, actually enjoy rentier incomes, largely attributable to the NEP and the climate it has fostered. These people are unlikely to give up such opportunities—perceived to have been provided

[21] Such arrangements refer to joint-ventures between ethnic Malays ("Ali") and ethnic Chinese ("Baba", a term used to refer to the "Straits Chinese" who settled in the port settlements of colonial Malaya before the mass immigrations into the tin-bearing hinterlands from the mid-nineteenth century), usually with a view to gaining advantage from the presence of the Malay partner, who is often seen as merely a front for the controlling Chinese interests.

by the NEP—without a fight. Hence, any government based upon such patronage and support is unlikely to be capable of riding roughshod over such interests, despite the better judgement of those with greater appreciation of the mixed legacy of the NEP.

The Mahathir government passed up two opportunities (in 1991 and 2001) to break with past policies in the interest of greater economic efficiency, more rapid growth and fairer distribution. It has been able to choose whether or not to announce that the NEP objectives, or more precisely the OPP targets, have been achieved. By doing so, the government could have made a clean break with the NEP in 1991 and embarked on new and different policies. Instead, the government chose to continue the basic thrusts of the NEP with some changes, reflecting Mahathir policy priorities, including greater emphasis on growth, industrialization and the emergence of the Bumiputera Commercial and Industrial Community (BCIC). This compromise formula sought to insert and assert Mahathir's priorities without excessively threatening his UMNO following, who are yet to be weaned off the NEP. Thus, the *Second Outline Perspective Plan for 1991–2000* was associated with the National Development Policy. This process continued in 2001 with the announcement of a new National Vision Policy to coincide with the *Third Outline Perspective Plan* period (2001–2010), an obvious reference to Mahathir's Vision 2020, first enunciated in February 1991.

Whether or not the new government policy represents any significant departure from the policies of the 1990s is difficult to gauge, but seems unlikely. In view of policy trends under Mahathir, which have mainly benefited the private sector, including foreign investors, there is little evidence of any significant advances in social policy to enhance the welfare of the majority. Unlike the first decade of the NEP in the 1970s, when social policy—albeit primarily based on ethnicity—became important, the last two decades have witnessed redistribution effects increasingly captured by politically-connected Malay business and middle-class interests while private sector promotion has primarily benefited politically well-connected rentier or crony interests.

The 1997 currency crisis and the unprecedented severe contraction of 1998 (Jomo 2001) drew attention to the cronyistic practices that have become an important feature of Malaysia's business landscape. Although the focus on cronyism as the cause of the 1997–1998 currency and financial crises was somewhat misplaced and served the proponents of financial liberalization and capital account openness, it is now recognized as a major problem distorting and retarding the development of Malaysian modernization and industrialization, as well as economic dynamism and competitiveness. After a strong recovery in 1999 and 2000, the Southeast Asian regional economic slowdown in 2001 underscored the weakness of Malaysia's domestic engines of growth and the mixed consequences of economic openness and dependence. The prospects for Malaysia's domestic engines of growth are increasingly recognized as weak, not least because of the economy's openness and strong outward orientation, as well as its historical reliance on foreign direct investment (FDI) for propelling its most dynamic industries.

One consequence of foreign domination of Malaysian manufacturing has been to encourage Malaysian investors to gravitate to other rentier activities, especially finance and property. As far as most Malaysian primary commodities are concerned, the major problems on the supply-side have been rising labour costs and the exhaustion of timber and land resources. Hence, for continued economic expansion, Malaysia desperately needs new investments, technology and market access, especially for manufacturers. FDI from abroad is supposed to sustain capital inflows, provided earlier by foreign borrowing in the early 1980s and by portfolio inflows before the 1997 crisis. But with the availability of China and other competitive investment locations, Malaysia appears less attractive to prospective investors.

For ethno-political as well as economic reasons, the Malaysian government favoured foreign investment, rather than (predominantly Chinese) domestic investment in the late 1980s. This strategy further enhanced foreign capital's dominance of Malaysian industry. However, in view of the post-1997 perception of lack of Malaysian policy consistency, it is unlikely that the massive foreign investments desired will be forthcoming, at least in the amounts desired in the near future. The government may then be tempted to either resort to foreign borrowing once again, or to offer even more attractive terms to encourage renewed foreign investment. It will be difficult to open the oil (and gas) tap much more, or to continue to cut down the already diminished forest, as happened in 1987. Needless to say, these options do not really offer sustainable, long-term growth and structural change for the Malaysian economy.

The debate over future Malaysian economic policy has recently surfaced again, after the economic and political crises of 1997–1998, causing considerable concern in various quarters. Decisions about future economic policies are probably not going to be decided by the interests or needs of the public, but are more likely to reflect the interests and desires of those in power and others of influence, including foreign economic advisors, who usually represent the interests of transnational corporations and international economic agencies.

While there is little doubt that the Mahathir regime's economic policy rhetoric had been decidedly nationalistic since 1998 and monetary policy has been somewhat independent, and although the ringgit has been problematically pegged to the US dollar since September 1998, there is little evidence of consistently sustained nationalistic economic policies. On the contrary, there have been a series of pragmatic policy reversals encouraged by the deteriorating situation since the strong recovery of 1999–2000.

After the economic policy shifts since the mid-1980s and Mahathir's retirement in 2003, economic policy has emphasized rapid growth, renewed redistribution efforts in favour of ethnic Malays—ostensibly to recover the Malay political ground—and greater deference to foreign business interests to enhance international acceptance in the wake of Mahathir's problematic reputation in the West.

Bibliography

Anand, Sudhir. 1983. *Inequality and Poverty in Malaysia: Measurement and Decomposition.* Oxford University Press, New York.

Fong Chan Onn. 1989. *Malaysian corporate economy restructuring: Progress since 1970.* Paper presented at the seminar, Dasar Ekonomi Baru dan masa depannya (New Economic Policy and Its Future), Malaysian Social Science Association, 24–26 July, Kuala Lumpur.

Gomez, E.T. and Jomo K.S. 1999. *Malaysia's Political Economy,* revised edition. Cambridge University Press, Cambridge.

Government of Malaysia. 2003. *Mid-Term Review of the Eighth Malaysia Plan, 2001–2005.* Government Printers, Kuala Lumpur.

———. 2001a. *Third Outline Perspective Plan, 2001–2010.* Government Printers, Kuala Lumpur.

———. 2001b. *Eighth Malaysia Plan, 2001–2005.* Government Printers, Kuala Lumpur.

———. 1999. *Mid-Term Review of the Seventh Malaysia Plan, 1996–2000.* Government Printers, Kuala Lumpur.

———. 1996. *Seventh Malaysia Plan, 1996–2000.* Government Printers, Kuala Lumpur.

———. 1994. *Mid-Term Review of the Sixth Malaysia Plan, 1991–1995.* Government Printers, Kuala Lumpur.

———. 1991a. *Second Outline Perspective Plan, 1991–2000.* Government Printers, Kuala Lumpur.

———. 1991b. *Sixth Malaysia Plan, 1991–1995.* Government Printers, Kuala Lumpur.

———. 1989. *Mid-Term Review of the Fifth Malaysia Plan, 1986–1990.* Government Printers, Kuala Lumpur.

———. 1986. *Fifth Malaysia Plan, 1986–1990.* Government Printers, Kuala Lumpur.

———. 1984. *Mid-Term Review of the Fourth Malaysia Plan, 1981–1985.* Government Printers, Kuala Lumpur.

———. 1981. *Fourth Malaysia Plan, 1981–1985.* Government Printers, Kuala Lumpur.

———. 1979. *Mid-Term Review of the Third Malaysia Plan, 1976–1980.* Government Printers, Kuala Lumpur.

———. 1976. *Third Malaysia Plan, 1976–1980.* Government Printers, Kuala Lumpur.

———. 1973. *Mid-Term Review of the Second Malaysia Plan, 1971–1975.* Government Printers, Kuala Lumpur.

———. 1971. *Second Malaysia Plan, 1971–1975.* Government Printers, Kuala Lumpur.

Jomo K.S. (ed.). 2001. *Malaysian Eclipse: Economic Crisis and Recovery.* Zed Books, London.

Kuala Lumpur Stock Exchange. Various years. *Annual Companies Handbook.* KLSE, Kuala Lumpur.

Merican, Malek. 1987. *The NEP from a Private Sector Perspective.* Paper presented at the Gemaputra Economic Congress, April, Kuala Lumpur.

Part IV
Fundamental Norms in the Protection of Minorities

[10]

Merit Principles

CHRISTOPHER McCRUDDEN*

Abstract—The 'merit principle' has long been an important term in discussions of the theoretical underpinnings of anti-discrimination law, and in particular in discussions of the appropriate scope of affirmative action measures in employment. Despite its centrality to these debates, the meaning of the term remains highly contested. Failure to appreciate its complexity of meaning has contributed to the political (and to some extent, legal) difficulties of resolving controversies to which anti-discrimination law gives rise. In this article, an attempt is made to disaggregate different meanings of the term, and the different weights accorded it, as a contribution to the wider debate about the pros and cons of affirmative action in particular.

1. *Introduction*

This is an essay about the use of what has been called 'the merit principle'.[1] The merit principle plays a crucial role in current north-American political debates on the permissible extent of affirmative action in employment. Fairly recently, for example, there have been major governmental reviews of affirmative action,[2] and the concept of 'merit' was to the fore of the political presentation of the results of these reviews.[3] That the use of the same concept could lead to

* Lincoln College, Oxford. I am grateful to the following for helpful comments on earlier drafts: Gerry Cohen, Heidi Feldman, Mark Freedland, Jack Getman, Lino Graglia, Sam Issacharoff, Andrew Kopplemann, Doug Laycock, Sandy Levinson, Dick Markovits, David Miller, David Rabban, Michael Rosen, Brian Simpson, Ted St. Antoine, and to participants at both the Faculty Colloquium at the University of Texas School of Law, and the Legal Theory Workshop at the University of Michigan Law School. Needless to say, none of those mentioned bear any responsibility for the view expressed.

[1] I shall argue subsequently that there are very different conceptions of the merit principle in common currency, hence the title of the essay. The most comprehensive attempt to engage in a similar task is that by Richard Fallon, 'To Each According to His Ability, From None According to His Race: The Concept of Merit in the Law of Antidiscrimination', 60 *Boston University Law Review* 815 (1980). My debt to Fallon's article will become apparent during the course of the article, as will my differences with him. In summary, I have adopted two of his three conceptions of merit, but have introduced additional conceptions which seem to me of considerable importance, and I have attempted to engage more fully the issue of what weight should be given to merit arguments, and the relationship between merit and other concepts, drawing on more recent philosophical work, published since Fallon's article.

[2] By 'affirmative action' I mean those programmes which use race or gender as an element in the decision whether to employ, promote, or lay off a person, in order to ensure increased representation of an underrepresented group.

[3] There have been three reviews of affirmative action which have come to radically different results with respect to its compatibility with the merit principle. Governor Pete Wilson's order revoking affirmative action programmes in California on the basis of their incompatibility with the merit principle was the first. Ed Mendel, 'Wilson to end some affirmative action programs. He says they prompted a new era of unfairness', *San Diego Union-Tribune*, 1 June 1995, A-3. The second was the White House Review. In its report, the White House review team set out the major underpinnings of the review, as follows: 'Because our ultimate goal is to perfect and realize this American ideal of opportunity, affirmative action cannot supersede the concept of *merit* – because to do so would unfairly deprive others of opportunity that is their due' *Affirmative Action Review: Report to President Clinton*, 19 July 1995, reprinted BNA, Daily Labor Report, 20 July 1995, para 1.2.1 (emphasis added). For a discussion of the development of the report, see C. Edley Jr, *Not All Black and White: Affirmative Action and American Values* (1996). A third

such different policy responses (one approving, two others disapproving of affirmative action), each justified as consistent with 'merit', should alone be sufficient reason to prompt a reconsideration of this concept.

The use of the 'merit principle' has not been restricted to the American *political* context. From the very beginnings of discussion on employment discrimination law, it has played a significant (if, for a long time a relatively marginal) role in the *scholarly* consideration of the theory of employment discrimination law generally.[4] Discussion of merit has become of particular significance in considering the permissible scope of race and gender-based affirmative action, the role of tests and testing in employment, in deciding the weight that should be given to seniority, in explaining pay differences between men and women, and in assessing non-race-based affirmative action.[5] Most recently, however, American law reviews have erupted into an impassioned debate which has brought the role of merit and the merit principle more to the centre of the scholarly stage. In particular, the apparent scepticism with which several of those associated with Critical Legal Studies and Critical Race Theory have greeted (some) arguments based on (at least some conceptions of) merit in the context of the hiring of law professors, has encountered robust criticism, including allegations of (unconscious) anti-Semitism.[6]

Impassioned though the political and scholarly debate is, these discussions of merit are often flawed by the absence of a serious attempt at understanding what merit is.[7] My argument in this essay is that at least some of the differences

review took place in Ontario, Canada. Under a previous government, 'employment equity' legislation had been passed, coming into operation in September 1994. Eliminating the legislation was a major plank in the campaign by the Progressive Conservative Party during the provincial general election, and was regarded as contributing to its subsequent election victory in June 1995. The main argument used by the Premier Michael Harris against the legislation was that the 'current legislation is quota-based'. 'It violates the merit principle.' *BNA Daily Labor Report*, 24 July 1995, 141 d8.

[4] Fiss, 'A Theory of Fair Employment Laws', 38 *University of Chicago Law Review* 235 at 241 (1971); Fallon, 'To Each According to His Ability, From None According to His Race: The Concept of Merit in the Law of Antidiscrimination', 60 *Boston University Law Review* 815 (1980); Fallon and Weiler, 'Firefighters v Stotts: Conflicting Models of Racial Justice', [1985] *Supreme Court Review* 1 at 15, fn 65.

[5] Kelman, 'Concepts of Discrimination in "General Ability" Job Testing', 104 *Harvard Law Review* 1158 (1991); Selmi, 'Testing for Equality: Merit, Efficiency and the Affirmative Action Debate', 42 *University of California Los Angeles Law Review* 1251 (1995); Riccucci, 'Merit, Equity and Test Validity: A New Look at an Old Problem', 23 *Administration and Society* 74 (1991); Overlaet, 'Merit Criteria as Justification for Differences in Earnings', 12(4) *Journal of Economic Psychology* 689 (1991); Fallon, 'Affirmative Action Based on Economic Disadvantage', 43 *UCLA Law Review* 1913 (1996).

[6] Critiques of merit include: Murray, 'Merit-Teaching', 23 *Hastings Constitutional Law Quarterly* 1073 (1996); Delgado, 'Rodrigo's Tenth Chronicle: Merit and Affirmative Action', 83 *Georgetown Law Journal* 1711 (1995); Shropshire, 'Merit, Ol' Boy Networks, and the Black-Bottomed Pyramid', 47 *Hastings Law Journal* 445 (1996); Kennedy, 'A Culturalist Pluralist Case for Affirmative Action in Legal Academia', 1990 *Duke Law Journal* 705; Johnson, 'The New Voice of Color', 100 *Yale Law Journal* 2007 (1991); Morrison, 'Colorblindness, Individuality, and Merit: An Analysis of the Rhetoric against Affirmative Action', 79 *Iowa Law Review* 313 (1994). Discussions of the critiques of merit include: Farber and Sherry, 'Is the Radical Critique of Merit Anti-Semitic?', 83 *California Law Review* 853 (1995); Carter, 'Academic Tenure and "White Male" Standards: Some Lessons from the Patent Law', 100 *Yale Law Journal* 2065 (1991); Kennedy, 'Racial Critiques of Legal Academia', 102 *Harvard Law Review* 1745 (1989).

[7] It is disappointing, for example, that the authors of the most recent, and controversial, critiques of the critics of merit, Farber and Sherry, above n 6, though recognizing that 'merit can be difficult to identify or even to define' (869) did not themselves analyse the different conceptions of merit in issue (882). The conception of merit which they regard as being under attack (865) is variously described as the 'current concept of merit' (857), the 'traditional conception of merit' (859), the 'conventional view of merit' (859), 'current concepts of merit' (p. 863), and 'current conceptions of merit' (883), without any further explication being offered.

apparent in the political and scholarly debates can be reduced by a more careful analysis of the concept itself, enabling the real differences in theoretical positions to emerge with greater clarity. My purpose in this essay is to try to reflect the complexity of merit, but to structure it – to try to provide a map by which the arguments about merit can be followed and situated, to provide a guide to the debate, a way through the maze. Some readers may think that the questions I consider here are somewhat esoteric, and academic, in the bad sense of the word. This would be a considerable misreading both of the extent to which the definition of merit is problematic,[8] and also of the importance of the issue of 'merit' in the current ideological battles surrounding affirmative action, and anti-discrimination law generally.

But does the North American debate have any relevance for the UK and Europe? I suggest that it does. The UK and the European Community (EC) have long had regard to American debates on the proper scope and meaning of anti-discrimination requirements, most recently in the context of the appropriate scope of affirmative (or positive) action for women under EC law.[9] In Northern Ireland, 'merit' has played a key part in the debate over affirmative action in the religio-political context, again drawing on American debates.[10] The debate over affirmative action in Europe (and Northern Ireland) shows no sign of tailing off in the near future.[11] More broadly, the change in the ideological approach adopted by the Labour Party in Britain shows clear signs of being influenced by American conceptions of 'merit'. And so I hope that an assessment of the central elements of the American debate on 'merit' will prove of some broader utility beyond the USA itself.

Before describing the map, let me begin at the end, with the conclusion. This essay will argue that the concept of 'merit' and 'the merit principle' are contested concepts, in that there are various competing conceptions which usually point in different, and sometimes incompatible, public policy directions.[12] The failure to resolve which conception of merit should guide policy has contributed, in part, to fundamental policy differences, in particular over affirmative action. Too often, discussions of merit assume one conception is the same as another because they are both called 'merit'.

8 See Parekh, 'A Case for Positive Discrimination', in B. Hepple and E.M. Szyszczak (eds), *Discrimination: The Limits of Law* (1992) 261 at 273.

9 *Kalanke* v *Freie Hansestadt Bremen*, Case C-450/93, [1995] ECR I-3051; *Marschall* v *Land Nordrhein-Westfalen*, C-409/95, [1998] IRLR 39 (ECJ).

10 McCrudden, 'Affirmative Action and Fair Participation: Interpreting the Fair Employment Act 1989', 21 *Industrial Law Journal* 170 (1990). See also, McCrudden, 'The Merit Principle and Fair Employment in Northern Ireland', in D. Magill and S. Rose (eds), *Fair Employment Law in Northern Ireland: Debates and Issues* (1996) 27 in which the author first developed some of the arguments discussed in this article.

11 McCrudden, 'The Legal Approach to Equal Opportunities in Europe: Past, Present and Future', 3 *International Journal of Discrimination and the Law* 193 (1998).

12 Such a view is hardly new. Compare Aristotle's view that the definition of merit (ἀξία) is contested, arguing that 'what is just in distribution must be according to merit in some sense, though they do not all specify the same sort of merit, but democrats identify it with the status of freemen, supporters of oligarchy with wealth (or with noble birth) and supporters of aristocracy with excellence'. Aristotle, *Nicomachean Ethics*, bk. V, ch. 3, p. 1131, col. A, ii. 26–29, reprinted in McKeon (ed.), *The Basic Works of Aristotle* (1941) 1006.

Lest this appear as directed solely against those who use merit arguments in order to limit affirmative action, some of those who attack merit arguments, perhaps particularly some writing in Critical Race Theory, fall into the same mistake in adopting an undifferentiated notion of merit as the basis of their rejection of any merit arguments.[13] This is a problem, therefore, which is too often common both to those who support, and those who oppose reliance on 'merit'. Future reform efforts in the area of affirmative action in particular are likely to be dogged by similar problems unless we can be clearer about the variety of ways in which the term can be, and is, used. It is unlikely, given its contested nature that we will agree that one conception of merit is the only appropriate one to use in debate.[14] We can, at least, attempt to prevent unintentional confusion by a clearer understanding of its different uses, and their implications. (Of course, those who intend to confuse do not share this interest.) I hope that those who currently use merit arguments, particularly those who use them approvingly, will conclude that such arguments are more trouble than they are worth, and stop using merit as a basis of argument in this area. Instead, I hope, that they will disaggregate the different conceptions, taking elements of merit arguments (and there are several which we shall see emerge out of the analysis) and concentrate on them in argument, whilst dropping use of the concept itself.

It is important, however, not to overemphasize the effect of drawing the sting of the merit argument on the debate over affirmative action. We can identify a multitude of related arguments against affirmative action, only one of which is explicitly 'merit-based'. While it is *necessary*, therefore, to consider the meaning and implications of merit arguments in the context of affirmative action, it is not *sufficient* to do so. To that extent, this essay should be seen only as a modest contribution to the wider debate about the pros and cons of affirmative action. The essay is, essentially, a ground-clearing operation to strip away one piece of the rhetoric which makes resolution of a fundamental problem more difficult.

That's the conclusion. How do I get there? In the following sections, I attempt first to introduce the structure of the merit argument, illustrating the radically different ways in which the merit argument can be used with two examples. I also identify where the principal disputes surrounding merit appear to arise. I am concerned primarily with the use of the term in the context of the distribution of jobs and employment opportunities. In the second section, there are several preliminary points which I make. In the context of the distribution of jobs, competition is inevitable. It is also practically inevitable that government will either want to, or will have to, answer the question of how jobs should be distributed. I distinguish, in addition, between negative and positive conceptions of merit, and I argue that the idea of merit in other areas of life where merit includes some idea of pure reward or penalty for past actions, should have no

[13] See Murray, above n 6 at 1079–80 for a discussion of the different positions such scholars may take.

[14] I thus disagree with the assumption of Shropshire, above n 6 at 457, fn 11 that 'what constitutes merit can be agreed upon'.

place in terms of what government requires in the distribution of employment. In the third section, I discuss some substantive questions, including what can count as merit. In the fourth section, I suggest five different conceptions of merit. In the fifth section, I consider the status of merit arguments, in the sense of what, if any, considerations can override merit arguments, and what, if any, moral weight merit arguments have. In the last section, I consider how we might begin to explain the attractiveness of merit to those who support it, and the venom with which its opponents attack it.

2. *What is Merit?*

A. *The structure of the 'merit argument' introduced*

A useful starting point, adapted from an excellent, if somewhat neglected, article by Richard Fallon, is to examine the structure of a merit argument. This can be represented in the form: S *merits X in virtue of M*, where S is a person, X a mode of treatment or an outcome, and M some feature possessed by S.[15] So, for example, we might say that John (S) *merits* the award of the sports prize (X) in virtue of having run faster than anyone else competing in the race (M). Or, that Mary merits admission to law school in virtue of her qualities of determination, clarity of thought, and ability to work hard, which we think are likely to make her a good lawyer in the future. What is involved, in other words, is selection of a person for the purposes of distribution of a benefit to that person.

B. *Two contrasting examples of the merit principle*

For the purposes of illustration, we can anticipate the various elements of the subsequent discussion by constructing two examples of how the merit principle might be formulated in order to see how the various separate elements may be combined to produce radically different results.

In the first example, '*S merits X in virtue of M*', might become: *S* deserves this particular job, indeed has an indefeasible right to it, when she satisfies better than anyone else the employer's criteria for selection of candidates for the job which involve qualities which are thought to be of general value in the society and are strictly job related, in the sense that they indicate how well someone will be able to perform the core elements of the job, conceived as the production of 100 widgets per hour.

In the second example '*S merits X in virtue of M*' might become: *S* should be considered for this particular job, and is qualified to be awarded it, provided she satisfies the features determined by society as relevant for carrying out the purposes of the job, broadly conceived to include the ability to work together

[15] See Fallon, above n 1 at 822. This conceptualization has been extensively used in discussing the concept of 'desert', see Lamont, 'The Concept of Desert in Distributive Justice', 44 *Philosophical Quarterly* (No. 174) 45–6 (1994).

with others, using criteria for selection which indicate general ability to carry out that purpose, whether contingently or not, and whether those features are thought to be of general value in the society or not. However, other considerations might be more important, in any specific case, in awarding the job than considerations of merit.

Put simply, probably too simply, we can identify at least five major differences surrounding merit in these two examples. First, there are differences in the limits and restrictions as to what 'merit' can consist of. In the first example, the qualities are those thought to be of general value in the society, but not in the second example. Second, there is a difference as to what 'the job' consists of. In the first example, 'the job' is narrowly defined as the production of widgets, and only the production of widgets, whereas in the second example 'the job' is conceived of as involving a much wider group of social skills. Third, there are disputes on the degree of 'fit' required between the job and the criteria of merit. In the first example, the qualities sought must be strictly related to the job, less so in the second example. Fourth, there are differences as to who is regarded as primarily deciding the criteria which define 'the job'. In the first example, it is the employer; in the second example, it is 'society'. Lastly, there is a difference over the relationship between 'merit' and other values. In the first example, the person is regarded as entitled to the job, implying that once she has satisfied the criteria of merit she should be awarded the job. This is not so in the second example, where other considerations are regarded as potentially trumping merit.

3. *Some Preliminary Considerations*

Before considering these issues in greater detail, however, there are several preliminary points which are worth considering: first, the issue of scarce resources; second, the role of the state; third, negative and positive conceptions of merit; fourth, the relationship between merit and virtue; and fifth, the relationship between merit and equality of opportunity. The way in which we approach these issues may constrain the way in which the debate about the meaning and place of merit will take place.

A. *Scarce resources and competition*

Someone might say that all the controversies to be discussed below assume that there will be a *competition* for *X*,[16] and that competition is (at least sometimes) inappropriate. Some years ago this might have given rise to a diverting discussion of whether competition was a good thing in general, whether competitiveness was to be encouraged, and so on. This was particularly likely to be the case given the use of the school sports-prize example, and even, conceivably, the example of admission to university. It would have been a 'diverting' discussion

[16] See, e.g. Fiss, above n 4 at 241: '. . . the choice among individuals *for scarce opportunities* should be the basis of the individual's merit' (emphasis added).

because, in the context with which we are primarily concerned, namely, the distribution of jobs, such competition is, given the existing social and economic structure of the West, inevitable, and therefore to say that we should assume a situation where there is no competition, is, at best, utopian.

That is not to say that we may not want to put into place social and economic policies which lessen competition, such as policies of job creation. Clearly, the more jobs there are, the less the competition for jobs, and thus the less pressing the distributional questions at the heart of the controversies surrounding the merit principle. But such policies merely lessen the importance of the distributional questions with which we are concerned, and at the margins only, and clearly do not render them irrelevant. Indeed, such policies themselves raise distributional questions of their own. Let us say, for example, that it would be good if a system could be put in place whereby funding could be located in particular geographic areas in order to stimulate economic development in those areas. The question of which areas should be targeted may well give rise to some at least of the distributional questions which arise in the individual employment context. In addition, how economic development of the area might best be stimulated may involve considerable discussion of what types of features the local labour market should reflect, such as the need to be 'flexible', which in turn may affect controversies over the idea of 'merit' in that labour market.

Nor does my rejection of a *general* argument based on the evils of competition mean that *certain Xs* should not be subject to competition. It might well be argued, for example, that basic health care, or welfare, should not be subject to competitive allocation. We might say that treatment for a heart attack should be available for everyone based on need, and that the form of the merit argument (*S merits X in virtue of M*) is inappropriate where *X* is 'health care'. Basic health care, we might say, should be distributed on the basis of '*S* needs *X*'. And there may well be other basic goods which we want to extract from competition, but I suspect that few will want to argue that the distribution of *individual* jobs can be among them, though some will want to argue that 'having a job' should be.

B. *Role of the state*

Turning now from the issue of scarce resources to the role of the state, some may argue that, in so far as the discussion on merit is regarded as relevant for the purpose of *public policy*, it is based on a fundamentally flawed premise: that the state should be attempting to influence, or determine, the content of the formula *S merits X in virtue of M*.[17] To put it bluntly, some will say that it is none of the state's business to try to influence, much less determine, the content of the formula in many situations, in particular perhaps in the private sector of employment, where employers should be free to determine the issue for themselves.[18] Such employers would be sensible, the argument goes, if they were to

[17] A position associated with Nozick, *Anarchy, State, and Utopia* (1974).
[18] Epstein, *Forbidden Grounds: The Case Against Employment Discrimination Laws* (1992) 163.

take into account the needs of economic efficiency in determining the content of the formula. But if they don't, we might say, then they will learn the hard way by going out of business. In either event, it is not the state's concern. To debate at length the merits of particular conceptions of merit as a guide to public policy, is therefore a pointless and dangerous exercise. The state should not be involved in the area in the first place. Such arguments have obviously been of considerable importance both intellectually and politically, not least during the last decade in the USA.

For several reasons, however, I will not be taking these arguments further. First, they are seldom adverted to in the current context of the appropriate distribution of jobs. Second, such arguments, by definition, cannot apply to employment in the public sector, where the state acts as the employer and must therefore determine the content of the formula. Third, in framing anti-discrimination legislation of even the most minimal kind, the state has already begun to take a stand on the content of the formula,[19] and as anti-discrimination law becomes ever more complex, the more the state is required to take increasingly complex stands. The political reality is that the state will be called on to make such choices for the foreseeable future. There seems to be a consensus that the state should have such a role, although the extent of such involvement is highly controversial.

There is, however, an important implication involved in the move away from a pure *laissez-faire* approach to a state-sponsored view of what merit involves. Under the market approach, the idea of merit is *subjective*, meaning that it involves only what each party to the contract is willing to accept (however dubious we might be about how free the consent of the worker is). Under a conception of merit imposed, or encouraged by the state, however, we 'assume that there is some *objective* measure that can be administered by an external agent who decides which types of agreements meet some standard of social acceptability and which do not'.[20]

C. *Public service employment and merit*

However controversial the role of the state in the context of the regulation of private employment, the state's role in the context of public employment is obvious and uncontested. But, being undisciplined directly by an effective market, and increasingly unwilling to appear to be perpetuating arrangements which could be justified only on the basis of party political advantage, civil service

[19] Fiss, above n 4 at 249.

[20] Epstein, above n 18 at 164 (emphasis added). As Epstein writes, this laissez-faire approach 'assumes that all elements of gain and loss are subjective, and that explicit measurement by external parties is not possible but is obtainable only by indirect inference. There is in a market exchange no objective test of merit on which any external observer can rely. There is only the subjective test of desire manifested in consent. Those things that tend to make a worker more desirable to the employer (and the employer more desirable to the worker) count as meritorious, while those that do not are not meritorious.' Epstein, above n 18 at 163.

employment has become increasingly regulated.[21] In the US federal civil service, the move from the spoils system began with the Pendleton Act 1883, which specified certain jobs as included within the merit system. For applicants for these positions, competitive examinations were used to decide who should be employed, and the Civil Service Commission was to oversee the system. Similar reforms were introduced at the state and city levels beginning around the same time.[22] Public standards for assessment and appointment have become accepted more and more. Central to these public standards is the concept of 'merit'.[23]

Unlike in the context of the legal regulation of private employment, where the term 'merit' is rarely used explicitly, in public service employment it is now regarded as central to recruitment, promotion and training, and the term is in constant use. There are several other reasons for considering, in particular, the role of merit in the public service. As applied to employment, the merit principle has been longest applied to public service employment, with a history in Britain stretching back to the middle of the last century, and in France to the Declaration of the Rights of Man in 1789. The length of time the principle has been applied in this context helps us to understand the evolution of the principle and its content in other contexts. The principle is one which is applied in many, if not all,[24] western public services, at least in theory, and this enables some degree of comparative experience to illuminate our considerations. In particular, it enables us to consider the different ways in which the merit principle has come into contact with various arguments based loosely on principles of equality of opportunity. This is not the place, however, even if there were time and space, for a full description of the merit principle in the context of the public service. We can, however, extract some relevant themes from the public administration literature which will illuminate our particular concern, the elucidation of the different conceptions of merit, and their differing implications.

We can see, to begin with, that though the term is one with a long history in the public service, it is also subject to considerable continuing debate as to its implications. In a modern civil service, at least three impulses seem to compete. The first is what we might think of as the 'Whitehall mandarin' conception of merit, where what is important is the ability of civil servants to be generalists, above the political fray, sufficiently clever to be able to lock horns with the

[21] Why merit systems were introduced remains controversial. A recent study of the introduction of the merit system into the US federal civil service (Johnson and Libecap, 'Patronage to Merit and Control of the Federal Government Labor Force', 31 *Explorations in Economic History* 91 (1994)) identifies several possible factors: 'moral outrage among progressives, ... the desire to provide tenure to party faithful ... changing demand for government services' (115) and (particularly) 'growing pressure from business groups to provide government services more effectively than was possible under patronage' (93).

[22] 1883, New York; 1884, Massachusetts; 1905, Illinois; Boston, 1885; New York, 1883; Chicago, 1895. See Johnson and Libecap, ibid at 112–13.

[23] For the federal civil service, see the Civil Service Reform Act of 1978 (PL 95–454), which codified merit system principles. For examples at the state level, see California Constitution, Article VII; New York State Constitution, Article V, section 6; Ohio Constitution, Article XV, section 10. See, in general, 15A Am Jur 2d Civil Service at 3.

[24] See *Rutan et al.* v *Republican Party of Illinois et al.* 497 US 62 (1989).

politicians who are the political heads of the departments, and with a well-developed sense of, and loyalty to, an idea of public service. The second is what might be called the 'entrepreneurial' conception of merit, where the skills required are those thought highly of in the business world – risk taking, flexibility, financial acumen, and there is an expectation that the civil servant is likely to be in the public service for only a limited amount of time. The third is what might be called a 'representativeness' conception of merit, where the role of the civil service is, in part, to reflect the makeup of society as a whole. I shall have more to say about some of these later.

D. *Negative and positive conceptions of merit*

Although I have framed the structure of the merit argument as '*S merits X in virtue of M*', *M* can be the *absence* of a particular quality or feature, or its *presence.* In the former case, the formula would be more accurately framed as '*S merits X in virtue of M* (*M* being any consideration other than *R*; *R* being the disfavoured quality or feature). This is probably the simplest conception of merit, where it is used negatively to rule out cronyism, political favouritism or nepotism, for example. I shall call this approach to the definition of merit, the 'negative approach'. Historically, 'the merit principle', both in the context of anti-discrimination law and in the public service employment context, usually started life in this negative sense. The 'positive approach' to merit tends, as we shall see, to be much more problematic in its meaning and implications. In the rest of this section, I shall concentrate largely on the positive approach to merit, returning to the negative conception only at the end of the section.

E. *Merit and virtue*

I am primarily concerned in this paper with the distribution of employment. In that context, one idea of merit should have no place, in terms of what the state requires. This is the idea of merit which is used in the context of rewarding someone *purely* for past 'attributes of conduct that make it deserving of praise, that is, the moral character of the action and not the value of the achievement'.[25] The role of the state is seldom one of rewarding, praising or expressing gratitude for such past achievement.[26] Indeed, the 'honours system' in some western European countries might be thought to be one of the few situations in which the state does so; even here, however, honours are given for achievement or public service, not for the person's moral motive. It would, therefore, be peculiar if this idea of merit was one which underpinned the merit principle in employment decisions. For the state, either directly or indirectly, to require employment

[25] Hayek, *The Constitution of Liberty* (1960) 94. This view appears to be adopted, for example, by Abrams who considers the appropriate role of anti-discrimination law to be one which is 'consistent with our meritocratic view of the relevant differences between individuals – a view through which our society *rewards* the individual for attainment' (emphasis added). Abram, 'Affirmative Action: Fair Shakers and Social Engineers', 99 *Harvard Law Review* 1312 at 1513–16 (1986).

[26] Davis, 'Race as Merit', XCII *Mind* (1983) 347 at 349.

decisions to be made on the basis of rewards for past virtue alone would surely be inappropriate, if only because of the costs in efficiency and productivity.

There seems to be an exception to this, however, which I shall consider at greater length. It is common practice for preference to be accorded, in public service employment, to those who served in the US armed services,[27] a preference which adversely impacts on women. The US Supreme Court, however, upheld the constitutionality of such preferences, rejecting a challenge on equal protection grounds.[28] What is interesting about the decision of the Court, however, is the extent to which the veteran's preferences were regarded as an exception justified by compelling public policy grounds, not merit.[29]

This is not to say that employment decisions are not, or should not be, made on the basis of taking achievement and effort into account, but rather that where this happens it should be done not to reward effort and achievement but in order to accomplish some other purpose: because effort and achievement are relevant to the job, or are proxies for other qualities useful for carrying out the job, or in order to create an incentive for others to become qualified etc.[30] These reasons are all *instrumental* uses of effort and achievement, rather than pure rewards for past effort and achievement.

F. *Merit and equality of opportunity*

Talk of merit often seems to raise issues of equality of opportunity, but the relationship between the two concepts is highly problematic, in part because of the contested nature of the concept of merit, in part because what constitutes equality of opportunity is, perhaps, equally contested. The result is that there is considerable controversy concerning the relationship between merit and equality of opportunity. For some, equality of opportunity as a principle of justice is defined in terms of merit: when the merit principle is satisfied, then there is equality of opportunity. For others, selection on the basis of merit only becomes an appropriate option when equality of opportunity has already been established: equality of opportunity must pre-exist in order for merit to become operational. This latter position is strongly argued by Bernard Williams in an influential essay, and usefully summarized by Gutmann: 'Institutionalization of the equal-opportunity principle is relied upon to create a distribution of positions according to merit. Only those societies that provide a thoroughgoing equality of opportunity can even hope to assess individual desert fairly in the end.'[31]

A third group would regard the concepts of merit and equality of opportunity as independent of each other, in the sense that neither is defined in terms of the

[27] 'Most civil service acts have sought to favor honorably discharged soldiers and sailors in the matter of appointments' 15 A Am Jur 2d Civil Service 36 (1995).

[28] *Personnel Adm'r* v *Feeney* 442 US 256 (1979).

[29] But contrast *Underwood* v *State of New York* 28 FEP 933 (US Dist Ct SDNY) 934: '... the preferential treatment they are accorded under state law indicates that the merit principle in civil service appointments is not so inflexible as to be entirely immune from equitable considerations'.

[30] Fallon, above n 1 at 824.

[31] Gutmann, *Liberal Equality* (1980) 109.

other. In that situation, however, given that there is the possibility of conflict, it is necessary to consider which has priority, with some taking the view that equality of opportunity should have priority, and others taking the view that merit should have priority. Kampe, for example, argues that 'merit is necessary for equal opportunity. Any adequate conception of competitive equal opportunity must allow a place, albeit a circumscribed place, for a merit principle in determining just distributions.'[32]

An attempt to elucidate the concept of merit by relying on a particular conception of equality of opportunity is more likely to lead to confusion, rather than clarification, and this possible strategy will not be further embarked on in this essay.

4. *Some Substantive Questions*

We can turn now to the substance of some of the questions I sketched out at the end of the second section: (i) the differences in the limits and restrictions as to what merit can consist of; (ii) the differences as to what 'the job' is thought to be; (iii) differences on the degree of 'fit' between the job and merit criteria; and (iv) differences as to what status should be attached to merit. This section will consider the first two of these; the third will be considered in the section following, and the fourth in the section following that.

A. *The role of relevance*

Are there limits and restrictions as to what merit can consist of? Often, those using the idea of merit will fall into one of two broad approaches. Some will take what I shall call a 'closed', or *a priori*, approach. An example would be where a person says that someone's race can never be an *M*, simply because it would be objectionable to award benefits, or burdens, on the basis of someone's race. *M* just cannot consist of someone's race, presumably because it is thought that a person's race is, or should be, always irrelevant to the doing of a job.[33] The negative conception of merit discussed above is often based on such stipulative constraints.[34]

A second approach is a more open-ended, continuing approach to the assessment of relevance. In contrast to the previous approach, the notion of what can constitute a relevant criterion for the award of a job requires and permits evaluations of relevance which may change over time, and type of job; what *M* can be is restricted by there having to be some connection between *X* and *M*,

[32] Kampe, 'Can There Be Equal Opportunity Without a Merit Principle', in S. H. Lee (ed.), *Inquiries into Values* (1988) 615 at 619.

[33] See also Edwards, *When Race Counts: The Morality of Racial Preference in Britain and America* (1995) 205. A good example is Kennedy, above n 6 at 1807: 'I do not want race-conscious decision-making to be assimilated into our conception of merit'.

[34] See, e.g. *State of Wisconsin* v *Dilhr* 14 FEP Cases 1189 (Wisconsin Supreme Court) (civil service requirements that the merit principle apply in public employment not consistent with an absolute preference being given to a person on the basis of their race or sex).

but that connection needs to be considered in an open way in each case. So, we might say that a statement 'John merits the sports prize by virtue of him being poor' is unacceptable because there appears to be no connection between the prize and the criterion for awarding it *in this case*, whereas experience of poverty may be a relevant criterion in the award of a job where such experience may help the person understand her clients better.

The question of what it is about the relationship between *M* and *X* that produces the conclusion that '*S* merits *X*' raises two further broad issues. First, what *degree* of relevant connection is desired; what is the 'closeness of fit' required between *M* and *X* (an issue which will be considered in the next section). Second, what is the *X* which we are trying to allocate, what does *X* consist of? It is to this second issue that I now turn.

B. *What is it that is being allocated?*

Because of the need for connectedness between *X* and *M*, of some sort, there may be considerable controversy in many real-life cases as to what *X is*, in other words, what is it that is being allocated. Let us take two examples.

My university wants to appoint a new president, and the short-listing committee meets to draw up the job description. Inevitably, we will have a fairly heated discussion as to what we think the function of presidents is and should be. Are they to be involved in fund-raising and therefore have good contacts; are they to give academic leadership by being active scholars; should they have had administrative experience outside academic life; should they be good on television; should they be able to make the university 'pull together'? Someone will inevitably say that all of these may be relevant, so let's put them all in the job description. And we probably will, but knowing that the precise mix, and the weight to be given to each relevant factor, will still have to be debated and considered at the short-listing stage, and at the stage of final appointment. What the example demonstrates, I hope, is that what the office of president *is*, is open to considerable debate, and so it is with X in many cases.

Or take the example of Mary's admission to law school. This is another example of where what the good is that is being awarded (*X*) is open to considerable debate.[35] When we are selecting law students, what are we selecting *for*? For the ability to benefit most from the course? For the ability to score highest in the final examinations? For the likelihood of serving the cause of justice after graduation?[36] For the ability to produce a range of opinions which will provide a stimulating academic environment?

On the other hand, some will say, these examples are fairly isolated examples (of academics being unable to make up their minds?). In the real world, it is quite clear what the essential nature of a job is. A bricklayer must be able to lay

[35] For penetrating discussions, see Williams, 'The Idea of Equality', in P. Laslett and W.G. Runciman (eds), *Philosophy, Politics and Society* (2nd series) 110 at 129–30, and Dhavan, Kibble and Twining, *Access to Legal Education and the Legal Profession* (1989) 29.

[36] See Dworkin, *A Matter of Principle* (1985) 299.

bricks; a plumber must be able to fix pipes; a typist must be able to type; an airline pilot must be able to fly airplanes (we hope!).[37] In this context, while the methods of satisfying oneself about how well someone lays bricks may be in dispute, at least the end to be pursued is clear. And in some sense this is true. We know that those personal characteristics which do not affect performance (eye colour, for example) just are not relevant. But in the case of other personal characteristics, it is not so clear that they are not relevant. Take age as an example. As Walzer argues: 'For most offices, the age of the candidate tells us nothing at all about the kind of job he will do. But it does tell us, roughly, how long he will do it. Is that a relevant consideration?' Trying to resolve the issue, he concludes, 'suggests forcefully how far we are from judgments about desert and how committed we are to controversy about relevance'.[38]

This debate over ends tends to become one which concentrates on how far the essential, or core, element of a particular job can be isolated, with some taking the view that what 'the job' is may be infinitely various as far as a particular employer is concerned, and others taking the view that in most cases a clear core of activities can relatively easily be identified. Key areas of dispute have arisen in public sector employment, and not just in the university context: what 'the job' of the police, or of civil servants, is, for example, has often aroused considerable controversy. My own view is that I am fairly sceptical whether there is any occupation where a core 'job' can be uncontroversially identified, and that we have moved so far beyond the simple job function approach that it is no longer a useful model. Take the case of the typist and the plumber mentioned above. In both these cases there is a plurality of considerations in issue. The typist should be able to type speedily, accurately, correct our spellings etc. There is therefore room for debate on the right amalgam of skills necessary in a 'good' typist. But I am anticipating some elements in my argument which need further explanation.

5. *Five Models of Merit*

On the basis of what has been said up to now, at least five different conceptions of merit can be identified.[39] By a 'model', I mean nothing more than a conception of merit which appears to be held by some individuals as the appropriate basis on which an 'objective' notion of merit might be formulated, and distinct from the others.

[37] Even in this context, however, problems arise. To what extent, for example, is it appropriate for us to consider that the bricklayer, the typist or the pilot should have the ability to work well with others, be friendly, be 'attractive'?

[38] Walzer, *Spheres of Justice* (1993) 146. But he would not go as far as Dworkin, whom he suggests adopts too loose a connection between jobs and the qualities relevant for doing them, and seems to deny any significant limits on the qualities that might count as qualifications (152).

[39] The second and third models derive from Fallon, above n 1 at 826. The fourth and fifth models are conceptions which disaggregate a further one.

A. *Merit as the absence of . . . (model 1)*

The term merit is sometimes used as a synonym for the *absence* of intentional discrimination, cronyism or political favouritism.[40] In this sense, the merit principle is satisfied if the process by which job allocation decisions are reached is not tainted by these factors, and a mechanism is created, as in the US federal civil service, for example, 'to preclude certain undesirable elements from entering the civil service'. At least from the point of view of the progressives pressing reform of the spoils system,[41] the emphasis was on the negative rather than positive factors, due probably to the recency and pervasiveness of the spoils system. Merit, in effect, 'became an expression of what was *not* wanted – keep the rascals out – but it had little to say about what *was* wanted for the civil service'.[42]

There is some difficulty with viewing this conception of merit as separate from the ones which follow. On the one hand, some view this model as 'free-standing', a complete, if limited, approach to what making a decision on the basis of 'merit' involves. On the other hand, others have seen this model as 'instrumental': an incomplete expression of another conception of merit. Even when it was first developed, it might be said, this idea of merit was introduced in order to serve an additional purpose, namely the greater efficiency of the delivery of public services.

B. *General 'common sense' merit (model 2)*

The second model requires that the qualities sought in order to accomplish the end pursued should be regarded as generally valuable in the society, a fomulation illustrated by a definition such as: 'The basic idea of meritocracy is that those who hold positions of authority and prestige should have earned them through the exercise of *some* skill, knowledge or talent *that the society desires or honors'*.[43] But this cannot be satisfactory. Do we really consider that Olympic athletes merit civil service jobs simply on the basis of their desired and honoured skills? Fallon's definition is therefore a more satisfactory definition of this second conception, introducing a relevance criterion which is satisfied by there being a general connection between the end pursued (doing the job) and the means chosen to achieve it (the selection criteria), describing merit (in this sense) as

[40] See, e.g. *State Personnel Bd* v *FEHC* 44 FEP 1051 (California Supreme Court) at 1058: 'the purpose . . . is to ensure that appointments . . . are made not on the basis of patronage'.

[41] For other considerations leading to reform, see above n 21

[42] Best, 'The Meaning of "Merit" in Canadian Public Administration', in R.F. Adie and P.G. Thomas (eds), *Canadian Public Administration: Problematical Perspectives* (2nd edn, 1987) 55 at 64. A recent British example of this is in the context of appointments to local government positions: see *The Conduct of Local Authority Business, Report* (Chairman: Mr David Widdicombe QC), (1986, Cmnd 9797) para 6.204. The Local Government and Housing Act 1989, s. 7(1) provided, following this report, that appointments to 'a paid office or employment' by a local authority 'shall be on merit'. There does not appear to have been any reported judgments in which the issue of what constituted merit has arisen.

[43] See Nielsen, *Equality and Liberty* (1985) chapter 8.

the 'possession of qualities that are thought to be of general value and *are reasonably likely to prove useful in carrying out a specific function*'.[44]

For example, a high IQ is generally a quality we admire. It is better to have a more intelligent civil servant than a less intelligent one. Thus we may say that George merits the award of his job in the Diplomatic Service in virtue of the fact that he has scored best in a general intelligence test, which is a way of generally determining the relative IQ of a person, and that he has shown himself willing and able to use that intelligence in carrying out the job.[45] This is the principal conception of merit upon which Michael Young constructed his famous novel *The Rise of the Meritocracy*, in which the term 'meritocracy' was first coined. The formula I+E=M (intelligence plus effort equals merit) was supposedly the guiding principle for the award of benefits in the society which he feared[46] Britain would become in the 21st century.

This may now seem to some a very unfashionable approach to merit. Yet that reaction is itself an indication of the changing nature of merit in our society. Young's 'novel' was not a flight of fancy, but one grounded in a view of the predictive capacity of testing, and a view of the appropriate role of intelligence in the allocation of jobs, and other benefits, in the Britain of his time. Nor, of course, was this a view confined to Britain. In the USA, too, the issue of IQ testing as a means of spotting 'raw talent' which should be developed has been of extraordinary significance. And the relationship between this development and the idea of 'merit' also appears to have strong links. Indeed, Fallows goes so far as to regard 'the idea that the state would scientifically seek out its most intelligent people and grant them extra rights' as having 'given us the modern meritocracy'.[47] One example he gives is of particular interest. Deferment from the draft was based in part on a test devised to spot educational aptitude (an interesting case of the general 'common sense' conception of merit being used to decide who should *not* be 'offered a job').

And, in some respects, it is an attractive conception of merit. Its benefit is to exclude most factors used intentionally to discriminate against particular groups on arbitrary grounds, such as gender or race. In particular, it begins to capture an important element in the appeal which merit arguments appear to have: it concentrates on attempting to identify 'objective' or 'neutral' elements which can form the basis of judgment, and it does so by concentrating on factors which

[44] Fallon, above n 1 at 826 (emphasis added).

[45] See, for example, Sanders, 'Might Britain be a Meritocracy', 29(1) *Sociology* 23 at 27 (1995): '... under conditions of perfect meritocracy, all ... would have been allocated to their class locations according to the differences between them in measured intelligence ...'.

[46] His fears are based on the effect such a formula would have on society in general (leading to increased inequality and severe social tensions) and on the inability of individuals to develop the full range of their capabilities, because of the narrow range of factors considered important.

[47] Fallows, 'A Substitute for Merit: the Case Against Credentialism', *The Atlantic* 49–67 (September 1985).

require the persons being assessed to be treated as individuals,[48] rather than as bearers of ascriptive criteria. It therefore has the appearance of enhancing autonomy, and of treating individuals as ends, rather than means.[49]

This conception of merit, however, involves recourse to very broad rules of thumb for selection, which may be stereotypical or out of date, or of insufficient predictive value. More problematic still, the second conception of merit appears to envisage the job being merited almost in the sense that a prize is merited. But this seems unconvincing, particularly when we admit the idea of some applicants for a job being 'overqualified' in the sense that 'although the candidates in question have an ample supply of the particular skills that the job requires, they also have other skills that will not be exercised, as a result of which they will predictably become bored and finally do the job less well'.[50] As Miller argues on the basis of this example, 'the aim [of job selection] is not to uncover talent *per se*, but to find the individual who on the basis of available evidence can be predicted to perform best in the particular role that the institution requires'.[51]

C. *Strict job-relatedness (model 3)*

The third model requires a much tighter 'fit' between means and ends. The quality M must be one which is *strictly* job related, and validated in such a way as to demonstrate that it accurately predicts the ability to do a specific, and identifiable, feature of the job. Using this idea of tightness of fit, then, the third model would want to have demonstrated that an IQ test actually does measure something which is specifically, and demonstrably, related to a particular job, not just generally so. In that sense it is an attempt to 'purify' the second approach.[52] In this conception of merit, as Fallon writes, merit becomes the 'possession of precisely those qualities of excellence needed to perform a functionally defined task'.[53] In seeking to achieve this, it coincides (at least) with the idea of 'scientific' management propounded by Fredrick W. Taylor who sought to move management from an art to a science. Jobs should be studied scientifically,

[48] See, e.g. the testimony of Shirley J. Wilcher, to the Senate Labor Committee considering affirmative action under Executive Order 11, 246, *Daily Labor Report* (16 June 1995) 1994 DLR 116 d31. See also Reynolds, 'Individualism vs Group Rights: The Legacy of Brown', 93 *Yale Law Journal* 995 at 1004 (1984): need to 'judge all applicants on their individual merits, *without discrimination*' (emphasis in original). See also Ginsburg, J in her opinion for the Court in *United States* v *Virginia* 116 S Ct 2264 (1996) where significant emphasis is given to the need to have individualized consideration of applicants to VMI, holding that the 'total disregard of their individual merit' was unacceptable (at 2282).

[49] McCaffrey points to a similar conclusion regarding the virtue some see in certain conceptions of 'efficiency': 'Slouching Towards Equality: Gender Discrimination, Market Efficiency, and Social Change', 103 *Yale Law Journal* 595 at 644, 646 (1993).

[50] Miller, 'Deserving Jobs', 42 (No. 167) *Philosophical Quarterly* 168 (1992).

[51] Ibid at 168. See further Pashman J (dissenting) in *Lige* v *Town of Montclair* 13 FEP Cases 1697 (New Jersey Supreme Court) at 1713.

[52] Edwards, *Positive Discrimination, Social Justice, and Social Policy* (1987) 154.

[53] Fallon, above n 1 at 826.

and systematic methods of selecting, training and supervising employees should be introduced.[54]

The most common way in which the merit principle is currently defined is that a position should be awarded to the most 'qualified' applicant for the position in question.[55] Three highly problematic aspects to the operationalization of this conception of the merit principle can be identified immediately. First, there is an issue of what the qualification criteria should be; second, there is the issue of what the exact job requirements are; and third, assuming agreement as to both these, there is the issue of what weight should be attached to each of the qualification criteria. Taking the simplest example to illustrate the point: there may well be considerable practical disagreement as to whether, for example, education or experience should be the criterion for the job in question. If the former, then 'best qualified' tends to mean 'best educated'. If the latter, 'best qualified' tends to mean 'most experienced'. If both are relevant, what weight should be attached to each of them, and in the event of conflict, which should predominate? 'Even when [those who are doing the evaluation] arrive at a unanimous conclusion, there is a good chance that each has made the choice for different reasons.'[56]

These problems have been exacerbated, though a model 3 conception of merit has been strengthened overall by the development of the legal concept of disparate impact discrimination by the US Supreme Court in *Griggs* v *Duke Power Co.* in 1971.[57] If minorities (and later women) are adversely affected by a particular selection device, then the onus is on the employer to show that the selection device is job related, and that no other alternative could be adopted that is less adverse to the aspirations of the affected group. The effect is to require that selection tests, for example, must not simply identify and compare the person's academic or other credentials but must attempt to use criteria which have proven important in doing the job. This is sometimes described as measuring the person for the job, not the person's qualifications or achievements in the abstract. This contributed to substantial rethinking, particularly in the US Civil Service, but also in other civil services, of whether traditional methods of selection were in fact necessary and effective in delivering the best person for the job. In part, this is because of the sheer technical difficulty of demonstrating job relatedness; in part, it is because no matter how 'objective' the selection criteria are, the subjective element will always be present, and thus the opportunity is there for intentional and unintentional biases and preferences to creep in.

One (unsatisfactory) way of conceiving the third model is simply to regard it (and indeed the second model) as ways of eliminating evasion of the first model,

[54] See Cascio and Thacker, *Managing Human Resources* (1994) 37–38. I am grateful to John Craig for this reference. Compare Slack, 'Affirmative Action and Merit in Public Administration', 18(4) *American Review of Public Administration* 377 at 379 (1988): 'The concept of merit originates in the reform and scientific management movements of the late 19th and early 20th centuries'.

[55] See, e.g. the testimony of Shirley J. Wilcher, to the Senate Labor Committee considering affirmative action under Executive Order 11, 246. *Daily Labor Report* (16 June 1995) 1994 DLR 116 d31.

[56] Best, above n 42 at 57.

[57] *Griggs* v *Duke Power Co.* 401 US 424 (1971).

by narrowing the area of discretion within which the employer will be able to put into effect discriminatory animus. One of the ways the *Griggs* case itself can be read, historically at least, is in precisely this way. The introduction by the Duke Power Co. of the high school qualification and the Wonderlic Test battery at the same time that Title VII of the Civil Rights Act 1964 was coming into effect just looked too much of a coincidence. The new requirements appeared to many to be a subterfuge to keep the existing exclusion of black workers effective.[58] But to read the *Griggs* case simply as a way of preventing the evasion of model 1 would be too limited. The third model which *Griggs* encapsulates embodies a genuinely different model of merit from the first.[59] Like the second model, it concentrates on the use of qualities, such as skills, intelligence, qualifications, which are considered independently valuable. It also builds on the ideas of objectivity and individuality present in model 2. The greatest strength of this approach is the extent to which it has been able to challenge the use of arbitrary or invidious criteria which impact adversely on a particular race or gender, such as nepotistic practices and word of mouth recruiting.[60]

We should not, however, ignore the financial and social costs involved in requiring validation of criteria to this degree, and the adverse effect of getting rid of all non-job-related social factors.[61] There are several possible effects of model 3 which make it an unlikely candidate for a generalized merit principle, however useful it is as a test for unacceptable racial and gender exclusion.

To begin with, this form of merit argument is too mechanistic in excluding those features of the job which are elusive, and cannot be measured. The tightness of fit required between means and ends will usually result in a rejection of a broad conception of what 'the job' involves, particularly the more social elements, because of the difficulty of measuring how someone performs those elements of the job better than others. Where required by law, it is potentially highly *dirigiste* in its implications, with the attendant disadvantages associated with the legal management of market transactions.

The model 3 conception of the merit principle is, in any event, unlikely to be applied strictly in practice, because of the difficulty of putting it into operation. In part this difficulty arises from the emphasis it gives to reliance on complex professional judgments and expertise. This is because, at least in the hiring context, the employer may often have to use proxies to assess whether the person has the exact skills necessary to do the precise job required to be done. So, for example, employers develop tests, or use interviews, or rely on recommendations. This *ex ante* method of assessing the presence of necessary skills raises the strong

[58] Delgado, above n 6 at 1723–4.
[59] Cp. Belton, 'Discrimination and Affirmative Action: An Analysis of Competing Theories of Equality and *Weber*', 59 *NC Law Review* 531 at 545 (1981): '...Griggs demands that employers and unions transform the theory of meritocracy into reality'.
[60] For example, Carter, above n 6 at 2069–70 who criticizes 'the favoritism and elitism that works to the disadvantage of leading candidates who are not white and who may be just as good as white candidates who are hired because they have the right friends'. See also Shropshire, above n 6 at 461: 'In sports ... being part of the network is an indication of merit'. See also at 470.
[61] Epstein, above n 18 at 215.

possibility that the proxies may actually test for the skills needed to do tests, interview well, or impress others, rather than test for the presence of skills needed to do the job (to the extent they are different).[62] Professional judgment and expertise may therefore be necessary to interpret the test results. Merit in the third sense is also unlikely to be applied in practice because (due to this) it is expensive and time-consuming to apply. The effect is that it is more likely in practice to slip back to something more closely approximating model 2. The difficulty of constructing, validating, and administering tests, for example, is such that it is by no means clear that acting on the results of such tests leads to merit results even in the sense supposed.[63]

D. *Merit as the capacity to produce particular job-related results (model 4)*

A fourth model is different again. In this there is no necessary requirement of a quality which is generally admired, as in the second and third models discussed above. There is a weaker notion of objectivity, not only in the sense that criteria are permitted which do not generally need to be conceived as societally valuable, but also because these criteria are themselves more open to interpretation and different methods of putting them into operation. It is also more open to ascriptive criteria being regarded as relevant, and therefore, arguably, it places less importance on individualizing employment decisions than models 2 and 3.

What is required is that there should be a feature of *S* which will be useful in the pursuit of *the doing of the job*; the feature need not necessarily be in itself something which we regard as generally valuable in the society. If it is instrumentally valuable in carrying out the job, then it can legitimately count as meritorious. For Edwards, 'the "best person for the job" . . . is not that person who has, and exercises, skills and talents for their own sake (and that are valued for their own sake), but rather [the person] who will apply them in a manner that will best get the job done . . .'.[64]

As importantly, the fourth model tends to take a much broader view of what 'the job' consists of, and is much more sympathetic to a view which includes within the idea of the job those features which *assist* in carrying it out rather than just those which are *necessary* in order to carry it out. So, for example, social and humanistic features of the job (such as good service delivery, acting as an effective 'role model', and customer satisfaction) could be considered within the concept of the job in this fourth model, but would be unlikely to feature in the second or third models. Edwards, for example, has developed a

[62] Kennedy's critique of merit, for example, is partially based on his scepticism of whether such proxies are accurate, Kennedy, above n 6 at 712, fn 22, and 717–18. Kraus, 'The End of Equality', *New Republic* (22 June 1992) 21–7 distinguishes between True Meritocracy (by which he appears to mean model 3) and Phoney Meritocracy (by which he appears to mean the use of proxies for the achievement of model 3).

[63] See Riccucci, above n 5; Kelman, above n 5 at 1253: 'employment tests are typically weak predictors of potential productivity and individual test scores are inaccurate measures of an individual's true abilities as those abilities are measures by the examination'.

[64] Edwards, above n 33 at 199. Compare Fiss, above n 4 at 241: 'In the employment context this commitment to the merit principle means that the individual businessman is expected to choose the most productive individual, that is, the best worker at any given wage rate'.

useful distinction between 'intrinsic functional relevance' and 'optimal service delivery'.[65]

The development of the fourth model in the public service employment context is particularly illuminating. Two explanations predominate for the introduction of the merit principle in public administration. One explanation is the desire for efficiency, in some relatively broad sense. So, in the famous phrase which justified the introduction of the merit principle into British public service, it was necessary 'to provide, by a proper system of examination, for the supply of the public service with a thoroughly efficient class of men (sic)'.[66] Another explanation, particularly in France, but also in Britain, was the desire to ensure greater democratic participation in public administration, 'by enlarging its ranks to all capable candidates regardless of political affiliation or government support. In this way, it was alleged, the situation of having public officials drawn from an élite (the aristocracy or those connected with a political party in power) would be avoided.'[67]

Some have argued, however, that there is a paradox in using the merit system to achieve the second objective, greater democratic participation in the public service:

> For, in replacing men of influence with officials from all social strata and thus making public power more democratic, a privileged caste – which owes its position to examinations and academic qualifications – is created ... [T]he bureaucracy not only managed to absorb the introduction of the merit system but turned it to its own advantage, using it as a means to constitute itself as a body in its own right. One might say that what appears to have been a process of democratization in fact became a process of a separately established bureaucracy defending itself from external influence. As such, it could not allow others to decide on admission to that body and so took over control of the selection procedures ... Thus the merit system works not so much towards making the administration more democratic and towards guaranteeing equal opportunity in the entrance procedures, as towards allowing the bureaucracy itself to secure control over these entrance procedures.[68]

Perhaps not unrelatedly, the traditional conception of the merit principle in the public service has been substantially rethought in several important respects, concentrating on the need to reconsider what 'the job' is about. Increasingly, in several jurisdictions, pressure from women and from various religious, ethnic, racial, and language minorities has contributed to a rethinking of the role of the public service and of public servants more generally. In doing so, the conception of 'merit' adopted in the public service of several countries comes much closer to the fourth conception of merit.[69] This approach has been most developed in the USA and Canada.

[65] Edwards, above n 33 at 216.
[66] Cassese and Pellew, 'The introduction of merit systems in various bureaucracies: a comparative account', in Cassese and Pellew (eds), *The Merit System* (Cahier d'Histoire de l'Administration no. 2) 19.
[67] Ibid.
[68] Ibid at 21–3.
[69] Best, above n 42 at 57–8.

In Canada, the language dimension has been to the fore, beginning in 1963. One way in which Canada (and indeed the USA) has sought to achieve this aim is by enforcing a strict conception of the disparate impact theory of discrimination set out in *Griggs*: critically evaluate any factor which has an adverse impact on these groups and (if it is not job related and necessary) then replace it.[70] However, in addition to the 'job-relatedness approach', both Canada and the USA have sought to build a more representative civil service in various other ways. In Canada, for example, the equal status of the French and English languages has been guaranteed; certain posts were designated as requiring bilingual capacity; special efforts have been made to increase the percentage of francophone speakers appointed through affirmative action measures to redress the imbalance.[71]

This has also been a long running approach in the USA, where the ethnic and racial dimension has been to the fore. The Civil Service Reform Act 1978 called for 'a work force reflective of the Nation's diversity'.[72] The current US Office of Personnel Management's (OPM) implementing regulations, which establish the principles that govern the employment practice of the federal government, specify that the purpose of competitive employment practices is, in part, to '[r]esult in selection *from among* the best qualified candidates'.[73] Each part of the government is required to 'conduct a continuing program for the recruitment of members of minorities for positions in the agency to carry out the [anti-discrimination] policy ... in a manner designed to eliminate underrepresentation of minorities in the various categories of civil service employment within the Federal service, with special efforts directed at recruiting in minority communities, in educational institutions, and from other sources from which minorities can be recruited'.[74] A further set of regulations have been issued by the OPM implementing a federal equal opportunity recruitment programme in furtherance of this requirement.[75] And the report to President Clinton on affirmative action considered the diversity argument an important reason for strong affirmative action in the federal civil service.[76] The study found that 'managers are encouraged to keep diversity and equal opportunity objectives in mind when conducting outreach and recruiting ...'.[77]

It has been argued by some, however, that implicit in the concept of a representative public service 'is the assumption that the public servant will actually function on behalf of, or in the interests of, the group from which he

[70] A good example of this approach is: Comptroller General of the United States, *Report to the Congress, Federal Employment Examinations: Do they Achieve Equal Opportunity and Merit Principle Goals* (US GAO, 15 May 1979). See earlier, United States Commission on Civil Rights, *The Federal Civil Rights Enforcement Effort – 1974*, Vol. V: To Eliminate Employment Discrimination (US CCR, July 1975) 18–19.

[71] Best, above n 42 at 72–6.

[72] 5 USC § 2301 (emphasis added).

[73] Code of Federal Regulations, Title 5, chapter 1, Part 300, § 300.102 (emphasis added).

[74] 5 USC § 7201(c).

[75] Code of Federal Regulations, Title 5, Part 720.

[76] 'Affirmative Action Review' Report to President Clinton, (19 July 1995), *BNA Daily Labor Report*, 20 July 1995, para 8.4.1.

[77] Ibid at para 8.4.1.

or she originally came',[78] to the extent that representativeness is justified by a view that policy will be better formulated by having a more diverse group involved. Although empirical studies are unclear to what extent this is the case, a recent American review of the literature concludes that 'a more representative bureaucracy may be a more responsive bureaucracy, at least in certain social policy areas', such as law enforcement and social work,[79] and some judges appear to adopt an equivalent view in their interpretation of what can constitute 'merit'.[80]

One way in which we can encapsulate the difference between the second and third models, on the one hand, and the fourth, on the other, then, is by asking whether someone's race can ever be counted as an *M*, in the sense that we could legitimately say: '*S merits X, in virtue of S's race*'. Since one's race is not a quality which society regards as generally valuable, race will not count as an *M* under models 2 and 3. Under model 4, however, independently valuable qualities are not required. Davis argues that in some circumstances being of a particular race may well be relevant: 'If looking the part [in a play] is a merit, then being black like Othello is a merit'.[81] The crucial question, therefore, in the context of the fourth model, is whether race is relevant, and if it is, it is neither wrong nor arbitrary to treat it as a merit.[82]

In permitting such features to count, however, the fourth model is seen by many as dangerously able to be misused, and to give the wrong signal about the role of race: '[I]t remains a dangerous business for the law to recognize – and a morally dubious business for the law to teach – the relevance of race to an individual's social worth'.[83] It is noticeable, for example, that race is not included as a *bona fide* occupational qualification in Title VII of the Civil Rights Act 1964 (though sex is).[84] The question of whether something can count as merit which is not independently valuable is thus highly controversial.

To some at least, the approach of treating a characteristic such as race as 'meritorious' just does not seem to ring true. So, they might argue, being tall is relevant for being a basketball player but we should not think of tallness as constituting 'merit'. It seems unacceptable to 'expand' merit to cover every conceivable asset which we have that may be useful in doing a job. But this

[78] Best, above n 42 at 78.

[79] Kellough, 'Affirmative Action in Government Employment', in Orlans and O'Neill (eds), *Affirmative Action Revisited, Annals of the American Academy of Political and Social Science*, 523 (September 1992) 117 at 121.

[80] For example, Pashman J (dissenting) in *Lige* v *Town of Montclair* 13 FEP Cases 1697 (New Jersey Supreme Court) 1714; *Baker* v *City of Detroit* 24 FEP Cases 1728. Contrast *Fountain* v *City of Waycross* 47 FEP Cases 976.

[81] Davis, above n 26 at 364. See also Fallon and Weiler, above n 4 at 45: 'There are contexts in which racial or minority status may enhance a person's ability to fulfil a particular function in employment'.

[82] See, for example, the discussion by Murray, above n 6, who argues for 'a more expansive meaning of merit' (1113) that would 'include Outsiders within its parameters' (1111) by including 'the valuable, concrete lived experiences of oppressed peoples' (1081).

[83] Fallon, above n 1 at 843. See also, Kennedy, above n 6 at 1794, and Carter, above n 6 at 2071.

[84] Similar approaches have been adopted in judicial consideration of state and city merit requirements. The New York Department of Civil Service, operating under merit requirements, may limit eligibility for examination to one sex when the duties of the position involved required a woman or a man, *Button* v *Rockefeller* (1973) 76 Misc 2d 701, 6 FEP Cas 588 (need for female state troopers). In *Higgins* v *City of Vallejo*, 44 FEP Cases 676 at 678, the Ninth Circuit rejected the 'unsupported premise that taking race into consideration is inconsistent with the merit principle (affirmative action plan promoted a black fire-fighter with the third highest test score over white firefighters with highest test score)'.

example perhaps allows us to develop an important variation on this approach. Whilst being tall does not itself constitute merit, it may be a necessary condition for what does constitute merit, namely, having the capacity to perform excellently on the basketball court. In the context of race, we would not treat race itself as merit, but rather view race as a proxy for another feature which the employer wishes to incorporate within her workforce. Duncan Kennedy, for example, has argued that while he does not consider race to be 'itself an index of merit', in the appointment of law professors[85] it should be regarded 'as a credential (as a proxy) for culture and community',[86] 'a rough but adequate proxy for connection to a subordinated community'[87] whose views should be represented in academic discourse. Membership of a subordinated community is hardly an independently valuable quality and thus does not qualify under model 2 or 3, but may be relevant in producing results, and hence be a candidate for inclusion under model 4.

E. *Merit as the capacity to produce beneficial results for the organization (model 5)*

The previous conception of merit, whatever its other differences, shares with the second and third conceptions of merit a sense of the job being filled as fairly well defined, and distinct from simply serving the needs of the organization as a whole. The fifth, and last, conception of merit does not hold to this limited conception of what it is that a person is being selected to do. Fallon encapsulates this approach by describing merit 'as the capacity to produce valued results within a specific context, regardless of whether the capacity arises from qualities generally esteemed as socially useful'.[88] So, under this conception of merit, the attributes of persons which will lead to them being able to contribute to fulfilling the goals of the organization in which they work would constitute 'merit'. Under the fourth conception of merit, what the attribute achieves is doing 'the job' better; under the fifth conception, what the attribute achieves is serving the organization better, in ways which one would be hard put to view as part of the job narrowly conceived.

There are two different senses in which the organization's goals may be better furthered. First, 'the job' may be placed more firmly in the wider organizational context. The idea that the employer is selecting employees not necessarily to do a well-defined task with clear job-performance expectations attaching to him or her is now increasingly put forward in more recent management and organizational theory, challenging the 'scientific management' approach discussed earlier. Employees should be viewed, it is argued, not as isolated individuals doing clearly defined tasks on their own, but as members of a complex social system in which cooperation, working as a team and the building of cohesion

85 Kennedy, above n 6 at 713.
86 Ibid at 716.
87 Ibid at 713.
88 Fallon, above n 1 at 827.

figure strongly.[89] Judged from this perspective, therefore, assessing merit on the basis of the third model appears increasingly anachronistic; an approach wedded to the 'scientific management' of the past.

Second, the organization may be better placed to take part effectively in the wider social context in which it operates. In this sense, being black may be 'meritorious' where having a more diverse workforce is 'good for business' because it will be pleasing to foreign investors, or keep the government from suing, or accord with the moral preferences of consumers. From as long ago as the mid-1970s, reports of the US Civil Rights Commission argued that a more representative civil service would 'more likely generate support for government programs by all groups in society'.[90]

The previous conceptions of merit may therefore be criticized as being much too abstracted to be convincing, perhaps particularly models 2 and 3, in which the organization is abstracted from its wider social context, the job is abstracted from its larger organizational context, and the job is reduced to the narrow qualities to do an 'abstractly and insularly defined job'.[91]

F. *The United States Supreme Court and merit*

The role of merit in the context of the US Supreme Court decisions on affirmative action is not immediately apparent. Whilst there has been significant use of the term in the American political and scholarly context, there has been infrequent use of the concept in the judicial context, perhaps surprisingly, given its political and scholarly prevalence, and the increased scepticism with which the majority of the Supreme Court now views affirmative action.[92] The preferred approach of a continuing majority of the US Supreme Court is not to resort to the merit principle as such (in any of the various conceptions identified above) in analysing the legality of affirmative action. Rather, the approach adopted has been to identify particular concerns which we have seen underpin particular conceptions of the merit principle, and to consider them specifically and independently, rather than resort to the 'catch-all' rhetoric of 'merit'. This strengthens the conclusion which I want to draw from my consideration of the different models of merit: they can neither come together to form a coherent concept (because they are mutually incompatible) nor does any one of them stand alone to form a satisfying conception of merit by itself. And (this is where the Supreme Court's approach is relevant) crucial debates which would appear likely to draw on merit arguments can quite easily (and in my view more profitably) be conducted without reference to the concept at all.

[89] O'Neil and Quinn, 'Applications of the Competing Values Framework', 32 *Hum. Res. Mngt* 1 (1993). Thanks to John Craig for this reference.

[90] United States Commission on Civil Rights, *The Federal Civil Rights Enforcement Effort ñ 1974,* Vol. V: To Eliminate Employment Discrimination (US CCR, July 1975) 6.

[91] Parekh, above n 8 at 273.

[92] See McCrudden, 'The Constitutionality of Affirmative Action in the United States: A Note on *Adarand Constructors Inc.* v *Pena*, 1 *International Journal of Discrimination and the Law* 369 (1996).

6. *Status of Merit Arguments*

Even assuming agreement that '*S merits X*' (however that is defined), there are further problems. For some, to say that '*S merits X*' means that *S* merits it in the strong sense that *S* should get *X*. Sometimes this is expressed in the form: *S deserves* it; and sometimes in the form *S* has a *right* to it. For others, however, to say that '*S merits X*' is only to say that *S qualifies* for *X*, and should be *considered* for the award of *X*. The importance of the issue is that it concentrates attention on what, if any, considerations can trump 'merit' (whatever it is).[93] When someone says that '*S merits X*', therefore, we need to press harder. What normative *weight* does the statement '*S merits X*' have?

The assumed connection between merit and strong moral entitlement is one of the aspects of merit which cause the most irritation among the sceptics.[94] Thornton has written, for example, that, 'The focus on individual worth means that the appearance of justice in allocations is maintained while major structural impediments to equality ... need not be addressed. Merit, therefore, also sometimes carries with it the moral quality of absolution.'[95] Nielsen has written (tongue in cheek): 'We need . . . a society genuinely open to talent, but a society in which equality of opportunity is still a genuine opportunity to be unequal in a fair structure of competition. And we need as well a proper civility which would be the unsullen acceptance by the lower orders of meritocratic hierarchies that result from this competition.'[96]

The case of the prize for sports day may seem to some a relatively straight forward example: we *ought to* award the prize to the person who runs fastest. This person has a legitimate grievance if she is not awarded the prize; we may even say that she has a moral right to it. Should we be concerned enough, we may even give the person a legal right too. But in many other situations, this implication may be less clear cut than in this example. In particular, to bring the issue back to the distribution of jobs, do we think of a job as equivalent to a prize, something which a particular person has a right to be awarded on the basis of qualifications? These are the issues we consider in this section.

A. *Merit and desert: some preliminary considerations*

There has been a significant theme in some recent *dissents* in the US Supreme Court that 'merit' is being sacrificed to affirmative action, and in many of these an underlying concern seems to emerge: that those who are 'losing out' are having their *rights* trampled on, that they are being denied jobs, or other positions which they *deserve*.

[93] Kelman, above n 5 at 1245.

[94] In pointing to the phenomenon of cognitive dissonance, Sunstein may provide an explanation for the linkage of merit with moral dessert. Sunstein, 'Three Civil Rights Fallacies', 79 *California Law Review* 751 at 759 (1991).

[95] Thornton, 'Affirmative Action, Merit and the Liberal State', 2 *Australian Journal of Law and Society* 28 (1985). See further, Best, above n 42 at 55.

[96] Nielsen, *Equality and Liberty* (1985).

One of the earliest examples is that of Douglas J in *DeFunis*: 'A DeFunis who is white is entitled to no advantage by virtue of that fact; nor is he subject to any disability, no matter what his race or colour. Whatever his race, he has a constitutional right to have his application considered on its individual merits in a racially neutral manner.'[97] Is this argument morally well grounded? Gross is one noted advocate for a strong desert claim based on merit. Restricting the sense of 'merit' so that a 'person's merit is simply his ability to perform a given task', Gross argues that a person 'deserve[s] a given post more than another if it is reasonable to believe that he will perform better in it. He thus merits (deserves) it more, since he has more merit.'[98] Cottingham has also argued for a strong connection between merit and desert: 'The plain fact is that "merit" in its standard, ordinary use, is logically tied to the notion of desert – it is a function of what people deserve by their achievements'.[99] He stresses, however, that he should not be interpreted as meaning that a person is rewarded on the basis of such undeserved characteristics as 'intelligence'. Rather the reward goes to 'his *efforts* in putting that intelligence to use'.[100]

There are several significant problems with arguments of this type. First, and perhaps most importantly, to rely on 'desert' to support an argument about the weight of merit may be to build uncertainty upon uncertainty, for the concept of desert is as controversial as the concept of merit.[101]

Second, assuming that desert has a stable meaning with a significant element of 'effort' in it, and with a strong moral weight attached to that effort, 'qualifications do not correlate neatly with effort', as George Sher, rightly, argues. 'If they did, we might appeal to the past efforts of the best qualified to account for their desert.... For often the best-qualified applicant is not the one who has worked the hardest but simply the most natively gifted.'[102] Everyday (academic) experience bears this out. Suppose a student comes to a professor to plead for a revision of the low grade he received in a recent examination. He argues that he worked hard, attended class assiduously, and participated energetically, whereas another student who got the highest mark was rude, lazy, and seldom attended class. We might agree that the student who is complaining is more deserving. Suppose all this is true. Should it lead the professor to change the grade? The answer is 'no'; when we grade we (usually, at least) grade on outcome, not effort.[103]

A third major problem with giving the merit principle such a strong moral weight is that to do so appears to ignore the *moral* (though not necessarily the

[97] *DeFunis* v. *Odegaard*, 416 US 312, 317, Douglas J (dissenting opinion).

[98] Gross, *Discrimination in Reverse* (1978) 114.

[99] Cottingham, 'Race and Individual Merit', 55 *Philosophy* 525 at 526 (1980).

[100] Ibid at 527 (emphasis added).

[101] The literature is substantial. For a recent discussion, see Lamont, 'The Concept of Desert in Distributive Justice', 44 *Philosophical Quarterly*, 45 (No. 174, 1994).

[102] Sher, 'Qualifications, Fairness, and Desert', in Bowie (ed.), *Equal Opportunity* (1988) 113 at 118. See also Edwards, *Positive Discrimination, Social Justice, and Social Policy* (1987) 156, who lays heavy stress on the 'moral arbitrariness' of the merit principle, as well as the fact that it is imperfectly applied.

[103] For a similar example pointing to a similar conclusion, see Overlaet, above n 5 at 690.

social) arbitrariness of the distribution of the characteristics that go to make up qualifications in many situations. As Rhode writes, 'Merit is a social construct that reflects a range of factors over which the individual has no control, including natural talent, family background, educational environment, economic resources, and gender-role socialization'.[104] Given that these will arise from genes, or other forms of luck, and may well be significantly influenced by past injustices, why should they bear any normative weight? They are, in Rawls' phrase, arbitrary from a moral point of view.[105] As Young has put it, 'being a member of the "lucky sperm" club confers no moral right to advantage'.[106] Nor is Cottingham's reformulation saved from similar criticisms, given the role which effort plays in building on existing intelligence.

Nevertheless, these arguments may prove too much to be wholly satisfying. Taken to an extreme, they seem to strip us of all our moral capacity, in that there is nothing we do that might not have been different if we had different genes and a different environment. The arguments, then, are perhaps too deterministic to be intuitively attractive.[107] George Sher, however, derives a stronger, more attractive conclusion from arguments similar to Gross and Cottingham. He considers that the 'best-qualified applicants ought to be chosen', not just that they should be seriously considered, but derives this conclusion as follows:

> When we hire by merit, we abstract from all facts about the applicants except their ability to perform well at the relevant tasks. By thus concentrating on their ability to perform, we treat them as agents whose purposeful acts are capable of making a difference in the world. Moreover, by concentrating on abilities that are internally connected to jobs and opportunities that exist to serve independent purposes, we affirm the applicant's involvement in the wider life of the community. For both reasons, selecting by merit is a way of taking seriously the potential agency of both the successful and the unsuccessful applicants. Conversely, when an applicant is selected on some other basis, there is a recognizable if elusive sense in which he and his rivals are not taken seriously. And this suggests that we may justify selection by merit by arguing that persons ought to be taken seriously in the relevant sense.[108]

He goes on to argue that this principle requires the selection of the best-qualified, not just a competently qualified person, because to do otherwise (for example, to seek to reduce underrepresentation by preferentially choosing a person from

[104] Rhode, *Justice and Gender* (1989) 186.

[105] See further, Sunstein, 'The Anticaste Principle', 92 *Michigan Law Review* 2410 at 2437 (1994).

[106] Young, 'Meritocracy Revisited', 31(6) *Society* 87 at 89 (October 1994).

[107] An interesting issue arises, which I do not want to try to resolve here, about what the relationship is between scepticism of Douglas, Gross, and Cottingham, and the justification of criminal punishment. I think I would want to argue that the act that is being punished where a crime has been committed is much more closely linked to the evil we seek to prevent than is the condition we seek to reward with the job we seek to have carried out. We are therefore more likely to argue convincingly that a criminal deserves to be punished than that a person deserves to be hired. For an interesting discussion of the relationship between desert and responsibility, see Feldman, 'Desert: Reconsideration of Some Received Wisdom', *Mind* 104, 413, 63 (1995); Smilansky, 'Responsiblity and Desert: Defending the Connection', *Mind* 105, 417, 157; Feldman, 'Responsibility as a Condition for Desert', *Mind* 105, 417, 165 (1996).

[108] Sher, above n 102 at 119–20.

the underrepresented group) is to risk treating an individual not as 'choosers or doers' but rather as 'mere bearers of needs or claims, as passive links in causal chains, or as an interchangeable specimen of larger groups or classes'.[109] '[O]nly selection by qualification accords all the applicants the respect they are owed as rational agents and . . . under such selection the best-qualified applicant, and he alone, is owed the position.'[110]

But, quite apart from the vagueness of what 'taking someone seriously' involves, what constitutes 'respecting' a person in the context of selecting for a job is notoriously difficult to pin down; it may have more to do with the fairness of the process[111] by which the person is selected, than the end result, a point I return to below. As important, Sher's argument, (put simply, that employing the less well qualified for social reasons is treating people as means rather than ends),[112] seems to prove too much. It is surely the case that in all employment selection decisions we treat individuals, to some extent, as means rather than ends even where we hire the best qualified (in the sense of effort plus credentials), because we are using that person as the means to achieve the efficient carrying out of the job tasks. Why is it less treating someone as a means rather than an end to do that, than preferring someone on the basis of wanting to achieve certain social goals?

A recent discussion by Miller introduces an alternative basis for the proposition that the best-qualified applicant deserves to be given the job. His argument is that if the most qualified person is passed over in preference to a person less well qualified, the first person is the victim of an injustice 'through being prevented from earning rewards commensurate with potential contribution'; she is deprived of the opportunity 'to become deserving'.[113] The argument makes an important assumption, however: that people are rewarded according to their contributions. However, this seems highly questionable, as recent economic analyses have amply demonstrated.[114] The weaker the correlation, the less force his argument has.

B. *Alternative approaches*

Four alternative arguments have been advanced for giving 'merit' some normative weight: we can sum these up as 'merit as a necessary underpinning of non-discrimination', 'merit as productivity', 'merit as qualification', and 'merit as legitimate expectation'. We can illustrate these different uses of 'merit' by discussing briefly the arguments of four authors. The first position is put forward by Alan Goldman; the second is taken by Norman Daniels; the third is taken by Michael Walzer; the fourth is adopted by John Rawls.

109 Ibid at 123–4.
110 Ibid at 124.
111 Compare Fishkin, *Justice, Equal Opportunity, and the Family* (1983) 22, who states the principle of merit as: 'There should be widespread *procedural* fairness in the evaluation of qualifications for positions' (emphasis added).
112 This is also a concern of Sandel, *Liberalism and the Limits of Justice* (1982) 141.
113 Miller, above n 50 at 162.
114 See the literature discussed by McCaffrey, above n 49.

(i) *Underpinning non-discrimination*

Goldman argues that a rule for awarding positions generally by competence is inductively supported by the principle that intentional discrimination against members of certain groups is morally wrong. If, he argues, we can never say that a person has a *prima facie* right to a position, because she is better qualified, how are we able to defend a prohibition on direct discrimination?[115]

But the answer is relatively straight forward: we do not need to base our moral repugnance of direct discrimination on a *right* to obtain a job for which one is best qualified, because there are several other better bases on which to build such a claim, ranging from the need to treat people with respect, through utilitarian justifications (such as efficiency), to considerations of redistributive justice.

(ii) *Productivity*

Daniels' argument is clear: '[C]laims of merit', he writes, 'in the restricted sense of that term relevant to meritocracies, are derived from considerations of efficiency or productivity and will not support stronger notions of desert'.[116] Merit, for Daniels, 'does not derive from having the abilities themselves, but only from the fact that abilities can play a certain social role. We focus on the relevant abilities because of their utility, not because there is something intrinsically meritorious about having them.'[117] The social utility which the merit principle advances, in his view, is productivity. 'To divorce the merit claim from all productivity considerations . . . makes it completely mysterious why job-related abilities are made the basis of merit in the first place.'[118] For Daniels, therefore, 'an individual merits a job if his or her placement in that job is part of an array of maximally productive job assignments. Such a merit claim does not presuppose that any kind of desert claim is present other than what can be derived from productivity considerations. Our obligation to honor a merit claim so derived is only as strong as the *prima facie* obligation to encourage productivity'.[119]

Other implications flow from this approach. First, the approach taken does not necessarily require the best qualified (in the sense of ability plus effort) to be hired. Productivity might not suffer by hiring someone who is qualified, but less well qualified, for example where the 'best qualified' person is so enthusiastic and able that they become frustrated with a hum-drum job.[120] Nor do we expect employers to go to endless lengths to search out the best qualified.[121] Nor will employers generally pay according to the increase or decrease in the individual's marginal productivity because, even if we could measure it, 'the costs of doing

[115] Goldman, *Justice and Reverse Discrimination* (1979) 33.
[116] Daniels, 'Merit and Meritocracy', 7(3) *Philosophy and Public Affairs* 206 at 207 (1978).
[117] Ibid at 210.
[118] Ibid at 211.
[119] Ibid at 213. Cp. Fiss, above n 4 at 241. See also Fallon and Weiler, above n 4 at 15, fn 65.
[120] The extent to which overall productivity might suffer is, of course, an empirical question, and one on which little empirical work has been done. For a controversial preliminary assessment of the evidence of the impact on productivity of affirmative action in the United States, see Herrnstein and Murray, *The Bell Curve* (1994) ch 20.
[121] Epstein, above n 18 at 37–8.

so, combined with the costs of the contracting process itself, would often make such arrangements infeasible'.[122]

Second, Daniels points to considerations other than ability plus effort which may be relevant in assessing productivity gains: 'A better mix of race and sex in such professions as the law, teaching, and medicine might well pay dividends in terms of services rendered to those who would not otherwise get them, inspiration to long-suppressed motivation, the overcoming of racial and sexual stereotypes which are unproductive in other ways, and so on'.[123] As Daniels argues, it is considerably less powerful to say 'An appeal to productivity supports my claim to have that job' than to say 'An appeal to just deserts backs my claim to have a right to that job'.[124]

Though initially somewhat attractive, Daniels' approach may, as he points out himself, backfire on someone supporting affirmative action, or even simple non-discrimination. If productivity is the key reason underpinning the merit principle, then if productivity is reduced by racist or sexist opposition to selecting a person who is black or female, who would otherwise be the most productive person for the job, then the productivity approach to merit 'might play a conservative role, capitulating to existing biases'.[125] Or, as Pitt has asked: 'What if there is clear evidence that all sections of society have more confidence in white male financial advisers?'[126] In so far as it conflicts with considerations of right or justice, therefore, Daniels does not consider that it should have priority.

(iii) *Qualification*

Walzer argues that in many, but not all cases, we should not regard jobs (he refers to them as offices) as capable of being 'deserved'.

> A prize, for example, can be deserved because it already belongs to the person who has given the best performance; it remains only to identify that person. Prize committees are like juries in that they look backward and aim at an objective decision. An office, by contrast, cannot be deserved because it belongs to the people who are served by it, and they or their agents are free to make choices they please. (...) [T]he competition for a particular office is a competition that no particular person deserves (or has a right) to win. Whatever an individual's qualifications, no injustice is done to him if he isn't chosen.[127]

Qualified candidates should, however, be given 'equal consideration', for to do otherwise would fail to take seriously the social meaning of jobs, that is the fact that their allocation involves questions of 'individuality and personal integrity'.[128]

Returning briefly to the public service use of merit, this latter role for merit is strongly represented. Some writers usefully distinguish between a 'merit system'

[122] McCaffery, above n 49 at 606.
[123] Daniels, above n 116 at 214.
[124] Ibid at 216.
[125] Ibid at 214.
[126] Pitt, in Hepple and Szyszczak (eds), *Discrimination: The Limits of Law* (1992) at 291–2.
[127] Walzer, above n 38 at 136.
[128] Ibid at 153.

and a 'merit principle'.[129] The former (the merit system) is the mechanism for achieving a goal which is the latter (the merit principle). Essentially a merit system aims to establish an open selection procedure, combining some sort of announcement of vacancies, and some sort of open competitive evaluation to ensure that candidates have the requisite knowledge and skills. The goal towards which the merit system works is the merit principle, which is the problematic issue which is the subject of our primary consideration. The two are worth distinguishing, however, since any condition or qualification could be openly operated and competitively tested, no matter how contrary to one or other conception of the merit principle, for example, if it was regarded as necessary for a candidate to be well-connected to a particular political party. A merit system in this sense is a useful and supportable way of adhering to the idea of according respect to those who are candidates for employment.

(iv) *Legitimate expectations*

Rawls argues that important, but limited, consequences flow from a course of conduct established by social institutions, concerning how particular goods are distributed. To the extent that social institutions choose people for certain jobs, say, on the basis of certain qualifications, others with those qualifications have a legitimate expectation that the social practice will continue: '. . . the more fortunate have a claim to their better situation; their claims are legitimate expectations established by social institutions, and the community is obligated to meet them'.[130]

Edwards, however, while recognizing the validity of some consequences flowing from the idea of legitimate expectations, gives them the status only of *expectations*. 'They do not give us a right nor even an entitlement to positions, but rather a "reasonable expectation" of being awarded a position under certain sets of circumstances.'[131] This claim is, moreover, a relatively easily defeasible claim, where, for example, the practice which has gained currency is itself unjust.[132] But, more generally, such expectations must surely be defeasible in many other circumstances as well, when, for example, the nature of the job changes, or more 'qualified' persons become available.[133] Two examples come immediately to mind: one is the position of movie stars just after the introduction of the 'talkies' when it was discovered that several had unsuitable speaking voices for the new medium. Surely, they had no legitimate expectations of continued employment. Or take the more recent situation of coal miners where the market for coal has collapsed; surely, they do not have a legitimate expectation of continuing employment.

[129] Best, above n 42 at 56.
[130] Rawls, *A Theory of Justice*, (1971) 103. See also Goldman, *Justice and Reverse Discrimination* (1979) 27–8.
[131] Edwards, above n 33 at 218.
[132] Daniels, above n 116 at 215.
[133] For a useful discussion, see Issacharoff, 'When Substance Mandate's Procedure: *Martin* v *Wilks* and the Risk of Vested Incumbents in Civil Rights Consent Decrees', 77 *Cornell Law Review* 189 at 231–6 (1992).

C. *Assessment*

None of the five models of merit discussed in section 5 identified the status of merit in relation to other concepts. In particular, they did not identify the weight to be accorded a merit argument. This section has considered various arguments which have been thought to underpin merit arguments, each of which gives a somewhat different status and weight to merit arguments. Put rather simplistically, they boil down to two contrasting approaches. On the one hand, there are those (like Goldman and Sher) who regard the merit principle as giving rise to a strong desert-based claim, and thus a strong moral obligation that the 'best qualified' should be awarded the job. But each of the arguments put forward to support this strong claim seems flawed. On the other hand, there are those (like Walzer, Daniels, and Edwards) who, more convincingly,[134] regard the merit principle as essentially justified on utilitarian grounds, providing no strong moral right but giving rise instead only to an obligation to give serious consideration to candidates ranked better under the concept of merit identified, an obligation which is itself capable of being overridden if in conflict with certain other values.

7. *The Virtues and Vices of Merit*

How can we explain the attractiveness of the merit argument to those who support it, and the venom with which its opponents attack it? Two explanations are possible. The first calls into question the *bona fides* of merit's supporters and opponents, viewing them either as using merit as a smoke screen for the continued exclusion of minorities and women from employment, or as covertly attempting to undermine any sense of excellence. To assume that the attraction of merit, or its opposite, lies simply in the bad faith of supporters and opponents would be neither sensible politically, nor honest. For the use of merit arguments do have certain attractive features, as well as clear pitfalls. Both need to be recognized for progress to be made on the appropriate role of merit.

A. *Virtues*

Historically, the merit principle has provided, in model 1, a strong basis on which to counteract cronyism, political favouritism, and direct discrimination in the public service and beyond. To weaken the merit principle might weaken the ability to stave off these evils. But those who support merit on these grounds should not feel that they are committed to merit in any other sense.

Use of a conception of merit (in the sense of model 2 or 3) may be important at some point historically because it indicates recognition by government of an important, if uncertain, moral intuition that fair consideration should be accorded to those seeking employment on an objective, individualized basis. The problem

[134] Cp. Fallon, 'Affirmative Action Based on Economic Disadvantage', 43 *UCLA Law Review* 1913 at 1922 and 1923 (1996).

lies, however, in identifying what the criteria are by which the desire to be 'objective' will be met. Or, even if we agree on those criteria , how to operationalize them.

The use of a conception of merit (particularly model 3) provides a clear link between anti-discrimination practice, and the ideology of some approaches to professional management, and, by providing strong support for such an ideology, establishes an important constituency in favour of anti-discrimination law, and its translation into effective practice. The creation of merit *systems* also provides an important emphasis on openness and transparency in identifying job content, and selection methods.

Publicly identifying anti-discrimination law with the merit principle also creates an identity of interest (and potentially practice) between the private sector and the public service (with its deeply embedded adherence to merit principle rhetoric), and enables the public sector to be seen to be leading the way, which may be of importance in minimizing some opposition from the private sector.

To underestimate these concerns seems wrong-headed. Indeed, the unwillingness of those most hostile to particular conceptions of merit to reject the concept in its entirety, appears to reflect a shared recognition of the appeal of some other conceptions of merit.[135]

B. *Vices*

Equally, however, it merely stokes the fires of suspicion, and generates further allegations of bad faith, for supporters of merit to ignore certain particular features of merit.

In particular, the meaning of merit has been the subject of considerable change over time, as we have seen above, and these changes reflect power struggles in the workplace and society. As Foster has put it, 'Recognizing that institutional standards and norms were developed in the context of the power struggles that have historically existed between certain groups in this society calls into question the assumption that they are neutral or universally constructed'.[136]

Given the range of its possible meanings, merit is open to political manipulation. What sometimes appears to be a model 1 conception of merit, suddenly seems to become transformed into model 2 or model 3, with little or no explanation, or perhaps even recognition, that a crucial move in the argument is being made.[137]

[135] Kennedy, above n 6 at 708: '[W]e just don't believe that it is *real* "merit" that institutions measure. ... This is not rejection of the idea that some work is better than others' (emphasis added). See also p. 720, fn. 30, distinguishing 'valuable' and 'corrupt' meritocratic systems. See also Johnson, above n 6 at 2052, fn 189: '... the *current* meritocratic evaluative model employed by the academy ignores and devalues the unique contributions provided by proponents of the voice of color ...' (emphasis added), and Delgado, above n 6 at 1746: '... cannot accept merit standards *as they are* ... we must fundamentally reevaluate merit standards and the way they are used ...' (emphasis added).

[136] Foster, 'Difference and Equality: A Critical Assessment of the Concept of "Diversity"', (1993) *Wisconsin Law Review* 105 at 157.

[137] An example illustrating movement between the first and second conceptions of merit can be found in the judgment of Judge Schreiber in *Liege* v *Town of Montclair* 13 FEP Cases 1697 (New Jersey Supreme Court) at 1704.

The use of the merit principle at this time rightly engenders suspicion that its introduction is sometimes hypocritical, in that even model 1 was for significant periods breached or ignored.[138] Now that structural change is possible, it might be argued, the importance of the merit principle is 're-discovered' in order to *limit* changes necessary to correct past breaches of the merit principle. The suspicion of the use to which the merit principle is put is strengthened too when we see the extent to which the merit principle (in the sense of models 1 and 3) is not applied consistently. There are significant breaches of these models when the (political) need is perceived to be strong (such as in the case of veterans' preferences), or where common sense dictates otherwise, as in the *bona fide* occupational qualification context.

A legitimate objection to merit arguments also lies in the degree to which merit is used to provide a moral underpinning for the *status quo*. The (unconvincing) linkage that some make between merit and desert, brings a moral, rights-based, flavour to the justification of inequality which is inappropriate and unjustified.[139] To underestimate these concerns about the use to which merit is put also seems wrong-headed.

C. *Persuasive definitions of merit*

The ideology of merit has a central place in American society, and most commentators recognize its popularity in the national imagination. For politicians (whether declared or not) 'merit' is something one must be in favour of; to be against it would be political suicide. But given the wide differences over its meaning and weight, it is open to (indeed positively *invites*) attempts to capture it and use it to shore up one's own political agenda. Not surprisingly, then, merit has become subject to 'persuasive definition'. The question remains, of course, whether there is anything other than a persuasive definition which is possible, whether there is a core conception of merit which is correct. My answer is that there is not.

As some have argued with regard to other concepts, disputes about merit cannot be resolved by analysis of the concept of merit itself. Rather, different conceptions of merit introduce different values external to merit in order to define them. The wide variety of such values and their conflicting nature explain why merit is contested. In other words, adoption of one or other conception of merit (or a decision on the appropriate weight to attach to it) is usually made in the light of other goals and values which are separate from merit itself: how should we view effort as opposed to productivity; how should we balance the interests of the individual and the interests of the organization; what does

[138] Cassese and Pellew, above n 66 at 18–19. Compare Delgado, above n 6 at 1721: 'Merit is what the victors impose'. Indeed, the use of 'merit' criteria to achieve the perpetuation of an elite is not restricted to this context, being considerably more widespread. We should not, for example, assume that the introduction of the merit principle in the public service, for example, was always motivated by laudable principles.

[139] Cp. Sunstein, 'Three Civil Rights Fallacies', 79 *California Law Review* 751 at 759 (1991).

distributive justice require; should we be seeking a colour-blind society, or embrace diversity?

Since we will have different answers to these questions, we will therefore adopt different conceptions of merit. The apparent debate about merit is in reality a series of debates about these other questions of value, not about merit itself. Merit has no one set of conceptual or moral requirements. In the public service employment context merit was, and is, 'a reflection of the times, and its changing nature would suggest that it is not an absolute, static concept but rather an evolving relative one.[140] And the point is true more generally. As Fallon and Weiler argue: '. . . merit is a concept intrinsically bound up with human interests, desires and purposes that are subject to change'.[141] The contexualized nature of merit is apparent not only from the historical change from negative to positive conceptions of merit. It is also apparent from changes in the content of the negative conception itself. The model 1 conception of merit has, in the past, been thought to be consistent with racial, gender, and religious bias of the most egregious and crude types; now it is not. It has been thought consistent with an age bar; now many think it is not (although the issue is controversial). It is still regarded as consistent with a preference for veterans, as we have seen. It is interesting to note, as does Thornton, that despite this significant variation over time in its meaning (or perhaps because of it), '[w]hen the word "merit" appears in legislation regulating public service employment, it is not defined but used as though it were a universal'.[142]

8. *Conclusion*

We can return, now, to where we started: to the relationship between affirmative action and merit. On the basis of the discussions of the use of merit in the past, we can predict that the merit principle is likely to be used for two related, but distinct purposes: as a general justifying aim for employment equality approaches, and as a background constraint on the use of certain methods of pursuing employment equality. If past experience tells us anything, however, it is that merit plays its most controversial, and political, role when it is used as a background constraint. In this context, it would be unsurprising, therefore, if the merit principle continues to play a critical role in responses to affirmative action.

What should we do about the merit principle in this context? In general, I suggest, we should not use the merit principle as shorthand for objections to particular types of affirmative action, unless we are prepared to spend a lot of

[140] Best, above n 42 at 59.

[141] Fallon and Weiler, above n 4 at 168. And this point appears to be a major area of agreement between critics and supporters of merit, compare Kennedy, above n 6 at 733: '[j]udgments of merit are inevitably, culturally and ideologically contingent', with Farber and Sherry, above n 6 at 882: '. . . our understanding of merit can change over time, and certainly has done so'.

[142] Thornton, 'Affirmative Action, Merit and the Liberal State', 2 *Australian Journal of Law and Society* 28 at 31 (1985).

time and effort in explaining and justifying the particular conception of merit adopted, and this is seldom done. If there are five basic conceptions of merit, and (at least) two different weightings are possible of each, simple maths leads to the conclusion that a person might be using a merit argument in one of at least ten different senses. And this is before we get to the issue of how to put it into operation. The problem with much of the political and scholarly debates mentioned earlier, is that despite (or possibly because of) their sound and fury, little of this complexity is actually reflected. On balance, therefore, more is lost than gained by the use of the 'merit principle' in these contexts. The use of the merit principle is also unnecessary, given that it is possible to identify those separate elements which appear to underpin different conceptions, and to discuss these separately, leading to a better focused debate, and consequentially better policy formulation, as indeed the US Supreme Court has done.

It is, however, unlikely that 'merit principle' rhetoric will be driven from political, or scholarly, debate. All that we can strive for, therefore, is that those who do wish to (or, in the case of the civil service, must) adopt the rhetoric of merit (either for or against) should be pressed to identify which model of 'merit' they are using (or defending), why that model is preferable to the other models in current use, what status they attach to the merit conception they are advancing, why that status is being attached, and how they intend to deal with the problems to which their chosen conception of the merit principle appears to give rise. For my guess is that despite (or perhaps *because* of) its centrality to American political discourse,[143] Americans are agreed neither on the definition of merit, nor on the extent to which it is desirable, nor (if it is desirable) on how to make it effective. We, in Europe, should be loath to follow Americans down such a treacherous, and uncertain, road.

[143] Kornhauser, 'Equality, Liberty and a Fair Income Tax', 23 *Fordham Urban Law Journal* 607 at 656 (1996): 'equality based on merit' is 'central to American ideology'.

[11]

REVERSING DISCRIMINATION

Sandra Fredman

REVERSE discrimination, or affirmative action, is inherently controversial. How can it be legitimate for an anti-discrimination policy to include measures which actively discriminate on grounds of race or sex? It is therefore somewhat surprising that it was not until 1995 that the lawfulness of reverse discrimination came before the European Court of Justice for consideration. In the famous *Kalanke*[1] case, the Court was required to judge the lawfulness of the City of Bremen's policy of preferring a woman over an equally qualified man in order to remedy conspicuous under-representation of women in specific job classes. The Court had no hesitation in declaring the policy to be an unlawful breach of the principle of equal treatment of men and women. Far from resolving the matter, the decision has fuelled fierce debate, precipitating the reference to the Court of a second and equally problematic affirmative action case. As the decision in *Marschall* is awaited, a glance across the Atlantic reveals an equally fierce but far more sophisticated and well-established controversy. In a series of cases before the United States Supreme Court, stretching from the well-known *Bakke*[2] case to the decision in the 1995 case of *Adarand v. Pena*,[3] the legitimacy of affirmative action has been tested repeatedly, culminating in the 1996 White House review of positive action. Such turbulence invites further examination of both the philosophical and the strategic dimensions of affirmative action.

Affirmative action denotes the deliberate use of race- or gender-conscious criteria for the specific purpose of benefiting a group which has previously been disadvantaged on grounds of race or gender. Its aims range from providing a specific remedy for invidious discrimination to the more general purpose of increasing the participation of groups which are visibly under-represented in important public spheres such as education, politics or employment. At its most controversial, it requires that individual members of the disadvantaged group be actively preferred over others in the allocation of jobs, university places and other similar benefits.

Given its deliberate use of race- or gender-conscious criteria, it is not surprising that the legitimacy of affirmative action is highly problematic. Much of the century has been spent convincing judges and legislators that race and gender are irrelevant and their use in the allocation of benefits or rights invidious. How then can it be legitimate to permit such use for purportedly remedial purposes? It will be argued in this article that the

---

1 Case C–450/93 *Kalanke v. Freie Hansestadt Bremen* [1995] E.C.R. I–3051; [1996] I.C.R. 314 (E.C.J).

2 *University of California v. Bakke* 438 U.S. 265 (1978).

3 *Adarand Constructors Inc. v. Pena* 115 S. Ct. 2097 (1995).

argument against affirmative action only seems unassailable because it is based on deep-seated but unspoken assumptions. Once these assumptions are exposed, it becomes possible to mount a convincing rebuttal. However, this is not, as is often assumed, the end of the argument. Even when the theoretical basis is established, it is still necessary to justify affirmative action on a strategic level. The mere presence of a handful of women or black people in positions of power is not necessarily of assistance in reversing discrimination against women or blacks in society in general. Thus it is crucial that affirmative action programmes be capable of justification in terms both of costs and of benefits. This article is in three parts. Part I deals with the theoretical debate; Part II considers the legal responses in the United Kingdom, European Union and United States; while Part III assesses the arguments and canvasses some of the strategic issues involved.

I. The Theoretical Debate

Responses to the controversy about reverse discrimination can be grouped into three broad camps. The "symmetrical" approach rejects reverse discrimination, the "substantive" approach largely supports it, and the "equal opportunities" approach uses arguments from each of the other two camps to permit positive action within strict limits.[4] Each will be dealt with in turn.

The "symmetrical" approach can be simply stated. On this view, the moral prohibition against using sex or race as a criterion for decision-making applies with equal strength regardless of whether it is directed against or in favour of a disadvantaged group. As the U.S. Supreme Court Justice Powell declared in *Bakke*: "The guarantee of equal protection cannot mean one thing when applied to one individual and something else when applied to an individual of another colour."[5] Discrimination on grounds of race is odious even if directed against a group that has never been the subject of governmental discrimination.[6] Notably, Justice Thomas, the only black judge on the Court, emphatically shares this view.[7] This symmetry is complemented by a vehement individualism. According to Justice Scalia, the view that there can be a "creditor or debtor race" is entirely alien to the focus in the constitution on the individual.[8] Moreover, argues Abram, any attempt to move from the individual to the group is bound to degenerate into a "crude political struggle between groups

[4] See also R. Fallon and P. Weiler "Firefighters v. Stotts: Conflicting Models of Racial Justice" in C. McCrudden (ed.), *Anti-Discrimination Law* (1991), pp. 140 *et seq.*

[5] *Bakke*, *supra*, n. 2.

[6] *Wygant v. Jackson Board of Education* 106 S. Ct. 1842 (1986).

[7] *Adarand*, *supra*, n. 3 at p. 2119.

[8] *Ibid.*

seeking favoured status."[9] Such a stance is further justified by reference to the principle of state neutrality. "Without doing violence to the principles of equality before the law and neutral decision-making, we simply cannot interpret our laws to support both colour blindness for some citizens and colour-consciousness for others."[10]

As the above discussion demonstrates, the "symmetrical" approach rests on three basic propositions. First, justice is characterised as an *a priori* concept, formulated independently of its historical or political contexts, and unaffected by the distribution of benefits and disadvantages in any particular society. The principle that it is unjust to discriminate on grounds of race or sex therefore applies in the same way regardless of whether the discrimination causes detriment to a disadvantaged or an advantaged group. Secondly, the symmetrical model asserts the primacy of the individual. This individualism has two dimensions: merit and fault. The "merit" principle requires that an individual be treated according to her or his own personal characteristics. Merit is assumed to be objective and quantifiable, to which race or gender are deemed irrelevant. The fault principle requires that individuals should only be responsible for their own actions, not for others. Thus no individual should be required to compensate for social ills which are not directly her or his fault. Affirmative action contravenes both merit and fault, according to this argument, by excluding a white person or a man from a benefit on grounds unrelated to merit and even though he or she is not responsible for the history of discrimination against black people or women. Finally, the "symmetrical" approach assumes that the state should be neutral as between its citizens, favouring no one above any other. The proposition that a group should be favoured on account of gender or race, even in a remedial sense, is therefore anathema. State neutrality also entails a state which intervenes as little as possible in the "free market." In its revived neo-liberal form, this version of state neutrality is used to oppose the use by the state or other public bodies of their contractual powers within the market to pursue public policies such as the elimination of discrimination. This necessarily outlaws the use of contract compliance or "set-asides" of state funds for the purpose of aiding minorities or women.

All three of these propositions are challenged by the "substantive" model. First, it is argued, formal justice substitutes the ideal for the reality. Because race and sex ought not to affect the individual, it is assumed that they do not. However, it is impossible to deny the continuing effects of discrimination against ethnic minorities or women in society. Justice therefore necessitates an asymmetric vision. As Dworkin argues, "The

[9] M. Abram, "Affirmative Action: Fair Shakers and Social Engineers" (1986) 99 Harvard L. R. 1312 at p. 1321.

[10] *ibid.*, p. 1319.

difference between a general racial classification that causes further disadvantage to those who have suffered from prejudice and a classification framed to help them is morally significant."[11] Nor can it be assumed that a formal, ostensibly non-interventionist notion of justice has no distributive effects: the maintenance of the status quo with all its uneven allocations of wealth is itself a distributive effect. The substantive approach is therefore based on an openly substantive and distributive notion of justice.

Similarly, the substantive approach rejects as misleading the aspirations of individualism. Certainly, the value of the individualistic principle should not be ignored: it is only because of a commitment to freeing individuals from status ascriptions that sexism and racism could eventually be exposed as morally and politically offensive. However, the ideal should not be confused with present reality, in which status ascriptions play a central role in determining an individual's opportunities. The substantive approach therefore insists that fairness take into account the extent to which opportunities are determined by individuals' social and historical status, which includes their race and gender. This argument extends to both merit and fault. In portraying merit as objective and quantifiable, it is argued, opponents of affirmative action are concealing the inherent subjectivity of decision-making processes and therefore making it difficult to root out prejudicial assumptions.[12] Where a "merit"-based process systematically excludes black people or women, it is necessary to reconsider the criteria themselves. For example, a stress on formal qualifications and work experience rather than acquired knowledge or informal experience is likely to undervalue women's skills. Dworkin goes further and permits merit to be redefined in order openly to include references to race or gender. If a black skin will enable a doctor to do a medical job better than a white skin, then that black skin validly counts as part of the calculation of "merit."[13] The fault principle is also seen to be flawed. Discrimination, on this view, is not merely a result of personal fault; it is deeply embedded in the structure of society. Thus the responsibility for correcting institutional discrimination should not lie only with those to whom fault or causality can be attributed: all members of the privileged class share the duty and may be expected to bear some of the cost of remedy. As the U.S. Supreme Court stated in *Fullilove v. Klutznick*, "As part of this nation's dedication to eradicating race discrimination, innocent persons may be called upon to bear some of the burden of the remedy."[14]

Finally, the "substantive" approach challenges the possibility of a neutral state. Rejecting the "symmetrical" vision of the state as separate

[11] R. Dworkin, *A Matter of Principle* (1985), 314.

[12] Dworkin, *supra*, at p. 299, B. Hepple "Discrimination and Equality of Opportunity—Northern Irish Lessons" (1990) 10 O.J.L.S. 408.

[13] Dworkin, *supra*, n. 11 at p. 299.

[14] 448 U.S. 448; 100 S. Ct. 2758 (1980).

from society with its current set of power relations, proponents of the "substantive" approach view the state as an emanation of the democratic process, the aim of which is to function as a conduit for or resolution of the cross-currents of social power. A government cannot, by definition, be neutral: a policy of non-intervention in a society which is rooted in discrimination inevitably favours the dominant groups by supporting the status quo. Similarly, the proposition that the state should not interfere with the "free" market is belied by experience. Thus the Thatcher government, committed as it was to minimalist state, saw no contradiction in the view that in order to "protect" the free market from contract compliance strategies, it was justified in legislating to limit local authorities' freedom of contract within the market.[15] The "substantive" approach therefore maintains that the state has a duty to act positively to correct the results of discrimination.

The approach based on "equal opportunities" is less clearly delineated. This model rejects a purely formal view of justice, recognising that certain distributive factors need to be considered. Its central tenet, therefore, is that true equality cannot be achieved if individuals begin the race from different starting points. This model also departs from the narrow individualism of the symmetrical approach, acknowledging the extent to which an individual's life chances are distorted by structural discrimination based on group membership. An "equal opportunities" approach therefore permits sex- or race-based policies if tailored to the purpose of equalising the starting point. It is, however, at this point that the traditional notions of neutrality, symmetry and the primacy of the individual reassert themselves. Once individuals enjoy equality of opportunity, it is argued, the problem of institutional discrimination has been overcome, and fairness demands that they be treated on the basis of their individual qualities, without regard to sex or race. This model therefore specifically rejects policies which aim to correct imbalances in the workforce by quotas or targets whose aim is one of equality of outcome.

It should be noted at this point that the metaphor of equal starting points is deceptively simple, possibly explaining why proponents of this model rarely spend much time defining "equality of opportunity." Is equality of opportunity merely a procedural requirement, which dictates changes of procedure intended to promote the desired outcome, but with no guarantee that this would in fact be the result?[16] Or does it, as Williams proposes, entail the far more substantive demand that persons from all sections of society have an equal chance of satisfying the criteria for access to a particular social good?[17] There are striking practical differences in these

[15] See Local Government Act 1988.

[16] See J. Waldron in S. Guest and A. Milne (eds.), *Equality and Discrimination* (1985), 97.

[17] Bernard Williams, "The Idea of Equality" in P. Laslett and W. G Runciman, *Philosophy, Politics and Society* (2nd ser., 1965) 110 at pp. 125–126.

abstract formulations, both in terms of their impact on disadvantage and the intensity of necessary state intervention and resource allocation. At their narrowest, procedural requirements demand only the removal of specific obstacles which inappropriately restrict or discourage participation by women or minority groups in certain jobs or positions.[18] Such measures have few resource implications for the state but make correspondingly little impact on the overall problem. For example, a requirement of high school qualifications for an unskilled job could be challenged if it excluded a high proportion of black people who have been discriminatorily denied education. However, this would do nothing to enhance the position of poorly qualified members of minority groups applying for skilled jobs which genuinely require high school qualifications. Similarly, the removal of demand-side obstacles to women's employment do nothing to change the underlying division of power within the family which leaves women with the primary responsibility for child care. A more proactive but still procedural version of an equal opportunities policy would include "outreach" measures, or measures requiring active encouragement of under-represented groups to apply for jobs or training places.[19] However, these, too, fail genuinely to equalise the starting points. Although they might overcome the "chill" factor and remove nepotistic practices and "old boy" networks, outreach measures would not increase the overall number of qualified applicants, or indeed the success rate of qualified applicants from under-represented groups.

Thus none of these measures would fulfil Williams's criterion for equality of opportunity, namely that all sections of the population have an equal chance of satisfying the grounds considered appropriate for the good. One of the main reasons is that, once the starting points are equalised, priority is given to the right of the individual to be treated according to her or his merit. Yet little attention is paid to the definition of merit. Even if prevailing notions of merit are accepted, one is not supplying genuine equality of opportunity if one applies this criterion to people who have been deprived of the opportunity to acquire "merit."[20] It is clear, therefore, that a thoroughgoing policy of equalising opportunities in fact requires a level of state intervention and resource allocation far beyond what most proponents of the equal opportunities model would envisage, including properly resourced education and training programmes,[21] investment in child-care facilities, and guarantees of flexible working opportunities available both to the mother and the father. As Williams argues, a system of allocation will fall short of equality of opportunity if the allocation in fact works out disproportionately between different sections of society, if

[18] See, *e.g.* Fair Employment (Northern Ireland) Act 1989 ("F.E.A. 1989"), s.58(1)(b).

[19] See, *e.g.* F.E.A. 1989, s.58(1)(a).

[20] Hepple, *supra*, n. 12 at p. 411.

[21] On Race Relations Act 1976, ss.37–38, see below.

this is because of a disadvantage which could be removed by further reform or social action.[22] The attempt, therefore, by proponents of an equal opportunities approach to combine a recognition of the limitations of formal justice with an individualistic, non-results oriented notion of equality inevitably yields a weak procedural compromise.

II. THE LEGAL RESPONSE

The arguments rehearsed above have been part of a lively debate in various jurisdictions about the legality of reverse discrimination. But the dominant model has differed widely as between countries, with U.K. raçe and sex discrimination law displaying strongly "symmetrical" tendencies, the European Community largely relying on an "equal opportunities" model, and the United States displaying the most sophisticated versions of both the "symmetrical" and the "substantive" models. Each of these will be examined in turn. I shall also discuss briefly the Northern Ireland Fair Employment Act which is a fascinating hybrid.

1. *The United Kingdom: the dominance of symmetry*

The pre-eminence of the symmetrical approach in race and sex discrimination legislation in the United Kingdom is clearly reflected in the House of Lords case of *James v. Eastleigh Borough Council.*[23] In this case, a man of 61 complained of unlawful discrimination on the grounds that he was denied concessionary rates for leisure facilities available to women of his age. This was because such concessions were only available when the individual reached state pensionable age, which was 65 for men and 60 for women. His claim was upheld. According to a majority of the House of Lords, the simple question to be considered was whether the complainant would have received the same treatment from the defendant "but for" his or her sex. In answering this question, the majority held, an affirmative answer was "inescapable." This line of reasoning explicitly relies on a formal notion of justice, abstracted from the social power relations within which it operates. Thus, Lord Ackner declared, "the reason why the policy was adopted can in no way affect or alter the fact that . . . men were to be treated less favorably than women, and were to be so treated on the ground of, *i.e.* because of their sex."[24] This can be contrasted with the substantive notion of justice expressed in the dissenting judgment of Lord Griffiths. In his view, concessions to persons of pensionable age were made available because such persons are almost always less well off than when in employment and less able to afford leisure and travel facilities. If women

[22] Williams, *supra*, n. 17 at p. 127.
[23] [1990] 2 A.C. 751.
[24] *James v. Eastleigh Borough Council*, *supra*, n. 23 at p. 769.

were in that position earlier than men, they required concessions earlier. Thus, he concluded, the reason for differential treatment was not the difference in sex, but the difference in economic well-being. Nor did he consider that the symmetrical result was dictated by the wording of the statute[25]: "What I do not accept is that an attempt to redress the result of that unfair act of discrimination by offering free facilities to those disadvantaged by the earlier act of discrimination is, itself, necessarily discriminatory 'on the grounds of sex'."[26]

While the effects of differential pension ages are now being dealt with,[27] the implications of the symmetrical principle are being felt in other arenas. Possibly the most important concerns the serious under-representation of women in positions of power within the decision-making process. The Labour Party decided to address the gross gender imbalance in the House of Commons by permitting women-only shortlists for Parliamentary selection as Labour Party candidates in a limited number of constituencies.[28] However, the symmetrical approach soon stifled this attempt. On a complaint by two men who wished to be considered as candidates in three such constituencies, an industrial tribunal struck down the policy as unlawful sex discrimination.[29] The case is notable for the absence of any of the sophisticated arguments on reverse discrimination found in other jurisdictions. The tribunal regarded the matter as conclusively decided by the "simple" answer to the "simple" test of whether the complainant would have received the same treatment but for his sex. "It is obvious direct discrimination on grounds of sex."[30] Instead, the main argument centred on whether the tribunal had jurisdiction over this issue. The tribunal confidently assumed jurisdiction under section 13 of the Sex Discrimination Act 1975, which makes it unlawful for an authority or body to discriminate on the grounds of sex in the terms on which it confers an authorisation or qualification needed to engage in a particular profession or trade. It went on to declare that the long experience of tribunals in employment cases was sufficient to dispel any doubts about their capability to adjudicate this case. However, it is doubtful whether an issue of such constitutional importance should be adjudicated by an industrial tribunal at all: it seems unlikely that section 13 was ever intended to include eligibility for party parliamentary candidature. Instead, the case should have proceeded by judicial review, with the court examining whether the response of the Labour Party was *Wednesbury* unreasonable in the light of the facts that women constitute less than 10 per cent of Members of Parliament; that

---

25 Sex Discrimination Act 1975, s.1(1)(*a*).

26 *James v. Eastleigh Borough Council*, *supra*, n. 23 at p. 768.

27 Pensions Act 1995, s.126.

28 50 per cent of constituencies which were either (i) marginal; (ii) new or (iii) where the sitting Labour M.P. was not standing at the next election.

29 *Jepson v. Labour Party* [1996] I.R.L.R. 116.

30 *ibid.*, at p. 117.

the male complainants were free to stand as independent candidates in the relevant constituencies, or apply for shortlisting in a large number of constituencies which did not maintain women-only shortlists, and that a woman applying in one of the ostensibly mixed constituencies stood little chance of gaining the candidature.

The stress on an abstract, formal notion of justice in the United Kingdom is complemented by an equivalent emphasis on individualism. This emerges primarily in response to attempted reformulations of the merit principle to take account of the specific needs of disadvantaged groups. The legislation contains a window of opportunity whereby merit could be redefined in this way: race is a "genuine occupational qualification" where, *inter alia*, the "holder of that job provides persons of that racial group with personal services promoting their welfare and those services can most effectively be provided by a person of that racial group."[31] The courts have permitted a limited redefinition of merit under this section, upholding the right of a community under-fives nursery to reserve one of five nursery worker posts to a worker of Afro-Caribbean origin with personal awareness of Caribbean culture,[32] the aim being to help in maintaining the cultural awareness of children of Afro-Caribbean origin at the nursery and to provide a link with their parents. However, any further incursions into the merit principle were rejected by the Court of Appeal in *London Borough of Lambeth v. Commission for Racial Equality.*[33] The case concerned a challenge of the council's decision to reserve two out of five managerial posts within its housing benefits department to applicants of Asian or Afro-Caribbean origin. This was justified on the grounds that over half of the tenants in Lambeth were of Afro-Caribbean or Asian origin, and that the appointment of two managers from these groups would be the most effective means of providing for the needs and experience of black people. In the Court of Appeal, Balcombe L.J. unequivocally dismissed the view that one of the two main purposes of the Race Relations Act was to promote positive action to benefit racial groups. Apart from the specific provisions permitting discriminatory training (see below), the purpose of the Act was solely to render acts of racial discrimination unlawful.

The final characteristic of the "symmetrical" model, the assertion of the neutrality of the state, is most apparent in the context of the controversy over the use by public bodies of their financial and contractual powers to further equal opportunities for women and blacks. Although contract compliance has chiefly been used for the purposes of advancing fair wages and promoting freedom of association, receiving official endorsement by

---

31 Race Relations Act 1976, s.5(2)(*d*). A similar exception applies in the case of sex: see Sex Discrimination Act 1975, s.7(2)(*e*).

32 *Tottenham Green Under Fives' Centre v. Marshall* [1989] I.R.L.R. 147, E.A.T.

33 [1990] I.C.R. 768, CA.

successive governments up to 1979,[34] it was also beginning to be used in the discrimination field in the early 1980s. However, since 1979 (and with the notable exception of the Northern Ireland Fair employment legislation), Conservative governments have actively expressed the familiar symmetrical argument that the state should not use its contractual powers to advance social policies in favour of particular groups, even if those groups have been systematically disadvantaged because of their race or sex. Hence, provisions included in the 1988 Local Government Act were expressly "designed to prevent abuses of the contractual process."[35] Among these is a specific proscription of attempts to promote equal opportunities for women by inclusion of relevant terms in local authority contracts,[36] with only a limited exception permitting the furtherance of equal opportunities on racial grounds.[37] Local authorities are not even permitted to use their contractual powers to enforce the law: only the remedies specified in the Act itself are permitted, however weak. This is evidenced by *R. v. London Borough of Islington, ex p. Building Employers Confederation*,[38] in which the Divisional Court struck down as unlawful a clause in the model contract issued by Islington specifying that any contractor should comply with the Sex Discrimination Act 1975.[39]

Despite the strict, even myopic, adherence to the symmetrical model, United Kingdom legislation does make two small but important gestures supporting positive action. First, in a provision which comes close to a substantive approach, the Sex Discrimination Act expressly permits trade unions, employers' organisations or professional organisations to reserve seats on an elected executive for persons of one sex where this is necessary to secure a "reasonable lower limit to the number of members of that sex serving on the body."[40] Secondly, some credence is given to the advancement of equal opportunities, by permitting a degree of sex- or race-conscious remedial action in training. If there are comparatively few or no members of one sex or racial group doing a particular type of work in Britain or in any particular area of Britain, it is not unlawful to reserve access to training facilities to members of that group to help equip them for that work. Similarly, measures encouraging an under-represented group to take advantage of opportunities for doing that work are declared to be lawful.[41] Finally, it is not unlawful to give specific training facilities to

[34] For a detailed discussion see S. Fredman and G. Morris, *The State as Employer* (1989), pp. 454–474.

[35] Nicholas Ridley, Secretary of State for the Environment in H.C. Deb., Vol 119, col. 86 (July 6, 1987).

[36] Local Government Act 1988, s.17(5)(a).

[37] Local Government Act 1988, s.18(2).

[38] [1989] I.R.L.R. 382, DC.

[39] "[The contractor] shall at all times comply with s.6(1)(*a*) and (*c*) [no discrimination in selection for employment] and (2) (*b*) [dismissal or other detriment] of the Sex Discrimination Act 1975."

[40] Sex Discrimination Act 1975 ("S.D.A. 1975"), s.49.

[41] S.D.A. 1975, ss.47, 48 (as amended by S.D.A. 1986, s.4.); Race Relations Act 1976, ss.37, 38.

those who are in special need of training because they have been fully engaged in family responsibilities.[42] Although these provisions provide a welcome break from the symmetrical approach, they also demonstrate the narrowness of the notion of equality of opportunity they espouse. Thus the permission to use positive action does not extend to the actual offer of a job or promotion. Nor is it permissible to offer gender-conscious training to existing employees.[43] Moreover, the measures are merely permissive rather than mandatory, and carry no commitment to government resourcing.

2. *The European Community: equal opportunities*

The outlines of an equal opportunities model are clearly visible in the Equal Treatment Directive.[44] According to article 2(4), the Directive "shall be without prejudice to measures to promote equal opportunity for men and women, in particular by removing existing inequalities which affect women's opportunities". This is backed up by the recognition that "existing legal provisions on equal treatment, which are designed to afford rights to individuals, are inadequate for the elimination of all existing inequalities unless parallel action is taken by governments, both sides of industry and other bodies concerned, to counteract the prejudicial effect on women in employment which arise from social attitudes, behaviour and structures."[45]

It has, however, been left to the judiciary to fill in the contours of the model. Early indications were strongly symmetrical. Thus in *Integrity*,[46] Advocate General Jacobs insisted that the principle of equal treatment "requires all discrimination on the grounds of sex to be abolished. Member States cannot therefore justify inequalities of treatment on the basis that the provisions at issue are favourable to women."[47] This was not, however, determinative of the issue: the case was concerned with the Social Security Directive,[48] which does not include an exception for equal opportunities, and the Court did not address the issue directly. *Kalanke*[49] was therefore the first explicit judicial statement on the issue. The case concerned the "tie-break" policy pursued by the City of Bremen whereby, if a man and a woman with the same qualifications applied for promotion, the woman was to be given priority if women were under-represented in that grade. When a man was passed over for a job in favour of an equally qualified woman in pursuance of this policy, he complained that he had been

42 S.D.A. 1975, s.47(3).

43 *ibid.*, s.47(4).

44 Directive 76/207 of February 9, 1976, [1976] O.J. L39/40.

45 Third recital to the preamble to Council Recommendation 84/635 of December 13, 1984, [1984] O.J. L331/34.

46 Case 373/89 *"Integrity" v. Nadine Rouvray* [1991] I.R.L.R. 176.

47 At p. 178.

48 Directive 79/7 of January 10, 1979 ([1979] O.J. L6/24).

49 *Supra*, n. 1.

discriminated against on the grounds of sex. Although the German Federal Labour Court (Bundesarbeitgericht) was willing to permit such a policy, the E.C.J. struck it down on the grounds of breach of the Equal Treatment Directive.

The decision epitomises the procedural version of an equal opportunities model. While recognising the limits of formal equality, the Court firmly set its face against substantive or results-oriented equality by focusing on the individual. Thus, the Court held, it is permissible to take measures which give an advantage to women with a view to improving their ability to compete equally with men in the labour market. However, this does not legitimate measures which depart from the principle of individual merit. "National rules which guarantee women absolute and unconditional priority for appointment or promotion go beyond promoting equal opportunities and overstep the limits of the exception in Article 2(4) of the Directive."[50] Substantive equality, or equality of results, is anathema, unless it is a natural result of equal opportunities. "In so far as it seeks to achieve equal representation of men and women in all grades and levels within a department, such a system substitutes for equality of opportunity as envisaged in Article 2(4) the equality of result which is only to be arrived at by providing such equality of opportunity."[51]

Advocate General Tesauro goes even further than the Court in stressing the primacy of the individual. "In the final analysis must each individual's right not to be discriminated against on grounds of sex . . . yield to the rights of the disadvantaged group, in this case, women, in order to compensate for the discrimination suffered by that group in the past?"[52] Such a formulation of the problem makes it inevitable that the answer be in the negative. The attainment of numerical equality, he concludes, violates the right of each individual to equal treatment. In any event, on his view, equality of results will remain illusory unless it is a natural consequence of equal opportunity measures.

There are two main problems with the *Kalanke*[53] approach. First, it assumes that there is a clear-cut and principled distinction between equality of opportunity and equality of results. The Advocate General took the view that measures aimed at removing obstacles preventing women from pursuing the same results on equal terms were legitimate, whereas measures giving them priority in attaining those results were not. The very fact that two candidates had equal qualifications indicated that they had had equal opportunities. No more was required by the Directive. However, there is a complex interaction between opportunities and results. The U.K. legislation makes specific provision for women-only training schemes.

[50] *Supra*, n. 1, para. 22; p. I–3078.
[51] *Supra*, n. 1, para. 23, p. I–3078.
[52] *Supra*, n. 1, para. 7. p. I–3057.
[53] *Supra*, n. 1.

Whereas these look like "equality of opportunities" strategies from the perspective of the job applicant, they are clearly "equality of results" strategies from the perspective of the training applicant. It is quite possible that a woman applicant only attained her equal qualifications as a result of results-oriented strategies at the training level.

The second problem with the *Kalanke* approach is that no attempt is made to consider the meaning of individual merit. Furthermore, even if merit is accepted as an objective distinguishing factor, it fails to yield an answer in cases where both parties competing for the particular job have, by definition, equal merit. Kalanke had no greater right to be selected than the woman; and there was thus no question of an "innocent" person suffering detriment on the grounds of his sex. In such cases, a choice can only be made on the basis of a criterion not related to merit. It is clearly desirable to eliminate traditional "secondary criteria", such as seniority, from the consideration of merit. But these would be eliminated by the provisions on indirect discrimination. In holding that gender cannot be used to tip the balance where merit is genuinely equal, the Court seems to imply that a random selection, such as spinning a coin, would be preferable to the social policy of achieving balanced representation of the sexes.

In attempting to salvage the Community's active affirmative action policy, the Commission sought to limit the *Kalanke* decision to cases where the preference for women was rigid and left no scope for consideration of individuals concerned. On its view, affirmative action programmes remained valid provided the preference was not automatic.[54] This view is at present being tested in the *Marschall* case,[54a] in which a requirement that equally qualified women be preferred to men was softened by a proviso allowing exceptions if "reasons specific to another candidate predominate". At the time of writing, the Court had yet to make a decision on the case. However, the attempt to circumscribe *Kalanke* on narrow technical grounds was given short shrift by Advocate General Jacobs in his opinion on *Marschall*. In substance, he argued, the rule at issue was no different from that in *Kalanke*: both aimed to promote equality of result rather than equality of opportunity, and only the latter was permitted by article 2(4). Moreover, the distinction between opportunity and result, was, in his view, clear. The proviso made no difference: not only was it too vague to be useful, it could itself function as a pretext for the reintroduction of discriminatory criteria such as seniority. Given his continued adherence to a strongly individualistic perspective—he asserts that the protection of the individual is the central concern of the Directive—it is not surprising that a results-oriented perspective is anathema. It remains to be seen whether the Court will accept this view.

---

[54] Proposal for a Council Directive amending Directive 76/207, [1996] O.J. C179/8.
[54a] Case C-409/95.

3. *Fair employment and Northern Ireland: equal opportunity or substantive justice*

Northern Ireland legislation promoting fair employment differs in crucial respects from U.K. sex and race discrimination provisions, instead incorporating a hybrid of all three of the approaches described above. The Fair Employment (Northern Ireland) Act 1989 is clearly symmetrical in the sense that its provisions for fair employment apply equally to Protestants as to Catholics. However, it moves beyond formal justice. Its main aim is to promote "fair participation in employment",[55] a term which, although "remarkably indeterminate"[56] and nowhere defined in the statute itself, is openly result-oriented. Indeed, one of the key motivations for its enactment was to reduce the striking differences in unemployment levels between Catholic and Protestants in Northern Ireland.[57] Moreover the "lawful pursuance of affirmative action" is specifically exempted from the principle of equality.[58] Similarly, the Act moves beyond individualism. Most conspicuous is the departure from fault: the employer is made responsible for promoting fair participation simply where disparities are apparent even though there is no proof that the employer was guilty of unlawful discrimination. The Act prescribes compulsory monitoring by employers of the composition of their workforces,[59] followed up by periodic reviews to ascertain whether members of each community are enjoying fair participation in employment in the employer's concern.[60] Where it appears to the employer that members of a particular community are not enjoying fair participation, the employer must determine what (if any) affirmative action would be reasonable and appropriate.[61] Fair participation is not available as a right of any individual, but only to members of the Protestant and Catholic communities.[62] Finally, the statute deviates from the notion of a neutral state. In marked contrast to the aversion to contract compliance as a remedial measure for race and sex discrimination, the Act explicitly provides that public authorities refrain from contracting with employers who are found to be in default of various provisions under the Act.[63]

Given that the Act has clearly moved beyond the first model, does it fall within the second ("substantive") or the third ("equal opportunities")

[55] *E.g.* F.E.A. 1989, ss.31(1), 32(5), 36(1)(c).

[56] C. McCrudden "Affirmative Action and Fair Participation: Interpreting the Fair Employment Act 1989" (1992) 21 I.L.J. 170 at p. 176.

[57] Catholics were more than twice as likely to be unemployed as Protestants with the same educational qualifications in 1991. (Fair Employment Commission, *The Key Facts: Religion and Community Background in Northern Ireland* (1995)).

[58] F.E.A. 1989, s.20(3).

[59] F.E.A. 1989, s.27. The duty is confined to employers employing more than 10 employees (25 in the first two years of operation of the Act) and all public employers: see sections 23 and 26.

[60] s.31(1).

[61] s.31(2)(3).

[62] McCrudden, *supra*, n. 56 at p. 181.

[63] F.E.A. 1989, s.41.

approaches? There are some visible gestures in the direction of a substantive approach, most notably the central role given to affirmative action.[64] However, closer examination places the Act squarely within the equal opportunities model. Its explicit aim is to promote equal opportunity[65]; which in turn is defined primarily procedurally, in the sense of being given equal consideration for a range of benefits, including jobs and training.[66] Similarly, "affirmative action" refers primarily to procedural changes, such as the adoption of practices encouraging participation.[67] Thus the obligation is confined to opening the relevant doors, rather than ensuring that disadvantaged groups are in a position to reach the doorway. This is underscored by the clear priority given to the merit principle: in all cases, "due allowance [must be] made for any material difference in ... suitability."[68] As Hepple perceptively comments: "We know ... that there is a connection between lack of educational and skill qualifications and belonging to the Catholic community. The appeal to 'merit' must appear disingenuous to members of the disadvantaged community who are rejected as 'unsuitable'."[69]

Nevertheless, the Act's regulatory scheme, requiring proactive steps to be taken by employers to correct imbalances in the workforce, has the potential to yield more substantive results than a simple exhortation to provide equal opportunities coupled with sanctions limited to proven acts of discrimination. Its emphasis on outreach measures and encouragement of applicants from different communities is particularly appropriate in addressing segregation of working places and high levels of sectarian harassment.[70] The Act has certainly yielded some concrete results: by March 1995, 4,062 private sector firms and 110 specified public bodies were registered, representing about 70 per cent of those in employment in Northern Ireland.[71] The Commission had sought written agreements to affirmative action programmes from 14 large private sector concerns.[72] Notably, these programmes were largely in firms in which Catholics were under-represented.[73] Moreover, the Catholic share of the workforce increased by about 2.4 per cent between 1990 and 1994 although the causal connection with the FEA is not easy to establish.[74]

[64] ss.1(2), 31(2), s.36.

[65] See Preamble. This aim is consistent with that recommended by the Standing Advisory Commission on Human Rights, *Religious Discrimination and Equality of Opportunity in Northern Ireland, Report on Fair Employment*, Cm. 237 (1987).

[66] F.E.A. 1989, s.20.

[67] s.58(1).

[68] s.20(2).

[69] Hepple, *supra*. n. 12 at p. 413.

[70] *Equal Opportunities Review* 70 (1996), p. 11.

[71] Fair Employment Commission, *Fifth Annual Report* (1993–1994).

[72] Fair Employment Commission, *Sixth Annual Report* (1994–1995).

[73] *Equal Opportunities Review* 62 (1995), p. 11.

[74] R. Cooper, "Fair Employment Review in 1996", (1996) 65 *Equal Opportunities Review* 14.

4. *The United States of America: "Symmetry" v. "Substance"*

It is in the United States that the debate has been most sophisticated. While a strong contingent of Supreme Court judges remain faithful adherents of the symmetrical stance, there are a large number of cases in which proponents of the substantive model have carried the day. Cases in this category are characterised by a preference for asymmetric, substantive justice; a rejection of individualism; and an explicit endorsement of the social responsibilities of a positive, non-neutral state.

It was the District Courts which quickly perceived that if cases of proven discrimination were to receive an effective remedy, affirmative action was essential. The trend therefore began with court-ordered affirmative action programmes (including reverse discrimination) prescribed as a remedy in cases of proven discrimination. This approach was endorsed by the Supreme Court first in respect of Title VII,[75] and then, in respect of the Equal Protection Clause. Thus in *U.S. v. Paradise*,[76] on a finding that the Alabama Department of Public Safety had for four decades systematically excluded blacks from employment as state troopers, the Supreme Court upheld a District Court order that 50 per cent of promotions should go to blacks (provided sufficient numbers were qualified) until black troopers constituted a quarter of each rank.

Similarly, there have been significant departures from individualism. Thus court-ordered reverse discrimination need not be restricted to the victim. Non-victims may also be beneficiaries provided they are members of a group previously suffering from invidious discrimination.[77] In addition, the Supreme Court soon began to accept voluntarily instituted affirmative action programmes, despite the lack of proven fault on the part of the employer. Instead, the Court has only required sufficient evidence of imbalances and segregation for which the employer appears responsible.[78] This approach is exemplified in *Johnson v. Santa Clara*,[79] a case which is strikingly similar on its facts to *Kalanke*.[80] *Johnson*, like *Kalanke*, concerned a voluntarily instituted affirmative action plan for hiring and promoting women and minorities in a context of severe under-representation of both groups in the workforce. The *Johnson* plan was more flexible than that of *Kalanke*, in that the sex of a qualified applicant was only a factor among several to be considered. It was also more controversial in that a woman could be promoted even if she was marginally less well qualified than a male applicant. The plan was challenged when a qualified woman was promoted ahead of a man to the position of road dispatcher, a

[75] *Franks v. Bowman Transportation Co.* 424 U.S. 747, 96 S. Ct. 1251 (1975).
[76] 480 U.S. 149, 107 S. Ct. 1053 (1988).
[77] *U.S. v. Paradise, supra.*
[78] *United Steel Workers v. Weber* 442 U.S. 193 (1979).
[79] 107 S. Ct. 1442, 480 U.S. 616. (1987).
[80] *Supra*, n. 1.

grade in which to date none of the 238 positions had been held by a woman. The male employee, who in fact had a marginally better test score, complained of sex discrimination contrary to Title VII. Far from facing judicial antagonism to its results-oriented focus, as did the plan in *Kalanke*, the *Johnson* policy received warm judicial endorsement. Justice Brennan giving judgment for the court, declared that it was no violation of Title VII to take sex into account in promoting a woman over a male employee where this was in pursuance of an affirmative action plan to remedy the under-representation of women and minorities in traditionally segregated job classifications.

Similarly, the Supreme Court of the United States has rejected the neutral view of the state, instead upholding both the right and the responsibility of the state to use its public and market powers in remedying discrimination. Thus in *Fullilove v. Klutznick*[81] the Court upheld a policy setting aside 10 per cent of federal funds granted for the provision of public works to procure services from minority-owned businesses, even if the latter were not the lowest bidder. Chief Justice Burger stated specifically that in a remedial context, it was not necessary for Congress to act in a wholly colour-blind way. One of the most important results of this judicial approach has been the continued vigour of the federal contract compliance programme,[82] which requires federal government contractors to establish goals and timetables to correct any under-representation of a specified group.[83] However, quotas are prohibited. It is noteworthy that, in 1993, these regulations covered establishments employing about 26 million people and receiving contracts of more than $160 billion.

The clearly visible triumphs of the "substantive" model do not, however, represent the full picture. In fact, proponents of the "symmetrical" model retain considerable influence, an influence which has arguably eclipsed that of the substantive model in more recent cases. The resulting tension has led to a level of debate of a sophistication not found in the United Kingdom or European Union. This is reflected in the controversies within the case law on three main issues: the "innocent" third party who is discriminated against on grounds of race or sex in the process of preferring minorities or women; the standard of scrutiny; and the role of the state.

The vexed question of how much of a burden it is fair to expect the "innocent" third party to bear has no easy answer. This is particularly so if that person is him- or herself disadvantaged. The "substantive" model suggests that it is acceptable to require members of the majority groups to contribute to the cost of rectifying disadvantage. Thus in *Franks v.*

[81] *Supra*, n. 14.

[82] See Executive Order No. 11246, 30 Fed. Reg. 12319 (1965).

[83] With certain exceptions, the Order applies to federal contractors and subcontractors employing more than 50 employees and with contracts worth more than $50,000.

Bowman,[84] Justice Brennan epitomised the "substantive" approach in holding that since there would always be a conflict of interests when scarce employment benefits had to be distributed, denial of a remedy on grounds of defeated expectations would frustrate the "make whole" aims of the anti-discrimination legislation. By contrast, Justice Powell has consistently used symmetrical arguments to assert the need to prioritise the vested interests of "innocent" employees.[85] The resulting tension has led to a finely tuned synthesis. Thus Justice Brennan has been careful to limit the encumbrance on "innocent" whites or men to cases in which the burden is diffuse; for example, where it forecloses one opportunity but leaves several others open, and where it is related to the denial of future opportunities, such as promotion or selection.[86] Since no one has an absolute right to a job or to promotion, the white man who is passed over in favour of a woman or black is not unduly burdened. However, he is prepared to bow to "symmetrical" arguments in the highly controversial context of layoffs, where the Court is asked to "allocate the burdens of recession and fiscal austerity."[87] In this context, the dominant principle has been that articulated by Justice Powell, namely that loss of a job is too serious a prospect to permit individual interests to be subordinated.[88] The result has been that, except in the case of identified victims of discrimination,[89] the vested interests of "dispreferred" workers to retain seniority rights and therefore remain in work have generally trumped the goals of achieving and maintaining a balanced workforce. The effects of this compromise are evident in *Wygant v. Jackson Board of Education*,[90] in which a collective agreement was struck down as contrary to the 14th Amendment because it gave preferential protection against layoffs to minority employees. The result was, however, largely to undermine the effects of positive action programmes incorporating under-represented workers: such workers were the "last in" and therefore inevitably the "first out".

The second controversial issue in U.S. case law concerns the standard of scrutiny which should be applied in affirmative action cases. The Supreme Court has a well-developed jurisprudence requiring "strict scrutiny" of any classifications which burden blacks: such a classification must serve a compelling governmental interest and be narrowly tailored to achieve that aim.[91] In practice, the insistence on strict scrutiny has outlawed most racist policies or practices discriminating against blacks. This raises the question:

---

84 *Supra*, n. 75.

85 *Wygant v. Jackson Board of Education*, *supra*, n. 6.

86 *Johnson v. Santa Clara*, *supra*, n. 79; *U.S. v. Paradise*, *supra*, n. 76; *United Steelworkers v. Weber*, *supra*, n. 78.

87 *Memphis Firefighters v. Stotts* 104 S. Ct. 2576 at p. 2592 (1984).

88 *ibid.*

89 *Franks v. Bowman*, *supra*, n. 75.

90 *Supra*, n. 6.

91 *Korematsu v. U.S.* 323 U.S. 214 (1944).

does an equally strict standard of review apply to racial classifications which benefit blacks at the expense of whites? U.S. case law is criss-crossed with deeply conflicting judicial statements on this point. In *Bakke* Justice Powell was unequivocal in his rejection of the argument that strict scrutiny applies only to classifications that disadvantage discrete and insular minorities. Instead, he argued, all kinds of race conscious criteria should be subject to the "most exacting of judicial examination."[92] By contrast, four judges (Justices Brennan, White, Marshall and Blackmun), taking a substantive asymmetric view, held that a less stringent standard of review should apply to racial classifications designed to further remedial purposes than to pernicious classifications. On this view, it was sufficient for the policy to be "substantially related" to the achievement of an important government objective, a standard known as intermediate review.[93] However, the case was inconclusive on this issue since four other judges, having decided the case on statutory grounds, did not address the standard. Similarly indecisive were the later cases of *Fullilove v. Klutznick*[94] and *Wygant v. Jackson Board of Education.*[95] It was not until the 1989 case of *City of Richmond v. JSA Croson*[96] that the symmetrical insistence on strict scrutiny received majority support in the Supreme Court, and then only in respect of local and state policy. It remained only to apply the same standard to action by the federal government. This was done, in the face of a strong dissent, in *Adarand v. Pena.*[97]

The triumph of strict scrutiny has not, however, signalled the end of substantive arguments: instead, symmetric and substantive arguments are both capable of expression within a strict scrutiny standard. Thus in *Fullilove v. Klutznick*,[98] Justice Powell held that the legislation passed the strict scrutiny test, and Chief Justice Burger declared that it ought to be upheld on either the intermediate or the strict scrutiny test. Yet the dissenters (Justices Stewart and Rhenquist) used strict scrutiny to strike down the plan. By contrast, it was the latter view which prevailed in *Richmond v. Croson.*[99] Using the standard of strict scrutiny, the Court struck down the city's policy of retaining 30 per cent of contracting work for minority businesses. Most complex are the judgments in *Adarand.*[100] Justices Thomas and Scalia upheld the strict standard from a strongly symmetrical and individualistic camp. However, Justice O'Connor, giving judgment for the Court, was at pains to dispute the notion that strict

[92] *Bakke, supra*, n. 2.
[93] *Fullilove v. Klutznick, supra*, n. 14, *per* Marshall J.
[94] *Supra*, n. 6.
[95] 476 U.S. 267 (1986).
[96] 488 U.S. 469 (1989).
[97] *Supra*, n. 3.
[98] *Supra*, n. 14.
[99] *Supra*, n. 96.
[100] *Supra*, n. 3.

scrutiny is strict in theory but fatal in fact.[101] Indeed, she held, the federal government might well have a compelling interest to act on the basis of race to overcome the "persistence of both the practice and lingering effects of racial discrimination against minority groups."[102] In this respect, her approach incorporates important elements of the clearly substantive view expressed in dissent by Justice Stevens,[103] who rejected the strict scrutiny standard by reasserting the fundamental difference between a policy designed to perpetuate a caste system and one seeking to eliminate racial discrimination. It should be noted that the effect of this judgment on gender is inconclusive, since cases of invidious discrimination against women have in fact not been subjected to the strict scrutiny test, but instead to an intermediate standard requiring only that the means "substantially relate" to the achievement of an important governmental interest.[104] The Supreme Court has held that the intermediate test applied whether the plan discriminated against women or in their favour[105] and Justice Stevens in *Adarand*[106] suggested that this remained the case for affirmative action programmes concerning women. However, the position is far from clear.

The third controversial issue concerns the role of the state. Strict scrutiny requires the Court to determine whether the asserted governmental interest is compelling, thereby opening up the question as to whether the state should remain neutral or take a positive role in correcting discrimination. *Fullilove*[107] endorsed the substantive insistence that the state has a responsibility to promote equity between the races. By contrast, more recent cases vehemently reassert the importance of state neutrality. Societal discrimination without more has been held to be too amorphous a basis for a racially based remedy[108]; race-based action is only legitimate if it aims to correct previous harm caused by the state actor in question.[109] A recent Court of Appeals decision epitomises this reassertion of state neutrality by holding that a state university could not take remedial action to remedy the admitted past discriminatory actions by the same state in its schools.[110]

Even if it is accepted that the state has a positive role, what aims is it permitted to pursue by means of affirmative action policies? As we have seen, Justice O'Connor, giving judgment for the court in *Adarand*[111]

[101] *Adarand*, *supra*, n. 3 at p. 2117.
[102] Rehnquist, Kennedy and Thomas JJ. all agreed.
[103] Joined by Souter, Ginsburg and Breyer JJ.
[104] *Personnel Administrator of Massachusetts v. Feeney*, 422 U.S. 256 (1979).
[105] *Mississippi University for Women v. Hogan*, 112 S. Ct. 3331 (1982).
[106] *Supra*, n. 3.
[107] *Supra*, n. 14.
[108] Powell J. in *Richmond v. Croson*, *supra*, n. 96.
[109] *ibid.*, and see *Wygant*, *supra*, n. 6.
[110] *Hopwood v. State of Texas*, 78 F. 3d 932 (1996).
[111] *Supra*, n. 3.

accepted that the state may have a legitimate interest in taking race-conscious measures to overcome the effects of past discrimination. She did not, however, specify whether other goals would be acceptable. Previous cases have touched on the legitimacy of such goals as racial diversity and the provision of role models. Thus Justice Powell in *Bakke*[112] declared that the goal of helping groups perceived as the victims of societal discrimination was clearly unconstitutional, but accepted as permissible the goals of supplying more professional people for under-served communities and of educational diversity. Neither of these last two legitimate goals, however, in his view, necessitated a quota system. The question was dealt with more conclusively in *Wygant.*[113] In this case, the defendant Board of Education argued, *inter alia*, that its policy of protecting newly hired minority teachers against layoffs was justified by the state's duty to reduce racial discrimination by providing minority role models for minority students. This was roundly rejected by Justice Powell, this time giving judgment for the Court, on the grounds that it would permit affirmative action long past the point of its remedial purpose. The legitimacy of diversity as a goal has now been rejected by the Court of Appeals.[114]

Despite the apparent ascendancy of the "symmetrical" approach in the U.S. courts, U.S. policy-makers have reaffirmed their commitment to the use of affirmative action, particularly in the form of federal contract compliance and set-aside programmes. *Adarand*[115] was quickly followed by a detailed Department of Justice memorandum which was, in many respects, strikingly similar to the European Commission's response to *Kalanke.*[116] A review of Federal affirmative action programmes, set up by President Clinton in February 1995, reported soon after. In his report, the President reiterated his support for affirmative action and, instead of suspending any particular programmes, instructed all Federal bodies to review their policies to ensure they did not create quotas, prefer unqualified individuals, use reverse discrimination, or continue after their purposes had been achieved. Programmes which set aside proportions of government contracts for minority businesses would be reformed so that they were specifically targeted on contractors from deprived areas, regardless of race.[117] Informed commentators predict, however, that such reviews are likely to result in minimal changes, and that, largely due to the commitment

---

[112] *Supra*, n. 2.
[113] *Supra*, n. 6.
[114] *Hopwood v State of Texas*, *supra*, n. 110.
[115] *Supra*, n. 3.
[116] *Supra*, n. 54.
[117] This account is taken from C. McCrudden "The Constitutionality of Affirmative Action in the United States a casenote on *Adarand v. Pena*" (1996) 1 *Int J. Discrimination and the Law* 369, and see also *Equal Opportunities Review* 63 (1995) pp. 31–33.

of the President himself, affirmative action is likely remain a vigorous area of activity.[118]

III. Assessment

Opposition to affirmative action is based on three main premises: formal justice, the primacy of the individual and the neutrality of the state. Yet, as the substantive critique has shown, each of these premises can be successfully challenged. Formal justice ignores the social fact that discrimination on the grounds of race or sex functions as a continuing and powerful constraint on the circumstances and opportunities of women and black people, a constraint which does not affect those of the privileged race or gender. Equal treatment of individuals who are not socially equal perpetuates the inequalities. This immediately exposes the fallacy of the symmetrical argument: since discrimination on grounds of race or sex has consistently worked to the detriment of black people and women, discrimination in their favour should be viewed quite differently from invidious and detrimental discrimination. A law which genuinely aims to narrow the disparities and eventually achieve equality must tolerate unequal treatment where necessary to achieve more equal results. With the rejection of formal justice comes a similar rejection of the "neutral" state. Ultimately, a state cannot truly be neutral; the real question is what role it should take in society. I would suggest, as does the substantive model, that this role should be one which includes intervention to narrow the disparities between the genders and the races, even where the causal connection with discriminatory action by the state or private actors cannot be established. This in turn requires a movement beyond pure individualism: a recognition of the role of group membership in shaping an individual's choices; and of the social responsibility of citizens regardless of individual fault. Taking race or sex into account is crucial in this enterprise.

This is not to say that the substantive model has resolved all the problematic issues. Proponents of affirmative action still need to face at least four inter-related questions. First, what is the aim of such action? Secondly, is it effective in achieving that aim? Thirdly, what role should merit play? Finally, are the costs fairly spread? There are no easy answers to these questions. Below, I hope merely to indicate the complexity of the issues, arguing ultimately that specific affirmative action plans need to be strictly scrutinised against a background of a substantive view of justice.

Of the various aims suggested in the case law and literature, the least controversial is the narrow remedial role, which permits affirmative action only to compensate for demonstrable past discrimination by the actor in question. However, to restrict the permissible goals so severely is to risk

[118] McCrudden, *supra*, n. 117.

rendering affirmative action programmes largely ineffective. This emerges clearly from the recent case against Texas Law School: the university was not permitted to use affirmative action to remedy past discriminatory action by the state of Texas in schooling[119]; yet poor schooling must have been a primary reason for the continuing under-representation of black people in that law school. In reality, the narrowness of this aim reflects the influence of the assumptions of a neutral state and individual fault. Instead of demonstrable fault, it should be sufficient to prove that there is a visible disparity in participation rates as between races or genders; a disparity which the state has a responsibility to counteract.

A move away from individualism also permits consideration of so-called non-remedial aims, such as diversity and role models. I would argue that in fact it is misleading to regard these aims as wholly non-remedial. While it may be true that a diverse student body is educationally enriching,[120] it is difficult to justify excluding a highly qualified white applicant simply on those grounds; nor can the argument be extended to employment. Instead, the desire for diversity must be seen as part of the wider remedial aim of achieving greater participation by black people and women in areas from which they have traditionally been excluded or absent. A student body or workforce which includes members of the disadvantaged group will be an arena in which prejudicial attitudes of the dominant group are challenged and bridges built. It is similarly misleading to classify the provision of role-models as a non-remedial aim. A long history of discrimination can lead to the internalisation of inferiority, so that members of the disadvantaged group believe themselves to be incapable of success in areas from which they are excluded. Visible success by other members of the same group helps to dispel such lack of confidence and feelings of inferiority.

These broader remedial aims have been best expressed by Chief Justice Dickson in a fairly recent Canadian case.[121] He declared that the aim of an employment equity programme is not to compensate past victims; but "an attempt to ensure that future applicants and workers from the affected group will not face the same insidious barriers that blocked their forebears".[122] He identified at least three ways in which such a programme is likely to be more effective than one which simply relies on equal opportunities or the proscription of intentional prejudice. First, the insistence that women be placed in non-traditional jobs allows them to prove that they really can do the job, thereby dispelling stereotypes about women's abilities. Secondly, an employment equity programme helps to

[119] *Texas v. Hopwood*, *supra*, n. 110.

[120] See "An Evidentiary Framwork for Diversity as a Compelling Interest in Higher Education" Note in (1996) 109 Harvard L. R. 1357.

[121] *Action Travail des Femmes v. Canadian National Railway Co.* [1987] 1 S.C.R. 1114, (1987) 40 D.L.R. (4th) 193.

[122] At p. 213.

create a "critical mass" of women in the workplace, overcoming the problem of tokenism, which would leave a few women isolated and vulnerable to sexual harassment or accusations of being impostors. It would also generate further employment of women, partly by means of the informal recruitment network and partly by reducing the stigma and anxiety associated with strange and unconventional work. Finally, a critical mass of women forces management to give women's concerns their due weight and compels personnel officers to take female applications seriously.

The second question, whether a gender- or race-conscious programme is effective in improving the position of the disadvantaged group, is more complex than might be expected. In particular, there is a clear danger of stigma and stereotyping which might perpetuate disadvantage.[123] This dilemma appears in stark form in social security cases, where women, particularly married women, have often been singled out for differential treatment. Do such measures respond to genuine needs experienced specifically by most women, or do they create financial incentives which perpetuate women's position as secondary breadwinners and homemakers?[124] Again, there is no generalised answer to such dilemmas. Specific policies or plans need to be carefully assessed to ensure that the risks of damaging stereotyping are outweighed by the possible gains of such criteria in reducing race or gender disadvantage.

Some of the most difficult remaining questions for proponents of affirmative action concern the merit principle. It is almost universally assumed that merit is the fairest method of selection, and therefore that affirmative action bears the onus of justifying any departure. Yet people do not "deserve" their talents,[125] and those born with greater talents do not necessarily "deserve" greater rewards. Therefore, as Fallon argues,[126] while it is arguably fairer than many other bases for distribution, such as nepotism or invidious discrimination, merit-based distribution is not morally required. Indeed, merit-based distribution is best justified not on moral but on utilitarian grounds, namely that society benefits from awarding educational opportunities or jobs to those who are most likely to perform best. Yet even the utilitarian argument is not conclusive. While some qualifications are often necessary for particular jobs or university places, a basic threshold of ability or qualification may well be sufficient, leaving no scope for the argument that the higher an individual's score, the better he or she will perform. This point is reinforced by the fact that

[123] See, *e.g. Mississippi University for Women v. Hogan*, *supra*, n. 105, where the majority held that an all women's nursing college operated to the detriment of women by reinforcing the stereotype of women nurses.

[124] See, *e.g. Integrity*, *supra*, n. 46.

[125] J. Rawls, *A Theory of Justice* (1971) pp. 101–104; 310–315.

[126] R. Fallon "Affirmative Action Based on Economic Disadvantage" (1996) 43 U.C.L.A. L. Rev. 1913 at pp. 1916–1923.

measures of ability are limited in their accuracy and might even be suspect. However, apparently scientific an assessment process might be, it is inevitable that some subjective decision-making takes place, and this may well include prejudicial stereotyping. In addition, even objective measures frequently systematically exclude groups who have been historically disadvantaged.

The above discussion opens up some possibilities for dealing with the question of merit. It is clear that some jobs cannot be done without certain qualifications and that university places would be wasted on those without the capacity to do them. Thus some notion of merit, or perhaps, in the Northern Irish legislative sense, "suitability" is a necessary condition for the allocation of particular benefits. Yet it is crucial to scrutinise the criteria for eligibility or suitability closely in order to root out both prejudice and exclusionary factors. The indirect discrimination provisions offer a well-established tool for determining whether exclusionary criteria are necessary for the job or benefit. At the same time, the recognition that merit is not an objective and quantifiable property facilitates the legitimate inclusion of social factors in the decision-making process. Thus the values of integrating diverse sectors of the community, of providing role models, of remedying past discrimination and of reducing inequalities in society are legitimate aims to be pursued in selecting students or employees; just as legitimate as making sure the person is suitable for the job.

This discussion also sheds some light on the question of whether the costs of affirmative action are spread fairly. Is the "innocent" white man expected to bear too great a cost for a problem beyond his making? Given that no one has an absolute moral claim to the award of a job, promotion or place at a university, the decision to use wide-ranging criteria for selection places no greater burden on these applicants than it does on any other disappointed candidates. It is in the context of layoffs that affirmative action programmes face their most severe test. It is clearly unfair to expect a handful of individuals to bear too great a share of the social responsibility for remedying discrimination, particularly by requiring them to surrender accrued seniority rights and therefore forfeit their jobs. On the other hand, as the facts of *Wygant*[127] demonstrate, the gains of an affirmative action programme boosting recruitment could easily be reversed if newly hired minorities are the first to be made redundant. There is no easy answer to this dilemma. Nevertheless, the problem need not be classified as a simple conflict of interests between a man and a woman, or a white and a black. Instead, the employer and the state could be called upon to share the burden, possibly by subsidising continued employment of both employees or helping the redundant worker to find another job.

[127] *Supra*, n. 6.

CONCLUSION

Ultimately, the most difficult questions surrounding affirmative action are not theoretical but strategic. I would suggest that affirmative action has a useful role to play, provided it is used sensitively and carefully monitored. The judgment of Justice O'Connor in *Adarand*[128] is a useful starting point. Strict scrutiny in the hands of a perceptive judiciary should be based on an asymmetrical, substantive model of justice which appreciates the deep moral differences between discrimination against a group which has been subject to historical and continuing detriment on the basis of their race or sex, and programmes which aim to remedy that discrimination. At the same time, such an approach should be alive to the dangers of stigma, stereotyping and exclusion.

Nor, however, should a defence of affirmative action overestimate its potential for achieving change. The E.C.J. in *Kalanke*[129] was correct in pointing out that numerical equality can be illusory if not accompanied by equality of opportunity. But, as argued above, equality of opportunity can itself be illusory unless it goes far beyond merely formal measures. A fully fledged equal opportunities programme requires a radical reshaping of the world of paid and unpaid work to accommodate the combination of paid and family work for both men and women. It also requires a sea change in both the quantity and quality of education and training available to ethnic minorities and women. Equalising the starting points therefore demands not only careful thought and planning but a high level of resource input reflecting a strong political commitment. The combination of such an equal opportunities strategy and carefully targeted affirmative action programmes could begin to yield the kind of progress not yet generated by anti-discrimination legislation.

SANDRA FREDMAN.*

[128] *Supra*, n. 110.
[129] *Supra*, n. 1.
* Reader in Law, Exeter College, Oxford. I am indebted to Dr. Christopher McCrudden and Judge Federico Mancini for their invaluable comments on an earlier draft.

[12]

COMPREHENSIVE EXAMINATION OF THEMATIC ISSUES RELATING TO RACIAL DISCRIMINATION

The concept and practice of affirmative action

Preliminary report submitted by Mr. Marc Bossuyt, Special Rapporteur, in accordance with Sub-Commission resolution 1998/5

Introduction

In its decision 1999/105, the Sub-Commission on the Promotion and Protection of Human Rights, recalling its resolution 1998/5 and noting Commission on Human Rights resolution 1999/81 and Economic and Social Council decision 1999/253, decided to renew its authorization to the Special Rapporteur on the concept and practice of affirmative action to request the United Nations High Commissioner for Human Rights to send a questionnaire to Governments, international organizations and non-governmental organizations, inviting them to provide all relevant national documentation on the subject of affirmative action.

On 6 June 2000, the questionnaire (annex) was sent by the Office of the United Nations High Commissioner for Human Rights (OHCHR), to Governments, international organizations and non-governmental organizations.

As the time available was too short to expect Governments to respond to a questionnaire sent to them, the present preliminary report will contain a first section providing an analysis of international conventions containing provisions relating to the concept of affirmative action and a second section, based mainly on the examination of legal doctrine, on the limits international law sets on affirmative action measures.

I. The Concept of Affirmative Action in International Law

The concept of affirmative action is generally referred to in international law as "special measures". The first mention of these "special measures" was made by the Government of India during the drafting of the International Covenant on Economic, Social and Cultural Rights (ICESCR). India suggested that an explanatory paragraph should be included in the text of article 2 specifying that:

> "Special measures for the advancement of any socially and educationally backward sections of society shall not be construed as distinctions under this article. Alternatively, the Committee might wish to insert in its report a statement, which would make that interpretation clear."[1]

The representative of India pointed out that the implementation of the principles of non-discrimination raised certain problems in the case of the particularly backward groups still to be found in many underdeveloped countries. In his country, the Constitution and the laws provided for special measures for the social and cultural betterment of such groups. Measures of that kind were essential for the achievement of true social equality in highly heterogeneous societies. As he felt certain that the authors of the draft covenant had not intended to prohibit such measures, which were in fact protective measures, he therefore thought it essential to make it clear that such protective measures would not be construed as discriminatory within the meaning of the paragraph. His proposal was withdrawn, although expressly supported by other representatives. However, it was felt that the "difficulty experienced by the Indian representative would best be met by the inclusion of an interpretative statement in the Committee's records, rather than insertion of an additional paragraph in the draft Covenant".[2]

According to Craven the ICESCR does not envisage an absolute equalization of result in the sense of achieving an equal distribution of material benefits to all members of society. It does, however, recognize a process of equalization in which social resources are redistributed to provide for the satisfaction of the basic rights of every member of society, based on the idea of equality of opportunity.[3] In its first General Comment, the Committee on Economic, Social and Cultural Rights states that an initial step towards the realization of the Covenant rights is to identify the disadvantaged sectors of the population, which should be the focus of positive State action aimed at securing the full realization of their rights.[4]

The idea of equality of opportunity is specifically to be found in articles 7 (c) and 13 (2) (c) of that Covenant. Article 7 (c), in particular, specifies that the only legitimate considerations in achieving equality of opportunity for promotion are seniority and competence. Craven argues that States would appear to be under an obligation to eliminate all other barriers to promotion that might exist both de jure and de facto. In particular, this may require the adoption of positive measures to promote the opportunities of groups in society that are under-represented in higher management positions. Article 13 (2) (c) provides that higher education shall be made equally accessible to all on the basis of capacity. That positive measure may be taken on behalf of certain groups in society is confirmed by the text of article 10 (2) and (3) of the Covenant that provides for special measures of protection to be accorded to mothers before and after childbirth and to children, especially in the workplace.

However, Craven further adds that all the articles do appear to rule out the possibility of quotas being imposed in the contexts of promotion in employment and access to higher education. They prohibit advantages being given on grounds other than seniority, competence and capacity. Craven believes, though, that a case could be made for the operation of quota

1 United Nations document A/C.3/SR.1182, para. 17.

2 United Nations document A/C.3/SR.1183, paras. 12 and 29.

3 M. Craven, The International Covenant on Economic, Social and Cultural Rights, a perspective on its development, Oxford, Clarendon Press, 1995, p. 158.

4 Committee on Economic, Social and Cultural Rights, General Comment 1, para. 3, in United Nations document HRI/GEN/Rev.4 (2000).

systems in each case on the basis that the terms of the articles are open to "progressive achievement". Thus, a system in which a proportion of places in higher education is set aside for students of a particular group could be justified, if it could be shown that it would ultimately contribute to the achievement of equal access on the basis of capacity at some stage in the future. Even then, that wider concerns of social utility could not be used as justificatory evidence means that the possibilities for imposing quotas with respect to higher education and employment are strictly limited.

Particularly interesting also are the general comments of the Committee on Economic, Social and Cultural Rights (CESCR). General Comment No. 5 has included "disability" as ground on which special treatment can be justified. An explicit disability-related provision in the ICESCR is absent, probably due to lack of awareness, but in its general comment, the Committee stated clearly:

> "The obligation of States parties to the Covenant to promote progressive realization of the relevant rights to the maximum of their available resources clearly requires Governments to do much more than merely abstain from taking measures which might have a negative impact on persons with disabilities. The obligation in the case of such a vulnerable and disadvantaged group is to take positive action to reduce structural disadvantages and to give appropriate preferential treatment to people with disabilities in order to achieve the objectives of full participation and equality within society for all persons with disabilities. This almost invariably means that additional resources will need to be made available for this purpose and that a wide range of specially tailored measures will be required."[5]

In General Comment No. 13, it is maintained that the adoption of temporary special measures intended to bring out de facto equality for men and women and for disadvantaged groups is not a violation of the right to non-discrimination with regard to education, so long as such measures do not lead to the maintenance of unequal or separate standards for different groups, and provided they are not continued after the objectives for which they were taken have been achieved. Therefore, in some circumstances, separate educational systems or institutions for groups shall be deemed not to constitute a breach of the Covenant.[6]

When the Third Committee of the General Assembly discussed the non-discrimination provisions of the International Covenant on Civil and Political Rights (ICCPR), the representative of India raised his point again and suggested that article 2 (1) of the ICCPR should be followed by an explanatory paragraph reading: "Special measures for the advancement of any socially and educationally backward sections of society shall not be construed as distinctions under this article."

He stated that, owing to past treatment or historical circumstances, a certain sector of the people had to be given greater privileges and protection only for a certain period of time in order to promote the rights of those people to re-establish their equality and conditions under which there would remain no need for such provisions, and equal opportunities would exist for all. If the Committee did not favour the insertion of that paragraph in the draft covenant, a passage of similar content should be included in the Committee's report. The Committee again endorsed the point made by the representative of India and stated that that interpretation,

---

5 Ibid., General Comment No. 5, para. 9.

6 Ibid., General Comment No. 13, paras. 32-33.

to which there was no objection, should be specially mentioned in the report.[7] The same views were held on article 26.[8]

In its general comment on article 26 of the ICCPR, which is a general non-discrimination clause, the Human Rights Committee pointed out that

> "the principle of equality sometimes requires States parties to take affirmative action in order to diminish or eliminate conditions which cause or help to perpetuate discrimination prohibited by the Covenant. For example, in a State where the general conditions of a certain part of the population prevent or impair their enjoyment of human rights, the State should take specific action to correct those conditions. Such action may involve granting for a time to the part of the population concerned certain preferential treatment in specific matters as compared with the rest of the population. However, as long as such action is needed to correct discrimination in fact, it is a case of legitimate differentiation under the Covenant".[9]

The practice of the Human Rights Committee confirmed its view on affirmative action. During the consideration of a report of Sweden, it was recalled that article 26 does not only refer to equality before the courts but also to equal protection of the law:

> "Article 26 of the Covenant referred not merely to the, as it were, negative or passive aspect of the prevention of discrimination through guarantees of equality before the law - an aspect already covered by article 14 of the Covenant - but also to the positive aspect of 'active protection against discrimination' on the various grounds enumerated."

The representative of the Government of Sweden replied that he "agreed that article 26 called for positive action for the elimination of discrimination, and not merely passive measures of prevention".[10]

In the case Stalla Costa v. Uruguay, the author complained of the preferential treatment, regarding the reinstatement to the public service of former public officials who had previously been unfairly dismissed on ideological, political, or trade union grounds. The author complained that this preferential treatment unfairly prejudiced his own chances of gaining a public-service job. The alleged discrimination was found to be permissible affirmative action in favour of a formerly disadvantaged group. The Committee considered the Act conferring such preferential treatment to be a "remedy" for persons who had previously suffered from violations of article 26.[11]

---

[7] United Nations documents A/C.3/SR.1257, para. 18; A/C.3/SR.1258, paras. 18, 38, 45, 47 (UAR); A/C.3/SR.1259, para. 33. See M. Bossuyt, Guide to the "Travaux Préparatoires" of the International Covenant on Civil and Political Rights, Dordrecht, Martinus Nijhoff Publishers, 1987, p. 55.

[8] United Nations document E/CN.4/SR.122, pp. 8 and 11.

[9] Human Rights Committee, General Comment No. 18, para. 10, in HRI/GEN/1/Rev.4 (2000).

[10] United Nations document CCPR/C/SR.189, paras. 15-16. J.J. Paust ("The permissibility of affirmative action in higher education under human rights law", New York City Law Review, 1998, pp. 95-96) agrees that "equal protection" should be interpreted in a manner that allows for certain measures of affirmative action to promote an "equal" and effective "protection" against ongoing discrimination.

[11] Communication No. 198/1985, in Selected Decisions of the Human Rights Committee Under the Optional Protocol, vol. 2 (United Nations publication, Sales No. E.89.XIV.1).

In Ballantyne, Davidson and McIntyre v. Canada, the Committee found that it was not necessary, in order to protect the vulnerable position in Canada of the francophone group, to prohibit commercial advertising in English. This protection may be achieved in other ways that do not preclude the freedom of expression, in a language of their choice, of those engaged in such fields as trade.[12] Thus, the affirmative action provision in this case was found to go too far, it was disproportionate to its ends.

The following inferences can be made on the basis of the two International Covenants. During the drafting of the ICRSCR and the ICCPR, it was generally accepted that a prohibition of discrimination and distinction, respectively, did not preclude positive measures being taken in favour of disadvantaged groups. It was generally agreed that the prohibition was only aimed at distinction of an unfavourable kind lacking any objective or reasonable basis. Moreover, it was also widely accepted that equality did not mean identity of treatment and that there were cases in which the law was justified in making distinctions between individuals or groups.

Therefore, according to Thornberry, it can be concluded that the concept of affirmative action is not contrary to the law of the Covenants.[13] In the same vein, Vijapur argues that the principle of non-discrimination in international human rights law clearly implies compensatory unequal treatment of individuals and groups who do not differ from the majority by their nationality, language or religion but only by their social and economic backwardness. He finds support for his conclusion in the inclusion of special protection clauses in human rights instruments.[14] Some authors even believe that the gist of the general comments is that affirmative action to implement the ICCPR's non-discrimination obligations is mandatory.[15] Yet, it should be stressed that neither of the Covenants has explicitly recognized the obligatory nature of affirmative action.[16] Nor are the form of affirmative action and situation in which such action must be taken defined, owing to the complexity of the issue.

The International Labour Organization (ILO) has been a pioneer in using mainly promotional conventions to realize defined objectives and policies. The ILO has also set out standards to be achieved, consequent with the principle of equal remuneration for work of equal value, incorporated into the ILO Constitution, and of equality of all human beings, irrespective of

---

12 Communication No. 385/1989, in Official Records of the General Assembly, Forty-eighth Session, Supplement No. 40 (A/48/40), vol. II, annex XII, sect. P

13 P. Thornberry, International Law and the Rights of Minorities, Oxford, Clarendon Press, 1991, p. 284. Referring to article 1 (4) of the International Covenant on the Elimination of All Forms of Racial Discrimination and article 4 (1) of the Convention on the Elimination of All Forms of Discrimination against Women, which do contain explicit statements about the legitimacy of affirmative action measures, he points out that a contrary interpretation in the context of the Covenants would display an "extraordinary lack of congruence".

14 A.P. Vijapur, "The principle of non-discrimination in international human rights law: the meaning and scope of the concept", India Quarterly, A journal of international affairs, 1993, p. 91.

15 A.F. Beyafsky "The principle of equality or non-discrimination in international law", Human Rights Law Journal, 1990, p. 27; Lord Lester of Herne Hill and S. Joseph, "Obligations of non-discrimination", in D. Harris and S. Joseph, (eds.), The International Covenant on Civil and Political Rights and the United Kingdom Law, Oxford, Clarendon Press, 1995, p. 579.

16 While recognizing this, M. Craven (op. cit., at note 3, p. 186) argues that, although the Committee on Economic, Social and Cultural Rights implicitly recognizes an obligation through the requirement that States concentrate upon the situation of vulnerable and disadvantaged groups in society, this is nevertheless a matter that ideally should be made clear in a future general comment.

race, creed or sex, as proclaimed in the 1944 Declaration Concerning the Aims and Purposes of the ILO, adopted by the International Labour Conference at Philadelphia.

The ILO Discrimination (Employment and Occupation) Convention of 1958 (No. 111), which was chiefly aimed at racial discrimination but is applicable to other forms of discrimination as well, engages each member State to undertake to pursue a national policy designed to promote equal opportunities and treatment in respect of employment and occupation with a view to eliminating any discrimination, enacting legislation to that effect and seeking the cooperation of employers' and workers' organizations and other appropriate bodies (arts. 2 and 3). Article 5 is one of the first articles in an international treaty to permit explicitly "special measures of protection or assistance" designed to meet the particular requirements of persons who, for reasons such as sex, age, disablement, family responsibilities or social or cultural states, are generally recognized as requiring special protection or assistance. It is clearly stated that these special measures will not constitute discrimination.

In 1960, a similar Convention relating to the field of education was adopted in the framework of UNESCO. The UNESCO Convention against Discrimination in Education singles out, in its article 1, as a discriminatory act the establishing or maintaining of separate educational systems. Article 2, however, qualifies that prohibition. It allows: (i) separate educational systems set up for pupils of the two sexes on an equivalent basis; (ii) educational systems separated for religious or linguistic reasons, offering an education which is in keeping with the wishes of the pupil's parent or legal guardians, on an optional basis and if the education provided conforms to certain standards; (iii) private educational institutions, if their object is not to exclude any group but to provide educational facilities in addition to those provided by the public authorities, under certain conditions. This article does not refer to special measures of favourable discrimination, but only determines when separate educational systems will not be deemed to constitute discrimination. Moreover, it does not explicitly provide for special public schools.

Article 5 of the same Convention relates to the right of members of national minorities to carry on their own educational activities, such as the teaching of their own language, provided that this right is not exercised in a manner which prevents the members of those minorities from understanding the culture and language of the community as a whole and from participating in its activities, or which prejudices national sovereignty. The standard of such education should not be lower than the general standard and attendance at such schools should be optional. States parties have to undertake all necessary measures to ensure the application of this right, but there is no suggestion that the State is obliged to provide financial or other assistance to the group. Thornberry labels this a case of negative rather than positive freedom.[17] The travaux préparatoires also indicate that special measures aimed at meeting special requirements of persons in particular circumstances, such as backward children, the blind, immigrants and illiterate populations, were not "unjustified" preferences, but would rather raise deprived persons to a condition of genuine equality.[18]

The International Convention on the Elimination of All Forms of Racial Discrimination (ICERD) adopted in 1966, deals in paragraph 4 of article 1 with what was called "favourable discrimination": measures taken in favour of certain racial or ethnic groups or individuals in order to ensure to them equal enjoyment or exercise of human rights and fundamental freedoms.

> "Special measures taken for the sole purpose of securing adequate advancement of certain racial or ethnic groups or individuals requiring such protection as may be necessary in order to ensure such groups or individuals equal enjoyment or exercise of human rights and fundamental freedoms shall not be deemed racial discrimination, provided, however, that such measures do not, as a consequence, lead to the maintenance of separate rights for different racial groups and that they shall not be continued after the objectives for which they were taken have been achieved."

This paragraph should be related to article 2, paragraph 2, of the same Convention which imposes on States parties the duty to take special measures to ensure the adequate development and protection of certain racial groups or individuals belonging to them, for the purpose of guaranteeing them the full and equal enjoyment of human rights and fundamental freedoms. It was underlined that protection of certain groups did not constitute discrimination, provided that such measures were not maintained after the achievement of the aims for which they had been taken.

Both articles find their origin in article 2, paragraph 3, of the United Nations Declaration on the Elimination of all Forms of Racial Discrimination adopted in 1963. The reason that the Convention deals twice with the same problem is that while article 1 defines discrimination and its paragraph 4 refers to a case in which the application of different treatment should not be deemed discriminatory, article 2 relates to duties which are imposed by the Convention on States parties; both insist upon the temporary character of the special measures, a reaction that was inspired by the then existing system of apartheid. In the debate on the paragraph on special measures, some representatives were concerned that special measures could be used as a weapon by Governments anxious to perpetuate the separation of certain groups from the rest of the population, or to justify colonialism. However, it was made clear that the aim should not be to emphasize the distinctions between different racial groups, but rather to

---

[17] Thornberry further states that this is reinforced by article 3 (d) of the Convention by which States undertake "not to allow, in any form of assistance granted by the public authorities to educational institutions, any restrictions or preference based solely on the ground that pupils belong to a particular group". He believes that the equality and non-discrimination promised by the Convention to minority groups is the equality and non-discrimination provided for the community as a whole, without regard to cultural differences. In any dispute involving an abuse of rights arising from an interpretation of the Convention, the balance is clearly in favour of the State, which can find ample scope to deny their practical exercise. P. Thornberry, op. cit., at note 13, pp. 289-290. He refers also to UNESCO General Conference document 11C/15 (see E/CN.4/Sub.2/210) according to whose analysis article 5 does not support the notion that States are obliged to provide public or publicly supported schools.

[18] UNESCO document 11C/15, annex III, para. 36 and E/CN.4/Sub.2/210, annex III, para. 13.

ensure that persons belonging to such groups could be integrated into the community, in order to attain the objective of equal development for all citizens.[19]

An application of article 1, paragraph 4, was made in the Australian case of Gerhardy v. Brown, where the 1978 Pitjantjatjara Land Rights Act was disputed as being racial discrimination.[20] The Land Rights Act aimed to prevent any person other than a Pitjantjatjara entering the Pitjantjatjara land, in the north-west of South Australia, without a permit from the corporate body of the Pitjantjatjara. The defendant Brown was an Aborigine, though not a Pitjantjatjara and thus not permitted to enter. The Australian High Court held that there was no discrimination, because the Land Rights Act was deemed to be a special measure within the meaning of article 1, paragraph 4, of the ICERD. However, five of the seven judges held that in the absence of article 1, paragraph 4, the provisions would have been discriminatory because they made a distinction between Pitjantjatjara and non-Pitjantjatjara, one element of which was the proposition that to be Pitjantjatjara was to be a member of a race. Thus, the judges rejected the argument that the Land Rights Act merely recognized traditional ownership and was therefore not discriminatory on the basis of race but a reasonable response to a traditional relationship with land.

According to Brown, the Australian judges treated article 1, paragraph 1, of the ICERD as being very much a prohibition on any formal discrimination by reference to a criterion containing any element of race irrespective of its "legitimacy".[21] It follows that any provisioncontaining notions of aboriginality will be prima facie discriminatory unless it can be categorized a "special measure". But, according to Brown, the fact that a primary criterion involves a reference to race does not make the rule discriminatory in law, provided the reference to race has an objective basis and a reasonable cause. It is only when the reference lacks a reasonable cause and is arbitrary that the rule concerned becomes discriminatory in the legal sense. In the case of the traditional ownership rights of the Pitjantjatjara, however, two other criteria were relevant, that of tribal origin and that of traditional ownership. The fact that this traditional ownership is peculiar to a particular group of Aborigines does not make recognition of such land rights discriminatory. The legal recognition has an objective basis; it is not arbitrary and is discriminatory only in the sense that a reasonable and legitimate policy coincides with racial origin. Secondly, the modalities of the different treatment must not be disproportionate in effect to other groups. This is a matter of assessment in relation to particular facts, specifically in the case of recognition of land rights, where the restriction on freedom of movement raises the issue of proportionality. In other words, Brown maintains, even when the different treatment is not discriminatory in a legal sense, the modalities, and the method of implementation, may be unreasonable and hence discriminatory at the second level.

---

[19] See N. Lerner, The UN Convention on the Elimination of All Forms of Racial Discrimination, Alphen aan den Rijn, Sijthoff and Noordhoff, 1980, pp. 32-39. P. Thornberry, op. cit., at note 13, pp. 265-268. India especially expressed strong support for the inclusion of special measures in the Covenant and referred to its own domestic situation, where the Constitution of India expressly authorizes special measures to protect backward groups, i.e. the Scheduled Castes and Scheduled Tribes.

[20] (1985) 57 ALR 472.

[21] I. Brown, "The rights of peoples in modern international law", in J. Crawford, The rights of peoples, Oxford, Clarendon Press, 1988, pp. 8-10.

The Seminar on the elimination of all forms of racial discrimination, held in 1968, undertook an important discussion on the legitimacy of reservations and quotas. According to one view, reservations and quotas were a fundamental means of promoting equality in law and in fact for persons who had been victims of discrimination, but others believed that it would be preferable to make special facilities available to backward groups in order to enable them to meet the general standards of merit. Though the second view is attractive, systems of reservations and quotas are not necessarily inconsistent with the principle of equality, as long as they are of a strictly temporary nature and are maintained no longer than is necessary to achieve the objectives for which they are imposed, i.e. the rescue of backward groups from their economic and cultural disabilities. The crucial point was made that although under certain circumstances reservations and quotas may be appropriate, they must always be of limited duration.[22]

The importance of the UNESCO Declaration on Race and Racial Prejudice of 1978, although only a declaration, cannot be underestimated as it was widely supported, being adopted unanimously by acclamation. It is considered to have become part of the international law of human rights, being a comprehensive international instrument that deals with the protection of cultural and group identity and the value of diversity. In article 1 of the Declaration, it is stated that all individuals and groups have the right to be different, to consider themselves as different and to be regarded as such. The right to be different should not, however, serve as a pretext for racial prejudice nor justify discriminatory practices, nor provide a ground for the policy of apartheid. Article 9, paragraph 2, requires that special measures be taken to ensure equality in dignity and rights for individuals and groups wherever necessary, while ensuring that they are not such as to appear racially discriminatory. This article does not mention "adequate advancement" as an aim of special measures, which makes the Declaration a bit less paternalistic and shows due respect to different groups.

The article further states that particular attention should be paid to racial or ethnic groups which are socially or economically disadvantaged, so as to afford them, on a completely equal footing and without discrimination or restriction, the protection of the laws and regulations and the advantages of the social measures in force, in particular in regard to housing, employment and health and to facilitate their social and occupational advancement, especially through education.[23] The fact that the article refers explicitly to social and economic measures is new; moreover, these measures also involve an obligation to respect the authenticity of the culture and values of the persons who are the object of the measures. In the same vein, the preamble strongly opposes any form of assimilation. The innovative aspect of this Declaration is that it asserts the need for affirmative action and at the same time recognizes the right to be different.

The Convention on the Elimination of All Forms of Discrimination against Women of 1979 had a precedent in article 3 of the International Covenants:

---

22 See United Nations document ST/TAO/HR.34, paras. 147-155.

23 See also article 5, paragraph 2, which points out the duties of States in education against racism and contains a clause on general affirmative action: States should take "appropriate steps to remedy the handicaps from which certain racial or ethnic groups suffer with regard to their level of education and standard of living and in particular to prevent such handicaps from being passed on to children".

> "The States Parties to the present Covenant undertaken to ensure the equal right of men and women to the enjoyment of all economic, social and cultural (civil and political) rights set forth in the present Covenant".

Many representatives thought that this article was merely a duplication of the general non-discrimination clauses in article 2 of the ICCPR and of the ICESCR, and in article 26 of the ICCPR. It was pointed out, nevertheless, that article 3 did not merely state the principle of equality but enjoined States to make equality an effective reality.[24] As such, the Human RightsCommittee asserted in its General Comment No. 4 that article 3, like articles 2 (1) and 26 insofar as those articles primarily deal with the prevention of discrimination on a number of grounds, of which sex is one, requires not only measures of protection but also affirmative action designed to ensure the positive enjoyment of rights. This cannot be done by simply enacting law.[25]

In 1975 the ILO adopted a Declaration on Equality of Opportunity and Treatment for Women Workers.[26] Article 2, paragraph 2, states unambiguously that positive special treatment during a transitional period aimed at effective equality between the sexes shall not be regarded as discriminatory.[27] According to MacKean, this formulation neatly summarizes the thesis that true equality sought by international instruments does not necessarily require identical treatment of all, but that special ameliorative measures are perfectly consistent with equality and do not constitute discrimination so long as they are not continued after the need has disappeared. In the same vein, UNESCO decided in 1979, in view of the handicaps facing girls and women, that until "full equality" of education and training opportunities was assured, there was a need for special programmes for girls and women, so as to enable them to reduce and eventually eliminate the gap.[28]

During the drafting of the Convention on the Elimination of All Forms of Discrimination against Women (hereafter "Women's Convention") the question of special measures was discussed. It was emphasized that the establishment of temporary conditions for women

---

[24] M. Bossuyt, op. cit. at note 7, pp. 75-79. The same arguments were used by those who considered a specific convention on women unnecessary in view of the texts already in existence. MacKean comments: "Some representatives considered that the paragraph might be taken to decree an 'absolute' or 'precise' equality or 'identity of treatment' but others urged that what was being sought was an effective equality in fact - not the abolition of differences between the roles of men and women in marriage, but rather the equitable differences of rights and responsibilities." There was certainly a feeling that de facto equality should be increased. As such, the representative of the USSR commented that the Third Committee was "elaborating principles of de jure equality; from these principles would arise the de facto equalization of human rights". He continued, "equality of rights went further than mere non-discrimination; it implied the existence of positive rights in all the spheres dealt with in the draft Covenant". W. MacKean, Equality and Discrimination under International Law, Oxford, Clarendon Press, 1983, p. 182.

[25] Human Rights Committee, General Comment No. 4, para. 2, in HRI/GEN/1/Rev.4 (2000).

[26] Adopted on 25 June 1975 by the 60th Session of the International Labour Conference. See United Nations document E/CN.6/603.

[27] The ILO had already undertaken efforts concerning equal remuneration for work of equal value. See ILO Equal Remuneration Convention, 1951 (No. 100), I. Brownlie, Basic documents on human rights, Oxford, Clarendon Press, 1981, p. 200.

[28] See United Nations document E/CN.6/632, para. 92.

aimed at establishing de facto equality should not be considered discriminatory. Article 4 provides explicitly:

> "1. Adoption by States Parties of temporary special measures aimed at accelerating de facto equality between men and women shall not be considered discrimination as defined in the present Convention, but shall in no way entail as a consequence the maintenance of unequal or separate standards; these measures shall be discontinued when the objectives of equality of opportunity and treatment have been achieved.
>
> "2. Adoption by States Parties of special measures, including those measures contained in the present Convention, aimed at protecting maternity shall not be considered discriminatory."

That this article was controversial appears from the reactions of France and the United Kingdom who insisted that the Convention should in no way require Governments to impose "reverse discrimination", by which they meant "discrimination in favour of women", since - save in certain carefully defined circumstances - this would represent a permanent departure from the objective of equal status and opportunities and would not be in the long-term interest of women themselves. On the other hand, the Convention should permit, but not require, temporary affirmative action measures in special fields to equalize opportunities for women in situations where it was necessary to overcome an undesirable historical link. States admitted that although this might appear to be discriminatory, it was necessary to right wrongs done against women in the past because of their sex. However, it was stressed that this should be seen essentially as a temporary measure which in the long term should become unnecessary. [29]

Problematic for some States were also the special protection measures concerning maternity. Some States felt that one's physical constitution was not a matter of sex but something that applied to both women and men. MacKean considers that the controversy was due to widespread confusion over terminology: "If 'equal treatment' always means the 'same' or 'identical' treatment, then of course special measures are unequal, but if equality is used in a normative sense then the difficulty disappears. Similarly, if discrimination means unjustifiable or unreasonable differentiations then the question arises whether certain measures are objectively justifiable. This can easily be shown for measures designed to protect women's physiological function, particularly childbearing, but as the ILO has shown, it is increasingly recognized that measures designed to protect women as such because of their physical nature might equally well be applied to some men."[30] Moreover, there was a lack of consensus during the drafting as to whether a convention should deal with equality between men and women or the elimination of discrimination against women.

Vogel-Polsky stated in her study, commissioned by the Steering Committee for Equality between Men and Women of the Council of Europe (CDEG), that States that had become parties to the Convention without making reservations on article 4 not only bound themselves to eliminate discrimination against women, but also took upon themselves the obligation to restore the balance between men and women in every aspect of social life through appropriate

---

[29] L.A. Rehof, Guide to the "Travaux Préparatoires" of the United Nations Convention on the Elimination of All Forms of Discrimination against Women, Dordrecht, Martinus Nijhoff Publishers, 1993, pp. 66-76.

[30] W. MacKean, op. cit. at note 24, pp. 190-191.

measures, more specifically affirmative action.[31] However, this position appears rather extreme. From the travaux préparatoires and the intention of the authors, it is important to note that this convention is promotional and programmatic and does not impose immediately binding legal obligations. Article 4 merely creates the possibility to achieve de facto equality through affirmative action, and acknowledges that affirmative action is not to be considered discriminatory.[32] The Committee on the Elimination of All Forms of Discrimination against Women, nevertheless, took note of the still present need for action to implement fully the Convention by introducing measures to promote de facto equality between men and women. It recommended States parties to make more use of temporary special measures such as positive action, preferential treatment or quota systems to advance women's integration into education, the economy, politics and employment.[33]

The subsequent articles of the Women's Convention guaranteeing diverse rights stipulate each in an intentionally repetitive way: that member States shall take "all appropriate" measures. Vogel-Polsky argues that because the Convention refers to "all appropriate measures" in an obligatory manner, it renders the "temporary special measures" referred to in article 4 not only indispensable but, combined with the fact that the Convention seeks equality in fact, the most appropriate measures to use. Vogel-Polsky maintains that this interpretation of the relationship between the various rights in the Convention and article 4 (which universally sanctions affirmative action) is directly inspired by the principle of "appropriate or full effect" ("effet utile") of international law.[34] The CEDAW seems to agree with this interpretation.

In its General Recommendation No. 23 on political and public life the Committee refers to temporary special measures in the following way:

> "While removal of de jure barriers is necessary, it is not sufficient. Failure to achieve full and equal participation of women can be unintentional and the result of outmoded practices and procedures which inadvertently promote men. Under article 4, the Convention encourages the use of temporary special measures in order to give full effect to articles 7 and 8. Where countries have developed effective temporary strategies in an attempt to achieve equality of participation, a wide range of measures [have] been implemented, including recruiting, financially assisting and training women candidates, amending electoral procedures, developing campaigns directed at equal participation, setting numerical goals and quotas and targeting women for appointment to public positions such as the judiciary or other professional groups that play an essential part in the everyday life of all societies. The formal removal of barriers and the introduction of temporary special measures to encourage the equal participation of both men and women in the public life of their societies are essential prerequisites to true equality in political life. In order, however, to overcome centuries of male domination of the public sphere, women also require the encouragement and support of all sectors of society to achieve full and effective participation, encouragement which must be led by States parties to the Convention, as well as by political parties and public officials. States parties

[31] E. Vogel-Polsky, Les actions positives et les contraintes constitutionelles et legislatives qui pèsent sur leur mise en oeuvre dans les Etats membres du Conseil de l'Europe

[32] See also A.W. Heringa, "Voorkeursbehandeling en moederschap", in A.W. Heringa, J. Hes and L. Linjnzaad, Het Vrouwenverdrag: een beeld van een verdrag ..., Antwerpen, Maklu, 1994, pp. 33-34.

[33] Committee on the Elimination of Discrimination against Women, General Recommendation No. 5, Temporary special measures, in HRI/GEN/1/Rev.4 (2000).

[34] E. Vogel-Polsky, "Les actions positives dans la théorie juridique contemporaine", in B. De Grave, (ed.), Positieve actie, positieve discriminatie, voorrangsbehandeling voor vrouwen, Tegenspraak-Cahier 8, Antwerpen, Kluwer, 1990, p. 79.

have an obligation to ensure that temporary special measures are clearly designed to support the principle of equality and therefore comply with constitutional principles which guarantee equality to all citizens."[35]

II. Limits Set on Affirmation Action Measures

International law sets major limits on affirmative action measures. These are:

(a) Affirmative action measures may not lead to discrimination;
(b) Affirmative action measures need to be temporary.

A. The prohibition of non-discrimination

Of particular importance when assessing affirmative action measures is their relationship with the principle of non-discrimination, which is the reverse formulation of the principle of equality and one of the most - if not the most - fundamental human rights. The principle of equality has been solemnly affirmed in the 1948 Universal Declaration of Human Rights, which states, "All human beings are born free and equal in dignity and rights", and in Article 1 of the Charter of the United Nations which asserts as one of the goals of the Organization "to achieve international cooperation (...) in promoting and encouraging respect for human rights and for fundamental freedoms for all without distinction as to race, sex, language, or religion". A similar provision is contained in all the human rights instruments of the international regional systems, such as the Council of Europe, the Organization of American States and the Organization of African Unity.

Non-discrimination is primarily a legal technique employed to counteract unjustified inequality, founded on the idea that a State may not legitimately disadvantage an individual on an arbitrary basis.[36] The prohibition of discrimination can be found in all international instruments.

---

[35] Committee on the Elimination of Discrimination against Women, General Recommendation No. 23, Political and public life, para. 15, in HRI/GEN/1/Rev.4(2000).

[36] Non-discrimination and equality constitute nowadays basic and essential principles relating to the protection of human rights. Consequently, they have also become principles of customary international law. Extensive support for this view is to found in various authoritative international instruments proclaiming the principle of non-discrimination, such as the International Covenant on Civil and Political Rights, the International Covenant on Economic, Social and Cultural Rights, the International Convention on the Elimination of All Forms of Racial Discrimination, the UNESCO Declaration on Race and Racial Prejudice, etc. Furthermore, authoritative legal institutions, such as the International Law Commission and the International Court of Justice, have made declarations in that sense. See, for example, the statements of the ICJ in its Advisory Opinion on the Legal Consequences for States of the Continued Presence of South Africa in Namibia notwithstanding Security Council Resolution 276 (1970), in the Barcelona Traction case (1970), and in its Advisory Opinion on Namibia (1971). The view is also supported by State practice and a strong opinio juris voiced atvarious international conferences and by authoritative experts.

Non-discrimination and affirmative action if not carefully framed may clash with each other. Where the non-discrimination principle removes factors such as race, gender, nationality, etc. from the society's decision-making processes, affirmative action seeks to ensure full and substantive equality by taking those factors into account.[37] However, affirmative action, in its desire to achieve equality, can sometimes use extreme measures and thereby violate the non-discrimination principle. Therefore, affirmative action policies must be carefully controlled and not be permitted to undermine the principle of non-discrimination itself. In order to understand when affirmative action becomes discrimination, it is worth while having a close look at the travaux préparatoires of several international instruments containing nondiscrimination principles.

During the preparation of the non-discrimination provision in article 7 of the Universal Declaration, the Chairman of the United Nations Commission on Human Rights, Eleanore Roosevelt, stated that equality did not mean identical treatment for men and women in all matters, for there were certain cases where differential treatment was essential. This was a clear reaffirmation of the idea that "equality" was not only to be understood in its normative sense but also in its formal sense. [38] According to Lauterpacht, it implies equality relative to the situation.[39]

The ambiguous terminology in the non-discrimination provisions of international human rights, which have used the terms "distinction" and "discrimination" interchangeably to cover the same concept, has created great confusion.[40] For example, there is an inconsistency in article 2 of the International Covenants: the International Covenant on Economic, Social and Cultural Rights guarantees that "the rights enunciated in the present Covenant will be exercised without discrimination of any kind", whereas the International Covenant on Civil and Political Rights guarantees "the rights recognised in the present Covenant without distinction of any kind".

---

[37] See United States Supreme Court Justice Blackmun's dictum: "in order to get beyond racism, we must first take race into account". Regents of the University of California v. Bakke, 438 U.S. 265, 1978.

[38] See United Nations document E/CN.4/SR.50, para. 9. For an explanation of the discussion on "distinction" and "discrimination", which reappeared later during the drafting of the International Covenants, see also J.T. Möller, "Article 7", in A. Eide, et al. (eds.), The Universal Declaration of Human Rights: A Commentary, Oslo, Scandinavian University Press, 1992, pp. 115-141.

[39] Sir Hersch Lauterpacht (An International Bill of the Rights of Man, New York, Columbia University Press, 1945, pp. 116-119) refers to section 1 of the Fourteenth Amendment of the Constitution of the United States, which states that the equal protection of the laws does not exclude distinctions between and classifications of persons so long as these are based on reasonable grounds. Early case law of the United States Supreme Court, therefore, does not forbid the segregation of blacks in schools, trains, railway stations and other public places. The Supreme Court stated that wide discretion in establishing classifications by reference to various factors is essential to and not inconsistent with the principle of true equality so long as the basis of classification is reasonable. This line of reasoning was later reformed. Lauterpacht admits that the interpretation of equality conceived as a mechanical equality of opportunity and advantage was stretched to the breaking point.

[40] On the history of this ambiguity, see M. Bossuyt, L'Interdiction de la discrimination dans le droit international des droits de l'homme, Bruxelles, Bruylant, 1976, pp. 7-27 ; N. Lerner, Group rights and discrimination in international law, Dordrecht, Martinus Nijhoff Publishers, 1991, pp. 24-28; B.G. Ramcharan, "Equality and nondiscrimination", in L. Henkin (ed.), The International Bill of Rights, New York, Columbia University Press, 1981, pp. 258-259.

Article 14 of the English version of the European Convention on Human Rights states: "the enjoyment of the rights and freedoms set forth in this Convention shall be secured without discrimination on any ground such as sex, race, colour, language, religion, political or other opinion, national or social origin, association with a national minority, property, birth or other status", while the French version uses the term "distinction".

Although no explicit explanation is offered in the travaux prėparatoires for these inconsistencies, it should be admitted that, whatever word was used, the drafters intended to include in both Covenants and in the European Convention the same level of protection. Both terms clearly exclude only "discrimination" understood as "arbitrary" or "unjust distinction".

The concept that not all distinctions are unlawful was crucial during the drafting of article 2, paragraph 2, of the International Covenant on Economic, Social and Cultural Rights, where an overwhelming majority endorsed a three-Power amendment (Argentina, Italy and Mexico) to replace the word "distinction" with the word "discrimination".[41] The stated purpose was to confirm that certain distinctions might be justified to promote the position of certain backward and underprivileged sectors of the population.

Similarly, in its General Comment on article 26, the general non-discrimination principle of the International Covenant on Civil and Political Rights, the Human Rights Committee added that "the enjoyment of rights and freedoms on an equal footing, however, does not mean identical treatment in every instance" and that "not every differentiation of treatment will constitute discrimination".[42]

In the same vein, the European Court of Human Rights affirmed in the Belgian Linguistics case that:

> "In spite of the very general wording of the French version ('sans distinction aucune'), article 14 does not forbid every difference in treatment in the exercise of the rights and freedoms recognised. This version must be read in the light of the more restrictive text of the English version ('without discrimination')."[43]

The concept of non-discrimination has further been clarified by a number of studies carried out by special rapporteurs of the Sub-Commission.[44] Modern legal doctrine makes the following conclusions:

(a) Nowadays, it is universally accepted that the term "discrimination" has to be reserved for

---

41 See United Nations document A/5365, p. 22.

42 Human Rights Committee, General Comment No. 18, Non-discrimination, paras. 8 and 13, in HRI/GEN/1/Rev.4 (2000).

43 European Court of Human Rights, Belgian Linguistics case, 23 June 1968, Ser. A, p. 34. The Court admitted that doing so would lead to absurd results - every legal provision which does not secure to everyone equal treatment would be contrary to article 14. This would be an untenable position, as law necessarily makes distinctions of many kinds.

44 See for a good summary Vijapur, op. cit. at note 14, pp. 73-74. MacKean, op. cit at note 24, pp. 94-96. For example, in 1949, the Secretary-General stated in his memorandum on the main types and causes of discrimination that discrimination is a detrimental distinction based on grounds which may not be attributed to the individual and which have no justified consequences. See United Nations document E/CN.4/Sub.2/40.

arbitrary and unlawful differences in treatment.[45] "Distinction", on the other hand, is a neutral term, which is used when it has not yet been determined whether a differential treatment may be justified or not. The term "differentiation", on the contrary, points to a difference in treatment, which has been deemed to be lawful;[46]

(b) Consequently, not every different treatment is prohibited - only those treatments that result in discrimination. This raises the question of when differential treatment becomes unacceptable, or when a distinction of any kind can be justified.[47]

International courts and authors looked for criteria which enabled a determination to be made as to whether or not a given difference in treatment contravened the non-discrimination principle.

In the South West Africa cases, Judge Tanaka affirmed that equality being a principle and different treatment an exception, those who refer to the different treatment must prove its

[45] Bossuyt, op. cit. at note 7, p. 27. MacKean, ibid., pp. 8-11.

[46] This is consistent with the international definitions on discrimination. "Discrimination" was not defined in the Universal Declaration or in the two International Covenants. The first definition of discrimination is to be found in the International Convention on the Elimination of All Forms of Racial Discrimination which provides that the term "racial discrimination" shall mean "any distinction, exclusion, restriction or preference based on race, colour, descent, or national or ethnic origin which has the purpose or effect of nullifying or impairing the recognition, enjoyment or exercise, on an equal footing, of human rights and fundamental freedoms in the political, economic, social, cultural or any other field of public life". Similarly, the Convention on the Elimination of All Forms of Discrimination against Women provides that "discrimination against women" shall mean "any distinction, exclusion or restriction made on the basis of sex which has the effect or purpose of impairing or nullifying the recognition, enjoyment or exercise by women, irrespective of their marital status, on a basis of equality of men and women, of human rights and fundamental freedoms in the political, economic, social, cultural, civil or any other field". The Human Rights Committee has used these definitions of specific forms of discrimination to construct a more general definition. According to the Committee discrimination should be understood to imply "any distinction, exclusion, restriction or preference which is based on any ground such as race, colour, sex, language, religion, political or other opinion, national or social origin, property, birth or other status, and which has the purpose or effect of nullifying or impairing the recognition, enjoyment or exercise by all persons, on equal footing, of all rights and freedoms". General Comment No. 18, para. 7. Other definitions are to be found in the ILO Convention concerning Discrimination in Respect of Employment and Occupation, 1958 (No. 111), which states: "For the purpose of this Convention the term discrimination includes - (a) any distinction, exclusion or preference made on the basis of race, colour, sex, religion, political opinion, national extraction or social origin, which has the effect of nullifying or impairing equality of opportunity or treatment in employment or occupation ...". The UNESCO Convention against Discrimination in Education (1960) asserts: "For the purpose of this Convention, the term 'discrimination' includes any distinction, exclusion, limitation or preference which, being based on race, colour, sex, language, religion, political or other opinion, national or social origin, economic condition or birth, has the purpose or effect of nullifying or impairing equality of treatment in education …".

[47] See C. Tomuschat, "Equality and Non-Discrimination under the CCPR", in I. Von Munch, Festschrift für Hans-Jûrgen Schlochauer, Berlin, Walter de Gruyter, 1981, pp. 712-716.

raison d'être and its reasonableness; it must not be given arbitrarily but be in conformity with justice.[48]

In the Belgian Linguistics case, the European Court, following principles which may be extracted from the legal practice of a large number of democratic States, held that

> "the principle of equality is violated if the distinction has no objective and reasonable justification. The existence of such a justification must be assessed in relation to the aim and effects of the measure under consideration, regard being had to principles which normally prevail in democratic societies. A difference of treatment in the exercise of a right laid down in the Convention must not only pursue a legitimate aim: Article 14 is likewise violated when it is clearly established that there is no reasonable relationship of proportionality between the means employed and the aim sought to be realised."[49]

These principles have been repeatedly applied in a great number of later cases.[50]

The United Nations Human Rights Committee has followed the European Court of Human Rights in its position, and declared in its views and General Comment No. 18 that:

> "not every differentiation of treatment will constitute discrimination, if the criteria for such differentiation are reasonable and objective and if the aim is to achieve a purpose which is legitimate under the Covenant".[51]

---

[48] Dissenting Opinion of Judge Tanaka, South West Africa cases, (2nd phase), ICJ Report 1966, pp. 284-316. Judge Tanaka keenly observed that the principle of equality requires that those who are equal be treated in an equal manner, and those who are different be treated differently. However, he asserted, the principle of equality does not mean absolute equality, but recognizes relative equality, namely different treatment proportionate to concrete individual circumstances. Although people have certain common characteristics, they nevertheless possess independent attributes and qualities, which may legitimately be taken into account in the distribution of social goods. The fundamental questions, however, remain: When can people be said to be equal or different, and which considerations may form legitimate justifications for differential treatment?

[49] European Court of Human Rights, op. cit. at note 43; M. Bossuyt, "Het discriminatieverbod van de Europese Conventie van de Rechten van de Mens in de Rechtspraak van de Commissie na het Belgisch taalarrest", Revue belge de droit international, 1972, pp. 503-528.

[50] The European Court's analysis of non-discrimination has been quoted with approval by the Inter-American Court of Human Rights in its Advisory Opinion oc-4/84, Proposed Amendments to the Naturalization Provisions of the Constitution of Costa Rica of 19 January 1984, para. 57: "There would be no discrimination in differences in treatment of individuals by a state when the classifications selected are based on substantial factual differences and there exists a reasonable relationship of proportionality between these differences and the aims of the legal rule under review. These aims may not be unjust or unreasonable, that is, they may not be arbitrary, capricious, despotic or in conflict with the essential oneness and dignity of humankind".

[51] See also, T. Opsahl, "Equality in Human Rights Law, with special reference to article 26 of the ICCPR", in M. Nowak, (ed.), Kehl, N.P. Engel Verlag, 1988, pp. 51-65. Case law: S.W.M. Broeks v. Netherlands, Communication No. 172/1984, Zwaan-de Vries v. Netherlands, Communication No. 182, 1984 Official Records of the General Assembly Forty-second session, supplement No. 48 (A/42/40), annex VIII, sects. B and D: because article 26 lays down a general principle of non-discrimination, the full range of this non-discrimination signifies that the Committee has competence to review any differential treatment, even in the field of economic, social and cultural rights, in order to determine if it amounts to discrimination.

Various authors have also analysed the different constitutive elements of discrimination.[52] One of these elements is the ground on which the distinction is based. The enumeration of the prohibited grounds in general human rights instruments is non-exhaustive. This follows clearly out of the enlargement of the four grounds enumerated in the Charter (race, language, religion and sex) to the 12 grounds in the Universal Declaration of Human Rights and both Covenants, to the 13 grounds in the European Convention on Human Rights, as well as from the use of the words "such as" which precede the enumeration of these grounds.

Consequently, a distinction based on another ground can be arbitrary and some distinctions based on some of the enumerated grounds are not necessarily illegitimate. The ground on which a distinction is based is nevertheless important in determining whether the E/CN.4/ Sub.2/2000/11 page 15 distinction is arbitrary or not. However, it is not the ground itself that is decisive, but the relationship or the connection between the ground and the right on which the distinction is practised. There needs to be a "sufficient connection" between the right and the ground or, in other words, the ground has to be deemed "relevant" for the specific right in which the distinction is practised. The general aim or the goal pursued by the legislation in question is not decisive, but the relevance of the particular ground with respect to the particular rights is. A distinction introduced by legislation in the pursuit of a perfectly legitimate goal can nevertheless be discriminatory - and as such constitute a violation of human rights - if the ground on which the distinction is based cannot be deemed relevant to the right in question.

Replacing the notion of "irrelevant" by the notion of "arbitrary" is not just substituting one word for another. The difference lies in the level at which the illegitimate character of the distinction has to be assessed. If this level were to be situated in relation to the general aims and goals of the legislation, the assessment would be purely political and inappropriate for judicial determination. The whole point, however, is that a legal rule is not necessarily legitimate because it pursues a legitimate goal. The law as a technique used to attain certain goals has to respect certain inherent requirements. The most fundamental of these is the respect of the equality principle, which prohibits the introduction of distinctions based on grounds which are irrelevant for the particular right or freedom.

While still requiring a value judgement, which can be influenced by political considerations, the evaluation of the relevance of the ground by assessing the connection between this ground and the right or freedom concerned remains a judicial act. The previous identification of the ground (on which the distinction is based) and of the matter (in which the distinction is practised) as a right reduces the political element to a strict minimum and safeguards the judicial character of the evaluation. The approach should not be basically different when evaluating distinctions introduced in the framework of a policy of "affirmative action".

There is no doubt that special measures may be necessary in order to ensure full equality for categories of the population which, sometimes for centuries, have suffered from a disadvantaged position in society. But it should be clear that not every measure taken in pursuit of such a policy should be accepted as legitimate regardless of the ground of distinction made or the nature of the right conferred. Even if it is established that the distinctions made in the

[52] Bossuyt, op. cit. at note 7, p. 262; M. Bossuyt, "The principle of equality in article 26 of the International Covenant on Civil and Political Rights", in A. De Mestral (ed.), The Limitation of Human Rights in Comparative Constitutional Law, Cowansville, Éditions Yvon Blais, 1986, pp. 283-284; E.W. Vierdag, The Concept of Discrimination in International Law with Special Reference to Human Rights, The Hague, Martinus Nijhoff, 1973, p. 176.

framework of an affirmative action policy are based on the same ground as the one which was the basis of previously unequal situations, the legal rules concerned should still be subject to the equality test.

The simple fact that a particular category of the population has suffered from disadvantaged economic or social conditions does not mean that in order to upgrade its material position any distinction based on the characteristic defining the group should be considered legitimate, even if this ground is irrelevant as a basis of distinction with regard to a particular right. It would not be justifiable to provide special social benefits to persons who do not need them but who belong to the category which used to be in a disadvantaged condition, and to refuse the same benefits to persons who do need them but belong to the category which previously enjoyed better conditions in society.

Affirmative action should be centred on taking measures expected to meet the particular needs of the category it is intended to favour, rather than on restricting the benefits of the measures on the basis of the element which distinguishes that category from the other members of the population, but which is not relevant for the right concerned. It is in choosing the measures, their timing and their location that the policy can favour the target category, without violating the rights - including their right to equal protection of the law without discrimination - of persons not belonging to that category. In no case may someone be deprived of a basic right under the pretext that doing so would help particularly disadvantaged groups better to overcome the consequences of previous discrimination.[53]

An affirmative action programme provision should not be interpreted as justifying any distinction based on any ground with respect to any right merely because its object is the amelioration of disadvantaged individuals or groups. Such an interpretation would justify absurd legislation in total disrespect of human rights and its fundamental principle of equality or non-discrimination.

B. Affirmative action measures need to be temporary

The requirement of "limited duration" of special measures has been continually stressed in international law. It has been maintained that although the acceptance of affirmative action is not contrary to international law, it does not allow ignoring the limits of affirmative action sanctioned by the Covenants.[54] The granting of affirmative action measures may not as a

[53] Lord Denning: "So here if this education authority were to allocate boys to particular schools according to the colour of their hair or, for that matter, the colour of their skin, it would be so unreasonable, so capricious, so irrelevant to any proper system of education that it would be ultra vires altogether and this Court would strike it down at once. But, if there were valid educational reasons for a policy, as, for instance in an area where immigrant children were backward in the English tongue and needed special teaching, then it would be perfectly right to allocate those in need to special schools where they would be given extra facilities for learning English". As quoted by MacKean, op. cit. at note 24, p. 246.

[54] Tomuschat, op. cit. at note 47, pp. 715-716, and Thornberry, op. cit. at note 13, pp. 281-286, refer to the travaux préparatoires of the International Covenants and the discussion on time limitation for affirmative action.

consequence lead to the maintenance of unequal or separate standards and they shall be discontinued after the objectives for which they have been taken have been achieved.[55]

It is absolutely to be avoided that affirmative treatment would lead to stigmatization or to a situation of "separate but equal", a doctrine previously used in the United States according to which Blacks were given the same rights as Whites but were forced to exercise these rights in isolation, or, worse, to a new apartheid.[56] The "limited duration" requirement reveals the difference between two overlapping notions in international law, i.e. the "protection ofminorities" and "prevention of discrimination".

Obviously, both minorities and disadvantaged groups can appeal to the non-discrimination principle protecting them against discrimination by reference to their race, colour, descent, national or ethnic origin, language. Likewise, they can be both beneficiaries of special measures, under the conditions mentioned, i.e. limited duration and the measures must not lead to discrimination themselves, to overcome past discriminatory treatment or structural discrimination.

However, it is clear that special measures of this kind are not sufficient to cover the issues raised regarding the exercise of the rights of persons belonging to minorities to enjoy their own culture, to profess and practise their own religion, or to use their own language. The exercise of these rights requires permanent measures of protection taken by States, which is a wider notion.

The concept of "protection of minorities" is one the oldest concerns of international law, finding its origin in the rise of the nation-State in the sixteenth and seventeenth centuries, which necessitated consideration for minority groups.[57] Many treaties were concluded for the benefit of specific groups, for example the Treaty of Paris of 30 March 1856 which contains provisions referring to the protection of Christian minorities in the Ottoman Empire. The Treaty of Berlin of 13 July 1878 is of particular interest because of the special legal status it accorded to some religious groups. The protection in these treaties was only partial and no machinery was established. Nevertheless, they served as a model for the "minorities system" that was subsequently established within the framework of the League of Nations.[58]

---

[55] See also articles 1, paragraph 4, ICERD and 4, paragraph 1, Woman's Convention. The Committee on the Elimination on Racial Discrimination, during the discussion on the fourthperiodic report of Fiji, pointed out that the special treatment accorded to certain racial groups did not appear to have a specified limited duration; in order to satisfy the Convention, a more categorical undertaking should have been given that the unequal rights of different racial groups would not be maintained after the objectives for which they were intended had been achieved. Official Records of the General Assembly, thirty-seventh session, supplement No. 18 (A/37/18), para. 101.

[56] Although the "separate but equal" doctrine appeared to violate the Fourteenth Amendment of the United States Constitution, the Supreme Court did not see it that way in 1896 when viewing the case Plessy v. Ferguson (163 U.S. 537, 1896). It involved a man who had been arrested for violating a Louisiana law that required railroads to provide "equal but separate accommodations" for "white and coloured" passengers. Half a century later, the doctrine was challenged in the case Brown v. Board of Education (347 U.S. 483, 1954) and the Supreme Court ruled that separate schools created a feeling of inferiority for Black students and for that reason violated the Fourteenth Amendment.

[57] See Thornberry, op. cit. at note 13, pp. 25-54, which deals extensively with the historical background.

[58] After the Congress of Vienna, treaty clauses for protection of minorities became more detailed and there was a shift away from the protection of religious groups to the protection of national minorities.

The treaties concluded under the "minorities system" were complex in their wording, but a survey of their provisions shows that they envisaged two aims:[59]

1. The principle of non-discrimination guaranteed nationals belonging to racial, linguistic or religious minorities enjoyment of the same treatment in the exercise of civil and political rights.
2. The principle that persons belonging to minority groups should be guaranteed a number of special rights which enabled the minorities to preserve and develop their national culture and consciousness. In particular, they had an equal right to establish schools and religious, charitable or social institutions at their own expense. They could use their own language, even in court, and freely exercise their own religion. Further, in towns and districts where there was a considerable proportion of citizens speaking a language other than the official language of the State, adequate facilities were to be provided for instruction to be given in that language to the children of such nations in primary school. Finally, the treaties provided that in those towns and districts where there was a considerable proportion of nationals of the country belonging to racial, religious or linguistic minorities, they were assured an equitable share in the enjoyment and application of the funds which might be provided out of public Treasury under the State, municipal or other budgets for educational, religious or charitable purposes. Some treaties also mentioned a limited right to autonomy.

Thus, the idea underlying the minority treaties signed within the framework of the League of Nations was twofold: to allow minorities to live alongside the rest of the population in a position of equality, and to preserve the characteristics and the separate identity of minorities.

Important case law on these special rights was developed by the Permanent Court of International Justice, which affirmed this double-track system. Five cases were submitted by the League Council to the Permanent Court for advisory opinions: three concerning German minorities in Poland, one concerning the Polish minority in Danzig and one concerning the Greek minority in Albania.

The judgement of the Court on the Minority Schools in Albania case is of great significance. The dispute originated with an amendment that was introduced into the Albanian Constitution whereby all private schools were abolished throughout the country. The Greek minority maintained that the amendment was in violation of the Albanian Declaration of 1921 concerning the protection of minorities. The Government of Albania contended that, since the abolition of the private schools constituted a general measure applicable to the majority as well as the minority, it was in conformity with the Declaration.

More in general, the Permanent Court stated:

> "Equality in law precludes discrimination of any kind: whereas equality in fact may involve the necessity of different treatment in order to attain a result which establishes an equilibrium between different situations. It is easy to imagine cases in which equality of treatment of the majority and of the minority, whose situation and requirements are different, would result in inequality in fact … .

---

59 P. de Azcárate, League of Nations and National Minorities: an experiment, Washington, Carnegie Endowment for International Peace, 1945, p. 216; McKean, op.cit. at note 24, pp. 14-45.

> The equality between members of the majority and of the minority must be an effective, genuine equality."[60]

As for the private schools of the Greek minority in Albania, the Court pronounced:

> "The institutions mentioned are indispensable to enable the minority to enjoy the same treatment as the majority, not only in law but also in fact. The abolition of these institutions, which alone can satisfy the special requirements of the minority groups, and their replacement by government institutions, would destroy this equality of treatment, for its effect would be to deprive the minority of the institutions appropriate to its needs, whereas the majority would continue to have them supplied in the institutions created by the State."

Because history showed that States such as Germany relied upon these minority provisions in the treaties to intervene militarily, most of the peace treaties signed after the Second World War contained non-discrimination clauses. Only a few treaties contained clauses protecting minorities, as the abuse of the minority treaties by Germany - and the consequent failure of the League of Nations - had left minority clauses with a poor reputation.

The emphasis in the protection of human rights shifted from group protection to the protection of individual rights and freedoms. The new approach applied only the non-discrimination principle, which meant that whenever someone's rights were violated because of a group characteristic, be it race, religion, nationality, etc., the matter was to be taken care of by protecting the rights of the individual on a purely individual basis. The principle of equality and the premise of non-discrimination became fundamental principles, enshrined in every human rights text written after the Second World War. This new approach was fully integrated in the establishment and workings of the United Nations. However, the notion of protection of minorities was still used in some international instruments.

At the first session in 1947 of the United Nations Sub-Commission on the Prevention of Discrimination and the Protection of Minorities, a discussion was held on the meaning of the terms "prevention of discrimination" and "protection of minorities".[61] It was indicated that there was a fundamental difference between them. "Discrimination" implied any act or conduct that denied to individuals or groups of people the equality of treatment they may wish. Protection of minorities was described as the protection of non-dominant groups which, while wishing in general for equality of treatment with the majority, wish for a measure of differential treatment in order to preserve basic characteristics which they possess and which distinguish them from the majority of the population. The protection belongs equally to individuals belonging to such groups and wishing the same protection. It follows that differential treatment of such groups or individuals belonging to such groups is justified when it is exercised in the interest of their contentment and the welfare of the community as a whole.

The notion of "protection of minorities" was further elaborated in a memorandum by the Secretary-General entitled, "The Main Types and Causes of Discrimination".[62] He argued that the protection of minorities, although similarly inspired by the principle of equality of

---

[60] Minority Schools in Albania, Advisory Opinion, PCIJ, 1935, Ser A/B No. 64, 19.

[61] This double-track system found its inspiration in the Advisory Opinion of the PCIJ on the Minority Schools in Albania, ibid. See United Nations documents E/CN.4/Sub.2/36 and E/CN.4/Sub.2/SR. 14 and 15.

[62] Op. cit. at note 44

treatment of all peoples, required positive action, such as establishment of schools where education is given in the native tongue, whenever the minorities concerned wished to maintain their difference of language and culture.[63]

The Secretary-General further maintained that while the goal of protection of minorities seems to differ from that of the prevention of discrimination, in reality there is no contradiction in aiming simultaneously at the protection of minorities and the prevention of discrimination. Indeed, in each case it is desired to obtain and effectively maintain equality of treatment of all peoples. Prevention of discrimination and the protection of minorities represent different developments of the same idea of equality of treatment for all peoples. One required the elimination of any distinction imposed, whereas the other required safeguards to preserve certain distinctions voluntarily maintained.

In his report on Protection of minorities, A. Eide[64] offered affirmative action as a solution to problems regarding minorities. However, he added that affirmative action can lead to group conflict, for which reason such measures should not be continued beyond the time when equality has been achieved.[65]

Affirmative action measures are temporary and compensatory, aimed at correcting conditions that impair the enjoyment of equal rights, while protective measures for minorities aim at conserving a group's identity.[66]

Annex

Questionnaire on Affirmative Action

1. What are the principal constitutional and legislative provisions relating to the principle of equality and the prohibition of discrimination? Please provide copies of the relevant provisions.

2. Provide landmark judgements relating to the principle of equality and the prohibition of

---

[63] Ibid.

[64] A. Eide, Protection of minorities: possible ways and means of facilitating the peaceful and constructive solution of problems involving minorities, (E/CN.4/Sub.2/1993/34, para. 172

[65] In its General Comment No. 18 on the non-discrimination principle, the Human Rights Committee stated that affirmative action, i.e. special measures, may be taken only for as long it is needed to correct discrimination in fact. On the other hand, in paragraphs 6.1 and 6.2 of its General Comment No. 23 on article 27, the minorities article, it admits that although the rights protected under article 27 are formulated in negativity terms positive measures by States may also be necessary to protect the identity of a minority and so long as they are only aimed at providing protection, they may constitute a legitimate differentiation under the Covenant. Here, no time limit is imposed. Notice also the different word use. This distinction is also made in State practice, for example, India has a different protection system for minorities, whose rights have an element of permanence, and for the Scheduled Castes and Scheduled Tribes, whose special rights are envisaged as temporary and exceptional measures to reduce the inequalities between communities.

[66] A.S. Akermark, Justifications of Minority Protection in International Law, London, Kluwer Law International, 1997, pp. 23-28.

discrimination.

3. Are there any provisions of a constitutional, legislative or executive nature referring to the concept of "affirmative action" and/or of so-called "positive" or "reverse" discrimination? If so, please provide copies of the relevant provisions.

4. What is, according to those provisions or to national case law, the relationship between the prohibition of discrimination and the concept of affirmative action?

5. Provide examples of national affirmative action schemes implemented pursuant to those provisions.

6. What groups are targeted by those affirmative action schemes (gender, racial groups, specific minorities, indigenous peoples, migrants, disabled persons, veterans, etc.)?

7. To what fields do those affirmative action schemes apply (education, employment, housing, transportation, ballot box, training, appointments to political, executive or judicial posts, awarding contracts or scholarships, others)?

8. What is the historical context in which those affirmative action schemes have been adopted?

9. What are the objectives stated in relation to those affirmative action schemes?

10. Are there any limits set to those affirmative action schemes and how will it be determined whether and when the objectives of those affirmative action schemes will be achieved?

11. Do the affirmative action schemes apply equally to all groups or are any distinctions made in favour of one or more specific groups over others? How are those specific groups defined?

12. Is there any national case law relating to those affirmative action schemes? If so, please provide copies of the principal judgements.

13. Are there any specific bodies, authorities, commissions, tribunals or courts competent to hear complaints in relation to the implementation and operation of affirmative action schemes?

14. Who is entitled to lodge complaints and start proceedings before such organs?

15. Provide, if available, statistics indicating the success of affirmative action schemes and particularly the progress made since their introduction.

Note: In the case where affirmative action schemes relating to different groups have been adopted, the answers should be given for each group specifically.

Part V
Specific Rights of Minorities

[13]

THE EMERGING RIGHT TO DEMOCRATIC GOVERNANCE

*By Thomas M. Franck**

> Legitimacy in 1991 flows not from the barrel of a gun but from the will of the people.
>
> *U.S. Secretary of State James A. Baker III*

> I know what real democracy is, what democracy is worth.
>
> *A thirty-seven-year-old Soviet lieutenant colonel who early on sided with anticoup forces*[†]

I. INTRODUCTION: THE POWER OF DEMOCRATIC LEGITIMACY

More than two centuries have elapsed since the signatories of the U.S. Declaration of Independence sought to manifest two radical propositions. The first is that governments, instituted to secure the "unalienable rights" of their citizens, derive "their just powers from the consent of the governed." We may call this the "democratic entitlement." The second proposition, perhaps less noted by commentators, is that a nation earns "separate and equal station" in the community of states by demonstrating "a decent respect to the opinions of mankind." The authors of the Declaration apparently believed that the legitimacy of the new Confederation of American States was not made evident solely by the transfer of power from Britain but also needed to be acknowledged by "mankind." This we may perceive as a prescient glimpse of the legitimating power of the community of nations.

For two hundred years, these two notions have remained a radical vision. The purpose of this essay is to demonstrate that the radical vision, while not yet fully word made law, is rapidly becoming, in our time, a normative rule of the international system. In the process, the two notions have merged. Increasingly, governments recognize that their legitimacy depends on meeting a normative expectation of the community of states. This recognition has led to the emergence of a community expectation: that those who seek the validation of their empowerment patently govern with the consent of the governed. Democracy, thus, is on the way to becoming a global entitlement, one that increasingly will be promoted and protected by collective international processes.

II. THE VALIDATION OF GOVERNANCE

Two recent events underscore this trend. The failure of the August coup in the Soviet Union, an event of inestimable human, political and historic import, demonstrates—for those sensitive to trends—that democracy is beginning to be seen as the *sine qua non* for validating governance. While President Boris Yeltsin of the Russian Republic and many Soviet citizens deserve primary credit for this

* Editor in Chief. The author wishes to express warm appreciation to many members of the Board of Editors for their helpful comments, as well as Paul Szasz, Robert Crouse, Gregory Fox, Dennis Sughrue, and the members of my honors seminar at the NYU Center for International Studies. Special thanks are due to the Filomen D'Agostino and Max E. Greenberg Research Fund of New York University School of Law.

† N.Y. Times, Aug. 22, 1991, at A15, col. 6; and *id.*, Aug. 21, 1991, at A9, col. 1.

triumph, it also derived considerable impetus from the new global climate, as evidenced by the vigor with which leaders of other democracies around the world aligned themselves against the coup's leaders. Equally significant is the reaction of governments in the Organization of American States and the United Nations General Assembly to the overthrow, in September 1991, of the elected President of Haiti, Jean-Bertrand Aristide, by a military coup. On October 11, the Assembly unanimously, without vote, approved a ground-breaking resolution demanding the return of Aristide to office, full application of the Haitian Constitution and full observance of human rights in Haiti.[1] The OAS, a week earlier, had unanimously recommended that its member states take "action to bring about the diplomatic isolation of those who hold power illegally in Haiti" and "suspend their economic, financial, and commercial ties" with the country until constitutional rule is restored.[2]

In both the Soviet and the Haitian cases, the leaders of states constituting the international community vigorously asserted that *only* democracy validates governance. This dramatic statement attains even more potency if, as in the Haitian case, it is transposed from political philosophy, where it is "mere" moral prescription, to law, where a newly recognized "democratic entitlement" was used in both the OAS and the UN General Assembly to impose new and important legal obligations on states. The OAS resolution, for one, stated that "the solidarity of the American states and the high aims which are sought through it require the political organization of those states on the basis of the effective exercise of representative democracy."[3] Undeniably, a new legal entitlement is being created, based in part on custom and in part on the collective interpretation of treaties.

This newly emerging "law"—which requires democracy to validate governance—is not merely the law of a particular state that, like the United States under its Constitution, has imposed such a precondition on national governance. It is also becoming a requirement of international law, applicable to all and implemented through global standards, with the help of regional and international organizations.

The transformation of the democratic entitlement from moral prescription to international legal obligation has evolved gradually. In the past decade, however, the tendency has accelerated. Most remarkable is the extent to which an international law-based entitlement is now urged by governments themselves. This is a cosmic, but unmysterious, change. For nations surfacing from long, tragic submergence beneath bogus "people's democracy" or outright dictatorship, the legitimation of power is a basic, but elusive, move in the direction of reform. As of late 1991, there are more than 110 governments, almost all represented in the United Nations, that are legally committed to permitting open, multiparty, secret-ballot elections with a universal franchise. Most joined the trend in the past five years.[4] While a few, arguably, are democracies more in form than in substance,

[1] UN Doc. A/46/L.8/Rev.1 (1991).

[2] Support to the Democratic Government of Haiti, OEA/Ser.F/V.1/MRE/RES.1/91, corr.1, paras. 5, 6 (1991).

[3] *Id.*, preamble.

[4] This enumeration was compiled by reference to reports in the *New York Times* and the *Country Reports on Human Rights Practices for 1990, infra* note 10, submitted by the Department of State to the appropriate committees of Congress. States that currently make legal provision for determining their governments by recourse to multiparty, secret-ballot elections are: Albania, Angola, Antigua and Barbuda, Argentina, Australia, Austria, the Bahamas, Bangladesh, Barbados, Belgium, Belize, Benin, Byelorussia, Bolivia, Botswana, Brazil, Bulgaria, Canada, Cape Verde, Chile, Colombia, the Comoros,

most are, or are becoming, genuinely open to meaningful political choice. Many of these new regimes want, indeed need, to be validated by being seen to comply with global standards for free and open elections.

That governments themselves now argue for the entitlement merely indicates their long-overdue recognition of an immutable fact of life: government cannot govern by force alone. To be effective, pace Austin,[5] law needs to secure the habitual, *voluntary* compliance of its subjects; it cannot rely entirely, or even primarily, upon the commanding power of a sovereign to compel obedience. Consequently, governments no longer blinded by the totalitarian miasma seek to validate themselves in such a way as to secure a high degree of voluntary public acquiescence in the governing process. Consent benefits the governing as much as the governed: that sociological truism is at last becoming a political axiom. In western industrialized nations, at least since the middle of the nineteenth century, such validation has increasingly been sought and achieved by governments. This is the hard-won tradition most of the world now seeks to emulate.

Since the beginning of the twentieth century, however, there has also been a countertendency. The notion of democracy as validation has been challenged, quite powerfully, first, by the notion of the "dictatorship of the proletariat" and, more recently, by a related theory of forced-march "modernization."

The doctrine of the dictatorship of the proletariat argued, with considerable force, that governing, especially in an industrial society, should not be an art but a science. It postulated, at least in theory, a dictatorship of trained and doctrinally correct economists, administrators, sociologists and political scientists capable of implementing correct policies. The complexities of governance were thought to be too great to be left to amateurs selected by the vagaries of popular passion.[6]

Congo, the Cook Islands, Costa Rica, the Côte d'Ivoire, Cyprus, Czechoslovakia, Denmark, Dominica, the Dominican Republic, Ecuador, Egypt, El Salvador, Estonia, Finland, France, Gabon, Gambia, Germany, Greece, Grenada, Guatemala, Guyana, Hungary, Honduras, Iceland, India, Ireland, Israel, Italy, Jamaica, Japan, Kiribati, Korea (Republic of), Latvia, Liberia, Liechtenstein, Lithuania, Luxembourg, Madagascar, Malaysia, Mali, Malta, the Marshall Islands, Mauritius, Mexico, the Micronesian Federation, Mongolia, Morocco, Mozambique, Namibia, Nauru, Nepal, the Netherlands, New Zealand, Nicaragua, Niger, Norway, Pakistan, Panama, Papua New Guinea, Paraguay, Peru, the Philippines, Poland, Portugal, Romania, São Tomé, Senegal, Singapore, the Solomon Islands, the Soviet Union, Spain, Sri Lanka, St. Kitts, St. Lucia, St. Vincent, Sweden, Switzerland, Tonga, Trinidad, Tunisia, Turkey, the Ukraine, the United Kingdom, Uruguay, Vanuatu, Venezuela, Western Samoa, Zambia and Zimbabwe. Several more states, such as Nigeria and Ethiopia, are committed to free, multiparty elections but have not yet enacted the necessary constitutional or legislative fiat. It must also be conceded that there are borderline cases, such as Morocco (included) and Jordan (not included), in which the elections are not necessarily decisive, depending on various factors, including the disposition of a monarch with substantial residual powers. In the large majority of cases, however, the decision to include or exclude is not seriously in doubt—though it should be recalled that the test for inclusion is whether the legal system establishes free and secret elections. Whether these are conducted fairly is another question.

[5] Austin defined law as the enforced command of a sovereign to a subject. J. AUSTIN, THE PROVINCE OF JURISPRUDENCE DETERMINED 201 (I. Berlin, S. Hampshire & R. Wollheim eds. 1954) (1832).

[6] *See, e.g.*, Theses on the Role of the Communist Party in the Proletarian Revolution Adopted by the Second Congress, in 1 THE COMMUNIST INTERNATIONAL: 1919–1943 DOCUMENTS 127 (J. Degras ed. 1971).

In 1920 Trotsky offered this response to a suggestion that the dictatorship of the Communist Party and the dictatorship of the proletariat were not identical:

> Today we received peace proposals from the Polish Government. Who decides this question? We have the Council of People's Commissars, but that too must be subject to a certain control. Whose

The contemporary theory of "modernization," which originated in the European fascist-charterist dictatorships of the 1930s, found new respectability among leaders of postcolonial Latin America, Africa and Asia, as well as some western friends of the Third World.[7] In the Third World, it was argued, the task of modern nation building—melding disparate tribes and clans to create new economies of scale—was said to warrant suspending imported bourgeois democratic values which, at any rate, were virtually meaningless in a largely rural, communal and illiterate society. The model was not a pompous Mussolini making Italian trains run punctually but Oliver Cromwell dismissing Parliament and getting Britain organized. In a few countries—Singapore, South Korea and Taiwan—the model seemed to work for a time, in the sense that much social and economic progress was achieved. In most instances, however, the implied promise was not kept.

Since the middle of the 1980s, both the "dictatorship of the proletariat" and the theory of "modernization" have collapsed under the weight of their evident failure. Throughout socialist Eastern Europe and in most of the dictatorships of Africa and Asia, the people have rejected both theories, together with the espousing governments, beginning with the televised popular revolution against Ferdinand Marcos in the Philippines. Instead, people almost everywhere now demand that government be validated by western-style parliamentary, multiparty democratic process. Only a few, usually military or theocratic, regimes still resist the trend. Very few argue that parliamentary democracy is a western illusion and a neocolonialist trap for unwary Third World peoples.

This almost-complete triumph of the democratic notions of Hume, Locke, Jefferson and Madison—in Latin America, Africa, Eastern Europe and, to a lesser extent, Asia—may well prove to be the most profound event of the twentieth century and, in all likelihood, the fulcrum on which the future development of global society will turn. It is the unanswerable response to those who have said that free, open, multiparty, electoral parliamentary democracy is neither desired nor desirable outside a small enclave of western industrial states.

The question is not whether democracy has swept the boards, but whether global society is ready for an era in which *only* democracy and the rule of law will be capable of validating governance. This may be a venerable philosophical issue known to Plato,[8] but it is also a functional question that can be, and now is being, stated in global legal terms. Are we witnessing the evolution of an international rule system that defines the minimal requisites of a democratic process capable of validating the exercise of power? What norms will such a rule system encompass? Is the international community capable of developing, consensually, an institutional and normative framework for monitoring compliance with those requisites? Is the community of nations able to define and manage appropriate consequences of noncompliance?

> control? That of the working class as a formless, chaotic mass? No. So we convened the central committee of the party to discuss the proposal and decide on the answer. . . . The same is true of the agrarian question, the food question, and all other questions.

Id. at 127–28.

[7] *Cf.* D. APTER, THE POLITICS OF MODERNIZATION (1965).

[8] Plato's effort, in the *Statesman*, the *Laws* and the *Republic*, to define the extent to which a ruler's legitimacy is validated by wisdom, on the one hand, and by his subordination to the laws, on the other, is analyzed in G. SABINE, A HISTORY OF POLITICAL THEORY 67–105 (rev. ed. 1953).

III. LEGITIMACY AND THE INTERNATIONAL SYSTEM OF RULES

These questions, in turn, raise two separate issues of legitimacy that are related but should not be confused: first, the legitimacy of national governments and, second, the legitimacy of the emerging international rules and processes by which the governance of nations is increasingly being monitored and validated. The latter issue is of primary interest to the international lawyer, but its importance is due to its manifest connection with the former. We are witnessing a sea change in international law, as a result of which the legitimacy of each government someday will be measured definitively by international rules and processes. We are not quite there, but we can see the outlines of this new world in which the citizens of each state will look to international law and organization to guarantee their democratic entitlement. For some states, that process will merely embellish rights already protected by their existing domestic constitutional order. For others, it could be the realization of a cherished dream.

Citizens, however, will not be the only beneficiaries. We have observed that the engine pulling the democratic entitlement is the craving of governments for validation. Without validation, the task of governance becomes fraught with difficulty. Regimes prize validation, then, as evidence of their legitimacy. Legitimacy, in turn, is the quality of a rule, or a system of rules, or a process for making or interpreting rules that pulls both the rule makers and those addressed by the rules toward voluntary compliance.

Western democracies have achieved legitimacy largely by subjecting the political process to rules, often immutably entrenched in an intrepid constitution. These lucky few nations have succeeded in evolving their own legitimate means of validating the process by which the people choose those they entrust with the exercise of power. To achieve such a system of autochthonous validation (and thus to facilitate governing), those who hold or seek political power have made a far-sighted bargain comparable to John Locke's social compact;[9] they have surrendered control over the nation's validation process to various others: national electoral commissions, judges, an inquisitive press and, above all, the citizenry acting at the ballot box. This collectivity decides whether the standards of the democratic entitlement have been met by those who claim the right to govern. In return, the legitimacy bestowed by that process gives back far more power to those who govern than they surrendered.

In many nations, unfortunately, no such bargain was struck. Those who claim to govern cannot demonstrate that they have fulfilled the requirements of the democratic entitlement, even if they purport to recognize that entitlement. Senegal, for example, is a multiparty state with universal franchise and a secret ballot, but the results of the 1988 national elections were rejected as fraudulent both by opposition parties and by other social institutions. The other parties subsequently boycotted the 1990 local elections and refused to accept the Government's legitimacy.[10] Increasingly, as will be demonstrated later in this essay, governments whose legitimacy is questioned are turning to the international system for that

[9] *See* J. LOCKE, TWO TREATISES OF GOVERNMENT 119–20, 164–66 (W. Carpenter ed. 1955) (1690).

[10] U.S. DEPARTMENT OF STATE, 102D CONG., 1ST SESS., COUNTRY REPORTS ON HUMAN RIGHTS PRACTICES FOR 1990: REPORT SUBMITTED TO THE COMMITTEE ON FOREIGN RELATIONS, U.S. SENATE AND THE COMMITTEE ON FOREIGN AFFAIRS, HOUSE OF REPRESENTATIVES 322–23 (Comm. Print 1991).

validation which their national *polis* is as yet unable to give. They do so to avoid the alternative—persistent challenge to authority by coups, countercoups, instability and stasis—and to enable themselves to govern with essential societal acquiescence. What they seek is legitimation by a global standard monitored by processes of the international system.

The capacity of the international community to extend legitimacy to national governments, however, depends not only on its capacity to monitor an election or to recognize the credentials of a regime's delegates to the UN General Assembly, but also on the extent to which such international activity has evolved from the ad hoc to the normative: that is, the degree to which the process of legitimation itself has become legitimate.

In any rule system, national or international, legitimacy has its own modalities. It is to the latter that the international lawyer's creative perspective must turn. Do the global requisites for democratic validation of governments now include, or are they evolving into, rules and procedures that are perceived as legitimate by those to whom they are addressed? In the international context,[11] legitimacy is achieved if—or to the extent that—those addressed by a rule, or by a rule-making institution, perceive the rule or institution to have come into being and to be operating in accordance with generally accepted principles of right process.[12]

Empirically, legitimacy can be demonstrated by observing rules, and the decisions of rule-making or rule-applying institutions. Some are habitually obeyed, without recourse to police enforcement, while others are largely ignored. Different rules exhibit varying degrees of compliance pull, which is the measure of a rule's legitimacy. However, the degree of a rule's pull to compliance cannot be measured solely by observing actual compliance. A more sensitive measure would have to take into account, additionally, the degree to which a violator exhibits deference to a rule even while violating it: for example, by lying about, or covering up, the violation or the circumstances in which the violation occurred.

Purely deductive research on rule legitimacy—pulse taking in the form of large-scale empirical investigation of compliance pull—is difficult to structure. Abstract/inductive reasoning about the nature of legitimacy is more feasible. Thus, one may postulate four indicators: *pedigree, determinacy, coherence* and *adherence.*[13] The content of these four indicators of legitimacy will be defined in ensuing sections of this essay. For this general overview, it is sufficient to summarize as follows: pedigree refers to the depth of the rule's roots in a historical process; determinacy refers to the rule's ability to communicate content; coherence refers to the rule's internal consistency and lateral connectedness to the principles underlying other rules; and adherence refers to the rule's vertical connectedness to a normative hierarchy, culminating in an ultimate rule of recognition, which embodies the principled purposes and values that define the community of states. A hypothesis may now be ventured: the degree to which a rule, or a rule-making process, exhibits these four qualities will determine the degree to which the rule or the process has matured and is perceived to be legitimate.

Those indicators provide a conceptual map with which to approach the previously posed questions. They afford a convenient way of sorting through the welter

[11] Legitimacy, in this as in all other contexts, is a matter of degree. Some rules and institutions enjoy more legitimacy than others.

[12] T. Franck, The Power of Legitimacy Among Nations 19 (1990).

[13] *Id.* at 50–194.

of data to reach some estimate as to whether the global system is evolving legitimate rules and institutions capable of validating national governance. That estimate, in turn, will help us understand and react appropriately to the inevitable counterindicative challenges: recidivist tendencies and totalitarian holdouts.

In seeking to assess whether an international democratic order is emerging, data will be marshaled from three related generations of rule making and implementation. The oldest and most highly developed is that subset of democratic norms which emerged under the heading of "self-determination." The second subset—freedom of expression—developed as part of the exponential growth of human rights since the mid-1950s and focuses on maintaining an open marketplace of ideas. The third and newest subset seeks to establish, define and monitor a right to free and open elections.

These three subsets somewhat overlap, both chronologically and normatively. Collectively, they do not necessarily penetrate every nook and cranny of democratic theory. For example, the three subsets do not yet address normatively the thorny issue of the right of a disaffected portion of an independent state to secede; nor, as we shall see, is it conceptually or strategically helpful—at least at this stage of its evolution—to treat the democratic entitlement as inextricably linked to the claim of minorities to secession. Still, these three increasingly normative subsets are large building stones, gradually reinforcing each other and assuming the shape of a coherent normative edifice. Moreover, regional subsets are adding some supernumerary buttresses, cornices and lintels to the new structure that dovetail with, and enrich, the emerging global architecture. Some examples of these will be included in our inventory.

IV. Pedigree: The Case of Self-Determination

Self-determination is the historic root from which the democratic entitlement grew. Its deep-rootedness continues to confer important elements of legitimacy on self-determination, as well as on the entitlement's two newer branches, freedom of expression and the electoral right.

Symbolic validation and pedigree provide legitimacy's cultural and anthropological dimension.[14] As with any rule, the capacity of the democratic entitlement to pull toward voluntary compliance depends, in part, on the strength of what W. Michael Reisman refers to as "the authority signal."[15] Specifically, the legitimacy of a rule reflects the durability, as well as the consistency, of its acknowledgment and application in practice.

Since self-determination is the oldest aspect of the democratic entitlement, its pedigree is the best established. Self-determination postulates the right of a people organized in an established territory to determine its collective political destiny in a democratic fashion and is therefore at the core of the democratic entitlement. Symbolically, it is signified by a long-evolving tradition of maintaining observers, on behalf of international and regional organizations, at elections in colonies and trust territories. Early observer missions developed operational procedures. They sent reports to their sponsoring international agency or committee, which helped the community's political organs and individual member governments make deductions about the legitimacy of the decolonization process. Gradually, with many variations, the observer missions' methods became the standard operating proce-

[14] *Id.* at 91.

[15] Reisman, *International Lawmaking: A Process of Communication,* 75 ASIL Proc. 101, 110 (1981).

dure for validating an exercise of self-determination. Later in this essay, we will recapitulate these rules and procedures. Here, however, we are concerned with the pedigree, the time frame within which those processes took root and matured.

The aspiration that underpins the principle of self-determination is of an antiquity traceable, in the West, at least to the Hebrews' exodus from Egypt,[16] estimated to have been approximately in 1000 B.C.[17] Its modern rise to the status of universal entitlement began when the Versailles Peace Conference[18] undid, or brought into line with late nineteenth-century European nationalist sensibilities, the work of the Congress of Vienna, which had utterly disregarded ethnic sensibilities in redrawing the map of post-Napoleonic Europe. Embarking on another redesign of Europe after the First World War, President Woodrow Wilson made self-determination his lodestar. To this end, firmly overriding the doubts of Secretary of State Robert Lansing,[19] he reinforced the U.S. team of negotiators with an unusual contingent of historians, geographers and ethnologists,[20] the more effectively to argue for the norm's supremacy over power politics and strategic or economic considerations. Consequently, the American delegation summoned up extensive data on demographics and evidence of ethnicity in advocating free choice by "peoples."[21]

Thus prodded, the conference authorized twenty-six on-site consultations with different European groups seeking self-determination.[22] The Danes of Schleswig, annexed to Prussia in 1864, were able to secure agreement that "the frontier between Germany and Denmark shall be fixed in conformity with the wishes of the population."[23] Wilson also prevailed in the view "that all branches of the Slav race" in what was to become Czechoslovakia "should be completely freed from German and Austrian rule"[24] in full consultation with Slavic representatives.[25] He resisted efforts by France's Premier Clemenceau to establish an independent Rhenish buffer state consisting of unwilling Germans.[26] Although the Versailles settlement also brought self-determination to Poland,[27] as regards the Upper Silesian and Czech boundary settlements, as well as Fiume, Wilson reluctantly came to concede that sometimes one had to consider "other principles"—strategic, economic and logistic—that could "clash with the requirements of self-determination."[28]

[16] *Exodus* 1:2.

[17] The author is indebted to Fr. Robert Crouse, Professor of Classics at Dalhousie University and King's College, for this approximation, one carefully hedged with caveats appropriate to so risky an enterprise.

[18] *See* H. HANNUM, AUTONOMY, SOVEREIGNTY, AND SELF-DETERMINATION 20–31 (1990). The use of self-determination at Versailles and subsequently is also discussed more fully in Franck, *Legitimacy in the International System*, 82 AJIL 705, 743–48 (1988).

[19] "[T]he phrase [self-determination] is simply loaded with dynamite. It will raise hopes which can never be realized." R. LANSING, THE PEACE NEGOTIATIONS, A PERSONAL NARRATIVE 97 (1921). *See* Brilmayer, *Secession and Self-Determination: A Territorial Interpretation*, 16 YALE J. INT'L L. 177 (1991).

[20] 1 R. S. BAKER, WOODROW WILSON AND WORLD SETTLEMENT 109 (1922).

[21] 1 S. WAMBAUGH, PLEBISCITES SINCE THE WORLD WAR 13 (1933).

[22] 1 R. S. BAKER, *supra* note 20, at 188.

[23] 2 A HISTORY OF THE PEACE CONFERENCE OF PARIS 203 (H. W. V. Temperley ed. 1920).

[24] 4 *id.* at 261.

[25] *Id.* at 262.

[26] 4 THE INTIMATE PAPERS OF COLONEL HOUSE 334–35, 345 (C. Seymour ed. 1928).

[27] 1 S. WAMBAUGH, *supra* note 21, at 16.

[28] M. POMERANCE, SELF-DETERMINATION IN LAW AND PRACTICE 4 (1982); D. FLEMING, THE UNITED STATES AND WORLD ORGANIZATION 152–55 (1938). For example, Czechoslovakia ended up with defensible boundaries only by denying self-determination to a large Sudeten-German minority.

Nevertheless, the principle of self-determination, as championed by Wilson and the minorities released from the embrace of the German, Russian and Austro-Hungarian Empires, was applied vigorously, if sometimes imperfectly, to the vanquished lands of postwar Europe. In the rest of Europe, however, it was applied only in Ireland. In denying self-determination to the Aaland Islands—which sought to join Sweden by breaking away from Finland, itself newly emancipated from Russia—a Versailles-created international commission of jurists observed that the Covenant of the League of Nations did not even mention the principle and that it had not yet attained the status of a positive rule of law.[29] More important, self-determination played little part in the disposition of the vast overseas lands and peoples of the former German Empire, which were doled out to Australia, Belgium, Britain, France, Japan, New Zealand and South Africa. It was applied badly, if at all, to the former Turkish dependencies in Asia. The League's mandate system evinced only muted concern for the wishes of those territories' inhabitants.

Remarkably, after the Second World War the principle of self-determination became the most dynamic concept in international relations. Former German, Japanese and Italian colonies were placed under the trusteeship of the victors (and, in one case, the vanquished), with the clear obligation "to promote . . . progressive development towards self-government or independence" in accordance with "the freely expressed wishes of the peoples concerned."[30] Conceptual evolution, however, did not stop there. Soon not only was self-determination recognized as a writ for obtaining decolonization but, by the terms of the very first article of the UN Charter, it achieved the status of a fundamental right of all "peoples" as a necessary prerequisite to the development of "friendly relations among nations." At least potentially, the concept was thus both universalized and internationalized, for it could now be said to portend a duty owed by all governments to their peoples and by each government to all members of the international community.

This was no random theoretical happenstance. In the postwar world of rising nationalisms, denials of self-determination were palpably no mere domestic matter. Repression tended to generate friction with neighboring states where liberation movements habitually sought sanctuary and succor. As in Bangladesh, Eritrea and the Southern Sudan, self-determination, denied, precipitated the flight of hordes of refugees, placing onerous economic, social and political strains on the neighboring states of refuge. Thus was self-determination firmly linked in theory and fact to the main UN task of preventing conflict among nations, a link that carries far-reaching, but ambiguous, implications for its future normative development (as this essay later seeks to demonstrate).

In the thirty-five years following the surrender of the Axis powers, self-determination transformed the world's political landscape. At this stage, the norm had clear, though limited, secessionist overtones, in the sense that it legitimated the secession of colonies from empires. Concurrently, the norm also evolved in a way that did not legitimate self-determination of minorities *within* a colony. The General Assembly warned against efforts to compromise a colony's "territorial integrity" by those—like Nigeria's Ibos—seeking to secede.[31] Beginning with India,

[29] L. BUCHHEIT, SECESSION: THE LEGITIMACY OF SELF-DETERMINATION 71 (1978).

[30] UN CHARTER Art. 76(b).

[31] Note, however, the decision of the political leaders of imperial India to partition the country, in effect permitting Pakistan to secede. On "territorial integrity," see Declaration on the Granting of

Burma and West Africa's Gold Coast, Britain acted in compliance with the norm's evolving requirements; it was followed, with more or less enthusiasm, by France, the Netherlands, Belgium, Spain, Portugal and South Africa. Imperial powers complained about the General Assembly's use of Charter Article 73(c) to monitor political developments in their colonies, but the resistance gradually abated. As a result of the impetus of decolonization, UN membership almost tripled. That this remarkable devolution could have been accomplished, for the most part, without recourse to war or revolution is a tribute to the normative legitimacy and primacy accorded self-determination by the consistent practice—despite lapses—of the community of states.[32] As we shall see, the growth of this process was facilitated by UN reporting requirements, the Organization's close scrutiny of the work of colonial administrations and the active involvement of the United Nations in monitoring elections and plebiscites in territories advancing toward independence. Self-determination was seen to require democratic consultation with colonial peoples, legitimated by an international presence at elections immediately preceding the creative moment of independence.

Today, the process of decolonization is nearly complete. Nevertheless, the principle of self-determination retains vigor, manifestly having contributed to the decision by the leaders of the Soviet Union, beginning in 1989, to withdraw their military forces and political suzerainty from Eastern Europe and, more recently, from the Baltic States. Its pull prompted South Africa's decision to give independence to Namibia and Morocco's *volte-face* regarding Western Sahara. When another vestige of imperfect decolonization, the Angolan civil war, ended in 1991, it was on the basis of an agreement to hold free, internationally observed elections, which, *nunc pro tunc,* would give Angola the legitimate regime it had failed to acquire at the chaotic moment of its independence.[33] Another UN-supervised process of popular consultation was created by the Paris agreement ending the civil war in Cambodia.[34] As we shall discuss in detail, the idea of self-determination has evolved into a more general notion of internationally validated political consultation, one that is beginning to be applied even to independent (postcolonial) states like Nicaragua and Angola, albeit without implying the community's right to validate secessionist movements within sovereign states.

The story of self-determination, as the first building block in the creation of a democratic entitlement, may thus be seen as a remarkable saga that tells of a rule that gradually augments its compliance pull, overcomes resistance and ultimately brings about an incontestable, historic transformation. Rules that acquire this

---

Independence to Colonial Countries and Peoples, GA Res. 1514, 15 UN GAOR Supp. (No. 16) at 66, UN Doc. A/4684 (1960); and Declaration on Principles of International Law concerning Friendly Relations and Co-operation among States in accordance with the Charter of the United Nations, Annex to GA Res. 2625, 25 UN GAOR Supp. (No. 28) at 121, UN Doc. A/8028 (1970), *reprinted in* 9 ILM 1292 (1970) [hereinafter Friendly Relations Declaration]. Note also GA Res. 1654 of 1961, in which, without dissent, the Assembly expressed itself as "[d]eeply concerned that, contrary to the provisions of paragraph 6 of the Declaration, acts aimed at the partial or total disruption of national unity and territorial integrity are still being carried out in certain countries in the process of decolonization." 16 UN GAOR Supp. (No. 17) at 65, UN Doc. A/5100 (1961).

[32] *See* Franck, *The Stealing of the Sahara,* 70 AJIL 694 (1976).

[33] As part of the cease-fire package, UNAVEM, the UN observer mission in Angola, oversaw the withdrawal of Cuban troops. The mission will culminate in the observance of elections in 1992. *See* N.Y. Times, May 26, 1991, §1, at 9, col. 1; and *id.,* June 1, 1991, at A1, col. 3.

[34] Final Act of the Paris Conference on Cambodia, UN Doc. A/46/608–S/23177, Annex (1991).

kind of pedigree have a unique claim to legitimacy. Moreover, the deeply embedded roots of self-determination also anchor the legitimacy claims of other, more recent, components of the democratic entitlement.

V. Determinacy: Its Function in Bestowing Legitimacy

Thus we see that the democratic entitlement has roots in the conduct of states dating back at least to 1918. From this beginning, practice has proliferated. But practice is not enough to legitimate new norms. The dots of practice must be connected by lines of enunciated principle—conceptualized reasons for acting—if the shapes of legitimate rules are to emerge. The production of legitimate norms depends on a combination of persistent practice and enunciated concepts. In addition, to legitimate a rule, the underlying principles must be enunciated in a way that makes their content determinate. In this section, then, we will look at the determinacy of those principles that stake out the democratic entitlement. Just as an enunciated principle needs to be implemented in common practice before achieving recognition as a binding rule, so a common practice, to be accepted as establishing a norm, needs principled enunciation.

By determinacy we mean the literary property of a rule: that which makes its message clear.[35] The determinacy of a rule directly affects its legitimacy because it increases the rule's transparency and thus its capacity to pull members of the international community toward voluntary compliance. It is true that all written communications, including rule texts, suffer from some degree of elasticity of meaning. It is also true that "moderate indeterminacy does not undermine the law's legitimacy."[36] Nevertheless, the more opaque and elastic the rule text, the less compliance pull it is likely to exert. Obviously, a rule that cannot be understood is unlikely to be obeyed. A rule that is vague opens itself to creative misconstruction by those whose conduct it is intended to regulate. Perhaps most important, the indeterminacy of a rule undermines its compliance pull by reducing the contingent expectation of reciprocity that helps pull states toward compliance. States, like persons, often obey rules even when it is to their short-run advantage not to do so, in the expectation that by denying themselves the gain that would accrue from noncompliance they will reinforce the power of the rule to pull others toward compliance, to the states' future benefit. This deferred-gratification rationale for rule compliance falls away, however, when the rule text is so indeterminate as not to support a reasonable expectation that compliance in one instance will reinforce the pull toward compliance in future contingent situations. Reciprocity affords little inducement to voluntary rule compliance if the rule is so fuzzy that its applicability to future cases will be easy to dispute and hard to demonstrate.

While the determinacy of a rule may initially be judged by examining the clarity of its text, even a quite elastic text may be rendered more determinate if it is subjected regularly to case-by-case interpretation, utilizing administrative or adjudicatory procedures accepted as legitimate in the community to which the rule is addressed. For example, the International Court of Justice, in interpreting Article 83(1) of the Convention negotiated by the Third United Nations Conference on the Law of the Sea, has taken a highly indeterminate text—one that calls for "an equitable solution" in apportioning an undersea coastal shelf among neighboring

[35] T. Franck, *supra* note 12, at 52–55.
[36] Kress, *Legal Indeterminacy*, 77 Cal. L. Rev. 283 (1989).

states—and has rendered it increasingly determinate.[37] So, too, as a result of litigation between Finland and Denmark currently before the Court, will we "discover" whether a tall, self-propelled oil rig constitutes a "vessel" under the right of unimpeded passage through straits as established by the Law of the Sea Convention.[38] The determinacy of a rule may therefore depend not only on its text, but also on the work of legitimate institutions charged with reducing textual indeterminacy in specific disputes.

Thus understood, how fares the determinacy of a normative entitlement to democracy? Are there rule texts that convey principles that are specific, or capable of being rendered so, by persuasive case-by-case interpretation and application? We shall now examine the determinacy of existing and emerging rules that bear on the previously identified main historic components of the democratic entitlement: self-determination, freedom of expression and electoral rights.

Determinacy and Self-Determination

As noted, self-determination is legitimated by its long pedigree. Despite lacunae, it also has a large and precise textual canon, refined by a growing "jurisprudence" of interpretation. In addition to the role of self-determination among the purposes of the UN Charter and in the UN trusteeship system, under Article 73, members responsible for administering non-self-governing territories pledged to "develop self-government, to take due account of the political aspirations of the peoples, and to assist them in the progressive development of their free political institutions." These provisions not only were implemented zealously by the UN system, but also were augmented by additional normative texts that concerned two issues essential to the determinacy of self-determination: *to whom* does it apply and *how* is it to be implemented? If rule texts establishing rights do not provide answers to these basic questions, they lack determinacy and the rule's legitimacy is diminished.

To whom does self-determination apply? The first serious effort to enunciate the applicable principles was undertaken by the fifteenth General Assembly in the annex to Resolution 1541 of December 15, 1960. It attempts to stipulate the test for determining whether a territory is non-self-governing within the meaning of Article 73(e) of the Charter. Under Principle IV of the resolution, non-self-governing status exists *prima facie* "in respect of a territory which is geographically separate and is distinct ethnically and/or culturally from the country administering it." Once that test has been met, Principle V states, "other elements may then be brought into consideration," including those "of an administrative, political, juridical, economic or historical nature. If they affect the relationship between the metropolitan State and the territory concerned in a manner which arbitrarily places the latter in a position or status of subordination, they support the presumption" that the territory is non-self-governing.[39]

[37] United Nations Convention on the Law of the Sea, *opened for signature* Dec. 10, 1982, UN Doc. A/CONF.62/122, *reprinted in* UNITED NATIONS, OFFICIAL TEXT OF THE UNITED NATIONS CONVENTION ON THE LAW OF THE SEA WITH ANNEXES AND INDEX, UN Sales No. E.83.V.5 (1983), 21 ILM 1261 (1982). For the Court's interpretation of Article 83(1), see Continental Shelf (Tunisia/Libyan Arab Jamahiriya), 1982 ICJ REP. 18 (Judgment of Feb. 24); Continental Shelf (Libyan Arab Jamahiriya/Malta), 1985 ICJ REP. 13 (Judgment of June 3).

[38] *See* Passage through the Great Belt, 1991 ICJ REP. 12 (Order of July 29).

[39] GA Res. 1541, 15 UN GAOR Supp. (No. 16), *supra* note 31, at 29.

The 1970 Declaration on Friendly Relations elaborated the Charter "principle of equal rights and self-determination of peoples" by reiterating the duty to end colonialism and to permit each colonial territory to assume a "political status freely determined by" the inhabitants. More broadly, the declaration attributes to "all peoples"—not merely the inhabitants of colonies—"the right freely to determine, without external interference, their political status."[40]

This broader concept of a *universal* right of self-determination is further enunciated in Article 1 of the International Covenant on Civil and Political Rights.[41] This treaty, ratified or acceded to by 113 states as of November 1991, but probably binding on other states as customary law,[42] states categorically: "All peoples have the right of self-determination. By virtue of that right they freely determine their political status and freely pursue their economic, social and cultural development." This provision has been called the "most controversial" in a document created and steeped in considerable controversy.[43] Western powers, in particular, at first argued that the right was only a political principle, that it was ill-defined and unsuited to a treaty enumerating individual—as opposed to collective—rights and thus inappropriate to the unique quasi-judicial enforcement machinery envisaged by the Covenant. Nevertheless, its proponents insisted that the norm of self-determination was fundamental, and a precondition, to the enjoyment of all other enumerated individual rights and freedoms. As a result, "the tide of political opinion in favour of including a right of self-determination proved irresistible"[44] and the principle was given pride of place among the designated entitlements. More significantly for the long term, the majority—including states that had opposed inclusion of the right—utterly rejected the notion that the entitlement applied only to colonial "peoples," declaring, rather, that if included, it must apply to peoples anywhere, whether in a politically independent state or a dependent territory.[45]

The Covenant clearly intends to make the right of self-determination applicable to the citizens of all nations, entitling them to determine their collective political status through democratic means. It also makes an important distinction between that right of each nation's collective *polis* and the rights of minorities within each state, which the Covenant elucidates in Article 27. Under Article 27, "ethnic, religious or linguistic minorities . . . shall not be denied the right, in community with the other members of their group, to enjoy their own culture, to profess and practice their own religion, or to use their own language."

Notably, not included among the enumerated rights of these minorities as defined in Article 27 is any entitlement to secede.[46] When the Covenant came into force, the right of self-determination entered its third phase of enunciation: it ceased to be a rule applicable only to specific territories (at first, the defeated European powers; later, the overseas trust territories and colonies) and became a

[40] Annex to GA Res. 2625, *supra* note 31, principle 4.

[41] International Covenant on Civil and Political Rights, Dec. 16, 1966, 999 UNTS 171, *reprinted in* 6 ILM 368 (1967) (entered into force Mar. 23, 1976) [hereinafter ICCPR]. The same provision is stated as Article 1 of the International Covenant on Economic, Social and Cultural Rights, Dec. 16, 1966, 993 UNTS 3, *reprinted in* 6 ILM 360 (1967) (entered into force Jan. 3, 1976).

[42] T. MERON, HUMAN RIGHTS AND HUMANITARIAN NORMS AS CUSTOMARY LAW 80–81 (1989); Sohn, *Generally Accepted International Rules,* 61 WASH. L. REV. 1073, 1077–78 (1986); Schachter, *International Law Implications of U.S. Human Rights Policies,* 24 N.Y.L. SCH. L. REV. 63, 68 (1978).

[43] D. MCGOLDRICK, THE HUMAN RIGHTS COMMITTEE 14 (1991).

[44] *Id.*

[45] *Id.* at 15.

[46] For a different view as to the legal status of the right to secede, see Brilmayer, *supra* note 19.

right of everyone. It also, at least for now, stopped being a principle of exclusion (secession) and became one of inclusion: the right to participate. The right now entitles peoples in all states to free, fair and open participation in the democratic process of governance freely chosen by each state. When such participation is denied, when a people that, in the terms of the aforementioned 1960 General Assembly resolution, "is geographically separate and is distinct ethnically and/or culturally" has been placed "in a position or status of subordination,"[47] perhaps a secession option may reemerge as an international legal entitlement. That aspect of self-determination, however, is far less clear at present than the entitlement to democratic participation in governance.

How is self-determination to be implemented? Gradually, answers to this question have also emerged. During the first forty years of the United Nations, members responsible for trust territories and colonies were charged with making periodic reports on their progress; these reports were subjected to increasing scrutiny by various UN bodies. Since the coming into force of the Covenant, reporting and scrutiny have been formalized, depoliticized to an extent, and welded to the process of case-by-case norm application. This development will help shape the postcolonial concept of self-determination and give it more determinacy. The Covenant thus foresees a continuing, growing body of law made by means of the interpretation and application of its provisions by an expert, independent, quasi-judicial body.

As usual, this process begins with a form of monitoring. The 113 states parties to the Covenant are legally obliged to "undertake to submit reports on the measures they have adopted which give effect to the rights recognized herein and on the progress made in the enjoyment of those rights."[48] These reports are scrutinized by a Human Rights Committee of eighteen members elected by states parties to the Covenant, who serve in their personal capacities[49] for a term of four years.[50] While the Committee is not a court, it does have the right to question the reports submitted by members. It transmits its reviews and such general comments as it thinks appropriate to the states parties to the Covenant and to the UN Economic and Social Council.[51] Under an optional procedure, parties may also agree to permit other parties to allege violations in a formal complaint.[52] An Optional Protocol permits individuals to lodge complaints against accepting states.[53] As of November 1991, sixty-three of the parties to the Covenant had agreed to give the Committee the competence to consider petitions. A recent study concluded that the Committee members have succeeded in establishing a high degree of independence and judiciousness.[54]

Formally, all petitions brought under the Optional Protocol are drawn to the Committee's attention by the UN Secretary-General.[55] More than a hundred such

[47] GA Res. 1541, *supra* note 39.

[48] ICCPR, *supra* note 41, Art. 40(1).

[49] *Id.*, Arts. 28, 30.

[50] *Id.*, Art. 32.

[51] For a discussion of this procedure, see D. McGoldrick, *supra* note 43, at 62–119.

[52] ICCPR, *supra* note 41, Art. 41. For a discussion of this procedure, see D. McGoldrick, *supra* note 43, at 120–246.

[53] ICCPR, *supra* note 41, Optional Protocol, *opened for signature* Dec. 19, 1966, Art. 1, 999 UNTS 302; *see also* D. McGoldrick, *supra* note 43, at 127.

[54] D. McGoldrick, *supra* note 43, at 45.

[55] Human Rights Committee, Provisional Rules of Procedure, Rule 78(1), UN Doc. CCPR/C/3/Rev.2 (1989). *See* Report of the Human Rights Committee, 44 UN GAOR Supp. (No. 40) at 179–82, UN Doc. A/44/40 (1989).

"cases" have been taken up and fewer than twenty were dismissed for lack of evidence of a violation. Some 150 more petitions are pending.[56] Although the Covenant envisages the possibility of voting, the Committee's decisions to date have been taken by consensus.[57]

The Committee, so far, has not had much occasion to explain the content of the right of self-determination. Only one petition-based case has been heard. While it rejected as inadmissible a claim by a Grand Captain of the Mikmaq tribal society that Canada was denying his people their right of self-determination, the Committee based its rejection on the applicant's inability to demonstrate that he was authorized to represent the tribe or that he, personally, had been deprived of a right protected by the Covenant.[58] As noted, the Covenant validates free and equal political participation as well as the cultural rights of minorities, but not necessarily secession. The Committee's finding leaves open the possibility that another individual might succeed in bringing a comparable petition if he or she can demonstrate having the *bona fides* to act in a representative capacity and alleges a denial of cultural autonomy or free and equal political participation.

The Committee does not merely consider reports and complaints. Periodically, it also makes more general findings on the state of civil and political rights and prepares summaries of the developing normative expectations arising from the Covenant. In its general commentary on Article 1, the Committee has been rather cautious, merely reiterating the primacy of self-determination among the human rights enumerated in the Covenant. "In accordance with the purposes and principles of the Charter of the United Nations," the Committee has written, "article 1 . . . recognizes that all peoples have the right of self-determination. The right . . . is of particular importance because its realization is an essential condition for the effective guarantee and observance of individual human rights and for the promotion and strengthening of those rights."[59]

The right to self-determination, in sum, may be said to be poised to move toward still greater determinacy. Its general normative content already has been spelled out in General Assembly resolutions to which a large majority of the international community has assented, and in several widely ratified treaties, beginning with the UN Charter and culminating in the Covenant. Equally important to the determinacy of the right of self-determination is the institutional potential for applying and clarifying the emerging rules; while the Committee's accomplishments have been modest, a systemic basis has been laid for more solid results. Now that the inhibitions of Cold War politics have been lifted and the liberal democratic sensibility is widely shared by the membership, what began as review by politicized, anticolonial committees of the General Assembly and by the Trusteeship Council may be expected to become a judicious process of principled rule interpretation by independent experts.

[56] D. McGOLDRICK, *supra* note 43, at 127. [57] *Id.* at 48.

[58] A.D. v. Canada, Report of the Human Rights Committee, 39 UN GAOR Supp. (No. 40) at 200, UN Doc. A/39/40 (1984). *See also* Ominayak and Lubicon Lake Band v. Canada, Report of the Human Rights Committee, 45 UN GAOR Supp. (No. 40), vol. 2, App. A, UN Doc. A/45/40 (1990). See discussion in D. McGOLDRICK, *supra* note 43, at 254–56; and McGoldrick, *Canadian Indians, Cultural Rights and the Human Rights Committee,* 40 INT'L & COMP. L.Q. 658 (1991).

[59] General Comments of the Human Rights Committee, UN Doc. CCPR/C/21/Rev.1, at 10–11 (1989). *See also* D. McGOLDRICK, *supra* note 43, at 247–48.

Determinacy and Free Expression

The second building block in constructing a normative entitlement to democracy is the right of free political expression. This right originated conceptually in the antitotalitarianism born of World War II and was first enunciated normatively in the Universal Declaration of Human Rights, adopted by the General Assembly on December 10, 1948.[60] As a mere resolution, the Universal Declaration does not have the force of a treaty; yet it was passed with such overwhelming support, and such prestige has accrued to it in succeeding years, that it may be said to have become a customary rule of state obligation. More to the point, its text manifests considerable determinacy, specifically recognizing a universal right to freedom of opinion and expression (Article 19), as well as to peaceful assembly and association (Article 20).

These entitlements reappear with even greater specificity in the legally binding Covenant on Civil and Political Rights.[61] Spelled out in that treaty are specific rights to freedom of thought (Article 18) and freedom of association (Article 22). Article 19(2) is an especially important component of the democratic entitlement. It states: "Everyone shall have the right to freedom of expression; this right shall include freedom to seek, receive and impart information and ideas of all kinds, regardless of frontiers, either orally, in writing or in print, in the form of art, or through any other media of his choice." While Article 19(2) is subject to restriction by law where "necessary . . . [f]or the protection of . . . public order . . . , or of public health or morals,"[62] these restrictions, like the rule itself, are subject to case-by-case review and application by the Human Rights Committee.[63]

Rights to opinion, expression and association contained in Articles 18, 19 and 22 look both backward and forward. They are a refinement of an aspect of the older right of self-determination; they also constitute the essential preconditions for an open electoral process, which is the newest component of the democratic entitlement. First mooted in the Universal Declaration, they became explicit treaty-based entitlements by incorporation into the Covenant and are likely to be made even more explicitly determinate by the review and monitoring of required national reports on compliance and specific petitions by complainants. The Human Rights Committee, for example, has been critical, albeit in a circumspect manner, of the compliance of Uganda and Zanzibar under Tanzanian control.[64] The Committee has also posed searching questions to representatives of Mali[65] and Jamaica[66] regarding the openness of their marketplaces of ideas. Professor Dominic McGoldrick has commended

> the close, detailed and critical analysis undertaken by members under the reporting process. The dialogue between the [Committee] and the States parties, in so far as it has developed, has been both direct and constructive. [Committee] members have in a diplomatic but forthright way criticized or expressed strong doubts concerning the compatibility with article 19 of specific ideological conceptions of and wide restrictions on freedom of expression.[67]

[60] GA Res. 217A (III), UN Doc. A/810, at 71 (1948).

[61] ICCPR, *supra* note 41.

[62] *Id.*, Art. 19(3).

[63] *See* D. McGoldrick, *supra* note 43, at 461.

[64] Report of the Human Rights Committee, 36 UN GAOR Supp. (No. 40) at 42–43, UN Doc. A/36/40 (1981) [hereinafter 1981 Report].

[65] *Id.* at 50–51.

[66] *Id.* at 56–57.

[67] D. McGoldrick, *supra* note 43, at 469–70.

In their tough questioning of the representatives of reporting states, the Committee's members are now aided regularly, behind the scenes, by a network of nongovernmental organizations.

While most of these critiques have occurred under the aegis of the general reporting requirement, a few case-by-case reviews have taken place under the Optional Protocol. The Committee found Uruguay's military regime in violation of Article 19(2) of the Covenant when it denied a petitioner the right freely to engage in political and trade union activities.[68] In *Perdoma and DeLanza v. Uruguay*,[69] the complainants alleged that they had been detained on account of "subversive association" based on their political views and connections. The Committee concluded that there was no evidence to substantiate the authorities' charge and that the arrest, detention and trial of the petitioners had not been justified on any of the grounds permitted in Article 19(3).[70]

When rules are impartially applied, whether by judges, administrators or experts, the determinacy of those rules increases and so, also, their legitimacy. Thus far, the Human Rights Committee's review of complaints regarding restrictions on expressive rights has just begun to have an impact, but in view of the end of the Cold War, the prognosis is much better. Moreover, other avenues for international protection of these rights are opening up, as evidenced by the requests of the intergovernmental Human Rights Commission to the UN Secretary-General that he appoint special representatives to report on alleged gross violations by various governments. In this respect, a significant new role for the Secretary-General was recently agreed upon by both the Government and insurgents in El Salvador. Under UN auspices, the parties consented to the establishment of ONUSAL, the UN Observer Group in El Salvador, which is to be controlled by the Secretary-General and is to supervise, and thereby seek to ensure citizens' rights to, free expression and association as part of a plan to create the circumstances for civil peace.[71]

In addition to such activity at the global level, parallel and reinforcing norm building and defining is under way at the regional level. The European Convention for the Protection of Human Rights and Fundamental Freedoms, the best-established regional normative system, provides in Article 10, paragraph 1: "Everyone has the right to freedom of expression. This right shall include freedom to hold opinions and to receive and impart information and ideas without interference by public authority and regardless of frontiers."[72]

Paragraph 2 of Article 10 does permit derogation in the form of

> restrictions . . . necessary in a democratic society, in the interests of national security, territorial integrity or public safety, for the prevention of disorder or crime, for the protection of health or morals, for the protection of the

[68] Alba Pietroroia v. Uruguay, Communication R.10/44, 1981 Report, *supra* note 64, at 153–59.

[69] Report of the Human Rights Committee, 35 UN GAOR Supp. (No. 40) at 111, UN Doc. A/35/40 (1980) [hereinafter 1980 Report].

[70] *Id. See also* Grille Motta v. Uruguay, Communication R.2/11, 1980 Report, *supra* note 69, at 132; Weinberg Weisz v. Uruguay, Communication R.7/28, 1981 Report, *supra* note 64, at 114; Hertzberg v. Finland, Communication R.14/61, Report of the Human Rights Committee, 37 UN GAOR Supp. (No. 40) at 161, UN Doc. A/37/40 (1982).

[71] Central America: Efforts Towards Peace: Report of the Secretary-General, UN Doc. S/22494 and Corr.1 (1991); *see also* N.Y. Times, Aug. 13, 1991, at A8, col. 3.

[72] European Convention for the Protection of Human Rights and Fundamental Freedoms, Nov. 4, 1950, 213 UNTS 221, Europ. TS No. 5 (entered into force Sept. 3, 1953) [hereinafter European Convention].

> reputation or rights of others, for preventing the disclosure of information received in confidence, or for maintaining the authority and impartiality of the judiciary.

The application of both the rule and its exceptions, however, is subject to review by a commission of experts and a European Human Rights Court.[73] These bodies have augmented the determinacy of the system. As in a mature regime, the European Commission and Court of Human Rights have made key decisions balancing the rights of individuals against specific exceptions. The Court has weighed freedom of the press against a defendant's right to an impartial trial.[74] It has drawn boundaries between free expression and obscenity[75] and sought a balance between a free press and the laws of libel and slander.[76] In so doing, it has made far more specific—hence legitimate—the Council of Europe's system of norms pertaining to expressive rights, just when it is rapidly expanding to include the newly freed nations of Eastern Europe.

Comparable progress is being made by the more recently established inter-American regional system. The 1969 American Convention on Human Rights[77] provides an elaborate textual basis for freedom of thought and expression (Article 13), the right of assembly (Article 15) and freedom of association (Article 16). Monitoring and enforcement is performed by two institutions created by the OAS Charter: the Inter-American Commission on Human Rights (Articles 34 and 64(1)) and the Inter-American Court of Human Rights (Articles 33, 62 and 64). The Court consists of seven judges elected by the states adhering to the Convention, who serve for a term of six years. As of May 1990, ten states—not including the United States—had accepted its jurisdiction.[78]

Determinacy and Electoral Rights

The third and newest building block in constructing the entitlement to democracy is the emerging normative requirement of a participatory *electoral* process. Despite its infancy, it, too, is rapidly evolving toward that determinacy which is essential to being perceived as legitimate. As early as 1948, the Universal Declaration of Human Rights, in Article 21, clearly enunciated the right of all persons to take part in government, as well as in "periodic and genuine elections which shall be by universal and equal suffrage and shall be held by secret vote or by equivalent free voting procedures." At the time, only UN members outside the socialist, Arab and Latin American blocs took this as a restatement of conditions already prevailing in their *polis.* With rapid decolonization, the proportion of UN members actually practicing free and open electoral democracy began to shrink further under the aegis of one-party modernizing authoritarianism in Africa and

[73] *Id.*, Art. 19, establishing the European Commission on Human Rights and the European Court of Human Rights. *See also* Arts. 20–55.

[74] The Sunday Times Case, 30 Eur. Ct. H.R. (ser. A) (1978).

[75] Handyside Case, 24 Eur. Ct. H.R. (ser. A) (1976); Case of Muller and Others, 133 Eur. Ct. H.R. (ser. A) (1988).

[76] Lingens Case, 103 Eur. Ct. H.R. (ser. A) (1986).

[77] American Convention on Human Rights, Nov. 22, 1969, OEA/Ser.K/XVI.1.1, doc. 70, rev.1, corr.1 (1970), *reprinted in* 1 THE INTER-AMERICAN SYSTEM, pt. II at 51 (F. V. García-Amador ed. 1983), 9 ILM 673 (1970) (entered into force July 18, 1978) [hereinafter American Convention].

[78] Argentina, Colombia, Costa Rica, Ecuador, Guatemala, Honduras, Peru, Suriname, Uruguay and Venezuela. *See* Current State of Conventions and Protocols on Human Rights, Annual Report of the Inter-American Commission on Human Rights, OEA/Ser.L/V.II.79, doc. 12, rev.1, Ann. A (1991).

Asia. Nevertheless, even in that relatively hostile atmosphere, few states were willing openly to block the textual evolution of a specific electoral entitlement, however many mental reservations their regimes may have harbored. Thus, two decades later, the Civil and Political Covenant was opened for signature,[79] entering into force in 1976 as a set of legal obligations now binding on more than two-thirds of all states. With the balance now heavily tilting toward the substantial new majority of states actually practicing a reasonably credible version of electoral democracy, the treaty-based legal entitlement also begins to approximate prevailing practice and thus may be said to be stating what is becoming a customary legal norm applicable to all.

Article 25 extends to every citizen the right:

> (*a*) To take part in the conduct of public affairs, directly or through freely chosen representatives;
>
> (*b*) To vote and to be elected at genuine periodic elections which shall be by universal and equal suffrage and shall be held by secret ballot, guaranteeing the free expression of the will of the electors.

Admirable as it is, this standard still needs greater specificity. Textual determinacy, once again, is gradually being augmented by process determinacy under the auspices of the Human Rights Committee, which is authorized to monitor compliance. That body has discussed the implications of Article 25 in connection with its review of national reports on implementation and a small number of petitions lodged under the Optional Protocol. In reviewing two citizens' complaints against the military regime of Uruguay, the Committee concluded that the complainants had been arbitrarily deprived of protected rights by decrees banning their political party and by being barred from running for office.[80]

During the Cold War, it was difficult to utilize the Human Rights Committee to hone the rule outlined in Article 25. Now the Committee is likely to perform that function more effectively as the members' ideological divisions narrow and citizens become more willing to risk submitting complaints. This evolution would be accelerated if, as seems likely, the United States ratified the Covenant. If, as seems *less* likely, the United States also ratified the Protocol permitting individual complaints,[81] the determinacy of the entitlement would be further legitimized, which, surely, must accord with our nation's interest and ethos.

The new climate has also permeated the General Assembly. At its forty-fifth session, that body adopted a resolution entitled Enhancing the effectiveness of the principle of periodic and genuine elections.[82] This nonbinding, yet important, document reaffirms and further specifies the electoral entitlement first outlined in the Universal Declaration of Human Rights and later embodied in Article 25 of the Covenant. It "stresses" the member nations'

> conviction that periodic and genuine elections are a necessary and indispensable element of sustained efforts to protect the rights and interests of the governed and that, as a matter of practical experience, the right of everyone to take part in the government of his or her country is a crucial factor in the effective enjoyment by all of a wide range of other human rights and fundamental freedoms, embracing political, economic, social and cultural rights.[83]

[79] ICCPR, *supra* note 41.

[80] Case 34/1979, 1981 Report, *supra* note 64, at 130; Case 44/1979, *id.*, Ann. XVI, at 153.

[81] *Supra* note 53.

[82] GA Res. 45/150 (Feb. 21, 1991).

[83] *Id.*, para. 2.

The resolution also declares "that determining the will of the people requires an electoral process that provides an equal opportunity for all citizens to become candidates and put forward their political views, individually and in co-operation with others, as provided in national constitutions and laws."[84] It commends "the value of the electoral assistance" the United Nations has provided member states at their request,[85] and asks the Secretary-General to seek the views of members and others on how the Organization can best respond to further such requests and to report his findings to the next Assembly, together with "an account of United Nations experience in election monitoring."[86]

At its next session the Assembly, with only four dissents, passed Resolution 46/137 of December 17, 1991, which declared that "periodic and genuine elections" are a "necessary and indispensable element" and a "crucial factor in the effective enjoyment . . . of a wide range of other human rights." The resolution established a procedure for authorizing the monitoring of national elections and endorsed the Secretary-General's decision to create an office, headed by a senior official, "to act as a focal point . . . in order to ensure consistency in the handling of requests of Member States organizing elections."

Parallel and reinforcing norm-generating activity occurring in regional frameworks has accelerated this evolution. The Charter of the Organization of American States, in Article 5, establishes the duty of members to promote "the effective exercise of representative democracy." The OAS Ministers of Foreign Affairs and the Organization's Permanent Council have issued a series of resolutions affirming this regional entitlement while censuring those committing apparent violations. For example, in June 1979, the Ministers demanded the "immediate and definitive replacement of the Somoza regime" in Nicaragua and the installation of a "democratic government" with the "holding of free elections as soon as possible."[87] Similarly, in December 1987, the Permanent Council took note of the "deplorable acts of violence and disorder" that had taken place in Haiti during that year's failed elections, expressed its "conviction that it is necessary to resume the democratic process" and urged the "Government of Haiti to adopt all necessary measures so that the people of Haiti may express their will through free elections."[88] In May 1989, the Ministers decided that "General Manuel Antonio Noriega . . . [had] abridged the right of the Panamanian people to freely elect their legitimate authorities" and thus had "seriously jeopardize[d]" an "essential purpose" of the OAS, which "is to promote and consolidate representative democracy." They further called for a "transfer of power in the shortest possible time" by means of "democratic mechanisms."[89]

On June 5, 1991, the Ministers adopted a crucial resolution on representative democracy. Its preamble states that the principles of the OAS Charter "require the political representation of [member] states to be based on effective exercise of representative democracy" and, in its operative sections, the resolution decides that the Secretary General shall

> call for the immediate convocation of a meeting of the Permanent Council in the event of any occurrences giving rise to the sudden or irregular interruption of the democratic political institutional process or of the legitimate exer-

[84] *Id.*, para. 3.

[85] *Id.*, para. 8.

[86] *Id.*, paras. 10, 11. The Secretary-General's report to the Assembly is UN Doc. A/46/609 (1991).

[87] OEA/Ser.F/II.17, doc. 40, rev.2 (1979).

[88] OEA/Ser.G/CP/RES.489, doc. 720 (1987).

[89] OEA/Ser.F/II.21, doc. 8, rev.2 (1989); *see also* OEA/Ser.F/II.21, doc. 45 (1989).

> cise of power by the democratically elected government in any of the Organization's member states.[90]

Within ten days, the Ministers of Foreign Affairs or the OAS General Assembly must convene so as to "look into the events collectively and adopt any decisions deemed appropriate."[91] It was this procedure that was invoked to bring about sanctions against the regime established by the military coup in Haiti in September 1991.[92]

Alongside these quasi-legislative developments, a regional quasi jurisprudence is germinating. In 1990, the Inter-American Commission on Human Rights, in considering a complaint of electoral fraud and other impropriety against Mexico, began to spell out in some detail the right of access, under general conditions of equality, to a nation's public functions.[93]

Even more dramatic are recent efforts by the nations of Europe to make the electoral entitlement explicit and specific. Article 3 of Protocol 1 to the European Human Rights Convention obliges the parties to "undertake to hold free elections at reasonable intervals by secret ballot, under conditions which will ensure the free expression of the opinion of the people in the choice of the legislature."[94] Finding the Greek colonels' regime in violation, the European Court of Human Rights interpreted this Protocol to require "the existence of a representative legislature, elected at reasonable intervals."[95] The European Commission, meanwhile, has rejected the purist argument that the Protocol requires states to adopt a system of proportional representation.[96]

As members of the Conference on Security and Co-operation in Europe,[97] the same nations, augmented by Canada, the United States and the nations of Eastern Europe, recently joined unanimously in spelling out the contents of the new right to participate in free and open elections. At a meeting in Copenhagen in June 1990, they affirmed that "democracy is an inherent element of the rule of law" and recognized "the importance of pluralism with regard to political organizations."[98] Among the "inalienable rights of all human beings," they decided, is the democratic entitlement, including "free elections that will be held at reasonable intervals by secret ballot or by equivalent free voting procedure, under conditions which ensure in practice the free expression of the opinion of the electors in the choice of their representatives"; a government "representative in character, in which the executive is accountable to the elected legislature or the electorate"; and political parties that are clearly separate from the state.[99] The thirty-five

[90] Representative Democracy, OEA/Ser.P/AG/RES.1080 (XXI–0/91), para. 1.

[91] *Id.*, para. 2.

[92] Support to the Democratic Government of Haiti, *supra* note 2.

[93] Annual Report of the Inter-American Commission on Human Rights, OEA/Ser.L/V/II.77, doc. 7, rev.1, at 97 (1990) (Mexico Report).

[94] Protocol 1 to the European Convention, *supra* note 72, Mar. 20, 1952, 213 UNTS 262, entered into force May 18, 1954, and, as of June 1991, had been ratified by all but one party to the Convention (Liechtenstein).

[95] The Greek Case, 12 Y.B. EUR. CONV. ON HUM. RTS. 179 (1969); *see also* Case of Mathieu-Mohin, 113 Eur. Ct. H.R. (ser. A) at 22 (1987).

[96] Application 7140/75, 7 Eur. Comm'n H.R. 95, 97 (1977).

[97] Conference on Security and Co-operation in Europe, Final Act, Aug. 1, 1975, 73 DEP'T ST. BULL. 323 (1975), *reprinted in* 14 ILM 1292 (1975).

[98] Conference on Security and Co-operation in Europe, Document of the Copenhagen Meeting of the Conference on the Human Dimension, June 29, 1990, *reprinted in* 29 ILM 1305, 1308, para. 3 (1990) [hereinafter Copenhagen Document].

[99] *Id.*, para. 5.

CSCE participants also linked recognition of the democratic entitlement by governments to the validation of their right to govern: "the will of the people, freely and fairly expressed through periodic and genuine elections, is the basis of the authority and legitimacy of all government,"[100] they declared, implying the illegitimacy of regimes that deny their citizens basic democratic rights.

According to Professor Theodor Meron, one of the public members of the U.S. delegation, the "language of Copenhagen goes far beyond any existing human rights instruments."[101] The document is detailed to an unprecedented degree, establishing a standard that the UN General Assembly might profitably emulate in a resolution. Citizens have the right to expect "free elections at reasonable intervals, as established by law"; a national legislature in which at least one chamber's membership is "freely contested in a popular vote"; a system of universal and equal adult suffrage; a secret ballot or its equivalent; free, nondiscriminatory candidature for office; freedom to form political parties that compete "on a basis of equal treatment before the law and by the authorities"; fair and free campaigning; "no legal or administrative obstacle" to media access, which must be available "on a non-discriminatory basis for all political groupings and individuals wishing to participate in the electoral process"; and a guarantee that the "candidates who obtain the necessary number of votes required by law are duly installed in office and are permitted to remain in office until their term expires or is otherwise" terminated in accordance with law.[102]

This unprecedented North Atlantic and Europe-wide initiative to endorse and define a popular right of electoral democracy[103] went on to commend the growing practice of involving foreign observers in national elections. The participating states invited "observers from any other CSCE participating States and any appropriate private institutions and organizations who may wish to do so to observe the course of their national election proceedings, to the extent permitted by law," and pledged to "endeavour to facilitate similar access for election proceedings held below the national level."[104]

Later in 1990, the leaders of the thirty-four CSCE states joined in Paris to declare "a new era of democracy, peace and unity."[105] Unanimously, they endorsed an extraordinary Charter, which commits them "to build, consolidate and strengthen democracy as the only system of government of our nations."[106] The Charter restates the older entitlement to free expression but adds the right of every individual, without discrimination, "to participate in free and fair elections,"[107] backed by the leaders' pledge to "co-operate and support each other with the aim of making democratic gains irreversible."[108] Although the Charter is not a treaty, its language is weighted with the terminology of *opinio juris.* It is deliberately norm creating. In particular, the Charter builds on the assumption

[100] *Id.* at 1309, para. 6.

[101] Meron, *Democracy and the Rule of Law,* 153 WORLD AFF. 23, 24 (1990). *See also* Steiner, *Political Participation as a Human Right,* 1 HARV. HUM. RTS. Y.B. 77 (1988).

[102] Copenhagen Document, *supra* note 98, at 1310, para. 7.

[103] Buergenthal, *The Copenhagen CSCE Meeting: A New Public Order for Europe,* 11 HUM. RTS. L.J. 217, 221–22 (1990).

[104] Copenhagen Document, *supra* note 98, at 1310, para. 8.

[105] Conference on Security and Co-operation in Europe, Charter of Paris for a New Europe and Supplementary Document to Give Effect to Certain Provisions of the Charter, Nov. 21, 1990, Preamble, *reprinted in* 30 ILM 190, 193 (1991) [hereinafter Paris Charter].

[106] Paris Charter, *supra* note 105, at 193. [107] *Id.* at 194.

[108] *Id.* at 195.

that electoral democracy is owed not only by each government to its own people, but also by each CSCE state to all the others. According to Judge Thomas Buergenthal, another U.S. participant in the Copenhagen meeting, today

> no domestic institution or norm, in theory, is beyond the jurisdictional reach of the CSCE. Here the traditional domestic jurisdiction doctrine, which has tended to shield the oppressive state practices and institutions from international scrutiny, has for all practical purposes lost its meaning. And this notwithstanding the fact that non-intervention in the domestic affairs of a state is a basic CSCE principle. Once the rule of law, human rights and democratic pluralism are made the subject of international commitments, there is little left in terms of governmental institutions that is domestic.[109]

In this connection, one should note that the United States *is* a party to this normative evolution of the CSCE process.

To safeguard the rights concerned, the Paris Charter establishes an institutionalized process for monitoring compliance with the electoral duties of states. It gives the CSCE several organs, including a secretariat at Prague[110] and an Office for Free Elections at Warsaw. The latter is to "facilitate contacts and the exchange of information on elections within participating States."[111] The Charter also envisages the eventual creation, after further consultations, of a "CSCE parliamentary assembly, involving members of parliaments from all participating States," to achieve "greater parliamentary involvement in the CSCE."[112]

The new Office for Free Elections and its functions are described in the "supplementary document" appended to the Charter.[113] The office is to "foster the implementation" of the provisions of the Copenhagen Document pertaining to electoral democracy and, to this end, is authorized to "compile information," including, but not limited to, reports by governments on elections and the electoral process in participating states, "as well as reports of election observations." It is also to "serve to facilitate contact among governments, parliaments or private organizations wishing to observe elections and competent authorities of the States in which elections are to take place."[114]

Most recently, in September to October 1991, these nations' representatives unanimously endorsed the Document of the Moscow Meeting of the Conference on the Human Dimension of the CSCE. It reaffirms "that issues relating to human rights, fundamental freedoms, democracy and the rule of law are of international concern, as respect for these rights and freedoms constitutes one of the foundations of the international order." The participating states "categorically and irrevocably declare[d] that the commitments undertaken in the field of the human dimension of the CSCE are matters of direct and legitimate concern to all participating States and do not belong exclusively to the internal affairs of the State concerned."[115] More important yet is the mechanism and procedure established in paragraphs 3–16, which envisages a "resource" of experts, up to three of whom may be named by a state requesting good offices or mediation services in connec-

[109] Buergenthal, *CSCE Human Dimension: The Birth of a System*, 1 COLLECTED COURSES OF THE ACADEMY OF EUROPEAN LAW, No. 2, at 3, 42–43 (forthcoming).

[110] Paris Charter, *supra* note 105, at 206.

[111] *Id.* at 207.

[112] *Id.*

[113] *Id.* at 214–15.

[114] *Id.* at 214.

[115] Conference on Security and Co-operation in Europe, Document of the Moscow Meeting of the Conference on the Human Dimension of the CSCE, Oct. 3, 1991, Preamble, at 2 (unofficial text of the U.S. delegation), *reprinted in* 30 ILM 1670 (1991). [hereinafter Moscow Document].

tion with any domestic dispute arising under the "human dimension." If a CSCE state poses a human dimension question to another member and that member does not itself invite such a mission of inquiry, the requesting state and five others may invoke the process, with one expert of the three-person panel to be selected from the "resource" list by the requesting state, one by the requested state, and the third by agreement between the other two or by the ranking official of the CSCE designated by its Council. These "rapporteurs" are to establish the facts and report on them, and they may give advice on possible solutions to the problems raised. Most important of all is part II of the Moscow Document, in which the members pledge that they

> will support vigorously, in accordance with the Charter of the United Nations, in case of overthrow or attempted overthrow of a legitimately elected government of a participating State by undemocratic means, the legitimate organs of that State upholding human rights, democracy and the rule of law, recognizing their common commitment to countering any attempt to curb these basic values.[116]

The evolution of textual determinacy with respect to the electoral entitlement is a relatively recent development. In practice, however, the monitoring component of the entitlement has a long history. The long record of UN election monitoring both in the former trusteeship territories and in some colonies immediately before they attained independence was already mentioned as instrumental in establishing pedigree. But that practice also honed the normative content of the entitlement. As early as May 1956, the Trusteeship Council sent monitors to the plebiscite in which the people of British Togoland chose to join Ghana.[117] Its monitors were involved in conducting the preindependence plebiscites in the British Cameroons in November 1959 and February 1961.[118] Similarly, following the November 1959 violence between the Hutu and Tutsi tribes in what was then Belgian-administered Ruanda-Urundi, the United Nations supervised a preindependence election and referendum that determined the separation of the linked indigenous kingdoms and the future of the monarchy.[119]

In 1961 the United Nations assisted New Zealand, the administering authority, in conducting a plebiscite in Western Samoa that endorsed a draft constitution and a form of association with the former trustee.[120] On June 17, 1975, the

[116] Moscow Document, *supra* note 115, para. 17, at 9.

[117] Report of the United Nations Plebiscite Commissioner for the Trust Territory of Togoland under British Administration, UN Doc. T/1258 and Add.1 (1956).

[118] *See* GA Res. 1350, 13 UN GAOR Supp. (No. 18A) at 2, UN Doc. A/4090/Add.1 (1959) (whether the Northern Cameroons wished "to be part of the Northern Region of Nigeria when the Federation of Nigeria becomes independent"); GA Res. 1352, 14 UN GAOR Supp. (No. 16) at 26, UN Doc. A/4354 (1959) (whether the Southern Cameroons wished to achieve independence by "joining the independent Federation of Nigeria [or] the independent Republic of Cameroons"); GA Res. 1473, *id.* at 38 (putting the questions posed in the GA Res. 1352 plebiscite before the Northern Cameroons); *see also* Report of United Nations Commissioner for the Supervision of the Plebiscites in the Southern and Northern Parts of the Trust Territory of the Cameroons under United Kingdom Administration, UN Doc. T/1556 and app. (1961).

[119] GA Res. 1579, 15 UN GAOR Supp. (No. 16), *supra* note 31, at 34 (elections); GA Res. 1605, 15 UN GAOR Supp. (No. 16A) at 8, UN Doc. A/4684/Add.1 (1961) (referendum).

[120] GA Res. 1569, 15 UN GAOR Supp. (No. 16), *supra* note 31, at 33 (whether the inhabitants of the territory accepted "the Constitution adopted by the Constitutional Convention on 28 October 1960" and endorsed "that on 1 January 1962 Western Samoa should become an independent State on the basis of that Constitution"); *see also* Report of United Nations Commissioner for the Supervision of the Plebiscite in Western Samoa, UN Doc. T/1564 and Add.1 (1961).

United Nations observed the vote in which residents of the Northern Mariana Islands endorsed a loose form of political confederation with the United States;[121] and, at various times in the 1980s, it supervised plebiscites in the rest of the U.S. Pacific Islands Trust that determined the future status of those several archipelagoes.[122]

The monitoring of political progress in trust territories led to the case-by-case enunciation of principles applicable to the democratic entitlement. Throughout the 1950s and 1960s, the Trusteeship Council and the General Assembly, on the basis of reports made by visiting missions, made recommendations to the states administering trust territories. These frequently specified the steps necessary to effect democratic participation by the inhabitants in choosing their political future. For example, in its 1959 report on Belgian administration of the Ruanda-Urundi Trust, the Council urged that the representation of inhabitants in the legislative body be increased and that it be given greater power. The Council also called for direct universal suffrage and an increase in the responsibilities of elected local authorities.[123] Such advice was influential both in determining the rate and direction of a territory's emancipation and in crystallizing a broadly shared expectation about the requirements of the democratic entitlement.

Although the United Nations had a specific legal ground for intervening in, and validating, the democratic process within trust territories, it also found bases for supervising colonial elections and referendums just prior to independence and this role gradually came to be an accepted element in legitimizing those crucial transitions. Thus, UN observers oversaw the referendum establishing a new constitution for the Cook Islands in 1965[124] and the preindependence referendum and elections in Spanish Equatorial Guinea in 1968.[125] The United Nations undertook similar monitoring of the referendum on the future status of West New Guinea (West Irian) from July 14 to August 2, 1969,[126] as well as of the November 1980 elections conducted in the New Hebrides under French and British administration, which led to the creation of independent Vanuatu.[127]

As the colonial era drew to a close, the significance of the UN election-monitoring role, instead of declining, appears to have increased, partly because the last

[121] Report of the United Nations Visiting Mission to Observe the Plebiscite in the Northern Mariana Islands, Trust Territory of the Pacific Islands, 43 UN TCOR Supp. (No. 2) at 24, UN Doc. T/1771 (1976).

[122] *See* Report of the United Nations Visiting Mission to Observe the Plebiscite in the Federated States of Micronesia, Trust Territory of the Pacific Islands, 51 UN TCOR Supp. (No. 1) at 14, UN Doc. T/1860 (1984) (June 21, 1983 plebiscite for the islands of Truk, Yap, Kosrae and Ponape); Report of the United Nations Visiting Mission to Observe the Plebiscite in the Marshall Islands, Trust Territory of the Pacific Islands, *id.* (No. 2) at 12–13, UN Doc. T/1865 (1984) (Sept. 7, 1983 plebiscite); Report of the United Nations Visiting Mission to Observe the Plebiscite in Palau, Trust Territory of the Pacific Islands, 53 UN TCOR Supp. (No. 2) at 14, UN Doc. T/1885 (1986) (Feb. 21, 1986 plebiscite).

[123] 24 UN TCOR Annex 1 (Agenda Item 3) at 21, UN Doc. T/L.928 (1959).

[124] GA Res. 2005, 19 UN GAOR Supp. (No. 15) at 7, UN Doc. A/5815 (1965); Report of the United Nations Representatives for the Supervision of the Elections in the Cook Islands, UN Doc. A/5962 and Corr.1 (1965).

[125] GA Res. 2355, 22 UN GAOR Supp. (No. 16) at 54, UN Doc. A/6716 (1967); United Nations Mission for the Supervision of the Referendum and the Elections in Equatorial Guinea, UN Doc. A/7200/Add.4, Anns. V, VI (1968). Independence was formally achieved on October 12, 1968.

[126] GA Res. 1752, 17 UN GAOR Supp. (No. 17) at 70, UN Doc. A/5217 (1962); Report of the Secretary-General regarding the Act of Self-determination in West Irian, UN Doc. A/7641 (1969).

[127] GA Res. 34/10, 34 UN GAOR Supp. (No. 46) at 199, UN Doc. A/34/46 (1979); Report of the United Nations Mission to Observe the Elections in the New Hebrides, UN Doc. A/34/852 (1979).

cases of decolonization were among the most difficult. In these, a UN "honest broker" role proved indispensable. A remarkable example is UNTAG, the UN transitional administration that acted as midwife in the birth of independent Namibia. Under South African administration since Germany's defeat in World War I, the territory was set on the road to independence first by the General Assembly's termination of South Africa's mandate in 1966, followed by a landmark advisory opinion by the International Court of Justice in 1971,[128] and by a decision of the Security Council in 1978 establishing the parameters for the territory's political development and democratic entitlement.[129] It took another decade, however, for the political climate in South Africa to change sufficiently to permit international implementation of self-determination through a UN-supervised vote. By that time, tribal and racial cleavages had become potential obstacles to a peaceful transition. Created by the Security Council precisely to prevent a preindependence civil conflict, UNTAG monitored the final months of South African administration and supervised the elections immediately prior to independence. But UNTAG did not merely monitor a vote. It took responsibility for maintaining peace, overseeing the South African military withdrawal and assisting in the drafting of a new constitution. It helped achieve the rapid repeal of discriminatory legislation, implementation of an amnesty and the return of political refugees; and it was instrumental in keeping the election peaceful and productive. Deploying more than seven thousand military and civilian personnel at a cost of $373 million, it prepared the November 1989 elections and conducted them so successfully that a risk-filled situation became, instead, a model of political transformation.[130]

The Security Council authorized a similarly complex role for the United Nations in a resolution of April 29, 1991, that established a United Nations Mission for the Referendum in the Western Sahara.[131] Under the plan negotiated by the Secretary-General with the Government of Morocco and the POLISARIO liberation movement, electoral monitoring is to be but one component of a project that gives the Organization predominant responsibility for governance of the territory in the period leading up to, and during, the crucial plebiscite. After almost two decades of war for control of the territory, the United Nations is to ensure security, facilitate large-scale repatriation of refugees, oversee the withdrawal of rival militias, and supervise the delicate process of determining who is eligible to vote.[132]

Even more remarkable than its monitoring in trust territories and colonies is the recent supervision by the United Nations of crucial votes in independent member states. In the first of these, the 1990 election in Nicaragua, UN monitoring was the culmination of the Secretary-General's far more extensive "good offices" negotiations, in cooperation with the OAS, aimed at ending the Central American regional conflict. This effort led, in August 1987, to the Esquipulas II agreement

[128] Legal Consequences for States of the Continued Presence of South Africa in Namibia (South West Africa) notwithstanding Security Council Resolution 276 (1970), 1971 ICJ REP. 16 (Advisory Opinion of June 21).

[129] SC Res. 435, 33 UN SCOR (Res. & Dec.) at 13, UN Doc. S/INF/34 (1978). It did not authorize the sending of UNTAG until 1989. SC Res. 628, 44 UN SCOR (Res. & Dec.) at 2, UN Doc. S/INF/45 (1989); SC Res. 629, *id.*

[130] *Namibia, Independence at Last,* UN CHRON., June 1990, at 4. Namibia formally achieved independence on March 21, 1990. *Id.*

[131] SC Res. 690 (Apr. 29, 1991).

[132] The Situation Concerning Western Sahara: Report by the Secretary-General, UN Doc. S/22464 (1991).

between five Central American Presidents, which established a blueprint for restoring peace and ensuring legitimacy in Nicaragua. In response to its call for free, internationally monitored elections, on March 3, 1989, the Nicaraguan Foreign Minister requested that the Secretary-General establish an observer mission.[133] The General Assembly had already authorized the Secretary-General to assist the Esquipulas process in appropriate ways,[134] but that resolution had made no mention of election monitoring. Nevertheless, the Secretary-General thought he had a "sufficient legislative basis" to comply with Nicaragua's request.[135] As a result, he established ONUVEN on July 6, 1989,[136] an initiative approved by the Security Council three weeks later.[137]

The active, far-reaching role of the UN observers in Nicaragua clearly illustrates how much the ground rules for international election monitoring had evolved in practice from the days of the missions to British Togoland and Ruanda-Urundi. The observers sent by the Secretary-General monitored the activities of the Supreme Electoral Council in drafting and implementing new laws applicable to nominating, campaigning and related activities. They were deployed throughout the electoral campaign and mediated disputes between candidates concerning access to funding, the media and even the streets. They oversaw the rights of political parties to organize and campaign, verified the campaigners' right of access to radio, television and newspapers, and investigated numerous charges of abuses and irregularities that might have undermined the legitimacy of the outcome.[138] At the final stage, ONUVEN observed the voting and established its own projection of the results.[139] Commenting on these varied functions, the head of ONUVEN, Elliot Richardson, noted that his group had decided early in its career "that responsibility for verification of the electoral process demanded more than merely recording the process, more than monitoring, and could not stop short of actively seeking to get corrected whatever substantial defects had been discovered."[140]

Creating a UN mandate for ONUVEH, the mission established on October 10, 1990, to oversee Haitian elections, was more controversial. The Haitian case—greeted by many but feared by others—was seen as a potential precedent for international monitoring in any independent state. While the same might have been said of ONUVEN, Nicaragua's long civil war could have been seen as sufficiently threatening to the peace to justify, exceptionally, a UN role in validating those national elections. In Haiti's case, however, there was no obvious threat to international peace and the elections did not constitute part of a regional program for internationally supervised postwar reconciliation. In fact, the UN monitoring role there resulted solely from a request in a letter to the Secretary-General from the Haitian Transitional Government.[141] In normative terms, Haiti may be understood as the first instance in which the United Nations, acting at the request of

[133] *See* The Situation in Central America: Threats to International Peace and Security and Peace Initiatives, UN Doc. A/44/642, at 2 (1989) [hereinafter First Nicaragua Report].

[134] GA Res. 43/24, 43 UN GAOR Supp. (No. 49) at 27, UN Doc. A/43/49 (1988).

[135] UN Doc. A/44/304, at 2 (1989).

[136] UN Doc. A/44/375 (1989).

[137] SC Res. 637, 44 UN SCOR, *supra* note 129, at 19.

[138] *See, e.g.*, The Situation in Central America: Threat to International Peace and Security and Peace Initiatives, UN Doc. A/44/927 (1990) [hereinafter Fifth Nicaragua Report]. *See also* First Nicaragua Report, *supra* note 133; UN Doc. A/44/834 (1990) (Second Report); UN Doc. A/44/917 (1990) (Third Report); UN Doc. A/44/921 (1990) (Fourth Report).

[139] Fifth Nicaragua Report, *supra* note 138.

[140] *Id.* at 3.

[141] UN Doc. A/44/965 (1990).

a national government, intervened in the electoral process solely to validate the legitimacy of the outcome.

Despite misgivings, ONUVEH secured the imprimatur of the General Assembly.[142] Once again, the monitors were authorized to do far more than oversee the ballot count. Their first report noted the lack of democratic traditions in Haiti and its long history of totalitarianism and violence, much of it government inspired and some of it quite recent.[143] In preemptive response to this problem, the Assembly had authorized the recruiting of observers "with solid experience in the public order field."[144] As ONUVEH soon discovered, the

> first task . . . was to help create a psychological climate conducive to the holding of democratic elections. . . . In this they were assisted by a radio and television campaign conducted by an ONUVEH information team. . . .
>
> . . . [They] inquired into difficulties encountered by the registration and polling stations in registering voters and into irregularities reported to them. They attended political meetings . . . and monitored radio and television broadcasts to make sure that all candidates had equal access to the mass media.[145]

Although the Secretary-General, in his final report on ONUVEH, expressed satisfaction with the fairness of the electoral process and the role played by the United Nations, he also noted the formidable obstacles that lay ahead for Haitian democracy and called for "launching a civil education campaign on the importance of the parliament and local authorities."[146] The Secretary-General rightly warned that, if electoral democracy is to be more than a one-time event in the history of a state with little experience in such matters, a far more sustained effort will have to be made under the auspices of the community of nations. This warning suggests the need for a long-term, preemptive assistance program. More, it at least implies the need for a longer-term international effort to create the grass roots elements of democratic political institutions and processes—a particularly challenging form of technical assistance—in nations without that tradition. This need, in turn, suggests an important future role for the nongovernmental, citizen-to-citizen organizations—at present, an underused, but invaluable, component of the UN system.

The military coup that ousted Haiti's elected Government on September 30, 1991, verified the Secretary-General's warning that elections are not necessarily a cure-all. The General Assembly responded less than two weeks later, passing by consensus a resolution that "[s]trongly condemns both the attempted illegal replacement of the constitutional President of Haiti and the use of violence, military coercion and the violation of human rights in that country" and "demands the immediate restoration of the legitimate Government." It also "[a]ppeals to the . . . Members" to "take measures in support" of action by the OAS to isolate Haiti diplomatically and economically.[147] By these provisions, the Assembly made clear its intention henceforth to regard the overthrow of a democratically elected

[142] GA Res. 45/2 (Oct. 12, 1990).

[143] First Report of the United Nations Observer Group for the Verification of the Elections in Haiti, UN Doc. A/45/870, at 9–10 (1990).

[144] GA Res. 45/2, *supra* note 142, para. 1(*d*).

[145] United Nations Electoral Assistance to Haiti, UN Doc. DPI/1120 (1991).

[146] Electoral Assistance to Haiti: Note by the Secretary-General, UN Doc. A/45/870/Add.1, at 23 (1991).

[147] GA Res. A/46/L.8/Rev.1, paras. 1, 2, 4 (Oct. 11, 1991) (italics omitted).

regime as an appropriate subject for censure and even for recommending collective measures.[148]

The Organization of American States has also engaged in election monitoring. Its members authorized the dispatch of a 435-person commission to Nicaragua in 1990 to observe 70 percent of the polling sites.[149] In addition, the OAS maintained a major presence during the Haitian elections,[150] not only to watch the polls, but also to assist in drafting the electoral law and organizing voter registration.[151] Over the past two years, OAS monitors have observed elections in Suriname, El Salvador, Paraguay and Panama as well.[152] As a result, in part, of such collective efforts,[153] the thirty-four OAS member states—with the lamentable exception of Haiti—all have governments chosen in accordance with the democratic entitlement.[154]

Monitoring by governmental and nongovernmental observers also became an important ad hoc part of the post-1989 transition from Communist to democratic regimes in Eastern Europe. These events foreshadowed the textual declarations regarding election standards and procedures in the Copenhagen and Paris documents. Once again, practice preceded the drafting of new principles. The United States sent an official mission to monitor Bulgaria's 1990 election, as did several other CSCE governments.[155] Several members of Congress observed the electoral campaigns in Bulgaria[156] and Czechoslovakia,[157] as did their counterparts from some Western European parliaments.

At the unofficial level, additional election monitoring has taken place in recent years. Emissaries of the Council of Freely Elected Heads of Government of the Carter Center observed the 1990 Nicaraguan and 1991 Zambian elections.[158] The (U.S.) National Democratic Institute for International Affairs has monitored elections in twelve countries since 1986.[159] At least half a dozen teams of foreign observers, including experts from the United States, the Philippines, Japan and the British Commonwealth, monitored parliamentary elections in Bangladesh on February 27, 1991.[160] International observers from Canada, France, Germany and the United States verified the propriety of elections held in Benin in March 1991.[161] Perhaps most remarkable was the authorized presence of sixty-five inter-

[148] The "secondary" role of the General Assembly in recommending collective measures by the members has been controversial, but was found to be justified by Article 17, paragraph 2 of the Charter. *See* Certain expenses of the United Nations (Article 17, paragraph 2, of the Charter), 1962 ICJ REP. 151, 163 (Advisory Opinion of July 20).

[149] N.Y. Times, Feb. 23, 1990, at A3, col. 4.

[150] OEA/Ser.G/CP/RES.537, doc. 805 (1990).

[151] Report of the Secretary General on the Assistance the Organization Is Giving to the Provisional Government of Haiti in its Electoral Process, OEA/Ser.G/CP/doc.2108/90, at 1.

[152] N.Y. Times, June 9, 1991, §4, at 2, col. 1.

[153] See, e.g., the OAS condemnation of General Manuel Noriega's usurpation of democratic electoral process in Panama's election of May 7, 1989, *supra* note 89. *See also* N.Y. Times, May 18, 1989, at A8, col. 3; *id.*, Aug. 16, 1989, at A9, col. 1.

[154] N.Y. Times, June 9, 1991, §4, at 2, col. 1. Cuba is not a member.

[155] N.Y. Times, June 6, 1990, at A10, col. 3.

[156] *See* Kahn, *Bulgaria's Different Pathway,* Christian Sci. Monitor, June 22, 1990, at 18. Helsinki Watch also sent monitors. N.Y. Times, June 11, 1990, at A1, col. 1.

[157] N.Y. Times, June 10, 1990, §1, at 31, col. 1.

[158] N.Y. Times, Aug. 9, 1989, at A13, col. 1; N.Y. Times, Nov. 1, 1991, at A3, col. 1.

[159] National Democratic Institute for International Affairs, Response to United Nations General Assembly Resolution 45/150: Developing a United Nations Elections Assistance Capability 2 (1991) (memorandum submitted to the Secretary-General).

[160] N.Y. Times, Feb. 28, 1991, at A5, col. 4.

[161] N.Y. Times, Mar. 12, 1991, at A11, col. 1.

national observers at the referendum on independence conducted in Latvia on March 3, 1991.[162]

Elliot Richardson, as head of the UN observers in Nicaragua, predicted that "the United Nations is likely in the future to be called upon for similar assignments in other countries."[163] "The results of such elections," as Professor Reisman recently observed, "serve as evidence of popular sovereignty and become the basis for international endorsement of the elected government."[164] Appropriately, President George Bush, in addressing the forty-fifth General Assembly, proposed the establishment of a standing UN electoral commission to assist nations, at their request, in guaranteeing that their elections will be free and fair.[165] A year later, as noted, the Assembly implemented that proposal.

Requesting international electoral monitoring thus will likely become an increasingly routine part of national practice, particularly useful whenever the democratic legitimacy of a regime is in question. Of course, there are still hard-core holdouts, such as the totalitarian governments of Myanmar, North Korea and China. Their number, however, is diminishing. The Government formed in Ethiopia in May 1991, after the end of the civil war, has undertaken to conduct "free, democratic and internationally monitored elections" within a year.[166] The insurgents who took power in Eritrea have committed themselves not to secede from Ethiopia until after a UN-monitored plebiscite, to be held within two years.[167]

A recent study by the UN Secretariat, noting the rising demand for monitoring, made a start at setting out the juridical, institutional, administrative and fiscal parameters of an expanded UN electoral monitoring service.[168] The OAS was authorized to prepare a similar study.[169] These begin the conceptually difficult task of sifting through the increasing body of practice to clarify the meaning of the normative concept signaled by the phrase "democratic entitlement." These data make it strikingly apparent that international election monitoring cannot be limited to guaranteeing citizens' right to vote, but rather must also ensure a far broader panoply of democratic rights of the sort enunciated in the Civil and Political Rights Covenant and the Charter of Paris. In case-by-case implementation and the distillation of that experience, greater determinacy will be achieved.

A study that seeks to connect the dots of practice with lines of enunciated principle must also look at the several instances when election monitoring was denied. For example, in 1990 the Secretary-General refused to monitor the Romanian elections on the ground that his participation had not been authorized by the General Assembly or Security Council. He added, perhaps even more persuasively, that he had not been invited to participate early enough in establishing the rules and methods to be used in conducting the election campaign.[170] In

[162] Fin. Times (London), Mar. 4, 1991, at 14.

[163] Fifth Nicaragua Report, *supra* note 138, at 3.

[164] Reisman, *Sovereignty and Human Rights in Contemporary International Law*, 84 AJIL 866, 868–69 (1990).

[165] N.Y. Times, Oct. 2, 1990, at A12, col. 1. [166] N.Y. Times, May 29, 1991, at A6, col. 5.

[167] N.Y. Times, June 22, 1991, at 3, col. 1.

[168] Principles for United Nations Observance of Elections, Confidential Memorandum (June 6, 1989) (in the possession of the author).

[169] OEA/Ser.G/CP/RES.421, doc. 606 (1985).

[170] *See U.N. Says It Won't Monitor Romanian Elections* (NEXIS, CURRNT Library, Reuters, Jan. 25, 1990).

1991 the Office of the Secretary-General rejected requests for election monitoring made by Lesotho and Zambia, again on the ground that he felt he was unauthorized, in the absence of special circumstances, to monitor elections in sovereign states. The political organs of the United Nations may have been too cautious, so far, in giving the Secretary-General authority to respond favorably to a bona fide request by a member. On the other hand, the office of the Secretary-General may have been too cautious in denying requests for monitoring without even presenting them for approval to the Security Council or the General Assembly.

There is reason, nonetheless, for some caution. Commentators have rightly warned that the bare monitoring of the act of voting may place observers in the position of seeming to legitimate an electoral victory that was not fairly achieved. This reservation need not implicate fraud or repression but, more likely, concerns the effect on free choice of the normal operation of entrenched social and political institutions. In the words of a recent report to the General Assembly by the Secretary-General:

> [R]equests should pertain primarily to situations with a clear international dimension; the monitoring of an election or referendum should cover the entire electoral process in order to secure conditions of fairness and impartiality; . . . there must be broad public support in the State for the United Nations assuming such a role; and, finally, there should be approval by the competent organ of the United Nations.[171]

In future, in keeping with Assembly Resolution 46/137 of December 17, 1991, all requests for monitoring will be considered by the Council or Assembly, which will have the task of evolving standards for accepting or refusing.

While no observation process can reach back far enough into a nation's history to extirpate the impacted roots of social and cultural inequalities, observers can do—and already have done—more than simply watch tellers count ballots. To make citizens' rights to free and open elections a legitimate entitlement, its parameters need to be made clear and specific. To that end, a robust repertory of practice, a canon of enunciated principles and an institutional framework for implementation are developing that are capable of giving the entitlement increasing determinacy.

As the entitlement becomes an accepted norm, a drawn-out debate in international law will draw to a close. Do governments validate international law or does international law validate governments? It is becoming apparent that each legitimates the other.

The capacity of the international system to validate governments in this fashion is rapidly being accepted as an appropriate role of the United Nations, the regional systems and, supplementarily, the NGOs. A recent study conducted by the Netherlands Minister of Foreign Affairs gives expression to the new normative expectation. It asked: what can reasonably be expected of a European state seeking to join the European Communities and the Council of Europe? The study finds that applicant states "must be plural democracies; they must regularly hold free elections by secret ballot; they must respect the rule of law; [and] they must have signed the European Convention on Human Rights and Fundamental Free-

[171] Enhancing the Effectiveness of the Principle of Periodic and Genuine Elections, Report of the Secretary-General, UN Doc. A/46/609, para. 79, at 25 (1991). *See also* Gelb, *The Free Elections Trap*, N.Y. Times, May 29, 1991, at A23, col. 1.

doms."[172] Such a test for validation of governance and entry into a society of nations would have been unthinkable even a decade ago; it is considered unexceptionable in the new Europe. Some comparable rule in future should, and undoubtedly will, become the standard for participation in the multinational institutions of the global community.

As a step in this direction, the UN General Assembly might adopt and adapt the guidelines in the CSCE's Copenhagen Document and Paris Charter and declare these applicable to Article 25 of the Civil and Political Covenant. Such a resolution, among other things, would guide and assist the Human Rights Committee in more efficaciously carrying out its monitoring of compliance by the large majority of states parties to that global instrument. It would also help to make more determinate the content of the evolving customary law applicable to national political practices. Bringing the evolution of UN practice approximately into line with that of the CSCE would endow the emerging democratic entitlement with greater specificity and coherence.

VI. Coherence of the Democratic Entitlement

Pedigree and determinacy, as we have seen, give a rule the pull to compliance that we have identified as evidence of its perceived legitimacy. So also coherence. Coherence is that quality of a rule which permits it to be seen holistically: that is, as part of a rule context in which the parts gather compliance pull from the purpose and meaning of a larger whole. A rule that can plausibly lay claim to being part of such a skein exercises a greater compliance pull than one that cannot.[173]

Another way of understanding coherence is to examine the extent to which the compliance pull of a rule, invoked in one case, is augmented by evidence that it has connections that lead beyond the specifics of that dispute. Such augmentation may appear in several forms. First, it may become apparent that the rule being tested is so intimately connected with a larger regulatory scheme—for example, as one clause of an entire treaty—as to bring into play the weight and purpose of the larger whole. Second, the rule being tested may evince an important principle—English common law abounds in such "maxims": *nemo dat quod non habet,* for example—on which many distinct rules depend. Third, the issues in one instance may resemble those in others, creating a form of imperative to treat likes alike by applying the same rule.

How coherent, thus understood, is the normative canon of the democratic entitlement? Our examination of global and regional texts and processes will reveal that the rules pertaining to self-determination, freedom of expression and the right to participate in free and open elections are closely interwoven strands of a single fabric. These three generations of democratic entitlement, reinforced by regional systems, not only share many of the same or similar norms, but also have developed common or comparable kinds of institutions, procedures and customs. Each thread reinforces, and is reinforced by, the weave of the cloth.

When it comes to shared underlying principles, however, the connections are less straightforward. The democratic entitlement, after all, rests on the still-radi-

[172] Letter from the Minister for Foreign Affairs (H. van den Broek) to the Advisory Committee on Human Rights and Foreign Policy (June 20, 1990), *reprinted in* NETHERLANDS ADVISORY COMMITTEE ON HUMAN RIGHTS AND FOREIGN POLICY, DEMOCRACY AND HUMAN RIGHTS IN EASTERN EUROPE 30–31 (1990).

[173] *See* T. FRANCK, *supra* note 12, at 150–82.

cal principle that the community of states is empowered to compose and apply codes governing the comportment of governments toward their own citizens. No doubt, some such assumption long ago justified "enlightened" colonialism; its relic is still on view in Article 38(1)(c) of the International Court's Statute, which authorizes the judges to consult "general principles of law recognized by *civilized* nations" (italics mine). The term "civilized" may still be tainted by association with Cecil Rhodes, but the notion that governments can be graded for deportment is not. The Charter limits UN membership to states that are "peace-loving" (Article 4(1)) and enjoins governments to respect the "equal rights and self-determination of [their own] peoples" (Article 1(2)). The Genocide[174] and Racism Conventions[175] certainly do qualify as rules of deportment imposed on all states by the community of nations. Having become customary as well as treaty law—if not also rules of *jus cogens*—these Conventions may be said to exemplify the principle that states collectively have the authority to determine minimum standards of conduct from which none may long deviate without eventually endangering their membership in the club.

Nevertheless, the notion that the community can impose such standards, on which the democratic entitlement is based, has always been challenged by reference to another, embodied in Article 2(7) of the Charter. It provides, as formal recognition of the centuries-old principle of state sovereignty, that the Organization shall not interfere in matters "essentially within the domestic jurisdiction of states." While, as noted above, this conflict may have been resolved within the regional context of the CSCE with the recognition by the Copenhagen Document and the Paris Charter of the paramountcy of the democratic entitlement, the clear-cut supremacy of that entitlement is not yet apparent in the global context. Of course, state sovereignty, by operation of technological advances as much as of heightened humanistic sensitivity, is not what it used to be. Even those who defend the continued vitality of the principle would probably concede that genocide does not fall "essentially" within the ambit of protected "domestic" government activity. Nor, certainly, do egregious racism and, at least since the 1960s, denials of self-determination. Since the coming into force of the Civil and Political Rights Covenant, aggravated denials of the right to free speech and to free and open elections also have become generally acknowledged exceptions to the principle of noninterference in states' domestic jurisdiction. Nevertheless, a residual conflict of principles still troubles many states.

The problem is not so apparent in general theory as in application. To proclaim a general right to free elections is less intrusive than monitoring any particular election in an independent state. Effective monitoring is even more intrusive than the mere observation of balloting. And collective action to compel states to adhere to a standard is the most intrusive of all. Thus, the conflict of principles needs to be recognized, made explicit, and reconciled to the general satisfaction of the large preponderance of states before the democratic entitlement's global legitimacy is demonstrated by real, as opposed to formulaic, coherence. That will require action to meet the practical concerns of states that still regard the nonintervention principle as of overriding importance to their national well-being.

[174] Convention on the Prevention and Punishment of the Crime of Genocide, Dec. 9, 1948, 78 UNTS 277 (entered into force Jan. 12, 1951).

[175] International Convention on the Elimination of All Forms of Racial Discrimination, *opened for signature* Mar. 7, 1966, 660 UNTS 195, *reprinted in* 5 ILM 352 (1966) (entered into force Jan. 4, 1969) [hereinafter Racial Convention].

Also unclear is the extent to which the various parts of the democratic entitlement can yet claim the legitimacy that derives from "treating like cases alike." Are virtually all states, for example, ready to have their elections monitored by a credible global process? This and other issues need to be examined in detail before the democratic entitlement can be said to have achieved universal coherence.

Significance of the Human Rights Connection

A bright line links the three components of the democratic entitlement. The rules, and the processes for realizing self-determination, freedom of expression and electoral rights, have much in common and evidently aim at achieving a coherent purpose: creating the opportunity for all persons to assume responsibility for shaping the kind of civil society in which they live and work. There is a large normative canon for promoting that objective: the UN Charter, the Universal Declaration of Human Rights,[176] the International Covenant on Civil and Political Rights,[177] the International Convention on the Elimination of All Forms of Racial Discrimination,[178] the International Convention on the Suppression and Punishment of the Crime of *Apartheid*,[179] the Declaration on the Elimination of All Forms of Intolerance and of Discrimination Based on Religion or Belief,[180] and the Convention on the Elimination of All Forms of Discrimination against Women.[181] These universally based rights are supplemented by regional instruments such as the European Convention for the Protection of Human Rights and Fundamental Freedoms,[182] the American Convention on Human Rights,[183] the African Charter on Human and Peoples' Rights,[184] the Copenhagen Document[185] and the Paris Charter.[186]

Each of these instruments recognizes related specific entitlements as accruing to individual citizens. These constitute internationally mandated restraints on governments. As we have seen, they embody rights of free and equal participation in governance, a cluster within which electoral rights are a consistent and probably necessary segment. The result is a net of participatory entitlements. The various texts speak of similar goals and deploy, for the most part, a similar range of processes for monitoring compliance, several of which have already become common usage in connection with the democratic entitlement. One can convincingly argue that states which deny their citizens the right to free and open elections are violating a rule that is fast becoming an integral part of the elaborately woven human rights fabric. Thus, the democratic entitlement has acquired a degree of legitimacy by its association with a far broader panoply of laws pertaining to the rights of persons vis-à-vis their governments.

[176] GA Res. 217A (III), *supra* note 60.

[177] ICCPR, *supra* note 41.

[178] Racial Convention, *supra* note 175.

[179] GA Res. 3068, 28 UN GAOR Supp. (No. 30) at 75, UN Doc. A/9030 (1973), *reprinted in* 13 ILM 56 (1974) (entered into force July 18, 1976) [hereinafter Apartheid Convention].

[180] GA Res. 36/55, 36 UN GAOR Supp. (No. 51) at 171, UN Doc. A/36/51 (1981), *reprinted in* 21 ILM 205 (1982).

[181] GA Res. 34/180, 34 UN GAOR Supp. (No. 46) at 193, UN Doc. A/34/46 (1979), *reprinted in* 19 ILM 33 (1980) (entered into force Sept. 3, 1981).

[182] European Convention, *supra* note 72.

[183] American Convention, *supra* note 77.

[184] African Charter on Human and Peoples' Rights, *adopted* June 27, 1981, OAU Doc. CAB/LEG/67/3/Rev.5, *reprinted in* 21 ILM 58 (1982) [hereinafter Banjul Charter].

[185] Copenhagen Document, *supra* note 98.

[186] Paris Charter, *supra* note 105.

Nevertheless, while we may well be moving in this direction, we may not have arrived. When, in November 1989, the UN Secretary-General was asked by the Nicaraguan Sandinista Government to monitor national elections, he felt compelled to link his acceptance not to the human rights framework but to older, perhaps better-established, norms of the international system. Indeed, he went out of his way to reassure the General Assembly that, while the United Nations had frequently supervised elections in the context of decolonization, "it has not been the practice to do so in respect of independent States." He even noted with pride that, "on a number of occasions over the years, we have declined invitations from Member States to that effect." Nevertheless, the Nicaraguan case could be distinguished because the request was not from "a single Member State, but one which has the support of the Presidents of Costa Rica, El Salvador, Guatemala, Honduras and Nicaragua," and thus "clearly belongs in the context of the Central American peace efforts."[187] The same effort to link the democratic entitlement and peacemaking is evident in the 1990 agreement negotiated by the Secretary-General between the Government of El Salvador and the insurgent Frente Farabundo Martí para la Liberación Nacional (FMLN).[188] It links the dispatch of UN monitors (ONUSAL) to observe human rights and the process leading up to Salvadoran elections with their larger role in ending the civil war.[189] Clearly, the content and scope of the democratic entitlement, in practice, will be shaped by whether it is connected to, and legitimized by, the relatively narrow *peacemaking*, or the much more expansive *human rights*, canon.

Coherence of Underlying Principles

So far, the Secretary-General's choice of the peacemaking linkage strategy has avoided a head-on conflict between proponents and opponents of election monitoring as a general normative democratic entitlement. Sooner or later, however, an unresolved conflict of deep-seated principles—the emerging right to free and fair elections and nonintervention in domestic affairs—is likely to generate a clash of political wills in the global and regional communities unless these dissonant principles are reconciled.

The very idea of general international monitoring of elections in sovereign states still arouses the most passionate ire, not only of the increasingly isolated residue of totalitarian regimes, but also of nations with long memories of humiliating interventions by states bent on "civilizing" missions. While they will accept occasional monitoring of elections to end a civil war or regional conflict, they consider it a necessary exception, not a normal manifestation of a universal democratic entitlement.

[187] UN Doc. A/44/210, at 2 (1989).

[188] Central America: Efforts Towards Peace, *supra* note 71.

[189] ONUSAL, the United Nations Observer Mission in El Salvador, will monitor the "release of individuals who have been imprisoned for political reasons . . . , the right of all persons to associate freely with others for ideological . . . political . . . or other purposes . . . , freedom of expression and of the press" and "freedom of movement." Agreement on Human Rights, Annex to Note verbale dated 14 August 1990 from the Charge d'affaires of the Permanent Mission of El Salvador to the United Nations addressed to the Secretary-General, UN Doc. A/44/971–S/21541, ann. at 4–5 (1990). For the March 1991 elections in El Salvador, however, the United Nations declined to mount an observer operation, dedicating its strained resources to other aspects of the peacemaking and monitoring process while letting the OAS take the lead, supported by nongovernmental organizations, in observing those elections. National Democratic Institute for International Affairs, *supra* note 159, at 14.

Conflict was clearly foreshadowed in 1990 when the General Assembly weighed the proposal to establish ONUVEH, the aforementioned observer group to monitor Haiti's elections. Since linkage between election monitoring and peace was much harder to demonstrate in the absence of armed hostilities, the creation of ONUVEH encountered significant opposition, notably from China, Cuba and Colombia.[190] The long specter of U.S. hemispheric interventions was invoked in the Assembly's corridors. Several months elapsed before suspicions could be assuaged by diplomatic assurances that the Haitian case, too, would set no general precedent. Cuba, in the debate prior to the vote authorizing ONUVEH, spoke emphatically against "any attempt to use this United Nations resolution or activity as a pretext for interfering in the internal affairs of Haiti"[191] and stressed that elections "can never be regarded as affecting international peace and security."[192] Mexico also went on record as denying any precedential value to the authorization of ONUVEH.[193] These states contended that UN election monitoring in an independent nation is unlawful *per se,* in the absence of exceptional peacemaking exigencies.

The International Court of Justice rebuffed this view indirectly in its 1986 *Nicaragua* decision. The majority stated, in connection with commitments binding a nation to electoral standards, that it could not

> discover, within the range of subjects open to international agreement, any obstacle or provision to hinder a State from making a commitment of this kind. A State, which is free to decide upon the principle and methods of popular consultation within its domestic order, is sovereign for the purpose of accepting a limitation of its sovereignty in this field. This is a conceivable situation for a State which is bound by institutional links to a confederation of States, or indeed to an international organization.[194]

There are thus no legal impediments to institutionalizing voluntary international election monitoring as one way to give effect to the emerging right of all peoples to free and open electoral democracy, but this is not to say that states as yet have a *duty* to submit their elections to international validation. Although the CSCE, in Europe, seems poised to pioneer a generalized duty to be monitored, even it has not made the duty mandatory for all. In the international community, while there may be a duty under Article 25 of the Civil and Political Rights Covenant and its regional and customary law analogues to permit free and open elections and review of national compliance by the Human Rights Committee, there is as yet no obligation to permit actual election monitoring by international or regional organizations. Indeed, one should expect resistance to any effort to transform an election-monitoring option, exercisable at the discretion of each government, into an obligation owed by each government to its own people and to the other states of the global community. Admittedly, however, a "rule" that only applies self-selectively has far less legitimacy than one of general application.

[190] The Security Council failed to reach consensus on the issue, with China threatening to veto. In the General Assembly, Cuba and Colombia argued that election monitoring in an independent state, unrelated to a threat to the peace, constituted a violation of Article 2(7) of the Charter. *See* UN Doc. A/45/PV.29 (1990).

[191] *Id.* at 62.

[192] *Id.* at 59–60.

[193] *Id.* at 64–65.

[194] Military and Paramilitary Activities in and against Nicaragua (Nicar. v. U.S.), 1986 ICJ REP. 14, 131 (Judgment of June 27) [hereinafter *Nicaragua* opinion].

This deficiency was demonstrated by the General Assembly's incoherent tiptoeing around the democratic entitlement at its session in the fall of 1990. The members passed two seemingly incongruent resolutions on monitoring, which reflect the concern of Third World states as they contemplate the seemingly inexorable evolution of an entitlement to democracy, including free elections and resultant international supervision. We have already noted the first of these resolutions, in which the democratic entitlement was restated by the Assembly and election monitoring commended as one way to ensure its implementation.[195] Almost in the same breath, however—and over the opposition of only twenty-nine states, mostly European, but also including Australia, Canada, Israel, New Zealand, Turkey and the United States—the second resolution affirmed "that it is the concern solely of peoples [of each state] to determine methods and to establish institutions regarding the electoral process, as well as to determine the ways for its implementation according to their constitutional and national legislation";[196] and it urged all states "to respect the principle of non-interference in the internal affairs of States."[197] The vast preponderance of states voting for this resolution did not do so out of concern to protect dictatorships. Rather, they were worried about the underlying principle.

When underlying principles are coherent, the rules manifesting them assume increased legitimacy. When rules exemplify principles in collision, those rules are perceived as of low legitimacy. The principle underlying a universal democratic entitlement is that the participatory rights of persons in shaping their civil society may not be abridged arbitrarily by governments. This principle has powered the rights of self-determination and freedom of expression and, now, energizes the move to provide international protection for electoral rights.

There was a time when international efforts to implement the right of self-determination were vigorously opposed as trenching upon the right of governments, under Article 2(7) of the UN Charter, to administer their colonies without outside interference. That opposition gradually abated, as the principle of self-determination gained in determinacy. Efforts to monitor compliance with the right to freedom of expression have encountered similar expressions of outraged *amour-propre* by states called to task for arbitrarily silencing their own citizens. It is not surprising that passionate resentments should also arise in some quarters at the prospect of seeing the international community insinuate itself into the intimate political process by which governments are empowered by the citizenry.

The opponents are mostly motivated by fear that monitoring will be used to reimpose a form of neocolonialism under the banner of establishing democracy. That fear must be addressed, but it must also be put in perspective. History has warned, repeatedly, that the natural right of all people to liberty and democracy is too precious, and too vulnerable, to be entrusted entirely to those who govern. John Stuart Mill once observed that the moral fiber of a nation is weakened if the intervention of outsiders spares its people the trouble of liberating themselves.[198] In view of the technological edge dictators nowadays enjoy over their people, this proposition is no longer wholly defensible. The opposite case was stated by Uganda's President Godfrey L. Binaisa, who, after the overthrow of Idi Amin's

[195] See *supra* text at and notes 82–86.

[196] GA Res. 45/151, para. 2 (Dec. 18, 1990).

[197] *Id.*, para. 4.

[198] 3 J. S. Mill, Dissertations and Discussions: Political, Philosophical and Historical 238–63 (1873).

bloody junta, went before the General Assembly to chide its delegates for their indifference to his people's plight. "In the light of the clear commitment set out in . . . provisions of the Charter," he said, "our people naturally looked to the United Nations for solidarity and support in their struggle against the Fascist dictatorship. For eight years they cried out in the wilderness for help; unfortunately, their cries seemed to have fallen on deaf ears." Acerbically, Binaisa observed that, "somehow, it is thought to be in bad taste or contrary to diplomatic etiquette to raise matters of violations of human rights by Member States within the forums of the United Nations."[199]

Where dictators can only be confronted effectively with the active support of the international community, inhibitions about interference in the "domestic jurisdiction" of states seem less compelling than they used to be. "We are arriving at the conclusion," then Soviet Foreign Minister Boris D. Pankin observed recently, "that national guarantees [of human rights] are not sufficient. So we have to review the principle of noninterference in affairs of other governments."[200] To this end, the Declaration of Human Rights and Freedoms, adopted by the Soviet Congress of People's Deputies on September 5, 1991, after the coup, states that "[e]very person possesses natural, inalienable and inviolable rights and freedoms. They are sealed in laws that must correspond to the universal declaration of human rights, the international covenants on human rights and other international norms and this declaration."[201] The OAS Foreign Ministers' 1991 resolution to the same effect has already been noted,[202] as have the CSCE heads' Paris Charter[203] and Moscow Document.[204]

It thus appears that support is increasing even—perhaps *particularly*—among former totalitarian states for the proposition that the democratic entitlement, enhanced by linkage with other basic human rights and the accompanying international monitoring of compliance, has trumped the principle of noninterference. Even the 1991 resolution of the General Assembly warning about outside "interference" in the electoral process[205] seemed to acknowledge this development, for it added an otherwise incongruous caveat,

> that only the total eradication of *apartheid* and the establishment of a non-racial, democratic society based on majority rule, through the full and free exercise of adult suffrage by all the people in a united and non-fragmented South Africa, can lead to a just and lasting solution to the explosive situation in South Africa.[206]

Surely, this assertion demonstrates not the supremacy of nonintervention but, rather, its opposite: that undemocratic electoral processes imposed upon a people by their government are now almost universally regarded as counternormative and not beyond the purview of the international community. In 1991 the UN Human Rights Commission further affirmed this view by voting unanimously to condemn the military Government of Myanmar for having failed to carry out its promise to return that country to democratic, civilian rule.[207] The junta's refusal to allow the elected legislature to meet and its arrest of many parliamentary

[199] UN Doc. A/34/PV.14, at 4–6 (1979).
[200] N.Y. Times, Sept. 10, 1991, at A13, col. 5.
[201] N.Y. Times, Sept. 7, 1991, at 5, col. 3.
[202] Resolution on Representative Democracy, *supra* note 90.
[203] Paris Charter, *supra* note 105.
[204] Moscow Document, *supra* note 116.
[205] *See supra* text at and notes 196–97.
[206] GA Res. 45/151, *supra* note 196, para. 7.
[207] N.Y. Times, Mar. 7, 1991, at A14, col. 1.

leaders were perceived as an international—not merely a domestic—issue, warranting a response from the community of nations.

Nevertheless, steps should be taken to meet the fear of some smaller states that election monitoring will lead to more Panama-style unilateral military interventions by the powerful, perhaps even for reasons less convincing than those which provoked the 1989 U.S. military strike against the Noriega dictatorship. That a new rule might authorize actions to enforce democracy still conjures up just such chilling images to weaker states, which see themselves as the potential objects of enforcement of dubious democratic norms under circumstances of doubtful probity. Of course, to give coherence to a general norm requiring free and open elections does not necessarily implicate military enforcement action.

If there is to be monitoring, some consequences could reasonably be expected to ensue for those who "fail the test." And if monitoring evolves into a systemwide obligation, perhaps some consequences will attach even to a refusal to be monitored. As Judge Buergenthal has observed about the effect of the Copenhagen Document and the Paris Charter, there is bound to evolve a "linkage of human rights to other questions (trade, security, environment, etc.). . . . Linkage permits the participating States . . . to condition their bilateral and multilateral relations in general upon progress in the human dimension sphere."[208] While perhaps true, today, only regarding the CSCE, this effect is likely to point the way toward the enforcement of the democratic entitlement in the global community, as well.

This prospect evokes hope, but also justified fears that must be abated. The coherence of the democratic entitlement ultimately will depend on whether most states, most of the time, freely agree to be monitored: whether, in short, the process is perceived as legitimate. To achieve this normative coherence, monitoring will have to be uncoupled, in the clearest fashion, from a long history of unilateral enforcement of a tainted, colonialist "civilizing" mission. If the duty to be monitored is to develop as customary law, it must be reconciled in the minds of governments with their residual sovereignty. This requires that all states unambiguously renounce the use of unilateral, or even regional, *military* force to compel compliance with the democratic entitlement in the absence of prior Security Council authorization under chapter VII of the Charter; such authorization, except for *regional* action under Article 53, would require a finding that the violation had risen to the level of a threat to the peace.[209] Such a pledge would merely reiterate the existing normative structure of the Charter, Articles 2(4), 51 and 53 in particular. Yet this reiteration is necessary, in view of the history of unilateral interventionism which has undermined that self-denying ordinance. Specifically, states must acknowledge that the evolution of a democratic entitlement cannot entitle a state or group of states to enforce the right by military action under the pretext of invoking Articles 51 or 53. *Ça va sans dire* is no answer to those demanding that assurance in the light of recent Soviet and U.S.-led unilateral or pseudoregional actions alleged to promote "democracy" in neighboring states and justified as "collective self-defense."

[208] Buergenthal, *supra* note 109, at 43.

[209] The General Assembly, in the case of the 1991 Haitian military coup, appears to have concluded that it is empowered to recommend action of an economic and diplomatic kind to its members. In approving regional military action under Article 53, the Security Council appears not to be limited to cases in which international peace has been threatened or breached.

A specific renunciation of unilateralism would obviously not obviate every possibility that some negative consequences might ensue for governments unwilling to be monitored or to hold free elections; nor should it. The international community long has asserted, in the case of South Africa, a right of all states to take hortatory, economic and—in extreme cases—even military action to enforce aspects of the democratic entitlement,[210] but only when duly authorized by the United Nations in accordance with its Charter. Article 2(7), in barring UN intervention "in matters which are essentially within the domestic jurisdiction of any state," stipulates that "this principle shall not prejudice the application of enforcement measures under Chapter VII." Rhodesia's Unilateral Declaration of Independence provoked a UN resolution permitting Britain to use military force.[211] It is no longer arguable that the United Nations cannot exert pressure against governments that oppress their own peoples by egregious racism, denials of self-determination and suppression of freedom of expression. That litany is being augmented by new sins: refusals to permit demonstrably free elections or to implement their results. However, if the sin is committed, the international community may only invoke collective enforcement measures such as sanctions, blockade or military intervention in limited circumstances—as when the Security Council finds that a threat or breach of the peace has occurred—or if it collectively determines that it is not engaging in enforcement *against* a member but is acting at the request of a legitimate government against a usurper. These prerequisite determinations, however, must be made by the appropriate collective machinery of the community and not by individual members.

This procedure is both legally required and politically essential. To obtain the general consent necessary to render the denial of democracy a cognizable violation of an international community standard, it must be understood that whatever countermeasures are taken must first be authorized collectively by the appropriate UN institutions. Collective action—so the tremulous must understand and the powerful aver—is not a substitute for, but the opposite of, unilateral enforcement. In this respect, as in many others, the principal enemy of the evolution of a new rule is fear of its vigilante enforcement.[212] For that reason, the entitlement to democracy can only be expected to flourish if it is coupled with a reiterated prohibition on such unilateral initiatives. Only then will the rule enjoy the degree of principled coherence necessary to the widespread perception of its legitimacy.

Treating Like Cases Alike

If voluntary acceptance of monitoring becomes the general practice of states, it will gradually evolve from an optional to a customary and, ultimately, mandatory means of satisfying the democratic entitlement. This transformation, surely, is to be encouraged, but it is unlikely to occur as a consequence of a global treaty. Too many states, especially smaller ones, still fear that it will erode the rule of nonintervention. It may occur, however, through gradual, incremental steps that make

[210] *See* Apartheid Convention, *supra* note 179. *See also* R. BISSELL, APARTHEID AND INTERNATIONAL ORGANIZATIONS 156–59 (1977).

[211] SC Res. 253, 23 UN SCOR (Res. & Dec.) at 5, UN Doc. S/INF/23/Rev.1 (1968).

[212] *See* Arend, *International Law and the Recourse to Force: A Shift in Paradigms*, 27 STAN. J. INT'L L. 1, 40–45 (1991).

voluntary submission an attractive option for most governments.[213] If the United Nations' concern to restore democracy in Haiti is grounded, in part, on the ousted government's having been legitimated by a monitored election, that constitutes a palpable inducement to governments to take up the option. When that option is generally taken, the international monitoring of an election will cease to be a special case and will have become normative, a rule that treats like cases alike.

We have already noted that the right of self-determination, as first enunciated and practiced at Versailles, lacked coherence because it applied only to the European territories of the former German, Austro-Hungarian and Turkish Empires. After the Second World War, the UN Charter, in Article 1(2), made "the principle of equal rights and self-determination of peoples" universally applicable. Nevertheless, for forty years thereafter, the right of self-determination was implemented only selectively, primarily in colonies and trusteeship territories. There may have been a reason it was applied to India but not to Hungary or Czechoslovakia, but, if so, no persuasive, principled distinction was advanced.[214]

Undoubtedly, this incoherence undermined its legitimacy. More recently, we have seen the right at last becoming—in theory and increasingly in practice—one of universal application as it merges with newer aspects of the democratic entitlement. Thus, we may conclude that self-determination is evolving from incoherence to coherence, which reinforces its legitimacy.

The same may be said of the right of free expression. We have already observed the work of the Human Rights Committee in implementing Article 19 of the Civil and Political Covenant and protecting citizens' expressive rights. In giving effect to the general reporting requirement, the Committee has begun to impart principled coherence to the textual provisions, in the sense of filling in the interstices and fitting the parts to the purposes of the whole.[215] With the end of the Cold War, the remnants of the "double standard" in applying expressive rights through international monitoring institutions will mostly wither away.

Coherence is being aided by parallel regional initiatives. These tend to monitor and implement the rules equally, regardless of "whose ox is gored." Notable in this respect is the aforementioned work of the European Court of Human Rights and the Inter-American Court of Human Rights, as well as the as-yet inchoate potential of the new African Human Rights Commission.[216] Equal application of the expressive entitlement is reinforced by the textual convergence regarding

[213] While it is true that General Assembly resolutions, state practice or even a subsequent treaty cannot vitiate a specific rule of the UN Charter, all three can affect a Charter rule's interpretation. *See* Czaplinski & Danilenko, *Conflicts of Norms in International Law*, 21 NETH. Y.B. INT'L L. 3, 35–41 (1990).

[214] *See* T. FRANCK, NATION AGAINST NATION 224–45 (1985).

[215] D. MCGOLDRICK, *supra* note 43, at 459–79. Under the procedure for review of country reports, the Committee has sought to

> examine, comment, and request clarification in respect of the different aspects of freedom of expression revealed in the State reports. This has involved, for example, such matters as general and specific banning or censorship, registration or notification requirements, governmental control and direction in its various forms, limitations applicable to particular groups, for example, armed forces, civil servants, prior restraints or subsequent penal responsibility for publications, rights of reply or correction, the applicable limitations embodied in the criminal law or penal codes for offences such as blasphemy or blasphemous libel, sedition, subversive propaganda, anti-State or anti-ideological propaganda, and the effective remedies demanded by . . . an individual who claims that his rights under article 19 have been violated.

Id. at 461.

[216] The Commission is established by part II of the Banjul Charter, *supra* note 184.

freedom of expression of the European Convention on Human Rights,[217] the American Convention on Human Rights,[218] and the African Charter on Human and Peoples' Rights.[219] The too-long failure of the United States to ratify the Civil and Political Rights Covenant and the American Convention nevertheless has detracted from this convergence and is only in part mitigated by the fact that the U.S. Constitution, as implemented by the courts and Congress, puts the United States essentially, if not wholly, in compliance with the international and regional standards.

So far, less uniformity of application, and thus less global coherence, can be ascribed to the emerging rule on citizens' right to participate in free and open elections. As we have observed, on-site monitoring remains voluntary and exceptional. If it is to become a more general obligation, likes must be treated alike, which means that the new majority of democratic states must submit to it. They, who have the least to fear and the most to gain, should want to participate in universalizing the practice, if only to help legitimize it. Few states are likely to volunteer as long as participation in international monitoring is tantamount to a government's admission that it does not have credibility with its own people. To induce a pull toward compliance in deviant and recalcitrant regimes—those that most need it—on-site monitoring must also be practiced by the states that least need it. It must become an unremarkable universal habit.

VII. Adherence and the Democratic Entitlement

Adherence refers to the vertical connection between a specific rule of obligation and other "higher" principles that define the objectives of the rule system or set out its normative standards. A particular rule ("cross on the green, stop on the red") is more likely to pull toward voluntary compliance if it is seen to be within the framework of a community's normative hierarchy than if it is a mere ad hoc arrangement.[220] The democratic entitlement also is more likely to be perceived as a legitimate rule if it can be seen as a necessary part of a normative hierarchy. As it happens, the right to democracy can readily be shown to be an important subsidiary of the community's most important norm: the right to peace.

With the exception of the principle *pacta sunt servanda*, no principle of international law has been more firmly established—first by the Kellogg-Briand Pact and, particularly since 1945, by the UN Charter—than that states "shall refrain in their international relations from the threat or use of force against the territorial integrity or political independence of any state."[221] Not only has this peace principle been featured in treaty law, but it has been resoundingly echoed in the jurisprudence of the International Court of Justice[222] and in *opinio juris* expressed in key UN resolutions.[223]

[217] European Convention, *supra* note 72, Arts. 9, 10, 11.

[218] American Convention, *supra* note 77, Arts. 13, 14, 15, 16.

[219] Banjul Charter, *supra* note 184, Arts. 8, 9, 10, 11.

[220] T. Franck, *supra* note 12, at 184.

[221] UN Charter, Art. 2(4). *See also* Treaty Providing for the Renunciation of War as an Instrument of National Policy, Aug. 27, 1928, Art. 1, 46 Stat. 2343, TS No. 796, 94 LNTS 57 (Kellogg-Briand Pact).

[222] *See Nicaragua* opinion, 1986 ICJ Rep. 14.

[223] The customary law is well summarized in the Court's *Nicaragua* opinion, *id.* at 98–105. *See, especially,* Friendly Relations Declaration, *supra* note 31; Definition of Aggression, GA Res. 3314, 29 UN GAOR Supp. (No. 31) at 142, UN Doc. A/9631 (1974), *reprinted in* 13 ILM 710 (1974).

Most recently, the Security Council, in its resolutions[224] and actions to reverse Iraq's attack on Kuwait, reiterated the primacy of the entitlement to peace and protection against aggression. More than thirty nations joined in liberating Kuwait because, at last, aggression against one has begun to be seen as a contingent violation of the common peace. Stopping aggression and maintaining the peace has become the central concern of a newly cohesive international community.

If that principle indeed stands at the apex of the global normative system, the democratic governance of states must be recognized as a necessary, although certainly not a sufficient, means to that end. Peace is the consequence of many circumstances: economic well-being, security, and the unimpeded movement of persons, ideas and goods. States' nonaggressiveness, however, depends fundamentally on domestic democracy. Although the argument is not entirely conclusive, historians have emphasized that, in the past 150 years, "no liberal democracies have ever fought against each other."[225] It has been argued persuasively that "a democratic society operating under a market economy has a strong predisposition towards peace."[226] This stands to reason: a society that makes its decisions democratically and openly will be reluctant to engage its members' lives and treasure in causes espoused by leaders deluded by fantasies of grievance or grandeur.

No one has stated this position more eloquently than the eighteenth-century German philosopher Immanuel Kant. He examined the correlation between democratic governance and nonaggressiveness in his essay *Perpetual Peace.*[227] There, he argued that democracy, leading to a "pacific union" among liberal states, would counteract the aggressive tendencies of absolutist monarchies by making government accountable to the majority. In contrast, a state of perpetual war would likely prevail between democracies and totalitarian states.[228] Moreover, Kant discerned a three-way linkage among democracy, peace and human rights.[229]

Neither Kant nor his modern interpreters make the argument that democracies will not fight: only that they are not disposed to fight each other. The historical record bears this out.[230] Consequently, one way to promote universal and perpetual nonaggression—probably the best and, perhaps, the only way—is to make democracy an entitlement of all peoples. This conclusion was eloquently and unanimously accepted as axiomatic by the CSCE representatives at their aforementioned 1990 Copenhagen meeting. Unanimously, they proclaimed "their conviction that . . . pluralistic democracy" is a prerequisite "for progress in setting up the lasting order of peace, security, justice and co-operation that they seek to establish in Europe."[231]

[224] SC Res. 660 (Aug. 2, 1990), *reprinted in* 29 ILM 1325 (1990), and subsequent resolutions. *See* Schachter, *United Nations Law in the Gulf Conflict,* 85 AJIL 452 (1991).

[225] Mearsheimer, *Why We Will Soon Miss the Cold War,* ATLANTIC MONTHLY, August 1990, at 35, 46.

[226] T. Smith, *Democracy Resurgent,* in SEA CHANGES 152, 157 (N. Rizopoulos ed. 1990).

[227] I. KANT, PERPETUAL PEACE 107–39 (T. Humphrey rev. ed. 1983) (1795).

[228] *See* Doyle, *Liberalism and World Politics,* 80 AM. POL. SCI. REV. 1151 (1986).

[229] Note, however, that the notion of human rights operates to limit not only totalitarian, but also democratic, excess. Thomas Jefferson underscored this with his oft-quoted observation that "an *elective despotism* was not the government we fought for." T. JEFFERSON, NOTES ON THE STATE OF VIRGINIA 120 (W. Peden ed. 1954).

[230] The point is well developed by Doyle, *An International Liberal Community,* in RETHINKING AMERICA'S SECURITY (G. Allison ed., forthcoming).

[231] Copenhagen Document, *supra* note 98, Preamble, at 1307.

The symbiotic linkage among democracy, human rights and peace is now widely recognized. Already in 1968, Security Council Resolution 253 invoked chapter VII of the Charter to impose military sanctions on Rhodesia. It expressly proceeded on the theory that gross denials of both human rights and the democratic entitlement can constitute "a threat to international peace and security."[232] At the regional level, the OAS Ministers of Foreign Affairs, in demanding the replacement of Nicaragua's Somoza dictatorship with a government chosen through free elections, declared in 1979 that democracy was the necessary precondition to "peace, freedom and justice." The dictatorship was characterized as "disrupting the peace of the Hemisphere."[233] A decade later, in condemning the fraudulent Panamanian elections staged by General Noriega, the OAS Ministers stated that this crisis of governmental legitimacy "involves internal and external factors . . . and could seriously endanger international peace and security."[234]

This understanding of the three-way linkage among democracy, human rights and peace is further illustrated by the recent cease-fire agreement negotiated by the UN Secretary-General between the Government of El Salvador and the FMLN.[235] As noted, it obliges the Government and the insurgents to work with yet another UN observer mission (ONUSAL), which is authorized to monitor and verify compliance with the basic human rights guaranteed by the signatories. The parties specifically recognized that compliance with human rights is a *sine qua non* to ending the war. They also accepted that the democratic entitlement must be guaranteed—and monitored by international observers—if peace is to be established.

Thus, it appears with increasing clarity, in normative text and practice, that compliance with the norms prohibiting war making is inextricably linked to observance of human rights and the democratic entitlement. The achievement of none of these basic objectives of the international community is possible, in any lasting sense, without the realization of them all. This interdependence suggests that the legitimacy of the democratic entitlement is augmented by its hierarchic relation to the peremptory norm of global peaceability.

A distinction needs to be noted here. As we have observed, some governments have argued that the international community's jurisdiction to intervene in the domestic affairs of states to secure compliance with the democratic entitlement is (or should be) limited to cases where its violation has given rise to breaches of the peace. Others have disagreed, claiming that the jurisdiction to intervene is also based on broader human rights law, which authorizes various intrusive forms of monitoring and even envisages sanctions against gross violators. One can prefer this latter view, while still agreeing that the democratic entitlement does have a connection to the United Nations' "peace" role, that the *legitimacy* of any collective international intervention to support a democratic entitlement is augmented by the entitlement's intimate link to peace. The substance of that link, however, is not merely the role of democracy in *making* or *restoring* peace after conflict has arisen but also—indeed preeminently—its role in *maintaining* peace and *preventing* conflict.

The World Court observed in the *Bernadotte* case that established rights and duties implicitly validate a penumbra of unenunciated, yet legitimate, means nec-

[232] SC Res. 253, *supra* note 211.
[233] OEA/Ser.F/II.17, doc. 40/79, rev.2.
[234] OEA/Ser.F/II.21, doc. 8/89, rev.2.
[235] Central America: Efforts Toward Peace, *supra* note 71.

essary to give them effect.[236] If the "end" of global peace demands the "means" of global democracy, a Charter-based system established to ensure peace must also be presumed to be authorized to ensure universal adherence to democratic political rights.

VIII. THE EMERGENCE OF DEMOCRACY AS A GLOBAL NORMATIVE ENTITLEMENT

The entitlement to democracy in international law has gone through both a normative and a customary evolution. It has evolved both as a system of rules and in the practice of states and organizations. This evolution has occurred in three phases. First came the normative entitlement to self-determination. Then came the normative entitlement to free expression as a human right. Now we see the emergence of a normative entitlement to a participatory electoral process.

The democratic entitlement, despite its newness, already enjoys a high degree of legitimacy, derived both from various texts and from the practice of global and regional organizations, supplemented by that of a significant number of nongovernmental organizations. These texts and practices have attained a surprising degree of specificity, given the newness of the entitlement and especially of its requirement for free and open elections.

It is easy to deconstruct this now commonly used set of textual formulations and the accompanying practice. The terms (e.g., elections, free, fair) inevitably convey different meanings in various political cultures but, remarkably, evoke an amply demonstrable degree of convergent expectations. They crisscross sociocultural and political boundaries. The entitlement now aborning is widely enough understood to be almost universally celebrated. It is welcomed from Malagache to Mongolia, in the streets, the universities and the legislatures, not only because it portends a new, global political culture supported by common rules and communitarian implementing institutions, but also because it opens the stagnant political economies of states to economic, social and cultural, as well as political, development. As the heads of European Community states and governments pointed out in the group's conclusions of June 1991, "suppression of individual freedoms impede[s] an individual from participating in and contributing" to "the process of development."[237] Economic development, as even the Chinese leadership must be discovering, is linked inextricably with political freedom. An economic free market cannot long flourish without creating pressure for a free market of ideas. At the same time, the problems of underdevelopment can only be addressed successfully in a world of stable, peaceable nations, which, in turn, also presupposes a world of open democracies.

The democratic entitlement's newness and recent rapid evolution make it understandable that important problems remain. We have considered these primarily under the rubric of coherence, indicating that this entitlement is not yet entirely coherent. The key to solving these residual problems is: (1) that the older democracies should be among the first to volunteer to be monitored in the hope that this will lead the way to near-universal voluntary compliance, thus gradually transforming a sovereign option into a customary legal obligation; (2) that a credible international monitoring service should be established with clearly defined

[236] Reparations for injuries suffered in the service of the United Nations, 1949 ICJ REP. 174, 179–80 (Advisory Opinion of Apr. 11).

[237] European Council, Presidency Conclusions, Doc. SN 151/2/91 (Ann. V) at 27 (1991).

parameters and procedures covering all aspects of voting, from the time an election is called until the newly elected take office; (3) that each nation's duty to be monitored should be linked to a commensurate right to nonintervention by states acting unilaterally; and (4) that legitimate governments should be assured of protection from overthrow by totalitarian forces through concerted systemic action after—and *only* after—the community has recognized that such an exigency has arisen. In the longer term, compliance with the democratic entitlement should also be linked to a right of representation in international organs, to international fiscal, trade and development benefits, and to the protection of UN and regional collective security measures.[238]

Both textually and in practice, the international system is moving toward a clearly designated democratic entitlement, with national governance validated by international standards and systematic monitoring of compliance. The task is to perfect what has been so wondrously begun.

[238] To limit collective security measures to cases of attack against democratic states is a change in the system's rules that is unlikely to come about in the near future. Yet it is worth contemplating. Would it help Kuwait to establish a democratic internal order if its future protection by UN-authorized collective measures depended upon such a transformation?

[14]

JUSTICE AND REPARATIONS

HOWARD McGARY JR.

A question that confronts America today is: how do we make just a society that has been plagued by racist and sexist ideologies and by discriminatory institutions. This is a very crucial question because of the enormous implications it has for public policy. It appears that any solution that we adopt will require that attitudes be changed, social goals be reexamined and that some of our basic institutions be either altered or abandoned. In this essay I will support the thesis that it is just reparation to afford preferential treatment in the areas of employment and higher education to black Americans who are and have been the victims of institutional injustice.

James Foreman raised the issue of black reparations at New York's Riverside Church in May 1969 (Lecky 1969, p. 114-26). During his interruption of the scheduled Riverside Church service, Foreman demanded $500 million as black reparations. Foreman said:

> Fifteen dollars[2] for every black brother and sister in the United States is only a beginning of a reparations due us as people who have been exploited and degraded, brutalized, killed and persecuted.

This spectacular pronouncement by Foreman is now known as the Black Manifesto. Unfortunately, Foreman's tactics and not the manifesto received attention from the news media. The issue of black reparations was pushed into a corner and virtually nothing has been said about reparations as a concept of social justice. It is important for philosophers to analyze the concept of reparations if we are to become clear about the morality of such an issue.

The justification for reparations is basically a backward-looking enterprise. Reparations by definition are due only when a breach of justice had occurred. Typically, people who made demands for reparations do so on the ground that they have been unjustly treated in the past. If we consider black and colonial people who have made demands for reparations, their demands are based on documented injustices done to them in the past and more importantly, an acknowledgement on the part of the transgressor's descendants that this is, in fact, true. In such cases, according to Locke and certain other social contract theorists, rectifications of past injustices are in order (Locke, TTG, 10).

A. COMPENSATION

Traditionally people who have been concerned with the justice of compensation have worried about placing the burden on the innocent or creating a distribution that is unfair. These feelings are enforced by the way we view theories of distributive justice. When we distribute something according to a principle we consider just, then we can't see any reason for a redistribution. For example, a person who is allotted three shares of some commodity according to some principle embraced by members of a society feels entitled to the three shares and is apprehensive of any redistribution that lessens his share.

The interesting thing about compensation seems to be that compensation might involve someone's being at fault or it might not. An important part of the right of compensation is the idea that we must ensure that each person has a right not to be hindered from arranging his life as he sees fit as long as it does not hinder others from doing the same.

B. JUSTIFICATION FOR BLACK REPARATIONS

I feel that the justification and intent of reparations is not the same as the justification and intent of compensation. In the case of reparation it *is* the case that someone is at fault. There are countless ways that the injustices might have occurred. The ways differ in detail, but they all are similar in one respect; namely that it is clear that an injustice has occurred.

The usual worry associated with the idea of giving reparations is not that one doesn't know that an injustice has occurred or who committed the injustice. This is merely a matter of fact. The difficult questions are: what are the ways that injustices have shaped present holdings? Do the beneficiaries of injustice who are not direct parties in the act of injustice have a duty of reparations? And what are permissible ways to rectify past injustices? (Nozick 1974, p. 152).

Before we can answer these questions we must be clear in our thinking concerning the idea of a community paying reparations to a group. In order to do this I shall analyze a less complicated case. Suppose a person X has the indisputable right to a certain watch. Let us further suppose that a person Y steals the watch from X. In this case we can clearly see that Y owes X a watch and an admission of wrongdoing. If we complicate the example we can get the following: after Y steals the watch from X he gives it to a person Z. This case has a pertinent similarity to the case of the demand for reparations by black Americans but they are different.

Now suppose Y steals the watch from X and Y dies; but before he dies, Y leaves a legal will that bequeaths the watch to his son W. In this case, we feel that W should return the watch to X and acknowledge the error by his father Y. This case is close, but not quite analogous to the demand for black reparations. In order for them to be analogous, both X and Y must die and both have descendants. The debt of justice in this case involves the descendants of X and Y. We believe that W should return the watch to the legal heir of X. It is a lot harder in this case than the other cases to see why the watch should be relinquished by W.

In our watch example we are able to trace the illegitimate holding transfer from person to person. Although this case has a pertinent similarity to the case of black reparations they are not identical. In our watch example the persons involved are individuals and the subject predicates would be either simple proper names like 'John' or 'Mary' or simple definite descriptions of the sort: the person who stole the watch from X at time t. The general principle that we follow in cases like our watch case appears to be: holdings that are illegitimately transferred insofar as possible should be returned to their rightful owners.

In the case for black reparations, unlike the watch case, reparations are not on an individual level, but involve groups. Blacks as a group are demanding reparations from the white community. Bernard Boxill in his article "The Morality of Reparations" explains why black people are owed reparations. Boxill says:

> The slaves had an indisputable moral right to the product of their labor; these products were stolen from them by the slave masters who ultimately passed them on to their descendants; the slaves presumably have conferred their rights of ownership to the products of their labor to their descendants; thus, the descendants of slave masters are in

possession of wealth to which the descendants of slaves have rights; hence, the descendants of slave masters must return this wealth to the descendants of slaves with a concession that they were not rightfully in possession of it (1972, p. 117).

Boxill's explanation is in the right direction. But those who deny that these are good reasons for affording reparations to black Americans would take issue with Boxill's views; and some who favor reparations would disagree with Boxill's formulation of the justification. An initially plausible objection against Boxill's line of reasoning can be stated in the following way: Why should I (a present day white) pay for the injustices of malevolent whites in the past? I don't own any slaves: and my parents and their parents didn't own any slaves. This is a challenging reply. But I think that Boxill anticipates this sort of objection by claiming that the descendants of slave masters have benefitted because of the unjust actions of their ancestors. This reply by itself is not enough to meet the force of this criticism. It can explain why the descendants of slave masters owe a debt of justice, but it fails to show how whites who are not the descendants of slave masters owe a debt of justice to black Americans. In order to argue that the total white community owes the total black community reparations, we must present an argument that shows how all whites, even recent immigrants benefitted from slavery and how all blacks felts its damaging effects.

Before we offer such an argument, we must be clear about what blacks are demanding as reparation. One of the most dramatic demands for black reparations can be found in James Foreman's Black Manifesto. This document is good in many respects and bad in at least one. Foreman's Manifesto was not meant as a justification or explanation of the concept of black reparations. Foreman's demand was just that: a demand, not a justification. When he asked for $500 million dollars in reparation from churches, people construed this to be repayment to blacks from whites for slavery. Such a conclusion is obviously false. Foreman had no such idea in mind. He realizes that to divide $500 million dollars among blacks in America would amount to about $23 dollars per person. This as reparation is an insult. Even if the money was invested in the behalf of all black Americans the resulting wealth would not be a proper reparation. Slavery and racial discrimination in this country damaged blacks in ways and on levels that require more than a cash outlay. A mere cash outlay alone cannot bring about cultural respect and self-determination. I think if reparations as a means of rectifying past injustices is to be taken seriously, more than money must be involved.

I want to support the position that white Americans have received certain advantages over black Americans because of the existence of slavery and other unjust discriminatory institutions in this country. Some of the advantages that whites enjoy are: access to better housing, better medical care and better schools than the typical black American has access to. Notice that it could be the case that because of slavery and racial discrimination that all Americans including white Americans have suffered. In this paper I won't detail my reasons for thinking that whites enjoy certain advantages over blacks because of slavery and racial discrimination, but I do want to say that I believe that this claim, if true, supports my view that white Americans have a duty of reparations to black Americans.

According to some people this argument leads to undesirable consequences. They feel that this line of reasoning would justify poor whites paying reparations to blacks who have a better financial lot. Let us assume for the sake of argument that poor whites can have a duty of reparation to blacks who have a better financial lot.

Are wealthy individuals like Sammy Davis Jr., and Red Foxx owed reparations? Their ancestors suffered the horrors of slavery, and they both suffered the sting of institutional racism. Because they have obtained financial success, does this make them ineligible for reparations? Let us consider the following hypothetical. Suppose John steals a car from Tom, and Tom is unaware that John stole the car. In this case Tom can make no demands on John because he doesn't know John stole his car. Let us suppose that Tom inherits an automobile dealership and then discovers that John stole his car. Tom can now demand that John return his car. Although he now owns hundreds of new cars and John only has in possession the car he stole from Tom.

C. REPARATIONS TO GROUPS AS WELL AS INDIVIDUALS?

A persistent problem with giving reparations is trying to decide whether reparations should be made to groups as well as individuals. J.W. Nickel (1973) argues that reparations are owed to groups as well as individuals. He argues that certain groups deserve reparations not because of any natural characteristics that makes them a member of a group but because they have suffered and still suffer because of those characteristics. In an earlier article Nickel argues that blacks as a group deserve reparations because of injustices and not skin color (1972). However, in both of these short essays Nickel fails to show why whites as a group have the duty of reparation to blacks.

Is it because of skin color? Of course not. Perhaps it is because of injustices. But has every white at some time acted unjustly toward some black? Here again we must answer no. Because we answer no to this question we should not conclude that whites as a group do not have a duty of reparation.[3] (See Bittker 1973, Chapter 8). However, some argument is needed to justify this duty. In section B of this essay I argued that because of unjust institutions and holding transfers, such as bequests to children and inheritances, whites have benefitted from injustices done to blacks even if they did not personally perpetuate the injustice. Many will object to this claim because they are not aware of the deep roots of racism in American institutions private and public (See Moreland 1970, Chapters 2, 7). Numerous governmental reports and publications have pointed out how racism pervades our society (See the National Advisory Commission Report on Civil Disorders 1968). If these reports are accurate then it is plausible to suppose that reparations can be made to groups as well as individuals. What about the specific demand for reparations by black Americans as a group?

D. THE DEMAND FOR BLACK REPARATIONS

People of varied political persuasions have argued that all people must have power over their own destinies. They all agree that anything less is a violation of liberty. I too accept this conclusion and feel that a black reparations program should serve this noble end. But how can providing reparations to blacks serve to give them power over their lives?

I think that a comprehensive reparation should be forward looking. For this reason I suggested that a purely financial reparation might not serve this forward looking end (Thalberg 1973-74). A major source of the damages that blacks suffered were the result of unjust institutions. These institutions are set up in ways that unjustly discriminate against blacks. Providing blacks only with money to cover the financial damages done to them will not suffice. There must be other things involved in the reparation. For blacks, power to make decisions that affect their lives is paramount. I feel that preferential hiring and educational programs might serve to give blacks this power (McGary 1974, p. 10). There are problems, both conceptual and technical, associated with such programs (See Cowan, Nickel, Nunn and Thomson). It is not the purpose of this essay to settle all these issues, but I think there are good reasons to believe that such programs will give blacks some of the means to obtain control over their own lives.

I think that James Foreman and others have realized that blacks lack political and economic power. The economic powerlessness of blacks in America is discouraging. Even with the hopeful trends that are beginning to develop in a few industries, blacks as a group still remain near the bottom of the social economic ladder.

John Rawls argues that a person needs primary social goods (like access to health care, decent income and social position) and fair equality of opportunity for self-respect. If Rawls is correct, and I think that he is, then many blacks in the country, lacking primary goods and fair equality of opportunity, lack two of the essential ingredients necessary for self-respect. A comprehensive preferential hiring and education program might give blacks this respect and control over their own destinies.

E. TYPES OF REPARATION PROGRAMS

Above we suggested that a preferential hiring policy could count as a proper reparations for blacks who have been the victims of injustice.[4] Our argument depended upon the claims that 1) reparations can be made to a group as well as individuals and 2) that all whites gained specific advantages from slavery and racial discrimination and that all blacks have felt its damaging effects. This argument I will call the reparation argument for preferential treatment.

The argument for the preferential programs that I sketched above depends upon the following general principle: those who receive unfair advantages from Institution I have a duty to those who are unfairly disadvantaged by I. In our case for black reparations the subject predicates involved might be: person put at a disadvantage by Institution I, the group of black Americans who are disadvantaged as a result of Jim Crow Laws, recent white immigrants who enjoy certain advantages over blacks as a direct result of racist institutions in America. These English subject predicates unlike the ones in our watch example connects the parties involved to some common institution or practice. We should also notice that in our watch example the holding in question is a material object. It is clear in this case what must be returned, namely the watch. Even over time, returning the watch to its rightful owner presents very few problems. We either physically hand over the watch that was stolen or pay fair market value for the watch if it cannot be returned. The case we sketched concerning black reparations is not so simple. Here in a real sense there is no object or material holding (exactly) to be returned. What is at stake or in dispute is one person or group gaining an advantage in competitive situations involving institutions.

Do our institutions tell us that applying our general principle brings about a just resolution in all cases? I think that if we follow our principle we can answer yes. Even the recent immigrant not void of contact with racist institutions in this country has received advantages that the typical black person does not enjoy. The case of the recent immigrant, however, does raise the following bothersome questions: should those who have received greater advantages because of slavery and other racist institutions in this country share a greater portion of the burden of reparations? I feel that they should. However, it is no easy task to determine the logistics of the problem. I won't here attempt to solve this problem but I feel that a satisfactory solution can be found.

Let us know review an argument that seeks to justify preferential programs not by looking to the past but on more forward-looking utilitarian grounds. I believe that this argument, although quite different from my own, supports my belief that preferential hiring and educational programs are just. Many reasonable people are not convinced that my reparation argument demonstrates that a preferential hiring policy as a reparation is not unjust to those who fail to get the job or fail to get into law school because of preferential programs (See Newton 1975, p. 311). They usually present an argument similar to the argument put forth by Defunis in the famous case of Defunis v. Odegaard and the University of Washington. Defunis argued that it was unjust and unconstitutional that black students be admitted to the University of Washington Law School with lower test scores than his.

Ronald Dworkin in a recent book review argues that Defunis' arguments are initially appealing, but in the last analysis that they are unsound. Dworkin claims that the faulty premise of Defunis' argument is his belief that Law Schools must use intelligence as the only criterion for admission to law school, and that he was denied fair equality of opportunity because the law school admitted blacks into the law school who had lower scores on tests that are claimed to measure intelligence and aptitude.

Dworkin considers the argument that the LSAT tests because they are culturally biased don't accurately measure the capabilities of black applicants. He admits that this argument deserves consideration, but chooses to rest his case on a quite different line of reasoning. He contends that the Defunis argument rests on the faulty premise that test scores are the crucial factor for determining who should be admitted to law schools. Dworkin argues that law school entrance criteria should not be limited to tests of intellectual capacity but should take into account other factors that will ensure that the best interest of the school and the community at large are maximized. In other words the law schools weigh all factors that they feel will help bring about good social ends.

Many schools use a similar argument when they admit football players with lower entrance exam scores, with the justification that a competitive football team is an important part of college life. These arguments are similar but not identical. They differ in that football players choose to be football players whereas people don't choose what racial group they will be members of. It is also true that people work to become football players, but people are born into racial groups. I realize that it is questionable whether or not football players should be given preferential treatment, but these cases give us a precedent for this sort of treatment.

Is this preferential treatment just? Can't we use Dworkin's utilitarian argument to justify actions that are clearly unreasonable? Dworkin cites the Sweatt v. Painter, 339 US 629, 70 S. Ct. 848 case involving a black man who was denied admission to a law school in Texas. Would not our utilitarian argument justify not admitting Sweatt to the Texas Law School on the grounds that it would not promote the public good. For example, racist alumni might not give contributions to the school if they admitted a black person. Is the justification for not admitting Defunis the same as the one used by racists for not admitting Sweatt? Dworkin very skillfully argues that they are not.

Dworkin's utilitarian argument does not rest on the old psychological utilitarianism of Bentham, but on the idea that the community's preferences should determine public policy. "If it can be discovered what each individual prefers, and how intensely, then it might be shown that a particular policy would satisfy more preferences, than alternative policies (Dworkin 1976, p. 32)". Reasoning in this manner the community's welfare is interpreted as that policy that satisfied the community's total collection of preferences.

Although law schools don't have a means for precisely evaluating the judgments about the preferences its admissions policies will effect, it is reasonable to believe that their judgments are plausible. This preference method appears to be fair to everyone to the extent everyone's preferences are considered. It appears that our utilitarian argument based on preferences gives each person the right to be treated equally.

However, when we look closer we discover that there are personal preferences and external preferences. Personal preferences are preferences for a person's own enjoyment of some goods or opportunities. External preferences are preferences for the assignment of goods to others. For example, a person might have a personal preference against a preferential educational policy because it will not enhance his own welfare. He might have external preferences against the policies because he hates black people or disapproves of the mixing of the races. The point is simply that external preferences can reflect prejudiced attitudes or beliefs about a person or group. Dworkin argues that basing public policy on the external preferences of the community causes some members of the community to be treated unjustly. I think that this line of reasoning shows us why the justification for not admitting Defunis is not identical to the justification for not admitting Sweatt. Defunis was denied admission because a judgment was made by law school officials that such actions supported the public good. They also made a further judgment that the particular preferential admission policy in question would in fact achieve the public good determined by assessing the personal preferences of the community. While failing to admit Sweatt could only be interpreted as supporting the public good if we use external preferences as a measure of utility.

I find Dworkin's argument compelling. I think if we conjoin my reparations argument with Dworkin's utilitarian argument, we are provided with good reasons for believing that preferential hiring and educational policies are just reparations.

F. BLACK REPARATIONS AND THE LAW

In this section I will review a part of that body of legal literature that is directly related to the subject of reparations and consistent with the philosophical position that I gave above. Boris Bittker in his helpful book *The Case for Black Reparations* suggests that a proper way to justify affording reparations to black Americans might be one that does not rest solely on damages done during slavery, but on those recent historical damages inflicted on blacks (1973, p. 9-11). In the last century there have been countless harms and injustices inflicted against blacks. Many of them have been condoned by law. Bittker explores section 1983 of Title 42 of the United States Code which says:

> Every person who, under color of any statute... Of any State or Territory, subject... to the deprivation of any rights... Secured by the Constitution and Laws, shall be liable to the party injured in an action at law, suit in equity, or other proper proceedings for redress (Bittker 1973, p. 31).

According to Bittker this statute's principal purpose was to deal with the terrorism perpetuated in the south by the Ku Klux Klan and similar terrorist groups. A question of great interest concerning section 1983 is whether or not it provides a system of reparations for at least one form of discrimination. Before we look at Bittker's answer to this question I should inform the reader that Section 1983 applies to liability for performance of official duties. The question is how should a citizen be compensated when a public official under law deprives him of his federal rights. On this question Bittker concludes that:

> Where damages for past misconduct are at stake, however, to remit the plaintiff (person seeking compensation) to an action against individual officials would have the consequences of denying an effective remedy if they are impecunious. At most, the "essential governmental function" exemption ought to go no further than to relieve the state from vicarious liability for unauthorized torts of its employees.

Section 1983 follows the traditional common-law approach to damages, that is, each plaintiff is treated as a discrete individual whose personal circumstances determine the amount he shall recover. This means that each black person must file an individual suit for damages under Section 1983. Bittker also tells us that the government should not be held legally responsible for the unauthorized actions of its agents.

Bittker contends that Section 1983 serves as a useful starting point for supporters and non-supporters of black reparations. He feels that an examination of this section will lay bare the relevant questions concerning reparations. Some of those questions are: 1) should reparations be made to individuals or groups? 2) will it be necessary to promulgate an official code of racial classification to administer a reparation program? 3) would it be unjust because it might divert funds that would otherwise be used to benefit the nation's poor? I won't explore Bittker's specific answers to these questions. However, I will recapitulate Bittker's answer to the relevant constitutional question — does the constitution permit the federal government to establish and finance a program of reparations whose benefits would go to black citizens exclusively[5]

People who argue against programs that serve the ends of a particular group exclusively usually make reference to the Fifth Amendment's guarantee of due process of law or to the Fourteenth Amendment's guarantee of equal protection of the laws. Speaking as a lawyer Bittker after reviewing housing and school desegregation cases, says that he is not sure whether or not a black reparations program would be constitutional. He feels that some judicial verdict would have to be rendered on the constitutionality of such programs. However, he points out that a judicial verdict rejecting the program's constitutionality would not in itself be a judgment on its fairness or wisdom (Bittker 1973, p. 126). If the constitution does not permit reparations programs, justice might require that we amend it to allow for such programs. If such programs are constitutional then we still must decide if it is just and wise to enact such programs. We must remember that to be legally responsible for injury is to be liable for damages or some official action. While on the other hand to be morally responsible does not necessarily entail any kind of official or unofficial action or liability. Feinberg writes:

> "To be morally responsible for some thing or action is to be liable not to overt responses, but to a charging against one's record as a person. This record in turn can be used for anyone of a variety of purposes — as a basis for self-punishment, remorse, or pride, for example; but a person can avoid putting it to these further uses, leaving responsibility simply a matter of record". (1970, p. 76)

Feinberg suggests that when we speak of liability in cases of compensation and reparation, we must realize that each case has a different intent. According to Feinberg, the term, 'reparation' has the intent of redressing wrongful injury, while compensation serves to remedy losses which might not be anyone's fault. He also feels that reparation restores moral equilibrium, as would an apology or expression or remorse. The notion of compensation does not necessarily involve this idea. A result of reasoning along these lines is that it allows one to conclude that some grossly immoral act cannot be rectified.

Reasonable and intelligent people worry about the legal and moral difficulties associated with providing groups with reparations to rectify past injustices. Mr. Justice Jackson of the U.S. Supreme Court in regards to the right of the Shoshone people to receive reparations said:

> It is hard to see how any judicial decision under a jurisdiction act can much advance solution of the problem of the Shoshone Indians. Any judgment that we may render gives to these Indians neither their lands nor their money. We would not be second to any other in recognizing that — judgment or no judgment — a moral obligation of a higher order rests upon this country to provide for decent shelter, clothing,

> education, and industrial advancement of the Indians. Nothing is gained by dwelling upon the unhappy conflicts that have prevailed between the Shoshones and the whites. The generation of Indians who have suffered have gone to the Happy Hunting Ground, and nothing that we can do can square this account with them.

Views like Justice Jackson's give some support to the claim that demands for reparations by oppressed members of our society such as blacks or Indians have no legal basis and that a duty of reparation or liability can't be established on moral arguments alone. I disagree with people who maintain that the demand for reparations by black Americans has no legal basis. However, I do agree that some injustices are so gross and far-reaching in their damaging effects that moral equilibrium cannot be restored, but this does not mean that we should sit on our hands and not attempt to make some effort to eliminate in part the moral imbalance caused by past injustices. The idea of settling injustices that have placed a group at a disadvantage in a society by acknowledging remorse, but not taking any official steps to rectify the past injustices that have placed the group in question at a disadvantage seems to be unjust.

In concluding, I would like to reiterate my defense against the charge that reparations, as here discussed, represent an injustice against those persons who are properly qualified for a position but not selected because of preferential treatment. Aren't these people entitled to complain? I think that they are entitled to complain because there are not enough places at college and positions in businesses for capable and willing persons, but not because some who have been the victims of injustices are selected over them. If everyone from the start had been treated fairly the competition for present positions would even be more intense, making it more difficult for everyone. If nothing can be done to assure that all who are capable and willing receive positions, then this unhappiness should fall on everyone, not just on those who have been historically disadvantaged.

Rutgers University at Livingston College

NOTES

1 I read versions of this paper at the University of Illinois at Chicago Circle and at the Illinois Philosophical Association meeting on Philosophy and Public Affairs in November 1976. I thank Irving Thalberg, John Dolan, Rolf Sartorius, Myles Brand and Debroah Brown for their reactions to a yet earlier draft of this essay.

2 There is some controversy over what the black population figures are in the U.S. Foreman estimates the black population in the U.S. at 33 million.
3 This line of reasoning does not preclude the possibility that certain whites deserve reparations from the more general white community.
4 A policy where qualified blacks are given preference over white males who have better qualifications.
5 The Supreme Court has consistently held that racial classifications must be a part of a program which furthers an "overriding" or compelling state interest.

REFERENCE BIBLIOGRAPHY

Aristotle. *Nicomachean Ethics*, translated by Martin Ostwald, New York: Bobbs-Merrill Company, Inc. (1962).

Bittker, Boris. *The Case for Black Reparations*, New York: Random House, (1973).

Boxill, Bernard. "The Morality of Reparation", *Social Theory and Practice*, Vol. II, no. 1, (1972).

Cowan, J.L. "Inverse Discrimination and Morally Relevant Characteristics", *Analysis, 33*, 1: (1972).

Dworkin, Ronald. "Defunis versus Odegaard and the University of Washington: The University admission case. The Record, ed. Ann Fagan Ginger, *The New York Review of Books*, Vol. XXIII, no. 1 February 5, 1976.

Feinberg, Joel. *Doing and Deserving*, New Jersey: Princeton University Press (1970).

Frankena, William K. *Ethics*, New Jersey: Prentice-Hall, Inc. (1973).

Lecky, Robert S., Wright, H.E. *Black Manifesto: Religion, Racism and Reparations*, New York: Sheed and Ward (1969).

Locke, John. *Two Treatises of Government*, edited by Peter Laslett, 2nd edition, Cambridge; Cambridge University Press (1967).

McGary, Howard, Jr. "Reparations and Inverse Discrimination", *Dialogue, 17*, 1 (1974).

Moreland, Lois B. *White Racism and the Law*, Columbus, Ohio: Charles E. Merril (1970).

Newton, Lisa H. "Reverse Discrimination as Unjustified", *Ethics*, Vol. 83, 4 (1973).

Nickel, J.W. "Discrimination and Morally Relevant Characteristics", *Analysis, 32*, 4 (1972).

Nickel, J.W. "Should Reparations be to Groups or Individuals", *Analysis, 34*, 5 (1973).

Nozick, Robert. *Anarchy, State and Utopia*, New York: Basic Books, Inc. (1974).

Nunn, William A. "Reverse Discrimination", *Analysis 34*, 5: (1974).

Rawls, John. *A Theory of Justice*, Cambridge: Harvard University Press (1971).

Thalberg, Irving, Jr. "Reverse Discrimination and the Future", *Philosophical Forum, 5*, 1-2 (1973-74).

Thomson, Judith Jarvis. "Preferential Hiring", *Philosophy and Public Affairs, 2*, 4 (1971).

[15]

Multiculturalism and Minority Rights: West and East

WILL KYMLICKA

Professor of Philosophy, Queen's University, Canada, and Visiting Professor in the Nationalism Studies Program, Central European University, Budapest

Are Western models of multiculturalism and minority rights relevant for the post-Communist countries of Central and Eastern Europe? This article describes a range of Western models, and explores the social and political conditions that have led to their adoption in the West. It then considers various factors which might make the adoption of these models difficult in Eastern Europe, and considers the potential role of the international community in overcoming these obstacles.

Introduction

Countries in post-communist Europe have been pressured to adopt Western standards or models of multiculturalism and minority rights. Indeed, respect for minority rights is one of the accession criteria that candidate countries must meet to enter the European Union (EU) and NATO. Candidate countries are evaluated and ranked in terms of how well they are living up to these standards (see EU Accession Monitoring Program OSI 2001).

There are two interlinked processes at work here. First, we see the 'internationalizing' of minority rights issues. How states treat their minorities is now seen as a matter of legitimate international concern, monitoring and intervention. Second, this international framework is deployed to export Western models to newly-democratizing countries in Eastern Europe.

This trend implicitly rests on four premises: (i) that there are certain common standards or models in the Western democracies; (ii) that they are working well in the West; (iii) that they are applicable to Eastern and Central Europe (hereafter ECE), and would work well there if adopted; (iv) that there is a legitimate role for the international community to play in promoting or imposing these standards.

All four of these assumptions are controversial. Western countries differ amongst themselves in their approach to ethnic relations, and attempts to codify a common set of minimum standards or best practices have proven difficult. Moreover, the success of these approaches is often deeply contested within Western countries. Many citizens of Western democracies view their domestic policies towards ethnic relations as ineffective, if not actually harmful. The wisdom of 'exporting' these policies to ECE countries is even more controversial, both in the

West and the East. Countries in post-Communist Europe differ significantly from Western countries (and from each other) in terms of history, demography, geopolitical stability, economic development and democratic consolidation. Given these differences, Western approaches may simply not be relevant or helpful, and attempts to impose them against the wishes or traditions of the local population can be counter-productive in terms of ethnic relations.

So the decision to make minority rights one of the criteria for 'rejoining Europe' rests on a number of controversial assumptions. This decision was taken by Western leaders in the early 1990s, almost in panic, as a response to fears that ethnic conflict would spiral out of control across the post-Communist world. There was relatively little public debate or scholarly analysis about the wisdom of this decision, and it seems clear in retrospect that it was taken without a full consideration of its implications, or of the difficulties it raised.

In my view, the time has come to have a vigorous and public debate about these four assumptions. Now that the initial panic about ethnic violence has subsided, and with relative peace throughout the region, we can afford to sit back and think more carefully about the potential and pitfalls of 'exporting' and 'internationalizing' minority rights.

In a recent volume (Kymlicka and Opalski 2001), I attempted to explore these four basic assumptions in some depth. In this short article, I can only give a brief sketch of my conclusions.

I. Western Trends Regarding Ethnocultural Diversity

First, then, what do we mean by Western standards or models of multiculturalism and minority rights? Efforts have been made by various international organizations to formally codify a set of minority rights or multicultural practices, including the 1992 Declaration of the United Nations, the 1992 European Charter for Regional or Minority Languages Charter and the 1995 Framework Convention of the Council of Europe, and various Recommendations of the OSCE's High Commissioner on National Minorities (1996, 1998, 1999). In theory, these embody the standards that ECE countries are expected to meet.

These documents are important, but are potentially misleading as a guide to Western understandings of minority rights (and hence to Western expectations about how ECE countries should behave). For one thing, these declarations are often quite vague. They typically assert broad principles of respect and recognition for minority groups, but then hedge them with multiple qualifiers about 'where appropriate' and 'within the framework of national law'. Also, these formal declarations are continually evolving, most recently in efforts to include minority rights in proposals for a new Constitution of the European Union.

In my view, these formal declarations are the surface manifestation of deeper trends that are occurring throughout the Western democracies regarding ethnic relations. In order to fully understand the forces at work in current processes of internationalizing and exporting minority rights, we need to look below these formal documents to the underlying social trends.

There have in fact been dramatic changes in the way Western democracies deal with ethnocultural diversity in the last thirty to forty years. In the volume, I highlight five such trends, but for the purposes of this paper let me focus on two.

The first concerns the treatment of substate/minority nationalisms, such as the Québécois in Canada, the Scots and Welsh in Britain, the Catalans and Basques in Spain, the Flemish in Belgium, the German-speaking minority in South Tyrol in Italy, and Puerto Rico in the United States.[1] In all of these cases, we find a regionally-concentrated group that conceives of itself has a nation within a larger state, and mobilizes behind nationalist political parties to achieve recognition of its nationhood, either in the form of an independent state or through territorial autonomy within the larger state. In the past, all of these countries have attempted to suppress these forms of substate nationalism. To have a regional group with a sense of distinct nationhood was seen as a threat to the state. Various efforts were made to erode this sense of distinct nationhood, including restricting minority language rights, abolishing traditional forms of regional self-government, and encouraging members of the dominant group to settle in the minority group's traditional territory so that the minority becomes outnumbered even in its traditional territory.

[1.] We could also include the French and Italian minorities in Switzerland, although some people dispute whether they manifest a 'national' consciousness.

However, there has been a dramatic reversal in the way Western countries deal with substate nationalisms. Today, all of the countries I have just mentioned have accepted the principle that these substate national identities will endure into the indefinite future, and that their sense of nationhood and nationalist aspirations must be accommodated in some way or other. This accommodation has typically taken the form of what we can call 'multination federalism': that is, creating a federal or quasi-federal subunit in which the minority group forms a local majority, and so can exercise meaningful forms of self-government. Moreover, the group's language is typically recognized as an official state language, at least within their federal subunit, and perhaps throughout the country as a whole.

At the beginning of the twentieth-century, only Switzerland and Canada had adopted this combination of territorial autonomy and official language status for substate national groups. Since then, however, virtually all Western democracies that contain sizeable substate nationalist movements have moved in this direction. The list includes the adoption of autonomy for the Swedish-speaking Åland Islands in Finland after the First World War, autonomy for South Tyrol and Puerto Rico after the Second World War, federal autonomy for Catalonia and the Basque Country in Spain in the 1970s, for Flanders in the 1980s, and most recently for Scotland and Wales in the 1990s.

This, then, is the first major trend: a shift from suppressing substate nationalisms to accommodating them through regional autonomy and official language rights. Amongst the Western democracies with a sizeable national minority, only France is an exception to this trend, in its refusal to grant autonomy to its main substate nationalist group in Corsica. However, legislation was recently adopted to accord autonomy to Corsica, and it was only a ruling of the Constitutional Court that prevented its implementation. So France too, I think, will soon join the bandwagon.

The second trend concerns the treatment of indigenous peoples, such as the Indians and Inuit in Canada, the Aboriginal peoples of Australia, the Maori of New Zealand, the Sami of Scandinavia, the Inuit of Greenland, and Indian tribes in the United States. In the past, all of these countries had the same goal and expectation that indigenous peoples would eventually disappear as distinct communities, as a result of dying out, or intermarriage, or assimilation. Various policies were adopted to speed up this process, such as stripping indigenous peoples of their lands, restricting the practice of their traditional culture, language and religion, and undermining their institutions of self-government.

However, there has been a dramatic reversal in these policies, starting in the early 1970s. Today, all of the countries I just mentioned accept, at least in principle, the idea that indigenous peoples will exist into the indefinite future as distinct societies within the larger country, and that they must have the land claims, cultural rights (including recognition of customary law) and self-government rights needed to sustain themselves as distinct societies.

We see this pattern in all of the Western democracies. Consider the constitutional affirmation of Aboriginal rights in the 1982 Canadian constitution, along with the land claims commission and the signing of new treaties; the revival of treaty rights through the Treaty of Waitangi in New Zealand; the recognition of land rights for Aboriginal Australians in the Mabo decision; the creation of the Sami Parliament in Scandinavia, the evolution of 'Home Rule' for the Inuit of Greenland; and the laws and court cases upholding self-determination rights for American Indian tribes (not to mention the flood of legal and constitutional changes recognizing indigenous rights in Latin America). In all of these countries there is a gradual but real process of decolonization taking place, as indigenous peoples regain their lands, customary law and self-government. This is the second main shift in ethnocultural relations throughout the Western democracies.

In the volume, I also discuss important shifts regarding other types of groups, including immigrants, guest-workers, refugees and African-Americans. In all of these contexts as well, we see shifts away from historic policies of assimilation or exclusion towards a more 'multicultural' approach that recognizes and accommodates diversity.

However, for the purposes of this paper, the cases of national minorities and indigenous peoples are particularly relevant. They help illustrate the extent to which Western democracies have moved away from older models of unitary, centralized nation-states, and repudiated older ideologies of 'one state, one nation, one language'. Today, virtually all Western states that contain indigenous peoples and substate national groups have become 'multination' states, recognizing the existence of 'peoples' and 'nations' within the boundaries of the state. This recognition is manifested in a range of minority rights that includes regional autonomy and official language status for national minorities, and customary law, land claims, and self-government for indigenous peoples.

These, then, are some of the deep trends that are shaping domestic practices and opinions in the Western democracies. The extent to which these two trends have been 'internationalized' differs. In the case of indigenous peoples, serious efforts have been made to codify these emerging practices at the level of international law. Land claims, customary law and self-government for indigenous peoples are all clearly affirmed in recent international documents, such as the draft declarations at the United Nations and the Organization of American States. In this case, emerging international law reflects the most advanced practices of Western countries in terms of accommodating indigenous peoples.

By contrast, only very modest minority rights, such as mother-tongue primary education, have been recognized in the case of substate national groups. No international document has affirmed any principle of territorial autonomy or official language status for substate national groups.[2] In this case, international law lags far behind the emerging practices of Western democracies in terms of the rights accorded to substate national groups. To oversimplify, we might say that while international law is attempting to codify 'best practices' in the case of indigenous peoples, it is only codifying the most 'minimal standards' or 'lowest common denominator' in the case of substate national groups.

These variations in the formal content of international documents are important, but they should not blind us to the underlying trends. An increasing number of citizens in the West have grown accustomed to the idea of living in a 'multination' state that accords substate nations and indigenous peoples the rights and powers needed to sustain themselves as distinct and self-governing societies into the indefinite future. Substate national groups do not have a *right* to multination federalism under international law, but many people in the West view this as the 'best' response to substate nationalisms. It is in any event viewed as a fully legitimate option. It is seen as natural and acceptable for substate groups to desire this sort of arrangement, and normal and appropriate for a free and democratic state to move in this direction.

[2] This idea was floated in Recommendation 1201 of the Parliamentary Assembly of the Council of Europe, in 1993, but was quickly dropped in subsequent European declarations, not least due to the vehement opposition of France and Greece.

II. Explaining and Evaluating the Western Models

So we see emerging trends in the West towards various forms of multiculturalism and minority rights. This raises two important questions. First, why have so many Western countries moved in this direction? And second, how should we evaluate this trend? Should we view these models as a 'success' or a 'best practice' to be celebrated, and perhaps even to be exported to other regions, such as the ECE?

Let me start with the first question. In my view, there are three central factors that have made these trends possible, and perhaps even inevitable in the Western democracies:

(a) *Demographics*: The first factor is simply demographics. In the past, many governments had the hope or expectation that ethnic minorities would simply disappear, through dying out or assimilation or intermarriage. It is now clear that this is not going to happen. Indigenous peoples are the fastest-growing segment of the population in the countries where they are found, with very high birth rates. The percentage of immigrants in the population is growing steadily in most Western countries, and most commentators agree that even more immigrants will be needed in the future to offset declining birth rates and an ageing population. And substate national groups in the West are also growing in absolute numbers, even if they are staying the same or marginally declining as a percentage of the population. No one anymore can have the dream or delusion that minorities will disappear. The numbers count, particularly in a democracy, and the numbers are shifting in the direction of non-dominant groups.

(b) *Rights-Consciousness*: The second factor is the human rights revolution, and the resulting development of a 'rights consciousness'. Since 1948, we have an international order that is premised on the idea of the inherent equality of human beings, both as individuals and as peoples. The international order has decisively repudiated older ideas of a racial or ethnic hierarchy, according to which some peoples were superior to others, and thereby had the right to rule over them.

It is important to remember how radical these ideas of human equality are. Assumptions about a hierarchy of peoples were widely accepted throughout the West up until World War II, when Hitler's fanatical and murderous policies discredited them. Indeed, the whole system of

European colonialism was premised on the assumption of a hierarchy of peoples, and was the explicit basis of both domestic policies and international law throughout the nineteenth century and first half of the twentieth century.

Today, however, we live in a world where the idea of human equality is unquestioned, at least officially. What matters here is not the change in international law *per se*, which has little impact on most people's everyday lives. The real change has been in people's consciousness. Members of historically subordinated groups today demand equality, and demand it as a *right*. They believe they are entitled to equality, and entitled to it *now*, not in some indefinite or millenarian future.

This sort of rights-consciousness has become such a pervasive feature of modernity that we have trouble imagining that it did not always exist. But if we examine the historical records, we find that minorities in the past typically justified their claims, not by appeal to human rights or equality, but by appealing to the generosity of rulers in according 'privileges', often in return for past loyalty and services. Today, by contrast, groups have a powerful sense of entitlement to equality as a basic human right, not as a favour or charity, and are angrily impatient with what they perceive as lingering manifestations of older hierarchies.

Of course, there is no consensus on what 'equality' means (and, conversely, no agreement on what sorts of actions or practices are evidence of 'hierarchy'). People who agree on the general principle of the equality of peoples may disagree about whether or when this requires official bilingualism, for example, or consociational power sharing. But there can be no doubt that Western democracies historically privileged a particular national group over other groups who were subject to assimilation or exclusion. This historic hierarchy was reflected in a wide range of policies and institutions, from the schools and state symbols to policies regarding language, immigration, media, citizenship, the division of powers, and electoral systems. So long as minority nationalist leaders can identify (or conjure up) manifestations of these historic hierarchies, they will be able to draw upon the powerful rights-consciousness of their members.

(c) *Democracy*: The third key factor, I believe, is democracy. Put simply, the consolidation of democracy limits the ability of elites to crush dissenting movements. In many countries around the world, elites ban political movements of minority groups, or pay thugs or paramilitaries to beat up or kill minority leaders, or bribe police and judges to lock them up. The fear of this sort of repression often keeps minority groups from voicing even the most moderate claims. Keeping quiet is the safest option for minorities in many countries.

In consolidated democracies, however, where democracy is the only game in town, there is no option but to allow minority groups to mobilize politically and advance their claims in public. As a result, members of minority groups are increasingly unafraid to speak out. They may not win the political debate, but they are not afraid of being killed, jailed or fired for trying. It is this loss of fear, combined with rights-consciousness, that explains the remarkably vocal nature of ethnic politics in contemporary Western democracies.

Moreover, democracy involves the availability of multiple access points to decision-making. If a group is blocked at one level by an unsympathetic government, they can pursue their claims at another level. Even if an unsympathetic right-wing political party were to win power at the central level, and attempted to cut back on the rights of minorities, these groups could shift their focus to the regional level, or to the municipal level. And even if all of these levels are blocked, they could pursue their claims through the courts, or even through international pressure. This is what democracy is all about: multiple and shifting points of access to power.

Where these three conditions are in place – increasing numbers, increasing rights-consciousness, and multiple points of access for safe political mobilization – I believe that the trend towards greater accommodation of ethnic diversity is likely to arise. Indeed, I think it is virtually inevitable. This is the lesson I draw from the experience of all the Western democracies. These trends have not depended on the presence or absence of particular personalities, or particular political parties, or particular electoral systems. We see enormous variation across the Western democracies in terms of leadership personalities, party platforms and electoral systems. Yet the basic trends regarding ethnic diversity are the same. And the explanation, I believe, rests in these three deep sociological facts about numbers, rights-consciousness, and opportunity-structures.

There may of course be disruptions in this general trend. Economic crises or considerations of state security can quickly override debates on minority rights. September 11th, for example, has reconfigured debates about the accommodation of Arab and Muslim immigrants in many Western countries. (I will return to the relationship between minority rights and state security later, since it is particularly important in the ECE context.) But in the West, such economic or geopolitical crises have been relatively rare, and led only to temporary deviations in the underlying trend towards accommodation.

So there are a variety of sociological factors that underlie the trend towards multiculturalism and minority rights in the West. But how should we evaluate this trend? Should it be judged a 'success'? Are the emerging Western models of immigrant multiculturalism, indigenous self-government and multination federalism something to celebrate, and perhaps to export?

Let me focus on the evaluation of multination federations, since they are probably the most relevant and also the most controversial for ECE countries. Are multination federations in the West working well? In some cases, it is simply too early to tell to judge their success. For example, the federalization of Spain and Belgium is comparatively recent, and devolution in the United Kingdom is only a few years old.

However, if we look across the broad range of cases, I think we can make some fairly firm judgements about their strengths and weaknesses. Multination federalism in the West has clearly been 'successful' along some dimensions, and equally clearly been a 'failure' along other dimensions.

Let's start with the successes. I would argue that multination federalism has been successful along at least five dimensions:

> (i) *peace and individual security* – these multination federations are managing to deal with their competing national identities and nationalist projects with an almost complete absence of violence or terrorism by either the state r the minority.[3]
>
> (ii) *democracy* – ethnic politics is now a matter of 'ballots not bullets', operating under normal democratic procedures, with no threat of military coups or authoritarian regimes which take power in the name of national security.
>
> (iii) *individual rights* – these reforms have been achieved within the framework of liberal constitutions, with firm respect for individual civil and political rights.

3. The Basque Country is the main exception, although of course the ETA campaign of violence began in the 1960s and 1970s as a response to the highly-centralized Fascist regime, and is unlikely to have emerged had Spain been a democratic multination federation.

(iv) *economic prosperity* – the move to multination federalism has also been achieved without jeopardizing the economic well-being of citizens. Indeed, the countries that have adopted multination federalism are amongst the wealthiest in the world.

(v) *inter-group equality* – last but not least, multination federalism has promoted equality between majority and minority groups. By equality here I mean non-domination, such that one group is not systematically vulnerable to the domination of another group. Multination federalism has helped create greater economic equality between majority and minority; greater equality of political influence, so that minorities are not continually outvoted on all issues; and greater equality in the social and cultural fields, as reflected for example in reduced levels of prejudice and discrimination between groups.

On all these criteria, multination federalism in the West must surely be judged as a success. These multination federations have not only managed the conflicts arising from their competing national identities in a peaceful and democratic way, but have also secured a high degree of economic prosperity and individual freedom for their citizens. This is truly remarkable when one considers the immense power of nationalism in the past hundred years. Nationalism has torn apart colonial empires and Communist dictatorships, and redefined boundaries all over the world. Yet democratic multination federations have succeeded in taming the force of nationalism. Democratic federalism has domesticated and pacified nationalism, while respecting individual rights and freedoms. It is difficult to imagine any other political system that can make the same claim.

However, there are two important respects in which multination federations have not succeeded. First, the lived experience of inter-group relations is hardly a model of robust or constructive intercultural exchange. At best, most citizens in the dominant group are ignorant of, and indifferent to, the internal life of minority groups, and vice versa. At worst, the relations between different groups are tinged with feelings of resentment and annoyance. Despite the significant reforms of state institutions in the direction of multination federalism, substate national groups still typically feel that the older ideology of the homogenous nation-state has not been fully renounced, and that members of the dominant group have not fully accepted the principle of a multination state (or have not fully accepted all of its implications). By contrast, the members of the dominant group typically feel that members of minority groups are ungrateful for the changes that have been made, unreasonable in their expectations, and are impossible to satisfy. As a result, inter-group relations are often highly politicized, as members of both sides are (over?)-sensitive to perceived slights, indignities and misunderstandings. As a result, many people avoid inter-group contact, where possible, or at least do not go out of their way to increase their contact with members of the other group. When contact does take place, it tends to reduce quickly to rather crude forms of bargaining and negotiation, rather than any deeper level of cultural sharing or common deliberation.

The result is sometimes described as the phenomenon of 'parallel societies', or even of 'two solitudes'. Consider the Flemish in Belgium or Québécois in Canada. Multination federalism has enabled these national groups to live more completely within their own institutions operating in their own language. In the past, these groups often faced extensive economic, political and social pressure to participate in institutions run in the dominant language. For example, all of the courts, or universities, or legislatures, were only conducted in the majority language. Yet today, as a result of adopting the ideal of a multination federation, these groups have been able to build up an extensive array of public institutions in their own language, so that they can access the full range of educational, economic, legal and political opportunities without having to learn the dominant language, or without having to participate in institutions that are primarily run by members of the dominant group. In effect, these sorts of multination federations allow groups to create 'parallel societies', co-existing alongside the dominant society, without necessarily much interaction between them.

The interactions between these parallel societies can be very minimal indeed. The French-speaking and English-speaking societies in Canada have often been described as 'two solitudes', which I believe is an accurate description. Francophones and Anglophones in Canada read different newspapers, listen to different radio programs, watch different TV shows, read different literatures. Moreover, they are generally quite uninterested in each other's culture. Few English-speaking Canadians have any desire to learn about internal cultural developments within French-speaking Canada, and vice versa. Anglophones are not interested in reading francophone authors (even in translation), or in learning about who are the hot new media stars or public intellectuals or entertainers within Quebec (and vice-versa).

This sort of parallel societies/two solitudes also exists in Belgium between the Flemish- and French-speaking groups. And also in Switzerland between the German, French and Italian-speaking groups. Switzerland has been described as composed of three groups that "stand with their backs to each other" (Steiner 2001: 145). The French-Swiss stand facing towards France; the Italian-Swiss facing towards Italy; and the German-Swiss facing towards Germany, each focused on their own internal cultural life and the media and culture of the neighbouring country whose language they share. Most members of all three groups accept the principle that Switzerland must be a multilingual state that recognizes and shares power amongst its constituent groups. But few people have much interest in learning about or interacting with the other groups.

In short, increased fairness at the level of state institutions has not been matched by improvements at the level of the lived experience of inter-group relations. The *state* has made itself accessible to all citizens, and affirms the important contribution that each group makes to the larger society. But from the point of view of individuals, the presence of other groups is rarely experienced as enriching. On the contrary, the level of mutual indifference in these countries (and hence the reduction of interethnic relations to mere bargaining) has been described as "nauseous" by one critic of multiculturalism (Barry 2001: 312). The state has become more just, inclusive and accommodating, but inter-group relations remain divided and strained.

Second, and perhaps more importantly, multination federations have not removed secession from the political agenda. On the contrary secessionist ideas and secessionist mobilization is part of everyday life in many Western multination federations. Secessionist parties compete for political office, and electors may even be given the choice of voting for secession in a referendum (as in Puerto Rico and Quebec). To date, no such referendum on secession has succeeded in the West. This suggests that the adoption of federalism has reduced the actual likelihood of secession, since it is almost certain that one or more of these countries would have broken up long ago without federalism. Had Canada, Belgium and Spain not been able to federalize, they might not exist as countries today.

But even if federalism reduces the likelihood of secession, it does not remove secession from the political agenda. Secessionists are on TV, in newspapers, and compete freely for elected office. And secessionist political parties often get substantial support in elections: e.g. 40 per cent in Quebec; 30 per cent in Scotland; 15 per cent in Belgium or the Basque country; 10 per cent in Catalonia; 5 per cent in Puerto Rico. This means that secessionists are present in parliament and on government commissions, and they use these platforms to articulate their views. So, while multination federalism may have reduced the actual likelihood of secession, it has not removed it from everyday political life, or taken it off the political agenda. It has not 'solved the problem of secession'.

So we have a mixed balance sheet, with both successes and failures. What then should be our overall judgement? In some eyes, the failures outweigh the successes. For some people – let's call them 'statists' – the key issue is secession. They believe that eliminating any threat of secession is the first and foremost criterion for evaluating state institutions. The first task of any state is to ensure the integrity of its borders, and so states must first remove secession from the political agenda, and only then think about how best to improve individual rights or democracy or equality. Viewed from a statist perspective, multination federalism fails.

For other people – let's call them 'communitarians' – the key issue is interpersonal relations between citizens. They believe that a political community should be precisely a *community*, united by strong feelings of fraternity and common identity. Viewed from this communitarian perspective, multination federalism abandons the goal of a united community. It accepts the existence of more or less permanent divisions within the polity, and indeed institutionalizes these divisions within state structures. Unwilling to accept this sort of division, communitarians reject multination federalism.

Many citizens in the West, however, have concluded that the successes of multination federalism outweigh the failures. From their point of view – let's call it the 'liberal-democratic' perspective – the fundamental criterion is neither the sanctity of state boundaries nor the strength of community feelings. Rather, political institutions should be judged by their impact on the lives of individuals, as measured by the basic liberal criteria of personal freedom and security, democratic rights, and economic security and prosperity. And on these criteria, multination federalism in the West does quite well. It enables citizens in both majority and minority groups to live freely and peacefully, to participate actively in government, and to enjoy comparatively high levels of economic security and prosperity.

From this liberal-democratic point of view, it may be a source of disappointment that the members of different groups stand with their back to each other. But they stand as free and equal citizens, leading lives of peace and prosperity, under a state that upholds their rights and operates even-handedly between the different groups. And that surely is the main task of a liberal-democratic state. It may also be a source of frustration that state boundaries are contested by secessionists. But so long as the secessionist mobilization occurs in a peaceful and democratic way, with respect for liberal rights and freedoms, then it must be tolerated. The only way to eliminate secessionist mobilization and communal divisions would be to eliminate substate nationalisms, and that in turn could only be achieved by restricting individual rights and democratic freedoms. As I have just noted, there are powerful sociological forces that underlie ethnic mobilization, and wherever the members of substate national groups and indigenous peoples are given the individual freedom and democratic space to mobilize against (what they perceive as) inherited hierarchies, they are likely to do so. And so the choice is between finding liberal-democratic means of institutionalizing that ethnic mobilization, or of adopting illiberal and undemocratic means of suppressing it. For liberal-democrats, the choice is obvious.

In any event, it is far from clear that attempts to suppress minority nationalism would actually work. They are likely to drive nationalist mobilization underground, and perhaps even into violent resistance. While statists and communitarians might be willing in principle to adopt illiberal or undemocratic means to suppress substate nationalism, they increasingly recognize that such efforts are likely to be futile, given the growing numbers and powerful rights-consciousness of the members of minority groups. Statists and communitarians in the West are, slowly and grudgingly, giving up on the dream that they can create political communities unblemished by secessionist sentiments or communal divisions.

In short, we see a growing consensus on the appropriateness of multination federalism in the West, but this support is hedged with ambivalence and reservations. Members of the majority group are disappointed and resentful that moving to multination federalism has not succeeded in eliminating secessionist mobilization and communal divisions. Members of the minority group typically feel that aspects of the old hierarchies remain in the habits and practices of the dominant group and in the institutions of the state, and resent the fact that the dominant group has not fully embraced the spirit of partnership. These feelings of resentment and misunderstanding wax and wane, but they are always close enough to the surface to make all sides wonder whether the whole effort was worthwhile, or whether the country will stay together.

Under these circumstances, it is potentially misleading to describe multination federalism as a 'success', let alone as something to 'celebrate'. Celebration is hardly the spirit with which most Western citizens view the institutions of multination federalism. And yet, beneath the reservations and ambivalence, there is also the sense that this is the best, and perhaps the only, way for liberal democracies to deal with substate nationalisms.

III. Relevance to Eastern Central Europe

Much more could be said about the strengths and weaknesses of multination federalism in the West, or about other forms of multiculturalism and minority rights. But let me turn now to ECE countries, and ask whether is feasible or desirable to 'export' these models to post-Communist Europe.

Both the practice and the discourse of minority rights in ECE is very different. There is enormous resistance in virtually every ECE country to the idea of federalism or other forms of territorial autonomy for national minorities.

In some cases, pre-existing forms of minority autonomy were scrapped: Serbia revoked the autonomy of Kosovo/Vojvodina; Georgia revoked the autonomy of Abkhazia and Ossetia; Azerbaijan revoked the autonomy of Ngorno-Karabakh. Indeed, the revoking of minority autonomy was often one of the first things that these countries chose to do with their new-found freedom after the collapse of communism. In other cases, requests to restore historic forms of autonomy were rejected (e.g. Romania refused to restore the autonomy to Transylvania which had been revoked in 1968). In yet other cases, requests to create new forms of autonomy were dismissed (e.g. Estonia rejected a referendum supporting autonomy for Russian-dominated Narva; Kazakhstan rejected autonomy for ethnic Russians in the north; Ukraine rejected a referendum supporting autonomy for ethnic Romanian areas; Lithuania rejected requests for autonomy by ethnic Poles; Macedonia rejected a referendum for autonomy for Albanian-dominated Western Macedonia in 1992). And in yet other cases, countries have redrawn boundaries to make it impossible for autonomy to be adopted in the future (e.g. Slovakia redrew its internal boundaries so that ethnic Hungarians would not form a majority within any of the internal administrative districts, and hence would have no platform to claim autonomy; Croatia redrew internal boundaries in Krajina and West Slavonia to dilute Serbian-populated areas).

The only cases in ECE where territorial autonomy has been accepted are cases where the national minority simply grabbed political power extra-constitutionally, and established *de facto* autonomy without the consent of the central government. In these situations, the only alternative to recognizing *de facto* autonomy was military intervention and potential civil war. This was the situation in TransDneister in Moldova; Abkhazia in Georgia; Krajina in Croatia; Crimea in Ukraine; and Ngorno-Karabakh in Armenia. Even here, most countries preferred civil war to negotiating autonomy, and only accepted autonomy if and when they were not able to win militarily. (Russia and Ukraine are the two exceptions.)

We see a similar trend with respect to official language rights. Despite the striking levels of linguistic diversity in many ECE countries, Belarus is the only one that has adopted a policy of official bilingualism. Taras discusses the 'paradox' that formerly monolingual countries in the West are moving towards greater respect for linguistic diversity, whereas formerly multilingual countries of the Soviet Union are "pressing ahead with unilingualism" (Taras 1998: 79).

In short, we see a dramatic difference between East and West in the basic approaches to substate nationalism and multination federalism. What explains this difference? In the volume, I explore a range of possible explanations that I can only briefly touch on here. Two common explanations can be quickly dismissed. Some people argue that whereas ethnonational groups in the West reside in homogenous territories, in the East they are dispersed and inter-mingled, and so territorial solutions that work in the West will not work in the East. I think this is simply incorrect as a generalization. The ethnic Albanians in Macedonia, or ethnic Hungarians in Slovakia, are no more or less territorially concentrated than the French in Canada, Puerto Ricans in the US or Catalans in Spain. In all of these cases, there is a region in which the substate national group is particularly concentrated, but there are both 'internal minorities' (i.e. people living in that region who do not belong to the substate national group) and a 'minority diaspora' (i.e. members of the substate national group who live outside the region). The size of these internal minorities and minority diasporas in many ECE countries is no more or less than in comparable Western countries.

A second common explanation for opposition to bilingualism and federalism in ECE is that they cost a great deal of money, and while rich Western countries can afford these costs, poorer countries in ECE cannot. But this too is misleading. Federal countries can be just as efficient as unitary states, and studies suggest that bilingualism has negligible effects on overall state budgets. In fact, forcing public institutions in regions dominated by a linguistic minority to shift to the majority language is often a costly and inefficient process.

So what then is the real explanation for the resistance to multination federalism? Why have people in ECE countries come to such different conclusions about its relative potential and pitfalls than in the West?

One possible explanation is that there are more statists and communitarians in the East than West, and fewer liberals. As a result, ideas about the sanctity of the state and the unity of the nation are more powerful in the region, and are invoked to pre-empt the democratic freedoms and spaces needed for multiculturalism and minority rights to emerge.

But that is at best part of the story. For the fact is that *both* liberals and statist/communitarians in the ECE are more likely to oppose multination federalism than their counterparts in the West. Liberal-democrats in the West assume that substate national groups will exercise their territorial autonomy in accordance with the basic principles of liberal constitutionalism, so that devolving power from the central state to a self-governing region does not threaten the basic respect for individual rights and democratic freedoms. This indeed is what we see throughout the Western multination federations. In the ECE, by contrast, many liberal-democrats worry that such substate autonomies will become petty tyrannies that flout the rule of law, deny human rights, and oppress internal minorities.

Statists and communitarians in the West have grudgingly come to accept that their dreams of constructing a united community within uncontested borders are simply unrealistic. Attempts to preserve the ideology of 'one language, one nation, one state' through the assimilation or exclusion of minority groups have proven futile. Minorities are too numerous, and too politically conscious of their rights, to simply disappear. In the ECE, by contrast, many statists and communitarians cling to the hope that minority nationalism will fade away. They believe that substate nationalism is really a transient by-product of some other problem that will disappear over time through the processes of modernization or democratic transition. Some people assume that minority nationalism will fade as the economy improves, or as democracy is consolidated, or as communications and media become globalized. On this view, if ECE states have the strength to hold out against minority demagogues and ethnic entrepreneurs, then the problem will gradually solve itself. This, of course, is precisely the expectation that Westerners have gradually relinquished, since minority nationalisms have in fact strengthened rather than weakened as Western states have become more democratic, prosperous and globalized.

In comparing East and West then, we see a curious set of contrasts. In the ECE, many intellectuals and politicians are deeply pessimistic about the prospect that substate national groups can exercise territorial autonomy in accordance with liberal-democratic norms, yet are surprisingly optimistic about the possibility that substate nationalism will simply disappear. By contrast, Western public opinion is optimistic about the capacity of substate national groups to govern within liberal-democratic constraints, but pessimistic about the likelihood that substate nationalism will disappear as a result of processes of modernization, democratization, development or globalization.

These differing forms of optimism and pessimism account for some of the differences between the West and East. But there is one other very important factor. As I mentioned earlier, the trend towards greater accommodation of diversity can be blocked or deflected by considerations of security. Whether in the East or West, states will not accord greater powers or resources to groups that are perceived as disloyal, and therefore a threat to the security of the state. In particular, states will not accommodate groups which are seen as likely to collaborate with foreign enemies. Most Western democracies are fortunate that this is rarely an issue. For example, if Quebec gains increased powers, or even independence, no one in the rest of Canada worries that Quebec will start collaborating with Iraq or the Taliban or China to overthrow the Canadian state. Québécois nationalists may want to secede, but an independent Quebec would be an ally of Canada, not an enemy, and would cooperate together with Canada in NATO and other Western defence and security arrangements. So too with Catalonia: if Catalonia becomes more autonomous, or even independent, it will still be an ally, not an enemy of Spain. So too with Scotland *vis-à-vis* the rest of Britain, Flanders *vis-à-vis* the rest of Belgium, or Puerto Rico *vis-à-vis* the rest of the United States.

In most parts of the world, however, minority groups are often seen as a kind of 'fifth column', likely to be working for a neighbouring enemy. This is particularly a concern where the minority is related to a neighbouring state by ethnicity or religion, so that the neighbouring state claims the right to intervene to protect 'its' minority.

Under these conditions, we are likely to witness what political scientists call the 'securitization' of ethnic relations (Wæver 1995). Relations between states and minorities are seen, not as a matter of normal democratic politics to be negotiated and debated, but as a matter of state security, in which the state has to limit the normal democratic process in order to protect the state. Under conditions of securitization, minority self-organization may be legally limited (e.g. minority political parties banned), minority leaders may be subject to secret police surveillance, the raising of particular sorts of demands may be illegal (e.g. laws against promoting secession), and so on. Even if minority demands can be voiced, they will be flatly rejected by the larger society and the state. After all, how can groups that are disloyal have any legitimate claims against the state? So securitization of ethnic relations erodes both the democratic space to voice minority demands, and the likelihood that those demands will be accepted.

This, I think, is precisely the situation we find throughout most of the ECE. State-minority relations have been 'securitized'. Dominant groups throughout the region feel they have been victimized by their minorities acting in collaboration with foreign enemies. We see this in the Czech Republic regarding the German minority; in Slovakia *re* the Hungarian minority; in the Baltics *re* the Russian minority; in Croatia *re* the Serbian minority; in Bulgaria *re* the Turkish minority, to name a few.

In all of these cases, minorities are seen (rightly or wrongly) as allies or collaborators with external powers that have historically oppressed the majority group. Hungarians in Romania and Slovakia may be a relatively small minority (10-15 per cent of the population in each country), but Slovakians and Romanians perceive them as the allies of their former Habsburg oppressors, and indeed as the physical residue of that unjust imperialism. The Russians who settled in Estonia and Latvia after World War II are seen by the state, not as a weak and disenfranchised minority group, but as a tool of their former Soviet oppressors. The Muslim Albanians in Serbia and Macedonia, or the Muslim Turks in Bulgaria, are seen as a reminder of, and collaborator with, centuries of oppression under the Ottomans.

This history of imperialism, collaboration and border changes have encouraged three interrelated assumptions which are now widely accepted by ECE countries: (a) that minorities are disloyal, not just in the sense that they lack loyalty to the state (that is equally true of secessionists in Quebec or Scotland), but in the stronger sense that they collaborated with former oppressors, and continue to collaborate with current enemies or potential enemies; therefore, (b) a strong and stable state requires weak and disempowered minorities. Put another way, ethnic relations are seen as a zero-sum game: anything that benefits the minority is seen as a threat to the majority; and therefore (c) the treatment of minorities is above all a question of national security.

In the West, by contrast, ethnic politics have been almost entirely 'desecuritized'. The politics of substate nationalism in the West is just that – normal day-to-day politics. Relations between the state and national minorities have been taken out of the 'security' box, and put in the 'democratic politics' box. Under these circumstances, the three factors I discussed earlier – demographics, rights-consciousness, multiple access points – to operate freely, and the almost inevitable result is the trend towards accommodation of diversity.

It is worth noting that this desecuritization of ethnic politics in the West even applies to the issue of secession. Even though secessionist political parties wish to break up the state, citizens in the West assume that secessionists must be treated under the same democratic rules as everyone else, with the same democratic rights to mobilize, advocate and run for office. The reason for this remarkable tolerance of secessionist mobilization, I believe, is precisely the assumption that even if substate national groups do secede, they will become our allies, not our enemies (and also govern their seceding state in accordance with human rights and liberal-democratic values).

IV. The Role of the International Community

So far, I have focused on three obstacles to multination federalism in ECE: (a) scepticism about the likelihood that substate autonomies will be liberal-democratic; (b) the belief that ethnic mobilization, including substate nationalism, will disappear over time as a result of modernization and development; and (c) the fear that minorities will collaborate with enemies of the state. By contrast, in the West most citizens are (a) optimistic about the liberal-democratic credentials of substate autonomies; (b) resigned to the long-term existence of ethnic politics and minority nationalist mobilization; and (c) confident that minorities will be allies not enemies in any larger regional or international security conflicts.

There are of course other obstacles to the exporting of Western models of multination federalism to the ECE, not least the unhappy experience of the failed Communist federations. But enough has been said, I think, to make clear the major challenges facing the international community in its efforts to promote minority rights in the region.

It is clear that the West has the power to impose any number of conditions on ECE countries, including minority rights conditions. Most ECE countries are sufficiently desperate to get into the EU and NATO that they would accept virtually anything the West demanded in this area. But these legal and political reforms will only be successful and enduring if they are accompanied by changes in people's underlying hopes, fears and expectations about state-minority relations. And the crucial change here, I believe, involves the acceptance that nationalist mobilization by substate national groups is a normal and legitimate part of everyday politics in a free and democratic society. So long as this central idea continues to be resisted, there is little hope for genuine progress in state-minority relations.

To my mind, this really involves two separate changes. First, it requires challenging the naive hope that minority nationalism will fade away with economic development and democratic consolidation. There is not a shred of evidence to support this hope, yet it remains remarkably widespread throughout the ECE, and so discourages people from recognizing the durability of the issue. Second, it requires challenging the 'securitization' of ethnic politics that arises from the fear that minorities will collaborate with neighbouring enemies. This is a more complicated issue, and probably can only be fully resolved by constructing viable regional structures of geo-political security, whether through the inclusion of ECE countries in NATO, or the construction of an alternate regional security body. But the successful negotiation and implementation of minority rights can only take place within democratic spaces that have been 'desecuritized'.

The central question, then, is whether the current activities of the international community are helping to 'normalize' and 'desecuritize' the democratic expression and mobilization of minority nationalism in Eastern Europe. In the volume, I attempt a provisional assessment of the activities of various Western organizations, including the OSCE, in this regard. My tentative answer, perhaps rather unsurprising, is that the record is mixed, and that much more could be done. While supporting the democratic rights of minorities in many respects, Western organizations are also, at times, feeding into myths and misperceptions about the nature and durability of substate nationalisms. They have had some success at pushing various ECE countries to live up to certain very minimal standards regarding minority rights, but have not effectively challenged dominant ideologies about the illegitimate nature of substate nationalist claims for territorial autonomy and official language status, and have not pushed to create meaningful democratic spaces to deliberate about these claims in a free and informed way.

However, my main aim is not to pass judgement on any particular international organization, but rather to stimulate greater reflection on the goals such organizations should be pursuing. As I said at the beginning of this paper, the original agenda behind the internationalizing of minority rights was driven by short-term concerns about avoiding violence and civil war. Today, we need to think more clearly about long-term goals. We need to think about the enduring conflicts that arise in multination states, about the institutions that can manage those conflicts in a peaceful manner, and about the underlying assumptions and beliefs that allow citizens to debate them in a free and democratic way.

References

Documents:

United Nations
Declaration on the Rights of Persons Belonging to National or Ethnic, Religious and Linguistic Minorities (1992)

Organization for Security and Cooperation in Europe
The Lund Recommendations on the Effective Participation of National Minorities in Public Life (1999)

The Oslo Recommendations Regarding the Linguistic Rights of National Minorities (1998)

The Hague Recommendations Regarding the Education Rights of National Minorities (1996)

Articles:

Barry, B. (2001). *Culture and Equality: An Egalitarian Critique of Multiculturalism.* Cambridge: Polity.

EU Accession Monitoring Program (2001). *Monitoring the EU Accession Process: Minority Protection.* Budapest: Open Society Institute.

Kymlicka, W. and Opalski, M. (2001). *Can Liberal Pluralism be Exported?* Oxford: Oxford University Press.

Steiner, J. (2001). "Switzerland and the European Union: A Puzzle". In M. Keating and J. McGarry (eds). *Minority Nationalism and the Changing International Order.* Oxford: Oxford University Press.

Taras, R. (1998). "Nations and Language-Building: Old Theories, Contemporary Cases". *Nationalism and Ethnic Politics.* 4/3: 79–101.

Wæver, O. (1995). "Securitization and Desecuritization". In R. Lipschutz (ed.) *On Security.* New York: Columbia University Press.

Biographical Note

Will Kymlicka is the author of five books published by Oxford University Press: *Liberalism, Community, and Culture* (1989), *Contemporary Political Philosophy* (1990; second edition 2002), *Multicultural Citizenship* (1995), *Finding Our Way: Rethinking Ethnocultural Relations in Canada* (1998), and *Politics in the Vernacular: Nationalism, Multiculturalism and Citizenship* (2001). He is also the editor of *The Rights of Minority Cultures* (OUP 1995), co-editor with Ian Shapiro of *Ethnicity and Group Rights* (NYU 1997), co-editor with Wayne Norman of *Citizenship in Diverse Societies* (OUP 2000), and co-editor with Magda Opalski of *Can Liberal Pluralism Be Exported?* (OUP, 2001). His most recent work focuses on the process of 'internationalizing' minority rights, and the prospects for achieving an international consensus on minority rights norms.

[16]

Equality and Non-discrimination: Fundamental Principles of Minority Language Rights

FERNAND DE VARENNES
Senior Lecturer in Law, Murdoch University
Director, Asia-Pacific Centre for Human Rights & the Prevention of Ethnic Conflict and Tip O'Neill Fellow in Peace Studies, INCORE

1. The Foundation of Human Rights: Tolerance, Coexistence and Integration

'A country should be judged on the basis of how it treats its minorities.'
Gandhi

A modern democratic State must be based on respect for fundamental human rights which also includes linguistic aspects. To understand this, it is necessary to consider the link between minority language rights and the values of tolerance, coexistence and integration. These values underpin the essential content of human rights, i.e. respect for the worth and dignity of human beings, and provide its foundation.

It is impossible for a State to be absolutely neutral in terms of cultural or linguistic preferences. All governments must use at least one language for the conduct of their affairs and to communicate with their population. By preferring an official, national or dominant language (or languages), the State is at the same time giving advantage to those people who speak the same language as that (or those) chosen by the State. The reality in most countries is that some parts of the population speak languages which differ from the official or dominant language(s) chosen by the State, and are therefore disadvantaged by the government's choice.

What should be done then? Some governments, mainly in the past, have tried to eliminate these minorities and their linguistic differences. However, this eliminationist or assimilationist approach has serious flaws — especially if coerced. In most cases, attempts to eliminate minority languages have understandably been resisted — in some cases precipitating violent conflicts. An analogy can be found in the wars of religion which swept through Europe many centuries ago. Although there were many factors involved in these conflicts, it should be remembered that the spark for conflict was often an attempt to eliminate religious differences. The monarch tried to impose his religion on an entire population in accordance with the principle *cuius regio, eius religio*.

Today, tension and conflict arises in cases where there are attempts to impose *cuius regio, eius lingua*. This is the approach of a State where the 'State-forming nation' (i.e. the linguistic, religious or ethnic majority) reigns supreme. In extreme cases, this approach has taken the form of forced assimilation, ethnic cleansing and even cultural or physical genocide. Clearly, it is based on rejection of the universal values of respect, justice and reasonableness that are reflected in human rights. The policy ideal of 'one language–one State' is usually divisive and destructive in States where it affects negatively members of a minority that are in significant numbers.

Human rights scholar Rodolfo Stavenhagen has pointed out that 'in most cases of open ethnic conflict in the world today, the State is not an impartial onlooker or arbiter, but rather a party to the conflict itself. Indeed, in multiethnic societies, the State is frequently either controlled by, or identifies strongly with, a dominant or majority *ethnie*.'[1] More recently, another scholar has concluded that '[I]t is not difficult to establish that violations of the rights of free exercise and non-discrimination intensify conflict... nor to project with reasonable confidence that the observance and implementation of those norms will serve to reduce conflict.'[2] As these observations suggest, peaceful coexistence can be achieved by respecting certain fundamental rights that have an impact on ethnic or linguistic interests. This is the logic which has been followed in international law since the Second World War with the acceptance of a 'faith in fundamental human rights, in the dignity and worth of the human person, in the equal rights of men and women and of nations large and small', to quote from the preamble of the *Universal Declaration of Human Rights*.

Human rights, including minority rights, are based on the acknowledgement and acceptance of the human person in all of his or her diversity. Just as one's colour of skin or religion should not diminish one's worth or dignity, so the State should not reject or be intolerant towards

[1]R. Stavenhagen, 'Ethnic Conflict and Human Rights – their Interrelationship' in: K. Rupesinghe, ed., *Ethnic Conflict and Human Rights* (Tokyo: United Nations University, 1988), p. 19.

[2]D. Little, *Belief, Ethnicity and Nationalism* (Washington: United States Institute of Peace, 1996), http://www.usip.org/research/rehr/belethnat.html.

minorities. International human rights standards such as non-discrimination, freedom of expression and religion and others are all founded on the recognition of the intrinsic value of the human person's dignity and worth. These rights are based on tolerance of human differences, such as linguistic and religious differences, and recognition and respect of human diversity. To deny persons belonging to minorities access to certain benefits, or to disadvantage them because of their religion or language is — under certain conditions — no longer permissible. That is what could be described as the basic premise of human rights, especially for States operating within a democratic framework. Tolerance of human differences permits the peaceful coexistence of people who have diverse ethnic and linguistic backgrounds.

But what does tolerance mean in practice? Does it mean that any minority demand regarding language matters must be accepted by the State, regardless of the costs or practical difficulties this may raise? The answer is no. There must be a balance between the different interests involved, such as those of individuals who may be disadvantaged by a government's linguistic preferences in terms of employment opportunities or educational consequences, as well as the legitimate interests of the State which may have to confront, *inter alia*, practical limitations to the provision of services in minority languages arising from a genuine lack of financial or human resources. Finding the right balance can and must be based on principles of tolerance, coexistence and integration. Integration does not mean the elimination of human differences, but rather taking them into account and accommodating them to the extent possible and practicable so that individuals may be able to participate in the life of the linguistic or cultural community to which they belong as well as in the life of the wider society of the State as a whole.

The balancing of the interests of the State and those of minorities in language matters does not mean that a State cannot adopt a common or official language. It only means that linguistic minorities must be accommodated as much as is reasonably possible given the situation of the minority and the conditions within the State. That is the very essence of the modern concept of the rights of persons belonging to minorities.

Building upon existing international standards, the independent experts who elaborated *The Oslo Recommendations Regarding the Linguistic Rights of National Minorities* emphasize — with a view to offering practical policy guidelines — exactly the elements of balance and integration as follows:

> The rights of persons belonging to national minorities to use their language(s) in public and in private as set forth and elaborated in The Oslo Recommendations Regarding the Linguistic Rights of National Minorities must be seen in a balanced context of full participation in the wider society. The Recommendations do not propose an isolationist approach, but rather one which encourages a balance between the right of persons belonging to national minorities to maintain and develop their own identity, culture and language and the necessity of ensuring that they are able to integrate into the wider society as full and equal members.[3]

In relation to a specific subject area, the balancing of interests can be found, for example, in Recommendation 12 of *The Oslo Recommendations Regarding the Linguistic Rights of National Minorities* which deals with economic life and urges a balance between a private individual's desire to use a minority language in his or her own economic activities and the State's interest in assuring the use of the official or dominant language in areas such as the protection of workers or consumers. Individuals are free to use their language of choice in private economic activities, but the government can also require the additional use of the official or dominant language. An individual's freedom of expression and the State's own interests (i.e. *public* interests) are thus balanced together and reasonably accommodated.

Documents such as the UN *Declaration on the Rights of Persons Belonging to National or Ethnic, Religious or Linguistic Minorities*, the Council of Europe's *Framework Convention for the Protection of National Minorities* as well as *The Oslo Recommendations Regarding the Linguistic Rights of National Minorities* are part of a tendency to increase understanding and respect for human rights which are anchored upon principles of tolerance, coexistence and integration. It is in this spirit that the rights of linguistic and other minorities must be seen: they are measures aimed at reaching a balance of inclusion and harmony rather than exclusion and conflict.

[3] *The Oslo Recommendations Regarding the Linguistic Rights of National Minorities*, Explanatory Note, p. 14; see below at p. 370.

2. The Principle of Non-discrimination in Relation to Language

Linguistic rights are connected to many fundamental human rights — in particular non-discrimination — in a way which is consistent with the values of tolerance, coexistence and integration. The same idea was long ago pursued in relation to other bases of discrimination, e.g. through elaboration of the *International Convention on the Elimination of All Forms of Racial Discrimination* and the *Convention on the Elimination of All Forms of Discrimination against Women* which extend the application of very general provisions on non-discrimination to a variety of relevant subject areas in relation to these specific categories of persons. Similarly, documents such as the UN *Declaration on the Rights of Persons Belonging to National or Ethnic, Religious or Linguistic Minorities*, the *Framework Convention for the Protection of National Minorities* and *The Oslo Recommendations Regarding the Linguistic Rights of National Minorities* provide more precision for the direct application of human rights in situations involving minorities. In particular, *The Oslo Recommendations* clarify how the principles of tolerance, coexistence and integration can be applied in relation to language use. Many of the recommendations offer general examples of the effect of human rights in language matters and, in effect, constitute policy guidelines as to how these matters may be addressed in such a way which respects relevant international standards.

To give a simple example of this interrelationship between international human rights and the content of *The Oslo Recommendations*, Recommendation 1 refers to the right of persons belonging to national minorities to use their personal names in their own language. This right is protected in international law under the *International Covenant on Civil and Political Rights* and the *European Convention for the Protection of Human Rights and Fundamental Freedoms* as part of the right to private and family life (Articles 17 and 8, respectively), as has already been confirmed by both the United Nations Human Rights Committee and the European Court of Human Rights.[4] According to Article 11(1) of the *Framework Convention for the Protection of National Minorities*, States parties are also bound to ensure 'official recognition' of the personal names of persons belonging to minorities.

[4]*Coeriel and Aurik v. Netherlands*, UN Human Rights Committee, Communication No. 453/1991, U.N. Doc. CCPR/C/52/D/1991 (1994); *Burghartz v. Switzerland*, European Court of Human Rights, Judgment of 22 February 1994, 181 E.H.R.R. 101.

Most fundamentally, language use is a matter of freedom of expression. The right of persons belonging to a linguistic minority to use their language with other members of their group, in private and in public, is guaranteed expressly under Article 27 of the *International Covenant on Civil and Political Rights*. According to Article 2(1) of the same Covenant, this right is to be guaranteed 'without distinction of any kind, such as... language...'. The same standard applies specifically for children pursuant to Articles 30 and 2(1) of the *Convention on the Rights of the Child*. In this connection, it is important to clarify what the right of non-discrimination means in international law in order to better understand what tolerance, coexistence and integration in a democratic setting means in specific situations. Essentially, the principle of non-discrimination means that there should be no unreasonable differentiation or limitation — assuming, in the first place, the existence of a legitimate public interest on the basis of which the State may interfere at all. In relation to language use, one may well imagine legitimate public interests justifying limits on certain *content* of language, but it seems difficult to imagine the existence of interests which would ever justify limits on language *as a vehicle of communication* (i.e. in the sense we are discussing 'language' here).

The right to have access to public services or to communicate with public entities in a minority language is an important point of intersection between minority interests and common interests of coexistence and integration. But, there are many practical implications to be taken into account. It is not enough to have a group to be entitled to these rights. There is balancing to be done between the interests of individuals who belong to minorities and the interests of the State (i.e. the general interest). Whereas a State may have any official language(s) it chooses, it must also, in situations where there are significant numbers and sufficient demand, use a minority language. In an effort to reach such a balance, Recommendation 14 of *The Oslo Recommendations* provides as follows:

> Persons belonging to national minorities shall have adequate possibilities to use their language in communications with administrative authorities especially in regions and localities where they have expressed a desire for it and where they are present in significant numbers. Similarly, administrative authorities shall, wherever possible, ensure that public services are provided also in the language of the national minority. To this end, they shall adopt appropriate recruitment and/or training policies and programmes.

When the number of speakers of a minority language is 'significant', a State's refusal to provide public services in their language would appear unreasonable and therefore discriminatory, since it denies them a benefit or advantage that is available to others, namely the benefit of public services in their own language. Of course, the principle of non-discrimination does not mean that a State cannot have an official or preferred language. The right of non-discrimination based on language means in general that while it is quite legitimate and even necessary to choose an official language or dominant language which is in effect more favourable for those persons for whom the chosen language is their own, there are situations where it would be unreasonable not to use *also* (under certain conditions) other languages. If the number of persons is high enough and the disadvantage or denial of a particular benefit to individuals is serious enough, then it is reasonable to use another language *as well*. For the government to refuse to do so would be discriminatory.

That is also exactly what is foreseen in Article 10(2) of the *Framework Convention for the Protection of National Minorities*. Not all national minorities have the right to public services in their language. Only when there are enough individuals who demand it and when they are in significant numbers in a particular region does it become necessary for the government to offer public services in a minority language. In those circumstances, it would be inconsistent with principles of tolerance, coexistence and integration, and therefore with non-discrimination, to disadvantage or deny to so many people the benefit and advantage of having their language used in public services to an appropriate degree and level.

3. The Case of Language Use in the Conduct of Democracy

> The Court considers one of the principal characteristics of democracy to be the possibility it offers of resolving a country's problems through dialogue, without recourse to violence, even when they are irksome.[5]

The foundation of democracy is that the will of the people is the basis of government. The crucial procedural elements of the expression of 'the will

[5] *United Communist Party of Turkey and Others v. Turkey*, European Court of Human Rights, Judgment of 30 January 1998, European Court of Human Rights Reports 1998-I, para. 57.

of the people' are the rights to vote and to stand for public office. Since democratic government is usually run by means of debate among elected representatives, language issues have arisen in specific situations in terms both of the language of proceedings and also the linguistic proficiency of candidates for election. With regard to the first issue, Recommendation 15 of *The Oslo Recommendations* asserts that 'the State shall take measures to ensure that elected members of regional and local governmental bodies can use the language of the national minority during activities relating to these bodies'. The idea is that the substance of deliberations, and the bases of decisions, should not be constrained by unnecessary language requirements, and that, moreover, they should be enhanced by the facilitation of commonly spoken languages so that ideas and positions may be fully expressed and considered. Of course, when Recommendation 15 indicates that elected members of regional and local governmental bodies can use the language of the national minority where significant numbers of people are involved, logically this implies that an individual who is a member of such a minority can be a candidate and can be elected. Yet, this is not always the case.

A number of countries have regulations that prevent individuals from being candidates or to sit if they are elected as officials in local, regional or even national elections unless they can demonstrate an appropriate knowledge of the official or dominant language. Such a linguistic criterion can exclude individuals who belong to linguistic minorities (and also other persons belonging to the majority) if their proficiency in the official or dominant language is deemed to be insufficient. According to Article 25 of the *International Covenant on Civil and Political Rights* (ICCPR), no such language proficiency criterion is permissible since the rights to vote and to stand for election are to be guaranteed to all citizens 'without any of the distinctions mentioned in Article 2 [of the Covenant]', i.e. including distinctions of language.

While the ICCPR is unequivocal with regard to language distinctions in the context of elections, Council of Europe standards are less clear. Article 3 of the *First Protocol of the Convention for the Protection of Human Rights and Fundamental Freedoms* guarantees 'the free expression of the opinion of the people in the choice of legislature'. However, the European Court of Human Rights has stated that 'States [have] considerable latitude to establish in their constitutional order rules governing status of parliamentarians, including criteria for disqualification',[6] as well as the right to vote and to stand for election. But these are subject to certain limitations:

> The Court reiterates that Article 3 of Protocol No. 1 implies subjective rights to vote and to stand for election. As important as those rights are, they are not, however, absolute. Since Article 3 recognises them without setting them forth in express terms, let alone defining them, there is room for 'implied limitations'...[7]

Dealing even more closely with linguistic criteria, the European Court of Human Rights had to decide in *Mathieu-Mohin and Clerfayt*[8] whether the exclusion of elected parliamentarians from the bilingual electoral district of Brussels was in breach of Article 3 of the *First Protocol of the Convention for the Protection of Human Rights and Fundamental Freedoms*. They had to submit to a test of eligibility consisting in a parliamentary oath to be sworn in the Dutch language. The applicants, being francophones, took their oath in French instead and were denied the right to sit on the Dutch-language Council in respect of certain matters. According to the Court, Article 3 by itself has no linguistic component, and the electors involved enjoyed the right to vote and the right to stand for election on the same legal footing as Dutch-speaking electors. They were not deprived of their Article 3 right sufficiently in this case since the limitation is not disproportionate to the point of thwarting the 'free expression of the opinion of the people in the choice of the legislature'.[9] However, in proceeding to examine Article 14 of the Convention taken together with Article 3 of the *First Protocol*, the Court came to the conclusion that Article 14 could be invoked, although in the circumstances the measure adopted by the State was not unreasonable nor disproportionate:

> The aim is to defuse the language disputes in the country by establishing more stable and decentralised organisational structures... In any consideration of the electoral system in issue, its general context

[6] *Gitonas and Others v. Greece*, Judgment of 1 July 1997, European Court of Human Rights Reports 1997-IV, para. 39.

[7] *Ibid.*, paragraph 39.

[8] (1987) *European Court of Human Rights*, Series A, No. 113, Judgment of 2 March 1987.

[9] *Ibid.*, at p. 25.

> must not be forgotten. The system does not appear unreasonable if regard is had to the intentions it reflects and to the respondent state's margin of appreciation within the Belgian parliamentary system — a margin that is all the greater as the system is incomplete and provisional.[10]

The comments of the European Court of Human Rights on the application of non-discrimination in this area suggests, therefore, a balancing of the competing interests and consideration of the objectives being sought, as well as the actual consequences of the governmental measures for affected individuals.

In *Mathieu-Mohin*, individuals could still vote for the candidate of their choice, and these candidates could be elected regardless of their linguistic capabilities. They did have to swear an oath in Dutch in order to be able to participate in certain functions, but this the Court considered not to be an unreasonable, disproportionate demand in light of the accepted aim of defusing the language disputes in Belgium by establishing more stable and decentralised organisational structures. This is clearly distinguishable from what can be found in some countries where there are regulations that go much further than what the Court was ready to accept in *Mathieu-Mohin* and which could be considered to be unreasonable criteria and therefore discriminatory under Article 14 of the *Convention for the Protection of Human Rights and Fundamental Freedoms* and Article 26 of the *International Covenant on Civil and Political Rights.*

For example, even if elected by a large majority in a free and democratic election, a person in some States in Europe will not be permitted to sit as a representative in a political body if s/he is not sufficiently fluent in the official language. This works clearly to the detriment of persons belonging to linguistic minorities, as the OSCE High Commissioner on National Minorities has pointed out in certain cases.[11] A better approach most common in open and democratic societies is to have no such linguistic criteria. If a person is duly elected, he or she should be permitted to represent the freely expressed will of the people — whatever his or her linguistic (i.e. oral) proficiency. This is because rules that require

[10]*Ibid.*

[11]See Letter of 19 December 1998 addressed from the OSCE High Commissioner on National Minorities to the President of Estonia, reproduced in R. Zaagman, *Conflict Prevention in the Baltic States: The OSCE High Commissioner on National Minorities in Estonia, Latvia and Lithuania* (ECMI Monograph # 1, Flensburg: European Centre for Minority Issues, April 1999), Annex 4, pp. 69–71.

an appropriate knowledge of the State language, or oral and written proficiency in the official or dominant language, especially to be a member of a local government, have a very serious consequence on the free exercise of one of the most fundamental human rights. Almost certainly, this should be deemed to be an excessive and unreasonable requirement, thus constituting a distinction based on language which is discriminatory in violation of both the *European Convention for the Protection of Human Rights and Fundamental Freedoms* and the *International Covenant on Civil and Political Rights.*

The relatively simple truth is that if someone not proficient in the official or dominant language is elected, it is either because that person represents many people who are in the same situation or, in any event, because the electorate indicated with their votes their confidence in his or her ability to represent their interests in the legislature. If anything, such an election is evidence of the social reality in that constituency. It should only be set aside for the most clear and pressing reasons which would (and should) in all likelihood be extremely rare, if at all possible.

4. Conclusion

> Does not the sun shine equally for the whole world? Do we not all equally breathe the air? Do you not feel shame at authorizing only three languages and condemning other people to blindness and deafness? Tell me, do you think that God is helpless and cannot bestow equality, or that he is envious and will not give it?
>
> Constantine the Philosopher (Cyril), 9th Century A.D.[12]

Human rights today are more than an 'interesting idea': they constitute an integral part of the moral fabric of the international community to which Europe and its constituent States belong. But because the appearance of international human rights is a relatively young phenomenon in historical terms, it also means that not every aspect of their application is fully understood or appreciated. This is especially true for issues involving minorities, including use of language. There is a continuing process going on to define more clearly how various international human rights standards, such as freedom of expression and non-discrimination, among

[12]Quoted in J. A. Fishman, ed., *Readings in the Sociology of Language* (The Hague: Mouton and Co. N.V. Publishers, 1968), p. 589.

others, may affect the private and public use of language by persons belonging to minorities, as well as government language restrictions or preferences. This process finds inspiration in values of tolerance, coexistence and integration that are part of the very foundation of a modern democratic State. Attention to these values does not involve a loss of sovereignty or a threat to unity. On the contrary, their careful application may help avoid and resolve tensions and conflicts involving language issues in a number of countries — tensions and conflicts which may threaten the State.

Inspired by these values, documents such as *The Oslo Recommendations Regarding the Linguistic Rights of National Minorities* are part of the world-wide process of clarifying how human rights can be applied in what are described as the linguistic rights of national minorities. They provide a balance between the different interests involved, trying to arrive at a fair and reasonable result. Individual freedom in private matters, practical difficulties for governments, advantages or burdens caused to individuals by State language preferences or restrictions, the objectives of integration and peaceful coexistence — all these must be taken into account in trying to achieve this balance.

It is perhaps important to repeat that the principle of non-discrimination does not prohibit all language distinctions and preferences. Distinctions that represent a proportionate balance between the different interests are seen in international law as being reasonable, and therefore not discriminatory. However, this means that if a State language preference or restriction is 'unreasonable', such as when the government refuses to provide public services in regions and localities where persons belonging to a national minority are present in significant numbers, then such a language distinction is discriminatory and unacceptable. Of course, such a conclusion can only be drawn upon assessment of the particular circumstances of a specific situation. However, in general, and so far as possible, policy and law should be elaborated and applied with a view to ensuring full and equal opportunities for all persons, including persons belonging to linguistic minorities.

Part VI
Human Rights Law and Minority Rights Law

[17]

A Critical Evaluation of International Human Rights Approaches to Racism

KEVIN BOYLE AND ANNELIESE BALDACCINI

I. INTRODUCTION

The focus of the Florence lectures has been on Europe, including the new legal obligations to be undertaken by EU member states on the elimination of racial and ethnic discrimination. The provisions of the Equal Treatment Directives are radical and far-reaching.[1] Yet these same states, with the exception of Ireland, have also been parties to the United Nations International Convention on the Elimination of All Forms of Racial Discrimination (hereinafter 'ICERD'), in most cases for decades.[2] They have been obligated under that treaty to act to eliminate race- or ethnic-based discrimination. The major obligations under the new Directives are paralleled under ICERD. The EU states have submitted many reports to the monitoring committee for the UN Convention. But it is clear that the decades of implementation of the global convention have proved insufficient to force the kind of comprehensive legislative protection against racial and ethnic discrimination now required under the new Directives.

Should one conclude that the UN Convention and other United Nations long-standing efforts to eliminate racism have been in vain? That regional approaches are the only effective way to persuade states to tackle racism? At the least such questions need to be asked. They are particularly appropriate in the context of the forthcoming United Nations World Conference on

[1] Council Directive 2000/43/EC of 29 June 2000 implementing the principle of equal treatment between persons irrespective of racial or ethnic origin; Council Directive 2000/78/EC of 27 Nov. 2000 establishing a general framework for equal treatment in employment and occupation.

[2] GA Res. 2106 A (XX) (1965). In United Nations, *A Compilation of International Instruments* (1994), i, Part 1, at 66. For the list of ratifications, accessions, and successions, see Office of the United Nations High Commissioner for Human Rights (OHCHR), *Status of Ratifications of the Principal International Human Rights Treaties,* available on the website of the OHCHR at <http://www.unhchr.ch> (treaty body mechanisms).

Racism.[3] The purpose of that Conference is (or should be) to take stock of achievement and to define what policies and strategies should be pursued for the future. The World Conference takes place against the unpalatable reality that racism, in all its manifestations, is pervasive in the world. Whether expressed in theories of 'natural' racial hierarchy, or in hostility and violence towards different ethnic groups within multiethnic states, or towards migrants and refugees, racism has not only survived the twentieth century's major idea of human rights but threatens its very achievements.[4]

A review of international human rights approaches to the elimination of racism and racial discrimination must begin with the acknowledgement that the world community is a long way from achieving one component of the basic message of human rights—that of the equal dignity of all human beings. At the outset of the new century, the challenge of securing the right to equality promised in the Charter of the United Nations to all individuals remains unfulfilled. Racism and racial discrimination is but one manifestation of the denial of equality. Sex discrimination that feeds violence against women, the hatred and discrimination suffered by people on grounds of their religion, and the suppression of cultural and linguistic minorities are all global facts. There have been advances. In the context of racism, the most important of the last half-century has been the end of colonialism through the achievement of independence and self-determination for millions of people. Another has been the dismantling of institutionalized white racism in Southern Africa and the United States. But fear and rejection of difference, alongside justifications of inequality in the treatment of human beings based on so-called race, ethnic origin, descent or colour, presents a continuing human rights challenge in all societies.[5]

The United Nations Charter gave as one purpose of the new world organization the achievement of international cooperation 'in promoting and

[3] A United Nations World Conference organized by the High Commissioner for Human Rights is to be held in South Africa from 31 Aug. to 7 Sept. 2001. A website devoted to the preparations of the World Conference can be accessed from the OHCHR home page <http://www.unhchr.ch>. See also Part VI *infra.*

[4] For a powerful and sobering analysis of the challenge of contemporary racism, see Report of the International Council on Human Rights Policy, *The Persistence and Mutation of Racism* (1999).

[5] The dilemma involved in using the term race has exercised many concerned with combating racism and racial discrimination. There is only one human race and there is no scientific biological basis as there was once believed to be for classifying human beings into categories called races. Physiological traits and differences of colour between people do not justify racial classifications. The differences between human beings are a function of different ethnic identities. Nevertheless racism constitutes a set of objectively false beliefs that biological differences do exist between humans that are linked to a racial hierarchy. It is the survival of these beliefs that justify discrimination and subordination of others. However, while it is not impossible to abandon completely the language of race used in the international standards, it is desirable to speak of racial or ethnic discrimination rather than racial discrimination. See further n. 77.

encouraging respect for human rights and fundamental freedoms for all without distinction as to race, sex, language or religion'.[6] The United Nations was to be a 'center for harmonizing the actions of nations in the attainment of these common ends'.[7] At the same time, the potential of the UN was deliberately constrained by the limitation imposed through Article 2(7) of the Charter, excluding intervention by the United Nations in matters 'essentially within the domestic jurisdiction of any state'. It has been on these contradictory foundations that international approach to the protection of human rights have been built over the last fifty years. That approach has involved securing agreement on common global human rights standards and having states accept these standards as binding commitments in international law. A crucial part of the international approaches has been to persuade states to accept international supervision in the implementation of such commitments. In addition, the UN has sought to develop its capacity to respond to serious violation of these international human rights standards through investigation and by creating limited avenues of complaint and redress for victims. But it remains an essential feature of the international human rights system that it is virtually impotent without the support and commitment of states. The central question for the future is how to sustain support and commitment from all countries. Elimination of racial, ethnic, and other types of discrimination, as forms of human rights violation, requires significant social change in most if not all societies. It cannot be achieved solely by the enactment of anti-discrimination laws, important as such laws are. There is little evidence that countries understand the full implications of racial or ethnic equality or are yet ready to embrace the long-term changes necessary to achieve it.

With these thoughts in mind this chapter will consider the origins of the international human rights approaches towards racism and racial discrimination. In addition, it will examine the activities and policies pursued at the international level in countering racism and racial discrimination, as well as the institutions through which such activities and policies have been pursued. A full account of international human rights approaches should embrace regional levels as well. These dimensions are covered elsewhere in the volume and this account will concentrate on the global human rights system developed through the United Nations. However, the need for the future to envisage a greater level of integration of national regional and global human rights approaches to the achievement of equality and non-discrimination will be discussed.

[6] United Nations Charter, Article 1(3). [7] Ibid., Article 1(4).

II. THE SIGNIFICANCE OF THE LANGUAGE OF EQUALITY IN THE UNITED NATIONS CHARTER

International efforts to tackle racism and racial discrimination should be first considered in the context of the UN Charter's endorsement of the principle of human equality. Reference to the human rights language of the UN Charter is often abbreviated to leave out the equally important language of equality. Thus, Article 1(3) of the Charter committed the new international body 'to achieve international cooperation in promoting and encouraging respect for human rights and fundamental freedoms *for all without distinction as to race, sex, language or religion*'.[8]

The revolutionary nature of the Charter was not alone that the promotion and encouragement of human rights was to be one of its purposes, but that that goal embraced all human beings equally 'without distinction as to race, sex, language, or religion'. Language linking the non-discrimination principle with the subject of human rights is to be found throughout the Charter.[9] The rejection of discrimination and the affirmation of the right to equality of treatment in the 1948 Universal Declaration of Human Rights, as well as in all later human rights treaties, underscores that human inclusiveness is a characteristic of the international human rights approach.[10] The early action taken to prepare instruments directed at the elimination of discrimination, in addition to conventions of a general character, is a unique feature of standard setting on human rights at the global level.[11]

Although the dominant approach, after 1945, to the promotion and protection of internationally recognized human rights was to be based on the defence of the rights of individuals, there was also recognition that individuals faced denial of rights because of group characteristics. The distinctions identified in the Charter—race, sex, language, and religion—were at the time seen as the main categories of discrimination or exclusion believed in, practised, and justified throughout the world.

[8] Emphasis added.

[9] See, in addition to Article 1(3), Articles 13(1)(b), 55(c), and 76(c). Other human rights provisions in the Charter are to be found in Articles 62(2) and 68 concerning the functions to be discharged in this field by the Economic and Social Council. See also W. McKean, *Equality and Discrimination under International Law* (1983), at 54–5.

[10] Universal Declaration of Human Rights (UDHR), adopted by GA Res. 217 A (III) (1948). In *International Instruments, supra* n. 2, at 1.

[11] Such early instruments are, for instance, the Convention on the Prevention and Punishment of the Crime of Genocide, GA Res. 260 A (III) (1948); the Convention for the Suppression of the Trafficking in Persons and of the Exploitation of the Prostitution of Others, GA Res. 317 (IV) (1949); the Convention on the Political Rights of Women, GA Res. 640 (VII) (1952); the Supplementary Convention on the Abolition of Slavery, the Slave Trade, and Institutions and Practices Similar to Slavery, GA Res. 608 (XXI) (1956). All in *International Instruments, supra* n. 2, Parts 1 and 2.

The emphasis on equality and the repudiation of discrimination resulted directly from the context in which the United Nations was established. The UN was born in the aftermath of the defeat of Nazism, a racist ideology. The Universal Declaration of Human Rights—the instrument that was to give content to the human rights provisions entrenched in the Charter—was drafted with the perversions of Nazism in mind. The first international human rights convention, the Genocide Convention of 1948, was aimed at stigmatizing as an international crime the ultimate expression of racism, the destruction of national, ethnic, racial, or religious groups.[12] In drafting the Universal Declaration, members of the United Nations Human Rights Commission, while divided over whether the Universal Declaration should be of a binding or declaratory nature, agreed from the outset that prominence was to be given to the principle of equality or the standard of non-discrimination as the starting point of all other liberties.[13] The early establishment of a Sub-Commission on the Prevention of Discrimination and the Protection of Minorities was a crucial reflection of this need for parallel work on the causes and extent of discrimination, as well as the need for new international instruments and standards to combat discrimination.

Article 1 of the Universal Declaration proclaims the positive principle that '[a]ll human beings are born free and equal in dignity and rights'. Article 2 proclaims the entitlement of everyone to the rights and freedoms in the Declaration 'without distinction of any kind such as race, colour, sex, language, religion, political or other opinion, national or social origin, property, birth or other status'. The Declaration thus aimed at the elimination of all forms of discrimination, adding categories not found in the Charter. Article 7 sets forth the principle of equality before the law and the entitlement of all to 'equal protection against any discrimination in violation of this Declaration and against any incitement to such discrimination'.

These principles were also firmly inserted in the subsequent two United Nations Covenants that along with the Universal Declaration of Human Rights make up the International Bill of Human Rights.[14] The two Covenants include a common Article 3 on equality between men and women, as well as prohibitions on discrimination on the grounds first elaborated in Article 2 of the Universal Declaration cited above. In addition, the Civil and Political Covenant in Article 26 sets out a free-standing equality clause based on Article 7 of the Universal Declaration. It was on these foundations, entrenching the norms of equality and non-discrimination, that all other

[12] Ibid., Part 2, at 673.

[13] J. Morsink, *The Universal Declaration of Human Rights: Origins, Drafting and Intent* (1999), at 92–116.

[14] International Covenant on Economic, Social and Cultural Rights (ICESCR) and International Covenant on Civil and Political Rights (ICCPR), both adopted by GA Res. 2200 A (XXI) (1966). In *International Instruments, supra* n. 2, at 8 and 20.

international human rights instruments created through the United Nations and the regional systems have been built.

The commitment to equality of treatment led to specific international instruments on the main types of discrimination aimed at their elimination. Racial and ethnic discrimination was one such field. Sex discrimination was another. The International Convention on the Elimination of All Forms of Racial Discrimination came into force in 1969 and the parallel Convention on the Elimination of Discrimination against Women in 1981.[15] Progress on elaborating standards in respect of victims of religious discrimination or discrimination experienced by cultural minorities, including on such grounds as language, proved more difficult. In 1981, the Declaration on the Elimination of All Forms of Intolerance and Discrimination based on Religion or Belief was adopted by the General Assembly.[16] A decade later, the Declaration on the Rights of Minorities was adopted.[17] In neither case has sufficient consensus been found to transform these texts into legally binding instruments. The claim to equality is a dynamic one and new forms of discrimination have been asserted and progressively recognized. The UN Declaration on the Rights of Disabled People 1975 is one example.[18] The proposed Declaration on the rights of Indigenous Peoples is another, as is the emerging concern with discrimination on grounds of sexual orientation.[19]

The links between different forms of discrimination and intolerance, including the links between racial or ethnic discrimination and other forms of discrimination, need for the future to be made more explicit. That can be achieved through a greater emphasis on the right to equality of treatment as a crosscutting concern in international human rights theory and practice. Such an approach can help to end the relative and unproductive isolation in which different international human rights instruments and mechanisms concerned with discrimination appear to operate.

[15] Convention on the Elimination of All Forms of Discrimination Against Women (CEDAW), GA Res. 34/180 (1979). In ibid., at 150.

[16] GA Res. 36/55 (1981). In ibid., at 122.

[17] Declaration on the Rights of Persons Belonging to National or Ethnic, Religious and Linguistic Minorities, GA Res. 47/135 (1992). In ibid., at 140.

[18] GA Res. 3447 (XXX) (1975). In ibid., Part 2, at 544.

[19] Draft Declaration on the Rights of Indigenous Peoples. E/CN.4/Sub.2/1994/2/Add.1 (1994). Discrimination against homosexuals has not been the subject of specific norms at the United Nations but has been progressively recognized as a prohibited ground of discrimination in many countries. Under the new Protocol 12 to the European Convention on Human Rights (ECHR) which provides for a 'free-standing' prohibition on discrimination, sexual orientation, while not explicitly mentioned, is included. See, Explanatory Report to Protocol 12, Council of Europe, Directorate General of Human Rights 1999, and *Salgueiro da Silva Mouta v Portugal*, European Court of Human Rights, judgment of 21 Dec. 1999.

III. THE CENTRALITY OF RACIAL DISCRIMINATION IN THE DEVELOPMENT OF INTERNATIONAL HUMAN RIGHTS LAW

The challenge of race and racism has had a profound influence on the international human rights protection system created through the United Nations over the last half century. Indeed, it was largely the search for an effective international response to racism that produced the main components of the UN human rights regime. The United Nations was established in the aftermath of the Holocaust. But it was also born at a time of the colonial empires of European powers that were based on explicit assumptions of racial superiority and inferiority. While the United Nations was centrally involved in the achievement of decolonization, in which the colonial powers for the most part cooperated, these same powers were deeply concerned that racial practices in their colonies would face challenge at the international level. The United States, which did not have colonies but did have racial segregation and disenfranchisement of its black minority in its southern states, had similar concerns with international scrutiny.

Opposition from a number of countries to the United Nations having authority to protect human rights (in addition to the function of encouraging and promoting them) stemmed in part from concern over likely scrutiny of domestic policies on race and immigration. Equally, the exclusion of UN involvement in member states' domestic affairs (Article 2(7) of the Charter) was in large part motivated by an unwillingness of such countries as the United States and the United Kingdom to envisage external scrutiny of their racial practices.[20]

(i) Racial Segregation in the United States

The race question was to prove a major factor in shaping US policy towards accession to the international conventions on human rights promoted through the UN. The importance of the human rights and equality language of the UN Charter was quickly seen by opponents of American apartheid. In 1946, a petition was submitted to the UN by the National Negro Congress expressed to be on behalf of 13 million oppressed Negro citizens.[21] In 1947, the National Association for the Advancement of Coloured People (NAACP)

[20] Lauren, 'First Principles of Racial Equality: History and the Politics and Diplomacy of Human Rights Provisions in the United Nations Charter', 5 *HRQ* (1983) 1, at 19.

[21] McDougall, 'Toward a Meaningful International Regime: The Domestic Relevance of International Efforts to Eliminate All Forms of Racial Discrimination', 40 *Howard Law Journal* (1997) 571, at 573.

submitted a similar petition calling for redress.[22] Civil rights lawyers sought to invoke the Charter in domestic challenges to racism with some initial success.[23] In 1950 in *Sei Fuji v State*, a Californian district court of appeal declared a land ownership statute unconstitutional because it discriminated against a Japanese national. The Court relied on the human rights clauses of the Charter in its decision.[24] On appeal, however, the California Supreme Court held that Articles 55 and 56 of the Charter were not self-executing.[25] In an earlier case, also involving discrimination against persons of Japanese origin, the Charter's non-discrimination clauses were raised before the United States Supreme Court.[26] The American Civil Liberties Union argued that the Charter established obligations on the United States government to reject racial discrimination. While the majority of the Court determined the case in favour of the petitioner on other grounds, one judge in a trenchant opinion invoked the Charter and its prohibition of racial discrimination.[27] These cases, although they proved the high water mark of attempts to apply the human rights provisions of the Charter in US courts, did trigger a campaign in the US Congress to restrict the power of the President to enter into human rights treaty commitments. Among the concerns was the likely infringement on the powers of the states and that such treaties would entail international scrutiny of racial segregation. In 1954, the Secretary of State, John Foster Dulles, gave an undertaking to the Senate that the US would not join any international human rights treaty.[28] It has only been in the 1990s that the US has ratified some of the international human rights treaties, including the International Convention on the Elimination of Racial Discrimination.[29]

(ii) South Africa and Apartheid

Notwithstanding the Great Powers' intentions, the race question burst on to the international level at an early point. The coming to power of the

[22] Janken, 'From Colonial Liberation to Cold War Liberalism: Walter White, NAACP and Foreign Affairs, 1941–1955', 21 *Ethnic and Racial Studies* (1998) 1074, at 1982.

[23] Lockwood, 'The United Nations Charter and United States Civil Rights Litigation: 1946–1955', 69 *Iowa Law Rev.* (1984) 900.

[24] 217 P.2d 481 (Cal.Dist.Ct.App. 1950).

[25] 38 Cal.2d 718 (1952). The Court held the Alien Land Act unconstitutional as a violation of the 14th Amendment. Article 56 UN Charter proclaims that '[a]ll Members pledge themselves to take joint and separate action in cooperation with the Organization for the achievement of the purposes set forth in Article 55.' Article 55(c) states that the UN shall promote 'universal respect for, and observance of, human rights and fundamental freedoms for all without distinction as to race, sex, language or religion'.

[26] *Oyama v California*, 332 US 633 (1948).

[27] Lockwood, *supra* n. 23, at 919.

[28] F. Newman and D. Weissbrodt, *International Human Rights Law Policy and Process* (1996), at 34–5.

[29] The US ratified ICERD on 21 Oct. 1994. See *Status of Ratifications, supra* n. 2.

Nationalist Government in the Republic of South Africa in 1948 with an avowedly racist policy of apartheid, and the racist policies in Southern Rhodesia, South West Africa, and the Portuguese colonies, presented the first human rights challenges to the new United Nations.

As early as 1946, when a complaint was lodged by the Indian Government over the treatment of persons of Indian descent in South Africa, that country's racial policies were on the agenda of the major United Nations organs.[30] It was not, however, until 1952 that the 'question of race conflict in South Africa resulting from the policies of apartheid of the Government of the Union of South Africa' was first discussed at the General Assembly. Overruling vehement objection from South Africa that the matter fell essentially within its domestic jurisdiction, the General Assembly voted to establish an ad hoc commission to study the racial situation in South Africa.[31] Reports of the ad hoc commission found that South Africa's racial policies were contrary to the United Nations Charter human rights provisions. The General Assembly noted these findings with 'concern'[32] and 'apprehension'.[33] It was to progressively adopt ever stronger language in condemnation of South Africa's racist policies over the following years.[34]

The resolutions passed by the General Assembly, based on the findings of the ad hoc commission, asserted the right to condemn, and to demand rectification of, breaches of the human rights provisions of the Charter.[35] In particular, the General Assembly determined that governmental policies not directed towards racial equality were inconsistent with Articles 55 and 56 of the Charter.[36] After the outrage provoked by the Sharpeville massacre in 1960, the Security Council joined the General Assembly in condemning South Africa's racial policy, holding implicitly that human rights provisions of the Charter prevailed over the domestic jurisdiction clause.[37] The International Court of Justice upheld the view that the Charter's human rights provisions, far from being simple statements of morality, laid down binding obligations for member states. The challenge of racism played a decisive role in this development. The legal and binding character of the non-discrimination norm enshrined in the

[30] Lauren, *supra* n. 20, at 24.

[31] GA Res. 616A (VII) (1952).

[32] GA Res. 721 (VIII) (1953).

[33] GA Res. 820 (IX) (1954).

[34] GA Res. 917 (X) (1955), Res. 1178 (XII) (1957), Res. 1248 (XIII) (1958), Res. 1375 (XIV) (1959). An overview of the General Assembly's early resolutions on South Africa is to be found in Dugard, 'The Legal Effect of United Nations Resolutions on Apartheid', 83 *South African Journal of International Law* (1966) 44, at 44–5.

[35] On the gradual restriction by the General Assembly of states' domestic jurisdiction, see Cassese, 'The General Assembly: Historical Perspective 1945–1989', in P. Alston (ed.), *The United Nations and Human Rights—A Critical Appraisal* (1992) 25, at 32–4. Also R. Higgins, *The Development of International Law Through the Political Organs of the United Nations* (1963), at 58–130.

[36] See *supra* n. 25 for the text of Articles 55 and 56 UN Charter.

[37] Res. S/4300 (1960). On the Sharpeville massacre see further below.

Charter was first tested with respect to the policy and practice of apartheid and racial discrimination.[38] In the *Namibia* case, the International Court of Justice held that racism and racial discrimination constituted a total negation of the purposes and principles of the Charter.[39] It is now established in international law that the prohibition of racial discrimination exists independently of the general obligation to respect human rights and is part of *ius cogens*.[40]

From the 1960s onwards, as a result of the pressure of the newly independent African and Asian countries, which had gained the majority of votes in the General Assembly, critical discussion of apartheid policy gave way to concrete, and over the years successful, attempts at imposing sanctions on South Africa.[41] Condemnation of apartheid led to the adoption, in 1973, of the Convention on the Suppression and Punishment of the Crime of Apartheid.[42] The General Assembly followed this in 1985, with the adoption of the Convention Against Apartheid in Sports.[43]

[38] See the dissenting opinion of Judge Tanaka in the *South West Africa* cases (Second Phase), who referred to Article 55(c) of the Charter to demonstrate that the rule of non-discrimination 'can be regarded as a source of international law'. ICJ Reports (1966), at 293.

[39] The Court stated that 'to enforce distinctions, exclusions, restrictions and limitations exclusively based on grounds of race, color, descent or national or ethnic origin which constitute a denial of fundamental human rights is a flagrant violation of the purposes and principles of the Charter . . .'. *Legal Consequences for States of the Continued Presence of South Africa in Namibia (South West Africa) notwithstanding Security Council Resolution 276 (1970)*, ICJ Reports (1971) 3, at 57. One year before, in *Barcelona Traction, Light & Power Co.*, the Court had referred to the outlawing of, *inter alia*, racial discrimination as obligation *erga omnes*. ICJ Reports (1970), at 3. See Rodley, 'Human Rights and Humanitarian Intervention: the Case Law of the World Court', 38 *ICLQ* (1989) 321, at 321–33.

[40] In 1986, the US (Third) Restatement of the Foreign Relations Law recognized that systematic racial discrimination constitutes a violation of peremptory norms of customary international law. Restatement (Third) § 702, n. 11 (1986).

[41] The first resolution by the General Assembly to call on states to break off diplomatic and economic relations with South Africa was voted in 1962 (Res. 1761 (XVII)). The same resolution requested the Security Council to take appropriate measures and, if necessary, to consider the expulsion of South Africa from the United Nations. A year later the Security Council recommended to the member states an arms boycott against South Africa (SC Res. 181 (1963)). The General Assembly thereafter repeatedly stated that the apartheid policy constituted a threat to international peace and, as early as 1973, it had suspended South Africa from participating in the work of the Organization. The Security Council's endorsement came after much hesitation in 1977 when it imposed sanctions by a binding decision acting under Chapter VII, thus characterizing apartheid as a threat to international peace in the sense of Article 39 of the Charter (SC Res. 418 (1977)). On the international legal and political aspects of apartheid, see Delbrueck, 'Apartheid', in R. Wolfrum (ed.), *United Nations: Law, Politics and Practice* (1995) i, 27, at 34–8.

[42] GA Res. 3068 (XXVIII) (1973). In *International Instruments*, *supra* n. 2, at 80. Article I(1) declares that apartheid is a 'crime against humanity' and a 'serious threat to international peace and security'. The Convention met objections particularly on the part of Western states because it was said that the vague language used in the definition of various crimes contained in the Convention did not meet the standards required by the rule of law. Delbrueck, *supra* n. 41, at 36.

[43] GA Res. 40/64 (1985). In *International Instruments*, *supra* n. 2, at 87.

Support in the General Assembly for action against apartheid and racial discrimination in Southern Africa brought a further and least expected change of policy with respect to domestic jurisdiction. This concerned the treatment of petitions from individuals over human rights violations. From the outset, it had been the position of the Commission on Human Rights—the body set up by the Economic and Social Council (ECOSOC) under Article 68 of the Charter with the task of promoting human rights—that it had no power to respond to the stream of petitions over human rights violations throughout the world received at the UN.[44] This policy suited the colonial powers and the United States precisely because of the issue of race. It also suited the Soviet Union, which was equally reluctant that the repressive policies pursued by Stalin would be ventilated on the international stage.[45] The Soviet Union, however, was prepared to support as part of the ideological contest the initiative of the African countries to change the Commission's practice on responding to complaints. What both the African countries and the Soviet Union had in mind was racism and colonialism in Southern Africa. In the event, the ECOSOC Resolutions 1235 and 1503, which created the mechanisms for responding to violations, were expressed to be primarily focused on apartheid and racial discrimination.[46] But the language adopted crucially provided for competence to consider violations of human rights *wherever they may occur.*[47] It was on these foundations that the competence of the Commission on Human Rights and its Sub-Commission to respond to gross violations of human rights in the world has developed.[48] One response of the Commission has been to establish special rapporteurs on specific themes of violation. One such is the Special Rapporteur on Contemporary Forms of Racism and Related Intolerance appointed in 1993 whose role is discussed below.

[44] What is known as the '1947 Doctrine', following the Commission on Human Rights adoption, at its first session in 1947, of a self-denying rule to the effect that it would take no action on individual human rights complaints. See ECOSOC Res. 75 (V). This rule was reaffirmed in 1959 by ECOSOC Res. 728 F (XXVIII).

[45] Alston, 'The Commission on Human Rights', in Alston, *supra* n. 35, 126, at 141.

[46] ECOSOC Res. 1235 (XLII) (1967) authorized the Commission and its Sub-Commission to 'examine information relevant to gross violations of human rights and fundamental freedoms, as exemplified by the policy of apartheid as practised by the Republic of South Africa . . . and racial discrimination as practised notably in Southern Rhodesia . . . and to make a thorough study of situations which reveal a consistent pattern of violation of human rights, and report, with recommendations thereon, to the Economic and Social Council . . .'. ECOSOC Res. 1503 (XLVIII) (1970) devises a greatly improved procedure for handling complaints from individuals and non-governmental organizations which appear to reveal a consistent pattern of gross and reliably attested violations of human rights.

[47] See GA Res. 2144 (XXI) (1966), which invited the Council and the Commission 'to give urgent consideration to ways and means of improving the capacity of the United Nations to put a stop to violations of human rights *wherever they occur*' (emphasis added).

[48] For an extensive study of the development of these non-treaty procedures, see Alston, *supra* n. 45, at 126–210.

(iii) The Pioneering Studies of the Sub-Commission on Prevention of Discrimination and Protection of Minorities

A crucial role in the development of international human rights law and its implementation was played by the Sub-Commission on the Prevention of Discrimination and the Protection of Minorities.[49] The Sub-Commission was set up in 1947 as an advisory body to the Commission on Human Rights.[50] The Commission from its inception was riven by bloc-voting and by the refusal of state delegates to allow their country or other members to be criticized. Members of the Sub-Commission, appointed as independent experts and—at least in theory—less vulnerable to political pressure, proved more willing to act as a human rights body. After contributing to the drafting of the anti-discrimination provisions of the Universal Declaration of Human Rights, the Sub-Commission turned its attention to implementation and enforcement action. Early attempts to pursue an active policy in this respect were, however, challenged by the Commission and ECOSOC. The Sub-Commission thereafter focused on research and standard setting particularly in the field of discrimination.[51]

While the subject of sex discrimination was taken on by the Commission on the Status of Women, the Sub-Commission conducted and forwarded to the Commission on Human Rights a number of studies on the problems of discrimination in other fields. The first such study concerned discrimination in education and became the basis of UNESCO's 1960 Convention on the same subject.[52] A study on discrimination in employment and occupation

[49] On the crucial role played by the Sub-Commission in its early years, see Humphrey, 'The United Nations Sub-Commission on the Prevention of Discrimination and the Protection of Minorities', 62 *AJIL* (1968) 869. For an overview on its more recent activities, see Koufa, 'Elimination of Racial Discrimination and the Role of the United Nations Sub-Commission on Prevention of Discrimination and Protection of Minorities', 10 *International Geneva Yearbook* (1996) 44. See also Eide, 'The Sub-Commission on Prevention of Discrimination and Protection of Minorities', in Alston, *supra* n. 35, at 211–64; McKean, *supra* n. 9, at 72–81.

[50] The Sub-Commission was authorized to 'undertake studies, particularly in the light of the Universal Declaration on Human Rights, and to make recommendations to the Commission on Human Rights concerning the prevention of discrimination of any kind relating to human rights and fundamental freedoms and the protection of racial, national, religious and linguistic minorities', *Report of the Commission on Human Rights*, UN Doc. E/1371 (1949).

[51] The difficult relation in the early years of the UN between the Sub-Commission and its referent bodies is well captured in the comment by a notable author that the 'crime of the Sub-Commission was that it had taken its job too seriously'. Humphrey, *supra* n. 49, at 875.

[52] *Study of Discrimination in Education*, by Charles D. Ammoun, appointed Special Rapporteur of the Sub-Commission. UN Doc. E/CN.4/Sub.2/181/Rev.1 (1957). For the UNESCO Convention against Discrimination in Education (1960), see *International Instruments*, *supra* n. 2, at 101.

was entrusted to the International Labour Organization. That also led to an important Convention.[53] Other studies were on discrimination in political rights,[54] on religious rights and practices,[55] on emigration and the right to return,[56] and on racial discrimination in political, economic, social, and cultural fields.[57] These studies were acted upon by the Commission on Human Rights and provided much of the basis for international instruments subsequently adopted in the field of discrimination. This early work of the Sub-Commission was also of enduring value for its analysis of different aspects of discrimination and its development of such concepts as that of indirect discrimination, justified distinctions, and special or positive measures.[58] These concepts were later incorporated in the anti-discrimination treaties.

Although its mandate and functions have considerably expanded, in recent years the Sub-Commission has continued to contribute significantly to work on equality and non-discrimination.[59] Its study on the exploitation of labour through illicit and clandestine trafficking, completed in 1975, led to the International Convention on the Protection of the Rights of All Migrant Workers and Members of Their Families, adopted in 1990.[60]

[53] ILO Convention (No. 111) Concerning Discrimination in Respect of Employment and Occupation (1958). In ibid., at 96.

[54] *Study of Discrimination in the Matter of Political Rights*, rapporteur Hernan Santa Cruz. UN Doc. E/CN.4/Sub.2/213/Rev.1 (1962).

[55] *Study of Discrimination in the Matter of Religious Rights and Practices*, rapporteur Arcot Krishnaswami. UN Doc. E/CN.4/Sub.2/200/Rev.1 (1960). This study sharply divided the Commission and despite the General Assembly's decision that there should follow a declaration and a convention on the elimination of religious intolerance, the first saw the light in the 1980s, while the latter never came into existence.

[56] *Study of Discrimination in Respect to the Right of Everyone to Leave Any Country, Including his Own, and to Return to his Country*, rapporteur José D. Inglés. UN Doc. E/CN.4/Sub.220/Rev.1 (1963). Interestingly, the Sub-Commission's intention to include in this study the controversial question of immigration was not accepted by the Council. Humphrey, *supra* n. 49, at 880.

[57] *Special Study of Racial Discrimination in the Political, Economic, Social and Cultural Spheres*, rapporteur Hernan Santa Cruz. UN Doc. E/CN.4/Sub.2/267 (1966).

[58] McKean, *supra* n. 9, at 94–6.

[59] To acknowledge the Sub-Commission's considerably expanded mandate, ECOSOC recently renamed it 'Sub-Commission on Promotion and Protection of Human Rights'. Dec. 1999/256 of 27 July 1999.

[60] GA Res. 45/158 (1990). In *International Instruments*, *supra* n. 2, Part 2, at 554. Further examples include the report on the rights of persons belonging to ethnic, religious, and linguistic minorities, conducted by Mr Capotorti and completed in 1977, that led to the 1992 UN Declaration on minorities, *supra* n. 17. The study of problems of discrimination against indigenous populations, conducted by Mr Eide in 1983, together with the pioneering work of the Sub-Commission's working group on the indigenous populations, resulted in the draft Declaration on the Rights of Indigenous Peoples, that is currently being considered for adoption by the Commission on Human Rights, *supra* n. 19.

(iv) Standard Setting and Racial Discrimination

As already noted, the late 1950s and early 1960s saw a growing number of newly independent countries taking seats at the United Nations, determined to see the development of new procedures to combat apartheid and racism. The Sub-Commission, as a result, became increasingly concerned with racial discrimination. In 1960, South Africa provoked a horrified international response when its police massacred sixty-nine peaceful protesters in the black township of Sharpeville. In the same year, widespread anti-Semitic incidents in West Germany and other parts of the world provoked a sharp reaction by the Sub-Commission, which was in session. It took the initiative—unprecedented in the UN subsidiary bodies—of adopting a resolution condemning these manifestations of anti-Semitism.[61] In the wake of these events, the need to put in place an effective instrument to combat racial discrimination as well as religious intolerance was widely shared and gave rise to a decision by the General Assembly to draft a declaration to be followed by a convention.[62] The intention had been to draft an instrument embracing both religious and racial discrimination. No consensus could, however, be reached in the Third Committee with regard to religious issues and it was eventually decided to aim at two different instruments, one dealing with religious discrimination and intolerance and one with racial discrimination.[63] The opposition to a joint instrument came from some of the Arab delegations, and the Soviet and Eastern Europe states. Arab countries were concerned over the inclusion of anti-Semitism lest it might be read as a recognition of the state of Israel. The Soviet Union for its own reasons was not prepared to have religious discrimination included but did want a focus on race.[64] Acrimonious controversy over the question of anti-Semitism as constituting racial as well as religious prejudice resurfaced in the Third Committee during the drafting of the Race Convention. As one source of the initiative to draft a Convention had been the outbreak of anti-Semitism some delegations, led by the United States, sought to have a specific reference condemning anti-Semitism, as well as

[61] UN Doc. E/CN.4/Sub.2/L.214. Humphrey, *supra* n. 49, at 882.

[62] Literature outlining the history of the adoption of the Race Convention is consistent in tracing its origins back to the events described above. See, among others, Schwelb, 'The International Convention on the Elimination of All Forms of Racial Discrimination', 15 *ICLQ* (1966) 998, at 997–1000. Meron, 'The Meaning and Reach of the International Convention on the Elimination of All Forms of Racial Discrimination', 79 *AJIL* (1985) 283, at 285–6.

[63] Sensitivity over religion had already emerged as a result of the study of discrimination in religious rights and practices conducted by the Sub-Commission's rapporteur, Arcot Krishnaswami, and submitted to the Commission on Human Rights in 1960. See *supra* n. 55.

[64] Schwelb, *supra* n. 62, at 999. Also, N. Lerner, *Group Rights and Discrimination in International Law* (1991), at 46.

apartheid.[65] While a number of delegations did refer in speeches to the Holocaust, Arab political sensitivities resulted in the reference being dropped. But not before the Soviet Union submitted a draft that would have added also a condemnation of Zionism and Nazism.[66]

While controversy over religious issues stranded for more than twenty years a parallel declaration on religious discrimination, the Declaration on the Elimination of Racial Discrimination followed speedily in 1963.[67] It was followed two years later by the Convention on the Elimination of All Forms of Racial Discrimination. That treaty marked the real beginning of the international protection of individual human rights. The UN had begun the treaty approach to combating human rights violations in 1948 with the Genocide Convention, but no progress could be made on the establishment of any international mechanism for the Convention's enforcement. ICERD had enforcement provisions including a procedure for individuals to complain against states, a breakthrough that stemmed from the Sub-Commission.[68] ICERD set an important precedent. It cleared the way for the later adoption of the International Covenants and the development of procedures for monitoring the extent of states' compliance with their human rights treaty obligations.

IV. THE INTERNATIONAL CONVENTION ON THE ELIMINATION OF ALL FORMS OF RACIAL DISCRIMINATION

The centrepiece of the international human rights approach to combating racism and racial discrimination is the International Covenant on the Elimination of All Forms of Racial Discrimination 1966 (ICERD). The Convention entered into force on 4 January 1969 and has therefore now been in force for over three decades. It was, until 1993, when it was overtaken by the Convention on the Rights of the Child, the most widely ratified international human rights treaty.[69]

[65] Schwelb, *supra* n. 62, at 1011–14.

[66] Such manœuvres, culminating in the condemnation of Zionism by a resolution of the General Assembly in 1975, have dogged the United Nations over the years and have damaged its credibility considerably. See van Boven, 'United Nations Strategies to Combat Racism and Racial Discrimination: A Sobering but not Hopeless Balance Sheet', in M. Castermans *et al.* (eds), *The Role of the Nation-State in the 21st Century* (1998) 251, at 253 and n. 236 *infra*.

[67] United Nations Declaration on the Elimination of All Forms of Racial Discrimination, GA Res. 1904 (XVIII) (1963). In *International Instruments, supra* n. 2, at 61.

[68] 'the first basic plan for the implementation of the convention was suggested by Judge José Inglés in the Sub-Commission. Had he not taken this initiative, it is unlikely that the General Assembly would ever have adopted measures for implementation of the convention', Humphrey, *supra* n. 49, at 883.

[69] 157 states are to date party to the Convention. See *supra* n. 2 for the status of ratification of the main international human rights treaties.

In assessing the impact of the Convention and its future potential the ideological and political context of its birth requires to be kept in mind. The Convention's provisions, although expressed to be concerned with the elimination of all forms of racial discrimination in all countries, sought at the same time to target colour discrimination and colonialism, in line with the wishes of its African and Soviet sponsors. Thus, the Convention condemns doctrines of racial superiority and singles out apartheid in South Africa, as well as segregation between white and black practised in the European colonies and the United States.[70] The monitoring body established under the Convention, the Committee on the Elimination of Racial Discrimination (hereinafter 'CERD'), was also given a function under Article 15 to comment upon petitions alleging racial discrimination received from the inhabitants of Trust and Non-Self Governing Territories by the Committee on Decolonization.[71]

The tension between the immediate concern with colonialism and apartheid and the objective of universal elimination of all forms of racial and ethnic discrimination finds reflection in the language of the Convention as well as in its interpretation, by both states parties and the Committee. It is a tension that has persisted over the history of the ICERD. The assumption that racism was solely about the consequences of Western imperialism inevitably placed the Convention in a fraught political environment. The other human rights treaties that followed ICERD had also to function in the Cold War years, but none had to function in quite such an emotional and ideological environment as had ICERD.

The ICERD was the prototype for the later international human rights conventions in its scheme of implementation.[72] In addition to fulfilling obligations at the domestic level, states undertake to report periodically to CERD on 'legislative, judicial, administrative or other measures' undertaken to fulfil the Convention's requirements.[73] The Convention scheme of implementation also provides for an inter-state and an individual complaint procedure. However, to date the main vehicle of implementation of the Convention, as with the other international instruments, is through state reporting, and the main activity of CERD is, and has been, the examination of such reports in conjunction with the states parties. Experience with these

[70] As noted above, the serious issue of the resurgence of anti-Semitism was sidelined for political reasons.

[71] For reasons of space this account will not consider the Committee's limited functions under Article 15. With the virtual achievement of decolonization, this always marginal duty of the CERD has accordingly dwindled. See Partsch, 'The Committee on the Elimination of Racial Discrimination', in Alston, *supra* n. 35, 339, at 348.

[72] On the treaty system as a whole, see P. Alston and J. Crawford (eds), *The Future of UN Human Rights Treaty Monitoring* (2000).

[73] Article 9(1) ICERD.

implementation procedures is discussed below as part of an analysis of the work of the Committee. But before considering implementation, the substantive provisions of the Convention require to be set out.

(i) The Definition of Racial Discrimination

At the time of the Convention's adoption most states understood racism politically, applying to cases such as the treatment of the black population of the USA, apartheid in South Africa, and to practices associated with colonialism. The general definition of racial discrimination in ICERD, however, does not focus exclusively on such state policies and practices. It covers all acts of discrimination based on motivations of a racial nature, including acts of individuals or groups, and calls the state to account whenever such activities impinge, either currently or potentially, upon the enjoyment of fundamental human rights.

The drafters of the Convention followed closely the definition of discrimination adopted by the ILO and UNESCO in the Conventions that dealt with discrimination in employment and education, respectively.[74] Article 1(1) defines racial discrimination as

> [a]ny distinction, exclusion, restriction or preference based on race, colour, descent, or national or ethnic origin which has the purpose or effect of nullifying or impairing the recognition, enjoyment or exercise, on an equal footing, of human rights and fundamental freedoms in the political, economic, social, cultural or any other field of public life.

The definition is concerned with racial discrimination, not racism as such. Doctrines of racial superiority, however, are condemned in the Convention.[75] Such doctrines at the time were based on biological theories that divided humankind into racial categories according to supposed genetic differences.[76] The efforts undertaken in the post-war era to discredit doctrines of racial

[74] The ILO Discrimination (Employment and Occupation) Convention No. 111 (1958), Article 1(a) defines 'discrimination' as including '[a]ny distinction, exclusion or preference made on the basis of race, colour, sex, religion, political opinion, national extraction or social origin, which has the effect of nullifying or impairing equality of opportunity or treatment in employment or occupation', *supra* n. 53. The UNESCO Convention against Discrimination in Education (1960), Article 1, defines 'discrimination' as including 'any distinction, exclusion, limitation or preference which, being based on race, colour, sex, language, religion, political or other opinion, national or social origin, economic condition or birth, has the purpose or effect of nullifying or impairing equality of treatment in education . . .', *supra* n. 52.

[75] See ICERD preambular para. 6 and Article 4.

[76] Racism as a systematic and rationalized hostility based on biological differences is a nineteenth-century phenomenon (Gobineau's *Essay on the Inequality of Human Races* appeared in 1854). See M. Banton, *International Action Against Racial Discrimination* (1996), at 52.

superiority as scientifically false were successful, but did not solve the question as to the nature of difference. Thus, the concept of race, a concept that is at odds with the idea of human unity that the UN intended to promote, survives.[77] While the concept of race could not be dropped altogether from the ICERD definition, it was broadened to include the core mischiefs at which the struggle against racism is aimed—discrimination based on colour, descent, national and ethnic origin.[78] Colour tackles discrimination based on physical criteria. 'Descent', a term unique to ICERD, has been interpreted to include the notion of caste and denotes social origin, while 'national or ethnic origin' refers to prejudice that stems from linguistic, cultural, and historical differences.[79] The definition is thus not limited to objective physical characteristics. It also captures subjective as well as socio-economic variables connected with racism. The definition is capable of addressing past, present, and future expressions of racism: be it white supremacism, casteism, ethnonationalism or what is called neo-racism, a version which no longer presupposes biological difference but emphasizes allegedly insurmountable differences between cultures. It also protects every group that has a defined collective identity and for the purpose of which self-identification is the relevant criterion.[80]

[77] Efforts at UN level to discredit doctrines of racial superiority started as early as 1948, when ECOSOC requested that the UNESCO develop a programme to disseminate scientific facts that would counter commonly held racial prejudices (ECOSOC Res. 116 (VI) B(iii)). UNESCO contributed with its work from the 1950s to the 1970s by convening committees of prominent scientists who were asked to discuss the racial problem and to make known the scientific facts about race. These efforts led to four statements on the concept of race (reprinted in the Encyclopedia of Human Rights (1996) 2nd edn. at 1215–23) and culminated in the adoption, in 1978, of the UNESCO Declaration on Race and Racial Prejudice, which states in the strongest terms that '[a]ll human beings belong to a single species . . . any theory which involves the claim that racial or ethnic groups are inherently superior . . . has no scientific foundation and is contrary to the moral and ethical principles of humanity'. In *International Instruments, supra* n. 2, at 132.

[78] During debates in the Sub-Commission it became clear that 'while, as UNESCO had shown, there was no such thing as race, the term "race" would have to be used in the draft convention', Lerner, *supra* n. 64, at 49.

[79] While the words 'colour', 'descent', and 'ethnic origin' did not represent major difficulties, a serious problem arose with regard to the term 'national origin' due to it being widely used as relating to nationality or citizenship. To avoid any misinterpretation, paragraphs 2 and 3 were added to Article 1 excluding distinctions between citizens and non-citizens from the ambit of the definition, ibid., at 49.

[80] See CERD General Recommendation VIII (38th session, 1990): '[T]he ways in which individuals are identified as being members of a particular racial or ethnic group . . . shall, if no justification exists to the contrary, be based upon self-identification by the individual concerned.' Thus, as a general rule, a group's consciousness of its own separate identity determines whether it is a 'race' for the purposes of the Convention's protections.

(ii) The Scope of the Convention's Substantive Provisions

The Convention's provisions are far-reaching. It obliges states 'to pursue by all appropriate means and without delay a policy of eliminating racial discrimination in all its forms and promoting understanding among races' (Article 2(1)). This general goal is then developed by reference to five objectives for the achievement of which states parties are required

- not to engage directly, or through their public institutions at all levels, in acts or practices of racial discrimination;
- not to sponsor, defend, or support racial discrimination by any persons or organizations;
- to amend, rescind, or nullify legislation which creates or perpetuates racial discrimination;
- to prohibit, by all appropriate means, racial discrimination by any persons, group, or organization;
- to encourage the elimination of barriers through integrationalist multiracial organizations and movements and discourage anything which tends to strengthen racial division.[81]

The prohibition of racial discrimination covers the full range of rights including civil, political, economic, social, and cultural rights. It includes rights pertaining to the private sphere, such as marriage, inheritance, as well as freedom of thought, conscience, and religion—a unique feature in those early days of standard setting.[82] The scope of Article 5, containing a non-exhaustive list of these rights, had to be clarified to allay apprehensions of states entering these obligations. The obligations of the states parties did not refer to the granting of these rights, but only to admitting no racial discrimination in their enjoyment to the extent that they were guaranteed in the domestic law of the states parties.[83] To ensure equality under the law and to guarantee effective protection, Article 6 calls for courts and other state institutions to provide for just and adequate reparation or satisfaction for any damage suffered as a result of racial discrimination.

A number of provisions were, and still are, considered radical in their application and attracted a high number of reservations. Assuring states parties' compliance has proven particularly difficult with regard to Article 4 requiring

[81] Article 2(1)(a)–(e) ICERD.

[82] On the drafting history of the substantive provisions of ICERD, see Partsch, 'Elimination of Racial Discrimination in the Enjoyment of Civil and Political Rights', 14 *Texas International Law Journal* (1979) 191.

[83] The Committee debated this issue extensively in 1973, adopting a statement for inclusion in its Report to the General Assembly. See Buergenthal, 'Implementing the UN Racial Convention', 12 *Texas International Law Journal* (1977) 187, at 207.

the prohibition and criminalization of hate speech and the suppression of organizations that incite racial hatred.[84] Article 4 has long been considered by CERD as the key article of the Convention.[85] It recognizes the power of hate propaganda to foster prejudice and racial discrimination. However, the assumption that ideas generate attitudes which can be dispelled mainly by legislation is arguably contradicted by the Convention itself, when it requires states to combat prejudices that lead to racial discrimination through measures in the fields of teaching, education, culture, and information (Article 7). The focus to date in the practice of the Committee on the duty of states to legislate to combat racial discrimination may account for its almost total neglect of Article 7. Yet the latter is the key provision under the scheme of the Convention if states are to address the root causes of racism.[86]

Unsurprisingly, a great deal of the Committee's early efforts to ensure compliance concentrated on what was the priority on the UN's human rights agenda and embodied in Article 3 of the Convention, the condemnation of apartheid and racial segregation. This resulted in the sometimes controversial practice of states being requested to submit information on political matters, i.e. regarding the status of their diplomatic, economic, and other relations with South Africa.[87]

(a) Justified Distinctions: The Case of Non-nationals

The Convention allows for distinctions to be made between citizens and non-citizens (Article 1(2)) and gives due regard to state sovereignty in matters of citizenship, nationality, and naturalization, provided states do not discriminate against categories of foreigners (Article 1(3)). However, other articles have been interpreted to ensure that non-citizens are not completely unprotected under the Convention. CERD's practice therefore has been to construe Article 1(2) narrowly.[88] The inclusion of non-citizens within the reach of Article 4 has never been disputed nor that equality before the law must be guaranteed to 'everyone' without distinction as to race or ethnic

[84] A conspicuous number of reservations and/or declarations were entered in respect of Article 4 by states acceding to the Convention. The issue is discussed further below.

[85] See CERD General Recommendation XV (42nd session, 1993), reiterating that '[w]hen [ICERD] was being adopted, Article 4 was seen as central to the struggle against racial discrimination.'

[86] See Farrior, 'The Neglected Pillar: The "Teaching Tolerance" Provision of the International Convention on the Elimination of All Forms of Racial Discrimination', 5 *Journal of International and Comparative Law* (1999) 291.

[87] See CERD General Recommendation III (6th session, 1972). The practice of asking states parties to report under Article 9(1) on their relations with South Africa had been formally endorsed by the General Assembly, which had been pursuing a policy of isolating South Africa since 1962. See *supra* n. 41, and Buergenthal, *supra* n. 83, at 195.

[88] Mahalic and Malahic, 'The Limitation Provisions of the International Convention for the Elimination of All Forms of Racial Discrimination', 9 *HRQ* (1987) 74, at 75.

origin (Article 5). The distinction established in Article 1(2) should have no impact on the implementation of Article 6 and access to remedies. The fact that many non-nationals, such as immigrants, are visibly different from the majority of the population makes them easier targets of racial discrimination and racism. The Convention would be undermined if the protections it affords did not extend to such categories of people.

CERD has recognized that states have the sovereign right to impose distinctions between citizens and non-citizens insofar as their purpose or effect contains no element of discrimination based on race, colour, descent, or national or ethnic origin.[89] It has also held that Article 1(2) 'must not be interpreted to detract in any way from the rights and freedoms recognized and enunciated in other [human rights] instruments . . .'.[90] CERD has been consistent in asking states to report on the status of non-citizens, particularly migrant workers and refugees, who usually belong to a single ethnic group and face hostility, contempt, and social and economic ostracism. Although CERD has no authority under Article 1(2) to require states parties to guarantee non-citizens rights comparable to those enjoyed by citizens, the social inclusion of migrants is pivotal in combating racism and xenophobia. Migrant workers suffer discrimination even when protective legislation is devised for them and their sense of security is seriously endangered by the threat of expulsion common to all aliens. Despite the many instruments adopted at international level to promote their rights and protect them from abuse, there is a stark reluctance to tackle discrimination against migrant workers.[91] None of the instruments has reached a significant number of ratifications and, most disconcertingly, are ignored by the main immigrant-receiving countries—the affluent Western countries.

The treatment of refugees has been discussed primarily under the ambit of Article 1(3). Committee members have asked for statistical breakdowns by race and country of origin of refugees having applied for, been granted, lost, or been refused asylum or citizenship. There have also been inquiries con-

[89] Ibid., at 76.

[90] CERD General Recommendation XI on non-citizens (42nd session, 1993), para. 3. Under international standards of human rights, justified distinctions between citizens and non-citizens are limited. With regard to the non-discrimination standards under ICCPR, see Human Rights Committee General Comment 15 on the position of aliens under the Covenant (27th session, 1986), para. 2: 'The general rule is that each one of the rights of the Covenant must be guaranteed without discrimination between citizens and aliens.'

[91] International protection for migrants is provided by ILO Convention No. 97 (revised) on Migration for Employment and ILO Convention No. 143 on Migrant Workers (Supplementary Provisions). Neither has been widely ratified. The International Convention on the Rights of All Migrant Workers and Members of Their Families, adopted by the General Assembly in 1990, provides more extensive rights than the ILO Conventions, but has not yet entered into force. For the status of ratification of this latter Convention, see Report of the Secretary-General, A/55/205 (2000).

cerning refugees' rehabilitation and resettlement programmes as well as measures to defuse racial tensions resulting from the presence of refugees.[92] States parties' restrictive immigration and asylum policies, including visa systems and other measures aimed at curbing illegal immigration, have been reviewed under this provision. The CERD has sought to assess their disparate impact on people, such as people of colour, or whether discrimination against refugees based on their country of origin was involved. Despite many evident abuses the Committee has been constrained in its criticism.[93] There has also been a reluctance to question naturalization laws, where they grant citizens of favoured nations preferential treatment. Denial to access to citizenship is, however, frequently directed against ethnic minorities, even when legislation does not say so. The absence of clear international norms on acquisition of citizenship complicates the problem considerably.[94] There is scope under the Convention for calling on states to facilitate naturalization of non-nationals as a means of combating prejudices. These are fostered by the legal status of longstanding residents from ethnic or other minority groups as second-class citizens. There is also a need to support and create more opportunities for legal migration and ensuring that international human rights standards are integrated into immigration and asylum policies and practices.

(b) Equality in Fact: Special Measures and Affirmative Action Under the Convention

Racial equality is a free-standing right in the Convention, extending to all human rights and fundamental freedoms, whatever their source.[95] The special feature of the Convention is that it promotes not only equality in law but also equality in fact, in order to allow different ethnic, racial, and national groups the same social development. The goal of *de facto* equality is reflected in several provisions of the Convention, calling for 'special measures' (Article 2(2)), allowing distinctions for the purpose of affirmative action (Article 1(4)), and prohibiting distinctions which have the purpose *or effect* of impairing the recognition, enjoyment, and exercise, 'on an equal footing', of human rights and fundamental freedoms (Article 1).[96] The latter provision addresses

[92] Mahalic, *supra* n. 88, at 81.

[93] European states commonly deflect criticism invoking the Schengen Agreement, that results in asylum and immigration policies becoming largely a community matter. See, for instance, at CERD's 56th session the consideration of the 12th, 13th, and 14th report, of France (continued), para. 10–11. CERD/C/SR.1374 of 6 July 2000.

[94] The right to a nationality is enshrined in Article 15(1) UDHR.

[95] Meron, *supra* n. 62, at 286. Cf. Article 14 ECHR (equality as auxiliary to substantive rights). However, the recently adopted Protocol 12 ECHR, which opened for signature on 4 Nov. 2000, provides for a free-standing equality right, *supra* n. 19.

[96] See also Article 2(1)(c) asking states parties to take effective measures to review policies and amend, rescind, or nullify laws and regulations which have the effect of creating or *perpetuating* racial discrimination. On affirmative action, see Fottrell, 'Ever Decreasing Circles:

indirect discrimination, the disproportionate impact of apparently neutral practices on individuals or groups who differ in race, colour, descent, national or ethnic origin from the majority of the population. The Convention thus advocates a notion of equality of outcome, which is sensitive to the starting point of people, to past disadvantages which have created systematic patterns of discrimination in many societies, the effects of which may be continued or even exacerbated by facially neutral policies.

The Convention's purpose of achieving substantive equality in principle goes beyond the formal equality concept where the majority of national constitutions stop and which assumes conformity with the dominant culture. It rather recognizes the need to accommodate diversity and to redress disadvantage emanating from past discriminatory policies and practices, which have developed into structural patterns of injustice. Where racism is institutionalized in society, as is often the case, claims to formal equality are of limited avail.

> More effective results may be expected from taking special measures or affirmative action policies with a view of affording opportunities for self-development and advancement of groups who following long periods of persistent racial discrimination and marginalisation, have been denied such opportunities.[97]

The reversal of the effects of historical inequities is a positive duty on states parties. Article 2(2) requires states to take 'when circumstances so warrant' special and concrete measures 'to ensure the adequate development and protection of certain racial groups or individuals, belonging to them for the purpose of guaranteeing them the full and equal enjoyment of human rights and fundamental freedoms'. However, the precise nature of the duty is unclear and CERD has done little to elucidate the scope of affirmative action under the treaty.[98] The lack of precision and standards in ICERD's provision is, however, common to other non-discrimination treaties that envisage affirmative action policies. International human rights bodies, other than stating the existence of the obligation under the relevant treaties, have not to date seriously debated on the merits or modalities of such policies.[99] Moreover, because the benefits of such policies cannot be immediately appreciated—the reversal of historical

Affirmative Action and Special Measures under International Law', in D. Fottrell and B. Bowring (eds), *Minority and Group Rights in the New Millennium* (1999) 183.

[97] Van Boven, 'Are Remedies and Reparations Effectively Available to Victims of Racial Discrimination?', 4 *Connect* (Fall 2000) 5.

[98] Fottrell, *supra* n. 96, at 192.

[99] See CEDAW, Article 4(1): 'Adoption by State Parties of temporary special measures aimed at accelerating *de facto* equality between men and women shall not be considered discrimination as defined in the present Convention, but shall in no way entail as a consequence the maintenance of unequal or separate standards; these measures shall be discontinued when the objectives of equality of opportunity and treatment have been achieved', in *International Instruments, supra* n. 15. With regard to the ICCPR, the Human Rights Committee General Comment 18 on non-discrimination (37th session, 1989), para. 10, addresses the question of

inequities being inevitably a long-term process—domestic implementation of affirmative action has exposed the concept to criticism as constituting positive or reverse discrimination, thus rendering it legally contested and politically intractable. The experience of the country which has done most to pursue affirmative action, the United States, is not encouraging in this regard.[100]

Compounding the lack of standards, Article 2(2) provides no safeguards against the use of measures that, in promoting the adequate development of racial groups, constitute assimilationist policies. The ICERD approach is integrationist, as reflected in the provision that the maintenance of separate rights for vulnerable groups is only admitted for a limited period (Article 2(2) second sentence). States are further enjoined under Article 2(1)(e) 'to encourage, where appropriate, integrationalist multi-racial organizations and movements and other means of eliminating barriers between races, and to discourage anything which tends to strengthen racial division'.

These provisions reflect the predominant focus of the Convention on discrimination based on colour. Increased attention to the interests of ethnic minorities has resulted in the adoption of specific international and regional instruments recognizing the right to maintain ethnic identity.[101] In line with these developments, CERD has recently endorsed the importance of recognition by governments of the concrete rights of ethnic or linguistic groups to the preservation of their identity.[102]

special measures, stating that 'the principle of equality sometimes requires states parties to take affirmative action in order to diminish or eliminate the conditions which cause or help to perpetuate discrimination prohibited in the Covenant. For example in a State where the general conditions of a certain part of the population prevent or impair their enjoyment of human rights, the state should take specific action to correct those conditions. Such action may involve granting for a time to part of the population concerned certain preferential treatment in specific matters as compared to the rest of the population. However as long as such action is needed to correct discrimination in fact, it is a case of legitimate differentiation under the Covenant.'

[100] On the legal and political debates in the US, the first country to have undertaken widescale affirmative action programmes over the last thirty years, see Fottrell, *supra* n. 96, at 193–202.

[101] See, e.g., UNESCO 1978 Declaration on Race and Racial Prejudice, *supra* n. 77; UN 1992 Declaration on the Rights of Persons belonging to National or Ethnic, Religious and Linguistic Minorities, *supra* n. 17; Council of Europe 1995 Framework Convention for the Protection of National Minorities, ETS 157. Compare also with Article 27 ICCPR that at least to a modest extent recognizes the interests of ethnic minorities, *supra* n. 14.

[102] CERD General Recommendation XXI (48th session, 1996) on the right to self-determination: 'In accordance with article 2 of the [ICERD] and other relevant international documents, Governments should be sensitive towards the rights of persons belonging to ethnic groups, particularly their right to lead lives of dignity, to preserve their culture, to share equitably the fruits of national growth and to play their part in the Government of the country of which they are citizens. Also, Governments should consider, within their respective constitutional frameworks, vesting persons belonging to ethnic or linguistic groups comprised of their citizens, where appropriate, with the right to engage in activities which are particularly relevant to the preservation of the identity of such persons or groups.'

(c) Public and Private Reach of the Convention

One central provision of ICERD, Article 2(1)(d), provides that '[e]ach state party shall prohibit and bring to an end by all appropriate means, including legislation as required by the circumstances, racial discrimination by any person, group or organization'.

The question of determining the reach of the Convention when non-governmental or private actors are involved has been much debated.[103] Reference is frequently made to the overarching definition of racial discrimination referring to racial discriminatory acts occurring within 'public life'. This appears to exclude private acts from the scope of the Convention. More convincingly, it has been suggested that public life in Article 1 should mean the opposite of private life, rather than referring only to governmental actions.[104] This interpretation is supported by the guarantees contained elsewhere in the Convention, such as the right of access to any place or service intended for the use by the general public (Article 5(f)), the right to work and to housing (Article 5(e)). CERD practice has made it clear that these guarantees extend to employment in private enterprises, to housing provided by private owners, or admission to private clubs. The Committee has stated that 'to the extent that private institutions influence the exercise of rights or the availability of opportunities, the State Party must ensure that the result has neither the purpose nor the effect of creating or perpetuating racial discrimination'.[105]

The issue of the private/public reach of the Convention's provisions is of continuing importance considering the extent to which governments, through programmes of privatization, are divesting themselves from regulating basic public facilities and services and the ever more prominent role played by private actors on a global level.[106] The phenomenon of 'shrinking government' blurs the distinction between spheres of public conduct that are the subject of governmental regulation and spheres of private conduct that are not. Such trends detract from states' accountability and go in the opposite direction to what is needed to counteract racism.

The dichotomy between private and public realms also bears upon other obligations in the Convention, such as the requirement not to 'sponsor, defend and support racial discrimination by any persons or organizations' (Article 2(1)(b)), or to penalize the dissemination of racist ideas and participation in organizations that advocate racial hatred (Article 4). The

[103] See, among others, Meron, *supra* n. 62, at 291–5. [104] Ibid., at 293.

[105] CERD General Recommendation XX (48th session, 1996), para. 5.

[106] For an analysis of these developments, see *Globalization in the Context of Increased Incidents of Racism, Racial Discrimination and Xenophobia*, Working paper submitted to the Sub-Commission by J. Oloka-Onyango as a contribution to the preparation of the World Conference against Racism. E/CN.4/Sub.2/1999/8 (1999).

Convention leaves open the question of how to strike a balance between individual freedom and government restriction in fulfilling these obligations.

(d) Governmental Interference in Private Conduct: Hate Speech

Article 4 requires that states prohibit not only advocacy of hatred, but also 'all dissemination of ideas based on racial superiority or hatred', and the provision of 'any assistance to racist activities, including financing thereof' (Article 4(a)). Organizations which promote and incite racial discrimination are to be declared illegal and prohibited by law, and participation in such organizations or activities is to be made punishable as well (Article 4(b)). Public authorities and institutions at national and local level are enjoined from promoting or inciting racial discrimination (Article 4(c)).

Article 4 mirrors Article 20(2) of the Covenant on Civil and Political Rights (ICCPR) which prohibits any advocacy of national, racial, or religious hatred that constitutes incitement to discrimination, hostility, or violence. But it goes further than Article 20. States must outlaw not only advocacy of hatred, but also 'all dissemination of ideas based on racial superiority or hatred'. The Article requires the suppression of organizations advocating racial hatred. It further requires that incitement be made an offence, as well as the financial support to racist activities of any kind.

CERD has consistently held that Article 4 is mandatory in that it requires comprehensive legislative action to implement its terms.[107] The prohibition of the dissemination of *ideas* based on racial superiority or *hatred* irrespective of intent or consequences has, however, proved in practice to be difficult for governments. In specific cases, proof of an intention to stir up racial hatred or proof that racial hatred was actually stirred up as a result is hard to obtain.[108] The same difficulty emerges with respect to outlawing racist organizations. Legal systems in which criminal intention alone is not sufficient to outlaw an organization before that intention is translated into action face difficulties in implementing the required preventive steps against incitement to racial discrimination.[109]

Criminalizing the expression of views—no matter how despicable—and participation in racist organizations clash with the rights to freedom of expression and association, recognized as fundamental human rights in all major

[107] On implementation of Article 4, see CERD General Recommendation I (5th session, 1972), General Recommendation VII (32nd session, 1985), and General Recommendation XV (42nd session, 1993).

[108] Hatred is a feeling, a state of mind and not a clearly established legal interest, as is the case of discrimination. See Lerner, 'Incitement in the Racial Convention; Reach and Shortcomings of Article 4', *Israel Yearbook on Human Rights* (1993) 1, at 8. See also Farrior, 'Molding the Matrix: The Historical and Theoretical Foundations of International Law Concerning Hate Speech', 14 *Berkeley Journal of International Law* (1996) 48.

[109] Lerner, *supra* n. 108, at 13.

human rights instruments.[110] The concern that these requirements for change in domestic law in the proposed Convention would impair freedom of expression and association resulted in the inclusion of the 'due regard' clause. States undertake to adopt immediate and positive measures designed to eradicate all incitement to, or acts of, racial discrimination 'with due regard to the principles embodied in the Universal Declaration of Human Rights and the rights expressly set forth in Article 5 of [the] Convention'.[111] Freedom of expression and association are among the rights to be given 'due regard' in fashioning legislation to implement Article 4. The due regard clause did, however, not dispel the concern among a number of states that Article 4 was too sweeping and a conspicuous number of reservations were entered on this Article upon ratification.[112]

The interpretation of the due regard clause and Article 4 as a whole is still unsettled. Some states have interpreted it as not imposing on a state party the obligation to take any action impairing the right to freedom of expression (notably, the United States), others have invoked the due regard clause to justify alternative sanctions to criminal liability. CERD considers that the due regard clause must be read in the light of the UDHR as a whole, where the right to free speech and association are not absolute but subject to limitations and arguably greater weight is given to freedom from discrimination.[113] However, the Committee has not always been unanimous with regard to the effects of the due regard clause in Article 4 and with the merits of criminalizing hate speech and racist organizations, recognizing that in some instances

[110] See UDHR, Articles 19 and 20(1); ICCPR, Articles 19 and 21; ECHR, Articles 10 and 11; American Convention on Human Rights, Articles 13 and 16; The African Charter on Human and Peoples' Rights, Articles 9 and 10. In I. Brownlie (ed.), *Basic Documents on Human Rights*, 3rd edn. (1992).

[111] ICERD, Article 4, first paragraph.

[112] Some eighteen states parties to ICERD have entered reservations and/or interpretative declarations in respect of Article 4. Interpretative declarations were lodged, among others, by members of the Council of Europe on recommendation of the Committee of Ministers of the Council of Europe. See Resolution (68) 30 adopted by the Ministers' Deputies on 31 Oct. 1968. For the full texts of the reservations and/or declarations, see CERD/C/60/Rev.3, 12 Feb. 1999.

[113] See limitation clauses in the UDHR, Articles 29 and 30. In particular, Article 29(3) provides that the rights and freedoms set forth in the Declaration may in no case be exercised contrary to the purposes and principles of the United Nations. Being one of the purposes, as articulated in Article 1(3) of the Charter, the promotion of human rights for all without distinction, among others, as to race, it follows that under Article 29(3) UDHR no individual or group may exercise their rights to freedom of expression or association in a manner which vitiates the rule against racial discrimination.

That the right to equality in international human rights law is so basic is confirmed, *inter alia*, by Article 4 ICCPR. While allowing derogation from substantive articles of the Covenant, among which those providing freedom of expression and association, it specifies that any measures taken in derogation of the Convention's provisions (where allowed) may not involve discrimination.

the effect may run counter to the desired goal.[114] Public proceeding in a court may in fact inadvertently provide the offender with the opportunity to publicize his racist views. An organization driven underground by repressive measures might be much more dangerous than one allowed to act openly.

A new challenge comes from the growth of racist propaganda on the Internet.[115] The particular characteristics of communication on the Internet makes state regulation relatively powerless to prevent the misuse of technology even in countries that want to do so. The discussion is largely limited to industrialized countries, where the overwhelming majority of Internet users are concentrated. There is a widening gulf across the Atlantic in attitudes toward curbing the Internet traffic that expresses racist extremism. Web sites banned in Europe, where in broad terms legislation against incitement to racial hatred is being used to cover expression on the Internet, are able to resurface from the haven of the United States, where they are protected under the constitutional guarantee of freedom of speech.[116]

The need for international minimum standards for the legal treatment of racial hatred and xenophobia in cyberspace as well as a draft code of conduct for the Internet community is being widely debated at the international and regional level.[117] Among the measures envisaged to counteract racist

[114] Divided comments from CERD members were, for instance, expressed over a hate speech case under the ECHR (*Jersild v Denmark*, ECHR (1978) Series A, No. 19, 1). In that case a television journalist was convicted of aiding and abetting the dissemination of racist speech through broadcasting an interview with young racists. Whilst some members of CERD welcomed the applicant's conviction as 'the clearest statement yet . . . that the right to protection against racial discrimination took precedence over the right to freedom of expression', others considered that 'in such cases the facts needed to be considered in relation to both rights'. In the event, the European Court, in finding that the conviction of the journalist violated Article 10 and the guarantee of freedom of expression, considered its judgment compatible with Article 4 ICERD. See report of the Committee to the General Assembly, A/45/18, p. 21, para. 56.

[115] Technical, legal, juridical aspects relating to the screening and prohibition of racist propaganda on the Internet have been extensively debated at the United Nations *Seminar on the Role of Internet in the Light of the Provisions of the International Convention on the Elimination of All Forms of Racial Discrimination*, Geneva, 10–14 Nov. 1997. See n. 239 *infra*. Moreover, OHCHR has recently conducted consultations with member states, United Nations bodies, specialized agencies, intergovernmental and non-governmental organizations, on the use of the Internet to incite racism, xenophobia, and intolerance. The resulting report has been submitted to the Preparatory Committee for the World Conference against Racism. A/CONF.189/PC.1/5.

[116] For an excellent overview on the legal and technical issues involved in counteracting the dissemination of racist messages via the Internet, see European Commission against Racism and Intolerance (ECRI), *Legal Instruments to Combat Racism on the Internet*, Report prepared by the Swiss Institute of Comparative Law, CRI(2000)27, Strasbourg, Aug. 2000.

[117] See, for instance, the Action Plan on Promoting Safer Use of the Internet, Decision No. 276/1999/EC of the European Parliament and the Council of the European Union of 25 Jan. 1999.

propaganda on the Internet are those which require ISPs (Internet Service Providers) to register web sites and their authors, and the introduction of Internet filtering programs.

(e) Remedies for Victims of Racial Discrimination

The right to a domestic remedy is a basic requirement of the international approach to human rights protection. Article 6 ICERD deals with effective protection and remedies, as well as just and adequate reparation or satisfaction for victims of racism and racial discrimination. The notion of effective remedies entails that recourse procedures should be simple, transparent, and accessible, based on awareness of the vulnerability of victims of racial acts, the fact that they are mostly ignorant of their rights and of linguistic and other barriers they often face in seeking legal remedies. The scrutiny of states' reports by CERD has brought home that in many cases effective remedies so defined are unavailable, particularly where victims belong to the most destitute and marginalized groups of society.[118]

Nevertheless agreement on the priority of establishing practical and effective remedies to victims of racial discrimination—for example by providing for legal aid and assistance, providing standing for non-governmental organizations to assist victims during the legal process, or by alleviating the burden of proof—is a welcome development in current policy recommendations at international and regional level.[119]

A new emphasis is being placed on the role of administrative or other bodies in enforcing anti-discrimination laws. In recent years there has been a growing number of specialized bodies set up in various countries aimed at combating discrimination and promoting equality. These bodies, according to the legal and administrative traditions of the countries in which they are established, have taken different forms—national commissions for racial equality, ombudsmen against ethnic discrimination, centres/offices for combating racism and promoting equal opportunities, or bodies having similar functions within a wider human rights mandate.[120] Their function varies from providing assistance in litigation to taking up the case on behalf of a

[118] A comprehensive analysis on the issue of remedies with regard to victims of racial discrimination is provided by a former Committee member, Theo van Boven. See his background paper on 'Common problems linked to all remedies available to victims of racial discrimination' (HR/GVA/WCR/SEM.1/2000/BP.5), prepared for the United Nations *Expert Seminar on Remedies Available to the Victims of Racial Discrimination, Xenophobia and Related Intolerance and on Good National Practices in this Field*, held in Geneva 16–18 Feb. 2000. See n. 239 *infra*.

[119] See, for instance, the report and recommendations of the *Expert Seminar on Remedies* above. A/CONF.189/PC.1/8. At the regional level, see ECRI, *Compilation of ECRI's General Policy Recommendations*, CRI(99)54, Strasbourg, Aug. 1999.

[120] See ECRI, *Good Practices: Specialized Bodies to Combat Racism, Xenophobia, Anti-Semitism and Intolerance at National Level*, CRI(99) 43, Apr. 1999.

victim, or adjudicating complaints through amicable solutions or in binding and enforceable decisions.

This approach shifts the focus from repressive measures and criminal sanctions to conciliatory measures and civil law remedies. It reflects an awareness that the reality of racial or ethnic discrimination is most often experienced in the denial of social and economic rights—especially in the fields of employment, housing, and health care. Alternative civil justice models may prevent the need to bring cases of discrimination to court and are often more effective than criminal prosecution in combating prejudice, promoting understanding and tolerance, and in protecting victims from retaliation.

There is also scope under the Convention for specifically tailored group enforcement mechanisms. Where collective rights are involved—such as the case of indigenous peoples, Roma/Sintis, or other minority groups that are victims of entrenched and deeply rooted racism—individual complaints with a view of obtaining reparation are unlikely to secure structural changes in economic and social life.[121] However, the advocacy of remedial actions of this nature, or of any kind, needs to be accompanied by national educational policies directed at majority communities to promote understanding and tolerance. Such duties, mostly neglected, are set out for states under Article 7 ICERD.

(f) The Need to Address the Root Causes of Racism—Article 7

The struggle against racism and racial discrimination over the history of ICERD has focused on the role of law. Priority has been given under the Convention to legislation intended to suppress propaganda, the dissemination of racist ideas, and the prohibition of organizations that advocate racist violence and hatred. States have been encouraged to rescind discriminatory statutes and regulations, to strengthen legal guarantees and remedies against racial discrimination and, more recently, to take positive or special measures designed to enable disadvantaged racial groups to enjoy their human rights and fundamental freedoms on an 'equal footing'. This approach was and remains an essential foundation. But law alone cannot address the problem of racism at its roots. Combating 'prejudices that lead to racism' is one of the goals of the Convention, which calls upon states 'to adopt immediate and effective measures, particularly in the field of teaching, education, culture and information'.[122] Efforts to implement this article both by the CERD and

[121] See, with regard to the rights of indigenous peoples, CERD General Recommendation XXIII (51st session, 1997) addressing the need of fair compensation for indigenous peoples, which should as far as possible take the form of lands and territories.

[122] Article 7 ICERD. Doubts about over-reliance on the impact of legislation in combating racism were forcefully expressed during the drafting process of the Convention by the United Kingdom delegate: 'Using legislation by itself was like cutting down a noxious weed above the ground and leaving the roots intact.' See Banton, *supra* n. 76, at 59.

reporting states have been meagre. After many years of total neglect, guidelines on implementation of Article 7 were developed with assistance from UNESCO, but states' reports have continued to treat it as a marginal issue, as does much of the literature on the Convention.[123]

Article 7 specifies the fields in which states parties are to adopt measures in order to end racial prejudice and promote understanding. The little that states have reported on implementation of Article 7 has tended to focus on the education of schoolchildren.[124] But Article 7 does not address educational measures only in the school setting. It includes broader education and training such as the training of teachers, law enforcement officials, judges, and other public figures.[125] The reference to culture and information addresses persons, associations, and institutions that shape opinions, through, for example, cultural events, in sport and, not least, the media. Article 7 deserves deeper attention both from governments and CERD. The duties it requires of states reflect the thesis that racist ideas are not innate, but are transmitted to the young through others: parents, peers, teachers, politicians, and other opinion leaders. Unless such ideas are tackled at their source, they will continue to be handed down from generation to generation.[126] The importance of full implementation of these provisions for the long-term success of the goals of ICERD and the right to equality cannot be underestimated.

(iii) The Committee on the Elimination of Racial Discrimination

The Committee on the Elimination of Racial Discrimination (CERD) was established in 1970. It comprises eighteen members elected by the states parties from among their nationals. The Convention requires that those elected as members be

> experts of high moral standing . . . who shall serve in their personal capacity, consideration being given to equitable geographical distribution and to the representation of the different forms of civilization as well as of the principal legal systems.[127]

[123] See Wolfrum, 'The Committee on the Elimination of Racial Discrimination', 3 *Max Planck UNYB* (1999) 489, at 504; Farrior, *supra* n. 86, at 294. CERD issued an early General Recommendation on the implementation of Article 7, but rather than specifying the types of steps states should take, it simply implores states to report on the measures they have taken. CERD, General Recommendation V (15th session, 1977).

[124] See *Joint Working Paper on Article 7 of the International Convention on the Elimination of All Forms of Racial Discrimination*, UN Doc. E/CN.4/Sub.2/1998/4 (1998), para. 46.

[125] See also CERD General Recommendation XIII (42nd session, 1993) on the training of law enforcement officials in the protection of human rights, urging states to include information on implementation of this recommendation in their periodic reports.

[126] See the *Study on the Implementation of Article 7 of the International Convention on the Elimination of All Forms of Racial Discrimination*, prepared by the Special Rapporteur, Mr Georges Tenekides. A/CONF.119/11 (1983).

[127] Article 8(1) ICERD.

Members or experts are elected for a term of four years that can be renewed.[128] The Committee is charged with the task of overseeing the implementation of the Convention and to report on its work to the General Assembly through the Secretary General. It can offer suggestions and general recommendations to the states parties on implementation.[129] It has the competence to receive and respond to complaints from states and individuals.[130]

Study of the Committee has been considerably aided by the existence of a substantial body of literature including the writings of former and serving Committee members.[131] One drawback is that all accounts of the functioning of the Committee have been written by members from Western countries. A fuller assessment would profit from the perspectives of those elected to represent other regional groupings.[132]

How effective has CERD proved to be? Any assessment of an international initiative over a period of thirty years to eliminate racial discrimination of every kind in over 150 states must inevitably be tentative, even speculative. That caveat made, it seems clear that conflicting ideas within the Committee as to the purposes of the Convention, the global geopolitical context in which it developed, and the attributes of Committee members combined to limit its capacities to achieve a great deal. That at least seems to be true for the first twenty years of the Committee's existence. The Committee had permanent members of the Soviet Bloc countries whose governments in their reports insisted that racism was a function of imperialism and colonialism and therefore did not arise in their jurisdictions. Experts from these countries did not question or challenge such submissions. On the other hand the other protagonist in the Cold War, the United States, remained aloof from the Convention while seeking to dismantle its own inheritance of racism and segregation suffered by black citizens through its own internal democratic and constitutional resources.

One of the most perceptive writers on the Committee, and himself a former member, divides its story into the three decades during which it has functioned.[133] During the first decade of the 1970s, states parties and the Committee came to terms with the full implications of the Convention especially for domestic legal change. Research has demonstrated that a substantial number of ratifying countries did incorporate at least some of the Convention's requirements in internal law. Thus, Australia passed the Racial

[128] Article 8(5)(a) ICERD. [129] Ibid., Article 9(2). [130] Ibid., Articles 11–14.

[131] For a book length study see Banton, *supra* n. 76. Also Banton, 'Decision-taking in the Committee on the Elimination of Racial Discrimination', in Alston and Crawford, *supra* n. 72, at 55–78; Partsch, *supra* n. 71, at 339–68. Wolfrum, *supra* n. 123.

[132] It is regretted that it did not prove possible for reasons of time and resources to interview members of the Committee in preparing these lectures. Advice in conducting our research given by Mr Michael Banton (UK) is gratefully acknowledged.

[133] Banton, *supra* n. 76, at 99–171.

Discrimination Act 1975 prior to ratifying the ICERD and adopted the Convention's definition of racial discrimination in that Act. Costa Rica and Egypt, among others, adopted constitutional changes to incorporate prohibitions on racial discrimination.[134] At the same time, however, other countries insisted that they had ratified the treaty as an act of solidarity with those subject to apartheid and similar practices and saw no need to alter their laws as racial discrimination was unknown in their countries.[135] A review of the first forty-five states' reports submitted found that over half the states in question emphatically denied that any form of racial discrimination existed on their territories.[136]

In the second decade, the 1980s, ICERD, and in particular its Committee, were rendered largely impotent due to the Cold War. There was extraordinary turnover in membership that militated against it achieving much impact through its dialogue with states.[137] The focus on the link between racism and anti-imperialism, both within CERD and the United Nations as a whole, frustrated any modest advances in the procedure and practice of implementation that might have been achieved.[138] ICERD sessions had to be cancelled on a number of occasions due to a lack of funds.[139]

From the end of the Cold War and throughout the 1990s, CERD has been able to recover momentum and to address its mandate with greater commitment and energy.[140] It became more involved with the other treaty bodies through the annual meeting of Chair Persons of the Treaty Bodies and has in consequence implemented a number of reforms and innovations in its work. These changes are reflected in the enhanced quality of discussion of state reports, in the adoption of improved concluding observations,

134 See N. Lerner, *The U.N. Convention on the Elimination of All Forms of Racial Discrimination* (1980), at 165–211.

135 Banton, *supra* n. 76, at 105.

136 Ibid., at 106.

137 Forty-three members occupied the eighteen seats between 1970 and 1978 and forty-one in the ten-year period from 1979 to 1988. The Convention allowed for casual vacancies to be filled by another expert from among the state's experts. There was no provision for election for such vacancies. In contrast, the Human Rights Committee under the ICCPR, which came into force six years after the ICERD, required an election to be held for casual vacancies. The ICCPR also directed that the need for lawyers on the Committee should be factored into the election of eligible Committee members. In the last decade the Committee has increased it effectiveness as a result of a considerably reduced turnover, Banton, *supra* n. 76, at 142.

138 Banton notes, referring to the first eighteen years of the Committee's existence, that 'CERD was in no position to act against any but a pariah state. Chile and Israel found themselves in such a position and South Africa would have done had that country become a state party. There was insufficient trust within the Committee for it to take decisions other than by consensus and this permitted any small minority to exercise a veto. Many members saw their obligations in diplomatic terms and perhaps could do little else while the opposition between East and West hung over so many of the decisions that had to be taken.' Banton, *supra* n. 76, at 137.

139 Partsch, *supra* n. 71, at 346.

140 Banton, *supra* n. 76, at 142.

as well as in the quality of recent General Recommendations adopted under Article 9. The CERD has also fashioned a preventive procedure and, reversing traditional attitudes, has become more open to involvement of non-governmental organizations (NGOs) in its work. Thus in August 2000, the Committee held a two-day seminar on discrimination against Roma in which for the first time NGOs were permitted to attend and make interventions.[141]

(a) Membership of the Committee

One characteristic of the Committee throughout its thirty-year existence has been the practice of many states to appoint civil servants, diplomats, or retired diplomats as members. The practice reflected the assumption of the large number of states, who swiftly ratified the Convention, that it was essentially about apartheid and institutional racism in countries other than their own. While the diplomatic presence has been said to have been useful in the early years of the Committee, especially in bringing governments to understand the nature of the legal obligations they had undertaken, it is also the case that the effective independence of the Committee was in constant question.[142] Concern that committee members, especially country rapporteurs, were subject to pressure from other diplomats led the CERD to adopt a General Recommendation expressing its alarm.[143] At its fiftieth session in 1996, CERD secured majority support from among its members for an amendment to its rules of procedure to ensure for the future that 'as a general rule' experts would not participate in the discussions of their home states' reports. It is current practice to agree the text of Concluding Observations in public session, a change intended to inhibit participation by a member who may be a national of the state under discussion.[144]

The range of professional backgrounds found on the Committee has often been cited a particular strength by its members.[145] However, the expanded range of the Committee's work, such as its focus on ethnic minorities and indigenous peoples, alongside the growing awareness of the complexity of the task of ending discrimination in many countries, suggests that there is a strong case for the appointment of new expertise. Such expertise should include specialists in anti-discrimination law as well as persons experienced in implementing anti-discrimination programmes including in the field of education.

[141] The discussion led to the adoption of CERD General Recommendation XXVII (57th session, 2000), outlining a number of measures that governments of relevant states parties should take to improve the situation of the Roma.

[142] Banton, *supra* n. 76, at 101; Partsch, *supra* n. 71, at 340–1; Wolfrum, *supra* n. 123, at 494.

[143] General Recommendation IX (38th session, 1990).

[144] Wolfrum, *supra* n. 123, at 509.

[145] Ibid., at 494.

(b) Committee Procedures

The Committee meets twice a year in March and August to review state reports. Since 1996 it has assessed on average ten reports in each session. A crucial early point of procedure was whether reports would be examined in the presence or absence of the states parties. At the direction of the General Assembly the procedure was settled that states should be present.[146] This decision, followed by the later treaty bodies, allowed what is perhaps the most important feature of the treaty monitoring system to develop, that of dialogue between the Committee and reporting states.[147] It is now hard to envisage that any impact could have been achieved by the CERD without face to face debate between the representatives of states and the experts.

Since 1988 the appointment of special rapporteurs from among its members with responsibility for leading the review of each country report has deepened the quality of the exchange between state representatives and the Committee. The disputed question of access to other information than that provided by governments—in particular information from NGOs—was a source of tension and disagreement as it was to become with other treaty bodies. The entitlement of members to have such access and to refer to it was achieved for CERD through following the precedent of the other human rights treaty bodies.[148] Some members also resisted the acceptance of written information from the specialized agencies, ILO and UNESCO, when dealing with state reports. A solution was found whereby these bodies provided their material to Committee members interested through the Secretariat.[149] ILO and UNESCO representatives attend CERD sessions as observers. It appears that the contribution which is valued by the CERD has been made by the ILO, especially in respect of its Convention on Discrimination in Employment.[150] The potential role of UNESCO in respect of Article 7 could have been considerable. But in practice that has not proved to be the case.[151]

From 1991 the Committee has also adopted a system in step with the reforms proposed by the Independent Expert on the functioning of the treaty bodies, in respect of Concluding Observations following its examination of a state report.[152] This document is now discussed and agreed in public session in the absence of the state party—and a longstanding contentious issue, already noted—without the participation of any Committee member who is

[146] A/RES/2783 (XXVI) (1971). [147] Partsch, *supra* n. 71, at 340–1.

[148] See Decision 1 (XL), 'in examining the reports of States parties, members of the Committee must have access, as independent experts, to all other sources of information, governmental and non-governmental' and Wolfrum, *supra* n. 123, at 507.

[149] Partsch, *supra* n. 71, at 344–5. [150] Ibid., at 344.

[151] Lerner, *supra* n. 134, at 148.

[152] See *Final Report on Enhancing the Long Term Effectiveness of the United Nations Human Rights Treaty System* (the Alston Report). UN Doc. E/CN.4/1997/74 (1996).

a national of the state in question. The Observations broadly follow a similar layout to the conclusions of the other monitoring committees and are comparable in their focus and quality to those of other treaty bodies.[153] They achieve their purpose of identifying for states exactly where further action has to be undertaken in the implementation of its Convention commitments.

(c) Overdue Reports

The Convention lays down that states parties must report every two years to the CERD.[154] That interval has clearly proved, in the light of the expansion of the treaty system, too onerous on states. The interval provided for periodic reporting by states in the later treaties was longer.[155] Not without hesitation the CERD agreed to a new practice requiring submission of a comprehensive report every four years updated by short reports every two years.[156]

This has been welcomed by states. It has enabled the CERD to reduce the backlog in consideration of reports it has received. But it has not solved the problem of non-submission of reports. ICERD is not alone in having this problem. Delay in the submission of reports by governments is shared with other monitoring committees. However, ICERD is the treaty with the most significant problems (see Fig. 1). Of the 1,235 reports from the main human rights treaties as of 31 March 2000, ICERD accounts for the greatest number.[157] Part of the explanation lies in the cumulative delays of a large number of reports, that are overdue from a number of states (see Fig. 2). Nevertheless, the disproportionate delinquency with regard to ICERD must raise the suspicion that states take their reporting requirement under ICERD less seriously than with respect to the other treaty bodies.

The CERD has taken action. In 1991 it proposed a procedure to the General Assembly that, in the case of states with seriously overdue reports, it would undertake a periodic review based upon the last reports submitted. This initiative was endorsed by the General Assembly and has had positive effects in inveigling some states to submit and to cooperate.[158] The CERD has also pressed that technical assistance be made available to states experiencing difficulties in preparing reports in which the Committee members would participate.[159] Nevertheless the problem remains unresolved and serious.

[153] See, for example, 57th Session, Concluding Observations of the Committee on the Elimination of Racial Discrimination: Norway. CERD/C/57/CPR.3/Add.12, 10 Aug. 2000.

[154] Article 9(1) ICERD.

[155] Cf. ICCPR, Article 40(1) 'whenever the Committee so requests'; Convention against Torture (CAT), Article 19(1) 'every four years'; CEDAW, Article 18(1)(b) 'every four years'; Convention on the Rights of the Child (CRC), Article 44(1)(b) 'every five years'.

[156] Partsch, *supra* n. 71, at 367.

[157] See *Recent Reporting History under the Principal International Human Rights Instruments*, HRI/GEN/4 of 27 Apr. 2000.

[158] GA Res. 49/178 (1994), para. 6 and see Banton, *supra* n. 76, at 152.

[159] General Recommendation XI (39th session, 1991).

Treaty	ICESCR	ICCPR	ICERD	CEDAW	CAT	CRC	Total
Overdue reports	160	142	430	236	112	155	1235
State parties	142	144	156	165	119	191	917
Percentage of total	14	12	34	18	12	10	

Figure 1. *Reporting status under the main international human rights instruments*

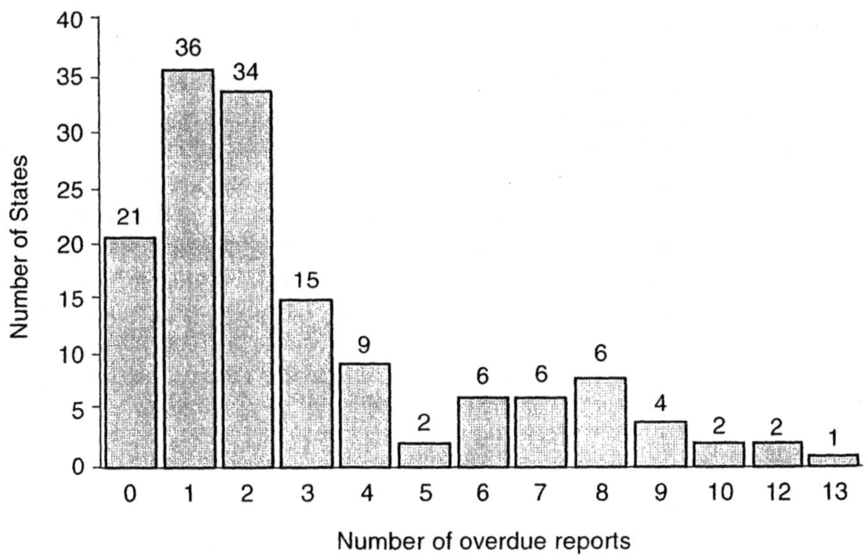

Figure 2. *ICERD overdue reports*

(d) General Recommendations

Under Article 9, paragraph 2, of ICERD the Committee may make suggestions and General Recommendations prompted by its work in examining state reports. Recommendations are to be reported to the General Assembly along with any comments on them from state parties. The Committee over its life has made some twenty-seven General Recommendations.[160] None appear to have provoked a response from the states' parties. As with similar

[160] For a compilation of the Committee's General Recommendations, see CERD/C7365 of 11 Feb. 1999.

statements by the other treaty bodies, the recommendations enable it to both indicate to states the Committee's view of the scope of Convention provisions as a guide in their reporting and to offer guidance on the legal interpretation of the Convention.[161] It is accepted that General Recommendations do not bind the states parties, but they do bind the members of the Committee who have agreed them.[162] The recommendations to date cover most provisions under the Convention and in recent years have also dealt with wider issues. In 1994, the CERD called for the establishment of an international tribunal to prosecute crimes against humanity in the light of 'racially and ethnically motivated massacres and atrocities occurring in different parts of the world'.[163] It has also drafted an important statement on self-determination, secession, and the claims of ethnic and religious minorities.[164] Other recent General Recommendations include two on indigenous peoples and one on gender related dimensions of racial discrimination.[165] Perhaps the largest gap to be filled concerns the definition of racial discrimination and Article 1 of the Convention. Given the history of the Convention and the priority given to combating apartheid, the CERD has shied away from comment on the definition of racial discrimination. It was plausible to assume that the definition offered in section I of the Convention offered adequate guidance. However, in the post-apartheid world there is a need for a comprehensive clarification and elaboration of the scope of the Convention's protections. This would provide not only clear guidance to states but also to others, including those who are targets of discrimination in many settings. Ideally, preparation of such a statement should be agreed with the Special Rapporteur on Contemporary Forms of Racism.

(e) Complaint Procedures

Inter-state complaint mechanism

Article 11 of ICERD enables any state party to bring to the attention of the Committee its concern that another state party is failing to give effect to the Convention. The procedure does not require a separate declaration of acceptance by governments.[166] The state-to-state complaint option under

[161] The ultimate arbiter of the meaning of the Convention is the International Court of Justice which, under ICERD Article 22, has jurisdiction over disputes between the states parties relating to the 'interpretation or application' of the Convention that are not settled 'by negotiation or by the procedures expressly provided for' by the Convention. Jurisdiction of the ICJ has been excluded via reservation by twenty-two states parties to ICERD. See CERD/C/60/Rev. 3 of 12 Feb. 1999.

[162] Meron, *supra* n. 62, at 285.

[163] General Recommendation XVIII (44th session, 1994).

[164] General Recommendation XXI (48th session, 1996).

[165] See General Recommendation XXIII (51st session, 1997); General Recommendation XXIV (55th session, 1999); General Recommendation XXV (56th session, 2000).

[166] As is the case, for example, with the ICCPR (see Article 41).

Article 11 of ICERD has never been utilized. As with similar procedures in other human rights instruments, it must be regarded, for now at least, as a dead letter. The theory on which it was based, that the states parties have both a collective interest and a responsibility for the elimination of racial discrimination including in other jurisdictions, has not been borne out in practice. The collective involvement of states parties arises only from their participation in elections of members of CERD and in their participation in the General Assembly to which CERD makes an annual report. On occasion the CERD has received notice of what it has termed 'disguised complaints' about other states' actions as part of the periodic report under Article 9 of the Convention.[167] The Committee has suggested in such cases formal resort to the Article 11 procedure but with no results.[168] It has been suggested that the explanation for the failure of states to have resort to the inter-state mechanism arises from their awareness that the Committee had no power to legally adjudicate on a state's complaint. The Committee may only recommend a friendly settlement and has no enforcement powers.[169] However, the more likely explanation, as with other state-to-state complaint mechanisms in the major human rights treaties, is political while also reflecting an unwillingness shared by states to empower any quasi-judicial mechanism at the international level.

Individual complaint mechanism

Under Article 14 of the Convention, a state may make a declaration recognizing the competence of the CERD to receive through the Secretary General communications from individuals or groups of individuals within its jurisdiction claiming to be victims of a violation of one of the rights set forth in the Convention.[170] The Article 14 complaint procedure came into force as early as 1982 with acceptance by ten states.[171] However, the increase since that date in the number of states providing recourse to the jurisdiction of the Committee has been minimal. To date thirty out of 156 states parties only have made a declaration under Article 14.[172] As a result there has been a disappointing and limited practice achieved to date. Over the almost two

[167] Disguised complaints have included Iraq's claim that it could not report on the operation of the Convention in northern Iraq because of the establishment of safe havens for Kurds during the Gulf War.

[168] See General Recommendation XVI concerning the application of Article 9 of the Convention (42nd session, 1993).

[169] See Wolfrum, *supra* n. 123, at 511. Also Buergenthal, *supra* n. 83, at 202.

[170] On the procedural rules governing Article 14 communications, see M. O'Flaherty, *Human Rights and the U.N. Practice Before the Treaty Bodies* (1996), at 104–7.

[171] Article 14(9) ICERD.

[172] As of 27 Aug. 1999, twenty-eight states had made the declaration under Article 14, A/54/18 paras. 1 and 2. The Yugoslav Republic of Macedonia and Portugal joined in 2000. CERD/C/SR.1372 and CERD/C/SR.1400.

decades the Committee has considered only a dozen communications.[173] All have been from developed Western countries. None have raised s ystemic issues of violation. However, several complaints about alleged racial discrimination in the operation of social security benefits, in housing,[174] or in respect of employment give a clear indication of the considerable potential of the procedure for victims.[175]

The explanation for the low level of acceptance of the individual complaint mechanism can only be a matter of speculation. But it is difficult to avoid the conclusion that states remain unconvinced that the CERD should develop such a quasi-judicial role. This is disappointing for the development of the Convention and international human rights protection as a whole. It could be argued that the individual complaint procedure under the First Optional Protocol to the International Covenant on Civil and Political Rights offers an alternative forum. The Human Rights Committee can address inequalities and racial discrimination under the Protocol. The Committee on Economic, Social and Cultural Rights may also address racial and ethnic discrimination in the future, should the proposed individual complaint mechanism under that Covenant come into effect. But neither body can interpret the ICERD and the duties imposed on states by that Convention. The international treaty system,

[173] See *Compilation of Opinions and Decisions Adopted under Article 14 of the Convention*, CERD/C/390 of 5 June 2000.

[174] One case involving, among others, alleged violations of the right to housing (Article 5(e)(iii)) and freedom of residence (Article 5(d)(i)) is *L.K. v The Netherlands* (No. 4/1994), Opinion of 16 Mar. 1993. The case concerned threats of racial violence by local inhabitants hostile to foreigners taking up residence in their neighbourhood. The facts were not disputed and the case focused on the expediency principle, thereby finding that instances of racial discrimination have to be prosecuted with particular attention, *inter alia*, by ensuring the speedy disposal of such cases by domestic judicial instances.

[175] See, for instance, *Yilmaz-Dogan v the Netherlands* (No. 1/1984), Opinion of 10 Aug. 1988, where the Committee found a violation of Article 5(e)(i) concerning equality before the law in respect of the right to work and protection against unemployment. The petitioner's dismissal from employment, after a prolonged period of absenteeism owing to illness and childbirth, was based on the employer's unwillingness to extend sickness-leave benefits to her because of prejudices against foreign women workers. Alleged violations of the right to work under Article 5(e)(i) were also dealt with by the Committee in *Diop v France* (No. 2/1989), Opinion of 18 Mar. 1991; *Z.U.B.S. v Australia* (No. 6/1996), Opinion of 26 Aug. 1999; *Barbaro v Australia* (No. 7/1995), Decision of Admissibility of 14 Aug. 1997; *B.M.S. v Australia* (No. 8/1996), Opinion of 12 Mar. 1999; *D.S. v Sweden* (No. 9/1997), Decision of Admissibility of 17 Aug. 1998. In *Ziad Ben Ahmed Habassi v Denmark* (No. 10/1997), Opinion of 26 Aug. 1999, the CERD found a violation of Article 2.1(d) with respect to the Danish Bank's loan policy *vis-à-vis* foreign residents and that it was necessary to ascertain whether or not the criteria applied involved racial discrimination, within the meaning of Article 1 of the Convention. In *B.J. v Denmark* (No. 17/1999), Opinion of 17 Mar. 2000, that concerned an alleged violation of Article 5(f), the Committee supported the petitioner's request for economic compensation for the humiliation of having been refused access to a place of service for the use of the general public.

as it has evolved, has established a separate role for the anti-discrimination instruments, on racial and sex discrimination, that is complementary to the other human rights conventions.[176] The encouragement of wider acceptance of the Article 14 procedure by states should be a priority for the Convention.[177]

(f) Early Warning and Urgent Procedures

In 1993, following a recommendation of the meeting of chairpersons of the treaty bodies, the CERD adopted new procedures concerned with prevention of violations of the Convention.[178] An early warning procedure was addressed to the prevention of ethnic or racial conflicts and an urgent action procedure was aimed at imminent or actual large-scale problems of serious racial or ethnic discrimination or conflict. In each case, the state in question is placed under the new procedure and remains on the agenda of the Committee at future sessions. These important initiatives have been invoked to date in respect of a range of situations in some fourteen countries, including Bosnia and Herzegovina, Kosovo, the Occupied Palestinian Territories, Algeria, Burundi, and Rwanda.[179]

The actions which the Committee can take under the procedures include requesting the submission of a report, bringing the situation to the attention of others, including the High Commissioner for Human Rights, the Secretary General or indeed the General Assembly and the Security Council. Members have also undertaken Good-Offices missions both to Croatia and Yugoslavia.

It is right that the CERD, given its mandate, should have sought to respond directly to some of the worst episodes of ethnic and racial conflict of the 1990s, such as have occurred in the Balkans and the Great Lakes region of east Africa. It is equally important for the future, given its accumulated knowledge and experience, that it should provide early warning to the international community over threatened ethnic conflict. But its capacity for positive influence on events must be acknowledged to be limited. CERD cannot itself become a vehicle for active conflict resolution. Its role should be rather to develop a more focused approach on the prevention of ethnic and racial discrimination based both on dialogue with reporting states and through the

[176] A proposed optional protocol to the Convention on the Elimination of Discrimination against Women providing for an individual complaint procedure is pending before the UN Human Rights Commission.

[177] A third procedure for monitoring implementation was created by Article 15 of the Convention, providing for cooperation between the Committee and competent United Nations bodies in matters of petitions from and reports concerning Non-Self-Governing Territories. See *supra* n. 71.

[178] UN Doc. A/48/18 paras.15–19 and Annex 3.

[179] For an account of the new preventive procedures, see Wolfrum, *supra* n. 123, at 513. Also Van Boven, 'Prevention, Early-warning and Urgent Procedures: A New Approach by the Committee on the Elimination of Racial Discrimination', in E. Denters and N. Schrijver (eds), *Reflections on International Law from the Low Countries* (1998) 165.

expansion of the individual complaint mechanism. Subject to its primary role as a treaty monitoring body, CERD can best make a contribution in response to gross violation or threatened ethnic violence where it acts as a partner with others, including any relevant national or regional body as well as the UN Human Rights Commission's Special Rapporteur on Contemporary Forms of Racism. However, the prospects of achieving such cooperative action in the short term among all such bodies can only be described as poor given experience to date.

(g) Funding

The capacity of the CERD to function effectively and creatively depends on its budget. That remains in crisis.[180] The finances of the CERD were entrusted under the Convention directly to the states who became parties, not to the UN regular budget. This decision apparently was intended to underscore the independence of the Committee. It has not worked out, however, quite like that. States, although subject to a modest levy, have been late or have failed to pay their contributions. This resulted in a series of sessions being cancelled in the 1980s, only halted when as a stop gap the Secretary General with General Assembly approval provided interim funding. An amendment to ICERD to enable its budget to be paid from the regular UN budget, although approved by the meeting of the states parties and the General Assembly, has still not come into effect.[181] The amendment requires approval in accordance with domestic legal procedures of all states which are parties to ICERD. But a decade later many states have yet to take the necessary steps.

Similar funding concerns afflict the one other UN institution established to respond to racism in the world in addition to ICERD, the Special Rapporteur of the Human Rights Commission, which will next be discussed.

V. THE SPECIAL RAPPORTEUR ON CONTEMPORARY FORMS OF RACISM, RACIAL DISCRIMINATION, XENOPHOBIA, AND RELATED INTOLERANCE

The institution of thematic rapporteurs by the UN Human Rights Commission, tasked with the investigation, analysis and, in some cases, the authority to respond to violation, has been a key innovation in the human rights competence of the United Nations. One such is the Special Rapporteur on Contemporary Forms of Racism, Racial Discrimination, Xenophobia, and

[180] ICERD is not alone in its long-term financing problems. All treaty bodies have similar problems. See Schmidt, 'Servicing and Financing Human Rights Supervisory Bodies', in Alston and Crawford, *supra* n. 72, at 481.

[181] This was proposed in the first report on treaty reform of the independent expert, Mr Philip Alston. UN Doc. A/44/668 (1989).

Related Intolerance, first appointed in 1993.[182] The selection of topics of human rights concern by the Commission justifying the appointment of rapporteurs is often infused by political considerations. The need for a thematic rapporteur on racism was pressed by Turkey. Among Turkey's concerns was the treatment of Turkish citizens in Germany. But there was a general concern shared by many developing countries that the focus on human rights violations, including ethnic discrimination in the developing world, should be balanced by attention to racism, especially against immigrants, in the developed world.[183]

The origins of the initiative can be traced to a report reviewing UN Decades against Racism undertaken for the Sub-Commission on Prevention of Discrimination and Protection of Minorities by Asbjorn Eide.[184] His study confirmed the grim reality of the rise of anti-Semitism as well as racism and extreme nationalism in Europe and the developed world as a whole, directed at minorities, indigenous peoples, migrant workers, and other vulnerable groups. The Sub-Commission thereafter sought an overview study from the Secretary General of current trends in racism discrimination, intolerance, and xenophobia.[185] The Secretary General's report, considered at the forty-fourth session (1992) of the Sub-Commission, confirmed the 'resurgence of racism and xenophobia throughout the world and more particularly in Europe, the United States and Australia'.[186]

At its forty-ninth session in 1993, the Commission, acting on a recommendation of the Sub-Commission, approved the appointment for a three-year term of a special rapporteur on contemporary forms of racism.[187] The discussion of the scope of the mandate in the Commission reflected horse-trading between the sponsors (Turkey and Pakistan) and the European Union states. The outcome was a mandate to cover all countries, but with a particular focus on developed countries and the situation of vulnerable groups, especially

[182] This account of the Special Rapporteur draws heavily on the research undertaken by Bernhard Schaefer, graduate student. We wish to acknowledge with gratitude his contribution. See Schaefer, 'The United Nations Struggle against Racism and Racial Discrimination—The Contribution of the Special Rapporteur on Contemporary Forms of Racism, Racial Discrimination, Xenophobia and Related Intolerance', *Papers in the Theory and Practice of Human Rights*, University of Essex, 2001 (forthcoming).

[183] According to a report in *The Times* (12 Dec. 1994), the appointment reflected the 'resentment many Third World countries felt at what they saw as the "disproportionate" focus on abuse in the developed world, and the relative silence over race relations in richer, industrialized countries. Turkey, especially, was piqued at the focus on its treatment of Kurds, and wanted more publicity for the treatment of Turkish migrant workers in Germany.' Cited in Banton, *supra* n. 76, at 41.

[184] *Study on the Achievements Made and Obstacles Encountered During the Decades to Combat Racism and Racial Discrimination*, E/CN.4/Sub.2/1989/8/ and Add.1. The UN Decades to Combat Racism are dealt with in Part VI, *infra*.

[185] Sub-Commission Res. 1990/2.

[186] E/CN.4/Sub.2/1992/11, para. 142.

[187] CHR Res. 1993/20.

migrant workers. Mr Robert Dossou (Benin) was initially appointed to the post but on his being made foreign minister, Mr Maurice Glele Ahanhanzo, also from Benin, was appointed on 7 December 1993.

From the perspective of the effectiveness of the UN approach to racism as a whole, it is depressing that this otherwise useful initiative was taken without any consultation with the long established treaty body—the CERD. That the proposal for a special rapporteur was promoted mainly by countries that were not parties to the ICERD is hardly an explanation. The Turkish sponsor stressed the limitations of the treaty mechanism in dealing with the reporting of racist incidents on an ongoing basis. He also argued for the need to monitor developments in countries that had not ratified ICERD.[188] These were legitimate points. The existence of a special thematic rapporteur alongside treaty bodies dealing with the same subject area is not unique.[189] But had the proposal been seen by the CERD and its reactions included in the Commission discussion, the potential contribution of the special rapporteur to a coherent UN human rights strategy towards new forms of racism might have been advanced. In particular, a plan of cooperative and complementary action between both mechanisms could have been endorsed by the Commission. Exchanges have occurred between CERD and the Special Rapporteur on cooperation. But they do not appear to date to have been successful. The question of cooperation is discussed further below.

(i) Anti-Semitism and Islamophobia

The Special Rapporteur's mandate was extended and clarified by the Commission in 1994. It now embraces 'incidents of contemporary forms of racism, racial discrimination, any form of discrimination against Blacks, Arabs, and Muslims, xenophobia, negrophobia, anti-Semitism, and related intolerance'.[190] This language reflects the Arab–Israeli conflict. It was not possible to get agreement to the Western group proposal that would have added anti-Semitism as one focus of the proposed mandate. The same issue had arisen in the same way in the 1960s over the drafting of ICERD.[191] Arab rejection then of a reference to anti-Semitism concerned any implication that it might involve political recognition of Israel.[192] In 1993, with the hopes for the Oslo peace process that began in that year, there appears to have been a change of attitude among states and a preparedness to end the often deliberate confusion between anti-Semitism, anti-Zionism, and other

[188] E/CN.4/Sub.2/1992/SR.11, para. 30–1.

[189] For example, the Special Rapporteur on Torture and the UN Convention Against Torture.

[190] CHR Res. 1994/64, para. 4.

[191] See Part III(iv), *infra*.

[192] Lerner, *supra* n. 134, at 2 and 72.

political disagreements with Israel. The diplomatic solution found for the Special Rapporteur's mandate was to balance the reference to anti-Semitism with other targets of contemporary discrimination, in particular Arabs and Muslims. The result can be criticized in technical terms as inappropriate.[193] Nevertheless on the principles of openness and of naming racism where it occurs or is perceived to occur, the solution has proved to be a positive one.

During the debate on the proposal to create the new position it was pointed out by the representative of the World Jewish Congress that the Commission had never before condemned anti-Semitism.[194] If this was true, the inclusion of anti-Semitism in the mandate constituted condemnation and the Special Rapporteur has in subsequent reports brought to the attention of the Commission the continuing shameful reality of hatred of and violence against Jews.[195] At the same time the Special Rapporteur has been able to also document discrimination against Arabs, a phenomenon captured in the new term 'Islamophobia'.[196] Although he has referred questions of 'discrimination against Muslims' in his mandate to the Special Rapporteur on Religious Intolerance, to avoid overlap he has recognized that, as with the case of anti-Semitism, it is not all that easy to distinguish religious and racially motivated prejudice.[197]

The Special Rapporteur gained some early experience on the sensitivities of discussing the facts and prejudices that inform racism in his first reports. His setting out of what was reported to him about Jews led to expression of concern by several Jewish organizations and the Israeli Government.[198] While praising his work in general, they noted that such statements 'reinforced hateful anti-Semitic stereotypes'. The Rapporteur, in his own defence, noted that he had adopted the same approach in reporting the facts of prejudice against Blacks.[199]

In his next report he set out an extended quotation from the Israeli Government that laid some of the blame for attacks against Jews in Europe at the feet of 'Muslim extremists' and a claim that the same extremists 'were turning to the Qur'an as a primary anti-Jewish source'.[200] This brought a protest from the Organization of the Islamic Conference, an unprecedented condemnation from the Human Rights Commission, and a decision of the Commission requesting its Chairman 'to ask the Special Rapporteur to take

[193] Specification can suggest that other forms of discrimination are excluded from the purview of a mandate that is in principle concerned with all contemporary forms of racial and ethnic discrimination.

[194] E/CN.4/1994/SR.9, para. 6. The Sub-Commission condemned anti-Semitism in 1960. See *supra* n. 61, and Banton, *supra* n. 76, at 53.

[195] Anti-Semitism is defined by the Special Rapporteur as 'the despising of Jews' which 'can be considered to be one of the root causes of racial and religious hatred'. A/49/677, para. 149.

[196] E/CN.4/1998/79, para. 39. [197] A/49/677, para. 17. [198] A/49/677, para. 111.

[199] A/50/476, paras 10–17.

[200] E/CN.4/1997/71, para. 27 and A/52/471, paras 6–7.

corrective action'.[201] While the Special Rapporteur commented that it was not for him to censor a government communication, he did delete a sentence of his report.[202]

This development in turn led to the meeting of special rapporteurs in 1997 at which it was recorded that there was a 'consensus among the participants that it was inappropriate for the Commission to request a special rapporteur to amend his report. It was clearly stressed that special rapporteurs were responsible for the content of their reports and that the Commission could criticize the substance of a report.'[203]

Professsor van Boven has commented, with no doubt an eye to the forthcoming World Conference on Racism, that 'such discord in the struggle against racism and racial discrimination is in stark contrast with the unity of action that the women's movement demonstrated in the process leading to the World Conference on Human Rights at Vienna in 1993 and the 1995 Fourth World Conference on Women in Beijing'.[204]

Nevertheless the fact that discord and disagreement exist needs to be faced, as does the depressing reality of pervasive ethnic and racial hostility in developed and developing world. The contribution of the Special Rapporteur, whether intentionally or not, has been positive in removing the diplomatic veil from that reality.

(ii) Assessment

The Special Rapporteur has had his mandate renewed and has been engaged upon it for six years. He has submitted annual reports to the Commission and to the General Assembly. He has also undertaken a range of country studies based on visits to those countries. What assessment can be made on his contribution to date?

There can be no doubt that the work carried out by Mr Glele Ahanhanzo has been useful. His initial or preliminary report offered some tentative definitions of the broad phenomena he had been asked to report, including racism, racial discrimination, and xenophobia.[205] Analytical depth may be wanting but the clear distinction between institutional racism, as reflected in governmental policies such as apartheid, and the multitude of racist practices that function without official sanction and despite legal prohibitions is useful for understanding contemporary racism. His initial reports are also important in conveying the complexity of racism and its often subtle and covert expression. Thus, while the core idea remains that of belief in a hierarchy of races,

201 CHR Dec.1997/125 of 18 Apr. 1997.

202 E/CN.4/1997/Corr.1.

203 E/CN.4/1998/45, para. 23.

204 Van Boven, *supra* n. 66, at 255.

205 E/CN.4/1994/66.

he notes that there has been a shift from biological to cultural explanations among those who espouse such doctrines. At the same time he notes that not all ethnic conflict and discrimination is the working out of belief in racial superiority. Ethnic groups differ and it can be competition over resources and the manipulation of awareness of difference that leads to discrimination, xenophobia, and violence.

(a) Annual Reports

His annual reports presented to the Commission and to the General Assembly provide a limited but undoubtedly authentic view of the reality of racial discrimination, prejudice, and violence experienced by ordinary people in many countries. The most useful function these reports perform is in keeping the Commission and the General Assembly aware of the manifold and ever-changing expressions of racism and racial intolerance. Typically annual reports include a summary of activities, a section on current examples of racism, xenophobia, and related intolerance in different countries, measures taken by governments and public institutions, the initiatives of civil society organizations in combating racism, along with conclusions and recommendations. He reports on incidents of racism and racial discrimination in general, as well as against Blacks and Arabs, and he details information on anti-Semitism, xenophobia, discrimination against women, and migrant workers. Following the appointment of a Special Rapporteur on the human rights of migrants in 1999, Mr Glele Ahanhanzo has dropped this subject from his report.[206] The Rapporteur has also included in his annual reports documentation on other targets of racial discrimination not specified in his mandate, including the Roma and indigenous peoples.

The annual reports lack depth and have other limitations that are related to the failure to provide the human resources the Special Rapporteur needs for his work. Six years into his mandate he has not had the resources he requested to undertake his work. Repeated requests have been made by the Human Rights Commission and the General Assembly to the Secretary General for such support to no avail.[207]A properly resourced mechanism could achieve much more.

(b) Country Missions

The Special Rapporteur has undertaken some eleven country studies to date.[208] These field missions are intended to allow him 'to assess the conditions actually

[206] The Special Rapporteur on the human rights of migrants, CHR Res. 1999/44, para. 3. For her first report, see E/CN.4/2000/82.

[207] See, for example, A/49/677, para. 50–1; E/CN.4/1995/78. All special procedures suffer similar administrative, financial, and personnel problems.

[208] In chronological order: USA, Brazil, Germany, France, the United Kingdom, Colombia, Kuwait, South Africa, Hungary, the Czech Republic, and Romania.

prevailing in a country by giving him direct access to first hand reports and to the dialogue established with the authorities of the countries in question and key figures in civil society'.[209] The authority to undertake such country studies deriving from a Special Rapporteur's mandate is one of the distinct advantages of this mechanism. The Special Rapporteur has taken full advantage of the opportunities provided in these missions both to meet governmental and non-governmental representatives, to visit prisons and holding camps, to meet with victims of racial discrimination and with the media.

It is not possible to consider these missions or the reports resulting from them in detail in the confines of this chapter.[210] Only a few will be noted here. The first mission undertaken was to the United States in 1994, producing the first UN study of racism and racial discrimination in that country.[211] The report is noteworthy for its in depth coverage of continued serious questions of racial discrimination, including in respect of the death penalty, the question of police violence, the activities of racist organizations, and the issue of hate speech.

The study resulting from his visit to Brazil deserves mention for the quality of its analysis.[212] As the Rapporteur notes, Brazil is perceived by the international community as a positive example of ethnic and racial integration. While it is true that intermingling of the races—'Whites', 'Blacks', and 'Indians'—has made classification by race difficult, the report shows that nevertheless pervasive and subtle economic and social discrimination persists, based on a 'colour hierarchy'. He was struck, as all observers must be, by the dramatic contrast between the rich and poor in Brazil and the link between poverty and colour.[213]

His reports on Germany, France, and the United Kingdom bring out common concerns over ever more stringent immigration and asylum legislation, as well as issues of anti-Semitism, police violence, and prejudice against racial minorities.[214]

Finally, reference should be made to the Rapporteur's visit to South Africa, a country whose former apartheid governmental system had been the focus of international anti-racism activities for almost half a century. His report records the continuing difficulties of transition to a democratic society, as well as new trends of racism and xenophobia. As regards the latter he noted that the presence of xenophobia directed at 'coloured' immigrants was increasing not only within the white population but also among the black majority.[215]

209 A/49/677, para. 46.

210 See for a detailed account, Schaefer, *supra* n. 182.

211 E/CN.4/1995/78/Add.1; (A/50/476, paras 18–20).

212 E/CN.4/1996/72/Add.1.

213 Ibid., para. 74(1).

214 See Germany, Sept. 1995, E/CN.4/1996/Add. 1; France, Sept.–Oct. 1995, E/CN.4/1996/72/Add.3; United Kingdom, Nov. 1995, E/CN.4/1996/72/Add.4.

215 Feb. 1995, E/CN.4/1996/72/Add.2.

In so far as one purpose of such visits is to inform the international community in more depth of the issues related to both racial discrimination and the efforts to abate or eliminate it, the country studies certainly succeed in that goal. It should also be noted that the Rapporteur, whose mandate was created primarily to focus on racism in the developed world, has in his country missions as in his annual reports chosen countries from different world regions.

The Special Rapporteur has made efforts to assess the impact of his recommendations and suggestions to governments arising from his country missions in follow up procedures. Given the restraint on resources, these efforts are impressive and the evidence provided on the impact of his work credible.[216]

(c) Cooperation with CERD and Other Bodies

Resolution 1993/20, establishing the mandate of the Special Rapporteur, encouraged him to 'have an exchange of views with the various relevant mechanisms and treaty bodies within the United Nations system in order to further enhance their effectiveness and mutual cooperation'. There have been such exchanges of views with a range of bodies, but they have not led to mutual cooperation or enhanced effectiveness of those working against racial discrimination at the UN level.

An initial meeting between the most relevant other body—the CERD—and the Special Rapporteur was held in March 1995.[217] There was agreement that the two mechanisms should work together in a complementary and reinforcing manner. The key advantages of the Rapporteur were that he had the authority to undertake visits to countries and, in addition, he could gather information on countries that had not ratified the ICERD. Concrete proposals for joint action in, for example, police training and mobilizing youth in the fight against racism were discussed. The Committee proposed that it could alert the Special Rapporteur to emergency situations through its new focus on the prevention of racial discrimination. The Special Rapporteur proposed that he could publicize the ICERD and the work of the Committee in his activities.

Little if anything of this positive thinking has come to pass. CERD has noted that since the 1995 meeting cooperation has 'faltered'.[218] One former member has noted that the Special Rapporteur's reports on Germany, France, the United Kingdom, Kuwait, and Colombia completely ignored the concluding observations of CERD with regard to the very same countries.[219] The

[216] On follow up, see A/51/301, paras 8–15 and 47 (field missions implementation of recommendations) and E/CN.4/1996/72, paras 62–5 (provisional evaluation). See also the CHR Res. 1997/74, para. 33, inviting governments that have ratified ICERD and which the Special Rapporteur has visited to include information in their periodic reports on measures they have taken to implement his recommendations.

[217] See A/50/476 and summary records of the meeting CERD/C/SR.1095.

[218] A/52/18, para. 666.

[219] Van Boven, *supra* n. 66, at 261.

Committee concluded in its 1999 report to the General Assembly that the Special Rapporteur 'appears to completely overlook the relevance of the Convention on the Elimination of All Forms of Racial Discrimination and the work of the Committee'.[220]

The Special Rapporteur also participated in a joint meeting of CERD and the Sub-Commission in August 1995.[221] In that year he also met with the Bureau of the European Commission against Racism and Intolerance and UNESCO, in both cases to discuss cooperation.[222] Little evidence is available of any practical outcomes of these contacts in the Special Rapporteur's work.

Some of the explanation for the failure of any synergy to develop with other bodies following the appointment of the Special Rapporteur may be found in the poor internal coordination between the relevant members of the human rights secretariat at the UN, a problem compounded by insufficient staff and funding. Given the seriousness of the human rights challenge that racism offers, it is unacceptable that the few mechanisms charged with responding to that challenge appear to function in isolation, and duplicate each other's role where they might build on their comparative advantages. Something is seriously wrong when, as admitted by the Special Rapporteur, a number of countries from whom he requested information replied by enclosing their periodic reports already submitted under ICERD which contained the information he had requested.[223] It is equally wrong that the Special Rapporteur's mission reports on the countries he has visited ignore data already available in periodic reports under the Convention.[224] As inexcusable is his failure to incorporate in a number of his own reports CERD Concluding Observations in respect of countries he has visited.[225] In contrast it should be noted that CERD members are provided with any relevant reports of the Special Rapporteur when considering a state report.[226] The credibility of the entire international human rights system is put at risk by such self-evident examples of lack of cooperation and of a common strategy.

VI. THE UN PROGRAMME OF DECADES AND WORLD CONFERENCES TO COMBAT RACISM AND RACIAL DISCRIMINATION

The United Nations has pursued an ambitious programme of international action, of Decades and World Conferences over the last thirty years with the

[220] A/52/18, para. 666. [221] See A/50/476, para. 33.

[222] E/CN.4/1996/72, paras 5–10. [223] E/CN.4/2000/16, para. 5.

[224] As noted by the CERD, A/52/18, para. 666.

[225] His reports on Germany, France, United Kingdom, Colombia, and Kuwait ignored the CERD recommendations on those countries.

[226] Van Boven, E.CN.4/1999/WG.1/BP.7, n. 25.

goal of the total and unconditional elimination of racism and racial discrimination throughout the world. The General Assembly, however, has acknowledged in repeated resolutions the failure of this vast programme.[227] On the launch of the Third Decade for Action to Combat Racism and Racial Discrimination in 1993, the Assembly noted with grave concern that 'the principal objectives of the previous two Decades have not been attained and that millions of human beings continue to this day to be victims of varied forms of racism and racial discrimination . . .'.[228] Other resolutions have lamented that 'at various levels . . . [racism is] showing signs of increase'.[229] As the Third Decade draws to an end, little interest or support has been shown by the international community in its fate, as evidenced by the paucity of funds contributed to the Trust Fund for the Decade's Programme of Action.[230]

These global activities stem from an initiative of the former Soviet Union beginning in 1971 when it succeeded in having that year declared the International Year to Combat Racism and Racial Discrimination.[231] As a follow-up to the International Year, the General Assembly designated the ten-year period beginning 10 December 1973 as the Decade for Action to Combat Racism and Racial Discrimination. It also approved a Programme of Action for the Decade calling upon member states to cooperate in every possible way in its implementation.[232] The programme set out activities to be undertaken at national, regional, and international levels, and included the idea of convening a World Conference on combating racism and racial discrimination. That conference was held in 1978.

[227] For the latest such admission, see GA Res. 54/154 of 29 Feb. 2000.

[228] GA Res. 48/91 (1993).

[229] See GA Res. 51/81 (1997); GA Res. 52/11 (1998); GA Res. 52/132 (1999); GA Res. 54/154 (2000).

[230] Lack of resources impeded the implementation of many activities of the Decades. A Trust Fund for the Programme for the Decade of Action was instituted in 1973 in application of para. 17 of the Programme of Action for the first Decade and re-established in 1983, in the framework of the Programme of Action for the second Decade. Contributions to the Fund have been scarce and remained below the levels hoped for, despite repeated appeals to governments (see A/47/77 of 1992 paras 12 and 20, A/50/136 of 1996 para. 22, A/51/81 of 1997 para. 16, A/52/111 of 1998 paras 11 and 12). Finally, A/53/132 of 1999, para. 22, requests the Secretary General to make provisions for financing the activities of the Programme of Action from the UN regular budget as a vital contribution to the World Conference.

[231] See also Resolution VII of the International Conference on Human Rights held in Tehran, Iran, in 1968 calling for the establishment of a new United Nations programme on racial discrimination. For the text of the Proclamation of Tehran, and resolutions, from the Final Act of the International Conference, see UN Doc. A/CONF.32/41. The Proclamation, adopted unanimously at the Tehran Conference, includes a reaffirmation of the Universal Declaration of Human Rights. It thus constitutes the first major endorsement of the UDHR by the Eastern Bloc, that had abstained when it was adopted in 1948, as well as by many newly independent countries.

[232] GA Res. 3057 (XXVIII) (1973) and the Programme of Action for the Decade annexed to the resolution.

A Second Decade (1983–93) was proclaimed on the recommendation of the Second World Conference to combat racism and racial discrimination, which took place in 1983.[233] The purpose of the Second World Conference was to evaluate the work undertaken during the First Decade and to chart new measures where necessary.[234]

Both World Conferences to date crumbled under political controversy. The agenda of both Conferences was dominated by South Africa and the Middle East. Highest priority was given to combating apartheid. Israel, along with South Africa, was singled out for special condemnation.[235] The Israel–Arab conflict was central to the failure not only of the Conferences but also of the Decades as a whole. In 1975 a General Assembly resolution described Zionism as a form of racial discrimination.[236] The 'infamous resolution' provoked the withdrawal of the US and Israel from the Programme for the First Decade. Other Western countries, while remaining involved, opposed what they considered a deliberate diversion from the fight against racism. The Second Decade commenced in 1983 with the international community divided along the same lines of confrontation. The comprehensive and far-reaching measures envisaged in the second Programme of Action—in the field of education, teaching, and training, in the protection of minorities, indigenous populations, migrant workers, and in the establishment of recourse procedures for victims—came to nothing. The Programme did not attract funds from those Western states that contributed most to the UN budget.

The onset of the Third Decade (1993–2003) held out hope of a new approach.[237] The Iron Curtain dividing East and West had fallen, a democratic transition was under way in South Africa, and the peace process in the Middle East had taken off. Discussion in the General Assembly reflected a change in tone, and a shift of focus from condemnation of racist regimes to a recognition that discriminatory practices based on culture, nationality, religion, or language affected states throughout the world. The 1993 World Conference on Human Rights in Vienna had moved the question of equality

233 GA Res. 38/14 (1983).

234 A study on the achievements made and obstacles encountered during the First Decade was entrusted by the Sub-Commission to Asbjorn Eide. E/CN.4/Sub.2/1989/8/Add.1 (1989). See *supra* n. 184.

235 See Reports of the 1978 and 1983 World Conferences to Combat Racism and Racial Discrimination, A/CONF.92/40 and A/CONF.119/26, respectively. Para. 18 of the 1978 Declaration (A/CONF.92/40) states: 'The Conference condemns the existing and increasing relations between the Zionist State of Israel and the racist regime of South Africa, . . .' . Para. 19 expresses deep regret for the situation of Palestinians, calling on Israel to cease all practices of racial discrimination against them. These statements are reiterated, although in a less strong language, in the 1983 Declaration, A/CONF.119/26, paras 18 and 19.

236 GA Res. 3379 (XXX) (1975), formally revoked by GA Res. 46/86 (1991).

237 GA Res. 48/9 (1993) and Programme of Action annexed. The Programme of Action was revised by GA Res. 49/146 of 1994 dropping measures related to apartheid.

up the human rights agenda and the conflict in the Former Yugoslavia brought home how racism could lead to such extreme practices as ethnic cleansing.[238]

The new (revised) Programme of Action for the Third Decade reflecting budget constraints is far less ambitious in scope than those that have gone before. But as its pared down programme still depends on voluntary contributions to the Trust Fund there is little scope for optimism. A review of the period 1994–2000 shows that out of a dozen seminars envisaged in the Programme, only five have so far been held.[239] Planned research into the causes of the new manifestations of racism and racial discrimination does not appear to have been undertaken.

The Third Decade may be rescued in its final phase by the momentum generated by the forthcoming (third) World Conference Against Racism, Racial Discrimination, Xenophobia, and Related Intolerance, to be held in South Africa in 2001, to the preparation of which the activities of the Decade's Programme have been focused.[240] The Resolution convening the Conference places emphasis on the need to address in a comprehensive manner all forms of racism and racial discrimination and to focus on action-oriented and practical measures to eradicate racism, including measures of prevention, education, and protection and the provision of effective remedies.[241] It stressed the importance of taking a gender perspective into account

[238] See Vienna Declaration and Programme of Action and the text concerning the elimination of racism, A/CONF.157/23 (1993), Part II B.

[239] These are: *Seminar on the Implementation of the International Convention on the Elimination of All Forms of Racial Discrimination with Particular Reference to Articles 4 and 6*, E/CN.4/1997/68/Add.1; *Seminar on the Role of the Internet in the Light of the Provisions of the International Convention on the Elimination of All Forms of Racial Discrimination*, E/CN.4/1998/77/Add.2; *Seminar on Immigration, Racism and Racial Discrimination*, E/CN.4/1998/77/Add.1; *Seminar of Experts on Racism, Refugees and Multiethnic States*, A/CONF.189/PC.1/9; *Expert Seminar on Remedies Available to the Victims of Acts of Racism, Racial Discrimination, Xenophobia and Related Intolerance and on Good National Practices in this Field*, A/CONF.189/PC.1/8. See also the final draft of the Model National Legislation for the Guidance of Governments in the Enactment of Further Legislation Against Racial Discrimination (HR/PUB/96/2). On the non-implementation of the Plan of Action, see also the recent reports submitted to the General Assembly by the Secretary-General, A/52/528 and A/53/305.

[240] The Office of the High Commissioner for Human Rights is to serve as a focal point of coordination. Before the decision of the General Assembly to convene the (third) World Conference against Racism, no focal point existed within the Office of the High Commissioner for Human Rights, which was in charge of the Third Decade. See GA Res. 54/154 (1999) welcoming the establishment of a racism project team within the OHCHR.

[241] GA Res. 52/111 (1998). The first PrepCom (1–5 May, Geneva) adopted the draft provisional agenda based on five major World Conference themes, which are: 1. Sources, causes, forms and contemporary manifestations of racism, racial discrimination, xenophobia and related intolerance; 2. Victims of racism, racial discrimination, xenophobia and related intolerance; 3. Measures of prevention, education and protection aimed at the eradication of racism,

throughout the preparations for and in the outcome of the World Conference. It encourages the organization of regional and national meetings in preparation for the event.[242] Unprecedented attention is given to the role of civil society and non-governmental organizations in contributing to a positive outcome for the Conference.[243] The year 2001 has been designated by the General Assembly as the 'International Year of Mobilization against Racism, Racial Discrimination, Xenophobia, and Related Intolerance'. This decision is intended to draw the world's attention to the objectives of the World Conference and give new momentum to the political commitment to the elimination of racism.[244]

VII. CONCLUSIONS

This chapter has reviewed international human rights approaches to the problem of racism and racial discrimination over the last fifty years. It is a review that must conclude with a mixed verdict in terms of achievement. If success is to be measured in terms of the ending of racist and colonial regimes in the world, then there have been positive results. Apartheid is no more and decolonization is virtually complete. But if success is measured in terms of the global rejection of racist theory or beliefs and the elimination of all forms of racial and ethnic discrimination, the record is dismal.

racial discrimination, xenophobia and related intolerance; 4. Provision of effective remedies, recourse, redress, [compensatory] and other measures at the national, regional and international levels, and; 5. Strategies to achieve full and effective equality, including international cooperation and enhancement of the United Nations and other international mechanisms in combating racism, racial discrimination, xenophobia and related intolerance, and follow-up. See the report of the Commission on Human Rights acting as the Preparatory Committee for the World Conference on its first session (1–5 May 2000), A/55/307 and annexed the decisions adopted by the first PrepCom.

[242] Expert seminars on regional themes were held in Warsaw, Poland (5–7 July 2000), Bangkok, Thailand (5–7 Sept. 2000), Addis Ababa, Ethiopia (4–6 Oct. 2000), Santiago, Chile (25–27 Oct. 2000). Four regional preparatory conferences are also scheduled in Europe, Africa, the Americas, and Asia. The first one—the European Conference against Racism—took place in Strasbourg from 11–13 Oct. 2000. See the General Conclusions of the European Conference against Racism, EUROCONF (2000) 7 final, 16 Oct. 2000.

[243] This is reflected in the appointment in late 1999 of an NGO liaison officer by the Secretariat for the World Conference against Racism, established within the Office of the High Commissioner for Human Rights. Another unprecedented aspect of NGO involvement in the World Conference is the funding of NGOs by OHCHR to support their participation at three of the four regional conferences—the conferences taking place in Santiago for the Americas, Dakar for Africa, and Tehran for Asia. In addition, the OHCHR is funding four networking meetings for NGOs to permit them to plan their input into the NGO Forum which will take place in South Africa just prior to the government conference. On the preparatory process for the World Conference, see A/55/285.

[244] A/53/132 1999, para. 37.

The pressure from the newly independent Asian and African countries, who became in the early 1960s the majority voice in the General Assembly, forced the pace on decolonization and apartheid. That pressure also laid the foundations of what has become the UN human rights system. But there was a cost. The struggle for racial equality and against discrimination became incorporated into the larger political and ideological conflicts of the Cold War. In the aftermath of the Cold War the issue of race threatens to be a continuing ideological battleground between developing and developed world. One indication was the clash at the first PrepCom held in Geneva for the 2001 World Conference, between the Western, African, and Latin American groups on the subject of compensation for the descendants of slaves and for indigenous populations.[245] The prospect of the World Conference reaching the necessary consensus for common action on a global basis towards the elimination of all forms of racial and ethnic discrimination appears remote.

Perhaps the most important if modest goal for the forthcoming World Conference would be the acceptance that new thinking is required. It should start from the premise that the subject is more complex than is often acknowledged and needs a long-term approach. A beginning has been suggested with the proposal that the CERD should agree a statement on the scope of the definition of racial discrimination in the Convention. In particular there is a need to bring out the distinction between discrimination based on colour and other differences, including cultural, which attract hostility and discrimination. Whether it is appropriate to label all forms of ethnic discrimination as racism in a normative definition requires study. Another element of a new approach should be a renewed emphasis on equality as a central component of international human rights law. In concrete terms that would require linking the goal of eliminating racial discrimination with the efforts to eliminate other forms of discrimination. Exploring the common links as well as the overlap between different forms of group discrimination may help to release the subject of racism and racial discrimination from its historical and politicized past. It would also identify the degree of progress or lack of it in removing other dimensions of discrimination, for example discrimination on grounds of religion or belief or sex discrimination.

The political and ideological environment in which the human rights activities directed at combating racial discrimination have been pursued in the past has served to isolate such efforts from other fields of anti-discrimination work. It also appears to have resulted in a distance between, for example, CERD and the bodies implementing the UN Covenants, the Human Rights Committee and the Economic, Social and Cultural Rights Committee. The

[245] See n. 241 *supra* and the confrontation over inclusion of the word 'compensatory' in the draft agenda for the World Conference between developed and Western countries, A/CONF.189/PC.1/21, 16 June 2000.

advancement of the international protection of human rights in the twenty-first century in theory and practice should be based on a new alignment between the promotion of equality and non-discrimination and the implementation of substantive human rights. A significant beginning has been made in the case of gender.[246] But there is also a need to address other categories of discrimination and exclusion as mainstream human rights concerns.

New norms strengthening protection against racial and ethnic discrimination are in prospect when the 1990 International Convention on the Protection of the Rights of Migrant Workers and Members of Their Families comes into force. The need for ratification of this Convention will be highlighted at the World Conference. The implementation of this important Convention provides an opportunity for the existing treaty bodies to rethink the relationships between the anti–discrimination treaties and the general human rights instruments. The Convention should not emerge as another unconnected initiative in the international protection of human rights.[247]

The fight against racial discrimination and prejudice needs above all a new emphasis on education. Education will be a topic at the World Conference. It is to be hoped that the need to bring together disparate initiatives in this field will be pursued. Thus, the efforts of the Special Rapporteur on Religious Intolerance to encourage the teaching of tolerance in schools and the activities generated by the current Decade on Human Rights Education (1995–2004) should be linked to any new UN initiatives on anti-racism education.[248] The experience of NGOs and of regional bodies such as the Council of Europe and OSCE in the fields of building tolerance and combating prejudice against minorities must be used in similar programmes at the global level.

The World Conference should also consider whether proclaiming another decade against racism and racial discrimination is called for. The idea behind decades has been to educate world opinion on the evils of racism. They have failed in that purpose. Fresh ideas are needed in the vital battle to involve public opinion on the side of tolerance and rejection of racism and xenophobia.

[246] Mainstreaming women's rights in UN activities dates from the Vienna World Conference on Human Rights 1993. See Vienna Declaration and Programme of Action, A/CONF.157/23, Part II B(3), para. 37, providing that '[gender] issues should be regularly and systematically addressed throughout relevant United Nations bodies and mechanisms'.

[247] The call by the Independent Expert, Mr Philip Alston, for radical rethinking of the working of treaty bodies, including his suggestion that the monitoring function for the Migrant Workers Convention ought to be undertaken by an existing treaty body in place of a new committee, is an excellent place to begin such discussion. See *supra* n. 152.

[248] The Special Rapporteur on Religious Intolerance will report on his educational work in an international conference to be held in November 2001 in Madrid. Press Release GA Third Committee 34th Meeting, 25 Oct. 2000. On implementation of the Decade on Human Rights Education see report of the High Commissioner on Human Rights to the General Assembly A/51/506 (1996).

The European experience of concentrating such activities over a year would seem to be a better alternative.[249]

The most important achievement of the international human rights approach to the elimination of racial discrimination has been to establish in international law a prohibition on racism as a state ideology and on the practice of all forms of racial or ethnic discrimination. Not only are these prohibitions part of international customary law but the majority of the world states that have ratified ICERD have embraced a range of duties obligating them to eliminate any such discrimination by legislative, educational, and other means. The encouragement of states in the pursuit of these goals will continue to be the vital and central role of CERD. The monitoring work of that body has expanded beyond discrimination on grounds of colour to include the full range of victims of discrimination, including ethnic minorities, immigrants, and indigenous peoples. CERD needs for the future to work more closely with national and regional anti-discrimination programmes and bodies, as well as to have access to leading research on ethnic relations and inter-cultural education in different parts of the world. CERD's increasingly complex mandate requires more specialist expertise to be added to the Committee's membership if it is to have influence on the policies of states parties. A committee with greater expertise would also in time encourage a wider acceptance by states of the Article 14 individual petition procedure as well as universal ratification of ICERD.

The Vienna World Conference on Human Rights urged the UN bodies to cooperate and avoid overlap in their activities.[250] That has not occurred in the field of racial discrimination. The Commission's Special Rapporteur appears to plough his own furrow without reference to the CERD. It is trite to say that such a situation serves only to undermine the credibility of the entire UN effort to offer leadership in the campaign to eliminate racial discrimination. In particular it makes even more difficult the task of persuading states to fully meet the financial needs of both mandates. It is to be hoped that a coherent United Nations strategy for the future on combating racial discrimination will emerge from the World Conference and that it will provide a coherent role for the Special Rapporteur that reinforces rather than undermines the work of the CERD.

249 The Council of Europe launched a European Youth Campaign against Racism, Xenophobia, Anti-Semitism and Intolerance, which was carried out from 1994 to 1996. See ECRI, *Activities of the Council of Europe with Relevance to Combating Racism and Intolerance*, CRI(99)56 final, Strasbourg, September 1999. Subsequent to this campaign, the European Union declared 1997 the 'European Year Against Racism'. See the report from the Commission on the implementation of the European Year Against Racism (1997), COM(1999)268 final.

250 See A/CONF.157/23 Part II A.

[18]

REINFORCING MARGINALIZED RIGHTS IN AN AGE OF GLOBALIZATION: INTERNATIONAL MECHANISMS, NON-STATE ACTORS, AND THE STRUGGLE FOR PEOPLES' RIGHTS IN AFRICA

J. OLOKA-ONYANGO*

* Associate Professor, Human Rights & Peace Centre (HURIPEC), Makerere University, Kampala; Visiting Professor, New York University Global Law School Program (Fall, 2002). Earlier drafts of this paper were presented to different audiences at the Washington College of Law, American University, Washington DC, and New York University School of Law. I am extremely grateful for the many useful comments that emerged from these discussions, and especially to Chidi Odinkalu, Danny Bradlow, and Sylvia Tamale for their critical reviews of the paper. Elizabeth Kennedy provided research assistance for which I am grateful.

INTRODUCTION

Despite the statement in the Vienna Declaration of 1993 that proclaims all human rights as "... universal, indivisible and interdependent and interrelated,"[1] certain categories of rights within the international corpus are marginalized. Civil and political rights are considered to belong to a first category, or 'generation,' of rights, while economic, social, and cultural rights have been relegated to a lower less important sphere.[2] The marginalization of the latter category can be discerned not only from the level of international attention paid to them, but also with respect to the approach of governments, judges, non-governmental actors, and even academics to the subject.[3] It is also reflected in the reluctance to accord the same weight or gravamen to the violation of these rights.[4] Thus, it is rare to hear of discussions of economic, social, and cultural rights in relation to the subject of genocide, or within the context of discussions about crimes against humanity.[5] Numerous arguments are advanced to differentiate the categories of rights, and the possibilities and mechanics of their enforcement.[6]

---

1. Vienna Declaration, art. 5, A/CONF.157/23, July 12, 1993.

2. *See* Shedrack C. Agbakwa, *Reclaiming Humanity: Economic, Social and Cultural Rights as the Cornerstone of African Human Rights*, 5 YALE HUM. RTS. & DEV. L.J. 177, 177 (2000) (arguing that economic, social, and cultural rights must be established and protected in Africa before human rights can be realized).

3. *See id.* at 178 (discussing the lack of attention paid to economic, social, and cultural rights).

4. *See id.* (imploring African states to enforce these rights, especially because of Africa's poor "socio-economic conditions").

5. *See* Sigrun Skogly, *Crimes Against Humanity-Revisited: Is There a Role for Economic and Social Rights?*, 5 INT'L J. HUM. RTS. 58 (2001) (asserting that civil and political rights are not the only rights involved in atrocities).

6. *See id.* at 66-75 (providing examples of different subcategories of these rights).

The roots of this marginalization can be retraced to the ideological standoff of the Cold War era, coupled with the processes of decolonization and the ensuing North/South divide in international politics.[7] Notwithstanding the demise of the Iron Curtain however, the generational approach continues to hold sway even today.[8] As the world's remaining global super power, the United States justifiably takes much of the blame for its continuing opposition to the enhanced recognition of economic, social and cultural rights.[9] Numerous other countries, however, are still reluctant to accord these rights the same level of domestic recognition and enforceability, raising the concern that they are content to make rhetorical statements about the marginalization of these rights, but not to do much by way of their realization.[10] Such an approach to economic, social and cultural rights reflects both duplicity and an inconsistency in the application of human rights standards.[11] It also raises questions

---

7. *See* Philip Harvey, *Human Rights and Economic Policy Discourse: Taking Economic and Social Rights Seriously*, 33 COLUM. HUM. RTS. L. REV. 363, 387-89 (2002) (discussing the process that resulted in the recognition of the right to work as a human right); *see also* Peter T. Muchlinski, *Human Rights and Multinationals: Is There a Problem?*, 77 INT'L AFF. 31, 34 (2001) (stating that "[t]he Cold War rules our discourse from its grave, as does a residual consciousness of imperial supremacy"), *available at* http://rru.worldbank.org/documents/human_rights_and_multinationals.pdf (last visited Mar. 4, 2003).

8. *See* Linda M. Keller, *The Indivisibility of Economic and Political Rights*, *in* 1(3) HUM. RTS. & HUM. WELFARE 9-14 (2001) (discussing the connection between political freedoms and economic development).

9. *See* Padideh Ala'i, *A Human Rights Critique of the WTO: Some Preliminary Observations*, 33 GEO. WASH. INT'L L. REV. 537, 545-548 (2001) (outlining the historical development of U.S. policy regarding the relationship between civil and political rights, and economic social, and cultural rights, and its past criticism of the United Nations for embracing economic, social and cultural rights).

10. *See* Ida Elisabeth Koch, *Social Rights as Components in the Civil Right to Personal Liberty: Another Step Forward in the Integrated Human Rights Approach?*, 20 NETHERLANDS Q. HUM. RTS. 29, 48-49 (2002) (explaining, for example, that under European Court of Human Rights case law there is no right to treatment for a detainee and "the Court has not been willing to recognize an obligation to provide for the medical or social care that is likely to shorten" detention).

11. *See id.* (stating that this type of approach to economic, social, and cultural rights creates a "catch-22 situation").

about the motives of those who more vigorously apply civil and political rights standards.[12] This approach also demonstrates the gendered character of international human rights law because it is generally women as a social class and as primary care givers who most acutely experience the violation and non-realization of this category of rights, particularly the rights to education, health care, work, and an adequate standard of living.[13]

The upsurge in concern about the phenomenon of globalization and its varied impacts on contemporary society has spurred the current increase in attention paid to economic, social, and cultural rights.[14] Consequently, a number of United Nations' agencies and institutions have taken up the issue of economic, social and cultural rights with increased vigor within the overall context of a "rights-based" approach to development.[15] Academic literature on the subject is growing, as is the number of civil society actors devoting attention to the issue. A growing body of case law (albeit in only a handful of countries) is reflective of an increase in litigation over these rights.[16] Despite these recent attempts, the focus unfortunately remains lopsided. To use the words of Christof Heyns, civil and political rights remain the "daily staple" of the mechanisms designed to enforce the observance of human rights.[17] Economic, social, and

---

12. *See* MICHAEL IGNATIEFF, HUMAN RIGHTS AS POLITICS AND IDOLATRY 19 (2001) (discussing different human rights cultures and their effects on the people under their direct control).

13. *See* HILARY CHARLESWORTH & CHRISTINE CHINKIN, THE BOUNDARIES OF INTERNATIONAL LAW: A FEMINIST ANALYSIS 234-44 (2000); *see also* Anne Gallagher, *Ending the Marginalization: Strategies for Incorporating Women into the UN Human Rights System*, 19(2) HUM. RTS. Q. 283, 285 (1997) (explaining that "women and their concerns remain on the sidelines of United Nations activity for the protection and promotion of human rights").

14. *See* Gallagher, *supra* note 13, at 285 (discussing some of the work done to increase recognition and protection of these rights).

15. *See, e.g.*, United Nations High Commissioner for Human Right, *A Human Rights Approach To Poverty Reduction Strategies*, Sept. 10, 2002 (providing an example of a U.N. agency that has issued draft guidelines integrating human rights into their poverty reduction strategies).

16. *See infra* notes 17-19 and accompanying text (discussing examples of such litigation).

17. Christof Heyns, *Civil and Political Rights in the African Charter*, *in* THE AFRICAN CHARTER ON HUMAN AND PEOPLES' RIGHTS: THE SYSTEM IN PRACTICE,

cultural rights are as much marginalized in the discourse, as they are in the enforcement.[18]

In such an atmosphere, it is important to monitor efforts to ensure that economic, social, and cultural rights gain more prominence on the burner of international attention. Does Africa offer some hope? The imaginative decisions of the South African High and Constitutional Courts, particularly with respect to the rights to education,[19] health[20] and shelter,[21] have been especially important in breaking down some of the philosophical and practical barriers that have been raised against the justiciability or enforceability of these rights.[22] For its part, the African Commission on Human and Peoples' Rights has attracted more criticism than praise, despite the innovative approach adopted in the Charter[23] to marginalized rights. However, a recent decision by the Commission should give cause for more positive reflection. This is the decision in *The Social and Economic Rights Action Centre (SERAC) and the Center for*

1986-2000, 137 (Malcolm D. Evans & Rachel Murray, eds., 2002) (discussing the traditional rights that comprise the basis of the African Charter).

18. *See id.* (asserting that civil and political rights are easier to enforce because they are more clearly defined).

19. *See In re: The Sch. Educ. Bill of 1995 (Gauteng)*, 1996 (4) BCLR 537 (CC) (Apr. 4, 1996) (interpreting the fundamental right of education in South Africa).

20. *See Ministry of Health & Others v. Treatment Action Campaign & Others*, CCT8/02 (July 5, 2002) (holding that the South African Constitution requires that the government establish programs that provide pregnant women with access to health care that will fight the transmission of HIV to the child); *Soobramoney v. Minister of Health (Kwa-Zulu Natal)*, 1997 (12) BCLR 1696 (CC) (adjudicating the issue of the right of access to health care services); *B v. Minister of Correctional Servs.*, 1997 (6) BCLR 789 (C) (Apr. 17, 1997) (deciding the issue of the right to be provided with adequate healthcare in prison).

21. *See Grootboom v. Oostenberg Mun.*, 2000 (3) BCLR 277 (finding that in this particular case the applicant parents are entitled to be accommodated with their children in the aforegoing shelter).

22. *See* Charles Ngwena, *The Recognition of Access to Health Care as a Human Right in South Africa: Is it Enough?*, 5 HEALTH & HUM. RTS. 26, 32-34 (2000) (providing a critique of the approach of the South African Courts to these rights).

23. *See* Organization of African Unity: Banjul Charter on Human and Peoples' Rights, June 6, 1981, 21 I.L.M. 58 (*entered into force* Oct. 21, 1986) [hereinafter Banjul Charter] (stating in Article 15, for example, that "[e]very individual shall have the right to work under equitable and satisfactory conditions, and shall receive equal pay for equal work").

Economic and Social Rights (CESR) v. Nigeria. The decision concerned the despoliation of the environment and other violations committed by the Nigerian government and several oil companies against the Ogoni peoples of the Niger Delta region.[24] Using the decision as our starting point, this paper seeks to develop some views on the broader issue of the relationship among the realization of marginalized human rights, the position of non-state actors, and the struggle for peoples' rights against the backdrop of the varied impacts of globalization.

A secondary mission of the paper is to examine the efficacy of international mechanisms, such as the African Commission, in addressing the rights of marginalized communities like minorities and indigenous people, and in handling non-state actors such as transnational corporations ("TNCs"). Our broader objective is to return to the essential promise of the Vienna Declaration, not only to reinforce the promotion and protection of economic, social and cultural rights, but also to reconnect them to the civil and political ones. This paper also seeks to revisit and draw attention to the other fundamental premise of Vienna, contained in the proclamation that the promotion and protection of human rights, ". . . is the first responsibility of governments."[25]

To achieve these objectives, the paper is divided into four parts. It begins with some conceptual and strategic questions and then provides a general background to Nigeria, as a prelude to reviewing the recent Ogoni case, both against the backdrop of its implications for the regime of human rights law, as well as in relation to the bigger picture of the international framework and the treatment of the issue of peoples' rights. Using that case as a foundation, the next section of the paper considers the place of prominent actors in the debate, such as state and transnational corporations. Questions

---

24. *See The Soc. & Econ. Rights Action Ctr. and Ctr. for Econ. & Soc. Rights v. Nigeria*, Communication 155/96 (African Commission on Human and Peoples' Rights Oct. 27, 2001) [hereinafter *Ogoni Decision*] (finding that Nigeria violated numerous provisions of the African Charter on Human and Peoples' Rights in its use of oil reserves in Ogoniland), *available at* http://www1.umn.edu/humanrts/africa/comcases/155-96b.html (last visited Mar. 3, 2003).

25. Vienna Declaration, art. 1, A/CONF.157/23, July 12, 1993.

relating to the responsibility of states and the accountability of non-state actors will be explored in greater depth here.

I. FOR WHOM DOTH THE BELL REALLY TOLL? SOME CONCEPTUAL AND STRATEGIC QUESTIONS

In 1981, the African Charter on Human and Peoples' Rights ("Charter") became widely recognized for breaking new conceptual ground in human rights law by including civil, political, economic, social and cultural rights in a single instrument.[26] Additionally, the Charter's exemplification of group rights, such as the right to development,[27] the right to peace,[28] and the right to a general satisfactory environment,[29] was viewed as a truly revolutionary re-articulation of rights discourse, and as providing much fodder to a holistic reading of human rights theory and practice.[30] The Charter's immediate effect at the conceptual level within the context of human rights analysis was to break the traditional hierarchy that had come to characterize the regime.[31] Furthermore, it added considerable momentum to the debate about group rights, as well as to the notion of "peoples" within the context of discussions about human rights.

This achievement was made in the first instance through the Charter's attempt to collapse the hierarchy of rights that had plagued the movement since the division of the Universal Declaration into Covenants, and the introduction of the ideas of 'progressive

26. *See* Frans Viljoen, *Review of the African Commission on Human and Peoples' Rights, in* HUMAN RIGHTS LAW IN AFRICA, 1997, 47 (Christof Heyns, ed., 1999) (discussing the creation of the African Commission on Human and Peoples' Rights).

27. *See* Banjul Charter, *supra* note 23, art. 22 (stating that "all peoples shall have the right to their economic, social and cultural development").

28. *See id.* art. 23 (proclaiming that "all peoples shall have the right to national and international peace and security").

29. *See id.* art. 24 (providing that "All peoples shall have the right to a general satisfactory environment favorable to their development").

30. *See* Heyns, *supra* note 17, at 137 (explaining that the Charter's inclusion of these rights was "intriguing").

31. *See id.* (discussing that the Charter's "unusual aspects" was difficult to ignore from an analytical perspective).

realization' and 'available resources' pinned to the enforcement of economic, social, and cultural rights.[32] It also presented wholly new possibilities in rights discourse through providing greater articulation to the concept of group and community rights.[33] Human rights could thus be viewed in holistic total: *what does it mean to have a right to vote if one is too hungry to lift the ballot paper? Conversely, does it matter that you have a right to food if your freedom to speak out on the lack of it is muzzled?* Put another way, what difference does it make if you are starved to death (a violation of your economic rights), or die from torture (a civic freedom violation)? The net effect is that you are dead, and the death is certainly not the result of natural causes. Ultimately, of what help is the categorization of rights if you are in a situation of conflict (a violation of the right to peace), your environment is despoiled, or you are dying from poverty, and consequently denied the right to development?

Unfortunately, the advance on the realization of economic, social and cultural rights, as well as on the rights of the '3rd generation' in Africa, has not lived up to the promise of the Charter.[34] The reasons for this are numerous, among them the perception that paying attention to this category of rights is principally a question of resources. Furthermore, for many African states at the time the Charter was drafted in the late 1970s and early 1980s, the notion of economic, social, and cultural rights was perceived within the framework of the *international*, much more than the *national*, context of realization. It was thus acceptable to make the demand for international reparation, while neglecting the domestic aspects of the

32. *See* International Covenant on Economic, Social and Cultural Rights, art. 2, Dec. 16, 1966 (*entered into force* Jan. 3, 1976) (stating that "Each State Party to the present Covenant undertakes to take steps. . .to the maximum of its available resources, with a view to achieving progressively the full realization of the rights recognized [by the Covenant]"), *available at* http://www.unhchr.ch/html/menu3/b/a_cescr.htm (last visited Mar. 3, 2003).

33. *See* U.N. CHARTER, arts. 1, 55; UNHCHR, Universal Declaration on Human Rights, Preamble, art. 20.3 (demonstrating that although the African Charter is often credited with the introduction of these rights, as a matter of fact they have a much older pedigree extending back to the United Nations Charter and the Universal Declaration), *available at* http://www.unhchr.ch/udhr/lang/eng.htm (last visited Mar. 3, 2003).

34. *See infra* note 27, at 396 (explaining that for all of its failures the Charter is a step in the right direction).

same problem. Additionally, civil society devoted most of its energies to addressing the violation of civil and political rights. Only recently, and following the backlash of the startling effects of the persistence of poverty and the demands of populations starved of basic necessities, have these approaches to the enforcement of human rights been revisited.

The African Commission ("Commission") has in many ways been a 'missing link' in the enforcement of economic, social and cultural rights on the continent. Criticized as insensitive, inept, and inefficient since its formation in 1987, the Commission has attracted more criticism than praise. In many respects, the great promise heralded by the Charter was not matched by the approach of the Commission to its mandate to promote and protect human and peoples' rights as stipulated in the provisions of Article 30 of the Charter.[35] In reality, the Commission lacks sufficient protective powers and enforceable remedies, and even mechanisms to encourage and track state compliance with its decisions. In the words of Amnesty International, ". . . the decisions it renders are non-binding, and attract little, if any, attention from governments of Member States."[36] This is why a protocol establishing an African Court has been adopted.[37]

So why focus on the African situation at all? Regardless of the limitations of the institutional framework, the Ogoni decision merits a fresh examination of both the relevance of the African Charter and of the Commission to contemporary debates about the enforcement of human and peoples' rights within a context of globalization.[38] As a site for the examination of the concerns raised by the marginalization of economic, social, and cultural rights, the African context is of

35. *See* Banjul Charter, *supra* note 23, art. 30 (stating that the Commission should be created "to promote human and peoples' rights and ensure their protection in Africa").

36. AMNESTY INTERNATIONAL, AFRICAN COURT OF HUMAN AND PEOPLES' RIGHTS: AN OPPORTUNITY TO STRENGTHEN HUMAN RIGHTS PROTECTION IN AFRICA 2 (2002).

37. *See* PROTOCOL TO THE AFRICAN CHARTER ON HUMAN AND PEOPLES' RIGHTS ON THE ESTABLISHMENT OF AN AFRICAN COURT ON HUMAN AND PEOPLES' RIGHTS art. 30, OAU/LRG/AFCHPR/PROT(III) (1998) (providing that States that are a party to the Protocol must comply with the decisions of the court).

38. *See supra* note 17 and accompanying text.

particular interest for several reasons. First, of all the regions of the world, Africa—devastated by the scourge of HIV/AIDS, confronting the problem of unsustainable debt, and largely excluded from the benefits of the 'knowledge economy'—is the one most in need of addressing the marginalized rights. Secondly, although so many countries on the African continent have followed the essential prescriptions of the globalization ethos—liberalization, de-regulation and the opening of their markets—the benefits of these prescriptions are yet to be registered. Finally, the African Charter continues to raise intriguing questions about marginalized rights, the place of the state, and the phenomenon of peoples' rights.

II. MILITARY DICTATORS, THE AFRICAN COMMISSION, AND PEOPLES' RIGHTS: THE CASE OF THE OGONI IN NIGERIA

The scourge of military dictatorship and undemocratic governance has long been an issue of concern to human rights activists and academics on the African continent.[39] Contemporary Africa's first military coup d'etat took place well before most countries on the continent had secured their independence. In the early 1950s, the nationalist elements in the Egyptian army overthrew the monarchy and established a military junta under the leadership of Abdel Gamal Nasser. Since that time, Africa has witnessed numerous coups d'etat in a considerable number of countries around the continent, stretching from Burkina Faso to Burundi, and from Libya to Lesotho.[40] Concern with the phenomenon of coups has assumed such prominence that during the formulation of the new African Union ("AU") to replace the Organization of African Unity ("OAU") in 2000, African heads of state and government undertook to condemn and reject "unconstitutional changes in government."[41] They also

39. *See* Philip C. Aka, *The Military, Globalization and Human Rights in Africa*, 18 N.Y.L. SCH. J. HUM. RTS. 361, 405 (2002) (discussing that the political leaders with the worst human rights records were products of the military).

40. *See id.* at 401-405 (describing the characteristics of certain African militaries).

41. *See* CONSTITUTIVE ACT OF THE AFRICAN UNION, art. 4(p) (2000) (rejecting the acceptability of unconstitutional changes in government), *available at* http://www.au2002.gov.za/docs/key_oau/au_act.htm (last visited Mar. 4, 2003).

empowered the AU to prohibit essentially illegal governments from further participation in the activities of the body.[42] The efficacy of the AU provisions on taking punitive action against violators is an altogether separate matter for analysis.[43] However, the significance in this proclamation lies in the distance that the institution sought to mark from the stance of absolute non-intervention established as a basic operational principle by the OAU at inception in 1963.[44]

Only a handful of countries on the continent have been subject to as much intervention by the military in the process of governance as Nigeria. Gaining independence in 1960, for the greater part of its post-colonial existence Nigerians have lived under the yoke of military governments, varying in the intensity and degree to which they have violated human rights in the country.[45] A central issue in the political development of Nigeria has been its federal arrangement of government, and the relationship between the central government and the individual states that make up the union.[46] Although the reasons for tension have varied, one of the most contentious issues in post-colonial Nigeria has been the struggle over the vast economic resources of the Niger delta, and in particular the impact of that

42. *See id.* art. 30 (stating that "governments which shall come to power through unconstitutional means shall not be allowed to participate in the activities of the Union"); *see also* Corrine A.A. Packer & Donald Rukare, *The New African Union and Its Constitutive Act*, 96 AM. J. INT'L. L. 365, 374 (2002) (discussing the damage that illegitimate governments and governance have done to the enforcement of human rights in Africa).

43. *See* Konstantinos D. Magliveras & Gino J. Naldi, *The African Union—A New Dawn for Africa?*, 51 INT'L & COMP. L.Q. 415, 423-24 (2002) (providing preliminary analysis of the use of punitive measures).

44. *See* Charter of the Organization of African Unity, May 25, 1963, art. 3, 479 U.N.T.S. 39 (providing that Member States agree to the "non-interference in the internal affairs of States").

45. *See* Bjorn Beckman, The Free Fall of the Nigerian State (paper presented at a workshop on the state of Nigeria, St. Peter's College, Oxford, May 30, 1996) (on file with author).

46. *See* Adebayo Oloukoshi & O. Agbu, *The Deepening Crisis of Nigerian Federalism and the Future of the Nation-State*, *in* CHALLENGES TO THE NATION-STATE IN AFRICA 74 (A. Olukoshi & L. Laaks, eds. 1996) (discussing obstacles in the development of Nigeria as a unified state following the resolution of the civil war).

exploitation on the peoples of the region.[47] Such a context is bound to generate social, political, economic, and cultural tensions. Unsurprisingly, the Delta region has been a hotbed of contention in independent Nigeria. Central to the discontent has been what is perceived to be the inequitable distribution of the proceeds of oil exploitation as well as the largely negative effects of that exploitation on the environment and the communities in the delta. Against this general background, we can now turn to a deeper examination of what this has meant for the protection of human rights in the country.

A. A BACKGROUND NOTE TO THE SITUATION IN NIGERIA, PAST AND PRESENT

Few issues relating to the Nigerian military dictatorship led by General Sani Abacha captured international attention as did the struggles by the peoples of the Niger Delta over the despoliation of their environment by the government and assorted oil companies. [48] The Sani Abacha government came to power in 1993 following a coup d'etat against the previous military junta led by General Ibrahim Badamasi Babangida, and lasted until 1998. While the Babangida regime which came to power in 1985 was notorious for its corruption and the cancellation of the results of an election that would have restored civilian rule to Nigeria much earlier than was to be the case. On its part, the Abacha government was noted for its human rights excesses, and for the systemic attempt to destroy all opposition to military governance and to eliminate any semblance of the rule of law. Abacha's dictatorship far exceeded the brutality and viciousness of anything that the Nigerian peoples had experienced in several decades of military governance. Abacha was on the verge of 'civilianizing' himself—resigning his army position so as to stand for elections as a civilian president—when he collapsed and died, allegedly from a massive heart attack. Abacha's death paved the way

47. Obijiofor Aginam, *Two Sides of a Coin—Human Rights and Multinational Investment in Africa: The Case of Nigeria*, AFRICA LEGAL AID Q., Jan.-Mar. 2000, at 23-6.

48. *See, e.g.*, Arvind Ganesan, *Human Rights, the Energy Industry, and the Relationship with Home Governments*, *in* HUMAN RIGHTS AND THE OIL INDUSTRY 54-60 (Asbjørn Eide, et al. eds. 2000) (examining Nigeria's struggle to balance economic and social interests in the development of its natural resources).

for a transitional program in which political prisoners were released and elections at local, state, and national levels were conducted between the end of 1998 and mid-1999. Olusegun Obasanjo, who ironically had led one of Nigeria's earlier military regimes, was elected as the first civilian president of Nigeria after a fifteen year hiatus of military governance.

One of the enduring paradoxes of Nigerian life is that unlike so many other situations of military dictatorship, civil society remained a resilient and committed opponent of both the Babangida and Abacha regimes.[49] Unable to make much headway through the domestic mechanisms of redress such as the courts because of an ouster of their jurisdiction over several matters,[50] Nigerian civil society increasingly turned to the African Commission in its attempt to reign in the excesses of the military dictatorship. Further, the creation of special tribunals to try many common and political crimes, often with the death penalty as a punishment, also raised considerable concern. Consequently, from the mid-1990s onwards, Nigerian human rights activists filed a series of cases with the African Commission in an attempt to find recourse through an international mechanism having been denied any space for maneuver domestically.

On its part, the African Commission had already demonstrated an increasing concern about developments in Nigeria. That concern was spurred by the several petitions filed by Nigerian civil society actors challenging laws passed or actions committed by the Nigerian government and highlighting the general deterioration of the human rights situation in the country. The attitude of the African Commission towards petitions from Nigeria must have also played a part in encouraging more of them to be filed. Reviewing the issue of whether a petition against the Nigerian government was admissible for having 'exhausted all domestic remedies,' in *Constitutional*

49. Julia Harrington, *The African Court on Human and Peoples' Rights*, *in* THE AFRICAN CHARTER ON HUMAN AND PEOPLES' RIGHTS: THE SYSTEM IN PRACTICE, 1986-2000, 320 (Malcolm D. Evans & Rachel Murray eds., 2002) (describing the Nigerian human rights community as "very active, well-informed and skillful").

50. *See* M.O. Ogungbe, *Ouster Clauses and Disobedience of Court Orders: A Judicial Impediment*, 5(2) EAST AFR. J. OF PEACE & HUM. RTS. 199-212 (1999) (examining the importance of the independence of a judiciary and the historical lack of such independence in Nigeria).

Rights Project & Civil Liberties Organization v. Nigeria[51] the Commission stated:

> Additionally, the jurisdiction of the [Nigerian] courts to entertain these actions in the first place is in serious question. Decree No.43, like almost all decrees promulgated by the military government, contains [an] ouster clause which specifies that the Decree cannot be challenged in the national courts. The ouster clauses create a legal situation in which the judiciary can provide no check on the executive branch of government. . . . However, it is fair to state that at the time the case came before the Commission no effective legal remedy existed in Nigeria of which the appellants could avail themselves.[52]

As a consequence, petitions that came from Nigeria during the Abacha period were deemed admissible by the African Commission almost as a matter of course.[53] Describing the ouster clauses as ". . .an attack of incalculable proportions on Article 7 of the African Charter," the Commission found the clauses a breach of the obligation imposed on states in Article 26 of the Charter to establish and protect the courts.[54] Thus, in the same vein, the Commission handled issues to do with the right to life,[55] arbitrary detention,[56] and

51. Communication 102/93, *Constitutional Rights Project v. Nigeria*, DOC. OF THE AFR. COMM. ON HUMAN AND PEOPLES' RIGHTS, Twelfth Activity Report, 1998-1999, Annex V, 712, (Rachel Murray & Malcolm Evans, eds. 2001) (examining jurisdiction in a case involving a challenge to the nullification of the 1993 presidential election results and the seizure of several newspapers).

52. *Id.* at 716.

53. *See* Viljoen, *supra* note 26, at 88-9 (discussing the Commission's history of acceptance of claims during this period).

54. Communication 129/94, *Civil Liberties Organization v. Nigeria*, Ninth Activity Report, 1995-1996, Annex VIII, *in* THE AFRICAN CHARTER ON HUMAN AND PEOPLES' RIGHTS: THE SYSTEM IN PRACTICE, 1986-2000, 452-55 (Malcolm D. Evans & Rachel Murray, eds., 2002).

55. *See* Communication 137/94, 139/94, 154/96, 161/97 *International PEN, Constitutional Rights Project, Interrights (on behalf of Ken Saro-Wiwa Jr.), Civil Liberties Organization v. Nigeria, in* THE AFRICAN CHARTER ON HUMAN AND PEOPLES' RIGHTS: THE SYSTEM IN PRACTICE, 1986-2000, 154 (Malcolm D. Evans & Rachel Murray, eds., 2002) (discussing the limits on the detainment of individuals under Article Six of the African Charter).

56. *See* Communication 102/93, *Constitutional Rights Project & Civil Liberties Organization v. Nigeria* (determining that three years detention without trial was a violation of Article Six of the African Charter).

the right to a fair trial,[57] to mention a few. In all instances, the findings were that the Nigerian government had violated specific provisions of the Charter. A number of country-specific resolutions on the Nigerian government were also made. Paradoxically, the brutality of the Nigerian regime was a fortuitous event in the development of the jurisprudence of the African Commission.

The African Commission's concern with Nigeria was heightened by the arrest and conviction of the famous poet and playwright Ken Saro-Wiwa, and his subsequent sentencing to death and execution despite a barrage of protest from various personalities and governments around the world. In what was only its second extraordinary meeting, the Commission met to exclusively examine the human rights situation in Nigeria in late 1995.[58] At that session, the Commission considered submissions from several non-governmental organizations ("NGOs") as well as a response from the Nigerian government regarding the Saro-Wiwa case.[59] Although it was a post-mortem occasion—Saro-Wiwa having been executed despite the entreaties of the Commission, several African governments, and international personalities—the session served to focus more attention on Nigeria. Apart from arranging to send a mission to Nigeria, the meeting examined the compatibility of internal legislation in Nigeria with certain articles of the African Charter and other practical measures that needed to be taken to address the situation.[60] The case of *SERAC & CESR v. Nigeria*

57. *See* Communication 129/94, *Civil Liberties Organization v. Nigeria, in* THE AFRICAN CHARTER ON HUMAN AND PEOPLES' RIGHTS: THE SYSTEM IN PRACTICE, 1986-2000, 155-56 (Malcolm D. Evans & Rachel Murray, eds., 2002) (holding the expungement of refugees without granting them an opportunity to be heard was a violation of Article Seven of the African Charter).

58. *See Final Communiqué of the Second Extraordinary Session of the African Commission on Human and Peoples' Rights,* Kampala, December 18-9, 1995 *in* THE AFRICAN CHARTER ON HUMAN AND PEOPLES' RIGHTS: THE SYSTEM IN PRACTICE, 1986-2000, 463-6 (Malcolm D. Evans & Rachel Murray, eds., 2002).

59. See *Human Rights Report on the Situation in Nigeria: Second Extraordinary Session, in* THE AFRICAN CHARTER ON HUMAN AND PEOPLES' RIGHTS: THE SYSTEM IN PRACTICE, 1986-2000, 476-86 (Malcolm D. Evans & Rachel Murray, eds., 2002) (documenting the gathering following the unjustified execution of a Nigerian artist).

60. *See id.* at 464-65 (describing the talks on human rights development in Nigeria that were held during this period).

(hereinafter referred to as "the Ogoni decision") thus arose within the general context of the crisis that culminated in the execution of Saro-Wiwa. More specifically, with respect to those dimensions of the case that had led the poet and playwright to begin his protest against the Nigerian government in the first place, that is, the despoliation of the Ogoni environment and its impact on their human and peoples' rights. Although it was not the first case on economic, social, and cultural rights handled by the Commission, it certainly is the most prominent.[61]

B. SERAC & CESR V. NIGERIA: A SYNOPSIS

The petition to the African Commission was filed in 1996, in the aftermath of the Saro-Wiwa execution and against a backdrop of a rapidly deteriorating human rights and security situation in the country. It specifically alleged that the operations of the Nigerian military government through its state oil company the Nigerian National Petroleum Company as majority shareholder in a consortium with Shell Petroleum Development Corporation had caused environmental degradation and health problems resulting from contamination of the environment among the Ogoni people.[62] Additionally, the petition alleged several acts of murder, intimidation and harassment committed by members of the Nigerian military. The communication focused on several violations to the African Charter, including the right to life (Article 4); the right to health (Article 16) and to a healthy environment (Article 24); the right to property (Article 14) and housing, the right to food,[63] and the protection of the family (Article 18). The communication was significant not only with respect to the scope of rights covered (transcending all 'generations' of rights), but also because it was the first time that

---

61. *See* Manisuli Ssenyonjo, *Justiciability of Economic and Social Rights in Africa: General Overview, Evaluation and Prospects*, *in* EAST AFR. J. OF PEACE & HUMAN RIGHTS (forthcoming 2003) (on file with author).

62. *See Ogoni Decision*, *supra* note 24, ¶ 1 (providing a factual background for the case).

63. *See* African Charter on Human and People's Rights, *in* THE AFRICAN CHARTER ON HUMAN AND PEOPLES' RIGHTS: THE SYSTEM IN PRACTICE, 1986-2000, 353 (Malcolm D. Evans & Rachel Murray, eds., 2002) (noting the lack of provisions either on the right to housing or the right to food).

many of the provisions of the Charter were being invoked for consideration by the Commission.

After addressing the preliminary issue of the admissibility of the communication,[64] the Commission turned to its merits, and outlined the duties expected of a state with respect to its human rights obligations, namely, the duty to *respect, protect, promote and fulfill* the human rights that it has undertaken to uphold by acceding to various international instruments, including the African Charter. Turning specifically to the right to environment provision of the Charter, the Commission stated that this requires a state to, ". . . take reasonable and other measures to prevent pollution and ecological degradation, to promote conservation, and to secure an ecologically sustainable development and use of natural resources."[65] Speaking to the issue of compliance with the 'spirit' of Articles 16 and 24, the Commission stated that this would include

> ordering, or at least permitting, independent scientific monitoring of threatened environments, requiring and publicizing environmental and social impact studies prior to any major industrial development, undertaking appropriate monitoring and providing information to those communities exposed to hazardous materials and activities and providing meaningful opportunities for individuals to be heard and to participate in the developing decisions affecting their communities.[66]

Focusing on Article 21, which is one of the prominent peoples' rights in the Charter and concerns the right of peoples to ". . .freely dispose of their wealth and natural resources,"[67] the Commission retraced the genesis of the provision to colonialism.[68] Pointing to the continuing vulnerability of Africa's resources to foreign misappropriation, the Commission stated that the intention of the

64. *See Ogoni Decision*, *supra* note 24, ¶¶ 34-43 (reasoning that there is no bar of admissibility for the case).

65. *Id.* ¶54 (deciding that the right to environment imposes obligations upon governments).

66. *Id.* ¶55.

67. Banjul Charter, *supra* note 23, art. 21.1 (stating that no person is to be deprived of the right to freely dispose of their wealth and natural resources).

68. *Ogoni Decision*, *supra* note 24, ¶ 58 (discussing the history behind Article 21).

drafters of the Charter was both to remind African governments of the continent's "painful legacy" and to "... restore co-operative economic development to its traditional place at the heart of African Society."[69] Consequently, citing the authority of several decisions of both the Commission and other international bodies like the Inter-American Court of Human Rights[70] and the European Court of Human Rights,[71] the Commission stated:

> [G]overnments have a duty to protect their citizens, not only through appropriate legislation and effective enforcement but also by protecting them from damaging acts that may be perpetrated by private parties. This illustrates the positive action expected of governments in fulfilling their obligation under human rights instruments.[72]

Again, in determining the extent of the government's obligation to human rights, the Commission unequivocally stated that Nigeria violated that obligation:

> The Government of Nigeria facilitated the destruction of the Ogoniland. Contrary to its Charter obligations and despite such internationally established principles, the Nigerian Government has given the green light to private actors, and the oil Companies in particular, to devastatingly affect the well-being of the Ogonis. By any measure of standards, its practice falls short of the minimum conduct expected of governments, and therefore, is in violation of the African Charter.[73]

An extensive part of the judgment examined the right to housing and the Nigerian government's obligations in this regard.[74] This is

---

69. *Id.*

70. *See* Velásquez Rodríguez v. Honduras, Judgment of July 29, 1988, Inter-Am. Ct. H.R. (ser. C) No. 4 (1988) (discussing the right of the Inter-American Court of Human Rights to investigate the Honduran government's role in the disappearance of a student following his arrest without a warrant).

71. *See* X and Y v. Netherlands, 91 Eur. Ct. H.R. (ser. A) at 32 (1985) (involving the claim of a rape victim under international human rights law for violations of protection against inhumane treatment and respect for individual privacy).

72. *Ogoni Decision*, *supra* note 24, ¶ 59.

73. *Id.* ¶ 60.

74. *See id.* ¶¶ 63-65 (describing the violation of the Ogoni people's right to housing by the Nigerian government).

important because the Charter actually does not contain an explicit provision on that right. Such an omission is striking, given that housing (or more broadly 'shelter') and its attendant rights are of particular concern in the African context,[75] ranging not simply from the basic right to have a roof over one's head, but also to the related issues of forced evictions and subsequent displacement, the conditions of shelter, and the vexed issue of compensation or other redress for its loss. On the matter of the right to housing, the Commission was unequivocal:

> Although the right to housing or shelter is not explicitly provided for under the African Charter, the corollary of the combination of the provisions protecting the right to enjoy the best attainable state of mental and physical health. . . the right to property, and the protection accorded to the family forbids the wanton destruction of shelter because when housing is destroyed, property, health, and family life are adversely affected. *It is thus noted that the combined effect of Articles 14, 16 and 18 reads into the Charter a right to shelter or housing[,] which the Nigerian Government has apparently violated.*[76] (emphasis added)

The Commission stated what it considered to be the two essential elements in the protection of the right to housing: not to destroy housing and not to obstruct efforts by individuals and communities to rebuild lost homes.[77] In this way, the Commission focused both on the cross-cutting and all-encompassing nature of this right—extending from individuals to communities—and also on its inter-generational character: individual dignity and integrity, and the ability to exploit available resources (in the developmental sense of the word). Additionally, according to the Commission, the right ". . .even goes further than a roof over [one's] head. It extends to embody the individual's right to be let alone and to live in peace—

75. *See* Kim Robinson, *False Hope Or A Realizable Right? The Implementation of the Right to Shelter Under the African National Congress' Proposed Bill of Rights for South Africa*, 28 HARV. C.R.-C.L. L. REV. 505, 508 (1993) (discussing the South African formulation of the right to shelter in the post-Apartheid era).

76. *See Ogoni Decision*, *supra* note 24, ¶ 63.

77. *Id.* ¶ 64 (stating that these elements are necessary for the state to fulfill its obligation to respect housing rights).

whether under a roof or not."[78] Consequently, the Commission stated that the state, its organs and agents must ". . .abstain from carrying out, sponsoring or tolerating any practice, policy or legal measure violating the integrity of the individual or infringing upon his or her freedom to use those materials or other resources available to them in a way they find most appropriate to satisfy individual, family, household or community housing needs."[79] The Commission drew considerable inspiration from the Committee on Economic, Social and Cultural Rights, and specifically from its General Comments on the relevant rights as outlined in the International Covenant on Economic, Social and Cultural Rights ("ICESCR").[80]

Finally, the Commission turned its attention to the right to food, which is another provision that does not appear in the Charter, but is well-articulated in the ICESCR.[81] In this respect, the Commission read the right to food into the Charter provisions on the right to life,[82] the right to health,[83] and the right to economic, social, and cultural development,[84] at an instant drawing a thread of connection between the so-called first, second, and the third generation of rights. In this way, the Commission gave full expression to the provisions of Article 5 of the Vienna Declaration: "all human rights are universal, indivisible and interdependent and interrelated."[85] The Commission further asserted that the right to food is "inseparably linked to the dignity of human beings and is therefore essential for the enjoyment and fulfillment of such other rights as health, education, work and

78. *Id.* ¶ 64.

79. *Id.*

80. *See id.* ¶ 66 (citing the ICESR conceptualization of "forced evictions" in discussing violations of the right to adequate housing by the Nigerian government).

81. *See* International Covenant on Economic, Social and Cultural Rights, 21 UN GAOR Supp. (No. 16) at 49, U.N. Doc. A/6316 (1966), art. 11 (stating that all parties to the ICESR include adequate food among the elements of a right to an adequate standard of living).

82. *See* Banjul Charter, *supra* note 23, art. 4 (enumerating an entitlement by every human being to respect for his life).

83. *See id.* art. 16 (proclaiming a person's right to mental and physical health).

84. *See id.* art 22 (granting a right to economic, social and cultural development for all peoples and giving states a duty to ensure this right).

85. *See* Vienna Declaration, *supra* note 1, art. 5 (noting that all human rights are universal and that all states are duty-bound to promote and protect these rights).

political participation."[86] In the view of the Commission, the Nigerian government's treatment of the Ogonis violated all three minimum duties to ensure the right to food because it destroyed food sources, allowed private oil companies to destroy food sources, and created significant obstacles impacting the ability of the Ogoni peoples' ability to feed themselves.[87] This background of the decision allows us to turn to a critical examination of its implications for the promotion and protection of human and peoples' rights.

C. THE IMPLICATIONS OF THE JUDGMENT: CONCEPTUAL, INSTITUTIONAL, AND COMPARATIVE

The importance of the Ogoni decision can be viewed on several levels: the conceptual, the institutional, and, in comparative terms with respect to the overall corpus of international human rights law. Obviously, its most immediate relevance is to the regional context of human rights struggles and to the place of the African Commission therein. Another dimension to the decision relates to the efficacy of the ruling within the framework of domestic action, because it is at the level of the national realization and enforcement of human rights that these issues will ultimately count. Decisions by international and regional mechanisms for the enforcement of human rights are important for what they add to the stock of interpretative material for the specific institution.[88] In short, they provide precedential value. However, they also supply significant material for other bodies to draw upon, whether in a judicial framework or not.[89] Civil society in particular recognizes the utility in creatively deploying international and regional human rights standards and decisions to the creation and

86. *See Ogoni Decision*, *supra* note 24, ¶ 68.

87. *Id.* ¶ 69 (chronicling the Nigerian government's failure to meet any of the three minimum duties contingent with the right to food).

88. *See generally* Cesare P.R. Romano, *The Proliferation of International Judicial Bodies: The Pieces of The Puzzle*, 31 N.Y.L. SCH. J. INT'L & COMP. L. 709, 751 (1999) (noting that international judicial bodies recognize and refer to precedents).

89. *See id.* (stating that international and regional judicial bodies render their decisions while recognizing that their actions will contribute to the larger body of the international legal order).

extension of democratic space in the domestic context.[90] It is also in this light that the Commission decision in the Ogoni case should be considered, particularly since it is not binding.

Needless to say, one might easily assert that the Commission's decision is of little utility to the corpus of human rights law or practice, either within the African context or within the wider comparative and international jurisprudence. The Ogoni decision took five years to finalize, mainly because of a lack of cooperation from the Nigerian government, but also on account of Commission inertia and inefficiency.[91] The Abacha government clearly deserved the label of an extreme human rights violator, but by the time the decision was handed down that government was no longer in power in Nigeria. Furthermore, as the Commission itself noted, the present Obasanjo government subsequently instituted several measures to address past violations, as well as to ensure the prevention of future occurrences of similar human rights violations.[92] Overall, the starkness of the violations catalogued assumes a different hue in a post-Abacha context. A cynical criticism might also claim that the Ogoni case was an 'easy' one to take on given the general outcry and opprobrium that the issue had attracted; the Commission could not but make a strong finding against the state.

A number of responses can be made to the criticisms listed above. Decisions of international bodies invariably take a long time,[93] and in the case of the African Commission, this problem is exacerbated by the fact that the members of the body serve on a part time basis. In

---

90. *See* Sylvia Tamale, *Think Globally, Act Locally: Using International Treaties for Women's Empowerment in East Africa*, 50 AGENDA 97, 99 (2001) (noting that international and regional treaties are useful instruments of accountability forcing governments to institute reforms).

91. *See* Viljoen, *supra* note 26, at 101 (describing inefficiencies deleteriously impacting efficient operation of the African Commission).

92. *See Ogoni Decision*, *supra* note 24, ¶ 72 ("The Commission does not wish to fault governments that are labouring under difficult circumstances to improve the lives of their people.").

93. *See generally* Jeffrey L. Dunoff, *Institutional Misfits: The GATT, the ICJ & Trade Environment Disputes*, 15 MICH. J. INT'L. L. 1043, 1091 (1994) (commenting on significant amount of time necessary for the International Court of Justice to render a decision notwithstanding its light case load).

addition, the Commission faces a host of logistical problems.[94] Consequently, a limited amount of business is completed in the two sessions per year that the Commission meets. However, notwithstanding these shortcomings of logistics and efficiency, the Ogoni decision represents a significant development for the Commission. Early communications by the body were sparse in reasoning and lacking in substantiation.[95] Over the years, the Commission's decisions have become more elaborate and extensive.[96] The Ogoni decision extends this practice, in that it is well-reasoned and broadly expansive of some of the most critical elements in the conceptualization of the African Charter. In this respect, the decision may represent a coming of age for the Commission.

Another criticism to consider is whether the decision is passé in that it was rendered against a government that is no longer in existence. Two responses address this critique. The first relates to the doctrine of state succession: decisions of this nature are against the state, not a particular government. Second, although the Ogoni case is unique to the particular history and political economy of Nigeria, the violations charted in the case resonate in many other African countries, and in states elsewhere around the world confronting the twin issues of resource exploitation and environmental protection in a fragile ecosystem, and where indigenous and minority communities and their rights are involved. This issue is presently manifested in the case of the planned Exxon/Mobil exploitation of the oil reserves in the Doba basin of Chad, one of Nigeria's neighbors.[97] The project, plagued by controversy from the start, is designed to exploit oil

94. *See* Viljoen, *supra* note 26, at 102 (detailing the African Commission's inability to overcome its significant backlog of cases).

95. *See id.* at 62-70 (chronicling the substandard level of quality of communications by the Commission in prior years).

96. *See, e.g.*, Communication No.212/98 *Amnesty International v. Zambia* (drawing upon African commission precedent relating to other nations in finding violations by Zambia of the African Charter), *available at* http://www.achpr.org/DECISIONS_25th_Session-_May_1999_eng.doc (last visited Feb. 20, 2003).

97. *See Useful Stuff, Maybe, For Once*, ECONOMIST, Sept. 14, 2002, at 49 (reporting on a new World Bank project in Chad designed to introduce transparency and accountability to oil exploitation efforts there).

reserves in a manner that does not lead to so many of the problems that have plagued the Niger delta.[98] The Chad project also introduced the World Bank to a process of soul searching over the most efficacious mode of intervention in projects of this kind.[99] Despite criticism of various aspects of the project by the Bank's Inspection Panel,[100] the Bank management appears determined to proceed with the investment.[101]

Oil companies and western governments are engaging in new strategic thinking about the countries in the Gulf of Guinea (off the coast of West Africa) and other locations around the continent as potential replacements of the Middle East as alternative sources of oil.[102] In particular, the island states of S•o Tomé and Principe, are

98. Jane I. Guyer, *The Chad-Cameroon Petroleum and Pipeline Development Project*, 101(402) AFR. AFF. 110 (2002) (describing the innovative nature of the Chad project's twin commitments to environmental management and institutional capacity-building).

99. *See* World Bank International Advisory Group, *Chad-Cameroon Petroleum Development and Pipeline Project: Report of a Mission, Sept. 28, 2001* (describing the challenge of making this complicated commercial project an instrument of development), *available at* http://www/worldbank.org/afr/ccproj/news/index.htm (last visited Feb. 17, 2003).

100. *See World Bank Inspection Panel, Investigation Report: Chad-Cameroon Petroleum and Pipeline Project (Loan No.4558-CD); Petroleum Sector Management Capacity Building Project (Credit No.3373-CD); and Management of the Petroleum Economy (Credit No.3316-CD)* (discussing certain of the alleged threats to local communities and environmental problems associated with the project), , *available at* http://www.worldbank.org/afr/ccproj/project/chad_Investigation_repor_final.pdf. (last visited Feb. 17, 2003).

101. *See International Bank for Reconstruction and Development International Development Association, Management Report and Recommendation in Response to the Inspection Panel Investigation Report, Report No.24667* (concluding that the project will continue as proposed with protections afforded by regular consultation and disclosure on environmental and social issues as necessary), *available at* http://www.worldbank.org/afr/ccproj/project/mgt_res_chad_Invest_repor_final.pdf . (last visited Feb. 17, 2003); Genoveva Hernández Uriz, *To Lend or Not to Lend: Oil, Human Rights and the World Bank's Internal Contradictions*, 14 HARV. HUM. RTS. J. 197, 199 (2001) (urging the Bank to more sensibly balance its approach to protecting civil and political rights with financial considerations surrounding its participation in the project).

102. *See* James Lamont & Michael Peel, *Human Rights Issue in Focus as US Interest in African Oil Surges: Concern Grows Over US Move in a Region Known for Corruption and Poor Governance*, FIN. TIMES, Oct. 29, 2002, at 13 (describing

touted as a 'replacement' to Saudi Arabia as a major source of oil resources for the United States.[103] The peace dividends in Angola[104] and the Sudan[105] will certainly raise afresh those issues relating to the link between exploitation of oil reserves and the conflicts in these countries.

Secondly, and more importantly, many of the problems that led to the filing of the complaint in the first instance remain. According to Ganesan:

> Soldiers remain deployed in the riverine areas of Bayelsa and Delta States. While there are genuine security concerns relating to kidnappings of oil workers and to inter-community conflict, especially in the Delta State, these soldiers are responsible for ongoing human rights violations. These violations range from routine extortion of money at roadblocks to arbitrary detention and torture. On a few occasions, individuals have also been summarily executed.[106]

Furthermore, the uprising of the peoples of the region is no longer confined to the Ogoni. Several other communities that were rather silent at the time the Ogoni 'troubles' commenced in the early 1990s have also found voice.[107] The issues considered in the Ogoni case are

---

the increasing interest level of United States and other Western oil executives for oil reserves in western and central Africa).

103. *See* Jon Lee Anderson, *Our New Best Friend: Who Needs Saudi Arabia When You've Got S•o Tomé*, NEW YORKER, Oct. 7, 2002, at 74 (noting that U.S. policy makers find S•o Tomé increasingly attractive as a source of oil because it is a stable democracy in West Africa).

104. *See, e.g.*, *Global Witness, All the Presidents' Men: The Devastating Story of Oil and Banking in Angola's Privatized War* (Mar., 2002) (describing the lack of transparency by oil companies in their dealings with the Angolan government and other troubled African nations), *available at* http://www.globalwitness.org/campaigns/oil/download/All_the_Presidents_Men.pdf (last visited Feb. 8, 2003).

105. *See* Adila Abusharaf, *The Legal Relationship Between Multinational Oil Companies and the Sudan: Problems and Prospects*, 43 J. OF AFR. L., 18, 19 (1999) (explaining that the oil industry is crucial to the development of the Sudanese economy).

106. *See* Ganesan, *supra* note 48, at 55.

107. *See* John Boye Ejobowah, *Who Owns the Oil? The Politics of Ethnicity in the Niger Delta of Nigeria*, 47 AFR. TODAY 29, 36 (2000) (chronicling the increasing amount of Niger Delta ethnic communities asserting ownership interests to the rich resources derived from their land).

thus still as much alive for the rest of the world and for Nigeria[108] as a country as they are for the peoples of the Niger delta.[109]

There is a final and fundamentally important issue that arises out of the Ogoni decision. This issue applies more generally to the corpus of international human rights law and the realization of marginalized rights. Specifically, the issue is the blindness to the gendered nature of virtually all the violations that took place in the Delta region. Nigerian women recently stormed oil facilities to make demands on the oil companies and thereby received significant international attention.[110] However, the action of women with respect to the situation in Nigeria's oil-producing areas enjoys a much longer, albeit less well-known and discussed, history. Well before Ken Saro-Wiwa and the Movement for the Survival of the Ogoni Peoples began to agitate for change in the Delta, women had organized protests against the oil industries dating back to the early 1980s.[111] Women as a social group continue to be among the most prominent critics of the oil industry and its impact on the delta economy. Why?

---

108. Human Rights Watch, THE PRICE OF OIL: CORPORATE RESPONSIBILITY AND HUMAN RIGHTS VIOLATIONS IN NIGERIA'S OIL PRODUCING COMMUNITIES, Jan. 1999 (exploring human rights violations associated with oil exploration and exploitation in the Niger Delta), *available at* http:///www.hrw.org/reports/1999/nigeria/index.htm (last visited Feb. 15, 2003).

109. *See Human Rights Watch, 14(7) THE NIGER DELTA: NO DEMOCRATIC DIVIDEND* (Oct. 2002) (describing the flawed relationship between oil companies and the Nigerian government and resultant discontent and suffering in the Niger Delta region) , *available at* http://www.hrw.org/reports/2002/nigeria3/ (last visited Feb. 17, 2003).

110. *See Women Storm Nigeria Oil Plant*, BBC NEWS, July 9, 2002 (describing the storming of an oil plant by hundreds of Nigerian women), *available at* http://news.bbc.co.uk/1/hi/world/africa/2118097.stm (last visited Feb. 18, 2003); *see also 'Deal Reached' in Nigeria Oil Protest*, BBC NEWS, July 16, 2002 (reporting on a deal reached between women protestors and oil officials with terms including hiring of local villagers at oil facilities, school construction, and construction of water systems and other utilities), *available at* http://news.bbc.co.uk/1/hi/world/africa/2129281.stm (last visited Feb. 17, 2003).

111. *See* Terisa E. Turner & M.O. Oshare, *Women's Uprisings Against the Nigerian Oil Industry in the 1980s* (examining revolts by local women against oil industry personnel and assets in Nigeria), *available at* http://www.uoguelph.ca/~terisatu/Counterplanning/c9.htm (last visited Feb. 8, 2003).

Initially, the kernel of their protests related to the manner in which the oil economy affected their land rights through the super-imposition of new regimes of land-holding.[112] Women, who do most of the farming in the area, were dispossessed by the oil industry from their farm lands.[113] Their protests have been directed at both the impact of oil production, as well as at the lack of social services to address fundamental questions of basic education, access to water and community amenities.[114] The Ogoni case is particularly sparse on rendering a gendered analysis of the manner in which women's human rights were specifically implicated and violated within the context of the general problems articulated in the decision.[115] There may be several explanations for this absence, including the fact that the issue was not specifically argued before the Commission.[116] However, is it enough to speak generally about violations done to the 'family,' to 'peoples,' and to the 'environment,' without exploring the manner in which these violations differentially impact men and women, and consequently amount to a specific violation of womens' human rights? Although the Commission made reference to the family and to Article 18 (the provision in the Charter that most explicitly deals with the issue of the rights of women),[117] the decision

112. *See id.* (explaining that Nigerian women participated in protests in 1984 and 1986 against land expropriation by the oil industry). It is not coincidental that the concern about the violation of these rights followed the unity of oil rights and land rights that was adjusted by the Land Use Act of 1978. *See* Cap. 202, Laws of the Federation of Nigeria (1990); *see also* Kaniye S.A. Ebeku, *Oil and the Niger Delta People: The Injustice of the Land Use Act*, 35 VERFASSUNG UND RECHT IN ÜBERSEE 201, 203 (2002) (relating that the Land Use Act placed state lands in a type of 'trust' held by that state's governor).

113. *See* Turner & Oshare, *supra* note 111 (reporting that industrialization by oil companies in the 1980s deprived Nigerian women of access to farm land).

114. *See 'Deal Reached' in Nigeria Oil Protest*, *supra* note 110 (relating that women protesters insisted on jobs and construction of community infrastructure from Chevron Nigeria).

115. *See Ogoni Decision*, *supra* note 24, ¶¶ 44-51 (referring to violations affecting the Ogoni community in general).

116. *See id.* ¶¶ 1-9 (stating that the complaint alleges harm suffered by the Ogoni community due to environmental destruction by the Shell Corporation and attacks by the Nigerian government in support of Shell).

117. *See* Lisa Kois, *Article 18 of the African Charter on Human & Peoples' Rights: A Progressive Approach to Women's Human Rights*, 3 E. AFR. J. PEACE &

focused on the general violation done by the Nigerian state to the family institution in Ogoni.[118] Ironically, the Commission did not elaborate on the violation of this specific right in the same manner that it did with the other provisions it examined, except to say that "family life" was "adversely affected" by the destruction of the Ogoni's shelter.[119]

Against this background, several points can be made with regard to the potential contribution of the case to a number of issues that are of concern to international human rights lawyers. Among them are the following:

*Demonstrating how international instruments can be more creatively interpreted in order to further break down the barriers between the different categories of rights;[120]

*Giving greater articulation to the right to a healthy environment in general, and specifically to Article 24 of the Charter, which provides that "all peoples" have "the right to a general satisfactory environment favorable to their development;"[121]

*Identifying actors other than the state in the commission of human rights violations;[122]

*Demonstrating how the collusion between the state and those actors can affect the protection of human rights and identifying the duties and obligations of the state in this regard;[123]

HUM. RTS 92, 92 (1996) (asserting that Article 18 is capable of functioning as a protective shield and promotion mechanism for women's rights).

118. *See Ogoni Decision*, *supra* note 24, ¶¶ 63-66 (finding that the Nigerian government harmed the Ogoni family structure by destroying Ogoni housing and property, and by harassing and killing Ogoni citizens).

119. *See id.* ¶ 63 (finding that the right to shelter, although not specifically mandated by the Charter, exists as a "corollary of the combination" of the rights to mental and physical health, the right to property, and the protection of the family).

120. *See* James Crawford, *The Rights of Peoples: Some Conclusions*, *in* THE RIGHTS OF PEOPLES 159, 163-168 (James Crawford ed., 1988) (discussing the relationship between peoples' rights and human and states rights).

121. Banjul Charter, *supra* note 23, art. 24.

122. *See* Dinah Shelton, *Protecting Human Rights in a Globalized World*, 25 B.C. INT'L & COMP. L. REV. 273, 321 (2002) (concluding that non-state actors, such as the media, corporations and international organizations, retain responsibility for human rights violations).

*Within the African context, for the first time providing an interpretation of Article 21 specifically, and the notion of peoples' rights in general, and thereby giving more strength to the struggle for the recognition and enforcement of group or community rights.[124]

These contributions must be viewed against the backdrop of the many criticisms that have been made over the realization and enforcement of second and third generation rights; that they are only aspirational; that they are non-justiciable, and that they are too general to be enforced.[125] Specifically with respect to the African Charter, scholars like Philip Alston have argued quite correctly that the relevant provisions on peoples' rights in the Charter have "come to little in practice" because of the dilemma about whether such rights belong to individuals, the state, or to "separate collective entities."[126] The same critique is aptly captured in the words of Inger Österdahl in a discussion of the new African Court.[127] She commences with a critique of the right to self-determination of which she says it would be "very difficult for the African Court to apply." She continues:

> Even more difficult than the right to self determination is to see how individual citizens will be able to use the African Court or the Commission to enforce their right to development, to a clean environment or to national or international peace and security. How would the African Court handle an individual complaint alleging the violation of any of these rights? When would it find that an individual has been the victim of

---

123. *See Ogoni Decision*, *supra* note 24, ¶ 60 (condemning the collusion between oil companies and the Nigerian government).

124. *See* Philip Alston, *Peoples' Rights: Their Rise and Fall*, *in* PEOPLES' RIGHTS 259, 286 (Philip Alston ed. 2001) (finding that the major obstacle to developing the rights of peoples' set out in the African Charter is the lack of a definition of 'peoples' in the instrument).

125. *See* Li-Ann Thio, *Battling Balkanization: Regional Approaches Toward Minority Protection Beyond Europe*, 43 HARV. INT'L L.J. 409, 458 n.320 (2002) (referring to third generation rights as being so broad that they "defy enforcement").

126. *See* Alston, *supra* note 124, at 286 (relating that the confusion concerning ownership of peoples' rights in the African Charter results from the absence of definitions in the instrument).

127. Inger Österdahl, *The jurisdiction* Ratione Materiae *of the African Court of Human Rights*, 7(2) REV. OF THE AFR. COMMISS'N ON HUM. & PEOPLES' RTS. 132-150 (1998).

> a violation of his or her right to development, to a clean environment, or to national or international peace and security?. . . Certainly the rights of the third generation are relevant in the African context. Practically every African citizen could claim to be denied of at least one but probably all three of these rights. The question is, however, how these rights will best be put into practice on the individual level.[128]

Two points should be made in response to this criticism, which in my view reflects an overly pessimistic view of the possibilities entailed by the group rights provisions in the African Charter and thus of the potential for the realization of peoples' rights. In the first instance, it is to recognize that the enforcement of collective, group, or peoples' rights is an important obligation on the international community and on states in and of itself.[129] This is clear in developments that have been made regarding the rights of minorities and indigenous peoples as both individuals and collectivities or communities.[130] It is quite clear that in reviewing the issues raised by the Ogoni petition, the African Commission viewed its mission primarily to deal with the *collective* violation of the rights that were under consideration.[131] Needless to say, communities are merely the collective expression of isolated individuals; the enforcement of community rights invariably will redound on the place of the individual within that context.[132] But does this mean that an *individual* cannot seek to enforce third generation rights?[133] Increasingly within a domestic context, rights such as the right to a healthy environment are being recognized and enforced as both

---

128. *See id.* at 48.

129. *See* Thio, *supra* note 125, at 458 n.319 (reporting that the 1996 International Covenants on Human Rights included peoples' rights).

130. *See* Alston, *supra* note 124, at 259-94 (discussing the evolution of the rights of minorities and indigenous peoples).

131. *See Ogoni Decision*, *supra* note 24, ¶¶ 44-69 (referring to violations committed against the Ogoni community).

132. *See* Richard N. Kiwanuka, *The Meaning of "People" in the African Charter on Human and Peoples' Rights*, 82 AM. J. INT'L L. 80, 100 (1988) (claiming that achievement of peoples' rights in the Charter depends on valuing individual rights).

133. *See* Alston, *supra* note 124 (reasoning that individuals will be reluctant to rely on peoples' rights for fear of undermining their individual claims against that of the " collective interest").

individual and collective constitutional rights,[134] with the most developed aspect of this right being the procedural.[135]

The other conceptual dimension to which the Ogoni case relates is with respect to the Commission's discussion of Article 24 concerning the right to a healthy environment. This is a right which still raises some contention among scholars of international law.[136] Aginam claims that Article 24 is "skeletal" and thus does not provide the necessary flesh that would be required to give effect to the provision.[137] He goes on to question the utility of Article 24, arguing that it is of "doubtful validity" particularly in the face of "powerful and influential multinational corporations."[138] Aginam compares the provision to Article XI of the Additional Protocol to the American

134. *See, e.g.*, S. AFR. CONST., art. 24 (stating that "everyone has the right" to a safe environment and that the government will take means to protect the environment).

135. *See, e.g.*, NIG. CONST., art. 91 (requiring that the Ombudsman investigate complaints and environmental exploitation and destruction); *see also* EDITH BROWN WEISS, IN FAIRNESS TO FUTURE GENERATIONS: INTERNATIONAL LAW, COMMON PATRIMONY, AND INTERGENERATIONAL EQUITY 107-08 (1992) (listing numerous constitutions that require the government to protect and conserve the environment).

136. *See* PATRICIA W. BIRNIE & ALAN E. BOYLE, INTERNATIONAL LAW AND THE ENVIRONMENT (1992) 191 (relating that scholars differ as to whether the right to a safe environment exists and, if it does, whether it is enforceable); *see also* R. D. MUNRO & J.G. LAMMERS, ENVIRONMENTAL PROTECTION AND SUSTAINABLE DEVELOPMENT: LEGAL PRINCIPLES AND RECOMMENDATIONS (1986) 7, 9 (asserting that the right to a sufficiently healthy environment should be considered fundamental for all human beings). This statement constituted Article 1 of the Legal Principles for Environmental Protection and Sustainable Development of the Experts Group on Environmental Law of the World Commission on Environment and Development. *Id.* at 7, 9; *see also* Dinah Shelton, *Human Rights and the Right to Environment*, 28 STAN. J. INT'L L. 103, 106, 138 (1991) (concluding that recognizing a right to environment would advance both environmental and human rights goals). *But see* Leslie A. Obiora, *Symbolic Episodes and the Quest for Environmental Justice*, 12(2) HUM. RTS. Q. 464, 473 (1999) (holding that political and socioeconomic reforms will lead to an active civil society and promotion and protection of environmental rights).

137. *See* Aginam, *supra* note 47, at 25 (arguing that the environmental rights provision of the African Charter is weak compared to equivalent provisions in the American Declaration of the Rights and Duties of Man).

138. *See id.* at 23 (commenting that the African Charter was the first international human rights agreement that includes a right to environment).

Convention on Human Rights[139] and the use made of that provision by the Inter-American Commission in upholding the environmental and health rights of the Yanomani Indians against the government of Brazil as an example.[140]

While recognizing the complexities of the 'right to environment' discussion, it is also important to focus on what has come to be recognized as some of the essential elements in the right, and specifically upon the manner in which human rights law and environmental protection interrelate.[141] Dinah Shelton identifies several levels on which the two overlap—utilizing human rights principles in the creation of environmental instruments, invoking environmental protection as an instrument to protect or preserve human rights, incorporating the environmental agenda fully into human rights through the formulation of a new human right to an environment that is both safe to humans and "ecologically-balanced and sustainable in the long term," and, finally, addressing environmental protection as a human responsibility.[142]

The approach of the African Commission to the right to environment appears to have combined several of Shelton's elements listed above.[143] It commenced with the assertion that Article 24 placed clear obligations upon the government with respect to the environment.[144] By adopting the "respect-protect-promote and fulfill"

---

139. Additional Protocol to the American Convention on Human Rights in the Area of Economic, Social and Cultural Rights, Nov. 14, 1988, 28 I.L.M. 156.

140. *See* Aginam, *supra* note 47, at 25-6 (finding that the African Commission's enforcement abilities are weaker than those of the Inter-American Commission on Human Rights).

141. *See* Kate Cook, *Environmental Rights as Human Rights*, 2 EUR. HUM. RTS. L. REV. 196 (2002) (finding that a right to environment in the context of human rights considers the environment's impact on a person's health and welfare).

142. *See* Dinah Shelton, *Environmental Rights*, *in* PEOPLES' RIGHTS 187-88 (Philip Alston ed., 2001) (expanding on the interconnectedness between international environmental and human rights law).

143. *See Ogoni Decision*, *supra* note 24, ¶ 53 (reasoning that Article 24 acknowledges the link between exercising social and economic rights and a healthy and safe environment).

144. *See id.* ¶ 54 (holding that Article 24 mandates that states "prevent pollution. . . promote conservation," and work towards "sustainable development and use of natural resources").

test,[145] the Commission clarified the distinction between a state taking proactive measures to ensure that the environment is not despoiled, and compensatory mechanisms in the event the destruction does take place.[146] In stating that states must order or facilitate independent monitoring, the Commission further emphasized that the obligation of states must include a preventative and promotional aspect, with a strong focus on the participatory rights of the communities that may be affected by any of the anticipated activities.[147] Certainly, these observations by the Commission help to clarify Article 24 and to allow a progressive articulation of the more concise elements of the right.

Finally, the "cross-generational" approach of the African Commission in rendering its decision on the issues raised in the Ogoni case is of further importance. [148] This approach adopts an interpretation of rights that seeks to both explore the essential character of the right in question and link the right to others within the corpus of international human rights law. As the Indian Supreme Court has demonstrated with its constructive interpretation of the right to life in a domestic context, this methodology of interpretation is essential to the objective of demarginalizing second and third generation rights, and in fortifying the interrelatedness and interconnection between the various categories of rights. In the instant case, the African Commission employs this technique quite adroitly with regard to both its analysis of the right to housing and the right to food, as well as in regard to the provisions of Article 24

---

145. *See id.* ¶¶ 45-7 (explaining the prongs of the respect-protect-promote-fulfill test).

146. *See id.* ¶¶ 53-54 (declaring that compliance with Article 24 included respecting and protecting the environment, but also responding to and acting on citizens' environmental claims).

147. *See id.* ¶ 55 (noting that Article 24 obligations include releasing environmental studies to the public and allowing individuals to participate in development decisions that affect their communities).

148. *See* Gino J. Naldi, *Future Trends in Human Rights in Africa: The Increased Role of the OAU?*, *in* The African Charter on Human and People's Rights: The System in Pracitce, 1986-2000, 9 (Malcolm D. Evans & Rachel Murray, eds., 2002) (commenting that the difference between generations of rights is less significant). This is because the Vienna Declaration on Human Rights emphasizes the universality and interdependence of all human rights. *Id.*

on the right to a general satisfactory environment.[149] The former rights are viewed as *both* individual and collective in that the actions of the Nigerian state and the oil companies deprived individual members of the community this right, and simultaneously violated the rights of the community *qua* a community.[150] In this regard, the Ogoni decision is important because of what it has to say about the issue of the interrelatedness of human rights.

There is no doubt that the Commission's opinion in the Ogoni case is important in terms of the enhanced promotion and protection of marginalized rights within the African context. However, it is also important because it permits us to examine a number of broader issues. For instance, how can we enhance the protection of peoples' rights from a non-statist perspective? What is the place of international mechanisms in the attempt to deal with the complexity of human rights violations in the age of globalization?[151] How can non-state actors such as transnational corporations be made more directly accountable for actions taken that lead to a violation of human rights?[152] These are questions to which we can now turn, while also recognizing that in many respects the decision in the Ogoni case does not go far enough, particularly when placed against the many challenges thrown up by the processes of globalization.[153]

---

149. *See Ogoni Decision*, *supra* note 24, ¶¶ 49-50 (citing that the right to a healthy environment overlaps with social and economic rights, while finding that the rights to housing and food are necessary for the enjoyment of social and economic rights).

150. *See id.* (holding that the Nigerian government and Shell violated the rights of individuals and the Ogoni community).

151. *See* Aginam, *supra* note 47, at 26 (recommending that the African Commission provide direction to the Nigerian government in lessening the destructive effects of development projects).

152. *See* Michael K. Addo, *Human Rights and Transnational Corporations*, *in* HUMAN RIGHTS STANDARDS & THE RESPONSIBILITY OF TRANSNATIONAL CORPORATIONS 31-33 (Michael K. Addo, ed. 1999) (discussing the problems surrounding enforcing human rights standards on transnational corporations).

153. *See* Kerry Rittich, *Transformed Pursuits: The Quest for Equality in Globalized Markets*, 13 HARV. HUM. RTS J. 231, 231-32 (2000) (describing that globalization has reduced state sovereignty, increased migration of peoples, increased the role of capital and international institutions, and widened economic inequality).

III. THE MULTI-FACETED CHALLENGES OF GLOBALIZATION: OLD ACTORS, NEW ISSUES

Few phenomena have so determined the trajectory of human progress in the late 20th and early 21st centuries than has the process of globalization.[154] While debate continues about precise definitions, certain key elements are recognized as basic to its operation: the increased flows of capital around the world, the phenomenal development of information and communications technology, the concentration of economic and political power at a supra-state level in multilateral trade, financial institutions, and in transnational corporations, and the growing movement of people.[155] Obviously, the implications of these developments are numerous, including determining a state's most appropriate response to a perceived diminution of its central power, ascertaining how to spread the benefits of globalization more equitably, establishing what can be done to enhance social equality and political participation, and achieving the enforcement of more effective mechanisms of accountability.[156]

For the debate about marginalized rights, globalization assumes a particular significance in terms of the degree to which it fosters their 'progressive realization' and thus minimizes their violation.[157] More crucially, it raises the issue of how to reinforce the processes of globalization from below, namely, how to ensure that those who are generally marginalized by processes of development and politics, including indigenous peoples, women, and minorities, are buttressed

---

154. *See* Vincent Cable, *The Diminished Nation-State: A Study in the Loss of Economic Power*, 124 DAEDALUS 23 (1995) (reasoning that economic integration's undermining of state sovereignty has influenced national economics and politics).

155. *See* Rittich, *supra* note 153, at 231 (remarking that the process of globalization has brought about "porous borders", powerful international economic institutions, and escalated capital flow); Cable, *supra* note 124, at 23 (noting that significant technological enhancement and improved communication has accompanied international economic integration).

156. *See* Rittich, *supra* note 153, at 231-32 (commenting that as a result of globalization, states must adapt to their weakening sovereignty and society is facing growing inequality and a lack of opportunity for reparation).

157. *See id.* at 231 (stating that globalization requires all social and political reform, no matter how local, to occur on an international plane).

from globalization's most debilitating effects.[158] All these developments are taking place against the backdrop of what can only be described as a crisis in global governance, wherein the existing instruments and mechanisms designed to address the issues raised by globalization are increasingly being placed under stress; the actors are old, but so many of the issues are new.[159] Not only is there a "democratic deficit" in the mechanisms that exist to manage or regulate the global economy, there are also serious issues of enforcement, particularly with respect to the most powerful among them.[160] With regard to Africa, these issues are exacerbated by latent as well as manifest conditions of conflict, renewed pressures for fundamental democratic reform and development, and a world growing increasingly more apathetic to the conditions that exist on the continent.[161] In many different ways, these issues were the subtext to the African Commission's examination of the violation of the rights of the Ogoni.

A. ON THE STATE AND THE STRUGGLE FOR PEOPLES' RIGHTS IN THE AFRICAN CONTEXT

The Ogoni decision raises numerous questions about the structure of the contemporary state, the impact of globalization on it, as well as the phenomenon of peoples' rights in Africa. Discussions of the impact of globalization on the state have focused primarily on the manner in which many of the policies pursued in the quest for economic reform have rendered the state incapable of fulfilling many

158. *See id.* at 232 (remarking that enhanced international market activity has exacerbated economic inequality).

159. *See id.* at 231-32 (deducing that the decline in state sovereignty along with economic inequality, both resulting from globalization, will negatively affect progressive social agendas).

160. *See* Jayati Ghosh, *The Democratic Deficit*, International Development Economic Association, Aug. 14, 2002 (reporting that the majority of people feel politically powerless while international institutions are free to institute economic policies unchecked), *at* http://www.ideaswebsite.org/news/aug02/news14_Democratic_Deficit.htm (last visited Mar. 4, 2003).

161. George Ayittey, *Obstacles to African Development*, *in* ISSUES AND TRENDS IN CONTEMPORARY AFRICAN POLITICS 321 (George Akeya Agbango, ed. 1997) ("[In the 1990s, Africa] was wracked by a never-ending cycle of civil wars, carnage, chaos, and instability.").

of its human rights obligations.[162] Thus, policies of restructuring and adjustment have had an impact on the right to work. Privatization and the removal of state subsidies have affected the realization of the rights to health, education, and to an adequate standard of living.[163] The increased emphasis on export-led production has placed a severe strain on the production of non-cash crop production, and thus on food security and the realization of the right to food.

But there is another side to the story. The structure of the African state inherited from colonialism was manifestly coercive and authoritarian.[164] Consequently, a much lower emphasis was placed on the participatory and accountability elements of statehood.[165] Independence may have removed direct foreign influence, but it did little to reform or re-design the essential features of the state.[166] The single-party state and military dictatorship reinforced the elements of coercion and authoritarianism.[167] While the processes of globalization have indeed diminished the regulatory functions of the state, ironically, in most cases, its coercive and authoritarian aspects have remained intact. In many instances these have been strengthened, even where there has been a "democratic" transition.[168] Coincidentally, Nigeria launched one of Africa's earliest programs of

---

162. *See, e.g.*, Cable, *supra* note 154, at 23 (concluding that globalization weakens state values and its commitment to its citizens' rights). *But see* Linda Weiss, *Globalization and the Myth of the Powerless State*, NEW LEFT REV. 1997, at 3 (arguing that states, at varying degrees, have used their power to adapt to globalization and economic internationalization, rather than being rendered powerless by transnational market forces).

163. *See* Kois, *supra* note 117, at 104 (explaining that in many African countries, national debt, currency devaluation, and rising unemployment have negatively impacted human rights standards).

164. *See* Ayittey, *supra* note 161, at 322 (asserting that "the authoritarian colonial state was never really dismantled after independence").

165. *See id.* at 322-33 (noting that elected African leaders imposed dictatorial regimes once they were in power).

166. *See id.* at 322 (commenting that the political systems instituted after independence were "strikingly similar" to those in place during the colonial era).

167. *See id.* (demonstrating that African regimes utilized colonial-era techniques to repress freedom movements).

168. *See id.* at 322-33 (relating that those elected to representative governments subverted the democratic institutions and installed repressive regimes).

economic structural adjustment.[169] However, as oil revenues grew, the amounts going to producing states lessened, necessitating a higher degree of coercion to suppress heightened disaffection with the increasing exploitation that was worsened by a state riddled with corruption.[170] The case of Nigeria may have been extreme, but it was by no means the exception.

Against the preceding background, it is important to review how the issue of states and peoples is treated in the African Charter.[171] As Alston points out, one of the main problems with the African Charter is the lack of definitional clarification of the words relating to group and peoples' rights.[172] In an early article on the same topic, Richard Kiwanuka also noted that the possible meanings of the word 'peoples' within the Charter are legion.[173] Moreover, those many interpretations of the word are not necessarily mutually consistent.[174] In my view, the approach of the Charter is reflective of what can only be described as an African schizophrenia on the issue of peoples and states.[175] Given the history of state formation on the continent, it is quite clear that there is a manifest disconnect between the peoples of the continent and the states that were imposed on them via the mechanisms of colonialism concluded at Berlin. When African

169. *See* Ayittey, *supra* note 161 (discussing that while imposing the Structural Adjustment Program or economic austerity, General Ibrahim Babangida was providing his military officers with expensive cars).

170. *See id.* at 327 (stating that a 1994 audit showed that more than one-third of Nigeria's foreign debt was wasted by its leadership).

171. *See, e.g.*, Kiwanuka, *supra* note 132, at 82 (concluding that the meaning of "people" changes with the context of the right in which it is used).

172. *See* Alston, *supra* note 124, at 286 (stating that the Charter's lack of a definition largely prevents the enforcement of peoples' rights).

173. *See* Kiwanuka, *supra* note 132 (discussing the various meanings of "peoples" in the Charter).

174. *See id.* at 100-01 (explaining that the Charter implies four different definitions "peoples" that may conflict); *see also* James Crawford, *The Rights of Peoples: 'Peoples' or 'Governments'?*, *in* Crawford, *supra* note 120, at 55-6 (discussing the conflicts between peoples, governments and states).

175. *But see* Thio, *supra* note 125, at 461, 461 n.338 (citing the Banjul Charter's definitional absence as part of a "trend" among international instruments to omit explanations of controversial terms); Kiwanuka, *supra* note 132, at 82 (remarking that the drafters of the Banjul Charter deliberately left out a definition to avoid "difficult discussion").

leaders designed the Charter, it was obvious that they viewed most of the provisions through a statist prism.[176] Especially with the implications of increasing marginalization in conditions of globalization, there is a need to revisit this perspective.[177] In other words, the choice is between creating more avenues for peoples' participation in the affairs of governance, and particularly enhancing their autonomous operation, versus retaining the essential nature of the state as we know it with all the consequences for the continued suppression and violation of human rights this implies.[178]

Much of the Ogoni case centered on Article 21, which in many respects represents the essence of peoples' rights articulated in the African Charter.[179] Article 21 is of particular interest because it combines so many of the tensions and conceptual difficulties that scholars like Alston and Kiwanuka complain about and brings to a head the disconnect between African states and their peoples.[180] Thus, clause 1 speaks of "peoples" having the right to "freely dispose of their wealth and natural resources."[181] This clause is strengthened by clause 2 that refers to a situation of "spoilation," in which case the "dispossessed people shall have the right to the lawful recovery of its property as well as to an adequate compensation."[182] On the other hand, clause 4 of the same article speaks about states "*individually*

176. *See* Alston, *supra* note 124, at 287 (reporting that the Organization of African Unity has long focused on state sovereignty and territorial integrity of "inherited colonial boundaries").

177. *See* Rittich, *supra* note 153, at 232 (explaining that globalization substantially reduces the possibility of succeeding in significant social and political change).

178. *See* Kiwanuka, *supra* note 132, at 101 (commenting that by minimizing the gap between peoples and their state, the notion of "peoples" and peoples' rights can be an "enabling tool").

179. *See* Banjul Charter, *supra* note 23, art. 21 (mandating that "all peoples" have the right to their own natural resources).

180. *See* Alston, *supra* note 124, at 287 (commenting on the potential contradiction in the Charter between peoples' rights and state sovereignty); Kiwanuka, *supra* note 132, at 95-97 (discussing the conflict between the Charter and domestic constitutions and other international agreements in terms of the right to natural resources).

181. *See* Banjul Charter, *supra* note 23, art. 21.1 (requiring that this right "shall be exercised in exclusive interest of the people).

182. *Id.* art. 21.2.

and collectively" being able to "exercise the right to free disposal of their wealth and natural resources."[183] Kiwanuka correctly connects the inspiration for this provision to the discussions about the New International Economic Order that dominated international debate in the 1960s and 1970s.[184] He also points to the problem that this entails, namely its state-centered perspective:

> However, equating states with "peoples" assumes that the interests of the people are adequately represented by their state—a rarity in most developing countries, as we all know. In consequence, equating peoples and states further strengthens the state and subjects the rights of the people to the whims of whoever controls the political process.[185]

While Kiwanuka was correct in identifying the inherent danger in the collapse in the provisions of Article 21 between the notion of 'peoples' and the state, certainly the article could be read with more flexibility.[186] Rather than privileging the interests of the state, it is possible to read the article as a direct boost to the rights and interests of the peoples *within* the state, and of the responsibility of the state to those peoples.[187] This is what the Commission implicitly did in the Ogoni case. Thus, the Commission was of the view that the Nigerian government failed to involve the "Ogoni Communities in the decisions that affected the development of Ogoniland."[188] The Commission is even more pointed in its subsequent statement: "The destructive and selfish role played by oil development in Ogoniland,

183. *See id.* art. 21.4 (including that the states parties shall dispose of their resources "with a view to strengthening African unity and solidarity").

184. *See* Kiwanuka, *supra* note 132, at 96-7 (explaining that state sovereignty over natural resources was mandated by United Nations resolutions in 1962 and 1974).

185. *See id.* at 97 (concluding that this critique has led to the New International Economic Order theory's lack of success).

186. *See id.* at 96 (reasoning that Article 21 requires the term "peoples" to be synonymous with the state).

187. *See* Thio, *supra* note 125, at 463-64 (suggesting that the term "peoples" in the Banjul Charter could constitute all persons within a state or the various minorities within a state).

188. *See Ogoni Decision, supra* note 24, ¶ 60 (stating that the complainants accused the Nigerian government of failing to "monitor or regulate" the oil companies' activities).

closely tied with the repressive tactics of the Nigerian Government, and the lack of material benefits accruing to the local population, may well be said to constitute a violation of Article 21."[189] Consequently, one can read into the view of the Commission an interpretation of Article 21 that does not equate the term 'peoples' with the state.[190] That interpretation is clear in the decision of the Commission on this matter. Nevertheless, a manifest weakness in the decision in this regard is that this interpretation of the provision is not clearly reasoned and spelled out.[191] Throughout the decision, the Commission does not deal with the issue of what kind of 'peoples' the Ogonis are—indigenous, a minority, or both? A more reasoned interpretation of Article 21 would have been a considerable contribution to the body of law on this subject.

Why didn't the Commission go further? Perhaps it was because it felt there was no necessity to do so. Having condemned the Nigerian government for its violations against the community, the necessary conclusions would follow.[192] But the more likely reason is an enduring reluctance to specifically address the logical implications of holding that peoples, and not the state, are allowed to "freely dispose of their wealth and natural resources."[193] In the instant case, this would go to the heart of the main issues of contention in the relationship between peoples and the state—the inequitable distribution of oil resources and the gradual reduction of the share of revenues going to the states of derivation, meaning the states where the oil is produced, which declined from fifty percent in 1966 to a

189. *Id.*

190. *See id.* (finding that the Nigerian government violated its responsibility to ensure persons enjoy their rights).

191. *See* Thio, *supra* note 125, at 464 (exploring various possible interpretations of the term "peoples").

192. *See Ogoni Decision*, *supra* note 24 (finding the Federal Republic of Nigeria in violation of Articles 2, 4, 14, 16, 18(1), 21, and 24 of the Banjul Charter).

193. Banjul Charter, *supra* note 23, art. 21 (providing that nobody shall be deprived of this right); *see also* Kiwanuka, *supra* note 132, at 95-6 (discussing the conflict between the state and the individual in terms of the right to development and use of natural resources).

paltry three percent by 1993.[194] The 1999 Nigerian Constitution revised the figure upwards to thirteen percent.[195] However, there are still many problems relating to the equitable redistribution of those revenues.

In current discussions in Nigeria about a new framework of constitutional governance, this issue is of critical concern. But it goes beyond the federal arrangement, which Nigeria designed to deal with the issue of dispossessed communities and even beyond the vexed issue of resource distribution. It is ultimately a question of the status of minorities within the federated states:

> The 1999 Constitution established Nigeria as a federal, democratic and republican nation. The question then is why are people still afraid of domination and marginalization? The answer, for the ethnic minorities is that the structure, powers and constitution of local government do not involve a deliberate framework that enable each of the constituent minority ethnic-nationalities to maintain their identity without being politically colonized, economically impoverished and culturally assimilated by a larger (sometimes contiguous) ethnic group. Thus, while the constitution provides for individual rights, it neglects minority group rights. The neglect derives from the assumption that protection of individual rights will be sufficient for the protection of individuals and groups against oppression, exploitation and 'internal colonization.'[196]

In other words, the issue would ultimately return to a question of civil and political rights; you cannot freely dispose of your wealth unless you have the necessary political power to do so. This calls into question the linkage between self-determination in its social, economic, and cultural context, and in its civic and political dimensions. We return once again to the level of participation by such communities in the affairs of state. Depending on one's point of

194. *See* Ejobowah, *supra* note 107, at 34-6 (relating that the 1967-1970 Nigerian civil war precipitated the decline of the states of derivation's revenue share).

195. *See* NIG. CONST. § 162(2) (providing that not less than thirteen percent of oil production revenue shall go to the states of derivation).

196. Etannibi E.O. Alemika, *Ethnic Minorities in Nigeria: Constitutional Democratic Framework for Autonomy and Self-Governance*, *in* League for Human Rights, THE RIGHT TO BE DIFFERENT: PERSPECTIVES ON MINORITY RIGHTS, THE CULTURAL MIDDLE-BELT AND CONSTITUTIONALISM IN NIGERIA, Lagos, 107 (1999).

view, the Commission's failure to tackle this issue is either a serious disappointment or simply a concrete reflection of African reality. At a minimum, it illustrates that economic self-determination is only one side of the coin and that the issue requires further problematization.

The African Commission is generally coy about addressing issues that relate to the question of self-determination, and given African history this may be understandable.[197] Prior to the Ogoni case, the Commission had only declared admissible one communication concerning the right to self-determination—a Charter right enshrined in the provisions of Article 20.1. [198] That case involved a claim of the denial of self-determination by a group seeking the recognition of the independence of Katanga, a mineral rich province in what was then southern Zaire, and is now the Democratic Republic of Congo.[199] In deciding that case, the Commission gave the following opinion:

> All peoples have a right to self-determination. There may however be controversy as to the definition of peoples and the content of the right. The issue in the case is not self-determination for all Zaireans as a people but specifically for the Katangese. Whether the Katangese consist of one or more ethnic groups is, for this purpose immaterial and no evidence has been adduced to that effect.[200]

---

197. *See* N. Barney Pityana, *The Challenge of Culture for Human Rights in Africa: The African Charter in a Comparative Context*, *in* THE AFRICAN CHARTER ON HUMAN AND PEOPLES' RIGHTS: THE SYSTEM IN PRACTICE, 1986-2000, 219, 233-34 (Malcolm D. Evans & Rachel Murray eds., 2002) (evaluating that the African Charter, an instrument replete with references to 'peoples', makes no mention of the terms 'indigenous peoples' or 'minorities' and the Commission is cautious in recognizing claims to self-determination).

198. *See* Frans Viljoen, *Admissibility under the African Charter*, *in* THE AFRICAN CHARTER ON HUMAN AND PEOPLES' RIGHTS: THE SYSTEM IN PRACTICE, 1986-2000, 70 (Malcolm D. Evans & Rachel Murray, eds., 2002) (relating the Commission's analysis of Communication 75/92 *Katangese Peoples' Congress v. Zaire*).

199. *See id.* (indicating that the Kantangese Peoples' Congress requested the Commission to grant its succession from Zaire under Article 20.1 of the African Charter).

200. Communication 75/92 *Katangese Peoples' Congress v. Zaire*, ¶ 3 [hereinafter *Katangese Peoples' Congress*], *available at* http://www1.umn.edu/humanrts/africa/comcases/75-92.html (last visited Mar. 4, 2003).

The Commission found no prima facie violation of the Charter, and deemed the complaint as having "no merit."[201] In so holding, the Commission viewed self-determination as able to be exercised only in the form of "independence, self-government, local government, federalism, confederalism, unitarism or any other form of relations that accords with the wishes of the people *but fully cognizant of other recognized principles such as sovereignty and territorial integrity.*"[202] This opinion mapped the dominant view in the OAU, of which it has been said, "it is highly questionable that the OAU genuinely believes in the principle of self-determination except when used in the colonial context."[203]

Caught between the doctrine of *uti posseditis*[204] and the fear of encouraging secession, the Commission's decision addressed only half of the complex issue of the implications of fully recognizing peoples' rights in the African context.[205] It is nevertheless necessary to acknowledge that the Commission took the first tentative steps in making distance between the collapse of the notion of 'peoples' and the state that many have argued is implicit in the Charter formulation of this right.[206] While the Commission could certainly have devoted more time and analysis to dealing with some of the conceptual problems relating to the term 'peoples,' consideration of the views given to Article 21 is an important step in the attempt to give this

---

201. *See* Viljoen, *supra* note 26, at 70 (indicating how the Commission interpreted the Katangese Peoples' Congress' claims).

202. *Katangese Peoples' Congress*, *supra* note 200, ¶ 4 (emphasis added).

203. James Crawford, *Right to Self-Determination in International Law*, *in* PEOPLES' RIGHTS 29-30 (Philip Alaston ed. 2001) (elaborating on the history of self-determination and its inclusion in the African Charter on Human Rights, adopted by the OAU and interpreted in its application to "people of the colony or non-self-governing territory").

204. *See* Black's Law Dictionary 1544 (7th ed. 1999) (defining "uti possidetis" under international law as "the doctrine that old administrative boundaries will become international boundaries when a political subdivision achieves independence).

205. *See Katangese Peoples' Congress, supra* note 200 (referring to the Commission's conclusions of the alleged violations to the community as a whole, not individuals)

206. *See* Pityana, *supra* note 197, at 231-32 (arguing that the African Commission interpreted "peoples" as a reference to the State and "to establish their rights as a collective within the State.").

term more precise definition, and more importantly, to provide a framework for redress and enforcement for the communities and individuals marginalized in the process of contestation.[207]

In this respect at least, the Ogoni decision helps us to move away from the pessimism that has engulfed much of the scholarship in this area, and the conclusion that the future of peoples' rights is ". . . not very bright."[208] It provides some hope that issues such as self-determination, minority rights and even the 'explosive' issue of secession can be approached in a more creative and non state-centric fashion.[209] What this implies is the need to seriously revisit the legacy of the authoritarian state that was born in the era of colonialism, and that has been perfected since independence under a variety of nationalist, single-party and military structures to rebuild and reinforce the mechanisms of participation and reign in the forces of coercion.[210] Only then will African states be better equipped to tackle the multifarious challenges of globalization, among which is the increasing prominence of non-state actors.

B. NON-STATE ACTORS AND THE HUMAN RIGHTS REGIME: THE QUESTION OF TNCS

While under traditional human rights law the state is the primary focus of accountability, globalization has sharply brought to the forefront the issue of the lack of accountability of non-state actors for human rights violations.[211] Most prominent among these actors are

---

207. *See id.* at 232 (realizing that although the Commission did not take an extensive look at the drafter's intentions regarding "all peoples," it was the first time it came close to recognizing "minority rights as 'peoples' rights'").

208. *See* Alston, *supra* note 124, at 292 (noting the continued bleak outlook on the fight for peoples' rights).

209. *See* J. Oloka-Onyango, *Heretical Reflections on the Right to Self-Determination*, 15 AM. U. INT'L L. REV. 151, 183-84 (1999) (recognizing that African interpretation of self-determination was an individual right for all peoples, and not limited to those having direct ties to the nation-state).

210. *See* Ayittey, *supra* note 161, at 321, 322-23 (describing the difficulties African states had in shedding the politics of colonialism and the need for government officials to justify their "repressive system" as one fostering unity).

211. *See* Robert McCorquodale, *Human Rights and Global Business*, *in* COMMERCIAL LAW AND HUMAN RIGHTS 89, 92-4 (Stephen Bottomley & David Kinley eds., 2001) (indicating that the primary responsibility of states in

transnational corporations ("TNCs"),[212] whose activities in international trade, finance, and investment have numerous implications for the observation and protection of human rights, particularly economic, social and cultural rights, and the rights of the so-called third generation.[213] With regard to the issue of oil exploitation (the subject-matter of the Ogoni case) there is growing evidence that in a number of poor but oil-rich developing countries, UNDP human development index rankings have fallen as oil revenues have increased.[214] The reasons for this trend may vary and include such things as corruption and the structure and control of the industry. From whichever direction the issue is viewed, the place of TNCs is an important one.

Some observers perceive the activities of TNCs as 'necessary evils' in the generation of power, the extraction of natural resources like oil or diamonds, or the production of goods for the export market.[215] However, increasing concern is being expressed about the

---

maintaining international human rights law and that this obligation remains that of the government even if the violator is a non-state actor, such as a corporation).

212. *See* El-Hadj Guissé, *Report of the Sessional Working Group on the Working Methods and Activities of Transnational Corporations on its Fourth Session*, E/CN.4/Sub.2/2002/13, Aug. 15, 2002 (defining a transnational corporation as "an economic entity operating in more than one country or a cluster of economic entities operating in two or more countries" in its attached Draft Norms on Responsibilities of Transnational Corporations and Other Business Enterprises with Regard to Human Rights).

213. *See* McCorquodale, *supra* note 211, at 97-8 (indicating that the activities of various transnational corporations ("TNCs") "[subject] peoples to 'alien subjugation, domination and exploitation'"); *see also* Anne Orford, *Globalization and the Right to Development*, *in* PEOPLES' RIGHTS 166-67 (Philip Alston ed. 2001) (recognizing that it is easy for TNC's to deny individuals economic, social, and cultural rights when their own government enters into international trade agreements that weaken domestic laws and policies, such as consumer safety and environmental protection, thereby infringing on the protections provided by international human rights law).

214. *See* Halima Ward, *Governing Multinationals: The Role of Foreign Direct Liability*, Briefing Paper of the Royal Institute of International Affairs (Energy & Environment Program), No. 18, Feb. 2001, at 1 (describing the difficulties in assessing the relationship among foreign direct investment, environmental protection, and human development).

215. *See* Orford, *supra* note 213, at 179 (referencing the historical debate pronounced by economic and industrial agencies to justify their role in

manner in which these activities affect peoples' access to and ownership of land, their rights to a healthy environment, and the conditions which they are forced to work under.[216] In sum, the whole gamut of human rights is being affected as globalization fosters the growth in the social and economic power of TNCs.[217] While many human rights violations committed by TNCs can be looked at through the prism of state responsibility, there are certainly gaps when issues of relative power and economic necessity are brought into the picture.[218]

Within the context of the debate about globalization, these imbalances have come to be viewed with increasing concern and have alerted governments, civil society actors and the United Nations system to the necessity of taking effective action to plug the gap.[219] Efforts in this regard extend from the United Nations Global Compact, to the draft guidelines of the United Nations Sub-Commission on the Promotion and Protection of Human Rights.[220] Several TNCs, spurred on by consumer and shareholder expressions of concern, have also drafted their own codes of conduct.[221]

decolonialization and the development of an industrialized state as one that advances and improves technology and wealth for developing nations).

216. *See* Guissé, *supra* note 212, at 17-8 (acknowledging the power of TNCs "to cause deleterious human rights impacts on the lives of individuals through their employment practices, environmental policies, relationships with suppliers and consumers, [and] interactions with Governments and other activities").

217. Muchlinski, *supra* note 7, at 31 (referring the increased economic and social power of corporations like Shell, BP, and Unocal and the need to hold multinational corporations accountable for human rights violations).

218. *See* McCorquodale, *supra* note 211, at 93-94 (advocating that states have the primary responsibility for human rights violations even when they occur through non-state actors, such as TNCs).

219. *See* Guissé, *supra* note 212, at 15-16 (citing the United Nations' concern that increased globalization and the rising influence of TNCs requires these businesses to promote and secure internationally accepted standards of human rights, as detailed in the Universal Declaration of Human Rights).

220. *See id.* (referencing the United Nations' efforts to expand accountability for human rights violations to include not only state actors but also TNCs and other business entities).

221. *See* McCorquodale, *supra* note 211, at 110-11 (indicating that shareholders challenge TNC's activities by filing shareholder resolution and consumers use boycotts, such as those used against Shell, to force TNCs to adhere to international human rights laws).

Domestic courts have also been drawn into the effort to secure greater accountability, whether through the civil actions pursued in a number of countries including the United States,[222] or through the filing of criminal charges against company officials, as in the recent landmark case in Lesotho involving bribery charges against the officials of the Canadian multinational, Acres International.[223]

How to approach the issue of the liability of TNCs for human rights violations is of course the subject of considerable debate.[224] At one end of the spectrum are those who argue that TNCs must play a much more active role in ensuring that the human rights issues in the countries in which they operate are fully addressed.[225] On the other hand, a number of scholars have been critical of attempts to create 'missionaries' out of TNCs whose primary raison d'etre is viewed as being the business of making a profit.[226] Marina Ottaway, for example, criticizes the campaign to get TNCs (particularly oil companies) to conform more to human rights standards.[227] She likens these efforts to the missionary crusades of last century, arguing that ". . . it is a singularly bad idea to cast oil companies in [the] role. . .of political and moral reformers by making them attempt to 'do' human

---

222. *See Doe v. Unocal*, 963 F. Supp. 880 (C.D. Cal. 1997) (citing the important precedent in setting civil actions against large corporations, although the decision was appealed).

223. *See Rex v. Masupha Ephraim Sole* (in the High Court of Lesotho; Ref. CRI/T/111/99, dated May 20, 2002; unreported); *see also Western Firm Fined for Lesotho Bribe*, BBC NEWS, Oct. 28, 2002 (explaining that Masupha Sole—the head of the Lesotho Highlands Development Authority—was found guilty of receiving more than $250,000 from Acres International, while the firm was fined more than US $2 million), *available at* http://news.bbc.co.uk/2/hi/business/2369103.stm (last visited Mar. 4, 2003).

224. *See* Michael K. Addo, HUMAN RIGHTS STANDARDS AND THE RESPONSIBILITY OF TRANSNATIONAL CORPORATIONS 25-6 (1999) (conveying the difficulty of "apply[ing] human rights standards to the commercial environment where individual and corporate goals sometimes conflict").

225. *See* McCorquodale, *supra* note 211, at 103 (citing decisions by various courts which held private actors responsible for certain human rights violations).

226. *See* Marina Ottaway, *Reluctant Missionaries*, FOR. POLICY, July/Aug., 2001, 44, 54 (focusing on the problem of making corporations and other business entities the models of morality with regards to international human rights law).

227. *See id.* at 44 (classifying oil companies as unfit for promoting notions of democracy that may come in direct conflict with the goals of capitalism and who easily circumvent the added responsibility of enforcing morality).

rights."[228] Among the several reasons she offers in opposition to the idea are the following: 1) TNCs are not the right organs to further moral causes; 2) It is arrogant and paternalistic to give TNC executives the task of "lecturing developing-country officials on human rights and democratic governance;" and 3) "Trying to put oil companies in the role of reformers creates a process where nobody wants to take responsibility."[229]

Other commentators have raised objections to what they consider to be the elevation of TNCs to the same status as states within the international corpus, stating that this runs the risk of removing the primary responsibility for the protection of human rights from states.[230] Questions may also arise over the appropriate fora for bringing actions against TNCs, in addition to raising issues of a diplomatic nature.[231] Ultimately, what these discussions point to is the often limited utility for the operation of human rights claims in a context where there is such a skewed relationship between those who are violating rights, and those who seek to have their rights recognized and validated.[232] In sum, the process of getting rights recognized and realized is an *intrinsically* political process.[233] This point further connects both to the ideological parameters in which this issue is located, as well as to the purely strategic choices that

228. *See id.* at 54 (indicating that the TNCs and other business entities are not suited to advance the human rights causes).

229. *See id.* at 53-4 (classifying the reasons for not placing TNCs in the role of regulating human rights violations).

230. *See* Orford, *supra* note 213, at 167 (reasoning that even when states align their interests with TNCs, such as in the form of trade agreements, it "weaken[s] the human rights guarantees of peoples within their states and globally").

231. *See* McCorquodale, *supra* note 211, at 104 (referencing cases where TNCs have argued *forum non conveniens*).

232. *See* Orford, *supra* note 213, at 176-77 (noting the complicated power relationships that emerge when interpretations of the right to development differ at the state and individual levels).

233. *See id.* at 173-74 (illustrating the various persons involved in effecting human rights stems from individual investors and currency speculators to global organizations and agencies such as the World Bank and IMF, and, of course, the interests of state governments and the TNCs, which all have their own political agendas and policy concerns).

scholars and activists must make.[234] Against the backdrop of this debate, what should be the role of international mechanisms like the African Commission in addressing this issue?

Much of the Ogoni case centered on the operations of the oil companies in the Delta region.[235] What the Commission said (and did not say) with respect to this matter is important for addressing some of the issues raised within the broader context of the challenges presented by globalization, and with particular regard to deciding the issue of the responsibility of TNCs for human rights violations.[236] The main target of the petition in the Ogoni case was the Nigerian National Petroleum Company, a company in which the Nigerian government held majority shares, in a consortium with the Shell Petroleum Development Company, which held a minority.[237] In comparison to the other oil companies, Shell is perhaps the most important actor given that it has the largest facilities, and has consequently been the target of most attention.[238]

The African Commission was particularly critical of the manner in which the Nigerian government related to the oil consortiums, stating that the government had failed to exercise the necessary degree of care required in the circumstances.[239] Additionally, the Commission

---

234. *See* Issa Shivji, *Perspectives on Human Rights*, PAMBAZUKA ELECTRONIC NEWSLETTER, No. 80 (explaining how the language of human rights is continually changing to include the "most pressing. . .conditions" and requiring those advocating new characterizations of human rights to understand how this effects the global outlooks and standards), *available at* *http://www.pambazuka.org/newsletter.php?issuedate=2002-09-19* (last visited Mar. 3, 2003).

235. *See Shell v. The Ogoni People of Nigeria* (describing the region of Nigeria at issue in the Ogoni decision), *available at* *http://www.clas.ufl.edu/users/bmcdade/GroupBioko/shellvs.htm* (last visited Mar. 3, 2003).

236. *See* Shelton, *supra* note 122 (realizing that globalization requires non-state actors to take responsibility for violations of human rights).

237. *See Ogoni Decision*, *supra* note 24, ¶ 1 (referencing the key players in the case and their relations to one another).

238. *See* McCorquodale, *supra* note 211, at 111 (citing the use of consumer boycotts, specifically those against Shell).

239. *See Ogoni Decision*, *supra* note 24, ¶ 56 (noting that although the Nigerian government had the right to produce oil for the benefit of its citizens' rights, it was

stated that the obligation of care extended to the design of "legislation and provision of effective remedies."[240] A government was thus under an obligation to protect its citizens from damaging acts "perpetrated by private parties."[241] By contrast, the Nigerian government had given these private actors the "green light" to "devastatingly affect the well-being of the Ogonis."[242] Similar criticisms of the actions and omissions of the Nigerian government were also made with regard to its examination of the right to housing[243] and the right to food.[244] In other words, the Commission laid the responsibility for the violations that had been committed by these non-state actors squarely on the shoulders of the state.[245] Indeed, this is the position long accepted under international human rights law: that the state is the primary actor responsible for the promotion and protection of human rights.[246] This is true irrespective of the size or relative economic clout of the state, or indeed of the status and standing of the private actor.[247]

The view of the African Commission in this regard was influenced by two cases[248] decided by the Inter-American Court (*Velasquez*

---

obligated to ensure that oil companies did not infringe upon the rights of the Ogoni people).

240. *See id.* ¶ 47 (indicating the government's duties in protecting its citizens).

241. *See id.* (requiring states to hold private actors responsible for human rights violations as part of their duty to protect citizens).

242. *Id.* ¶ 60.

243. *See Ogoni Decision*, *supra* note 24, ¶ 63 (referring to the Committee on E/S/C rights' requirements of the African charter).

244. *See id.* ¶ 68 (stating the Commission's view that the Nigerian government "should not allow private parties to destroy or contaminate food sources, and prevent peoples' efforts to feed themselves").

245. *See id.* ¶ 71 (noting that the Nigerian government did not live up to the minimal expectations pronounced in the African charter).

246. *See* McCorquodale, *supra* note 211, at 92 (advocating the primary responsibility for human rights as traditionally the State's role).

247. *See id.* at 93-4 (arguing that even when the State does not have direct control over non-state actors they are still responsible for any human rights violations stemming from those actors).

248. *See Ogoni Decision*, *supra* note 24, ¶ 59 (relying on the referenced decisions to hold States responsible when they "[allow] private persons or groups to act freely and with impunity to the detriment of the rights recognised").

Rodriguez v. Honduras[249] and the European Court (*X and Y v. Netherlands*).[250] The two decisions were path-breaking in the identification of the obligation of states vis-à-vis private actors. However, a number of distinctions need to be drawn between the earlier cases if only to point out that the Ogoni case raises additional issues. The decisions in *Rodriguez* and *X & Y* quite rightly drew their rationale from the long-standing proposition in international human rights law and restated by the Vienna Declaration proclamation that human rights is the "first responsibility of governments."[251] There is consequently an obligation on states to *prevent* private actors from abusing human rights (a due diligence duty) and a further duty to *respond* to violations that may be committed by them (a reparative duty).[252] However, the distinctions I wish to draw relate to the nature of the violations in the previous cases (civil and political rights), the nature of the actors (irregular armed groups in the former case, and a hospital for the mentally-handicapped in the latter), and ultimately the relations of power between the state and those actors.

Drawing those distinctions requires a deeper examination of how the violations of the kind committed in the Ogoni case required more than simply holding the state accountable for the violations of private actors. Clearly, there is a distinction in the type of private actors that commit human rights violations.[253] With particular respect to the relationship between TNCs and countries in the less developed and developing parts of the world there is an added dimension, that of inequality of power.[254] As Duruigbo points out:

---

249. Case No. 4, Inter-Am. C.H.R., OEA/ser. C, PP 159-88 (1988).

250. 91 Eur. Ct. H.R. (ser.A) para. 18 (1985), *reprinted in* 8 Eur. H.R. Rep. 235 (1985).

251. *See* Vienna Declaration, *supra* note 1 (pronouncing that primary legal responsibility regarding human rights and their violations rests with the state).

252. *See* ANDREW CLAPHAM, HUMAN RIGHTS IN THE PRIVATE SPHERE 120 (1993) (outlining two essential State obligations with relation to private actors operating within the State).

253. *See supra* notes 246-247 (expressing the problems of holding private organizations or actors accountable for human rights violations).

254. *See* Orford, *supra* note 213, at 175-77 (relating the power of corporate advertising in creating consumer demand and creating a right to development for individuals coinciding with westernized notions of development and advancement).

> The situation is even worse in the case of developing countries which, in their quest and scramble for economic investments of multinational companies, are too enfeebled to regulate or control the multinationals. Indeed, the companies are more likely to show a preference for those countries with lax regulations over multinational business activity. The absence in developing countries of the technical expertise and legal development necessary to monitor or regulate complex activities such as environmental pollution also militates against any efforts by these countries to control the activities of multinational corporations.[255]

In this sense therefore, the decision in the Ogoni decision is limited because it is only directed to the state in question, omitting consideration of the accountability of the non-state actor, particularly where the criminal law or the regulatory mechanisms of the host state are inadequate to tackle the problem.[256] Perhaps the Commission was influenced by the fact that both within the domestic Nigerian context and internationally, people who believe that the oil companies violated their rights have sought recourse through the mechanism of civil trials.[257] Some of these measures have been successful. However, these mechanisms of redress focus primarily on violations of civil and political rights, and on environment-related harms such as the effects of pollution.[258] With specific regard to the cases brought in the United States, there are several constraints to using the Alien Tort Claims Act, among them the narrow scope of the 'law of nations' as interpreted by US courts, and issues of

255. Emeka Duruigbo, *Multinational Corporations and Compliance with International Regulations Relating to the Petroleum Industry*, ANNUAL SURVEY OF INT'L & COMP.L.101, 139 (2001).

256. *See* Clapham, *supra* note 252, at 198 (referencing *X and Y v. Netherlands,* where the court recognized the violations that occurred did not constitute human rights violations, but also recognized the lack of criminal sanctions for such violations).

257. *See* Jedrzej George Frynas, *Legal Change in Africa: Evidence from Oil-Related Litigation in Nigeria*, 43 J. OF AFR. L. 121 (1999) (giving examples of suits brought within Nigeria for human rights violations at the hands of corporate entities). *But see* Duruigbo, *supra* note 255, at 141-42 (arguing that the costs of bringing litigation along with political concerns and inherently weak judicial systems are major deterrents to individuals or other groups pursuing human rights claims).

258. *See* Shelton, *supra* note 142, at 185, 187 (linking human rights law and environmental protection in globally protecting such rights).

jurisdiction.[259] The hurdles to bringing claims about violations of economic, social, and cultural rights (which are barely recognized in even the most sensitive of domestic jurisdictions) would invariably be higher.

This places an additional obligation on international mechanisms that deal with the alleged violation of marginalized rights to delve deeper when confronted with cases involving their violation. In the instant case, the African Commission could have gone further because the conditions for a finding of liability on the part of Shell were all present in the instant case. Where a TNC is directly involved with the host country in human rights violations, direct liability should be found. A number of domestic courts have answered this question affirmatively, most prominently, the court in *Doe v. Unocal.*[260] How does this relate to the Ogoni situation? Peter Muchlinsky argues that where there is a 'joint enterprise' or 'joint venture' between the state and the firm liability accrues:

> If it can be shown that [a multinational enterprise] obtains a material economic benefit from operating in an environment where it knows that the business venture in which it is engaged involves state-sponsored violations of human rights, or where, in extreme cases, the firm itself engages in such violations in the course of operating the venture, that firm will be directly liable for those violations on a joint and several basis with the host state.[261]

The evidence in the Ogoni situation points to the fact that the oil companies knew that their business ventures were involved in state-sponsored violations.[262] Moreover, the joint venture company

259. *See* Terry Collingsworth, *The Key Human Rights Challenge: Developing Enforcement Mechanisms*, 15 HARV. HUM. RTS. J.183, 202-03 (2002) (indicating the significant limitations on enforcement of human rights through use of the Alien Tort Claims Act alone).

260. 963 F. Supp. at 888 ("Where the policies underlying the doctrine militate against its application, the act of state doctrine should not apply, even to claims that a foreign government's actions are or were invalid.").

261. Muchlinski, *supra* note 7, at 45.

262. *See* HUMAN RIGHTS WATCH, *supra* note 108, at 13 (indicating witnesses having reported that company staff has been present when security force officers threatened communities with retaliation if there was disruption to oil production).

committed several violations itself.[263] Several reports that tracked the activities of the oil companies in the Delta region illustrate that the companies were not mere bystanders as the state and its agents wreaked havoc on the peoples of the area.[264] The evidence provided to the Commission supported this fact.

Given these circumstances, it is thus clear that the Commission could have examined the issue of the direct liability of the oil companies more extensively. For many countries in the developing world (even for those such as Nigeria), considerable economic and political power bears on the relationship.[265] In the Delta region, Shell and the other companies made most of the decisions. While this kind of situation is no excuse for the state to abdicate its human rights undertakings, should the 'first responsibility' obligation act as a barrier to the accountability of other actors who have an almost equal power and capacity to violate human rights? The following section of the paper further analyzes direct liability by looking at the issue of how the human rights regime in general, and the African Charter in particular, treat the issue of duties or responsibilities within the context of the protection of human rights.

C. GLOBALIZATION IN AN ERA OF BOTH RIGHTS AND RESPONSIBILITIES

The discussion in this paper has mainly focused on the contribution of the African Charter to the reinforcement of the relationship between different categories of rights, and of the African Commission's role in fostering this connection through the decision in the Ogoni petition. However, the African Charter is of significance

263. *See id.* (noting that some companies have called for security force intervention, especially by notoriously abusive forces, during citizen protests and when people tried to raise grievances with the oil companies).

264. *See, e.g.*, Shell, *Statement of General Business Principles*, Dec. 1997 (noting that Shell was committed to "conduct business as responsible corporate members of society, to observe the laws of [the countries in which they operate], to express support for fundamental human rights"), *available at* http://www.shelloman.com/st_generalbusiness.htm (last visited Feb. 11, 2003).

265. *See* Abusharaf, *supra* note 105, at 20-22 (illustrating the influence of political and economic power even while though recognizing that relations of power have changed from the traditional concession regimes that dominated early mining contracts).

to the human rights debate in another respect—the area of duties and responsibilities.[266] Attacked by many scholars and activists (the present author included) as a slippery-slope down which states could easily travel to effectively curtail the very rights supposedly recognized, the introduction of duties into a human rights instrument was generally viewed as a retrogressive step.[267] Part of this can be explained from the time at which the Charter was promulgated. In 1981, Mobutu Sese Sekou was still president in what was then Zaire (now the Democratic Republic of Congo), and Kenya, Guinea, Mozambique, Algeria, and a host of other countries across the continent were either single-party dictatorships or were governed by military juntas.[268] Adding more duties to the burden carried by citizens in these countries seemed like a sure step to enhancing the violation of human rights rather than promoting their increased protection. Moreover, the phraseology employed in the African Charter with respect to some of the duties listed is certainly still cause for concern.[269] In a post September 11 era where a disturbing number of governments are using the notion of state security to

---

266. Makau Mutua, *The Banjul Charter and the African Cultural Fingerprint: An Evaluation of the Language of Duties*, 25 VA. J. INT'L L. 339, 339 (1995) (noting that the Charter codifies people's rights as well as imposes duties on individual members of African societies).

267. *See, e.g.*, J. Oloka-Onyango, *Beyond the Rhetoric: Reinvigorating the Struggle for Economic and Social Rights in Africa*, 26 CAL. W. INT'L L.J. 1, 64 (1995). Stating:

> The stronger elements of the Banjul Charter, such as those contained in Articles 25 and 28, can form the basis for articulating a firm state duty to eliminate discrimination and to protect disadvantaged social and political minorities. In addition, however, there is a need to develop new instrumentalities for the control of governmental excess, and to protect the essential parameters of a decent human existence.

Id.

268. *See* Chidi Odinkalu, *Analysis of Paralysis or Paralysis of Analysis? Implementing Economic, Social and Cultural Rights under the African Charter on Human and Peoples' Rights*, 23.2 HUM. RTS. Q. 327, 328-30 (2001) (noting that the Charter was adopted at a time in which major human rights violations were going on throughout Africa).

269. *See* Banjul Charter, *supra* note 23, art. 27, 29.3 (outlining every individual's duty to exercise his or her freedoms with regard to collective security and not to compromise the security of the state whose national or resident he or she is).

wantonly violate human rights, concerns about emphasizing duties over rights assume even greater prominence.[270]

However, the notion of duties and responsibilities is not a creation of the African Charter. Indeed, its origins can be traced to the Universal Declaration, reflecting an explicit need for a balance to be found between rights and duties.[271] The American Declaration of the Rights and Duties of Man is even more extensive.[272] More recently, several efforts reflect a growing concern with the need to revisit the manner in which rights relate to responsibilities.[273] The attempted promulgation of an International Declaration on Human Responsibilities by the InterAction Council ("IAC") in 1998 was the result of a multi-national effort to address what was perceived as a

270. *See For Whom the Liberty Bell Tolls*, ECONOMIST, Aug. 29, 2002 (describing violations of rights in the United States following September 11); Rotimi Sankore, *September 11- And Its Implications For Africa*, 79 PAMBAZUKA ELECTRONIC NEWSLETTER (Pambasuka Organization), Sept. 12, 2002 (detailing the response of African governments to the Sept. 11, 2001 terror attacks and their implications for the protection of human rights), *at* http://www.pambazuka.org//newsletter.php (last visited Feb. 11, 2003). The former U.N. High Commissioner for Human Rights, Mary Robinson, former U.S. President Jimmy Carter, and Amnesty International have raised similar concerns. *See, e.g.*, Amnesty International Canada, *September 11: A Global Human Rights Agenda, Frequently Asked Questions*, Jan. 26, 2002 (stating that fundamental human rights must be protected without condition or exception, even post Sept. 11), *available at* http://www.amnesty.ca/sept11/faq1.htm (last visited Feb. 12, 2003).

271. *See Universal Declaration of Human Rights,* G.A. Res. 217A(III) (1948), art. 30 (stipulating that "nothing in this Declaration may be interpreted as implying for any [s]tate, group, or person any right to engage in any activity or to perform any act aimed at the destruction of any of the rights and freedoms set forth herein"), *available at* http://www.un.org/Overview/rights/html (last visited Feb. 12, 2003).

272. *American Declaration of the Rights and Duties of Man,* O.A.S. Res. XXX, Chap. 2, art. XXIX-XXXVIII, adopted by the Ninth International Conference of American States (1948), *reprinted in Basic Documents to Human Rights in the Inter-American System*, OEA/Ser.L.V/II.82 doc.6 rev.1, at 17 (1992), *available at* http://www1.umn.edu/humanrts/oasinstr/zoas2dec.htm (last visited Feb. 12, 2003).

273. *See* International Commission on Intervention and State Sovereignty, *Commission Report: Responsibility to* Respect (discussing the issue of responsibility), *available at* http://web.gc.cuny.edu/icissresearch/Final.Report/index.html (last visited Feb. 11, 2003). Although directed in the main to the subject of humanitarian intervention, the issue can apply to several other areas of international concern. *Id.*

contemporary and very real problem.[274] Despite serious problems with its thrust, content, and continuing disagreement on the place of duties within the corpus of international human rights law,[275] there is no doubt that the issue of duties and responsibilities is of fundamental importance to the human rights struggle today.[276] In the words of Andrew Clapham, the IAC draft declaration "responds to an ideological vacuum. The driving competing ideologies, which sought to prioritize freedom and equality, are no longer locked in combat at the United Nations and elsewhere."[277]

Clapham faulted the draft for being deficient and for not going far enough in pointing to the increasing power and responsibility of key international economic and financial actors such as TNCs and the multilateral financial institutions for the protection of human rights.[278] Concern over the issue of duties remains prominent on the agenda; in 1999, the United Nations passed a declaration

---

274. *See* The InterAction Council, *A Universal Declaration of Human Responsibilities*, Sept. 1, 1997, (stating the several objectives of the Declaration), *available at* http://www.asiawide.or.jp/iac/UDHR/EngDec11.htm (last visited Feb. 11, 2003). The objectives were:

> to bring freedom and responsibility into balance and to promote a move from the freedom of indifference to the freedom of involvement. If one person of government seeks to maximize freedom but does it at the expense of others, a large number of people will suffer. If human beings maximize their freedom by plundering the natural resources of the earth, then future generations will suffer.

Id.

275. *See, e.g.*, Ronald Rich, Universality, the Individual and International Law, Presented at the Responsibility in World Politics Workshop, Faculty of Law, Australian National University (Nov. 20, 1998) (arguing that although human rights are inalienable, their enforcement depends upon the action of states), *at* http://www.cdi.anu.edu.au/speeches/speeches_downloads/iacRichNov98.pdf (last visited Mar. 4, 2003).

276. *See* Sigrun Skogly and Mark Gibney, *Transnational Human Rights Obligations*, 24.3 HUM. RTS. Q. 781 (2002).

277. Andrew Clapham, *Globalization and the Rule of Law*, 61 REV. OF THE INT'L COMM'N OF JURISTS (1999), *available at* http://www.business-humanrights.org/Globalization-and-the-Rule-of-Law.htm (last visited Mar. 4, 2003).

278. *Id.* at 27 ("Those who are interested in tackling the effects of globalization on the vulnerable should concentrate on enforcing the rule of law against non-State actors.").

highlighting the issue.[279] In the wake of the recent economic crises in Argentina[280] and its repercussions in other Latin American countries like Uruguay and Brazil,[281] the issue of the obligations, responsibility and accountability of international financial institutions such as the International Monetary Fund is brought into bold relief.[282] Equally dramatic in terms of the responsibility debate has been the corporate accountability scandals associated with WorldCom and Enron.[283] The reaction of the U.S. government in passing legislation to address some aspects of corporate responsibility illustrates that even for states that very strongly support the process of globalization, there is a limit to corporate malfeasance.[284] Rather than diminishing concern over duties and responsibilities, globalization has heightened attention to the activities of such actors in a context of seemingly unstoppable economic power.[285] It is fundamentally important to

279. *Declaration on the Rights and Responsibility of Individuals, Groups and Organs of Society to Promote and Protect Universally Recognized Human Rights and Fundamental Freedoms*, G.A. Res. 53/144, Mar. 8, 1999, *available at* http://www.hfhrpol.waw.pl/EN-RTF/en-12-1.htm (last visited Feb. 11, 2003).

280. *A Decline Without Parallel*, ECONOMIST, Mar. 2, 2002, at 26 (detailing the economic collapse in Argentina); James E. Mahon, Jr., & Javier Corrales, *Pegged for Failure? Argentina's Crisis*, CURRENT HISTORY 72 (2002) (describing the riots and looting that accompanied Argentina's financial crisis).

281. *Lifelines for Brazil and Uruguay*, ECONOMIST, Aug. 10, 2002, at 33 (describing how Argentina's crisis had a detrimental impact on the political and economic arenas in Brazil and Uruguay).

282. *See* SIGRUN SKOGLY, THE HUMAN RIGHTS OBLIGATIONS OF THE WORLD BANK AND THE INTERNATIONAL MONETARY FUND (2001) (asserting that of the human rights obligations recognized in the international regime to respect, promote, protect, and fulfill, IFIs only have the obligation to respect).

283. *See, e.g.*, *The President's Leadership in Combating Corporate Fraud* (outlining the government's response to corporate scandals), *available at* http://www.whitehouse.gov/infocus/corporateresponsibility/ (last visited Feb. 15, 2003). The response of the U.S. government to the corporate scandals, inadequate though it may be, illustrates that even for states that strongly support globalization there must be some limits. *Id.*

284. *See id.* (detailing the Corporate Corruption Bill, which was passed in response to recent corporate scandals).

285. *See* Meaghan Shaughnessy, *The United Nations Global Compact and the Continuing Debate About the Effectiveness of Corporate Voluntary Codes of Conduct*, 2000 COLO. J. INT'L ENVTL. L & POL'Y 159, 162 (2001) (noting that many corporations have no incentive or legal obligation to set up codes of conduct that will protect human rights).

ensure that human and peoples' rights are not diminished within such a context.[286] However, the issue of responsibility is of serious concern for the promotion and protection of human rights in an era of globalization, and assumes several dimensions not quite on the front-burner when the African Charter emerged onto the scene in 1981.[287]

It is thus somewhat surprising that the Ogoni decision is almost completely silent on the issue of duties and responsibilities of anyone other than the state, despite the fact that the African Charter is well known for its articulation of such duties.[288] Was the Commission being careful so as not to deflect the burden of responsibility in addressing the plight of the Ogoni from the state? Did the Commission feel the Charter provisions and those elsewhere in the regime of international human rights law were inadequate to make a finding of such responsibility? Or was there a fear of a slippery slope, such that ascribing duties to corporate individuals could lead to their stricter application to natural persons in conditions that ultimately lead to a curtailment of their rights. None of this is clear from the decision, because the focus was wholly on the responsibility of the state.[289] While it is obvious that many of the duties stipulated in the relevant provisions of the Charter can only refer to natural persons (e.g. the duties to family), just as corporate bodies are not denied the exercise of rights that are recognized in international and domestic law (ranging from proprietary to associational rights), so too can duties be ascribed to them. The term "every individual" covers both natural and artificial persons. Moreover, corporate ascription of liability is not something new in the international law context. In the words of Dinah Shelton, "the international legal system can no longer be described as one governing states alone."[290]

286. *See id.* (urging the development of a legal mechanism to enforce compliance with codes of conduct in order to protect the human rights of developing countries in which corporations operate).

287. *See, e.g.*, International Council on Human Rights, TAKING DUTIES SERIOUSLY: INDIVIDUAL DUTIES IN INTERNATIONAL HUMAN RIGHTS LAW (1999) (describing the historical context of human rights duties).

288. *See* Banjul Charter, *supra* note 23, Chap. II (laying out the duties of each individual person).

289. *See Ogoni Decision*, *supra* note 24, art. 44 (stating that the communication alleged that the government of Nigeria violated various rights).

290. *See* Shelton, *supra* note 122, at 307.

To conclude, a more concise engagement with the issue of duties would greatly assist in dealing with the various dimensions of corporate malfeasance that were dramatically demonstrated in the case of the Ogoni, as well as bring corporate responsibility more precisely within the human rights framework. The Ogoni case suggests that regional and international human rights mechanisms should more directly confront the abuses committed by non-state actors as such, rather than continuing to focus wholly and solely on the responsibility of the state. In this respect, such mechanisms need to consider the provisions within the instruments they administer that speak to the issue of responsibility and duty, and seek an appropriate balance between state liability and the responsibility of the non-state actor. Creatively approaching this issue will enable them to both uphold the Vienna Declaration's dictum on the first responsibility of states, while recognizing that in the contemporary world, there are additional actors which need to be held accountable. As international mechanisms turn their attention to this issue, more attention nevertheless still needs to be given to the development of supra-state mechanisms of holding non-state actors accountable.[291]

CONCLUSION

The African Charter commenced life on a note of considerable promise. Born in the aftermath of the brutal dictatorships of Idi Amin in Uganda, Macias Nguema of Equatorial Guinea, and that of Jean Bedel Bokassa in the Central African Republic, the Charter promised to lead to a new chapter on the African continent.[292] This hope related not only to the protection of civil and political rights, but more specifically to the demarginalization of economic, social, and

291. *See* Deepak Nayyar, *The Existing System and the Missing Institutions*, *in* GOVERNING GLOBALIZATION (Deepak Nayyar ed. 2002) (suggesting that as part of the creation of an international system of governance, attention should be paid to the establishment of an international regime of anti-trust laws and a binding code on restrictive business practices).

292. *See* Julia Swanson, Note, *The Emergence of New Rights in the African Charter*, 12 N.Y.L. SCH. J. INT'L & COMP. L. 307, 307 (1991) (stating that the African charter was considered a remarkable document that is responsive to Africa's unique circumstances).

cultural rights, and the rights of the so-called 'third' generation.[293] That promise seemed to have been dashed by institutional inertia and inefficiency and the apparent lack of the necessary political will and creative intellectual flair that is always essential to turn the black letter of the law into an effective instrument to address the lived reality of the dispossessed.[294] African civil society and academia hold as much of the blame for this problem as the African Commission.

The Ogoni decision can be viewed as part of an on-going struggle to recapture the essential spirit of the African Charter, an instrument that was designed to *both* ensure that universal human rights standards are given expression within the regional context, *and* to convey the uniqueness of the African experience to the rest of the world.[295] The words of the Commission convey the important point as to why there is still a great need to be sensitive to the kinds of rights articulated in the Charter within the African context:

> The uniqueness of the African situation and the special qualities of the African Charter on Human and Peoples' Rights impose upon the African Commission an important task. International law and human rights must be responsive to African circumstances. Clearly, collective rights, environmental rights, and economic and social rights are essential elements of human rights in Africa. The African Commission will apply any of the diverse rights contained in the African Charter. *It welcomes this opportunity to make clear that there is no right in the African Charter that cannot be made effective.*[296]

Human rights are the site of constant struggle. Consequently, it is imperative that bodies such as the African Commission be positively

---

293. *See generally id.* at 309-25 (discussing in detail the peoples' rights in the African Charter).

294. *See* Shebdrack C. Agakwa, *Reclaiming Humanity: Economic, Social, and Cultural Rights as the Cornerstone of African Human Rights*, 5 YALE HUM. RTS. & DEV. L.J. 177, 177 (2002) (criticizing the government of Africa for its failure to successfully implement the African Charter and protection of human rights).

295. *See* Jim Lobe, *People Versus Big Oil: Rights of Nigerian Indigenous People Recognized*, FOR. POL'Y IN FOCUS, July 5, 2002 (billing the decision as "the strongest and most articulate statement on the validity and enforceability of economic and social rights emanating from any intergovernmental human rights body"), *available at* http://www.fpif.org/commentary/2002/0207nigeria.html (last visited Mar. 4, 2003).

296. *Ogoni Decision*, *supra* note 24, ¶ 71.

identified with that struggle. This need is all the more important as future contests over the realization of human rights assume different and more complicated dimensions, particularly under the framework of globalization. To borrow the words of Aginam, the synergy of human rights lies in a realization of the interdependence of all categories of rights.[297] It also lies in pushing the parameters of the conceptualization of human rights to their logical limits. Many issues remain unresolved, but the Ogoni decision is a critical turning point both for the Commission and for human rights law on the African continent. The decision is an important addition to the jurisprudence of the international regime of human rights.

297. Aginam, *supra* note 47, at 25.

[19]

"RIGHTING," RESTRUCTURING, AND REJUVENATING THE POSTCOLONIAL AFRICAN STATE: THE CASE FOR THE ESTABLISHMENT OF AN AU SPECIAL COMMISSION ON NATIONAL MINORITIES

Obiora Chinedu Okafor[*]

1. Introduction

The special theme of this volume of the *Yearbook*, i.e. "*Reflections on Some Forms of Statehood in Africa*," invites contributor and reader alike to grapple with an abstract concept that has nevertheless proved to be highly consequential to the lived experience of virtually every African – at least since the mid-nineteenth century. Despite the increasingly extensive literature on the subject,[1] both within and

---

[*] Associate Professor, Osgoode Hall Law School of York University, Toronto, Canada. Ph.D, LL.M (University of British Columbia, Vancouver, Canada); LL.M, LL.B (Hons) (University of Nigeria, Enugu Campus). I should like to thank Dr. Tiyanjana Maluwa, the H. Laddie and Linda P. Montague Professor of Law at the Dickinson School of Law, The Pennsylvania State University, Carlisle, Pennsylvania, USA, for inviting this article; and Chikeziri Igwe for his able research assistance.

[1] For a few samples, see Mutua (M.), "Why Redraw the Map of Africa: A Moral and Legal Inquiry" (1995) 16 *Michigan Journal of International Law* 1113; Wallace-Bruce (N.L.), "Africa and International Law – The Emergence to Statehood" (1985) 23 *The Journal of Modern African Studies* 575; Zolberg (A.R.), "The Specter of Anarchy: African States Verging on Dissolution" (1992) Dissent 303; Beissinger (M.R) and Young (C.), *Beyond State Crisis? Postcolonial Africa and Post-Soviet Eurasia in Comparative Perspective* (Washington D.C.: The Johns Hopkins University Press, 2002); Murithi (T.), *The African union: Pan-Africanism, Peacebuilding and Development* (Aldershot: Ashgate, 2005); and Okafor (O.C.), *Re-Defining Legitimate Statehood: International Law and State Fragmentation in Africa* (The Hague: Martinus Nijhoff, 2000) (hereinafter "Re-Defining").

without the legal academe, the topic is so complex, so controversial, so socially relevant, and so widely misunderstood still, that it does deserve further attention in a *Yearbook* such as this.

The objective of this article is to contribute in a modest way to the process of producing ever more accurate scholarly and policy understanding with regard to this very complicated socio-legal subject. To this end, the article will develop systematically an analytical case for the establishment of an African Union (AU) Special Commission on National Minorities as a way of beginning a viable process of resolving the national minority problem that underlies the structural legitimacy crisis that has afflicted the postcolonial African state from its very beginning as the successor of the colonial African state. In order to make this case, the article has been divided into five sections, including this introduction. In section 2, the nature of the national minority problem within the postcolonial African state is explicated. In section 3, the normative imperative of rejuvenating the postcolonial African state through its righting[2] and restructuring is discussed. Thereafter, section 4 develops – in as full a fashion as space allows – a case for the establishment of a particular kind of inter-African institution, i.e. the Special Commission on National Minorities, to facilitate and bolster the normatively imperative process of righting, restructuring – and therefore rejuvenating, the postcolonial African state. Section 5 concludes the article.

At the outset, it must be noted that the argument that is made in this article in favour of the establishment of a new institution that can make an important contribution to the peaceable management of the state legitimacy crisis that afflicts the postcolonial African state and which has almost completely crippled a few such states, is not in any way a suggestion that the postcolonial African state should be reconstituted in its present form with the help of this proposed institution. If anything, it is an argument that this state should be

---

2 I have borrowed the term "righting" from the work of Karen Knop. See Knop (K.), "The 'Righting' of Recognition: Recognition of States in Eastern Europe and the Soviet Union" in Le Bouthillier (Y.), McRae (D.M.) and Pharand (D.) (eds.), *Selected Papers in International Law: The Contribution of the Canadian Council on International Law* (The Hague: Kluwer, 1999) at 261.

*re*configured peaceably through a process that is framed by international human rights law and ordered in part by a process that is created by this institution, lest that state continue to be reconfigured in as conflict-ridden and violent a way as it so far has, at least for the most part.[3] Surely, even when ideally operated – which has not been the case – the current structure of the postcolonial African state cannot be the only viable way of configuring statehood in Africa?

Another caveat that must be entered at the outset is that the author's cautious faith in the value-added of the institution the establishment of which is proposed in this article does not imply the promotion of the uncritical reliance on international institutions and procedures as panaceas. The pitfalls of such an approach are well documented.[4] What the author's cautious confidence in the capacity of such an institution to make a difference does imply, however, is a limited faith in such institutions as *resources* in the hands of the human agents (such as local activists, the leadership of minority groups, and even diplomats). Viewed as resources, our expectations regarding the possible achievements of these institutions will become more limited, and therefore more realistic and accurate.

Needless to say, this article – especially its first two substantive sections – draws from some of my previous work in this general area. However, the article seeks to add value to the debate on statehood in Africa not just by deploying to the current terrain of enquiry important insights from that previous work, but also by offering a fresh perspective on some of the arguments in support of my earlier proposals for the establishment, within the structures of the defunct Organization of African Unity (OAU),[5] of a *Special Commission on*

---

3 See Mutua (M.), "Putting Humpty Dumpty Back Together Again: The Dilemmas of the Post-Colonial African State" (1995) 21 *Brooklyn Journal of International Law* 505, at 536.

4 For example, see Kennedy (D.), "A New World Order: Yesterday, Today and Tomorrow" (1994) *4 Transnational Law and Contemporary Problems* 329, at 339-357; and Kennedy (D.), "The Move to Institutions" (1987) 8 *Cardozo Law Review* 841.

5 Pursuant to the adoption of the *Constitutive Act of the African Union,* on-line: (http://www.africa-union.org/root/au/AboutAu/Constitutive_Act_en.htm) (visited 24 May 2006), on 1 July 2000, the OAU was formally dissolved in 2002 and replaced by the AU. See also *Decision of the Assembly of Heads of State of the African Union*, OAU Doc. AHG/AU/AEC/Dec. (I) (9-10 July 2002). On this

National Minorities.[6] The other important way in which value is added to the relevant body of literature by this article is through its further development, within the more contemporary context of the new African Union,[7] of my previously offered argument for the creation of this institution.

2. The National Minorities Problem within the Postcolonial African State

It is hardly controversial to argue that the relationship between almost all postcolonial African states and the national minorities who form the bulk of the sub-state groups that constitute nearly every one of these states has, to say the least, been highly problematic. Less well recognized in the literature is the fact that this problematic situation has been, and will for the foreseeable future remain, the central problem of post-colonial African statecraft.[8] Nevertheless, most observers of African politics would agree that as the *Constitutive Act of the African Union* has itself declared "the scourge of conflicts in Africa constitutes a major impediment to the socio-economic development of the continent."[9] Yet, since nearly every single one of these conflicts in Africa has quite remarkably been internal, or better still intra-state in nature,[10] and since virtually all of these intra-state conflicts have involved tensions over the practical enjoyment (or the

---

and similar issues, see Udombana (N.J.), "The Unfinished Business: Conflicts, the African Union and the New Partnership for Africa's Development" (2003) 35 *George Washington University International Law Review* 55, at 55-56 (hereinafter "Unfinished Business")..

6 See Okafor (O.C.), "Re-Defining", supra note 1 at 183-192. See also Okafor (O.C.), "The African System on Human and Peoples' Rights, Quasi-Constructivism, and the Possibility of Peacebuilding *within* African States" (2004) 8 *International Journal of Human Rights* 413 at 443; and Okafor (O.C.), "Convention Refugeehood, Early Warning Signs, and the Structural Crisis of Legitimate Statehood in Contemporary Nigeria" (2003) 9 *Buffalo Human Rights Law Review* 1 at 6.

7 See the Constitutive Act of the African Union, supra note 4.

8 See Okafor (O.C.), "After Martyrdom: International Law, Sub-State Groups, and the Construction of Legitimate Statehood in Africa" (2000) 41 *Harvard International Law Journal* 503 (hereinafter "Martyrdom").

9 See the Preamble of the Constitutive Act of the African Union, supra note 4.

10 See Udombana (N.J.), "Unfinished Business", supra note 4 at 59.

lack thereof) of group rights/interests within the relevant states, it appears that inter-group conflicts (mostly of the majority/minority type) have at the very least been one major impediment to the effectiveness of the postcolonial African state. What is more, based on my own careful observation of the dynamics of the politics of state formation in Africa, I am of the view that the seemingly incessant inter-group tensions that underlie almost all of the intra-state conflicts that occur within the postcolonial African state is – at least in terms of its scale, prevalence and consequences – *the* key African state-building problem of our time. This point is easily illustrated.

Throughout its postcolonial history, and even before, the postcolonial African state has been typically beset by inter-group tensions, crises, and violence. As Makau Mutua has brilliantly argued, viewed from the perspective of the desirability of generally cohesive or widely accepted states with a reasonable chance of attaining effectiveness, the postcolonial African state never really had a chance in the first place.[11] A brief review of a sample of such states will serve to illustrate the nature of the structural illegitimacy that has seriously threatened the viability of the postcolonial African state. In the Democratic Republic of the Congo (i.e. the former Zaire), "multiple secessions and inter-ethnic conflict followed [its] independence" from Belgium in 1960.[12] Chief among these tensions and conflicts was the secessionist rebellion of the people of the Katanga (later Shaba) area.[13] That some, if not all, of these tensions and conflicts have survived to this day, mostly via their exacerbation, manipulation and reification by certain political leaders is in part ably illustrated by the minority rights and secession claims made before the African Commission on Human and Peoples' Rights in the now famous and relatively recent *Katanga Case*.[14] In Rwanda, longstanding tensions, conflicts, and violence between the Hutu numerical majority and Tutsi minority eventually escalated into one of the most well-known

---

11 See Mutua (M.), supra note 2.

12 See McNulty (M.), "The Collapse of Zaire: Implosion, Revolution or External Sabotage?" (1999) 37 *The Journal of Modern African Studies* 53, at 54.

13 *Ibid.* at 62.

14 See *Katangese Peoples' Congress v. Zaire* (1996) 3 *International Human Rights Reports* 136.

genocidal episodes in human history.[15] While, Rwandan society has to some extent begun the long process of recovery and reconciliation, there is as yet no reliable evidence that the underlying tensions that led to the genocide have fully died down. The conflict in Burundi, which has lasted some ten years and killed well over two hundred thousand people and has, in Udombana's fitting words, left that country "paralyzed", is similarly based on structural tensions between a fearful but powerful Tutsi minority and a less powerful but far more populous Hutu majority.[16] While this conflict is now formally over, there is little evidence to suggest that the inter-group resentment and tensions that spawned it are no longer prevalent, even if in a slightly milder form. In Nigeria, the recent upsurge in violence in the oil-rich Niger Delta region, instigated for the most part by the militant wings of the various minority rights movements that populate that area, only underlines the intensity of much inter-group tensions in Africa's vastly most populous country.[17] The Biafran war that was fought mostly in the Igbo-dominated Eastern region of Nigeria in the late 1960s is perhaps the most negative consequence so far of this sort of intense tension.[18] Just as the decades old inter-group conflict in the Sudan between the somewhat "Arabized" North and the "non-Arabized" South waned and ended in a peace deal, a similarly destructive inter-group conflict broke out in the Darfur region of that same country.[19] While a peace deal was signed in mid-2006 by some of the sides to the Darfur conflict (the central regime in Khartoum included), there is little room for so optimistic an assessment that would declare most inter-group tensions "dead and buried" in that vast

15 See Hintjens (H.M.), "Explaining the 1994 Genocide in Rwanda" (1999) 37 *The Journal of Modern African Studies* 241.

16 See Udombana (N.J.), "Unfinished Business" supra note 4 at 61-62.

17 See Human Rights Watch, *They Do Not Own This Place: Government Discrimination Against 'Non-Indigenes' in Nigeria* (New York, Human Rights Watch, 2006) at 7-8; "Militants Kill 4 Policemen in Port Harcourt" *Thisday*, 15 May 2006, on-line: (http://www.thisdayonline.com/nview.php?id+48166&printer_friendly=1) (visited 15 May 2006).

18 See Forsyth (F.), *The Dogs of War* (New York: Viking Press, 1974).

19 See Human Rights Watch, *Darfur: Humanitarian Aid under Siege* (New York: Human Rights Watch, 2006) at 6.

but deeply troubled country.[20] More generally, Joel Ngugi was correct when he noted that Africa's "indigenous peoples" (who are almost always also minority groups) have been subjected to very serious ill-treatment that has too often generated high tension, conflict and violence.[21] While the foregoing is by no means a comprehensive rendering of the inter-group tensions and conflicts that afflict the post-colonial African state, it suffices to illustrate the centrality of such tensions and conflicts to statecraft in Africa, as well as its status as the key challenge of contemporary African state-building praxis.[22]

It is important, however, to note, as I have shown elsewhere, that contrary to the conventional wisdom, this tendency to be characterized by tensions, crisis and violence – one which has marked and marred the history of the postcolonial African state – is not uniquely African and has less to do with the much touted incapacity of Africans to govern themselves or to build large and effective centralized states than with the daunting challenges of state-building posed by the particular character of the state-formation processes that produced the postcolonial African state as we currently know it.[23]

Thus, the serious national minority problems that face the postcolonial African state are mostly structural in nature.[24] This does not of course discount the role of human agency in the generation of these problems. The structural nature of this problem stems for the most part from the structural illegitimacy of almost all such states in Africa.[25] In the main, such illegitimacy has derived from the postcolonial African state's lack of sufficient affinity with its constituent sub-state groups, and its origins as a generally unalloyed external *imposition* rather than as a largely organic entity created

20 *The Guardian* (Nigeria), 17 May 2006.

21 See Ngugi (J.), "The Decolonization-Modernization Interface and the Plight of Indigenous Peoples in Post-Colonial Development Discourse in Africa" (2002) 20 *Wisconsin International Law Journal* 297.

22 For other examples, see Jinadu (L.A.), "Explaining and Managing Ethnic Conflict in Africa: Towards a Cultural Theory of Democracy," Lecture Delivered at the Uppsala University Forum for International and Area Studies, 5 February 2004 (on file with the author).

23 See Okafor (O.C.), "Martyrdom," supra note 7 at 504.

24 *Ibid.*, at 504-514.

25 *Ibid.*, at 504.

through an internal process of consensus-building.[26] And although all states are a product of conflict, consensus and contrivance, it must be remembered that the postcolonial African state is by far the most contrived of all!

3. "Righting", Restructuring and Rejuvenating the Postcolonial African State:

I have argued in my previous work that certain doctrinal tendencies of international law (such as the facilitation of *homogenization*[27] and *peer-review*[28]) have traditionally facilitated the process via which the postcolonial African state has tended to coercively retain its restive sub-state groups, almost always with profoundly negative implications for the legitimacy, stability, peacefulness, and effectiveness of the relevant states.[29] Given the deep socio-cultural cleavages and serious structural tensions that characterize the postcolonial African state, this conflictual and often violent result is not all that surprising.[30] However, as I have also shown elsewhere, international law is in many senses slowly beginning to turn slightly in the direction of alternative doctrines and tendencies, such as *autonomy*[31] (rather than homogenization) and *infra-review*[32] (instead of peer-review). This

26 *Ibid.*

27 As used here, "homogenization" refers to the tendency in international law to facilitate the largely coercive attempts by states to "form cohesive, culturally unitary nations out of their distinct, diverse component polities." See *ibid.*, at 518.

28 As used here, "peer review" refers to the tendency in international law to facilitate "the process of determining state legitimacy... according to the *ipse dixit* or "say so" of pre-existing states. This determination is not necessarily made with reference to the nature or qualities of the would-be state, or of any of its constituent sub-state groups." See *ibid.*, at 515.

29 See Okafor (O.C.), "Re-Defining" supra note 1 at 53-77.

30 See Okafor (O.C.), "Martyrdom" supra note 7 at 505 and 521-526.

31 As used here, the term "autonomy" refers to the slight turn in favour of more respect in international law and society for the rights, desires and wishes of the sub-state socio-cultural groups that constitute most states (especially for their minority and self-determination rights). See *ibid.*, at 520-521.

32 As used here, the term "infra-review" refers to the requirement that the decision-making process regarding state legitimacy pay significant attention to the "say-so" and rights of the socio-cultural groups that constitute a given state. See *ibid.*, at 515.

turn may allow international law and institutions to avoid contributing in nearly as much measure to the generation of tensions and violence within the post-colonial African state.[33]

As these linkages among these specific traditional doctrines and tendencies of international law, the structural illegitimacy of the postcolonial African state, and the generation of conflict within many such states, have already been well explicated in other books and articles, I will not dwell of them here.[34] Rather, what I propose to do briefly in this section is to show how the international legal regime (and to a much lesser extent, certain domestic regimes within African states) have begun to contribute to the righting, restructuring – and therefore to the eventual rejuvenation – of the post-colonial African state. The promotion and sustenance of these righting and restructuring tendencies is seen as key to countering the negative effects that the homogenization and peer-review tendencies have had on the postcolonial African state, and in also facilitating the incipient – if still shaky – turn toward the relatively more desirable autonomy and infra-review tendencies.

Righting the Postcolonial African State

The need to "right" the postcolonial African state refers primarily to the international legal imperative of utilizing and adhering to international human rights law norms (especially those relating to self-determination and minority rights) in the processes of state-formation or even state-disintegration in Africa (as elsewhere). The use of the term "righting" also refers to a normative standard; i.e. it suggests that adherence to these minority rights and self-determination norms is in fact the right thing to do from a policy and moral perspective. As obvious as the necessity of adherence to such norms in statecraft may seem to some, international law has until recently tended to favour, rather than counter, attitudes that detracted from the observance of the requirements of these norms. As we have seen, the law has tended to favour the coercive retention of sub-state

33 *Ibid.*, at 517-518 and 520-521.

34 For example, see Okafor (O.C.), "Re-Defining" supra note 1; and Okafor (O.C.), "Martyrdom" supra note 7.

groups within established and generally homogenizing states, while paying scant attention to the "say so" or infra-review of such groups regarding the legitimacy of their continued membership within these established states. These two attitudes (i.e. homogenization and peer-review) tend to negative rather than adhere to the minority and self-determination rights that are becoming entrenched in international law. Thankfully, as strong and dominant as they remain, these attitudes have begun to wane in significant though still slight measure.[35]

International human rights law, especially articles 1 and 27 of the International Covenant on Civil and Political Rights; article 1 of the International Covenant on Economic, Social and Cultural Rights; articles 19-23 of the African Charter on Human and Peoples' Rights; and the Declaration on the Rights of Persons Belonging to National, Ethnic, Religious and Linguistic Minorities, imposes reasonably clear obligations on states to respect the rights of their constituent sub-state groups, especially those who are minorities within those states.[36] It is no secret that most African states have at the formal level consented to be bound by most of these obligations. These minority rights include the right of such groups to use their own languages, to participate fully in political and economic life, to self-determination (at least in the form of local autonomy), to maintain their own associations, and to non-discrimination. In particular, the African Charter, to which every African state, with the sole exception of Morocco, has adhered, mandates, *inter alia*, the equality of all the sub-state groups that constitute each African state,[37] outlaws the "domination of a people by another,"[38] guarantees the right of all peoples to "existence," and "self-determination,"[39] guarantees the

[35] See also Orentlicher (D.F.), "Separation Anxiety: International Responses to Ethno-Separatist Claims" (1998) 23 *Yale Journal of International Law* 1, at 3-4.

[36] See the *International Covenant on Civil and Political Rights*, 1966, 999 *UNTS* 171*; the International Covenant on Economic, Social and Cultural Rights*, 1966, 993 *UNTS* 3; the *African Charter on Human and Peoples Rights*, 1981, (1982) 21 *ILM* 58; and the *Declaration on the Rights of Persons Belonging to National, Ethnic, Religious and Linguistic Minorities*, GA Res. 47/135. 18 December 1992.

[37] See article 19.

[38] *Ibid.*

[39] See article 20(1).

right of all peoples to freely control their wealth and natural resources,[40] and clearly states that "colonized *or* oppressed peoples shall have the right to free themselves from the bonds of domination."[41] Clearly, these rights, even when they involve self-determination, apply even within established states such as postcolonial African states.[42] The term "all peoples" has been applied to the internal context in at least one official interpretation of the African Charter. And that expression has also been so applied in a fairly recent Canadian decision. This reading of that term was rendered in the *Katanga Case* as well as in the *Quebec Reference Case* in Canada.[43] What is more, a small number of African states have begun to include minority rights and the self-determination norm in their own domestic constitutions, albeit to varying degrees.[44]

The effect of this application of self-determination and minority rights to the internal sphere of states is that under contemporary international law, these states cannot now stand lawfully configured or in future be re-configured in ways that violate these minority rights and self-determination norms. Statecraft ought henceforth to be framed and shaped by the dictates of these norms. Thus, if statehood is to be "righted" in Africa (both in terms of adherence to the relevant

---

40 See article 21.

41 See article 20(2).

42 See Umozurike (U.O.), *The African Charter on Human and Peoples' Rights* (The Hague: Martinus Nijhoff, 1997) 53-54.

43 See *Reference Re Secession of Québec* (1998) 2 *S.C.R.* 217. See also Okafor (O.C.), "Entitlement, Process, and Legitimacy in the Emergent International Law of Secession" (2002) 9 *Inter national Journal on Minority and Group Rights* 41.

44 See section 235 of the South African Constitution which states that: "The right of the South African people as a whole to self-determination, as manifested in this Constitution, does not preclude, within the framework of this right, recognition of the notion of the right of self-determination of any community sharing a common cultural and language heritage, within a territorial entity in the Republic or in any other way, determined by national legislation." See (http://www.strategicassessments.org/library/resources/South_Africa_Constitution.pdf) (visited 20 May 2006). See also Henrad (K.), *Minority Protection in Post-Apartheid South Africa* (Westport, Connecticut: Praeger, 2002) at 116. And article 39 of the Constitution of the Federal Democratic Republic of Ethiopia contains self-determination (up to and including secession rights), language, cultural and political representation rights for all its constituent "nations, nationalities and peoples." See (http://www.ethiopar.net/English/cnstiotn/conchp32.htm) (visited 20 May 2006).

international law imperatives and in the sense of doing the right thing) those who lead the processes of state-formation or state-disaggregation on the African continent must begin to pay far greater attention to the dictates of the international and African self-determination and minority rights norms that seek to peaceably order state-building on the continent.

Yet, as is widely recognized, like statecraft elsewhere, African statecraft has generally not been as attentive as it ought to be to this imperative of "righting" the state. For the most past, the postcolonial African state continues to muddle through and endanger its corporate future by coercively retaining its constituent groups, and scarcely attending as adequately as it ought, to the infra-review of its constituent sub-state groups. This is one good reason to focus, as we will in the section that follows, on the necessity for the restructuring of the postcolonial African state along the lines dictated by the same norms that must guide its righting.

Restructuring the Postcolonial African State

Given that the international legal entitlement of the sub-state groups that constitute the postcolonial African state to some form of autonomy, as well as to infra-review of the acceptability to them of their continued membership within their current states, and given the intensity of the intra-state conflicts over autonomy and the like that has been experienced within almost every postcolonial African state, there appears to be a need to find peaceful ways of restructuring the state in Africa in order to better satisfy the yearnings of its constituent peoples.[45] As Makau Mutua has previously, and insightfully, warned us, confronted as it has always been by an intense structural legitimacy crisis, the postcolonial African state will be reconfigured one way or the other, either peaceably or violently.[46] The task is to make that reconfiguration as peaceable as it can be.

---

[45] For another scholar's argument that the righting of statecraft in Africa, via the application of the African Charter to the area, justifies the restructuring of African states based on power-sharing arrangements, see Jinadu (L.A.), supra note 21 at 23.

[46] See Mutua (M.), supra note 10 at 536.

Much as this imperative has been long recognized by other scholars such as Makau Mutua, African statecraft has yet to come close to an adequate recognition of this imperative. Indeed, the dominant tendency is for African states to reject self-determination claims,[47] and to view even less consequential minority rights claims with some suspicion. Far-too-many African states are still configured in highly centralized and homogenizing ways that allow far too little autonomy to the socio-cultural groups that constitute them, actually guarantee too few minority rights to their constituent sub-state groups, and provide far-too-little real avenues for meaningful infra-review of the structural legitimacy of the relevant states. Nigerian and Ethiopian quasi-federalism,[48] and the power-sharing arrangements in Ethiopia (i.e. special representation in parliament for minorities) and in Nigeria (as per the federal character principle)[49] are some of the mild exceptions to the generally centralizing trend within the postcolonial African state. And even many of the relatively few states that have quite commendably subscribed to federal constitutions and political arrangements have in practice all but neutralized the autonomy allowed by such federal arrangements, and have in reality remained overly centralized. And few, if any, African states brook even the most harmless discussions about infra-review, fearing that it would lead to rampant secession (and – as they see it – much chaos).

This tendency to over-centralize and homogenize the postcolonial African state is, as we have already seen, a major cause of the structural tensions that lead to conflict and violence on the continent. That is the chief reason why the state in Africa needs rejuvenation via its righting and restructuring; not simply to reconstitute it in its prevailing form, but to re-jiggle its structures in ways that have a greater chance of earning it the widespread legitimacy of its constituent peoples.

---

47 See Ankumah (E.), *The African Commission on Human and Peoples' Rights* (The Hague: Martinus Nijhoff, 1996) at 163.

48 See Gana (A.T.) and Egwu (S.G.) (eds.), *Federalism in Africa: Framing the National Question* (Trenton, New Jersey: Africa World Press, 2003) at 35. See also Jinadu (L.A.), supra note 21 at 24-30.

49 See Jinadu (L.A.), *ibid.* at 24-30.

Rejuvenating Postcolonial African State

Implied in much of the foregoing is the fact that the rejuvenation of the currently troubled and weakened postcolonial African state would depend quite heavily on the extent to which it is righted and accordingly restructured. As I have argued elsewhere, put summarily, the argument in favour of rejuvenating the postcolonial African state *through its righting and restructuring* is that an international legal move from homogenization toward multinational statehood would inhibit leaders in Africa from relying on the rules and norms of international law in their bids to forcibly homogenize their states.[50] African states would thus be encouraged by the new stance of the law (which pays more heed to self-determination and minority rights) to seek more peaceful means of securing their post-colonial borders and population composition.[51] Referenda regarding the integrity of African states, their structural organization, and the relationship among their different sub-state groups might then become more common and accepted.[52] And truly con-federal and federal structures and practices may take far deeper root in more African countries.[53] This would then lead to a reconfigured postcolonial African state that is better able to avoid the structural tensions and consequent conflicts that have characterized it since its very beginnings.

As this imperative task of righting, restructuring – and therefore rejuvenating – the postcolonial African state is far too important and consequential to be left to the affected states alone, and because of other important reasons that will be discussed in the next section, a suggestion is made in that section for the establishment of a new mechanism that will focus on, facilitate and foster the kind of state-building renaissance on the African continent that is hoped will be generated by attempts to right and restructure the postcolonial African state.

---

50 See Okafor (O.C.), "Martyrdom" supra note 7at 527.
51 *Ibid.*
52 *Ibid.*
53 *Ibid.*

4. Toward an AU Special Commission on National Minorities

How can the ongoing, if as yet very weak, trend toward the righting, restructuring – and thus the rejuvenation – of the postcolonial African state be facilitated, bolstered and sustained in order to prevent, manage and even resolve many of the conflicts that afflict the postcolonial African state? As we have seen, by writing self-determination or minority rights norms into their constitutions and by establishing federal and power-sharing state structures, a few African states have begun – albeit mostly at a formal level – the effort to right, restructure – and thus rejuvenate – the postcolonial African state. For example, South Africa has established a *Commission for the Promotion and Protection of the Rights of Cultural, Religious and Linguistic Communities*;[54] and Nigeria now operates a functional *Federal Character Commission*. Yet, as important, necessary, and commendable as these domestic efforts are, the structural crisis of state legitimacy in Africa that has been generated by the national minority problems that have afflicted the postcolonial African state since its very beginnings is far too serious and far too key and widespread as a source of conflict and violence on the continent to be left entirely to the vagaries of domestic politics. As such, there is a need for a meta-state mechanism to be devoted to the imperative and urgent task of helping to rejuvenate the postcolonial African state via its systematic righting and restructuring. The amelioration of so central a statebuilding challenge as the national minority problem (and attendant state legitimacy crisis) in Africa deserves the concerted efforts of all interested parties on the continent. It certainly deserves the attention of our continental institutions.

Aside from the seriousness of the state legitimacy crisis in Africa, another reason that commends the establishment of such a meta-state mechanism is the need to deploy relatively *triadic* structures in the attempt to manage or resolve the national minority questions that have led to the structural legitimacy crisis that afflicts the post-colonial African state. By a triadic structure is meant the management or

[54] See Section 181 of the Constitution of Republic of South Africa; and the *First Periodic Report of South Africa to the African Commission on Human and Peoples' Rights*, 2001 (submitted 2005) (on file with the author).

adjudication of disputes by "a relatively detached and independent third party."[55] In contrast to a triadic model, a *dyadic* conflict management structure is one that is limited to the parties to the dispute themselves or to the parties and an institution that is controlled by one of them. A good, and in fact common, example of such a dyadic structure is a situation in which a dispute between a majority group that extensively controls and dominates the central government of a country and one of the minority groups in that country is referred to an organ of that same central government. In the intensely multi-national African state context, as elsewhere, where majority sub-state groups often exert extensive control over the central government much to the detriment of the minority groups, and where inter-group trust is – to say the least – lacking, triadic structures (i.e. the injection of an external institution or body as the central dispute manager or arbiter) are likely to be significantly more effective than the inevitably dyadic structures of the kinds of domestic mechanisms deployed toward the management of inter-group tensions and conflict within such states. This is because among the weaker sub-state groups within these states, triadic dispute management mechanisms tend to inspire far more confidence than dyadic models regarding the fairness – and therefore the legitimacy – of the process of dispute management, and of its outcomes. And since the very tensions and conflicts that are to be subjected to dispute management tend to originate from a sense of deprivation, unfair treatment, and being dominated, and are unlikely to be doused or ameliorated when the dissatisfied minority or less powerful sub-state group is not fully confident of the fairness and legitimacy of the dispute management process and outcomes, it is only reasonable to conclude that non-triadic dispute settlement models are less likely to be effective in such circumstances. This much is recognized in Tim Murithi's conclusion that: "There is therefore a vital *third party role* that the African Union [a meta-state institution] can play in all future crisis situations on the continent, by intervening in the tense situations before they escalate."[56]

55 See Okafor (O.C.), "Entitlement" supra note 42 at 56.
56 See Murithi (T.), supra note 1. Emphasis supplied.

Also embedded in Murithi's call for the deployment of more triadic mechanisms toward the management of inter-group tensions and the structural crisis of legitimacy that afflicts the postcolonial African state is an expressed preference for the deployment of an inter-African institution to do this job. Despite the budgetary difficulties that such inter-African bodies often face, this is – in my view – the correct posture to adopt. For, to be optimally effective, the proposed meta-state mechanism must still be inter-African and "owned" by Africans. It must *not* be perceived as a foreign body imposed on Africans by those with whom Africa has not had a happy history of intervention. This is largely because of the well-documented incidence of post-colonial "immune reaction" within virtually every African state to foreign, especially unilateral non-African interventions.[57] The point here is that far-too-many interventions fail on an African continent that has only recently been decolonized largely because of their perceived excessive foreignness and illegitimacy as somewhat analogous to the colonial plunder and misrule of most African polities by a few European states, many of whom continue to exert a disproportionate level of power within non-African international institutions.

As such, other than because of the budgetary problems that it often faces, being the foremost inter-African institution of our time, the African Union is well suited to host and provide the kind of mechanism that is being suggested here. For one, the Constitutive Act of the African Union recognizes the imperative "need to promote peace, security and stability"[58] in Africa. Clearly, there is no more important way to promote peace, security and stability within Africa than the effective management of the deep-seated and large scale national minority problem that afflicts the postcolonial African state through the preventive righting, restructuring – and eventual rejuvenation – of that state. Secondly, since the African Charter on

57 See Deng (F.), "State Collapse: The Humanitarian Challenge to the United Nations" in Zartman (I.W.) (ed.), *Collapsed States: The Disintegration and Restoration of Legitimate Authority* (Boulder: Lynne Rienner, 1995) at 211.

58 See the Preamble of the Constitutive Act of the African Union, supra note 4. On the identity and nature of the AU's institutions, See Udombana (N.J.), "The Institutional Structure of the African Union: A Legal Analysis" (2002) 33 *California Western International Law Journal* 69.

Human and Peoples' Rights, the African Commission on Human and Peoples' Rights, and the African Court on Human and Peoples' Rights (the primary norms and processes relating to the vindication and enjoyment of self-determination and minority rights in Africa) are all AU institutions,[59] the AU can help right the postcolonial African state by facilitating the application of these norms in the domestic context. Thirdly, as a relatively detached third party which enjoys significantly greater legitimacy in Africa than other such international institutions, the AU can play a key triadic and preventive role in ensuring the fairness, legitimacy – and therefore effectiveness – of negotiated attempts to restructure specific African states according to the dictates of the relevant international norms, especially as mandated in the self-determination and minority protection clauses of the African Charter. It is in these ways that the AU can play a key role in the rejuvenation of the postcolonial African state.

However, in order to be able to play this historic role effectively, the AU ought to establish a new, dedicated, semi-autonomous sub-institution that will be devoted to the national minority question that has seriously troubled the postcolonial African state since its very beginnings. Aside from the fact that a crisis that is so central and consequential for Africa as the state legitimacy crisis (that has resulted from the national minority problem) in most African states deserves far more attention than it can get from any institution that multi-tasks and is not focused on this one basket of issues, existing AU institutions are simply not suitable for the task. Focused as it is on the adjudication of legal disputes, the new African Court on Human and Peoples' Rights is not equipped to serve as a preventive body and is simply not suited to the intensely political task of attempting to douse inter-group tensions within states well before they escalate into conflicts. Although more of a political animal (if still quasi-judicial in nature), the African Commission on Human and Peoples' Rights is clearly more suited to reaction (in deciding cases brought before it) than active direct intervention in tense situations as a way of preventing conflict and violence. And although there is little that

[59] For more on this point, see Murray (R.), *Human Rights in Africa: From the OAU to the African Union* (Cambridge: Cambridge University Press, 2004).

prevents it from developing its incipient preventive capacity, it is better for it to focus on its more developed adjudicatory function. What is more, the African Commission is already burdened with a multitude of tasks to an extent that obstructs its ability to focus squarely on the national minority question in Africa. This is of course not to discount the ways in which both the African Court and the African Commission can empower minority groups in Africa by providing them with an avenue for highlighting their claims of deprivation and oppression at the hands of majority groups and/or the state.[60] As importantly, even though they are equipped with some preventive capacity and charged t with the performance of some preventive functions, other AU bodies such as the Assembly of Heads of State and Government, the Executive Council, and the Peace and Security Council are simply far too politicized or much too broadly focused to perform fairly, legitimately, and effectively, the kind of focused, dedicated and specialized function that is needed to tackle squarely the national minority question in Africa.[61] The AU organ that comes closest to fitting the bill here is the Peace and Security Council.[62] Upon its physical establishment in 2004, this council replaced the defunct OAU/AU Mechanism for Conflict Prevention, Management and Resolution.[63] Supported by the AU Commission, a Panel of the Wise and a Continental Early Warning System, the Peace and Security Council is an important avenue for AU preventive and reactive action in the area of peace and security. However, this Council is far too politicized and too broadly focused to serve the purpose of ameliorating the national minorities' problem that is chief source of Africa's state legitimacy crisis. In any case, it is instructive

[60] See Murithi (T.), supra note 55 at 105.

[61] For a description and analysis of the nature of these organs, see Udombana (N.J.), "Unfinished Business" supra note 4 at 67-87.

[62] See the Protocol Relating to the Establishment of the Peace and Security Council of the African Union, adopted on 9 July 2002, in force since 26 December 2003, on-line: (http://www.africa-union.org/root/au/organs/psc/protocol_peace%20and%20security.pdf) (visited 19 June 2006).

[63] This mechanism was established in 1993 by the *Cairo Declaration*, OAU Doc. AHG/Decl.3 (XXIX), 28–30 June 1993). It has been incorporated into the new AU order by the *Decision on the Implementation of the Sirte Summit Decision on the African Union*, OAU Doc. AHG/Decl.3 (XXXVII), 11 July 2001.

that despite the fact that the Peace and Security Council has been in existence since 2004, Tim Murithi – a keen observer of inter-African politics – felt able to declare in 2005 that African statebuilding practice has so far tended *not* to be preventive. If prevention rather than reaction is the *raison d'être* of the proposed new institution, it is clear that the existing conflict prevention mechanism has so far not played, and is unlikely to play, that role effectively. It is for all of these and other such reasons that I am of the view that, at the very least, existing AU institutions need to be buttressed through the creation of a new, specialized and dedicated institution.

Much in line with my earlier call for an OAU Special Commission to undertake the same kind of tasks, it is proposed here that this new body, this new dedicated, focused, and specialized preventive inter-African institution, be styled the *AU Special Commission on National Minorities*. Recognition of the necessity for the creation of this type of avenue for the ventilation and management of sub-state group (especially minority group) grievances within states is not new. For instance, Gudmundur Alfredsson and Danilo Turk had long called on states to allow such groups increased access to both international policy-making and implementation bodies.[64] Similarly, Diane Orentlicher has also called for "binding arbitration procedures" to perform this kind of function.[65] More specifically, Tim Murithi has recently urged the appointment of an AU Special Representative on Peacebuilding, to perform somewhat similar, if broader, functions as the proposed special commission.[66]

This proposed commission should be composed of five eminent and influential African leaders (defined to include not just serving or former heads of state), whose identities must reflect the geographical, racial, religious, and gender diversity of the African continent. Such a composition, and the semi-autonomous character of the commission, would likely make it to be more effective than existing AU institutions

64 See Alfredsson (G.) and Turk (D.), "International Mechanisms for the Monitoring and Protection of Minority Rights: Their Advantages, Disadvantages and Interrelationships" in Bloed (A.), Leicht (L.), Nowak (M.) and Rosas (A.) (eds.), *Minority Human Rights in Europe: Comparing International Procedures and Mechanisms* (Dordrecht: Martinus Njhoff, 1993) at 181.

65 See Orentlicher (D.), supra note 34 at 74-77.

66 See Murithi (T.), supra note 1 at 109.

at tackling the national minority question in Africa. The eminence and moral authority of the five special commissioners would endow the commission with a reasonable degree of influence on the relevant African Governments. The fact that the commission is to be composed of five eminent persons rather than a single commissioner has the advantage of facilitating the greater institutionalization of its dispute prevention/management process rather than its over-personalization. This is an important feature given the struggle in many African states to overcome their own unhappy postcolonial histories of personal rule, and also given the need for the Commission's decisions to be subjected to internal checks and balances. In this way will the proposed Commission differ from the High Commissioner on National Minorities established by the Organization for Security and Cooperation in Europe (OSCE).[67] Furthermore, the autonomy of the AU Special Commission from African states, and even from the main political Organs of the AU, will also help bolster and cement its triadic character, thus enhancing the perceived legitimacy of its processes and decisions, and enhancing its effectiveness in the long run. The Commission will also have the significant advantages of specialist expertise, resulting from its dedication to a single basket of related issues. Such expertise will be important if the commission is to quickly become effective in tackling this central and devastating problem of the postcolonial African state. Given how urgent and imperative the resolution of the national minorities question is in Africa, and how devastating to the continent its ill- or non-resolution has been thus far, these advantages – no matter how slight they may seem – are important nevertheless.

5. Conclusion:

In conclusion, I have argued that given the status of the nationality minority problem that confronts the postcolonial African state as the key cause of the state legitimacy crisis that confronts that state, and given the fact that this structural legitimacy crisis that has afflicted

---

67 See Brenninkmeijer (O.), *The OSCE High Commissioner on National Minorities: Negotiating the 1992 Conflict Prevention Mandate* (Geneva: PSIO, 2005).

almost all African states from their very beginnings is by far the principal cause of high tensions, conflicts and violence on the continent, it is Africa's key state-building challenge. As such, it deserves far more focused and systematic attention from inter-African institutions than it has so far received. I have also argued that in order to rejuvenate the postcolonial African state, it must in effect be saved from itself. It must be "righted" and restructured in accordance with the increasing if still slight tendency in international law to pay attention to minority rights and self-determination norms in the conceptual ordering of state-formation and disaggregation. It was thereafter suggested that if this process of righting and restructuring – and therefore rejuvenating – the postcolonial African state is to be facilitated, bolstered and sustained, the African Union (AU) needs to – as a matter of urgency – appoint a Special Commission on National Minorities to guide and order this process. That this process must be allowed to happen and must be systematic and preventive (rather than chaotic and reactive) is underlined by Makau Mutua's accurate warning, with which I am in complete agreement that over time the postcolonial African state will definitely be reconfigured, and that the task is to as much as possible avoid further violent reconfigurations of that state by preemptively finding ways to allow its peaceable reconfiguration. It is hoped therefore that this discussion has contributed, however modestly, to the search for peaceable ways of reconfiguring and therefore ennobling the postcolonial African state.

[20]

MINORITIES, POVERTY AND THE MILLENNIUM DEVELOPMENT GOALS: ASSESSING GLOBAL ISSUES

IMPLEMENTATION OF GENERAL ASSEMBLY RESOLUTION 60/251 OF 15 MARCH 2006 ENTITLED "HUMAN RIGHTS COUNCIL"

Report of the Independent Expert on minority issues,*

Gay McDougall

* The present report is submitted after the deadline to reflect the most recent information.

Summary

The mandate of the Independent Expert on minority issues was established by the Commission on Human Rights in its resolution 2005/79. The Independent Expert is required inter alia to promote implementation of the Declaration on the Rights of Persons Belonging to National or Ethnic, Religious or Linguistic Minorities, to identify best practices by States and possibilities for technical cooperation by the Office of the High Commissioner for Human Rights. The Independent Expert submitted her initial report to the Human Rights Council in January 2006, in which she addressed the scope of her mandate, her methods of work, and identified key thematic priorities for the initial period of her mandate: minorities in the contextof poverty alleviation and the MDGs; and promoting inclusion and stability.

In the period following submission of her initial annual report the Independent Expert has undertaken two official country missions, to Hungary (25 June-3 July 2006), and to the Federal Democratic Republic of Ethiopia (28 November-12 December 2006), to consult on minority issues and consider national legislation, policy and practice relating to national or ethnic, religious and linguistic minorities.

The Independent Expert has conducted extensive consultations in regard to all elements of her mandate. She has attended expert seminars and conferences, has convened consultations, held bilateral and multilateral discussions, including with Member States of the United Nations, engaged with agencies of the United Nations system and regional intergovernmental organizations, and consulted widely with civil society and directly with minority communities. She has prioritized gender issues related to her mandate and has held dedicated forums for minority women during her country missions. She has conducted focused consultations and research on the key thematic priorities identified in her initial report.

In every region of the world, there are minorities that are the poorest of the poor, often having faced long-standing discrimination, exclusion, denial of their basic rights, and sometimes violence. Minorities face high and disproportionate levels of poverty and the dynamics of that poverty are often more complex in nature for minority groups and defy the rationale of common denominator policies of poverty alleviation. Often minorities are neglected or excluded from efforts to achieve the Millennium Development Goals (MDGs). Recognizing the urgent need to address the situations of minorities more fully in international and national efforts to alleviate poverty and achieve the Goals, the Independent Expert has decided to focus her second annual report on this subject.

Targeted as well as mainstreamed approaches and policies are required to address the particular circumstances of poverty experienced by persons belonging to national or ethnic, religious and linguistic minorities. Governments in designing, planning and implementing poverty alleviation and MDG policies, must give high priority to ensuring that disadvantaged minorities are considered in relation to their unique conditions of exclusion and discrimination, and consequent high levels of extreme and persistent poverty. To assist such efforts, in the contexts of MDG Country Reports and in Poverty Reduction Strategy Papers (PRSPs), Governments are urged to provide detailed consideration of the situations of minority groups and statistical data that helps to reveal the status of minorities in relation to other groups.

Introduction

The Independent Expert is pleased to submit to the Human Rights Council her second annual report, which provides an overview of her activities from January 2006. Since the presentation of her initial report (E/CN.4/2006/74), she has undertaken two official country missions, to Hungary (26 June-3 July 2006), and to the Federal Democratic Republic of Ethiopia (28 November-12 December 2006) (A/HRC/4/9/Add.2-3, respectively). The Independent Expert expresses her thanks to the Governments of Hungary and Ethiopia for their cooperation and assistance extended to her in the preparations and conduct of these visits.

In her initial report the Independent Expert identifies key thematic priorities for her work as: minorities in the context of poverty alleviation and the MDGs, and promoting inclusion and stability. Persons belonging to disadvantaged minorities are likely to suffer high and disproportionate levels of poverty in every region. The present report focuses on minorities in the context of poverty alleviation, and the need for programmes and strategies for achieving the MDGs that take into account the situations of minority communities uniquely affected by racism, discrimination, exclusion and often violence. Confronting poverty is a key component in policies for social inclusion and the promotion of stability.

The Independent Expert has held numerous consultations with government representatives from every region, regional intergovernmental organizations, civil society and academic and research institutions, international financial institutions including the World Bank, and United Nations agencies. At the regional level, she has consulted with the minority mechanisms of bodies including the Council of Europe, and the High Commissioner on National Minorities of the Organization for Security and Cooperation in Europe (OSCE), and will conduct further dialogue with such bodies in early 2007. She has engaged in consultations with the

Organization of American States (OAS) and the Inter-American Commission on Human Rights, and held initial dialogue with available senior staff of the African Union during her visit to Ethiopia. She has held initial consultations with representatives of the Organization of the Islamic Conference.

In taking forward her stated intention to enhance mainstreaming of minority issues within the work of the United Nations, she has consulted widely with United Nations agencies and bodies, including the Office of the United Nations High Commissioner for Human Rights (OHCHR), and the United Nations Development Programme (UNDP). During the course of her official missions she has also held briefings with country and regional staff of OHCHR, UNDP, the Office of the United Nations High Commissioner for Refugees (UNHCR) and UNICEF, and now seeks to enhance dialogue with such entities of the United Nations system, both in the context of wider inter-agency initiatives and in carrying out her country visits.

In her initial report, the Independent Expert stated her desire for close collaboration with United Nations treaty bodies, and particularly the Committee on the Elimination of Racial Discrimination (CERD). In August 2006 she held an official dialogue with CERD, during which she discussed possibilities for collaboration, including in regard to the Committee's early warning, urgent action and follow up mechanisms, and with a view to enhancing the Committee's capacity to consider minority issues within its work. A second substantive dialogue has been requested by the Committee. The Independent Expert has also requested official dialogues with the Human Rights Committee and the Committee on the Rights of the Child in 2007.

The Independent Expert is required to cooperate closely, while avoiding duplication, with regional organizations. As an example of her regional engagement, in its resolution entitled "Combating Racism and All Forms of Discrimination and Intolerance and Consideration of the Draft Inter-American Convention against Racism and All Forms of Discrimination and Intolerance" (AG/RES.2168 (XXXVI-O/06)), the OAS General Assembly requests the Inter American Commission on Human Rights "to continue intensifying dialogue and cooperation with" the Independent Expert on minority issues, including on the Draft Inter-American Convention against racism. She has also engaged in consultations with OAS member States, and supported by OHCHR, held an international expert consultation in January 2007 aimed at assisting regional and national institutions in regard to standard setting and effective mechanisms to combat discrimination and protect the rights of minorities.

Of considerable benefit has been the opportunity for the Independent Expert to meet directly with representatives of minority communities from all regions, notably at the twelfth session of the United Nations Working Group on Minorities, in August 2006. During this session she held a forum for minority representatives to consult directly with her, raise questions, and bring issues to her attention. She has benefited greatly from information provided to her by civil society, academic and research organizations. During official missions to Hungary and Ethiopia, she has equally made it a priority to meet with representatives of minorities in order to solicit their views.

The Commission on Human Rights, in its resolution 2005/79, decided to amend the mandate of the Working Group on Minorities so that it may, inter alia, focus its work on "conceptual support of, and dialogue with the independent expert, who shall participate as an observer". The Independent Expert has benefited from formal and informal consultations with the members of the Working Group and its Secretariat, and highlighted her support for a dedicated forum for minority issues. She notes the Working Group's unique functions, including important conceptual development work and the provision of access for minorities themselves to attend sessions and make their voice heard within the United Nations. During the Working Group's twelfth session, the strong potential for constructive collaboration was demonstrated, and the issue of policing, security and criminal justice in multi-ethnic societies was identified amongst areas of future joint initiative.

The Independent Expert has devoted close attention to the particular situations faced by women from minority groups. Women and girls from disadvantaged minority groups experience multiple and intersectional forms of discrimination based on both their minority status and their gender. Such multidimensional discrimination may make them particularly vulnerable to violation and denial of their rights in both public and private life, including violence and sexual assault. To mark International Women's Day in March 2006, the Independent Expert issued a statement calling for greater attention to the situation of minority women who face multiple discrimination.

She has held forums for minority women to hear their issues and concerns, and consulted with senior government officials responsible for gender and women's affairs. While visiting Hungary, she held a forum for Roma women to consult with her and interviewed women from Roma communities. During her visit to Ethiopia, she devoted attention to the particular situation of minority women and held consultations with women from groups including the Anuak and Nuer communities in the Gambella region. This attention to women's issues is reflected in her mission reports and specific recommendations.

Pursuing her work in the area of poverty alleviation and realization of MDGs for minorities, the Independent Expert has held numerous consultations with development agencies, including UNDP, the World Bank and national and international non-governmental organizations (NGOs). In close cooperation with UNDP, she initiated and co-convened an international consultation "UNDP's Engagement with Minorities in Development Processes" held on 18 and 19 October 2006 in New York, with the aim to strengthen consideration of minority issues in the areas relating to poverty/MDGs, democratic governance and crisis prevention and recovery. A commitment to the development of a UNDP policy/guidance note on minorities was a key outcome.

Promoting the rights of minorities, including through policies of equitable development and the rule of law in regard to anti-racism and anti-discrimination, for example, offers a vital means of promoting inclusion, stability, and conflict prevention. The Independent Expert has participated in seminars and forums in the field of social and human development indicators, early warning and conflict prevention, and held consultations with a variety of actors including the Special Adviser to the Secretary-General on the Prevention of Genocide. In November 2006 she was keynote speaker and participant in a high-level seminar "Preventing Ethnic and Religious Conflict" convened by Minority Rights Group International.

To assist in gathering information relating to State legislation, policy and practice on minority issues, in March 2006 the Independent Expert sent all Member States of the United Nations a questionnaire, for completion by national authorities. Their responses will greatly assist her in various aspects of her ongoing work. The questionnaire has proven useful including to identify best or successful practices on the part of States. She benefited considerably from the response of the Government of Hungary prior to her official mission,detailing legislation on minority issues and its unique system of minority self-governments.

The Independent Expert is required to identify best practices and possibilities for technical cooperation by OHCHR. As a practical measure she has begun focusing on three priority areas of work: policing and maintenance of security in multi-ethnic societies (in collaboration with the Working Group on Minorities); the arbitrary denial or deprivation of citizenship to certain minority groups as a tool to exclude minorities from due benefits or reasonable participation; and equal access to quality education and other education-related issues, including access to education in minority languages.

The Independent Expert has sent communications to States regarding specific situations and issues relevant to her mandate that have been brought to her attention. Such communications have been undertaken jointly with other Special Procedures mandate holders, with a view to verifying information, to establishing facts, to seeking additional information, and to raising issues of concern with Governments and establishing constructive dialogue.

I. Minorities, Poverty and the Millenium Development Goals: Assesing Global Issues

On Human Rights Day (10 December 2006) the Independent Expert was among the 37 Special Procedures mandate holders who issued a statement highlighting the urgent need to address the persistent poverty trapping many millions of people globally, as a grave human rights challenge. This statement made clear that "Poverty is part of a vicious cycle of marginalization, social exclusion and discrimination … often a cause, as well as a result, of a complex system of human rights denials."

In her initial report the Independent Expert states: "Minority groups that face widespread discrimination or exclusion are much more likely than other groups to be impoverished. […] The poorest communities in almost any region tend to be minority communities that have been targets of long-standing discrimination, violence or exclusion. As such, poverty within minority communities must be viewed as both a cause and a manifestation of the diminished rights, opportunities, and social advancement available to the members of that community as a whole. And efforts to reduce poverty are essential to larger efforts to promote the full range of civil, political, social and economic rights for minority communities.

"Poverty in this context involves more than just a lack of income or a daily struggle for basic sustenance. Poor communities are generally less able to participate effectively in political decision-making or to access mechanisms of justice when their rights are violated. They suffer from unequal access to education, health care, employment and land. Without a targeted focus on their needs and rights, they will remain disproportionately impoverished. And without a more coherent effort to reduce poverty through targeted strategies that specifically reach out to minority communities, the international community will fail to achieve, or sustain, the important targets set within the Millennium Development Goals …" (E/CN.4/2006/74, paras. 64-65).

The Independent Expert approaches the issue of poverty using the same four-point framework she has identified for the general protection of minority rights: protecting a minority's existence, including the physical integrity of persons belonging to minorities; protecting and promoting cultural and social identity; ensuring non-discrimination and equality, including ending structural or systemic discrimination; and ensuring effective participation of minorities in public life, especially in decisions that affect them.

The Independent Expert has conducted dedicated research on minorities and poverty-reduction strategies. She has received information from and consulted with a wide variety of expert sources, including States, development agencies, international financial institutions, United Nations agencies, and minorities themselves. She commissioned a survey and review of 50 MDG Country Reports and selected PRSPs, which are contained in addendum 1 to the present report (A/HRC/4/9/Add.1). MDG Country Reports and PRSPs offer a useful starting point for reflecting on cross-regional practice in integrating minorities positively into development processes.

The Independent Expert reiterates that in using the term "minorities", the focus of her work is on distinct groups that have faced long-term discrimination and disadvantage on the basis of identity as national, ethnic, religious or linguistic groups. Under her mandate "minority" status is not defined by numerical factors alone. She acknowledges that distinct groups that are numerically a minority in society may at the same time have dominance over the economy or other sectors. This thematic report on minorities and MDGs focuses on groups that are disproportionately disadvantaged and otherwise denied the power to protect their rights.

There is a genuine risk that the strategies used to achieve MDGs will be less beneficial for minority groups, and might even increase inequalities and further harm some minority communities. Greater effort is needed to ensure that minorities who are poor benefit fairly from the international commitment to reduce poverty and meet MDGs by 2015. This analysis seeks to contribute to this effort by providing an overview of key minority issues and concrete recommendations.

A. The disproportionate poverty of disadvantaged minorities

Poverty occurs in all countries, both developing and developed. Minority groups commonly have higher and disproportionate levels of poverty in all regions of the world and this poverty is often structurally and causally distinct, requiring both targeted and mainstreamed policies to overcome it.

Poverty-related data disaggregated by ethnicity, religion or language is hard to find. Household surveys on income and human development indicators do not usually gather information necessary to correlate this data to membership in a particular social group as defined by ethnicity, religion or language. This means that statistics on relative incomes and human development of minority groups are not available for many countries or, if available, are not frequently published. However, a sample of available statistics is revealing.

In 2002 income figures for Brazil, the proportion of whites living on less than $1/day is 4.3 per cent; for non-whites (predominately Afro-Brazilians), the figure is 8.3 per cent; at the level of $2/day the gap persists - 8.6 per cent of whites and 19.4 per cent of non-whites live on this income.[1]

In Nepal, the lowest consumption levels are among low-caste Dalits with poverty incidence of 46 per cent, Muslims with 41 per cent and hill Janajatis (ethnic indigenous communities)

[1] Matías Busso, Martín Cicowiez and Leonardo Gasparini, Ethnicity and the Millennium Development Goals in Latin America and the Caribbean, Working Paper 27, Centro de Estudia Distributivos, Laborales y Sociales (CEDLAS), Universidad Nacional de La Plata, (Bogota, Colombia: UNDP, 2005): Table 2.4, p. 77.

with 45 per cent. Low-caste Dalits, in particular, have a 15 per cent higher incidence of poverty than the average rate.[2]

In the United Kingdom, a third of British Indians and British African-Caribbeans, half of British Black Africans and two thirds of British Pakistanis and British Bangladeshis are living in poverty. This compares with less than a quarter of the British population overall living in poverty.[3]

In Namibia, the per capita income in a household where the mother tongue is German is 23 times higher than in a household where the main language is San (an indigenous minority group).[4]

The poverty gap between ethnic minorities and the Kinh majority in Viet Nam is said to be growing. Ethnic minorities are 14 per cent of the population of Viet Nam but constitute 29 per cent of the poorest.[5]

In some member States of the European Union (EU), immigrants and ethnic minorities from non-Western countries (e.g. non-European migrants in Denmark and the Netherlands, Turks in Germany, North Africans in France, Bangladeshis and Pakistanis in the United Kingdom) have labour-market activity rates that are 15 to 40 per cent below that of natives or western migrants. Roma in most EU member States and Travellers in Ireland have particularly low activity rates and are largely excluded from labour market.[6]

The 2000 United States of America census reveals that poverty rates for non-whites were on average much higher than for whites. Whereas non-Hispanic whites had the lowest poverty rate at 8.1 per cent, African Americans had average poverty rates of 24.9 per cent, American Indians and Alaska Natives had average rates of 25.7 per cent and Hispanic or Latinos had average poverty rates of 22.6 per cent.[7]

The manifestations of poverty are not only income-based. Aggregate human development indicators for minorities are similarly consistently lower than for non-minority groups.

For example, in India, the literacy rate of women from scheduled tribes in rural communities was only 16 per cent in 1991 and for scheduled castes the rate was 24 per cent; this is in comparison with a national average for women of 39 per cent.[8]

Survey data collected in the 1990s in 11 sub-Saharan African countries showed particularly striking results for Kenya, where the likelihood of mortality for Kikuyu (Kenya's most

[2] Nepal MDGs Progress Report 2005, (Kathmandu, Nepal: HMG Nepal, National Planning Commission, September 2005): p. 10.

[3] Lucinda Platt, Parallel Lives: Poverty Among Ethnic Minority Groups in Britain, London: Child Poverty Action Group (CPAG), December 2002.

[4] Namibia 2004 Millennium Development Goals, (Windhoek, Namibia: Office of the President, National Planning Commission, August 2004): p. 5.

[5] Roger Plant, Indigenous Peoples/Ethnic Minorities and Poverty Reduction Regional Report, (Manila, Philippines: Asian Development Bank, 2002): p. 32.

[6] International Centre for Migration Policy Development, Migrants, Minorities and Employment: Exclusion, Discrimination and Anti-Discrimination in the 15 Member States of the EU (European Monitoring Centre on Racism and Xenophobia, October 2003): p. 5.

[7] 7 Alemayehu Bishaw and John Iceland, Poverty 1999: Census 2000 Brief (Washington: U.S. Census Bureau, May 2003): p. 5 and Table 6.

[8] UNDP, Human Development Report 2000 (New York, NY: UNDP, 2000): p. 110.

populous ethnic group) infants was 65 per cent lower than for children of other ethnic groups and 74 per cent lower for children under 5.[9]

In the United States, 21 per cent of Hispanic children were not covered by health insurance (public and private) compared with 7 per cent of white non-Hispanic children; 12 per cent of Asian and Pacific Islander children; and 14 per cent of African American children also had no health insurance (figures from 2003).[10]

In South-East Europe, "three quarters of Roma women do not complete primary education (compared with one in five women from majority communities) and almost a third is illiterate (compared with 1 in 20 women from majority communities)". [11]

Only 13 per cent of children in Africa have access to primary education in their mother tongue compared to 62 per cent of children with this access in East Asia and the Pacific, a region with an even higher diversity of languages than Africa.[12]

The figures for minorities are not always worse. In Britain, 75 per cent of British Indians are in full-time education at age 18 compared to 42 per cent of the population as a whole.[13] In Malaysia, ethnic Chinese constitute 3 per cent of the population but control about 70 per cent of the private economy.[14] The negative trend, however, is clear. Even in cases where minorities may be advantaged in one sphere they may continue to face exclusion in the social or political spheres that may affect their human rights and human development.

Conventional poverty analysis often misses these trends for minorities because the focus is on individual or household levels rather than groups and on material measurements of poverty rather than the social dimensions. While the spatial dimensions of poverty across the urban and rural divide gain attention, the analysis rarely goes deeper to connect spatial and social dimensions and ask "who is poor, where, and why?". These measurements of vertical inequalities are important but they do not give an adequate picture of the dynamics of poverty across groups.

Mainstreaming of collection of data on gender has been important to uncovering the systematic exclusion of women in access to development and political participation, including how this may be different in urban and rural lives. This trend has been responded to through targeted programmes for women, adoption of gender-based analyses, introduction of gender advisors and even an MDG aimed at overcoming gender inequality (Goal 3). The changes in development that have resulted - albeit slowly and inconsistently - demonstrate that looking at development from a "group" perspective can improve outcome possibilities for specific targeted groups.

---

9 Chronic Poverty Research Centre, Chronic Poverty Report 2004-05 (Manchester, UK: Chronic Poverty Research Centre, 2005): p. 19.

10 Growing up in North America: Child Well-Being in Canada, the United States and Mexico (Baltimore, MD, USA: Canadian Council on Social Development, Annie E. Casey Foundation in the US, and Red por los derechos de la infancia en México, 2006): pp. 26-27.

11 Andrey Ivanov et al., At Risk: Roma and the Displaced in Southeast Europe (Bratislava: UNDP Regional Bureau for Europe and the CIS, 2006): p. 27.

12 UNDP, Human Development Report 2004 (New York, NY: UNDP 2004): p. 34, Figure 2.4.

13 Parallel Lives: Poverty Among Ethnic Minority Groups in Britain, see supra note 3.

14 Supra note 12, Human Development Report 2004, p. 29.

Mainstream development research and policy[15] has to date also given more attention to other categories of excluded groups[16] (e.g., children, older persons, persons with disabilities). Indigenous peoples have also gained attention to their issues in development, as evidenced in part by the fact that several international development agencies have policies on indigenous peoples; dialogues on development between the United Nations agencies and the Permanent Forum on Indigenous Issues have also been helping to establish good practice.

Attention to national, ethnic, religious and linguistic minorities is significantly weaker. Poverty research using the horizontal inequality[17] (which examine measurements of political, social, economic and income inequalities along identity lines) and social exclusion perspectives, finds that inequality between ethnic, religious or linguistic social groups is common. The Minorities at Risk Project,[18]which collects various indicators on the political, social and economic disparities experienced by more than 284 minority groups globally, estimates that some 750 million persons belonging to minority groups face serious economic discrimination and disadvantage and 832 million face political exclusion.[19]

The Minorities at Risk data set finds a correlation between horizontal inequalities and conflict along ethnic, religious or linguistic identity lines. Such inequalities are a major factor motivating groups or leaders to mobilize for change. The persistence of inequalities and the growth in the inequality gap can be destabilizing factors, in particular where the Government is seen to be failing to address these issues (or causing them). Conflict prevention is one reason why monitoring poverty alleviation among persons belonging to minorities is crucial: if strategies are successful for some groups but not for minorities, inequalities will increase and so too may tension. Inclusive participation strategies for poverty reduction are proven and effective conflict prevention measures.

There is a strong economic case for supporting the inclusion of minorities. Minorities with high or average levels of education are often underemployed, limiting their opportunities to contribute to economic and social life of society. Minorities with poor levels of education represent a vastly underutilized human capacity. One study has shown the economic benefits that come from better use of existing skills and capacity of minorities and investment in decreasing skills and capacity gaps (e.g., through improving access to education). It concludes: "The economies of Bolivia, Brazil, Guatemala and Peru would potentially expand at least by 36.7, 12.8, 13.6 and 4.2 per cent respectively, as a result of ending the long-term social exclusion of Afro-descendant and indigenous groups."[20] Another study demonstrates that

---

[15] Laure-Helene Piron and Zaza Curran, Public Policy Responses to Exclusion: Evidence from Brazil, South Africa and India, London: Overseas Development Institute, 2005, p. 1.

[16] Minority Rights Group International, An examination of approaches by international development agencies to minority issues in development (E/CN.4/Sub.2/AC.5/2004/WP.5).

[17] Frances Stewart, Horizontal Inequalities: A Neglected Dimension of Development. Working Paper 1, Centre for Research on Inequality, Human Security and Ethnicity (CRISE) (Queen Elizabeth House, University of Oxford, 2001).

[18] See http://www.cidcm.umd.edu/inscr/mar/.

[19] Supra note 12, Human Development Report 2004, Feature 2.1 "The Minorities at Risk data set - quantifying cultural exclusion", p. 32.

[20] 20 Jonas Zoninsein, The Economic Case for Combating Racial and Ethnic Exclusion in Latin American and Caribbean Countries (Inter-American Development Bank, May 2001): p. 2.

investing in Roma education in Hungary would bring economic and fiscal benefits of up to 70,000 euros per Roma student.[21]

The production capacity of minorities denied equal access to land and credit is also restricted. Addressing the health-care inequalities experienced by minorities can expand the national pool of healthy able workers to keep the economy growing. Where incomes of persons belonging to minorities expand, so does their consumption and thus the national (and international) economy benefits. Ethnic and religious diversity must not be seen as a hindrance to development: the hindrance comes where significant parts of the population lack the opportunity to contribute to development on an equal basis.

More research is urgently needed to uncover the extent of inequalities and poverty faced by minority groups and to provide a resource for shaping policies which recognize and respond to these inequalities.

B. The crucial impact of denial of the right to non-discrimination and equal treatment

The impact of discrimination on the basis of an individual's ethnic, religious or linguistic identity is usually a potent causal factor in the disproportionate poverty experienced by many minority groups and a key impediment in preventing minorities from benefiting from mainstream poverty reduction and social inclusion strategies.

The dynamics of poverty are more complex for minority groups. Racism often defies the rationality of a common denominator development policy, conceived to benefit all. A Roma family in poverty will not find a solution solely in national economic growth, when employers shut the door in Roma faces. They will not find a cure for their poverty in education systems that systematically segregate their children into inferior schools simply because they are Roma. Equally, in times of crisis essential humanitarian assistance and recovery efforts may fail to reach those communities who are most often forgotten or excluded even under normal conditions.

Living in remote regions, lower levels of human development, and psychosocial barriers (e.g., language barriers, low self-esteem) also contribute to the "chronic" poverty of many minorities, which is frequently structurally and causally distinct from poverty experienced by other groups. This demands a carefully considered response which takes into account the structures and causes that are unique or prominent in minorities' experiences. A mainstream social inclusion approach, hoping to reach all marginalized groups with the same policies, cannot fully address the rights and needs of minorities.

This is not to say that mainstreamed social inclusion approaches are entirely ineffective for marginalized minorities. As the 2005 Chronic Poverty Report notes, "People trapped in persistent poverty tend to experience multiple capability deprivations, such as poor education, illiteracy, bad health, inadequate nutrition, lack of human rights and civil rights. These constrain opportunities and choices and intergenerational benefits."[22] This is equally the case for chronically poor minorities. When examining the "capability deprivations" of

---

[21] Roma Education Fund, Expected Long-Term Budgetary Benefits to Roma Education in Hungary, Working Paper No. 1, September 2006.

[22] Supra note 9, Chronic Poverty Report 2004-05, p. 40.

minorities, theparticularities of their experiences quickly become evident and the need for parallel-targeted policies is conclusive.

One compelling factor contributing to the reduction of poverty levels of disadvantaged minorities is equal access to quality education. Minority children commonly lack equal access to quality education because of discrimination or live in regions with poor educational facilities. Lack of access to instruction in their own language also disadvantages them. Because of experiences of discrimination, minorities may not have confidence in the educational system and children may remain in the community rather than gaining formal education. This is particularly the experience of minority girls, where traditional or religious practices of early marriage, gender-specific roles or limited resources for school fees means their access to education is less valued.

Lower income levels of minorities may be the result of discrimination in access to employment and fewer opportunities for progress to secondary or higher education and attainment of specialized skills. Persons belonging to minorities on average may be paid less and be more likely to lose their employment in periods of economic hardship because of discrimination. Women belonging to minority groups will be disadvantaged further because of the additional impact of gender discrimination in employment, an example of intersectional discrimination against minority women. Lower incomes may also exist because minorities live in areas with fewer economic opportunities.

Lower incomes are often related to the lack of assets of persons belonging to minorities. Their land and property are often the first to be appropriated for development or conservation purposes, aided by the weak social, economic and political situation of minority communities to defend their land and property rights. Minorities find themselves displaced to less fertile land or to urban centres, without their consent, without adequate compensation and with little or no consideration of the impact on their livelihoods and cultures. Equitable market access for minorities is also difficult to secure and they may be discriminated against in access to credit and other financial services. The physical infrastructure in their regions may be suffering from underinvestment partly as a result of lack of effective political representation at the national level.

Lack of investment in hospitals, housing and municipal services in regions with large minority populations has led to consistently lower levels of life expectancy and adequate living conditions for minorities. For example, the Government of Hungary is concerned that the life expectancy of Roma is over 10 years less than the average. Some States have used policies of forced displacement from remote regions in which minorities live in order to improve access to social services, but the result has typically been decrease, rather than increase, in human development due to radical alteration of traditional lifestyles and livelihoods.

Even where discrimination is evident and understood to be a causal factor of chronic poverty, it is important to distinguish between direct and indirect discrimination, the former implying a specific intent to discriminate and the latter an "effect" of discrimination that needs not be intentional per se, but is a negative consequence that replicates itself unless there is an intervention. Discrimination should be considered and analysed as a potential factor in each case where minorities are experiencing inequalities. While direct or indirect discrimination may be a factor, the policy response demands a more nuanced understanding of the development context.

Discrimination manifests in both public and private spheres. Employers that offer fewer employment opportunities, or lower wages to minorities, are discriminating against them and increasing their likelihood of poverty. These practices should be addressed through strong anti-discrimination laws and mechanisms that vigorously enforce them. Research suggests that the psychosocial effects of living with discrimination decrease the ability of individuals to improve their situation even with assistance programmes if those are not sufficiently sensitive. Discrimination in education and employment over generations results in families with no formal wage earners and perceptions that there is little benefit from education, or no opportunity to find skilled employment.

At every level, discrimination against minorities creates obstacles that make benefiting from poverty reduction strategies difficult. To tackle these obstacles, appropriate targeted mechanisms are needed in both the public and private spheres. Discrimination results in poverty which is often more pervasive, more deeply entrenched, and which is more persistent in comparison to that faced by others. Mainstreamed social inclusion policies alone cannot tackle these issues. Confronting this poverty requires acknowledgement that it is uniquely fuelled by discrimination, and often a deliberate intention to exclude certain groups.

C. Current deficiencies in integrating minorities into poverty reduction strategies

The Programme of Action of the World Summit on Social Development (1995) recognized, in its paragraph 19, eight characteristics of poverty that are experienced universally: "lack of income and productive resources sufficient to ensure sustainable livelihoods; hunger and malnutrition; ill-health; limited or lack of access to education and other basic services; increased morbidity and mortality from illness; homelessness and inadequate housing; unsafe environments; and social discrimination and exclusion. It is also characterized by a lack of participation in decision-making and in civil, social and cultural life."[23]

The Millennium Development Goals were set to address the first six points on this list of manifestations of poverty and established ambitious targets to be met by 2015. However, the Goals do not comprehensively address, "social discrimination and exclusion" and "lack of participation in decision-making and in civil, social and cultural life", which are of particular relevance to marginalized or disadvantaged minority groups and have a direct causal relationship with the other six manifestations of poverty.

These issues are noted in the Millennium Declaration itself; in Section V on "Human rights, democracy and good governance", States make several pledges, including:

- To strive for the full protection and promotion in all our countries of civil, political, economic, social and cultural rights for all;
- To strengthen the capacity of all our countries to implement the principles and practices of democracy and respect for human rights, including minority rights;
- To work collectively for more inclusive political processes, allowing genuine participation by all citizens in all our countries (emphasis added, see A/RES/55/2).

[23] 23 Report of the World Summit for Social Development, Copenhagen, 6-12 March 1995 (United Nations publication, Sales No. E.96.IV.8), chap. I, resolution 1, annexes I and II.

Each of these points is vital for overcoming poverty and underscores the centrality of human rights in achieving this goal. This same idea is embodied in the human rights-based approach to development (HRBA). HRBA offers a useful and effective framework for devising a development policy which has a positive impact on human rights in both the process and the outcome.

Minority rights are human rights and consequently form an integral part of HRBA. The fact that minority rights are highlighted in the Millennium Declaration is significant. It is a clear recognition that protection of minority rights is an important foundation for building peaceful, equitable and democratic societies.

Respect for minority rights can improve the effectiveness of poverty reduction strategies because the causes of poverty for minorities are often linked to the violation of these rights. Many examples illustrate this. A person belonging to a minority may encounter employers who will not hire people noticeably from minority groups. When applicants complain about this practice, appropriate authorities fail to investigate. Under-resourced schools lack instruction in the mother tongue of minorities, so minority dropout rates are high. The Government offers financial benefits to the poorest, but details are not published in minority languages. When municipal government is deciding where to invest resources, there are no minority representatives and the desperate need for improved services in areas where minorities live is not discussed.

These are daily challenges for poor minorities in all countries. Using HRBA can help to identify how these challenges are linked to a range of human rights issues such as discrimination, access to justice and education, freedom to express a cultural identity or participation in decision-making. Through HRBA, overcoming poverty is understood as more than a question of economic growth. Including a minority rights perspective in HRBA gives an even stronger formula for beginning to address the complex factors that cause poverty for minorities globally.

Two key aid modalities shape international development cooperation today - the targets contained in the universally agreed MDGs and the nationally owned PRSPs. The two modalities are understood to be intertwined: PRSPs are the vehicle for achieving MDGs which provide concrete targets for PRSPs. They are particularly useful vehicles that should be used to improve the lives of minorities and ensure their inclusion in poverty alleviation policies.

All countries have committed to working towards achievement of MDGs by 2015. Both donor countries and countries receiving development assistance produce periodic reports on the steps they are taking to reach MDGs. A total of 143 States have submitted one or more MDG Country Reports.[24] Some 52 countries have produced PRSPs (or Interim PRSPs) and donors seek to assist such countries with the realization of the policies set forth in the PRSP.

MDG Country Reports and PRSPs are intended to be summary documents of a much more complex set of actions and policies. They nevertheless serve as useful proxies to identify the priorities and processes of a given State in its efforts to eradicate poverty and promote human development. A review of MDG Country Reports and PRSPs can give insight into the kinds of issues and interventions that governments have identified as important for their national policy on human development. This in turn can help reveal whether problems faced

[24] As of 1 November 2006.

by particular groups or regions are being overcome through specially-considered programmes on the ground.

The findings of a survey commissioned by the Independent Expert (see A/HRC/4/Add.1), demonstrate that only a handful of countries currently devote particular attention to minorities in their MDG reports. Even in those reports where minorities are mentioned, there is a lack of discussion on how and, crucially, why minorities are experiencing disproportionately high levels of poverty and other serious inequalities. While some countries disaggregate needs by region, few include any disaggregated data by ethnicity. Women belonging to minority groups remain particularly invisible in discussion of most of the MDGs. It is positive that several countries discuss the situation of indigenous peoples; however it is evident that those same countries fail to note that other minority groups within the State face similar or higher levels of exclusion and poverty. While resources and capacity are vital factors, the starting point for improving the impact of poverty reduction on minorities is strong political will.

Devising effective poverty reduction strategies requires understanding of the extent and dynamics of poverty in a given context. Monitoring progress also requires some data that forms the baseline from which to assess who is benefiting from poverty reduction and who is not. Monitoring data enables strategies to be changed where they are having a weak or negative impact. Virtually every country collects some kind of census data that can be used in this regard. There is no universal standardized system of data collection since governments will have differing priorities and differing capacities for gathering data. Over time, pressure to publish data disaggregated by sex has had a positive effect, with the result that the Human Development Index now includes some tables disaggregated by sex.

A recent project under the auspices of the Statistics Division of the United Nations on ethnocultural data revealed a serious gap in disaggregation of data by ethnicity or religion. In roughly 37 per cent of cases, censuses collected no ethnocultural data. Among 138 national census questionnaires surveyed, only 87 countries or 63 per cent employed some form of ethnic census classification. North America, South America, and Oceania demonstrated the greatest propensity to include ethnicity on their censuses. While Asia's tendency to enumerate by ethnicity was close to the sample average, both Europe and Africa were much less likely to do so (only 44 per cent of censuses in each region collected ethnocultural data).[25]

The reasons for the absence of data are varied. Governments may have concerns about data protection and privacy of citizens. Asking people to identify their ethnicity, mother tongue or religion may be socially sensitive, particularly where these identities have been used in the past to target individuals or groups for violence or exclusion. In other cases, the capacity to gather accurate data in a highly ethnically or religiously diverse country may be weak or not a budgetary priority. Even when data is collected it may not be published.

Data is important for effective poverty reduction and it is therefore surprising that, within aid modalities on poverty, the collection of ethnocultural disaggregated data is not uniformly supported. UNDP has noted that "showing and analysing data on specific ethnic groups may be a sensitive issue". However in 2005 UNDP published the MDG Monitoring and Reporting: A Review of Good Practices, wherein it recommends that, "wherever possible, disaggregated

[25] Ethnicity: A Review of Data Collection and Dissemination (Social and Housing Statistics Section, Demographic and Social Statistics Branch, United Nations Statistics Division, August 2003): p. 4.

data should be used to highlight disparities across gender, ethnicity, geographical location, age or other dimensions of inequality".[26]

The EU Race Directive, designed to address direct and indirect discrimination on the basis of racial or ethnic origin, indicates that discrimination may be monitored using statistical evidence (para. 15). However, many EU studies on social exclusion and poverty have not generally disaggregated data by ethnicity. EUROSTAT, the body that aids States with data collection, does not advocate strongly for ethnic data in its Income and Living Conditions Survey, which is the main source for social exclusion data and provides the basis for policy design.[27]

D. Promising practices in development policies

There are some good policy practices in evidence, although much remains to be done if minorities are to see significant poverty alleviation by 2015. The process is as important as the outcome. Where minorities are not consulted on poverty reduction strategies that will affect them, the outcome of well-intentioned programmes may be a null change or even a decline in human development. Minorities have a right to participate in decision-making that will affect them and respecting this right is paramount for development interventions.

There is no one-size fits all for successful poverty reduction, including for minorities. Nevertheless, it is useful to share experiences across countries with a view to stimulating successful practice, beginning with a focus on data collection. The Independent Expert welcomes additional information from States on their experiences and examples of successful practice in minority sensitive poverty reduction strategies.

The Permanent Forum on Indigenous Issues has taken important steps to engage intergovernmental and non-governmental organizations and Governments in dialogue on improving data collection on indigenous peoples' issues. This work has been undertaken in the context of strategies to achieve the MDGs for indigenous peoples, a major focus of recent sessions. The United Nations system, through the Inter-Agency Support Group on Indigenous Issues, has undertaken a review of existing indicators that may directly or indirectly concern or relate to indigenous peoples. Workshops were organized to feed into this process.[28]

Indicators must be relevant to the communities surveyed and the collection of data should be undertaken with direct involvement of minorities. UNDP Regional Bureau for Europe and the Commonwealth of Independent States is training Roma to act as survey managers to gather information to be used in poverty reduction strategies. This may make some community members more comfortable in sharing their concerns and self-identifying as minorities.

Collection of disaggregated data has long been established in the Compilation of guidelines on the form and content of reports to be submitted by States parties to the international human rights treaties (HRI/GEN/2/Rev.2). The treaty bodies request information about the "main ethnic and demographic characteristics of the country and its population" along with information on religion and mother tongue languages (ibid., para. 1). More specifically, the

---

[26] MDG Monitoring and Reporting: A Review of Good Practices (UNDP Bureau for Development Policy, Poverty Reduction Group, August 2005): p. 18.

[27] Kathryn Ramsay, Disaggregated Data Collection: A Precondition for Effective Protection of Minority Rights in South East Europe (London: Minority Rights Group International, 2006): p. 6.

[28] See www.un.org/esa/socdev/unpfii/news/news_workshop_doc.htm.

Committee on the Elimination of Racial Discrimination stresses the importance of ethnic data in monitoring progress on eliminating discrimination in its own reporting guidelines.

An important initiative under the auspices of OHCHR has been summarized in the report of the High Commissioner containing a draft basic document on the development of a racial equality index. The Index would provide a country-specific view of inequalities along key human development indicators based on ethnicity, information that is currently absent from, for example, UNDP annual Human Development Report and Human Development Index (see E/CN.4/2006/14).[29]

The Inter-American Development Bank (IDB) is helping to raise the profile of the need for more ethnocultural data. The Bank's project for monitoring the equity and social indicators for MDGs - Eqxis - includes information on the situation of indigenous peoples and Afro-descendants.[30] The data collected reveals wide gaps in available data for many countries. To fill this gap the Bank is funding national statistics strengthening programmes, for example, in Nicaragua. This effort has emerged from regional level dialogues on how to improve data collection on ethnicity. The last round of censuses in the region demonstrated increases in the collection of ethnocultural data.

In Europe, where exclusion of immigrants is a major problem, a European Inclusion Index has been developed to measure EU policy in five key areas relevant to Third Country Nationals: labour market inclusion, long-term residence, family reunion, nationality and anti-discrimination. In 2005 the findings showed that the then 15-EU member States had practices that were, on average, "less than favourable" to immigrant inclusion across all five areas. The second edition will be published in 2007 including all 27 EU member States plus Canada, Switzerland and Norway. Future editions will also be able to track countries' progress over time.[31]

Policy and programme options for addressing poverty among minorities can be broadly categorized either as targeted policies, tailored to the specific needs of minorities as the principal direct beneficiaries, or "mainstreamed" policies (especially for social inclusion) that do not differentiate between the particular needs of varied groups of beneficiaries in a common denominator approach. Governments and international development actors often favour mainstreamed social inclusion policies since these are understood to benefit a wider constituency. Moreover, where disaggregated data along ethnic lines is absent, it may be considered difficult to justify targeting specific groups for poverty reduction programmes. Resentment from other (poor) groups may further isolate those intended to benefit.

While mainstreamed social inclusion policies may help minorities to some degree because they are disproportionately among the poor, the generalized approach to poverty reduction can fail to address the particular structures and causes of the poverty experienced by minority groups. For example, adopting a mainstream social inclusion strategy to raise the minimum wage may benefit minorities who are more likely to be employed at this wage in addition to helping all people living on minimum wage; however, such a policy will not tackle the fact

---

29 The experts agreed that a global ranked index like the human development index would not be feasible.

30 See http://www.iadb.org/xindicators/.

31 Laura Citron, "How to measure integration: the European Inclusion Index", in Equal Voices, Issue 19, (Oct. 2006): pp. 11-16.

that minorities are disproportionately among those earning the minimum wage. The inequality gap may remain and in some circumstances, it may increase.

Tackling that inequality will require adopting and enforcing strong anti-discrimination labour laws, strengthening social support mechanisms or considering how to improve the average educational attainment of minorities. Affirmative action policies including quotas or reservations in education and in employment may be considered as temporary measures to address long-term inequalities and lack of access.

The decision on whether to use targeted or mainstreamed social inclusion policies requires consultations with minorities. The establishment of advisory committees or similar consultative bodies with representatives of minorities is a vital tool in devising successful poverty reduction strategies. The establishment of consultative mechanisms from below has been a priority for many minority groups. Through grass-roots mobilization, minorities can form coalitions to advocate at a national level on poverty reduction issues.

In Honduras such a mechanism was established in 2003 as part of the P*rograma de Apoyo a los Pueblos Indígenas y Negros de Honduras*. Under the auspices of the central Government it includes representatives of the 10 federations of Afro-descendants and indigenouspeoples. The programme will initially focus on small infrastructure projects identified locally by Afro-descendants and indigenous peoples. Other components will focus on: strengthening the regulatory framework for the protection of the rights of these communities; sensitization of Afro-descendant and indigenous representatives and government staff to each other's perspectives on development; and devising evaluation and monitoring tools. It is hoped that the cooperation can be replicated and enlarged.

In Kenya pastoralist representatives came together to input into drafting Kenya's PRSP. The Pastoralist Thematic Group (PTG) emerged out of a traditional gathering, the shirka, where poverty and the PRSP were discussed. PTG gained some attention to their issues and engaged government officials in dialogue about their concerns for the PRSP. While the final PRSP does not adequately reflect their concerns, PTG is a viable structure for continued advocacy. UNDP has established the United Nations Indigenous Peoples Advisory Committee of Kenya as an important focal point for indigenous minorities to liaise with UNDP and other United Nations agencies on priority issues. The municipal government has an equal responsibility to ensure minorities are engaged in decision-making.

In Aarhus, Denmark, 9.4 per cent of the population are minorities originally from non-EU countries. In 2005 Aarhus City Council adopted principles for a new integration policy and will be conducting a series of consultations in 2006 and 2007 with ethnic minority representatives (plus the existing "Integration Council") to devise better systems for minorities to access local services. In 2000, the Council adopted a 10-year employment strategy for refugees and migrants that have worked with local businesses to bring employment levels of refugees and migrants to that equal to other groups.[32]

National strategies for Roma have figured prominently in Central and Eastern Europe, in particular under the auspices of the Decade of Roma Inclusion, in which nine participating States are Bulgaria, Croatia, Czech Republic, Hungary, The former Yugoslav Republic of

[32] Anne Marie Larsen, "Integration at local level - the example of Aarhus/Denmark", in Equal Voices, Issue 19, (October 2006): pp. 24-28.

Macedonia, Montenegro, Romania, Serbia and Slovakia.[33] States pledge to achieve stated goals for the improvement of the socio-economic status of Roma by 2015 (coinciding with MDGs). Roma representatives have inputted into the process from the early stages and have been involved in the international Steering Committee of the Decade and preparation of country action plans. The capacity of Roma and Governments to make this Decade a success needs to be greatly strengthened.

In Brazil, a National Affirmative Action Programme to implement the Durban Declaration and Programme of Action was adopted in 2002, resulting in development specific programmes to address inequalities experienced by Afro-descendants and indigenous peoples. A Special Secretariat for the Promotion of Racial Equality (SEPPIR) was created in 2003 to advise on implementation of the national strategy. The proposed legislation on a Statute on Racial Equality (PL 6264/2005) provides for affirmative action in the form of quotas for Afro-Brazilians and indigenous people in higher education and public service. Under the Statute, 20 per cent of the spaces in public and private universities would be reserved for Afro-Brazilians. One study reports that educational inequalities can explain the 48 per cent wage gap and some 26 per cent of income inequalities.[34]

Where they exist, national strategies for improving the human development of persons belonging to minorities will often combine mainstreamed and targeted programmes. It is important that majority communities feel they too can benefit from these processes. Transparency about policy is key and disaggregated data helps to mandate targeted policies. Engaging majority communities alongside minority communities in community-level development initiatives can also be extremely valuable. Evaluation of development programmes in Romania found that by addressing Roma and non-Roma living in close proximity, project interventions could create stronger community cohesion.[35]

In Nepal, UNDP community development projects have earmarked a proportion of project resources for excluded groups. In the Decentralized Finance and Development Program, a minimum of 30 per cent of project funds are to be used to benefit women and Dalits. Direct support to minorities themselves can also be effective. The European Commission devised a major budget line to support civil society activities for minorities. The European Democracy and Human Rights Initiative set as one of its four funding priorities for 2002-2004 "Combating racism and xenophobia and discrimination against minorities and indigenous peoples". In 2002, some 21,000,000 euros were allocated to 32 projects under this funding line, mainly for activities in developing countries or countries in transition.

An appropriate legal and regulatory framework is vital for supporting poverty reduction strategies. Access to justice for persons belonging to minorities will often be weaker at all stages of the legal process, from support from police to investigate crimes against their businesses, to strong anti-discrimination legislation to safeguard labour rights. Constitutional provisions that recognize diversity and equality of all citizens are a good foundation. Detailed legal frameworks for non-discrimination should be accompanied by legal and regulatory

33 See www.romadecade.com.

34 Barrios et al., cited in supra note 15, Public Policy Responses to Exclusion: Evidence from Brazil, South Africa and India, p. 10.

35 35 UNDP Romania, Evaluation of Programmes Targeting Roma Communities in Romania, (Cluj-Napoca, Romania: UNDP Romania, 2006).

mechanisms to enforce the legislation, including labour tribunals, ombudspersons and equal opportunities policies.

Under the Racial Equality Directive and the Employment Equality Directive, EU member States have to strengthen their national non-discrimination laws. In the United Kingdom, the Employment Equality (Religion or Belief) Regulations 2003 make it unlawful to discriminate on grounds of religion or belief in employment and vocational training. They prohibit direct discrimination, indirect discrimination, victimization and harassment. Equally, newly acceded EU States are required to adopt new legislation, such as Hungary's comprehensive Act No. CXXV on Equal Treatment and the Promotion of Equal Opportunities.

E. The work of the United Nations and other institutions in the area of minorities, poverty alleviation and Millennium Development Goals

Governments bear the primary responsibility to ensure that minorities can overcome poverty, however, the United Nations and international development agencies can be important partners. The response of agencies to the recommendations of representatives of indigenous peoples has been positive, in the form of adoption of special policies and targeted programming and projects. However similar efforts for other ethnic, religious or linguistic minority groups have been much less pronounced.

While many international development agencies have dedicated policies or programmes for indigenous peoples, no agency has a corresponding programme for other minorities. The UNDP, EU, Danish International Development Agency (DANIDA), International Fund for Agricultural Development (IFAD), Norwegian Agency for International Development (NORAD), Netherlands Ministry of Foreign Affairs, Swiss Agency for Development and Cooperation (SDC), World Bank, Asian Development Bank and IDB have all taken specific steps - typically the articulation of policy statements or guidelines, or targeted cooperation projects - on indigenous peoples.[36] Indigenous peoples can use these as a basis both to engage in dialogue with these agencies and to hold them accountable to established standards or objectives. Minorities are sometimes mentioned in lists of "vulnerable groups", but rarely are the circumstances of their vulnerability analysed or responded to with separate measures.

UNDP is one agency taking the lead on working with minorities. In 2006 UNDP has collaborated closely with the Independent Expert regarding its future work on minority issues and the elaboration of a policy note/guidance note on minorities. This would complement the existing UNDP Policy of Engagement with Indigenous Peoples adopted in 2001. A budget line for work on minority issues has been included in the new Global Human Rights Strengthening Programme of UNDP, which calls for collaboration with the Independent Expert.

The IDB adopted an Action Plan for Combating Social Exclusion Due to Race or Ethnic Background in May 2001, with the long-term goal to integrate fully and consider race and ethnicity in IDB operations, programming and policies. The next phase seeks to build its institutional framework to address social exclusion and will focus on building the capacity and role of country offices through training, hiring practices, outreach, and project development.

[36] For further details see Minority Rights Group International, An Examination of Approaches by International Development Agencies to Minority Issues in Development, (E/CN.4/Sub.2/AC.5/2004/WP.5).

The IDB is reaching out to other agencies, through the Inter-Agency Consultation of Race and Poverty in Latin America and the Caribbean[37] and has convened workshops on issues including how to create economic development opportunities for Afro-descendants.

Among bilateral development agencies, SDC supported a three-year backstopping mandate with Minority Rights Group International to build the capacity of staff and support the organization as a whole to include minorities in development cooperation more effectively. Several training workshops on various aspects of working with minorities were held and country-specific policy support offered.

Private sector businesses must contribute fully to confronting poverty and enabling minorities to access employment. Where businesses make a serious commitment to equal opportunities policies, the diversity and strength of their workforce will grow and the benefits to communities are significant. Governments should be proactive in extending non-discrimination legislation and affirmative action policies to the private sector and robustly enforcing such policies. Multinational corporations should act in conformity with international human rights law and demonstrate leadership in regions in which they work.

II. CONCLUSIONS AND RECOMMENDATIONS

A. Conclusions

In all countries, developed and developing, the high levels and disproportionate poverty of persons belonging to minorities requires dedicated attention and concerted action. The initial step for States in designing development policies must be to assess their obligations under human rights treaties and customary law. Within the wider framework of a human rights-based approach to development, the rights to non-discrimination, to participation in decision-making and to protection of cultural identity are crucial to addressing the inequality and exclusion faced by many minorities.

The Millennium Declaration establishes an overarching commitment in Goal 8 to "develop a global partnership for development". Developed countries and the international community have a shared responsibility to address more fully the structural issues facing developing countries in eradicating poverty in general and specifically disproportionate poverty among minorities.[38]

The situation of minority women demands particular attention. The intersection of discrimination on the basis of gender and minority identity should be considered systematically in the reform of policies aimed at poverty elimination. It is well accepted that women from marginalized populations are the overwhelming number of those living in poverty worldwide.

---

[37] This group included the Inter-American Dialogue, the World Bank, PAHO, OAS/Inter-American Human Rights Commission, UNDP, the Ford Foundation, among others.

[38] Philip Alston, "Ships Passing in the Night: The Current State of the Human Rights and Development Debate Seen Through the Lens of the Millennium Development Goals", Human Rights Quarterly, 27.3 (2005) pp. 775-777.

B. Recommendations

The Independent Expert recommends that States:

(a) Gather data on key economic and social indicators concerning the human development of persons belonging to minorities, including through censuses or sampling surveys, to establish sufficient baseline data to design appropriate policy responses. The data, disaggregated by different specific ethnic, religious and linguistic group and also by gender, should be made public.
(b) Establish mechanisms for meaningful dialogue with representatives of minority communities about development policies, particularly at the local government level. At the national level, the creation of statutory bodies composed of representatives of minority communities mandated to review and monitor government policy as it may affect minorities has proved useful.
(c) Strengthen the legal and regulatory framework for addressing direct and indirect discrimination in both public and private spheres. Effective non-discrimination laws in key sectors such as employment and education can reduce obstacles that minorities face in overcoming poverty. Remedies and recourse procedures in discrimination cases should be readily accessible to minorities with penalties that are substantial and vigorously enforced.
(d) Adopt targeted and aggressive affirmative action policies for addressing the social exclusion of minorities, including a specific social and economic development plan for all marginalized groups. Affirmative action programmes should include the private sector as well as the public sector.
(e) Establish monitoring and evaluation mechanisms that can effectively measure the results of poverty reduction strategies that target minorities.
(f) Ensure that the MDG Country Reports and PRSPs, systematically reflect the situation of minorities, and that all review procedures monitor the impact of policies on minorities. Data disaggregated by social group and gender should be included in all PRSPs and MDG Country Reports.

Long-term success in poverty reduction for minorities requires an investment in tackling the root causes. In particular, States should consider measures in the following key areas:

(a) Education: Measures should include; addressing situations that result in segregation of minority children into different classrooms or facilities on the basis of their identity; increased access to education in mother-tongue languages; consideration of targeted financial assistance, or reserved places in secondary and higher education; curriculum development to reflect human rights education, minority cultures, and contributions of minorities to wider society.
(b) Employment: Measures to promote minority access to employment should include targeted skills training, investment in regions where minorities live, robust enforcement of anti-discrimination laws with respect to hiring, promotion and retention of minorities in the labour sector, penalties for violations of such laws that are sufficiently harsh to be a deterrent, targeted credit schemes and other support for small businesses. Affirmative

action measures in public and private sector employment should be implemented to address long-term discrimination and exclusion of minorities.

(c) Land and property rights: Governments should adopt and enforce laws that safeguard the equal rights of minorities to land and property. Land laws should recognize a variety of forms of ownership, both individual and collective. Minorities should be enabled to register legal title to their land. Legal remedy and/or compensation should be made available to those previously displaced from their homes or traditional lands. The rights of women belonging to minority groups to own and inherit land must be equal to that of men.

(d) Participation in decision-making: minorities have a right to participate effectively in decision-making on local or national issues and development plans that affect them or the regions in which they live. Support for participation, such as through reserved seats in governance or dedicated consultative institutions, should be prioritized.

The Independent Expert recommends that International development agencies:

(a) Adopt policy guidelines on minority issues which specifically address the particular issues faced by persons belonging to a broader array of minority populations in addition to Indigenous peoples.

(b) Build institutional capacity and knowledge on the situation of minorities, particularly in respect to poverty and other human development indicators. This may include training for staff on the human rights of minorities and applying human rights-based approaches to development.

(c) Undertake dialogues with minorities on development priorities, including through the establishment of minority advisory groups. Regional dialogues on minority issues may also be facilitated by international development agencies.

(d) Collect disaggregated data on the impact on minorities of policies, programmes and projects and support national statistics offices to build their capacity to collect and disseminate such data.

(e) Monitor budgetary support to ensure that resource allocations are appropriately targeting minorities or the regions in which they live and raise such approaches as matters of priority in consultations with government decision-makers.

(f) Support States in the preparation of MDG Country Reports, PRSPs and all review procedures associated with these modalities to ensure that the impact of policies on minorities is appropriately covered.

(g) Commission further research on the impact of development and poverty reduction strategies on minorities and ensure that country strategy papers for development cooperation reflect the situation of minorities and are published in minority languages.

(h) Establish budget lines to support work on minority issues in development. This may include funding to minority groups within civil society, investment in key sectors, or investment in regions where the poorest minorities live.

The United Nations, regional and national human rights institutions are recommended to:

(a) Provide necessary technical support on the drafting, implementation and enforcement of laws on non-discrimination and on laws and standards to protect the rights of minorities including the Declaration on the Rights of Persons Belonging to National or Ethnic, Religious or Linguistic Minorities.

(b) Integrate consideration of minority rights into research, dialogue and training on the human rights-based approach to development.

(c) Ensure that efforts to establish human rights-based indicators of human development include the elaboration of indicators with relevance to minorities.

The 2003 Guidance Note on Country Reporting on the MDGs of the United Nations Development Group should be revised to clearly reflect a requirement for the collection and inclusion of disaggregated data by race, ethnicity and religion, and guidelines in this regard.

The Independent Expert's mandate requires her to identify best practices. She strongly encourages States and international development actors to share with her further information on positive practices undertaken to develop strong policies and technical cooperation initiatives on poverty reduction in communities of historically marginalized minority populations.

Name Index

For Product Safety Concerns and Information please contact our EU representative GPSR@taylorandfrancis.com Taylor & Francis Verlag GmbH, Kaufingerstraße 24, 80331 München, Germany

Batch number: 10726296

Printed by Printforce, the Netherlands